PRIMA® GAMES

WE ARE STRATEGY

FREE eGUIDE!

Enter this code at primagames.com/code to unlock your FREE eGuide:

JXU4-2YD6-8GDH-DB98

Bonus content for this eGuide includes:

➤ **INTERACTIVE AREA MAPS**

➤ **BONUS BOSS FIGHT VIDEOS**

Mobile Friendly:
Access your eGuide on any web-enabled device.

Searchable & Sortable:
Quickly find the strategies you need.

Added Value:
Strategy where, when, and how you want it.

CHECK OUT OUR eGUIDE STORE AT PRIMAGAMES.COM!

All your strategy saved in your own personal digital library!

BECOME A FAN OF PRIMA GAMES!

Subscribe to our Twitch channel twitch.tv/primagames and join our weekly stream every Tuesday ~~1 /~~ EST!

D1127466

Prima GAMES

www.primagames.com

The Prima Games logo and Primagames.com are registered trademarks of Penguin Random House LLC, registered in the United States. Prima Games is an imprint of DK, a division of Penguin Random House LLC, New York.

DARK SOULS III

A SPARK FLICKERS

Dark Souls III beckons. Its world is filled with darkness and death, and there are few who remain with any strength to resist the pull of time and decay. Can you awaken the slumbering lords of this grim world? Which Covenant will you herald? Can you survive against monsters and the dark invaders that are waiting to attack you in your most vulnerable moments?

If you've played games in this series before, you understand what you're getting into. The precision of *Dark Souls* combat. The need for practice, the rewards of mastery, and that feeling that everything you face is tough but still fair. For you, this guide is a tool to find ideal weapons and styles for completing the game without as many trials and errors. We'll help you find the hidden pathways and the best upgrades, and we'll give you tips as you push through the game and start again with even greater challenges awaiting.

For newcomers, there is all of that and much more. This series can definitely be intimidating at first. The death system can hurt your progress if you don't know how to handle it. Upgrades are expensive, and level grinding isn't really a thing (certainly when compared to a traditional RPG). Instead, progress is often based heavily on learning how to fight, avoiding attacks, and knowing when to dodge, parry, or even run away.

We'll do everything in our power to make your training days as fun and enjoyable as you'd like them to be. *Dark Souls* loves to challenge, but it's just as happy to reward you when you take the time to do things correctly. We have pages of tips, suggestions, and tutorials to make your hardest hours much easier to overcome.

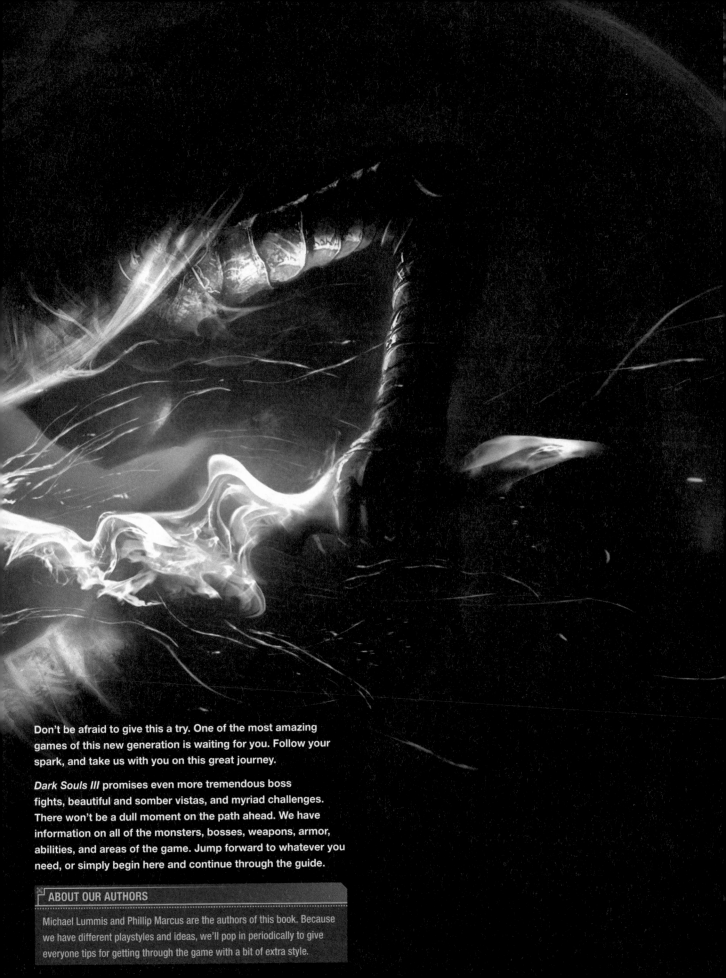

Don't be afraid to give this a try. One of the most amazing
games of this new generation is waiting for you. Follow your
spark, and take us with you on this great journey.

Dark Souls III promises even more tremendous boss
fights, beautiful and somber vistas, and myriad challenges.
There won't be a dull moment on the path ahead. We have
information on all of the monsters, bosses, weapons, armor,
abilities, and areas of the game. Jump forward to whatever you
need, or simply begin here and continue through the guide.

ABOUT OUR AUTHORS

Michael Lummis and Phillip Marcus are the authors of this book. Because
we have different playstyles and ideas, we'll pop in periodically to give
everyone tips for getting through the game with a bit of extra style.

A WORLD OF ASH & CINDERS

Dark Souls games tell their story without resorting to exposition or lengthy dialogue. Instead, they allow the player to uncover tidbits about the world indirectly. Item text descriptions and engaging your foes while getting brief glimpses into their motivations are all that you get. For some players, the history of the world will remain a mystery despite multiple playthroughs.

It isn't this guide's place to reveal all of the world's secrets; spoilers do not make for a very enjoyable guide. However, this chapter is designed to lead you toward the story and show you how to figure out the world.

One of the few ways to get information directly is chatting with the characters you meet at the Ashen Shrine and out in the area around Lothric. The first time you talk to each NPC, you often hear about their lives and whatever it is that they're doing. You're free to walk away at that point.

However, you can also stick around and continue talking to each character that you meet. They'll have multiple things to say to you if you keep talking to them. Sometimes this grants physical rewards (gifts from the characters you've met) or additional wisdom about the surrounding territory and its dangers.

It's suggested that you exhaust every NPC's conversations by talking to them until they repeat themselves. It's well worth your time, and players without patience can tap their buttons to hurry the conversation along.

Every item in the game has two screens' worth of information. One of them lists the stats for the item in question. These are certainly important for combat and utility, but press the "Show Item Info" button at the bottom of the screen to switch to the other page of info.

The descriptive page has a picture of the current item and some text that explains the function and often the lore of the item you're examining.

This is good for finding out the game's history, and it's also useful because there are sometimes hints about things that you can do with specific items. As an example, look at the descriptions for your keys. They'll lead you toward the area where you're supposed to use them.

Sacred Flame

Pyromancy taught amongst savages.
Flame burrows inside foes and ignites.

Originally used in a ceremony for cleansing
sacrificial impurities, thereby lending the spell its name.

As barbaric as it seems, this may in fact be
quite fitting for the savage pyromancers
who consider themselves servants of the divine.

WATCH THE INTRO MOVIE AGAIN

The movie that begins the game is beautiful, dark, and exciting, but it won't have much relevance to you initially. Try going back after playing 10 hours of the game or so, and the voiceover and visuals will start to have deeper meaning. The factions involved there are the same ones that you will be dealing with as you progress through the story.

PLAY THE REST OF THE SERIES

Dark Souls games don't take place in a new world each time. Instead, they're all linked together as part of one great (albeit sad) story of a world that has seen many better days.

There are even some characters that return from previous games. Keep an eye out for them; they're probably all trustworthy…

The *Dark Souls* story is an interesting experience. Every person who plays through these games comes away with a slightly different impression.

Because the story is fragmented and presented piecemeal, and there are many optional encounters, items, NPCs, and even entire areas, no two experiences are exactly the same.

You can talk to a friend who completed the game and come away with two different interpretations of events easily, and if you go online, you'll find pages of discussion and hours of videos where other players try to dissect the overall storyline.

There are also many smaller stories presented: sometimes short tales of single NPCs, sometimes factions or nations that only exist in the background on item descriptions or even item names.

The heart of the story in each *Dark Souls* game tends to be relatively straightforward, but there are always little loose ends and threads that you can pull and look deeper if you so choose.

How far you go down this rabbit hole is entirely up to you—there's no wrong way to experience the story. If you're the type who simply enjoys soaking in the atmosphere and letting it settle, you may not even want to delve too deeply into other theories. On the other hand, if you can't stand an unresolved mystery, you'll find mountains of speculation online about how all the pieces fit together.

Fair warning, though—many aspects of the story and world are missing pieces, so there will always be some aspects of the world that are left up to your interpretation. This is entirely by design, and your particular experience and interpretation of the world is always going to be a unique one. Enjoy it: few games tell a story or present a world in this manner.

CONTROLLING THE GAME

If you're experienced with the series, it shouldn't be hard to pick up the controller and get back into *Dark Souls III*. The system has a few changes from the earlier titles, but the general feel of the game and most of the commands are similar. You can probably skip this chapter unless you have any questions or want to re-familiarize yourself with all of the controls in the game.

New players should stop here and take in everything that you can. It takes quite a few fights to really get used to the *Dark Souls* combat system, and this chapter is likely to cut some time off of your learning curve.

THE HUD

The HUD shows you many things about your character, so you never have to look far to receive a wealth of information. Your character stays in the center of the screen, and you have control of the camera to look around. In the upper corner, you have bars for your health (in red), your FPs (in blue), and your Stamina (in green). These fill or deplete depending on the actions you take, and that lets you track whether you need to keep fighting, back off to rest, heal, or simply flee.

If your health gets too low, you're in great danger. Use your Estus Flask to heal, or get out of combat entirely if that isn't an option.

If your FPs bottom out, use the Ashen Estus Flask to restore them, or resort to basic attacks that don't rely on FP. Keep in mind that you can use many Weapon Skills even if your FP is depleted, but they drain more Stamina and often execute more slowly without FP. Spells, on the other hand, simply cannot be used without FP.

Stamina is the easiest to restore. Back off and lower your shield to get Stamina flowing back to your character. It only takes a few seconds to fill, and then you're ready to perform more actions.

Your Souls indicator is in the bottom-right area. The higher it goes, the more you have to spend. Think about returning to the Fire Keeper or a vendor so that you can invest those Souls into something worthwhile.

The bottom-left area shows your weapons and tools. The items in your hands are on the left and right. The tools you have readied are on the bottom. The top slot is for your spells.

Use the D-pad to swap around these items with others in the same slots that you have prepared. To see what you have, go into the Equipment screen to swap these items around ahead of time.

It's always good to have your Estus Flask and Ashen Estus Flasks equipped on the bar, but be sure to leave room for other staples like Homeward Bones, thrown weapons, buff items, or anything that raises your resistance against the major types of damage in the area.

Remember to shift your tools around depending on the situation that you're handling. If you go into an area that is filled with poison, change your tools to focus on that. When you leave, take those back off of the bar so that you're not always cycling through tons of items to get to the one you need.

CONTROLS

MOVEMENT

The left analog stick controls your movement. Normally, you turn and then move in whichever direction you push. Press back on the stick to move toward the camera, left to strafe left, and so on. Turn your camera to make it easier to see where you're going, or keep it focused on something specific if you're trying to dodge ranged attacks or watch an incoming enemy.

It's possible to lock on to enemy targets by clicking the right analog stick. When you're locked on to an adversary, you face them at all times. Consequently, moving left or right causes you to sidestep, and pressing down backs away from your target. This is slower than your standard run speed, but it makes things much easier when you're trying to aim your attacks at the foe in question.

It's useful to switch between lock-on and regular movement frequently. It's easier to run away and get distance from your enemies when you aren't locked on. Do this to get to safety, earn time for your Stamina to regenerate, or look for a place to hide and use your Estus Flask.

When you're on the attack, it's easier to line up attack combos when you're locked on. It requires less effort to stay on target and land shot after shot against your enemy. Your character strafes around the victim, avoiding some of their attacks without even using Stamina.

Move normally when you're exploring, lock on to take out your foes, but click the right analog stick again if you need to drop your lock and get away from an enemy that is gaining the upper hand.

Target locks disappear when your opponent is slain, but you can quickly shift them to other targets by pressing left or right on the right analog stick. This is useful if you change your focus on multiple targets, or for going through groups and slaughtering one after the other without needing to lock on to each one.

TARGET LOCKING

Target locking can be a trap on some very large enemies and some bosses. Because it slows your movement and locks your field of view on a specific point, you may find it harder to avoid some massive and dangerous attacks.

If you're having particular trouble with a specific enemy or boss battle, try disabling your lock-on and simply running around the target, dodging when necessary, striking when you see an opening. For most of the game, locking on to "normal" enemies out in the world is totally fine. Just be aware there are some situations where you should try disengaging it.

CATEGORY	ACTION	PS4 CONTROLLER	XBOX ONE CONTROLLER	NOTES
MOVEMENT	Move	Left stick	Left stick	
	Dash	Left stick while holding down ◯ button	Left stick while holding down Ⓐ button	
	Jump	**L3** button while dashing	Push in left stick while dashing	
EVASION	Backstep	◯ button	Ⓐ button	
	Roll	Left stick + ◯ button	Left stick + Ⓐ button	
INTERACTION	Open door	✕ button while facing door	Ⓑ button while facing door	
	Use lever	✕ button while facing lever	Ⓑ button while facing lever	
	Hold onto ladder	✕ button while facing ladder	Ⓑ button while facing ladder	
	Climb/descend ladder	Left stick (up or down)	Left stick (up or down)	
	Slide down ladder	Hold down ◯ button while holding onto ladder	Hold down Ⓐ button while holding onto ladder	
	Attack upwards on ladder	**R1** button while holding onto ladder	Right bumper while holding onto ladder	
	Attack downwards on ladder	**R2** button while holding onto ladder	Right trigger while holding onto ladder	
CAMERA	Control camera	Right stick	Right stick	
	Reset camera	**R3** button	Push in right stick	If no enemies are nearby.
	Toggle lock-on	**R3** button	Push in right stick	If there are enemies nearby.
EQUIPMENT	Toggle right weapon	Right directional button	Right on directional pad	
	Toggle left weapon	Left directional button	Left on directional pad	
	Toggle spell	Up directional button	Up on directional pad	
	Toggle item	Down directional button	Down on directional pad	
ITEMS	Use item	◯ button	✕ button	
STANCE	Two-hand right weapon	△ button	Ⓨ button	
	Two-hand left weapon	Hold down △ button	Hold down Ⓨ button	
ATTACKING	Right weapon: attack	**R1** button	Right bumper	
	Right weapon: strong attack	**R2** button	Right trigger	Can charge an attack by holding button down.
	Right weapon: guard	**L1** button while two-handing	Left bumper while two-handing	
	Right weapon: Skill	**L2** button while two-handing	Left-trigger while two-handing	
	Right weapon: dash attack	**R1** button while dashing	Right bumper while dashing	
	Right weapon: strong dash attack	**R2** button while dashing	Right trigger while dashing	
	Right weapon: backstep attack	**R1** button at the end of a backstep	Right bumper at the end of a backstep	
	Right weapon: strong backstep attack	**R2** button at the end of a backstep	Right trigger at the end of a roll	
	Right weapon: rolling attack	**R1** button at the end of a roll	Right bumper at the end of a roll	
	Right weapon: strong rolling attack	**R2** button at the end of a roll	Right trigger at the end of a roll	Can charge an attack by holding button down.
	Kick	Tilt left stick forwards + **R1** button	Tilt left stick forwards + right bumper	
	Right weapon: jumping attack	Tilt left stick forwards + **R2** button	Tilt left stick forwards + right trigger	
	Right weapon: plunging attack	**R1** button while falling	Right bumper while falling	
	Left weapon: attack	**L1** button	Left bumper	
	Left weapon: Skill	**L2** button	Left trigger	
	Right weapon: cast spell	**R1** button	Right bumper	
	Left weapon: cast spell	**L1** button	Left bumper	
	Left weapon: guard	**L1** button while suitable item is equipped	Left bumper while suitable item is equipped	When equipped to left hand.
	Backstab	**R1** button while behind enemy	Right bumper while behind enemy	
OPENING MENUS	Open menu	OPTIONS button or touch pad button (right)	Menu button	
	Open gesture menu	Touch pad button (left)	View button	
	Toggle action (Examine, Open, etc.)	△ button	Ⓨ button	
	Pick up item	✕ button	Ⓑ button	

Remember also that you can change lock-on targets during battle by flicking the right analog stick in roughly the direction of the desired target. Use this to prioritize dangerous single enemies, or even change body part targets on very large enemies.

Finally, if you ever find yourself walking on dangerously narrow terrain, target locking can get you into trouble by causing you to strafe off an edge, if your position suddenly shifts relative to your lock-on target. Consider disabling lock-on if your footing is unsure.

CAMERA CONTROL

The right analog stick controls your camera. Reposition this to see around corners, to keep your line of sight on a particular target, or to look all over a room when searching for treasure or threats.

THE SHOULDER BUTTONS

All four of the shoulder buttons control your equipment. The item in your right hand is used with **R1/RB** (attack) and **R2/RT** (strong attack). The item in your left hand gets **L1/LB** and **L2/LT**. If you're wielding an item in both hands, all four of the shoulder buttons have different actions for whatever you're wielding. Shields are set to **L1/LB**.

Each weapon and shield has its own timings and moves, so you don't really know what you're going to get out of them until you practice. The general rule is that **R1/RB** and **L1/LB** are for the basic uses of those items, and **R2/RT** and **L2/LT** deal with more specialized behaviors.

For example, a shield in your left hand is used to block with **L1/LB**. Hold down the button to keep your shield ready, and let go when you're done with it. **L2/LT** lets you parry with most smaller shields, but it also allows you to access special moves with your main weapon on shields that can't parry.

Try different uses of these moves. Hold down the button for a heavy attack to see if you can charge it for even more damage, and to mix up your timings. This is a very complex aspect of the game, and it is discussed in more detail in the Gameplay chapter.

WEAPON SKILLS

New to *Dark Souls III*, Weapon Skills are special moves that are specific to different pieces of equipment. You can find swords that allow you to perform lunging strikes and shield-breaking rising stabs, staves that buff your magic power briefly, and many more. You typically activate Weapon Skills by holding or pressing **L2/LT**, with the specifics for a given weapon showing up in the description of the item itself.

Keep in mind that shields can "interfere" with the Weapon Skill of your right-hand weapon. If your shield has a shield bash or parry on the **L2/LT** button, you need to two-hand your weapon by pressing ⊕/**Y**. You can then access the Weapon Skill ability of your weapon with **L2/LT** again.

Not all shields behave in this manner, however: quite a few allow you to execute the Weapon Skills of your held weapon without interference. Just keep that quirk in mind when you're examining shields.

THE MENU

Though you can't pause the game, you can bring up a menu with the Options/Start button. Try this to see what's available.

This is how you get to several important screens: System, Status, Inventory, Equipment, and Message.

The System screen has a number of options to explore. Take your time playing around with them until you find the control scheme that is ideal for your playstyle. Focus especially on Camera Speed, Brightness, Camera Axis, and lock-on behavior. All of these choices influence the game considerably, so you need to find the setup that you enjoy the most.

The Status screen lets you look at your character and his or her stats.

The Inventory screen allows you to use some of your tools and to read descriptions for all of the goodies that you find.

Check out the Equipment screen to set up your hotbars, change armor, choose weapons, etc.

The main menu also lets you assign several tools as quick-use shortcuts. These are items that you use fairly frequently, but you don't want them cluttering up your toolbelt in combat. You can freely assign these items from the Inventory screen, and use them directly from the Options/Start menu.

INTERACTION

Use ⊗ on the PS4 and Ⓐ on the Xbox One to interact with objects. This lets you pick up items, open doors, turn cranks, etc.

USE TOOL

Press ◎ on the PS4 and ⊗ on the Xbox One to use whatever tool you have selected. Throw your knives, use an Estus Flask, etc.

DODGE

Tap ◎ on the PS4 and ⓑ on the Xbox One to dodge in whichever direction you're currently moving. If you're standing still, this move causes you to suddenly backstep. Both of these maneuvers are infinitely useful for saving your life. Practice dodging all the time, as it's one of the best ways to survive attacks. Roll behind your enemies, jump back to avoid a heavy attack, or use this to quickly get out of the way of anything that is about to turn you into pudding.

Advanced players learn when it's best to dodge, shield block, and parry, but this is something that takes days or even weeks of play to master. When you're first playing *Dark Souls* games, just dodge the heavier attacks and block the lighter ones. It's a safe way to start your journey toward mastery.

That said, one of the most interesting aspects of dodging is that it does more than get you to quickly move out of the way. There is a small window during your dodge where you won't take damage even if an enemy is swinging at you. This invulnerable period lasts only a fraction of the animation time for the dodge, but it's vital for avoiding massive attacks that are common from invaders and bosses alike.

The dodge action has invulnerability frames: these are the number of visual frames during which your character has invulnerability while dodging. Thinking about things in terms of visual frames for determining timing is a tradition borrowed from other high-skill fighting games.

As a rule of thumb, practice dodging as late as possible when your enemies attack. If you dodge too early, it's still likely that you will take damage.

SPRINTING AND JUMPING

If you hold down ◎/ⓑ, you use Stamina to sprint in whichever direction you're traveling. This lets you explore faster and get away from pursuers. Be careful using all of your Stamina just before a fight begins, but otherwise, feel free to use it frequently.

When you're already sprinting, click the left analog stick to jump. This is rarely needed in the game, but there are a few gaps that you can jump. Often, these lead to extra treasure but are not required for getting through major regions.

ALTERNATE 1H AND 2H

Press ⓐ on the PS4 and ⓨ on the Xbox One to alternate between one-handed and two-handed use of your current item. This makes it easy to switch to heavier attacks briefly, and then go back to using a shield or another weapon when your enemy recovers.

If you press and hold the button, you switch to two-handed use of an item that is in your left hand instead.

It is incredibly powerful to master this switching process. If you're not using a shield at any given moment, swap to your two-handed stance, and deal more damage until you need your shield again. When mastered, you'll find yourself doing this in the middle of battles, even against single foes. Block, swap to the two-handed stance, and beat on your target. Once your enemy is ready to swing again, back off and get your shield ready.

SELECT ITEMS, WEAPONS, AND SPELLS

The D-pad controls your tools, spells, and equipment. You're allowed to equip multiple tools, weapons, shields, and spells, but only a few of them are prepared at a given time. Press down on the D-pad to shift between your equipped tools. Press left to switch items in your left hand, and right for changes to equipment in your right hand. Press up to select from currently Attuned spells.

Practice switching quickly between these items so you have more flexibility in how you approach situations. As a bare minimum, have access to a ranged spell or weapon, a melee weapon, and flasks to heal and restore FPs. This is a baseline that can be expanded based on the region that you're exploring. Are there multiple enemies with the bleed effect down there? Keep a Bloodred Moss Clump on your bar. In poisoned areas, switch that out for a Purple Moss Clump.

Keep in mind that equipped weapons, catalysts, ranged weapons, and shields all affect your total weight, and thus the speed of your dodges. If you're trying to stay nimble, packing six left- and right-hand pieces of equipment isn't a good idea.

Tools do not have an impact on your weight or speed beyond the real time it takes you to cycle through your toolbelt items if you have many selected. Try to keep your toolbelt items list fairly short. You don't want to cycle to a consumable fire-buffing item when you really need to drink from your Estus Flask!

GESTURES

Gestures are normally used as a roleplaying aspect of the game. You start with a modest selection of gestures that let your character animate an action, but various NPCs teach you more of them throughout the game.

These help you cheer on allies that come to help you defeat enemies, or warily give respect to invaders before dueling. Watch out when using any gesture around an invader; it's good to be polite, but not everyone is trustworthy. In fact, you should only bow when opponents keep healthy range before battle. Never expose yourself to an invader that gets a little too close for comfort.

If you realize that you're in danger, roll out of animations. This is certainly better than taking any free shots, although it still leaves you at a slight disadvantage because you've used Stamina and lost the initiative in an encounter.

GAMEPLAY

Now we're getting into the thick of it. This chapter is where the game comes alive. We'll cover combat, movement, evasive tricks, creation your character, and improving them over time.

UNDERSTANDING YOUR STATS AND ATTRIBUTES

Character attributes are very important in *Dark Souls III*. You use Souls to improve your attributes throughout the game, and that is how you are able to deal more damage, survive stronger enemy attacks, use better equipment, and wield the best spells. Read on to learn what all of these attributes do so that you can start planning what you want to do with your character.

The sections ahead talk about scaling, which is the amount of value that you get out of your attribute improvements. Most of the attributes have sweet spots that you really want to get to. Afterward, they'll be useful but not as powerful to improve.

As a general rule, attributes often get a huge amount of improvement up to 20. Between 20 and 40, the scaling improvement is still worthwhile, especially when they're a major focus of your character. After 40, many attributes taper off badly and give you only a little bonus for your hard won Souls.

LEVEL

Your character level is a reflection of the amount of power you've gained. Unlike many roleplaying games, you do NOT get experience or power automatically when you defeat enemies. Instead, you gain Souls. These act as a hybrid of currency and experience. You use them to buy goods, repair items, raise your level, etc. And they can be lost, too! Dying causes you to drop all of your Souls, which means that there is a serious risk of losing all of your current money/experience if you play recklessly.

Your level only rises when you visit the Fire Keeper at Ashen Shrine and invest Souls in your character. This gives you permanent bonuses and prevents those invested Souls from being lost if you die.

The higher your level gets, the easier it is to play the game because you have better and better stats. However, each level costs more and more Souls to purchase, so you can't stay in a weaker area and build up your character without investing a massive amount of time.

GAINING LEVELS

Because the cost for gaining levels increases every time you raise an attribute, it's important to keep in mind that while you can reach the "soft cap" on every attribute eventually, for the bulk of your first playthrough on any character, your starting stats and your target stats matter quite a bit.

You don't need to plan out your character in hard detail; just keep in mind that spreading yourself too thin across a ton of stats tends to make the game a bit harder your first time through.

SOULS

As stated earlier, Souls are a resource that you gain throughout the game. Killing enemies and using special items generate Souls for your character. Do your best to avoid death and to spend your Souls as often as possible. You do not lose items or levels when you die, so these are both safe ways to invest your resources.

REQUIRED SOULS

Required Souls lets you know how many Souls need to be invested for you to gain a level. You cannot partially gain a level, so it's impossible to invest your Souls in an attribute until you reach this threshold.

SPENDING WISELY

If you find yourself close to a level, it's usually worth it to burn a few consumable Soul items to reach the required amount.

On the other hand, if you're a lot further away, investing in extra consumables (arrows, curatives, and the like) is often a good idea. This minimizes the risk of losing a large number of Souls while exploring dangerous new ground.

When it comes to boss fights, you shouldn't be carrying a large Soul load against them to begin with!

HOLLOWING

Hollowing is only acquired by dying while you have a Dark Sigil in your possession. The more Sigils you have when you die, the more Hollowing you gain. Hollowing accrues from your deaths and investigation of the world. Your character looks more and more like a corpse as this stat rises, and there are some events that can only be triggered if you have a certain amount of Hollowing.

The NPCs chapter ("A Few May Help You on Your Path"), discusses the quests that interact with this stat. To remove all Hollowing (but not any carried Dark Sigils), you can use a Purging Stone.

VIGOR

VIGOR SCALING	VIGOR	10	15	20	25	30	35	40	50	99
	HP	523	715	993	1231	1372	1483	1576	1689	1819

HPs and Frost Resistance are controlled by your character's Vigor. Thus, this attribute is a major aspect of your survivability. It's very good for almost all characters to have some investment in Vigor so that you don't die in one or two hits.

That said, you should carefully avoid the temptation to overinvest in Vigor. Longer fights are never going to be in your favor; you want to be able to kill your foes, and Vigor is not going to help you deal more damage, cast better spells, or help you on offense. The goal with this attribute is to have "just enough" to get by. Your skill level and comfort with the game determine that margin, so newer players are probably going to need more Vigor than returning veterans.

It's best if you stop putting Souls into Vigor from 20-27, depending on your comfort with defensive techniques. After this, diminishing returns really hit Vigor hard. Highly skilled players won't need to even push up to 20 Vigor, but you aren't hurting yourself by reaching this moderate range.

For reference, above are a few sample Vigor values to give you an ideal of the scaling. Look how great everything is until you hit the point between 25 and 30. It slows considerably at that time, but it still gives you decent increases for a little bit longer.

INVESTING IN VIGOR

If you're on your first character, raise your Vigor. The difference between two or three hits before death on bosses is often the difference between victory or defeat, and in normal exploration, extra Vigor is super helpful for letting you stay out in the field longer between Bonfire stops.

ENDURANCE

ENDURANCE SCALING	ENDURANCE	10	15	20	25	30	35	40	50	99
	STAMINA	94	102	112	122	134	146	160	161	170

Endurance controls your Stamina and Resistance to lightning and bleeding. Stamina is a very powerful offensive and defensive attribute. Without high Stamina, you cannot block, dodge, or attack as effectively. All of these actions drain your Stamina, and when it's gone, you are a sitting duck for several seconds while you recover.

Once you gain more skill with this game, Endurance becomes just as important for surviving fights as your Vigor. If you have tons of Stamina, it's so much easier to avoid attacks outright by raising your shield or leaping out of the way. No matter how many HPs you have, it's better to avoid damage in the first place.

All characters need Endurance and, over time, you want to have more and more of it. Characters with weapons that have fast melee combos are going to get a great deal out of Endurance because they can stick to an enemy and slice continually whenever the enemy is caught off guard.

Endurance has interesting scaling. Unlike many attributes, it's somewhat slower early on, hits a peak in growth after 30, and then hits a brick wall after 40. This attribute is very useful in New Game Plus and during the late game on any playthrough.

INVESTING IN ENDURANCE

The visible numeric gains to your Stamina from raising Endurance seem small, but really, it just boils down to "Does more Endurance give me an extra swing before exhausting my Stamina bar?" And most of the time, it does with just a few points of investment.

Because openings during boss fights are often limited, you want to be able to pile on as much extra damage as possible in those brief moments, and Endurance lets you do that more effectively than any other stat. Strength might raise your per-hit swing, but what's better: 50 more damage on a strike, or 500 more damage from another strike?

In normal exploration, Stamina is a bit less important since you're usually not in quite as many do-or-die situations like boss fights.

Oh, and don't make the mistake of assuming that "Stamina = melee character." Even if you're focusing on magic, you still need to be able to dodge and attack efficiently with melee weapons for a good portion of the game before your spells become truly lethal, and many enemies are simply dealt with more quickly with a few melee strikes.

ATTUNEMENT

ATTUNEMENT SCALING AND SLOTS

ATTUNEMENT	1-9	10	14	18	24	30	40	50	99
SPELL SLOTS	None	1	2	3	4	5	6	7	10
FP	67	93	120	150	189	233	296	326	450

Attunement raises your FPs and the number of Attunement slots that you receive. This is an attribute for spellcasters. The more you want to push in that direction for your character, the more of this you need. Heavy physical damage dealers can skip Attunement entirely, while hybrid casters and full casters need to get a very solid amount of it.

Though FPs are always useful, the number of slots that you need should heavily determine the Attunement value that you shoot for with your build. Figure out the exact number of spells that you need to prepare, and only get the Attunement that you require. If you aren't going to work with magic at all, remember to create a character with the lowest possible Attunement and never put a single Soul into it.

INVESTING IN ATTUNEMENT

Because FP can be used for Weapon Skills as well as spells, a side benefit to playing a character looking to use magic heavily is an automatic gain in the number of Weapon Skills you can use.

It's generally not worthwhile to raise Attunement solely to use Weapon Skills on a more physical-focused character, simply because your basic attacks are still going to be your primary offense, and Weapon Skills are most often a supplement to your offense, not your primary source of damage.

VITALITY

VITALITY SCALING

VITALITY	10	15	20	25	30	35	40	45	50	99
EQUIP LOAD	50	55	60	65	70	75	80	85	90	139

This attribute controls your Equip Load and Resistance to Poison, and it helps your defense, as well. The heavier your equipment, the more of this you need. This is a very defensive attribute because heavier equipment is essential for your survival against high-damage enemies. If you can't equip that gear, you're not going to benefit from it.

Vitality is another attribute where you're shooting to have just enough of it. Look at your Equip Load and see if it's getting dangerously high. Raise Vitality so that you have your best equipment on and still have a fair bit of headroom.

Do not estimate your necessary Equip Load based on having close to 100% of your total value. Equip Load is trickier than that. At higher percentages, you can still walk, dodge, and sprint. However, your dodge speed and distance become horrible. This affects jumping, as well, so remember to take off your armor if you're having trouble with a given jump.

The lower your Equip Load percentage, the better. If you want to wear really heavy armor, there is only so much you can do. It takes a huge amount of Vitality to compensate for a suit of Winged Knight armor.

Make sure that you have enough Vitality to wear at least a decent lighter suit of armor and have a melee weapon, a shield, and a ranged weapon without topping 50% of your Equip Load. That's a good balance. Stack more Vitality as needed or wanted.

Vitality has a straight line of growth; it never gets any better or worse as it rises. Get what you need, and don't worry about the scaling.

INVESTING IN VITALITY

Low Equip Load and a quick dodge makes you feel more nimble when you're actually playing through the game and is just plain more pleasant than being a lumbering brick wall.

That being said, there are some advantages to being a brick wall at times—if you find yourself struggling with a boss, try changing up your gear.

Swap your light armor load for a full heavy suit of thick plate and a Tower Shield. This isn't the right medicine for every boss, but sometimes, being able to sponge and block a few more hits can make a fight more manageable.

The same goes the other way—if you've been playing as a brute, try swapping to a light suit of armor with a fast dodge and simply avoiding incoming attacks.

LUCK

LUCK SCALING

LUCK	10	15	20	25	30	35	40	45	50	99
ITEM DISCOVERY	110	115	120	125	130	135	140	145	150	199

Luck has a very small impact on the Bleed and Poison 'damage' of your weapons, but the effect is fairly weak.

One other slight benefit is that Luck increases the damage of Hollow Gem infused weapons, and there are a few weapons that gain some damage scaling from Luck.

In general Luck is a luxury stat, it's nice to have, but other attributes are more important for most first time players and fir

IMPORTANT! CHANGING YOUR STATS

Your stats are fixed once you invest in them by spending Souls, but it is possible to reassign all of your Soul Levels by visiting the NPC Rosaria in the Cathedral of the Deep. This can be done a limited number of times each playthrough. If you really don't like how your character turned out, you can fix it.

STRENGTH

Strength raises your Resistance to fire. It is also the primary attribute that determines which heavier weapons you can wield and how much Attack Power you gain when using them. Strength is a major attribute for melee characters. It is either taken in conjunction with Dexterity, or it is more exclusively focused if your build is dedicated toward specific heavy weaponry.

For the easiest melee build, get enough Dexterity to wield the weapons that you find yourself enjoying, and then stop investing in Dexterity after that. Put the rest of your Souls into Strength, and look for weapons that have strong scaling based off of Strength.

If you have high Strength and good weapon scaling, your bonus damage is sometimes much higher than the base damage of the weapon itself!

Regardless of these things, all Strength suffers from diminishing returns after a certain point. Even heavy Strength builds need to support their raw damage with other attributes; otherwise, they can't wear better armor, swing as many times, etc. After getting to 40 in Strength, even weapons with very high Strength scaling start to get tepid results. Make sure that your supporting attributes are up to par before you go much further.

DEXTERITY

Dexterity also adds Attack Power to many weapons. It improves your spellcasting times, reduces falling damage, and is required for wielding a number of items. Several high-speed weapons are based on Dexterity more than Strength, so this can still be the primary damage attribute for quite a few character builds. Dexterity helps with some of the speedier weapons and with your ranged weaponry.

Dexterity builds are often trickier to master compared to pure Strength melee characters. If you are a newcomer to the series, feel free to dabble here, but recognize that this is usually a more challenging path until you've gotten the game mechanics down to a science.

As with all damage attributes, you need to make sure that your Dexterity balances with your other attributes. Once you start to see the damage improvements weakening, put a number of levels into other attributes.

INTELLIGENCE

Intelligence improves spell effects and is required for using Sorcery and some Pyromancy spells (one Blessing requires Intelligence, too). This is a totally disposable attribute for physical damage dealers, but it's the mainstay for dedicated Sorcery casters. Pyromancers need Intelligence, too, but they can afford to treat it as a secondary attribute along with Faith and something for melee damage.

Get enough Attunement and Intelligence to wield the spells that you need the most. Pair this with rings that increase the power of your Sorceries or Pyromancy, and you're going to be in good shape. Modify your melee weapons with Crystal and Simpleton Gems so that they gain Intelligence scaling. This way, you still have some viable damage in melee to complement your spells.

FAITH

Faith is similar to Intelligence in that it is required for certain spells. In this case, Miracles and Pyromancy benefit from Faith (but Sorceries do not). Faith also influences your Resistance to magic and dark-based attacks.

Even if you aren't going for a massive Miracle-based build, it's possible to have a very minor amount of Attunement and Faith and still receive some good benefits from it. There are lower-tier Miracles that heal your character, remove ailments, and buff your weapons. It's very doable to create a character that primarily focuses on physical damage while still benefiting from a minor push into Faith.

An Attunement of 10 gets you a single spell slot, and a Faith of 8 lets you heal and remove ailments. That's almost no Souls invested for a very useful utility bump to your character.

STAMINA

Stamina is like your energy level. It falls when you block, dodge, or launch various attacks. It replenishes quickly once you stop blocking and attacking. You can still move around while restoring your Stamina, so back away from your enemies and let your Stamina return while they try to pursue you.

The green bar at the top of your screen shows your Stamina. Pay close attention to it because running out of Stamina can get you killed very quickly.

You still regenerate Stamina while blocking, but at a reduced rate. Move or roll away and drop your guard to refill your Stamina faster. Several Rings, some armor, and a few spells and consumables can enhance your Stamina regen rate, useful for tough fights.

HP

HPs are your life force. If they're totally depleted, you die, drop your Souls, and return to the last Bonfire that you visited. All of those are troublesome, so you never want to lose your HPs.

The red bar at the top of your screen is a reflection of your current and maximum HPs. Use your Estus Flask to restore lost health, and return to a Bonfire if you start running low on your Estus Flask uses. Some rings can provide limited healing. Miracles are also used to restore health, and a Pyromancy spell can heal you over time. In some areas, there are cauldrons of Estus Soup that you can also drink to restore yourself.

Equipping a Blessed Gem infused weapon or shield grants slight HP regen over time. Should you perish, you lose your Ember and a portion of your maximum health. Using an Ember consumable item, defeating a boss, or successfully participating in multiplayer (co-op or PvP) all restore your Ember and return you to full health.

FP

FPs control your ability to cast spells and use skills. In *Dark Souls III*, even physical damage dealers have need of FP because some of their abilities draw off of it, too.

The blue bar at the top of your screen shows your current and maximum FPs. It's possible to divide your Estus Flask uses so that you have uses that replenish FPs instead of HPs. The more you become a caster, the higher this ratio needs to be so that you can keep your spells going throughout longer and harder engagements.

DIVIDING ESTUS AND ASH ESTUS

For exploring (vs. going after bosses), it's not a bad idea to skew your Estus a little more toward the Ash Estus Flask if you have access to healing magic.

If you can cast healing Miracles or Pyromancy, you can greatly extend your survivability in the field, which is particularly useful earlier in the game when your total Estus charges are limited.

Just keep in mind that healing magic is not the same as near-instant healing from Estus, which is why you usually want a bit more pure Estus when you're tackling a new boss.

EQUIP LOAD

Equip Load is your capacity for carrying and using your equipped weapons and armor. The more you have, the heavier your gear can be without messing up your movements.

To judge whether your Equip Load is in good shape, go into the Equipment screen. On the right side, you find two numbers under your Equip Load: your current value and the maximum value. You want to have your current Equip Load be well under 100% of your maximum. Your character's movements, such as dodging, are influenced by your ratio of weight to maximum Equip Load. If you're over 100%, you can't even try to dodge. That's very, very bad. In the higher percentages of 70-100, you still face some serious penalties. You can dodge, but the movements are sluggish. Instead of gaining a defensive advantage, you might very well end up just as bad off as if you didn't dodge at all.

Your character feels much more mobile when dodging below 50% Equip Load, and the benefits continue to improve as you get lighter and lighter. Rather than looking for a specific value, you always have to wrestle between superior gear and having enough dodge speed and distance to stay safe.

If forced to choose, take the best weapons you need to survive. Don't compromise on that choice.

Then, figure out the Equip Load percentage that feels right to you for dodging. Once you're happy with that percentage, find the armor that gets you the most protection for that percentage, and upgrade to heavier gear whenever you get to raise your Equip Load.

In short: weapons > dodge > heavy armor.

POISE

Poise determines how much damage you can take without having your actions interrupted. Too little of this makes your character quite vulnerable to interruption. If you have fast weapons and great reflexes, this isn't quite as important (though it's always good to have). For weapons with longer animation times, it's vital. Being interrupted in the middle of your slow attacks puts you at a massive disadvantage.

Heavier, high-end armor helps you get your Poise up. If you're going to use extremely heavy weapons and armor, make sure that you have plenty of Vigor and high Poise, and load up on regular Estus Flasks. Your fights won't be pretty, but they'll splatter enemies that dare to stab you.

ITEM DISCOVERY

Item Discovery controls the chance that an item will appear after you defeat a monster. Due to more frequent drops, higher Item Discovery gets you access to more materials for upgrading equipment (among other things), so your character's progression is aided by very high Luck.

The Covetous Gold Serpent Ring raises this value when it's equipped, and using Rusted Coins or Rusted Gold Coins temporarily improves this value by a large amount.

TANKING AND POISE

Dark Souls is not a game where you can simply tank through damage and then retaliate. Poise lets you take hits and continue your offense, but even the heaviest armor can be flinched with hard hits, and absorbing all the punishment that foes can dish out is not a winning strategy.

Poise is another tool in your arsenal for dealing damage, not avoiding it.

By trading out light weight and quicker dodges for thick armor and slow dodges, you also gain more Poise, which can be used to ram home your attacks.

This is particularly important with heavy weapons, but it's also relevant for continued attack strings with lighter weapons.

Poise is also meaningful in PvP fights, where a flinch can interrupt a critical attack or let a killing blow through.

Poise generally works best on small to medium-sized enemies. Truly massive foes and bosses usually hit hard enough to interrupt even high Poise loadouts. In those situations, block or dodge.

ATTACK POWER

Attack Power shows the total damage inflicted by your various weapons if they strike a target without any Reduction. This value is a combination of all damage types that the weapon inflicts (physical, magical, etc.). A higher value here is always a good thing. To raise the value, have the Blacksmith upgrade the item and increase any attributes that contribute to the weapon's damage output.

Total Attack Power for a weapon might involve quite a few things. The base value is simply a matter of the weapon itself and the number of times it has been reinforced. Then, you add in a scaled amount of damage based on any pertinent attributes (this can include any or all of the following: Strength, Dexterity, Intelligence, Faith, and Luck).

Even with this information, you still don't know all the factors about a weapon's damage output. Unlisted are a weapon's swing time and Stamina cost per swing. These heavily impact your damage totals, as well. A weapon that deals 500 damage per swing might pale in comparison to another weapon that deals 350 a swing but takes half the time and Stamina to finish its attack.

Never judge your weaponry just by the numbers. In *Dark Souls* games, the movelist of a weapon is everything. You don't know a thing about each weapon until you've tried it out. You'll probably read that statement a number of times, but it's one of the most important pieces of advice that can be given.

"GOOD WEAPONS"

One quirk (and it's a good one) of the *Dark Souls* series is that almost any weapon is viable for a full playthrough.

Now, this does not mean that every weapon is just as easy as any other, or that any one weapon is "the best" against every target—only that you can take any basic weapon in the game, upgrade it, and upgrade your stats to suit it and use it effectively.

The cool part about this is it leaves a ton of room for personal exploration of weaponry. Using a spear feels very different from using a greatsword, the same with a mace vs. a dagger.

RESISTANCES AND ARMOR

Resistances and armor determine how affected your character is by bleeding, poison, frost, and curses. Resistances are controlled by your attributes, and your armor value is equipment-based. The more you have of each, the better. All of these are situational because not all enemies inflict these status effects. When dealing with adversaries that have them, prioritize equipment with the highest possible armor values against the effect in question.

Bleeding causes sudden sharp spikes of HP loss. Poison and Toxic effects deal damage over time, though Toxic nastier and harder to cure.

Frost slows your character, and dampens Stamina regen, making it very hard to avoid enemy attacks and respond in kind. This indirectly gets you killed because you can't get out of the way when foes attack you.

Curse effects are quite rare, but they're also frightening. If your curse bar fills all the way up, your character dies immediately.

DEFENSE AND REDUCTION

These defensive stats show you how strong your character is against specific types of attacks (strike, slash, thrust, magical, etc.). Your defense against each is determined by your character's attributes, whereas your equipment controls your Reduction. In both cases, higher is better, and you want to get as much as you can of each.

DEFENSIVE PLANNING

Continuing the discussion about defenses in *Dark Souls*, it's worth noting that even the heaviest armor in the game can only help you tank an extra few hits from truly nasty opponents.

Good defense does help you survive a lot of weaker hits, though, and you can definitely feel a difference in survivability against enemies earlier in the game if you return later at a higher level wearing stronger armor.

Remember that raising your level with any stat increases your defenses, so simply leveling up as you play through the game makes you a bit tougher, even if you stick to lightweight armor.

Don't obsess too much over small changes in the raw defense on armor, though. The weight and its extra status defenses are often more important than a few extra points of physical defenses.

If you do want to focus on heavy defense, you really need to load up to move the needle. If you're struggling in an area or against a specific boss, try changing your armor suit and see if a different approach feels better.

ATTUNEMENT SLOTS

This determines the number of spells that your character can have prepared simultaneously. Note that more powerful spells take up multiple slots. Therefore, it's useful to have a little bit more than you think you need in case you find something especially good and don't want to drop anything else in your arsenal.

COVENANT

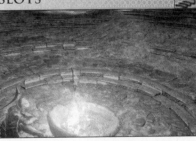

The Covenants in *Dark Souls III* each have useful rewards, and you improve your relations with the factions by earning items their masters approve of. You deliver these items to the shrines or NPCs of that faction, earning rewards when you deliver 10 and 30 of their favored items.

The Covenant line on your status page simply shows which Covenant you're currently serving. This is determined by the Covenant item that you equip in the appropriate slot on your character page.

CREATING YOUR CHARACTER

Now that you know what the stats do, it's time to create a character. In *Dark Souls* games, this process has a great deal of bearing on your first hour or two of play, but the choices you make only have limited relevance after that. Instead of being locked into a character class, you're merely deciding on a gender, visual appearance, and a starting set of attributes that you can modify to a great extent as you level.

STARTING CHOICES

Select New Game, and watch the introductory movie when you're ready to begin. This takes you to a screen where you figure out your first character. You can make others later if you want, or you can stick with your first character for multiple plays through the game.

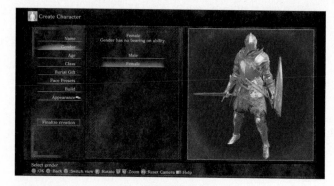

BASIC CUSTOMIZATION

Choose a suitable name for your character, their gender, and an age. These have no influence on the game's progression.

If you want more control over the aspects of your character, use Face Presets and Build for major changes, or click on Appearance to go into the main engine for selecting your voice and visual attributes.

Make a character you like looking at, you'll be spending a lot of time with them! Later in the game, the Covenant leader Rosaria allows you to change your appearance a limited number of times per playthrough.

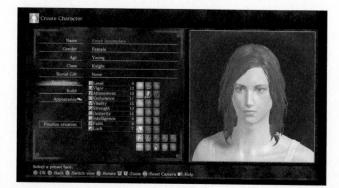

CLASSES ONLY MATTER FOR A SHORT TIME

This leaves class and Burial Gift as the only two things that remain. Burial Gifts are starting items. You can take one from this list, or nothing at all. There aren't any powerful items. The Life Ring gives you bonus HPs and its usage lasts longer than most of these items because it's a ring instead of a tool. Diving Blessing is hard to obtain otherwise, so that is a decent choice, as well. No matter what you take, you're not going to hurt your character or regret your choice.

BURIAL GIFT ITEM	ADVICE
None	There is no real reason to pick this, unless you want more of a challenge right off the bat.
Life Ring	An excellent choice because it is a permanent item. This helps you for hours of the early game.
Divine Blessing	A single-use item, but with the power to fully restore HPs and to cure ailments. This is a very good choice if you're confident in your early game and want something for later.
Hidden Blessing	Fully restores FPs. Similar to the Divine Blessing, this is a good later-game choice if you're unconcerned about your starting needs.
Black Firebomb	A decent thrown weapon, but it doesn't have any lasting value.
Fire Gem	Used to upgrade weaponry. Add Fire to an early melee weapon.
Sovereignless Soul	For a person who just wants extra Souls for the first time they get to the Firelink Shrine, this is very solid. A good choice for anyone who wants an early game boost but doesn't need tools or equipment.
Rusted Gold Coin	A single-use item to help with Item Discovery. This won't get you very much by itself.
Cracked Red Eye Orb	Gives you a single chance to invade another player. Ideal only for hardcore PvPers who want to get their blades wet that much sooner.
Young White Branch	Not a powerful option. It's a single-use item that lets you hide.

You might already know this, but your class is just a starting point in *Dark Souls III*. It determines your initial gear and attributes, but everything is still possible over time. The way you build your attributes and the equipment you use is everything. Any starting class can become a melee fighter, a ranged attacker, a spellcaster, or a hybrid of everything. Always plan ahead, but know that it's possible to shift your strategy midstream if it's absolutely essential.

The starting classes are listed below.

KNIGHT

Best start for:	LEVEL	9
Beginners	Vigor	12
	Attunement	10
	Endurance	11
	Vitality	15
Equipment:	Strength	13
Long Sword,	Dexterity	12
Knight Shield,	Intelligence	9
Knight Armor Set	Faith	9
	Luck	7

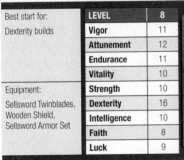

One of the easiest starting classes to begin with, the Knight has a decent shield, strong armor, and stats that favor a direct approach to problems. You can invest in a basic Miracle without changing your stats, and basic melee and ranged combat are both doable.

There isn't a single downside or tough spot for Knights; they're a wonderful starting point for beginners. You get a very good shield, higher-quality armor than your rivals, and a completely solid weapon, as well. You're tough, and you can still deal damage.

MERCENARY

Best start for:	LEVEL	8
Dexterity builds	Vigor	11
	Attunement	12
	Endurance	11
	Vitality	10
Equipment:	Strength	10
Sellsword Twinblades,	Dexterity	16
Wooden Shield,	Intelligence	10
Sellsword Armor Set	Faith	8
	Luck	9

Mercenaries are a fast melee class with the potential to get involved in ranged damage as soon as they get a bit of equipment. You're likely to go in this direction if you're interested in trying lighter armor, Dexterity builds, and perhaps a tiny amount of magic. Not as survivable as the Knight, nor as aggressive as a Warrior, this is a tougher choice unless you know from the beginning that you want to favor a Dexterity character.

If you want to check out dual-wield weaponry as soon as you begin, a Mercenary's Sellsword Twinblades can do that for you. They're a lot of fun.

WARRIOR

Best start for:	LEVEL	7
Strength builds	Vigor	14
	Attunement	6
	Endurance	12
	Vitality	11
Equipment:	Strength	16
Battle Axe, Round	Dexterity	9
Shield, Northern	Intelligence	8
Armor Set	Faith	9
	Luck	11

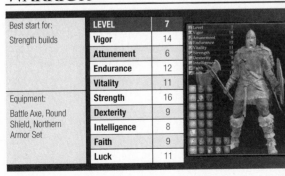

With high health, damage output, a strong weapon, and decent armor, Warriors are likely to be quite popular. Their extremely low Attunement means that it's going to take them a long time to become even weak casters, so avoid these characters if you want to dabble in any magical spells.

Warriors are ideal for a pure Strength character. If you favor heavy melee and direct solutions, you're going to be pleased with your choice. The Battle Axe is somewhat slow for a traditionally one-handed weapon, but it's high on damage. The Round Shield and Northern Armor Set aren't wonderful, but they'll serve you just fine.

HERALD

Best start for:	LEVEL	9
Melee/Faith hybrids	Vigor	12
	Attunement	10
	Endurance	9
	Vitality	12
Equipment:	Strength	12
Heal Aid Spell, Spear,	Dexterity	11
Talisman (Catalyst),	Intelligence	8
Kite Shield, Herald	Faith	13
Armor Set	Luck	11

Heralds give you options for healing and some survivability straight from the beginning. They're a decent option for players who want to try out melee and Miracles without dedicating themselves fully to either route.

Having a longer weapon and healing means that your Herald is more likely to survive engagements than some of the other options. Your damage output isn't stellar, but you are hard to burst down. The downside is that you have longer fights.

THIEF

Best start for:	LEVEL	5
Exploring ranged and	Vigor	10
melee combat	Attunement	11
	Endurance	10
	Vitality	9
Equipment:	Strength	9
Bandit's Knife, Short	Dexterity	13
Bow, Iron Round	Intelligence	10
Shield, Deserter Armor	Faith	8
Set, 30 Wood Arrows	Luck	14

Thieves begin with a dagger and a bow. This lets you practice ranged combat and melee without having to wait. Your learning curve will be steeper than some, but this pays dividends later as you become proficient in more combat types very quickly.

Thieves start at a lower level than almost any other class, but that isn't necessarily a problem. Although your first boss fight may be tougher, you have a huge amount of flexibility in determining your early build. Thieves aren't very strong outside of their starting Dexterity, which means that you can go anywhere with them almost immediately and not feel like there are many wasted Souls. Like the Deprived, there are upsides and downsides to this.

Thieves do have a modest problem that should be mentioned. Having Luck as a high starting attribute is a bit of an issue. Luck is fun and is good for farming items, but it doesn't help your survivability very much, nor does it end battles any faster. So, you won't have a strong character in the early stages. You must learn how to fight intelligently as soon as you begin (though maybe that's a hidden virtue in its own way).

ASSASSIN

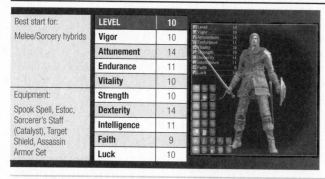

Best start for:	LEVEL	10
Melee/Sorcery hybrids	Vigor	10
	Attunement	14
	Endurance	11
	Vitality	10
Equipment:	Strength	10
Spook Spell, Estoc,	Dexterity	14
Sorcerer's Staff	Intelligence	11
(Catalyst), Target	Faith	9
Shield, Assassin	Luck	10
Armor Set		

Assassins have basic melee and Sorcery as soon as the game begins. They get to start with two Attunement slots (a rarity), and they know how to cast Spook.

Assassins get a good thrusting weapon that is fast and makes up for moderate hits with good combos of blows. To enhance this further, your Spook spell lets you creep up on enemies and start fights greatly in your advantage. You have weak armor, so this is important because Assassins don't do as well against groups of foes that rush together.

SORCERER

Best start for:	LEVEL	6
Full Sorcery hybrids	Vigor	9
(challenging)	Attunement	16
	Endurance	9
	Vitality	7
Equipment:	Strength	7
Soul Arrow, Heavy Soul	Dexterity	12
Arrow, Mail Breaker,	Intelligence	16
Sorcerer's Staff	Faith	7
(Catalyst), Leather Shield,	Luck	12
Sorcerer Armor Set		

Sorcerers are dedicated Sorcery characters. Their initial Attunement and Intelligence makes them a very awkward choice unless this is the route that you want to push. They have two slots and two spells, weak armor, and very low HPs. Even if magic is your planned forte, consider taking another caster unless you already know what you're doing. The Sorcerer is one of the harder choices in the beginning in *Dark Souls III*.

Your weak armor and poor shield mean that direct combat is very dangerous until you learn how to dodge well and keep foes away from you.

Pyromancer

	LEVEL	8
Best start for:	Vigor	11
Melee and magic hybrids	Attunement	12
	Endurance	10
	Vitality	8
Equipment:	Strength	12
Fireball, Hand Axe,	Dexterity	9
Pyromancy Flame (Catalyst), Caduceus	Intelligence	14
Round Shield,	Faith	14
Pyromancer Armor Set	Luck	7

Pyromancers are interesting characters. They need both Intelligence and Faith to a fair degree, and they also have to put points into some of their direct melee stats. This hybrid build takes a while to figure out, but the results are potentially quite powerful because of the flexibility that you gain.

Pyromancers start off with very nice offense options. Your ranged spell deals quite a bit of damage, and your Hand Axe is easily good enough to get the job done in short-range combat. You need to watch out for return attacks, but otherwise, you're in good shape. Win by taking the initiative and killing enemies quickly so that they don't outlast your modest HPs and armor.

This build promotes very specific types of weapon upgrades. If you follow this all the way through your game, make very careful choices when you're infusing your weaponry. You need to find gems that take advantage of your complex, mixed attributes. Don't get something that pushes your weapon into a single-attribute scaling set if it robs the item of your other decent attributes.

Cleric

	LEVEL	7
Best start for:	Vigor	10
Miracle builds	Attunement	14
	Endurance	9
	Vitality	7
Equipment:	Strength	12
Heal, Force, Mace,	Dexterity	8
Cleric's Sacred Chime (Catalyst), Blue	Intelligence	7
Wooden Shield, Cleric	Faith	16
Armor Set	Luck	13

This dedicated Miracle character will usually build with Strength, Faith, and at least a decent amount of Attunement. Because of a Cleric's higher survivability compared to a Sorcerer, this is not as unfriendly a choice for new players. It's still harder to try out than a basic Knight, but if you love the idea of a Miracle-based character, you aren't going to waste any stats. The Knight and Herald, on the other hand, already have way more invested in attributes that you won't use as much. This lets a typical Cleric build toward their goals a bit faster.

Balance your FP use carefully. If you cast Force too often, you won't have anything left to heal your character. Save Force for emergencies, and let most of your early FPs work toward healing and sustainability.

Deprived

	LEVEL	1
Best start for:	Vigor	10
Masochists	Attunement	10
	Endurance	10
	Vitality	10
Equipment:	Strength	10
Club, Plank Shield,	Dexterity	10
Loincloth	Intelligence	10
	Faith	10
	Luck	10

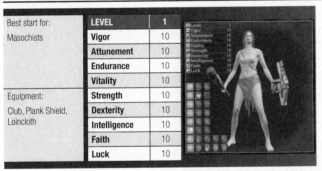

If this is your first time playing a *Dark Souls* game, just go ahead and stop looking at this class. Deprived begin the game at the lowest possible level and can build toward anything they want. Their early hour or two in the game is potentially very tough because they have no good equipment and no particular skills, and there aren't any great rewards for being them. They're simply there as a challenge.

You might think that they have an advantage by being "level one" in terms of building in the direction that you want. That's sort of not true, though; it's half true. Stop for a second and look at their starting attributes. Everything is a 10. Though you get a few easy levels to invest anywhere you want, you don't have the advantage of dumping a weak stat that you don't care about. This is a bit complex, so more explanation is warranted.

Look at the Warrior. Notice that they have very low Attunement, and somewhat low Dexterity, Intelligence, and Faith. That is why they have such high Vigor and Strength. Every class, when adjusted for level, has the same amount of attribute points. The Deprived doesn't really benefit from being level 1 because their flat attribute starting points ensure that they can't min-max at all. It's good to have low stats in some areas because that lets you have higher starting points for the attributes that you really care about. Flat 10s make your career tougher throughout the entire playthrough of the game.

To make a long story short—Deprived are very tough to play unless you want the game to kick you around a lot.

FINISHING

When you're happy with all of the starting elements, finalize your character, and load into *Dark Souls III*. Prepare yourself for battle.

CHARACTER BUILDS

Deciding how to level your character can be intimidating if you're new to *Dark Souls*. This section is here to provide you with some guidance.

While *Dark Souls* leans heavily on the "action" part of "action RPG," there is still very meaningful growth and development of your character over the course of the game.

Straight power gains tend to be fairly modest individually as you gain levels and upgrade weapons, but their overall impact by the end of your first playthrough is significant. You can revisit old areas to flex your new muscles occasionally to see just how much tougher you are.

Beyond simple numeric gains in your power, however, the breadth of options available to you for customizing your character is immense.

The massive amount of equipment you can find in the world of *Dark Souls III* and the range of options that you have for developing your stats over the course of a single playthrough allow for an absolutely huge number of possible builds.

While these generally boil down to fairly simple choices (Str or Dex weapons, heavily using one of the three magic types, which four rings you equip, which armor you wear), the specifics tend to feel quite different in practice.

A heavily armored character with a hefty Greatshield is typically sluggish but sturdy, as you usually can't get your weight limit high enough to have fast movement until much later in the game.

Likewise, a lightly armored character emphasizing Dex and using a quick Straight or Thrusting Sword and a fast bow with some supportive Sorceries plays and feels very different.

You can also make use of two-handed or dual-wielded weapons, eschewing the use of a shield in favor of straight evasion and devastating counterattacks when your foes leave openings.

Even simply changing your primary weapon and making use of unique Weapon Skills can feel different on a second playthrough.

All three of the magic branches (Sorcery, Pyromancy, and Miracles) offer useful utility spells for any character, and with a significant investment in magical attributes and some rings and armor, you can gain more special effects that amplify your magic power.

YOUR BUILD IS NOT YOUR CLASS!

Remember, your build is defined by your stat allocations as you level, the equipment you wear, and the upgrades you invest in your equipment.

Your class only serves as a jumping off point, giving you an early start on the stats that you want to prioritize and possibly some key early equipment that you might not be able to find in the game until later.

At very high Soul Levels, once you have raised many attributes up to their soft caps, characters are defined almost entirely by the equipment you choose to use. This tends to happen once you push into New Game Plus territory on a single character.

However, on your first playthrough, your starting attributes and stat choices as you level do matter quite a bit because you aren't likely to have enough Souls to simply raise everything equally for quite some time.

GENERAL BUILDS

For a brand-new player, either the generalist jack or the thuggish brute are probably the two easiest styles of build to play.

The generalist is a little tougher, but you get to experience all facets of the game, and that's both a good time and a great way to explore how different weapons, spells, armor sets, and shield types actually feel.

Casters can be strong, but they typically require a lot more levels to even use the more powerful spells to begin with. Because you don't unlock many of the spells and supporting gear until later (sometimes very late) in the game, you are likely to find that playing a caster for much of the early game amounts to throwing a few Soul Arrows or Fireballs occasionally.

In general, a pure caster works best on a New Game Plus run once you have access to the majority of the spells in the game and enough Attunement and Int/Faith to make use of your magical arsenal.

Don't let this dissuade you from choosing to pursue magic on your first run if that's what you enjoy, however. You can always shift gears with a character at any point in the game if you have a lot of trouble. At worst, you need to do some Soul farming to move your stats around a bit.

If you really don't like how your build turned out, you can visit the NPC Rosaria and completely reassign your attributes.

ARCHETYPES

THE JACK OF ALL TRADES

The dabbler, the dilettante, this style of build invests a little bit into a lot of areas.

Raise your stats just enough to equip a shiny new weapon, just enough to wear a favored suit of armor comfortably, and just enough to test out a new spell.

Playing this way means you gain less benefit from scaling effects on upgraded weapons. Also, you are likely to have a bit less raw HP and Stamina than a more focused character, and certainly less FP and Int/Faith than a heavy caster.

However, in exchange, you gain the ability to do just about anything in the game, at least to a degree. You can use Str or Dex weapons, even some Int/Faith weapons; you can use bows and crossbows; you can use specialized Catalysts; and you can make use of all three schools of magic.

WEAPONRY

Whatever you like! Try to keep both a one-handed and a two-handed weapon around that you enjoy using. If you're having any trouble against a specific enemy or boss, switch to the other weapon and see if you have an easier fight.

As far as upgrades go, because the heavy stat scaling upgrades won't give you as much benefit, you may want to look at upgrades that have little (or even no) scaling effects and simply give strong raw damage values.

Mix up your damage types, as well: both basic physical attacks and your elemental damage. Keeping a magic weapon in your back pocket for fighting flame demons or a fire weapon to incinerate flammable foes is just a good tactic.

For ranged weapons, try to make use of specialized elemental ammo; it can make up for some of the damage boosts you don't gain from straight stat scaling on your bow. You could also go with Raw, Fire, or Deep weapons and crossbows to commit wholeheartedly to ignoring scaling altogether.

ARMOR

If there's any build that skews toward a non-committal, middle of the road weight limit, this is the one. A sturdy regular shield with 100% physical absorption and a mix of armor that keeps you somewhere below 70% load should suit you just fine for the majority of the game.

Likewise, your ring set can essentially be anything that supports your current favored loadout. General-purpose rings work best, but you can always try out specialized rings that benefit ranged combat, magic, parrying and counterattacks, or whatever suits your current gear.

This is another area where playing a generalist can benefit you down the line when you try other character concepts, as this archetype is most likely to have the stats available to dabble in every area of play that rings can enhance.

THE BRUTE

Pump your Str, your HP, your Stamina, and occasionally your Vitality if your burden is getting too high. Smash everything under heavy clubs and massive swords. You can pretty much ignore Attunement, Int, Faith, and Luck.

If your chosen class happens to be very close to a stat requirement for useful early spells, go ahead and grab them—same goes for bow/crossbow usage. But don't go out of your way. At most, you want a backup healing spell or support buff; otherwise, everything gets pounded into dust.

Simple, straightforward, and very effective, this is probably the easiest build to progress through the game. If you are both new and you don't find a generalist approach appealing, this sort of focused setup can cruise through early game fights that late-blooming builds may struggle with, and it still scales perfectly well into the late game, if perhaps not with quite as much finesse.

WEAPONRY

Hammers and Great Hammers are ideal for this, with natural Str requirements and scaling. However, you can also take a meaty Greatsword or Ultra Greatsword or any solid one-handed weapon you enjoy using and slap a Heavy Gem on it to maximize its Str scaling.

ARMOR

Find the heaviest armor you can bear to use and the earliest Greatshield with 100% physical absorption and high Stability.

As you progress through the game, keep boosting your armor's weight as your Vitality improves, and keep an eye out for tougher Greatshields with higher Stability.

Once you have some spare materials and Souls for upgrades aren't a strain on you, go ahead and max out your shield's upgrades. Shield upgrades don't provide much of a statistical benefit, but they do boost Stability slightly. If you're going for your best impersonation of a brick wall, you want all the defensive benefits you can get.

If you want to double-down on your defenses, you can equip rings that provide defensive benefits just to squeeze every bit of possible mitigation and effective HP out of your build.

If you find that really heavy armor and a Greatshield is too much to handle early on either in terms of speed or stats, just go for heavier mid-weight armor and a normal shield with good defenses and block values. You can always squeeze into the heavy stuff later as your Vitality increases, or equip it for specific boss fights or tough areas when you don't mind the decreased mobility in favor of better Poise, defense, and shield-blocking Stability.

THE FENCER

Nimble and agile, this archetype focuses on using Dex-based weaponry, bows, Weapon Skills that provide mobility or rapid attacks, and added status effects from hitting enemies repeatedly.

To maximize your mobility, keep your weight as low as possible. Emphasize dodge rolls, parries, and backstabs to get the most out of weapons with enhanced critical damage.

Other than Dex, you want to raise Vigor and Endurance for HP and Stamina, but your Vitality requirements are generally going to be lower because you aren't wearing or using as much heavy gear.

You can dump the saved points from Vitality directly back into Dex/Vigor/Endurance if you want, or consider investing in either Sorcery or Miracles, with a bit of Int or Faith. Examine the spell lists and see if any relatively cheap spells appeal to you.

Another option is to invest some points in Luck, which provides slight benefits to bleeding and poison application. A few weapons are also influenced by Luck, so there are some gear loadouts that can benefit from this approach.

WEAPONRY

High Dex scaling weaponry like Daggers, Thrusting Swords, Curved Swords, Katanas, or even Claws are all suitable. You want light, fast weapons that let you stay mobile in combat. Look for weapons that have critical values above 100. Added bleed, poison, or frost (as well as elemental damage) are all desirable because you can stack up added effects quickly with a flurry of blows.

Additionally, the high Dex bows work great with this setup, and you can get some pretty solid ranged damage as a "free" benefit of focusing heavily on Dex.

You can also use the Sharp Gem to convert a weapon to stronger Dex scaling, or if you really want to push the status effect gimmick hard, apply a Blood or Poison gem to push bleeding or poison application even higher.

Another viable option is making use of the paired dual-wield weapons. The majority of them are Dex-focused; only the Twin Axes and Hammers lean toward Str.

ARMOR

Look for lightweight armor and a light one-handed shield, selecting anything that can keep you under 50% load. If you are choosy about your gear and raise Vitality a bit, you can potentially even go under 25% load for really nimble movement.

A shield with parry is a good choice if you plan on really emphasizing counterattacks. If you find that parrying is simply too difficult, go with a shield that allows Weapon Skills so you can make use of your main hand arts while keeping your shield active.

Keep an eye out for rings that provide boosts to critical damage effects (backstabs and parry counterattacks), as well as rings that grant benefits for rapidly and continuously attacking.

THE CASTER

Any character focusing heavily on spellcasting falls under the caster archetype, though whether you make use of Sorcery, Pyromancy, or Miracles (or even a mix of all three) heavily influences how your character feels and the types of weapons and equipment that you use.

This is by far the most difficult archetype to get off the ground if you insist on trying to use spells as your primary offense. Late in the game, with a developed character, high stats, lots of gear, and access to many spells, this becomes considerably easier.

Early on, however, you are typically constrained to one or two basic attack spells and a single support spell, with a limited FP pool at a time when your Estus Flask charges are restricted, as well.

The main trick to playing a caster is to recognize that you don't need to only cast spells to progress. You can and should still make heavy use of melee combat, ranged weapons, and tools, just like other archetypes.

There are non-scaling weapons you can find or create using Raw, Fire, or Deep gems. Once your Int, Faith, or both are at a higher level, you can pursue caster-focused gem upgrades (Crystal, Chaos, Blessed, and the like).

Using a non-scaling weapon early eases some of the pain of not having a high Str or Dex to gain "free" damage from. Also, you can start the game with a Fire Gem as a Burial Gift, giving you easy access to a solid weapon immediately.

Having access to ranged offensive spells can be quite useful against some enemies that are vulnerable to elemental damage. While you may find that some foes are simply too fast (or some bosses too dangerous) to use attack magic against easily, you can always make use of utility spells.

Be careful not to overinvest in Attunement and Int or Faith early in the game. Try to get your Vigor and Endurance to a comfortable level so you can still fight enemies with reasonable HP and Stamina.

SPELLCASTING SPEED

Dexterity provides a very small boost to spellcasting speed. It generally isn't worth focusing on as a pure caster, but if you happen to be playing a fencer-style character with naturally Dexterity, consider it a fringe benefit.

The only other sources of casting speed increases are two different Catalysts (the Witchtree Branch for Sorceries and the Saint-tree Bellvine for Miracles) and the Sage Ring, which provides a hidden bonus to Dexterity that only applies to casting speed.

The differences tend to be a handful of frames of animation for any combination of boosters, but when you're trying to dodge nasty incoming attacks, even fractions of a second can save you from incoming pain.

WEAPONRY

Make use of non-scaling weapons early in the game, followed by caster-attribute weapons later. There are also caster-specific weapons that can act as Catalysts while still allowing you to keep a weapon at the ready. These special tools generally have less Spell Buff than equivalent Catalysts, but they are more flexible and allow for quick spell usage mid-combat while still letting you use a shield or two-hand wield the weapon.

There are quite a few different Catalysts that provide unique benefits for Sorcery and Miracles, though only Pyromancy has the single Flame item.

Experiment with your equipment positioning. If you keep your Catalyst in your right-hand slot, you can keep your shield up in your left; if you use your Catalyst in your left hand, you can keep a weapon up in your right.

Depending on the spells you are using (and how comfortable you are with dodging vs. blocking), you may find that you prefer to have your magic always at hand. Alternately, you may be comfortable swapping it in and out, to either your left or right hand.

ARMOR

Because your points are stretched by investing in Attunement and one or more caster stats, you will likely find investing heavily in Vitality problematic, at least early in the game.

Consequently, favoring lighter armor is natural, as well as a small or medium shield.

There are quite a few rings that provide benefits to one school of spellcasting. Combining various weapons, Catalysts, rings, and even some armor that gives magical benefits can all boost the power of your spells.

Unfortunately, most of these won't be accessible to you until fairly far into the game, so really stacking them up is limited to the late game (or New Game Plus).

Again, don't overemphasize "caster gear" over other options that are likely to help you more in early game combat. Keep a keen eye on the damage output of your offensive spells compared with the weapons you have access to, and swap around your gear appropriately.

CHOOSING EQUIPMENT

WEAPONS

Your weapon has a huge impact on how your character plays. Each of the major weapon categories (from Daggers to Greatswords to Hammers to Spears) has completely different movesets, speeds, and Weapon Skills. Within those categories, the individual weapons also have their own quirks, sometimes varying the moveset slightly, requiring different attributes than the norm, providing some unique magical benefit, or possessing an unusual or entirely unique Weapon Skill.

There is no wrong choice of weapon. It can be overwhelming to worry that you might be messing up by choosing to level your basic Broadsword or Mace early in the game, but don't worry— you're not.

PVP WEAPON CHOICE

However, we'd be remiss in not noting that some weapons are definitely easier to use than others in PvP. Generally, common weapons with easy reads are more easily parried and evaded by veteran players.

Weapon categories a bit off the beaten path can be useful PvP toys, though this is more relevant if you're heavily into dueling—run-of-the-mill invasions against most players aren't always going to pit you against a hardened PvP target.

Any weapon in the game can see you through, even the humble Dagger. You may certainly struggle against some foes or bosses, but in the absolute worst case, you can always farm up more Souls and materials to level another weapon.

In the course of a single playthrough without much farming but with fairly thorough exploration, you can expect to level several weapons comfortably to high level, and at least one weapon to max without trouble.

Early in the game, spend time experimenting with different weapon categories just to get a feel for their basic movesets. Once you find one you like, pick a weapon in that category, and then go ahead and enhance and infuse it.

Later, after you are more experienced and you have seen more of the weapons offered in the game, you can start a new character with a specific weapon in mind that you want to build around stat-wise.

RANGED WEAPONS AND TOOLS

A bow should be a weapon used by any build, unless you have a very specific reason to avoid doing so. You don't need to invest heavily into Dex to use the earlier bows in the game, and any bow and a stack of cheap arrows can make some really difficult or annoying encounters become considerably easier or entirely trivial.

A more serious Dex build with a leveled bow and a stack of more powerful arrows can inflict some serious damage at a distance—definitely explore such a build at some point, even if it's not on your first character.

As far as tools go, don't skimp out on consumables. Later in the game, when you are leveled and have a good set of equipment and useful support spells, simple Firebombs and Throwing Knives are less important. But early in the game, magical coatings for your weapons and throwing weapons can be a huge boon against difficult enemies.

Throwing weapons gain stat-scaling effects in *Dark Souls III*, so a highly skilled character can get some extra mileage out of the basic throwing weaponry.

Early consumables are generally pretty cheap, and farming up enough Souls to buy big stacks of them isn't excessively time-consuming.

Later in the game, you have no excuse for fighting enemies with nasty status attacks without a stack of curatives on hand.

ARMOR

Your chosen armor set largely boils down to a simple choice: light or heavy?

Light armor typically lets you stay under 50% weight limit, giving you quick dodge rolls and better mobility. It also often has higher elemental Resistances than heavier armor.

Heavy armor gives better physical protection, and the toughest heavy armor can make normal enemy encounters a lot less threatening when you have a deep HP pool. The downside here is that keeping your burden level low is tough without really high stats.

There aren't really armor classifications, as far as actual light/medium/heavy armor. It's generally relative to your personal weight limit and what sort of mobility and dodge roll you find most comfortable.

Likewise, shields are generally a tradeoff between weight, total protection percentages, and Stability, a key stat for blocking powerful attacks.

If you're super confident in your dodging and parrying, a suit of light armor and a basic Buckler may be all you need throughout the entire game. On the other hand, if you find certain enemies, areas, or bosses difficult to evade, a heavier suit of armor and a tougher shield may make for easier combat.

There's nothing stopping you from swapping armor around at any time, so feel free to mix and match armor pieces from different sets to reach a comfortable weight level. If you have trouble with a specific fight, try raising or lowering your weight and defense, and see how you fare.

POISE

Heavier armor also typically grants more Poise, which is your ability to keep an attack going without flinching, even if you take some damage.

Even the highest Poise levels won't stop you from getting knocked on your butt by hard-hitting enemies, but moderate to high Poise levels can prevent interruptions from glancing hits or slight area damage.

Wearing light armor keeps you more nimble, but it's very easy to be interrupted by any enemy attack.

Favor higher Poise values if you are planning on using weapons with hard-hitting but slow attacks—you don't want to get interrupted when you're swinging a massive chunk of metal at your target's head.

RINGS

Rings provide a bevy of useful supportive abilities, increasing your defense or offense, providing various useful utility effects, and generally acting to enhance any style of play (heavy physical, ranged, spellcasting, evasive, and so on).

There's rarely "One True Set" of rings to wear. What you use depends on what you have available to you first and foremost, then what suits your build, and finally, whatever you personally prefer using.

Some rings provide simple, basic, and useful benefits, such as the Chloranthy Ring's Stamina regen boost, which is helpful for pretty much any character.

It's easy to slot all of your ring slots with such generalist buffs, and there's nothing wrong with that. However, you should make an effort to experiment at least a little with every new ring you find, unless its effect is totally wrong for your build (Sorcery boosters when you aren't using Sorcery and the like).

COMBAT

Combat is at the core of all *Dark Souls* games. Timing, positioning, building the best weapons, and selecting the ideal build is your only way to survive. It's time to go through these concepts, one by one.

SHIELD/PARRY

Not all shields are able to parry. Instead, some shields give you access to your equipped weapon's Weapon Skill. Other shields can knock aside light and moderate blows if you master the timing of your parry window. So, you get to experiment with your shields to figure out whether you like the versatility of being able to block and still have your Weapon Skill, or whether parrying is really the be-all and end-all for your combat style.

Some heavier and specialty shields have the Shield Bash skill, allowing you to use your shield a weapon!

WEAPON SKILL

Weapons have special moves that require FPs and are very powerful. These attacks usually have superior damage, cover ground more capably, or have other advantages that help you win a variety of encounters.

Weapon Skills cost FPs to use, and if you are a caster, you have to juggle your FPs between your equipped skills and spells. Skills can be activated without FP, unlike spells, but drain more Stamina and often execute slower or only partially without FP.

Because even melee characters use FPs, you need to balance your Estus Flasks. The more FPs you use, the more Ashen Estus Flasks you need. This means that you won't be able to carry as many swigs from your regular Estus Flask. This balancing act is very tricky, especially for magic-heavy characters.

USING SKILLS

Weapon Skills shake up equipment variety nicely, giving new options to old favorite gear and new cool toys to the more unique and rare items in the game.

Like spells, Weapon Skills can be ignored if you so choose, but it's generally worthwhile to experiment with different weapons as you find them to see if you like the way their moveset and their Skill handles.

Unlike spells, Weapon Skills can be used even if your FP is drained. They cause an increased drain on your Stamina, and for complex, multi-step moves, they may only partially execute.

Generally, this means that using Weapon Skills aggressively (particularly against very dangerous foes or bosses) is still limited by your FP. But if your Weapon Skill has a unique property (say, breaking shield guard or an evasive maneuver), you may still get some extra mileage out of your Skill before your next Bonfire rest.

There are some rings in the game that influence FP and Weapon Skill usage, so it's possible to work toward a build that emphasizes the use of your Weapon Skill. You may want to go for a full playthrough first before you attempt such a build, however, because acquiring all the pieces for such a loadout is usually going to be near the beginning of a New Game Plus playthrough anyway.

BAITING AND TRADING

Baiting is a potent combat tactic. You don't always want to be the first person to launch an attack in *Dark Souls* games. Just like your character, enemies aren't able to constantly spam their attacks. They have movesets and end up vulnerable if they miss, are parried, or even if they're blocked. Because of this, you sometimes want to bait an adversary into attacking you.

Bait a target that has long cooldowns between their attacks. If you know their range, you can frequently back off and launch your own attack a fraction of a second after their blow whiffs. Another classic is to dodge forward and attack from their flank while they're still engaged in their own swing; just don't try this when the target has a wide enough arc to hit you!

Once you know an enemy well enough, it's even possible to lock on to the target and walk around some of their attacks. Though this feels risky, you can keep your Stamina full, walk comfortably around your foe, and lay into them with everything you have.

Baiting a predictable attack is a core aspect of *Dark Souls* combat, and it's a vital skill whether you plan on dodging, parrying, or simply moving aside.

Trading is a crude form of baiting. Enemies with weaker attacks won't stagger you with their hits. Because of this, you're able to take their blows and respond with even more damage against them before and after their attacks land (as well as during the attack). Characters with high HPs, Poise, and Stamina can trade very effectively. This isn't a subtle or sustainable solution, but it works in a pinch.

WATCHING ENEMY ANIMATIONS

You should treat every single enemy in *Dark Souls* games with respect. Basic monsters, bosses, invaders: they're all more than capable of killing you if you make any mistakes. Don't try to rush, especially when you're entering new areas. Instead, treat each foe with care. Block, observe their attacks, and learn their movements. Being able to predict their motions and capabilities allows you to dodge, parry, and block with much greater skill. You won't need to have perfect reflexes once you know what's coming.

It's worth your time to master every type of enemy that you encounter. Not only does this raise your chance of survival against that target, but it also reduces the number of Estus Flask hits that you need to get through each area. That helps tremendously when you reach the boss because you have more resources to bring against them.

BOSS MECHANICS

Bosses usually have a couple of stages during your encounters with them. They'll get harder to beat, typically around the halfway point in the battle. The moves you learn to avoid and counter in the early fight will be outshined by even scarier abilities once your target realizes that it's either them or you.

As you practice against each boss, look for the animation that triggers this change. You can sometimes exploit this brief period with a rush of attacks while your foe is distracted. Just remember not to get too greedy!

HEALING IN BATTLE

Healing when you're in melee range is risky, but sometimes, you are going to die if you don't heal. For your best chance of survival, bait an enemy attack, and then dodge backward or to the side. If you have low Equip Load, this lets you put considerable distance between your character and the foe. Use the remainder of their animation time to drink from your flask or cast healing Miracles. Repeat the technique as needed.

An easier but less powerful way to heal in battle is to sprint away from your adversary. Drop your lock-on if that is engaged, and run away. Turn around a corner, heal, and wait for the opponent to come back to you. Breaking line of sight prevents most of their ranged attacks from threatening you, and that is especially important if there are additional ranged enemies helping their melee allies kill you.

DOUBLE-DRINK

If you tap the Use button again while you are drinking from the Estus Flask, you can perform a double-swig that is much faster than doing two separate full drinking animations.

The timing on the second drink is fairly specific, so test it out a few times near a Bonfire to get it down.

Early in the game, this isn't an issue. But later, when your health pool expands, you will find that even an upgraded Estus Flask cannot heal you fully in a single drink.

This is most important against really hard-hitting bosses that can deal crushing damage in a single hit. You need to recover and get back into the fight quickly, and performing a double-drink helps.

PULLING

Pulling is the act of getting enemy attention and drawing them back to a safer spot. This is most important in rooms with multiple opponents and wandering monsters, though it's also nice when you're trying to avoid fighting in rough terrain or near cliffs.

Pull enemies by shooting them at long range. Or, if you have to, slowly approach the first foe of a group. Wait until it sees you, and then back off to your safer battle spot. Fight it there, return, and then kill off anything else. Repeat your pulls as necessary.

Regardless of your build, pulling is a major technique. Going into a room that's filled with monsters is a great way to die. If you have any concerns about the fight ahead, pull each enemy back to a cleared room. This takes longer, but it's the best way to ensure your survival in new or tough areas.

MASTERING DODGE

Dodging is amazingly powerful. It costs way less Stamina to dodge an attack than it usually does to block it with a shield. You also get to roll into a new position, which often gives you an advantage over your enemy. Roll beside or behind your foe to get even more opportunities to attack before they recover. Or, dodge away to gain distance and time to react and heal, or to escape from a bad situation.

During the early portion of your roll, you become immune to most damage. This allows you to avoid attacks that would otherwise be guaranteed to rip you apart or drain all of your Stamina if you block. Wait until the last possible moment, dodge through the enemy attack, and come up tapping your Attack button to start hacking as soon as possible.

DON'T GET HIT!

Dodging really is that important, and while it can be a bit scary to rely solely on dodging for your defense (instead of using a shield some or all of the time), using dodge heavily has a lot of benefits.

The most obvious is simply improving your own timing over time. Attacks that seemed unavoidable become trivial to dodge with practice, and eventually, you learn to read enemy attacks as they occur and dodge in the correct direction with the right timing to evade them completely.

The other is that dodging opens up other offensive options, specifically two-handing or dual-wielding weapons. Across all of the weapon sets, large two-handers and rapid attacks from dual-wields typically deal more damage than an equivalently leveled one-hander used with a shield.

Even if you are using a shield, knowing when to two-hand your weapon and toss your shield on your back to crank out some extra damage is an important skill to master.

Dodging is key; learn to love it.

SHIELD BLOCKS

Shields are easy to use. Hold them high to defend against ranged and melee attacks, and make sure that you get time to recover your Stamina before the next wave of attacks comes your way. The upside to blocking is that it absorbs most or all damage from the enemy attack. Blocking works as long as you're facing your attacker.

The downsides of blocking are that it takes time, prevents Stamina regeneration while you're holding the shield up, and drains additional Stamina when you get hit. Light, fast attacks are the best ones to block; they don't drain much Stamina or delay you. Heavy attacks from larger creatures are the worst to block; they'll leave you staggered and winded. Without Stamina, you can't fight back, deal any damage, or continue blocking.

Ranged attacks are usually very easy and safe to block, provided they aren't dealing heavy damage of a type that the shield doesn't absorb. Even players who like two-handed weapons sometimes carry a shield and swap it in while approaching ranged targets.

The Stability value on your shield affects how hard of a hit you can absorb without having your guard blown out. You can enhance this slightly by upgrading it at the Blacksmith, though in general Greatshields always have more Stability than lightweight Small Shields.

BLOCKING SANS SHIELD

It's possible to block with two-handed weapons in addition to shields. If you look at the stats for any weapon in your inventory, you can see they have the same defensive statline as shields—these are used if you block with the weapon itself.

Generally, blocking with a two-hander isn't a great idea over simply dodging. But if you know you cannot evade an attack by dodging, blocking can at least save you some of the pain of eating the hit.

PARRYING

Parrying requires a shield that is parry-friendly, or a weapon that is made for parrying (like a Parrying Dagger). You use the alternate Attack button for these items to parry, but you need to wait until the last moment. Parrying early is often ineffective and causes you to take damage.

A proper parry requires you to face your opponent. Lock on to ensure that you stay in the proper position. Keep yourself close to the target so that you are in range for the parry and the counterattack. Then, hit the button when the enemy is just about to strike you. Once completed successfully, use the normal attack button to counterattack and deal heavy damage against your target.

Practice parrying against weaker monsters that aren't likely to kill you even if you make mistakes. Creatures around the Ashen Shrine and High Wall of Lothric are good candidates. The more comfortable you are with the parrying system, the easier it becomes to do this during clutch battles when a single mistake can end your life.

Parrying is way more aggressive than blocking. You aren't trying to simply avoid some damage. Blocking is already good for that and is way easier to pull off.

Not all enemy attacks can be parried, so with each major attacker, you must engage in some experimentation. However, most attacks can be parried and countered.

Parries are definitely the most difficult defensive tool in your arsenal. The payoff is extremely high counterattack damage.

Parry timing doesn't have to be totally perfect. There's a bit of leeway where if you just miss a parry, you "block" the attack without taking damage, but also without triggering the staggered counterattack animation.

Parrying is a key part of PvP. If you learn to anticipate attacks, you can deal heavy or fatal damage with a single move.

Because parrying is harder to use than dodging or blocking, it's usually something you might want to explore on a second playthrough if you're new, but definitely give it a try early. You may find that some enemies that are otherwise tough to handle become trivial to defeat when you parry their moves that have obvious wind-up animations.

Parrying works quite well on humanoid enemies using "normal" weapons. It's difficult (or impossible) to use on more monstrous opponents that have tougher tells or may not allow parries at all.

A parry-only playthrough is a great challenge run and will absolutely sharpen your skills.

BACKSTABS

If you get into position behind a humanoid enemy and attack, you perform a backstab. This lethal attack deals increased damage and locks you into a fixed animation that leaves you invulnerable to basic attacks from nearby enemies.

Perform backstabs on unaware adversaries by sneaking up on them. You can also use backstabs in combat if you can strafe behind your foes or stun them from the front and then strafe behind them.

Some weapons (typically dagger-class weaponry) deal increased damage when used for backstabs. This also applies to parry counterattacks.

Backstabs are great when you can land them, but be wary about trying to strafe around every humanoid you encounter. It's time-consuming to fish for backstabs, and that can get you in trouble when you're fighting multiple enemies.

One other warning: certain martially trained foes can perform special attacks designed specifically to punish strafing behind them.

RANGED COMBAT

Bows, crossbows, and many tools give you the ability to deal damage at range. Quite a few of your enemies lack that, which means that you often get a huge advantage when you mix ranged techniques into your repertoire.

Once you have a ranged weapon selected, make sure that you wield it two-handed, and then use the normal attack button to zoom in on your foes. This is needed for pulling and for sniping distant targets that would otherwise be very hard to hit. There are a couple of dragons in the game that you can kill without any trouble if you shoot from long range and never get close enough for their deadly breath to harm you.

It is very intuitive for Dexterity-based characters to rely on some ranged damage to soften their targets or to kill them outright, but don't make the mistake of ignoring ranged damage as a Strength-based character. Free damage is free damage, and ranged attacks are best used when they're safe and free.

Keep a ranged weapon in your second weapon slot so that you don't need to fiddle with menus to get one ready. Keep a healthy supply of arrows or bolts, and make sure to save your best ones for heavy targets. Use the cheap stuff when you're farming items, clearing levels, and generally fighting enemies that don't worry you too much.

Combine these ranged attacks with thrown weapons and bombs so that you can ravage heavy opponents during their approach. Also, remember to pull enemies away from their allies so that you're fighting one-on-one the majority of the time.

USING MAGIC

Magic takes more time than physical attacks, so treasure your positioning and stay away from monsters until you're ready to unleash spells safely. Make sure that you set up your Attunement so that spells have an intuitive progression on your bar. Have a primary attack spell next to any follow-up attacks. Leave support spells and general healing toward the end of your list so that you don't have to jump over them when switching from your mainline attacks to any follow-ups.

Don't be afraid to attune different spells when going into a new region. Sometimes, there are spells that are amazing in one place but almost useless in the very next area. Being able to cast Miracles that remove ailments can save your life constantly when you're dealing with poisonous monsters and environments, but why even have it on your bar when you're in High Wall of Lothric?

Customize your spells for the battles at hand. This takes a little more time, but it prevents you from needing as high of an Attunement. Those spare points can go into Intelligence or Faith and secure you even better spells.

DON'T RELAX. EVER.

Even if you've cleared a few rooms and have tons of space to relax, you might not be safe. The threat of invasion from another player demands that you pay attention at all times. Do not leave your game unattended. There is no pause; there is no respite. Unless you're playing offline, you need to keep the possibility of invasion in the back of your mind at all times.

IF YOU GET FRUSTRATED

This game is going to be hard, especially if you're new to *Dark Souls*. Don't get upset with yourself. Dying is very, very normal. Even extremely skilled players make mistakes here and there, and they've been playing these games for years. The rest of us are going to mess up more—much more. That's fine; it's built into the game, and you're not going to totally wreck yourself with your deaths, even if you end up dropping some Souls from time to time.

If you are getting past that comfortable point of frustration, try a few things:

TAKE BREAKS

A clear head makes every fight that much easier. A good night's rest does, too, as goofy as that sounds. How many times have you come back to a game and blown through something that was giving you impossible trouble the night before?

FARM SOULS

Level building is not as crucial to these games as in most action RPGs, but that doesn't mean that it won't help a little. Gathering Souls for a few extra levels makes it easier to survive, and it also gives you time to relax instead of taking on new encounters.

CHECK OUT ANOTHER PLAYER'S STREAM

You can take on *Dark Souls III* by yourself, and that's super cool. But it's also okay to watch other people play through areas and fight bosses. If you're just getting annoyed and want to push through to a new section of the game, few things help more than seeing another player's successful tactics in the fights that are messing you up.

USE ALL YOUR OPTIONS

It's easy to overlook your toolkit, but don't! Use your consumable items, or farm up some Souls and buy a big fat stock of them—temporary elemental buffs for your weapons, arrows, firebombs, curative items, etc.

Use your spells. Even if you aren't focusing on Sorcery, Pyromancy, or Miracles, a few points of Int or Faith are often enough to cast some very useful support spells.

Experiment with your equipment loadout. If you were light, try heavy. If you were one-handing, try two. If you were dodging frequently, try blocking, or vice versa.

Examine your ring options, as there are many useful rings that can give you a bit of an edge. Most won't provide huge power shifts, but taken together, a good set of ring bonuses can be very useful.

HEALTH AND SURVIVAL

HPs and FPs let you take damage and cast spells. Both of these limited resources are fixed; they won't regenerate over time. You either have to visit a Bonfire to restore them, or you need to use Estus or Ashen Estus Flasks to recover. There are a few spells and some equipment that can provide recovery, as well. It's time to quickly discuss these options.

BONFIRES

Every time you stop at a Bonfire, you get to restore all of your HPs and FPs, free of charge. You can do this as often as you like, so it's possible to return after every fight if you want. Monsters replenish whenever you visit a Bonfire, so you can't really abuse anything with this system. It's just there to make sure that you always have a fighting chance against the enemies that surround you.

If you find a great area for farming Souls or items, it's completely acceptable to run through a few fights, hurry back to a Bonfire, and rest to regenerate the monsters. Rinse and repeat, as needed.

SPELLS AND EQUIPMENT

While exploring the world, you can use several Miracles and a Pyromancy spell to restore your health.

Casting healing magic in combat is generally riskier than drinking from your Estus Flask due to casting speed. However, being able to restore your health using your FP can significantly extend the time you can spend in the field before you need to return to a Bonfire and heal.

Certain equipment (both rings and weapons) can provide some healing or regenerative powers for both HP and FP. Most of these heal too little to help you survive in the middle of a dangerous fight, but they can extend your survivability overall.

ESTUS FLASK

You start the game with an Estus Flask that restores health when you drink from it. You only have so many uses of the flask, but they are restored when you visit a Bonfire. This is usually going to be one of the items that you keep on your quickbar because it gets used all the time.

Because it takes a couple of seconds to drink from your flask, be careful. Do this in the middle of combat only when you must, and always put some distance between you and your enemies before you drink. If possible, block any foes' line of sight with a wall so that they can't even launch ranged attacks while you're vulnerable. You cannot dodge or move while drinking, so you're liable to take damage if anything gets the drop on you.

If you're badly wounded, it's possible to take a couple of swigs back-to-back by pressing the item key again while you're already drinking. This saves on the animation time and thus gets you healed much faster than if you drank, did something else, and then took another pull off of your flask.

THE ASHEN ESTUS FLASK

The Ashen Estus Flask works similarly, but it restores your FPs instead of health. Use it when you need to keep casting spells or using skills but have run out of juice. You find this flask only seconds into the game.

FLASK RATIOS

Estus Flask uses (both regular and Ashen) are not unlimited. When you're resting at the Ashen Shrine, talk to the Blacksmith and determine how many flask uses are for health and how many are going to be for FPs. This can be a tough decision for certain character builds. Experiment heavily with these numbers, and find out which resource is tapping out first. If it's always one of them, try changing the ratio to favor that flask a bit more.

UPGRADES

Your flasks improve throughout the game. There are special items that let you drink more often and gain more per drink from your flasks. Be tireless in your search for these items because they'll save your life time and time again.

Estus Shards grant you more sips from your flasks. Give these to the Blacksmith to increase your total count of flasks to assign.

Bone Cinders are burned in the Bonfire at the Ashen Shrine. They increase the power of each sip from the flask. In a very real way, they're just as important as the Estus Shards. Not only do they make your flasks last longer, but they reduce the amount of time you need to spend drinking during boss battles. That is huge because drinking leaves you vulnerable, sometimes even giving bosses the opportunity to finish you off before you're able to restore yourself.

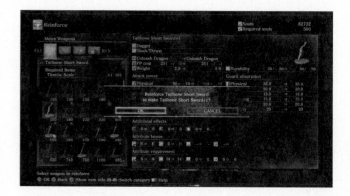

DEATHS, SOULS, AND LEVELING

Death is a constant threat throughout this game. Dangerous falls, poison, monster attacks, and traps are happily waiting to end you. Bosses are the worst threats of all, but it's entirely possible to die (often) when fighting against even the regular inhabitants of the world. This is especially true when you're getting used to the game since it does not play like most action RPGs.

If you lose all of your health, you'll immediately perish unless you're using a very finite and select type of accessory. When you die, you lose all of your Souls and then respawn at the last Bonfire that you used. This has two major consequences. First, there's the loss of time as you retrace your steps to return to where you were. Second, you will lose all of the Souls that you drop forever if you die again before making it back to the place where you initially fell.

Dragonslayer Armour

RESPAWNING

When you respawn at a Bonfire, your Estus Flasks are restored. This means that you can heal yourself again as you travel back to your bloodstain and are brought back to almost your maximum health. The problem for fallen characters is that they lose some of the spark that makes them human. Because of this, your maximum health diminishes if you die, making survival even harder in the future. This sounds scary, and it is a major problem, but there is a way to combat it.

Embers are items that you find from time to time, and they allow you to restore yourself to your ideal health total. You don't need to use these each time you die, as that would be very wasteful. Instead, it's best to wait until you're at a particularly difficult boss area before using an Ember. A solid technique is to explore each new region, dealing with whatever losses you take. Then, find any bosses that are nearby, fight them a few times to learn their mechanics, and then use an Ember when you feel like you're ready to beat the encounter. If you win during your practice sessions, then you obviously didn't need to use the Ember anyway!

EMBER RESTORED

Another aspect of respawning is that all of the normal monsters in the area return, as well. Special NPCs or bosses that are slain remain dead, but everything else will be waiting to stop you. This lets you farm regular monsters for extra Souls. It also forces you to learn efficient routes through most areas so that you don't get into too much fighting if you're trying to pass by or get to a boss. This way, you don't use your Estus Flasks too often before the important fights.

NEW AREAS AND RISK

It's totally normal to die while exploring a new area. Expect it; don't stress over it.

I like to prioritize each fresh run into a new area. First, I go for general exploration—pick up as many items as I can (those are all permanent benefits to your character that you can't lose), and finding new equipment, rings, and spells all help make the area easier.

Next, unlocking Bonfires and shortcuts is a huge boon. These make travel and recovery from death much easier. There are few areas in the game that aren't close to a Bonfire, a shortcut, or both.

Finally, charting a path to the boss. When you're ready to tackle a boss, figure out what combination of Bonfire and shortcuts lets you run to the boss without dealing with monsters on the way.

As for normal enemies? While they initially appear to be a huge obstacle, after a few scouting trips, you're going to be looking for areas where you can kill enemies that give a decent Soul return for a short-time investment. Bash those monsters, return to a nearby Bonfire (or Homeward Bone), repeat!

It's rarely necessary to farm for any extensive amount of time to "level up." *Dark Souls* doesn't really work that way.

Instead, when you find a new area that has relatively easy enemies that are giving you considerably more Souls per kill than a previous area, take the opportunity to gain several levels quickly to unlock new gear, stock up on consumables, and upgrade your equipment.

RETRIEVING YOUR SOULS

If you make it back to the area where you fell, you will see a bloodstain and a glowing green light above it. This is the game's way of saying, "Get this!" It's very easy to see, even from a distance, which is a godsend in dark areas.

Even if you're under attack, it is usually wise to sprint over to the pool of Souls and collect them before risking your life. This comes up most often in boss areas, where you might die repeatedly and have to pick up your Souls a few times before you master the encounter.

The best way to minimize the risk of Soul loss is to spend your Souls as soon as possible. Very early in the game, after defeating the first boss, you find a shrine with the Fire Keeper. This NPC lets you spend Souls to increase your stats. These changes are permanent, so you've effectively gotten rid of your Souls and gained power improvements in return.

Never walk around with more Souls than you're willing to lose. If dying would cause you to lose tons of time and work, don't risk it! Return to a Bonfire, warp to the Firelink Shrine, and spend those Souls. Even though it takes a few minutes to do this, you will be much better off than you would with even occasional deaths that don't let you retrieve your Souls.

You might have a few questions about Soul retrieval. If you die from a fall, do your Souls get lost forever? No—they'll appear very close to the spot where you fell. They should always be retrievable.

If you die in a boss' lair, the bloodstain will indeed be inside of that room. You can't get your Souls back without approaching the boss and starting the fight again. However, this does not mean that you have to defeat the boss to safely get your Souls back to a Bonfire. Homeward Bones return you to the last Bonfire that you used. Though risky to use when a boss is nearby, it is possible to escape from a boss fight. If you've built up many thousands of Souls, it can be worth the risk and the use of a Homeward Bone to get back to a Bonfire.

If you die twice without getting back to your bloodstain, the Souls from the first death are gone forever. Period. Instead, the new bloodstain will have only the Souls that you were carrying during your attempt to reach your first bloodstain. Be very, very careful when retrieving bloodstains with a large number of Souls.

Another trick for reducing risk is to hold on to items that generate Souls. You find these special Soul items throughout the game, and they don't slow you down or take up excess space. As such, you should hoard them until you're standing right next to the Fire Keeper. That way, you don't risk them at all! They'll be generated and spent in a safe place.

Also, keep at least one Homeward Bone on your character at all times. Although you shouldn't use them willy-nilly (because they do cost a modest amount of Souls each), they'll save you massive amounts of time and Souls later in the game. Once you start getting tens of thousands of Souls per run, you should use Homeward Bones exclusively. When you earn more Souls per minute than it takes just to run back to a Bonfire, it's time to start buying Homeward Bones in bulk!

GAINING LEVELS

Levels are not the be-all and end-all in *Dark Souls* games. Sure, it's always nice to have more Hit Points, better damage, and so forth. But sloppy techniques get you killed even with superior leveling. By contrast, tight, well-executed mechanics allow you to survive fights even with mediocre gear and leveling.

That said, most players are going to enjoy leveling and will appreciate the benefits that this provides. Certain PvPers may limit their growth at a specific level, and there are also players who set personal challenges for themselves. These games can be (and have been) beaten by people who avoided leveling. Have respect for those scary, scary players.

Assuming that you're not someone in one of those camps, then your goal is to accrue Souls and level as often as possible. The stronger you get, the easier most challenges become. However, it is still extremely important to plan out your leveling. Each time you invest enough Souls to gain a level, you do so by adding one point to your character's attributes. Never be casual with your choice here. Going after the "wrong" attributes for your intended playstyle can be detrimental.

For example, a good melee character might be made with Strength, but how much do you need? Just put all of your points in there? No. In fact, you might not need much at all, depending on the weapons that you prefer. Strength and Dexterity are both required for many advanced weapons, and investing too heavily in one might leave you deficient in the other (and thus, unable to wield some of the items that you want).

To further complicate matters, most attributes have diminishing returns. Overinvesting in any single attribute is foolish unless you have a strong reason to push hard in that area. This gets confusing quickly until you're very comfortable with the game.

All of this combines to reward players the most when they specialize but still boost a few supporting attributes for their build. A pure melee character who blows levels on Intelligence, Faith, and Attunement just for the sake of having them is not helping himself/herself. The same character with tons of raw Strength but no Vitality, Vigor, or any Dexterity will also have problems.

Focus on your most important attribute, and then make sure that you have enough in your peripheral attributes to get by.

USING EQUIPMENT

There are hundreds of tools, weapons, and pieces of armor in *Dark Souls III*. This section doesn't discuss all of them, but you can read about the major categories and how to understand their statistics.

TOOLS

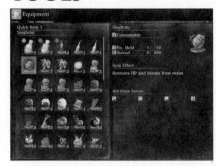

Tools are usable items that have a huge range of effects. Some of them generate Souls (Souls of various bosses, people, etc.). Others are single-use weapons, such as Firebombs and Throwing Knives. There are things to let you invade other worlds, help others, and leave messages in various locations.

To find out what you're carrying, open your menu and select Inventory. This takes you into a screen with many tabs (one for each category of equipment). You don't need to worry about weight for most things in this game; your equipped weapons, tools, and armor count, but everything else is kept available without any restrictions.

Go to the Tools tab, which is normally the first one shown. At the bottom of the screen, a legend shows you which buttons to use. There is a "Show Item Info" button that gives you a better picture of each tool. You also get a description that explains more about the tool's background and function.

Remember to use your tools during difficult fights. Some players hoard items for a rainy day, and then forget to use them while going against bosses. Bosses ARE your rainy days. Anything that buffs your survivability and damage output is amazingly useful when you're attacking bosses.

MATERIALS

These items are required for upgrading your weapons and armor. As such, they're incredibly valuable. You can find them on a variety of monsters, or sometimes grab them from specific areas as you explore. Always search bodies when you see a glowing white object beside them. You never know what you're going to find, unless you have a walkthrough to tell you what to expect.

Hoard materials and spend them only on the equipment that you're using the most. It costs Souls to upgrade equipment (in addition to the materials), so you should consider every upgrade with care. You make these improvements by talking to a Blacksmith. Look for the Ashen Shrine to meet an NPC who can help you with this.

There are several tiers of materials, so you can't take a piece of equipment to its maximum just by farming Titanite Shards.

KEY ITEMS

Some set items are required for progress through the game. These items include keys, crests, and other special pieces that you find during your time in *Dark Souls III*.

CATALYSTS

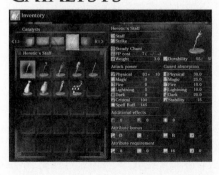

Catalysts allow you to use your spells. They can be equipped in either hand, and are a requirement for spellcasting. A few special weapons also act as Catalysts.

SPELLS

Spells allow characters to accomplish a variety of powerful effects. Each one has to be found or purchased, and then you unlock Attunement slots for them so that you can use each while you're adventuring.

The higher you raise your Attunement attribute, the more spells you can prepare simultaneously. This is very important for characters who are focused on magic builds, but it's far less important for melee and ranged weapon users. Hybrid builds can be very successful but are more challenging and should be attempted only after you have a strong foundation for playing the game.

To change the spells that you have prepared, go to a Bonfire and select Attune Magic.

MELEE WEAPONS

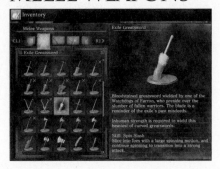

Melee weapons don't require ammunition, so they're free to use at almost any time. They require a fair amount of Stamina to wield, so you always have to balance between Stamina for dodging, blocking, and attacking.

Melee weapons primarily require Strength or Dexterity (or both) to deal damage, so these are major attributes to raise when you're wielding good melee gear.

When you look at a weapon in your Inventory screen, it shows a ton of information under Attack Power. This reveals the damage that a basic attack from that weapon does. Physical, magic, fire, lightning, and dark are all potential damage types, and the total weapon damage output is the sum of all of these categories.

After the damage number is often a bonus. It might say something like, "Physical 125 +30." This is telling you that the weapon does 125 as a base value, and then +30 due to your attributes.

Weapons let you know which attributes raise their damage output. Look lower on the page, where it says "Attribute Bonus." The higher the letter value under each attribute, the more influence that attribute has on your bonus damage. This gives you important information about the weapons that you should focus on with your given build. If you have very high Strength, look for items that have an S, an A, or a B under Strength. The same applies for any attribute that is shown.

Weapons can also have additional effects (Bleed, Poison, and Frost). The higher the value shown by each icon, the greater a chance the weapon has of causing that effect.

Attribute requirements heavily restrict your ability to use a weapon unless you meet or surpass certain values. Not all weapons have these requirements, but many do. Make sure to build your character toward the items that you're planning on wielding.

Weapons and armor have Durability, which is a stat that lowers as you use your equipment. Blacksmiths can repair equipment if it breaks.

RANGED WEAPONS

Ranged weapons have similar statistics, but they require that you purchase or find a considerable amount of bolts or arrows to fire them. This means that ranged weapons are sometimes more expensive to use (requiring you to spend Souls), but they are safer weapons and give you a fair advantage over certain foes.

Even characters who aren't building for high Dexterity should keep a ranged weapon around for pulling purposes. Keep a cheap type of ammunition in one of your quivers at all times, and have a more expensive or situational type of ammo in the other. This lets you poison or otherwise mess with more dangerous foes as much as possible before they close in against you.

You can purchase arrows and bolts at the Ashen Shrine. A few of the NPCs there carry these important pieces of ammo.

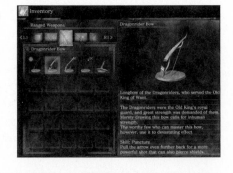

SHIELDS

Shields are one-handed items that give you a tremendous amount of defensive power. They absorb a percentage of damage from various types of enemy attacks. For the best survivability, look for shields with a physical value of 100. This means that they'll take all of the damage from physical attacks that come your way. Anything less than that, and you will still get hurt when you're blocking.

Obviously, the other guard power values can be important, as well, depending on what you're fighting against. Magical and elemental attacks often get a decent bit of damage through, so characters must be more mobile against targets that are using those effects.

Stability determines the amount of Stamina that you lose when you block attacks from foes. You want this to be as high as possible so that you can block with impunity against most enemy strikes.

As with melee and ranged weapons, shields may have attribute requirements and attribute bonuses, as well.

Shields are held up to block damage. If you don't know your target's timings very well, hide behind the shield as soon as their attack wind-up starts. Lower the shield afterward to regain Stamina, and maneuver until you get an advantageous position for your attacks.

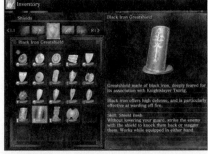

Once you know an enemy really well, it's possible to use shields with the Parry skill to block at the last moment. This creates a parry, an advanced defensive technique that stuns targets and leaves them extremely vulnerable to a riposte counterattack.

ARMOR

Armor is used to protect your head, chest, hands, and legs. The items that you find for this have stats for Reduction (the amount of direct damage they mitigate) and Resistances (to improve your ability to withstand bleeding, poison, and such). Armor also has weight that goes against your Equip Load.

You need to keep your maximum Equip Load high enough so that you can use strong defensive equipment. There is no advantage to having a bunch of excess Equip Load, so don't focus on this heavily until you start getting equipment that is heavier and has improved stats to warrant the investment.

RINGS

You have several slots for accessories. Rings are loaded into these four slots, and they'll give you a variety of special effects.

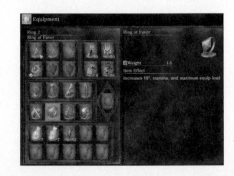

UPGRADING EQUIPMENT

Improving your equipment is at least as important as leveling when it comes to *Dark Souls* games. The benefits that you receive from finding better gear and then improving those items are impressive. Using the correct gear for each occasion turns encounters from brutal down to livable.

SEARCH EVERYWHERE

Your starting gear is usually fairly good, though certain classes get much better items and others start without any benefits whatsoever. On the whole, you're going to have decent weaponry and enough armor to get by. However, you find amazing things as you explore the game world. Some of them aren't even that far from the start of the game, although you have to know where to look.

Searching carefully is the first rule of upgrades. Off the beaten path are extra weapons, pieces of armor, items with bonus Souls, spare tools, and much more. You are heavily rewarded for looking around every corner, for dropping off of ledges, and for turning over everything in the scenery that isn't nailed down.

Look for messages wherever you go. Helpful players like to leave them near hidden items or pathways. Not all of these are trustworthy messages, but most will be. When you're exploring, keep your Soul count low so that you aren't risking much if you die trying to do something interesting.

Each time you find something new, examine it thoroughly. It's not always clear which items are the best. Higher stats are never a bad thing, but the moveset and bonuses for each weapon have the potential to turn plenty of things into hidden gems once you realize what they're good at doing.

SECRET DOORS

Attack suspicious walls if a corridor doesn't seem to lead anywhere. Secret entrances appear when you attack special walls. Go through these to find rare and often wonderful treasure.

REINFORCEMENT

Once you find superior weapons and armor, hunt for Titanite and other upgrade items, and bring everything to your Blacksmith. He'll take a moderate sum of Souls and then use those upgrade items to add pluses to your equipment. You get very substantial bonuses from these upgrades.

Normal weapons and shields are upgraded from +1 through +10. Some items have more powerful upgrade tracks and can only be upgraded to +5, but they'll be very powerful by the end of their path.

MODIFICATIONS

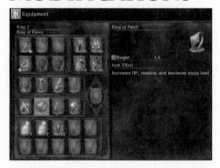

You can also add certain elemental effects to your items. Consider these upgrades very carefully because they aren't always going to help you accomplish your goals. Make sure that you're adding things that help your items do what they're meant to do. It sounds awesome to add an entire type of elemental damage to a weapon, but if you sacrifice your Strength bonuses on the item to get that element, it might not pay off in the long run. It's usually better to have a lot of damage from one type than two moderate types of damage.

Basic modifications are available as soon as you meet the Blacksmith in the Ashen Shrine, but there are four special items that you can return to him to improve the range of modifications that he masters.

All modifications exist to focus the types of damage that your weapons and shield are based on. Look at your attributes, and try to push the scaling of your weapons in a direction that plays off of your best ones.

MODIFICATION	POSITIVE EFFECT	NEGATIVE EFFECT
Heavy	Improves Str scaling	Destroys Dex scaling
Sharp	Maximizes Dex scaling	Lowers Str scaling
Refined	Improves Str and Dex Scaling	Requires high Str and Dex to exceed other infusions
Raw	Improves base damage	Destroys Str and Dex scaling
Crystal	Improves Int scaling, adds magic damage	Lowers Str and Dex scaling and base weapon damage
Simple	Improves Int scaling, regenerates FP slowly	Lowers Str and Dex scaling and base weapon damage, weaker Magic scaling than Crystal
Fire	Adds fire damage	Destroys Str and Dex scaling
Chaos	Improves Int and Faith scaling, adds fire damage	Lowers Str and Dex scaling and base weapon damage
Lightning	Raises Faith scaling, adds lightning damage	Lowers Str and Dex scaling and base weapon damage
Blessed	Raises Faith scaling, deals 20% bonus damage to Reanimated foes, regens HP slowly	Lowers Str and Dex scaling and base weapon damage
Deep	Adds dark damage	Destroys Str and Dex scaling
Dark	Raises Int and Faith scaling and adds dark damage	Lowers base weapon damage
Blood	Increases bleeding	Lowers Str and Dex scaling and base weapon damage
Poison	Increases poison	Lowers Str and Dex scaling and base weapon damage
Hollow	Adds Luck scaling	Lowers Str scaling
Shriving	Removes Infusion, does not affect Reinforcement level	—

IMPORTANT! NPC QUESTLINES

We do not discuss NPC storylines heavily here in the walkthrough.

However, if you wish to follow as many of the NPC plots as possible, please visit the NPC chapter ("A Few May Help You On Your Path") near the end of the book. Be aware that for obvious reasons, the chapter contains heavy spoilers.

Many of the NPC quests (and even their appearances) are tied to extremely specific actions in specific sequences, and some are mutually exclusive, so if you're trying to see a lot of them in a single playthrough, you need to decide early which you want to tackle and how you want to resolve them.

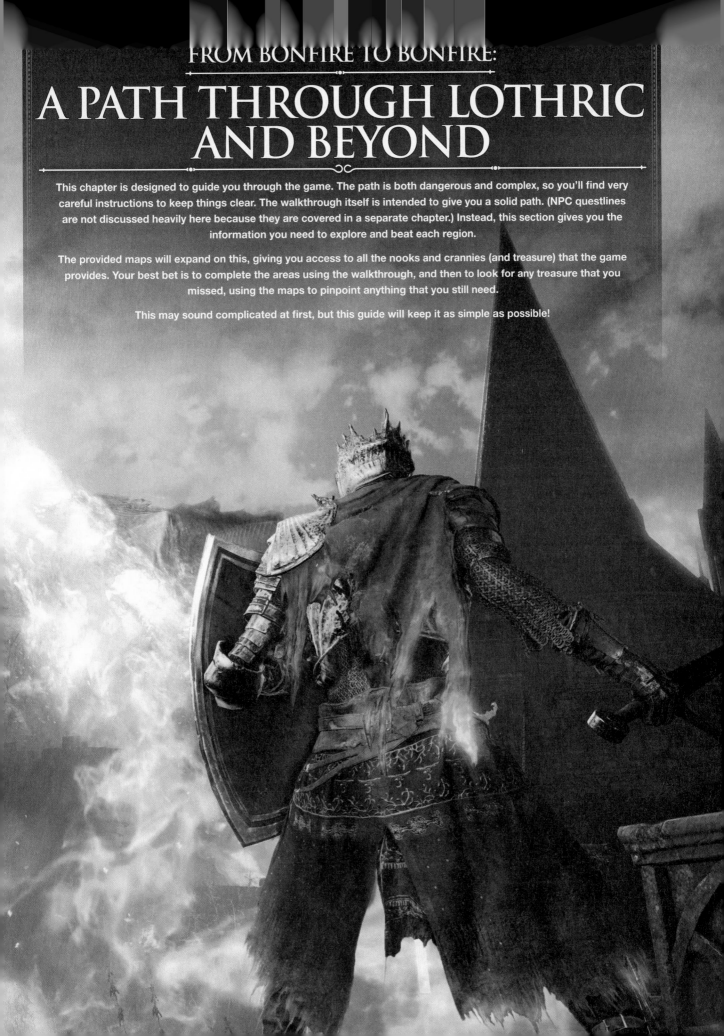

FROM BONFIRE TO BONFIRE:
A PATH THROUGH LOTHRIC AND BEYOND

This chapter is designed to guide you through the game. The path is both dangerous and complex, so you'll find very careful instructions to keep things clear. The walkthrough itself is intended to give you a solid path. (NPC questlines are not discussed heavily here because they are covered in a separate chapter.) Instead, this section gives you the information you need to explore and beat each region.

The provided maps will expand on this, giving you access to all the nooks and crannies (and treasure) that the game provides. Your best bet is to complete the areas using the walkthrough, and then to look for any treasure that you missed, using the maps to pinpoint anything that you still need.

This may sound complicated at first, but this guide will keep it as simple as possible!

CEMETERY OF ASH

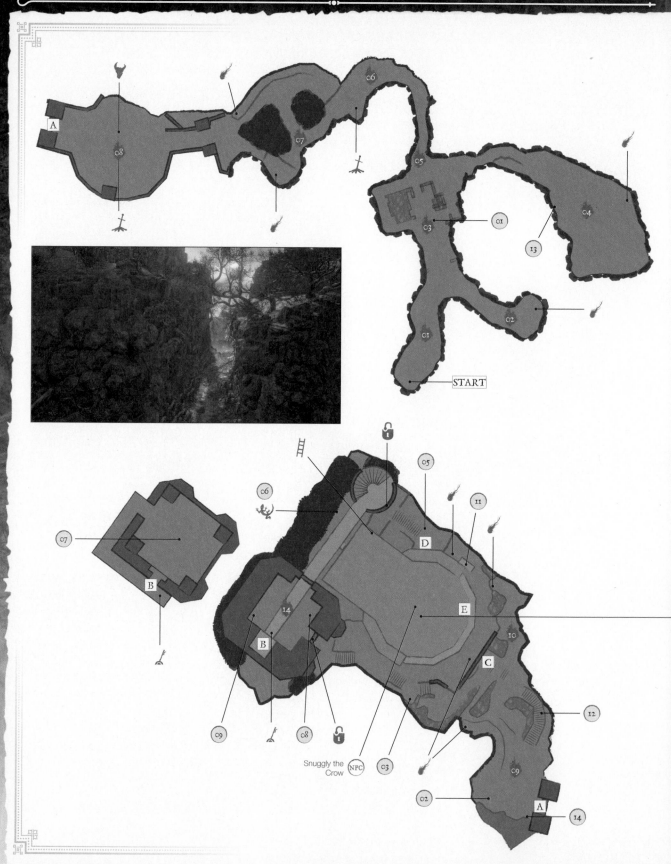

A

08

07

06

05

04

01

03

13

02

01

START

06

07

B

14

B

09

09

08

Snuggly the
Crow

NPC

03

D

05

11

E

10

C

12

02

A

14

MAP KEY

	Walkthrough Event
	Bone Shard
	Bonfire
	Boss
	Chest
A	Connector
	Crystal Lizard
	Dark Spirit
	Fog Gate
?	Hidden Door
	Ladder
	Lever
	Locked Door
∞	Major Item
	Mimic Chest
NPC	NPC
	Soul Shard
T	Trap
	Treasure

MAJOR ITEMS

1. Ashen Estus Flask
2. Broken Straight Sword
3. East West Shield
4. Estus Shard
5. Seed of a Giant Tree (occasionally)
6. Twinkling Titanite
7. Fire Keeper Soul
8. Fire Keeper Armor (full set, on ledge)
9. Estus Ring
10. Covetous Silver Serpent Ring
11. Hawkwood's Shield (after defeating Abyss Watchers)
12. Sunset Shield (after aiding Sirris against Hodrick)
13. Speckled Stoneplate Ring +1 (New Game +1)
14. Wolf Ring+2 (New Game +2)

BONFIRES LOCATED HERE

Cemetery of Ash
Iudex Gundyr (Boss)
Firelink Shrine
Untended Graves

ENEMIES

Grave Warden
Ravenous Crystal Lizard
Starved Hound
Iudex Gundyr
Crystal Lizard

KEY DISCOVERIES

Meet the Fire Keeper
Meet the Blacksmith
Meet the Shrine Handmaid
Meet Ludleth

VISITORS

The NPCs Sirris, Eygon, Anri, and Horace all visit the Shrine at various times if you pursue their questlines.

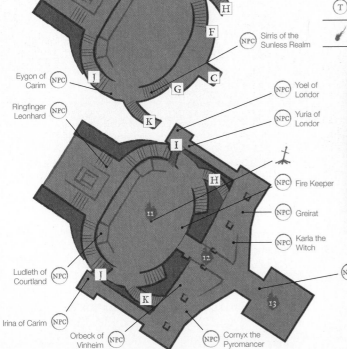

NPC — Unbreakable Patches

NPC — Hawkwood the Deserter

NPC — Sirris of the Sunless Realm

Eygon of Carim — NPC

Ringfinger Leonhard — NPC

NPC — Yoel of Londor

NPC — Yuria of Londor

NPC — Fire Keeper

NPC — Greirat

NPC — Karla the Witch

Ludleth of Courtland — NPC

NPC — Andre the Blacksmith

Irina of Carim — NPC

Orbeck of Vinheim — NPC

NPC — Cornyx the Pyromancer

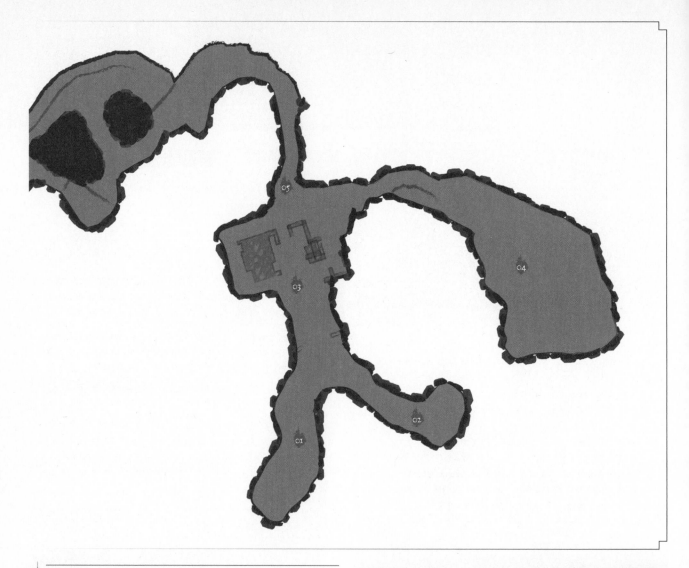

01

You wake and arise from the cold ground with your weapon in hand. There are only a few difficult enemies nearby, and none of them has seen you yet. This is your chance to get used to the commands that control your character.

MESSAGES ON THE GROUND

Messages are left by other players (and by the game's creators) to give you suggestions and warnings. Pay heed to these—they are often a good way to figure out what you need to do or where you should search, or a warning of what lies ahead.

Read all of the messages that you encounter. The ones in this area primarily tell you how to move, attack, and dodge.

Walk forward along the main path and approach the first enemy of the game. This Grave Warden is an easily vanquished combatant. Worn away by time, it barely has enough intelligence to realize that you are a threat. It won't even attack unless you provoke it or spend a great deal of time moving around trying to alert it to your presence. Avoid doing that.

Instead, approach it quickly and execute a single attack with your weapon, using a normal attack to deal lethal damage.

Steel yourself, and continue forward. Another Grave Warden is sitting nearby on the ground. Try using a strong attack against this foe. As before, this target is weak and won't do much to defend itself unless you give it time.

DON'T LET MERCY STAY YOUR HAND

Even though these enemies seem weak and vulnerable, you cannot afford to be sentimental. Given enough time, almost everything in this game will try to kill you. Many can succeed. Kill these enemies to put them out of their suffering, and collect their Souls so you can grow stronger.

Practice moving your character and turning the camera to keep a good eye on the targets that you're approaching. Also, use the lock on feature to target your enemies. This makes combat markedly easier because your movement and attacks all center on the adversary that you've selected. Likewise, dodging and attacking become much easier. Combine this practice with sprinting and dodging to make sure that these movements become second nature.

Where the path splits, take the short route to your right. At the end of that corridor, a corpse lies in the water. Above it, a glowing white light shines, beckoning you to approach. Walk over to the light and interact with it to pick up an item. Searching for items this way gets you extra tools, items to break into free Souls, equipment, and a variety of upgrades (for your weapons, flasks, and so forth). The more thoroughly you search, the easier this game becomes.

Return to the main path and proceed onward. The next Grave Warden is more alert. Attack as quickly as you can to dispatch the enemy before it comes after you. Failing that, dodge backward to avoid its strike, or raise a shield (if you have one). All of these methods are useful throughout the game. Aggressive attacks give you the initiative and can dispatch some foes before they are able to fight back. Dodging works against almost anything, but it requires proper positioning and timing. You don't want to roll into an enemy's strike or place yourself so far away from your target that you don't gain any advantage.

After your quick battle, look for another item on the ground. You can find it ahead, by a dilapidated fountain. Search the body you see to pick up an **Ashen Estus Flask**. To the right, there is also a **Dagger**.

FLASKS

The default item on your toolbar, the Estus Flask heals you when you use them. You start with three uses of the Estus Flask, which are refilled every time you stop at a Bonfire. The red bar at the top of the screen depicts your health.

This new Ashen Estus Flask restores FPs (indicated by the blue bar that is also located near the top of the screen). FPs are used to cast spells and use skills. You only have one swig of that flask for now, so avoid using it until you are low on FPs.

The next Grave Warden has a shield and guards a junction in the path. Approach cautiously, and then unleash a flurry of blows to beat through this foe's defenses. Enemies with more health, armor, or shields are able to take extra hits.

Take several attacks at once, and then roll backward to restore your Stamina. Repeat this as needed to dispatch your enemy without giving them a chance to counterattack. You can often kill foes with shields by whacking them until they are staggered. Once their shield is out of position, they take significantly more damage.

A few more Grave Wardens are located to the left or right of the central path. Kill them and explore briefly. The way ahead leads deeper into the region. A longer passage to the right takes you to an optional area that contains a tougher monster to beat. If you're looking for a challenge, head that direction. If you're worried, skip the fight and walk forward instead.

RAVENOUS CRYSTAL LIZARD

Monsters made out of crystal are often wonderful targets because they drop upgrade items for your weaponry. The beast that you find at the end of the path is no exception! This enemy has substantial health and requires multiple hits from you to kill it. Although these adversaries aren't that serious of a threat later on, they can be quite a dangerous to an inexperienced player without upgrades or gear.

Dodge out of the way whenever the creature rolls toward you or spins to knock you down. The Ravenous Crystal Lizard also has a breath weapon that freezes the area and deals damage if you are caught in it.

Roll around to the creature's flank, and make two or three attacks to wound it badly each time you successfully dodge. Repeat this action to kill the monster, but understand that death will take you if you cannot win quickly. You don't have many resources to fall back on.

When you're ready, return to the fork in the path and walk toward the break in the cliff walls. You can see open sky in that direction, which looks promising. If you have a shield, keep it raised as you approach an Grave Warden Archer. This creep fires its crossbow at anything that comes near. Shields block the damage from these attacks. If you don't have a shield, roll forward to avoid the shot, and hack through this creature before it can reload and fire again.

THEY DON'T COLLECT TAXES HERE, BUT DEATH IS A CERTAINTY

If you die, you return to your starting point (or to the last Bonfire you used, once you've unlocked one). Death reduces your total HPs until you defeat a boss or can use an Ember to restore your fire.

Also, your Souls drop to the ground and must be recovered before you die a second time. Failure destroys your lost Souls forever.

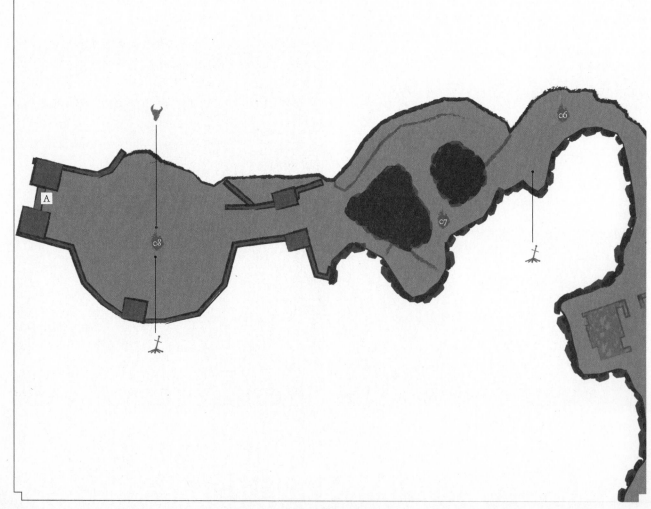

BONFIRE—CEMETERY OF ASH

 Follow the winding path up the mountain and rest at a Bonfire. This teaches you a new gesture (Rest), and it restores your Estus Flasks.

This guide does not mention every single item that you might encounter; refer to the maps for at the beginning of each area for this information. There are usually several ways to proceed through an area, but the safest or fastest route is discussed in this walkthrough.

Here, the best course of action is to take the path left as you pass the Bonfire. Kill a Grave Warden Swordsman on the way, and hug the wall on the left as you continue. Drop to a lower ledge, and then do so again to ambush a tougher enemy at the bottom of the route. This Grave Warden has more health, but a normal attack from above can put the target in bad shape before it even knows you're there. This is called a Plunging Attack, and it's an excellent way to deal high damage when you're falling.

Kill the monster, and sprint past two more enemies in the yard close by. You can fight them if you want, but a boss is ahead; it's best to take a fast route to the enemy boss so you can return here easily in the future. Finding quick paths to the bosses allows you to save your Estus Flasks and return to the bosses without delay if they kill you.

Once you get into the arena at the bottom of the path, any remaining enemies will stop chasing you. They know what's waiting in there, and they fear it! But you are ready for this, and it's time to face this guardian: Iudex Gundyr must be defeated.

MAJOR BATTLE

 Start your first serious battle by interacting with the slumbering warrior. This lets you pull the sword out of the gigantic knight, waking him.

IUDEX GUNDYR

STAGE I

Attack quickly before Iudex Gundyr has time to steady himself. It's quite possible to deal almost half of the boss' health in damage before the fight really gets going. Swing until you're almost out of Stamina, and then dodge to get away before his reprisal slams you into the ground.

Always Buff if You Have Time

As a Warrior, you start with a Battle Axe. The special skill for that weapon buffs Attack Power. It's very effective to use this buff immediately after pulling the sword out of Iudex. Buff yourself for bonus damage, attack quickly, and laugh as the boss gets nearly sent into Stage II right off the bat.

Iudex Gundyr has massive, sweeping attacks. Blocking costs you too much Stamina here, so work on your dodging. Dodge later than you think you'll need to, and feel free to dodge multiple times if you misjudge the attacks and still have time to keep rolling.

For extra damage, it's useful to switch from one-handed use of your weapon to two-handed use. This is particularly important for shield users because you won't be able to rely on your shield much in this fight anyway. The boss' hits deplete your Stamina pool and then cut you in half. It's better to dodge, counterattack, and deal as much damage as possible before escaping.

For a few extra tips, try to roll back from the boss' leaping attacks. Going underneath sometimes gets you hit. Also, it's better to wait for a real opening and perform multiple attacks rather than get a plink here and there between every swing that Iudex Gundyr does. Pick your moments well, and make them count. Sometimes, you need to simply get Stamina back; in that case, ease away from the boss and ensure that your gauge is full before you make any additional attacks.

If you're rolling toward the boss and avoiding his strikes, use a normal attack to come up swinging. Don't waste any time. Always stay a step ahead of your character's animations so that your actions remain tight and efficient.

STAGE II

Between half- and one-third-health, Iudex Gundyr stops in place and begins to change. Attack relentlessly when he does this, as he becomes much nastier after the transition. Try to kill him before he's able to react.

If he's still up and fighting, back off to get your Stamina and ready your shield. In this stage, the boss can hit suddenly and at long range, but he doesn't hit as hard with each strike. It's worth losing Stamina to absorb his early shots, which gives you time to move closer, strike, and get away. It won't take much longer to win this fight!

Roll or sprint far away if/when you need to use your Estus Flask. Never stop to heal when your enemy can simply smash you and take off all of the health that you're getting back (or more).

When Iudex Gundyr falls, you're rewarded with quite a few Souls and a **Coiled Sword**. Use the Coiled Sword to light the Bonfire there, and then rest. You've already done some great work, but this is only your first big fight. With many more battles ahead, along with thousands of smaller skirmishes, it's not going to get easier.

Open the double doors at the far side of the arena. They'll take you out to a hill that rises toward a very special location. There are more Grave Wardens on the way, but there aren't too many other obstacles for now.

Climb the hill and attack the monsters as you meet them. You encounter two along a small strip of land to your left, and more are waiting on the main path. The only change from what you've already seen is that the enemies are now grouped. Make sure that you rush into the packs and attack quickly to kill one or two targets before they get up and become organized. Prompt action makes the fights much easier.

A Starved Hound is at the top of the hill, on the right. This is a new enemy, and they're worth taking a moment to observe. Starved Hounds are very fast. They leap at their targets to knock them around, and they can get free hits by hitting you and dashing away as you recover. Use shields to block their leaping attacks, and then come back for a deadly counter when a Starved Hound is exposed. There isn't much time to do this, but you can always back off, get your Stamina back, and try again.

There's an entrance into the Firelink Shrine at the top of the hill. Don't explore the route to your left; there is a tougher fight over there, and it's better to unlock the Bonfire inside the shrine before you attempt anything tricky.

BONFIRE—FIRELINK SHRINE

Go into the building and talk to the NPCs inside. Then, use the Coiled Sword to light the Bonfire. You can now use the Storage Box here to store or retrieve items. You also use this Bonfire to Attune Spells and add bonuses to your Estus Flasks by burning Undead Bone Shards, which are only found in specific areas of the game.

Get your bearings here, because there is a lot to take in. The Fire Keeper is the most important person in the game. She'll allow you to invest Souls into your character. Every level gets you another attribute point, so you can customize your character however you see fit. This guide mentioned earlier that your starting class doesn't matter for long, and that's true. You can start as a Warrior and build toward Dexterity, Faith, or even Intelligence. Your stats and equipment determine everything about your character going forward. "Class" is only a starting point.

Of course, you are in better shape if you stick to the path that you begin with; your starting attributes give you a decent leg up on that style of play.

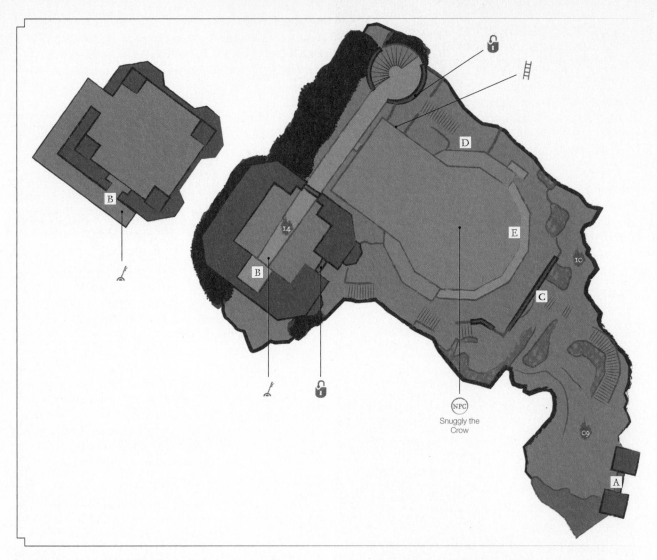

SHRINE HANDMAID

Another important woman is the Shrine Handmaid, who buys and sells items. She's located down a side corridor, on the way toward the Blacksmith. Her starting inventory is only decent, but she'll accept Ashes that you find throughout the game. Each time she gets new Ashes, she'll improve her wares! Sadly, everything still costs Souls, so you can't buy everything all at once. Pick and choose what you need the most. For now, note that she sells Wood Arrows for a trivial sum. You'll return to buy these very soon.

ANDRE THE BLACKSMITH

Blacksmith Andre has myriad functions. If you find the correct upgrade items, he'll reinforce your weapons and shields. For basic gear, Titanite Shards will do. As soon as you have two of these, come back to the Blacksmith and improve your favorite weapon. This is worth multiple levels of investment because weapon upgrading is a major part of your advancement. In fact, you may notice more benefits from good weapon upgrades than most of your leveling!

Andre also infuses equipment so that it scales in different ways. After you find special Coals, he can eventually turn weapons into much better, focused implements. You can make your items deal more damage based on Strength, Dexterity, Intelligence, or Faith. The more you focus, the better the results, as long as your character is focusing on the same attribute. This process can also add special effects to weaponry.

If you find Estus Shards, bring them to Andre to increase the number of Estus Flask uses. He'll also help you Assign Estus Flask uses between HPs and FPs. If you're not much of a caster, do that now so that you have a full complement of regular Estus Flask uses. Some melee characters need more FPs than others. Experiment to find the best combination for your playstyle, regardless of the archetype that you are playing.

A small man sits on a throne above the main chamber. His name is Ludleth, and he'll soon be able to transform the special Souls that you get from most bosses. He can fashion these Souls into special items. For now, simply talk to him.

Later, you can bring many more NPCs here, and others will come of their own volition. Not all of them will be friends, but most can help you on your way. All of these characters are covered in the NPC chapter at the end of this book.

Now that you have a base of power, you should explore new regions. The Bonfire here in the shrine has unlocked a new location. Go to the Bonfire and select Warp. The High Wall of Lothric is one of the places where you can travel, and it leads to treasure, monsters, and new mysteries.

After you've explored the area fully, read the following note to find some tricky treasure. These items are very powerful, and they can be easy to miss.

![Map of the Cemetery of Ash area]

D

E

F

G

I

NPC Hawkwood the Deserter

H

F

J

G

C

Ringfinger Leonhard

NPC

K

NPC Yoel of Londor

I

NPC Yuria of Londor

H

11

NPC Greirat

12

NPC Karla the Witch

J

K

13

NPC
Ludleth of Courtland

NPC
Irina of Carim

NPC
Orbeck of Vinheim

NPC
Cornyx the Pyromancer

NPC
Fire Keeper

NPC
Andre the Blacksmith

COLLECTING LOOT IN THE AREA

The tower sits above the shrine. You reach it by purchasing a Tower Key from the Shrine Handmaid for 20k Souls. Leave the shrine afterward, using the topmost exit. There's a tree outside that drops "**Seeds of a Giant Tree.**" These seeds turn monsters against Invaders, so they're very useful when you're fighting against other players and want them to die at the hands of creatures that they may be hiding near.

The seeds only fall on rare occasions. There is a 10 percent chance that one will drop after an invasion. If a seed doesn't fall at that time, the chance increases by 10 percent (up to a maximum of 50 percent per invasion). This chance resets to 10 percent each time a seed appears.

Unlock the tower and go inside. This leads you up and out to a bridge—cross it. Enter another building at the far side. From there, you can jump off the edge in that dark area and collect the Shrine Keeper set of clothing from a grave halfway down. It's a very difficult landing, and you'll die if you miss it. Don't try this when you have a full Ember going. Wait until you've already died at some point in the future, and then experiment with getting this loot.

The bottom features even more treasures.

Take a lift to the top of the newer tower, and look for the bell at the very top of this route. Get a **Fire Keeper Soul** there. This is something special that you give to the Fire Keeper so that she gains the ability to remove your Dark Sigils, if you have any.

Leave the new tower, and walk onto the damaged stone bridge. Look off from its left side, and then jump down to the roof of the shrine. Knock a ladder door so that you can easily return in the future, and then cross to the other side of the roof. Drop one tier down and look for an entrance back into the shrine. A small opening grants you access. Cross the rafters to collect an **Estus Shard**.

Don't leave the rafters yet. Cross to the side of the room and hit the wall there with your weapon to reveal a secret door. Carefully stay on the beams, proceeding toward the far end of the one you're walking on. Drop into a tiny hallway to find a chest that contains a very useful item. Later in the game, if you've met Patches, he'll also come here.

HIGH WALL OF LOTHRIC

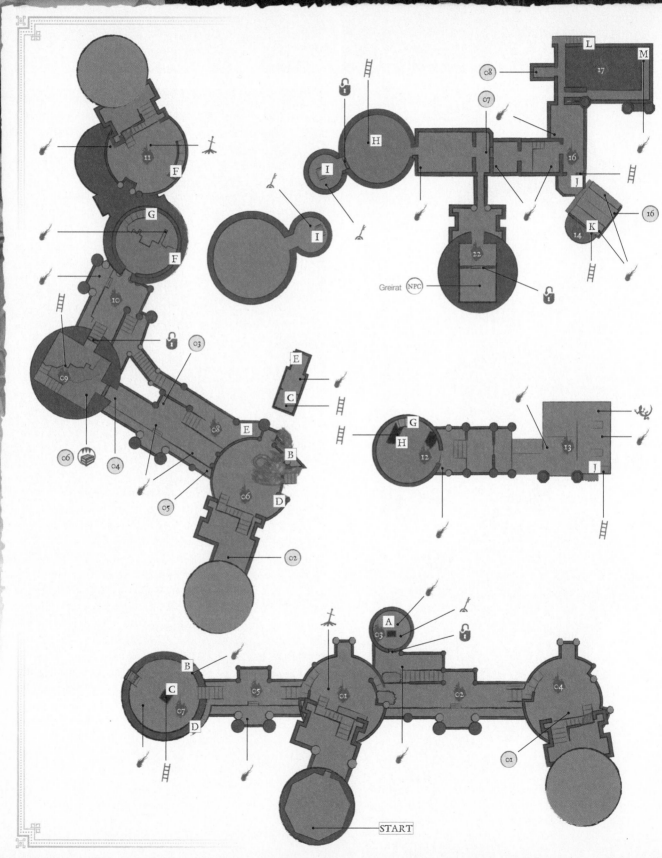

Greirat (NPC)

START

1	Longbow
2	Binoculars
3	Club
4	Steel Soldier Helm
5	Claymore
6	Deep Battle Axe
7	Mail Breaker
8	Broadsword
9	Silver Eagle Kite Shield
10	Astora Straight Sword
11	Estus Shard
12	Rapier
13	Ring of Sacrifice
14	Lucerne
15	Cell Key
16	Fleshbite Ring +1 (New Game +1)
17	Ring of the Evil Eye+2 (New Game +2)

BONFIRES LOCATED HERE

High Wall of Lothric

Tower on the Wall

Vordt of the Boreal Valley

Dancer of the Boreal Valley

Oceiros, the Consumed King

ENEMY NAME

Starved Hound

Large Hollow Soldier

Hollow Soldier

Praying Hollow Soldier

Lothric Knight

Hollow Assassin

Pus of Man

Winged Knight

Dragon

Crystal Lizard

Avaricious Being (Mimic)

Vordt of the Boreal Valley

Dancer of the Boreal Valley

KEY DISCOVERIES

Free Greirat the Thief

Acquire Red Eye Orb from Darkwraith

Acquire Small Banner of Lothric

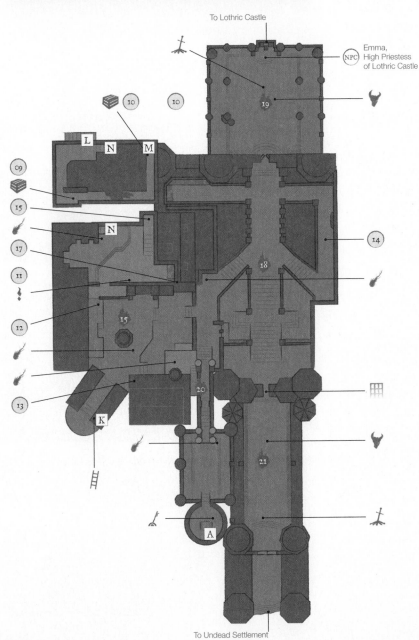

To Lothric Castle

Emma,
High Priestess
of Lothric Castle

To Undead Settlement

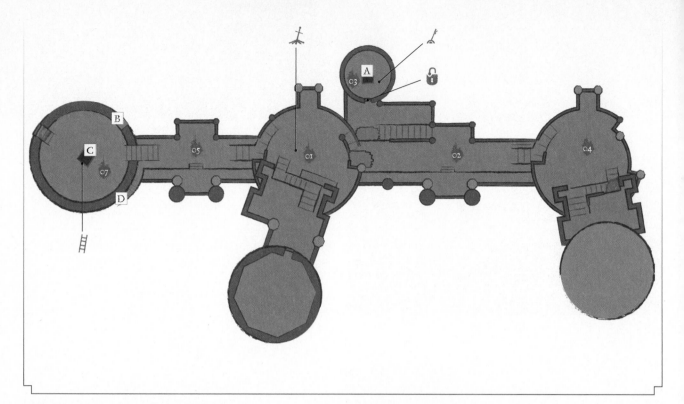

BONFIRE—HIGH WALL OF LOTHRIC

 Warping from the Firelink Shrine deposits you here, in a quiet chamber high on the walls above the Lothric Castle grounds.

Step forward and open the door onto the battlements to reach the High Wall of Lothric proper. Once outside, make your way down the steps and activate the Bonfire. This is your new home base as you tackle the next challenge on your quest to locate the Lords of Cinder.

You are immediately faced with a choice of how to leave this small tower—you can go left toward the ominous dragon in the distance, or right toward an otherwise unremarkable tower. The left path (toward **5**) is slightly easier. If you have trouble going right, just return later. The right path dead-ends for now, but you can find a few useful items along the way. If you're up for it, that's a good place to start.

Now That You're Getting the Hang of It

This guide is easing up on the full tutorial-style walkthrough here slightly, but only slightly. This is your first "real" taste of what *Dark Souls III* is going to throw at you. Take these lessons to heart, because it's only going to get harder from here.

Almost every encounter in the High Wall area is designed to teach you something useful, including basic combat against multiple enemies, how non-humanoid opponents fight, the judicious application of ranged weaponry, using your tools wisely, or sometimes simply running away (or past!) enemies.

Even this early in the game, you are going to find a few places that you can't yet reach. That's normal! You can and should backtrack frequently to revisit areas and reach previously inaccessible items or secrets.

If you're a veteran, you shouldn't need much handholding here. Just cherry-pick the best items you need for your build, and move on to the boss! Once you have access to Greirat, stocking up on consumables and arrows is a good idea for the fights to come.

After you've completed most of the High Wall of Lothric area, the route becomes a shortcut. It takes you down toward a lift that goes most of the way toward a boss (Vordt). For now, this path doesn't go very far into the level, but there is a bit of treasure on the way.

TAKE OUT THE ARCHER

As you proceed toward this area, a Hollow Soldier Crossbowman fires at you from above. It's possible to kill this enemy before you are exposed. Starting from the last Bonfire, look for a break in the wall on the right side. From there, hop onto the enemy's platform, kill him, and proceed safely.

A few particularly unpleasant Starved Hounds protect this pathway. They're identical to the one that you met outside of the Firelink Shrine. Expect them to be fast. They'll cover distance quickly and often attack a couple of times in a row. Use a shield to block their light strikes, and then counterattack for your kills. There are also Praying Hollow Soldiers, but they aren't a serious threat.

Below this initial stretch is the lift entrance, where a couple of Large Hollow Soldiers await. They have substantial health, so save your Stamina for bursts of attacks to kill them quickly.

○3   The stairs from **(2)** lead down toward the lift that was mentioned previously. You open the door to this lift by traveling all the way down toward the Winged Knight's area, and then taking the small side stairways that lead back up to here.

○4   This side area has multiple Hollow Soldiers, a Large Hollow Soldier, and a Praying Hollow Soldier. Most of them are somewhat distracted, so you don't have to fight them all at once. Focus on the Large Hollow Soldier with the axe, since he is the nastiest opponent of the group.

Beware the Pus of Man guarding the **Longbow** here, the bow is a very useful find for most characters, but this is a challenging enemy if you face it as one of your first encounters. Firebombs work well on these foes!

Because many don't start out with a ranged weapon, the Longbow allows you to begin getting your attributes ready for both ranged and melee combat. Whether you're a caster or a Strength-based fighter, it's useful to have enough Dexterity to wield these basic weapons. Their ammunition is cheap and can be purchased from the Shrine Handmaid back in Firelink Shrine.

If you're really determined to minimize Dexterity, then wait until you get a crossbow before working on ranged attacks. Crossbows don't require much Dexterity at all, allowing you to keep it at 10 or so instead of pushing it up to 14 (which still isn't that high).

○5   Back at the first Bonfire, you head left to reach this parapet. There are many Hollow Soldiers and Praying Hollow Soldiers here. Most of the Praying Hollow Soldiers won't attack you, except for specific, rare members of their kind. The majority of them just want to sit and pray to their dragonic gods.

BEWARE THE LANTERN BEARERS

Hollowed foes carrying lanterns act as lookouts for their kin. They'll scream when they see you, and any enemies that are already prepared to be hostile will come running to see what's going on. Try to eliminate these watchers quickly, or be ready for a fight if you hear them yell!

The Hollow Soldiers are another story. Watch for the one on the right, and for a couple of patrollers, as well. If you wait until the patrollers are farther away, you can clear out most of the area without facing more than one hostile target at a time.

○6   From **(5)**, there is a tiny stairway on the left. It's very easy to miss because there are larger stairs leading down toward **(7)**. Take these stairs up, and fight through a larger horde of Hollow Soldiers. One of the group has a lantern; remember that he's a lookout and will call on the others to assist him.

Also, one of the enemies above and to your left is a Hollow Soldier with Fire Bombs. Thus, you must choose to pull these adversaries back down the stairs, endure an occasional shot in the side, or sprint up the stairs to kill the bomber as soon as possible. He has another melee foe with him, so the direct route is the most dangerous one.

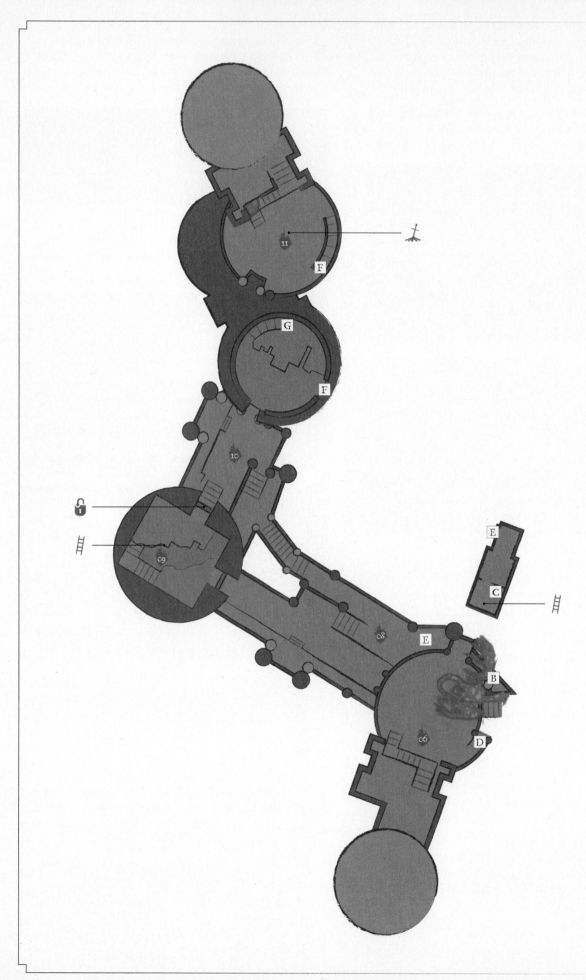

A dead dragon is here, slain upon the walls of the castle. Examine it for a moment, and then go around to the other side of the creature. A short drop leads down to a smaller parapet. You can survive this fall as long as you have any decent amount of health. Walk over the edge, get down below, and grab the Gold Pine Resin in the small window. This window drops you into **(7)**.

C7 Loot the **Firebombs** here, then use a ladder to descend to a lower section of the area. There are two Hollow Soldiers inside the tower, but both are unaware when you enter and can be dispatched without much difficulty. If you came from **(6)**, you enter the room a bit awkwardly and are more likely to get attention from both enemies at once, so be careful!

Major Battle

C8 The tower takes you back out to a larger stone walkway. This place is well guarded. A Hollow Soldier with a spear and shield is up front, and another one has a crossbow. If you want to be really cautious, pull the spearman back with a ranged attack or thrown weapon, and fight it inside the tower. Kill the crossbowman afterward.

LET THE DRAGON WORK FOR YOU

Many more Hollow Soldiers and some Large Hollow Soldiers are ahead. Stairs lead up, and the pathway continues on the right. For easier kills against the undead below, take the stairs up. This triggers a Dragon to land on the castle and start breathing fire everywhere.

Go back down the stairs, and start approaching the undead on the lower level. The Dragon breathes down there, too, killing most of your enemies!

The Dragon that lands on the upper wall has quite a bit of health. If you buy plenty of arrows back at the Firelink Shrine and use the Souls that you've gained to grab a bit of Dexterity (as needed), you can wield the Longbow and kill the Dragon quite safely.

To do this, bring your Longbow and arrows, and get onto the stairs that lead up toward the Dragon's area. Aim your Longbow (see the Controls chapter for details), and fire at long range to hit the creature's wings. You can't be hit by its breath from there, so the kill is purely a matter of time. It costs under 500 Souls to get more than enough Wood Arrows to do the job. You can get the farming completed for that in just a few moments, even this early in the game.

The Dragon's wing on the right takes a bit more damage than its main body and can easily be hit while you're hugging the left side of the stairs. This is safe, repeatable, and nets you a **Large Titanite Shard**. The area above has a large soul, an **Ember**, a **Steel Soldier Helm**, a **Club**, and a **Claymore**.

The Claymore is your first solid strong two handed weapon, with a good moveset for dealing heavy, cleaving blows in an area. The Club, though seemingly a simplistic weapon, is in fact an excellent starter weapon for a purely Strength focused character.

C9 This small room contains little other than a ladder leading to a door that connects to **(10)**, but there is an innocuous chest in the corner… a chest that is actually a Mimic.

This is an extremely nasty foe this early in the game, but you can defeat it with some clever terrain usage—climb the ladder and drill it full of holes with arrows from a distance.

Your reward is a very useful **Deep Battle Axe**. You can't make Deep weapons until much later in the game, and the Deep infusion gives this weapon inherent Dark damage. Deep weapons don't scale with stats, *but* they also don't *require* any significant stats to deal hefty damage. Deep weapons have the same power progression as Fire weapons, but with a different damage type. This is a great weapon for any character build where you aren't planning on investing heavily in Str or Dex!

Unlock the door that the ladder leads to. This connects you to **(10)** directly, allowing you to bypass the enemies below the Dragon at **(8)**.

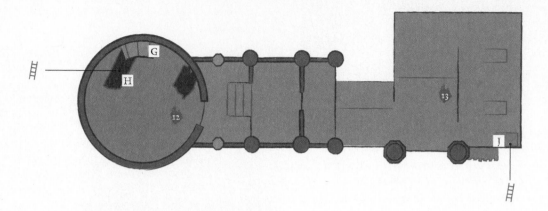

This is a small ledge with two resting Hollow Soldiers and a Lothric Knight. Kill the resting foes before they rise and before the heavier threat realizes that

you're there. This way, you have more room to maneuver against the Lothric Knight. As suggested earlier in the tower section, you can exploit ranged advantages against these armored enemies because they don't have anything to respond to that type of threat. If you're really worried, shoot from inside the tower and flee. You can return to repeat this after the Lothric Knight returns to its original area.

Or, charge the Lothric Knight and practice baiting its attacks. Lure the tough foe to launch a few of its own attacks, and then respond aggressively as soon as it whiffs or is parried. There are knights throughout the game with similar tactics, but better stats. Mastering your anti-armor techniques now will pay for itself many times over.

BONFIRE—TOWER ON THE WALL

The other side of that walkway leads into a larger tower with several floors. This is a very important area, so clear it carefully. A side stairway goes up the

outside of the tower and takes you to the second Bonfire of the area. This is the Tower on the Wall Bonfire, which is very useful for extending your foothold in this area.

Hollow Assassins guard the two middle platforms inside the tower. They have daggers and only moderate health, so you can cut them down quickly before they're able to attack you. Leap off of the stairs to make a Plunging Attack into an enemy below.

You can continue through the region from the next floor down by exiting the tower. Or, you can climb all the way to the bottom. This takes you down to the dungeon, which has an NPC that you'll be able to unlock later. Avoid this for now, and go outside to **(12)**.

The middle portion of the tower exits onto rooftops. Walk forward, and keep your weapons ready. Two weaker undead are praying on the ledge in front of you, but two Hollow Soldiers are also converging here. One climbs the ladder in front, and the other comes over the wall to your right. For an easier fight, hang back and pull the ladder climber. He'll come alone if you do this; the one who comes over the wall won't trigger until you actually get onto the platform.

Follow the rooftops, and observe a large party of praying undead. These enemies have been quite weak so far, but this group is much more dangerous than you might think.

A SINISTER SECRET

The standing member of this cult is your target. Soon after you're spotted, that one will transform into a Pus of Man. It gains more health, along with better range and damage, and it can be a serious threat to your survival. If you don't have a ranged option, it's best to fight this foe with a weapon and shield. If you do, back off to the ladder behind you, climb it, and plink at the enemy from range to weaken or kill it.

To avoid this encounter completely, rush to the next ladder and descend off of the roof, or dash and kill the transforming cultist before it's able to become a Pus of Man.

The only advantage of letting this thing turn is that they are worth a few more Souls and have good treasure drops if you farm them.

Tucked away behind one of the windows that jut out from this rooftop is a hidden Crystal Lizard. As it is located near the edge, it can be tricky to dispatch before it flees. Sprint at it and strike it with any weapon that can aim down far enough to hit it reliably. Doing so allows you to stun it and keep it in place long enough to kill it, netting a **Raw Gem**.

Raw Gems let you create weapons with *no* stat scaling, and no element either (unlike Fire or Deep Gems). Like the Deep Battle Axe earlier, this is a potentially useful weapon upgrade for any character that won't be investing heavily in Str or Dex, and because it deals pure Physical damage, you don't have to worry about elementally resistant foes when using a Raw weapon. The tradeoff to all these benefits is less *potential* damage compared to a scaling weapon with good stats.

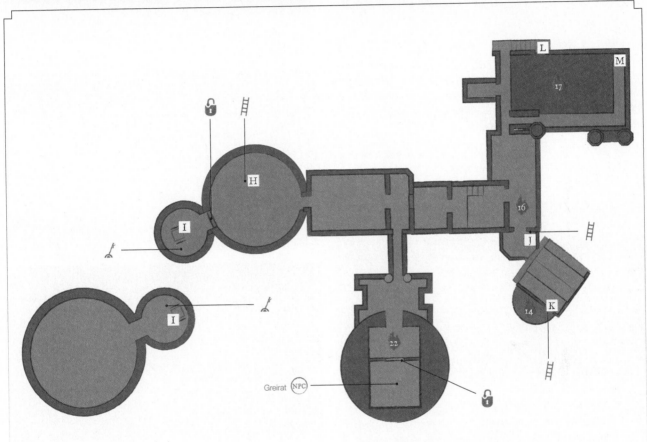

Greirat (NPC)

Below the transforming cult are ledges that look out over the Winged Knight's courtyard. You have a choice here, and both routes lead to the same place. It's best to go through both routes eventually to ensure that you collect all of the loot in the region.

The path to the right (toward **15**) is faster. It takes you through a few Grave Wardens and other weak monsters that climb over the railing. Keep a shield ready to handle the enemies with crossbows, but it's still mostly an easy route toward the Winged Knight that you must pass one way or the other.

The path to the left (toward **16**) is much more difficult, but it has a wealth of treasure.

If you check the rooftops nearby towards **(15)**, you can find a small set of **Black Firebombs**. These more potent versions of the basic Firebomb are useful for dealing some ranged damage to enemies you don't want to tangle with in melee, and very useful against enemies (and bosses!) vulnerable to fire. Likewise, heading towards the ladder scores you a set of regular **Firebombs**.

MAJOR BATTLE

15 A Winged Knight patrols through a large courtyard. Another foe is a resting Grave Warden in a corner of the yard, who won't be a major problem unless you back into it while fighting the main target. Above, another enemy waits on a ledge. If it spots you fighting, it'll jump down and help the Winged Knight. Try to keep the battle either in the middle of the yard or toward the tunnel that serves as a major entrance to the area.

The Winged Knight is kind of a beast. It can cover distance quickly, deal high damage, blow through Stamina if you block its attacks, and kill your character easily if you aren't careful. Ranged attacks weaken it well if you're willing to put in the time to attack, run, and return. For those who are less patient, walk behind the enemy while it patrols, and unleash an initial wave of attacks to weaken it before rolling away.

Watch out for the Winged Knight's short-range burst of magic, and also for the combos of wide swings that it makes. Dodge more than you think you'll need to, and treat this opponent like a mini-boss. If you put most of your efforts into avoiding its hits, the few quick counters that you score can dispatch it rather well. Don't try to burst the Winged Knight down from 100 percent to 0 percent in a single combo unless you're way overpowered.

Whether you choose to face the Winged Knight or not, there is a **Rapier** tucked away in the northwest corner of the yard by the Hollow Soldier. This is an excellent Thrusting Sword for any Dex focused character.

16 This alternate treasure route takes you toward the Winged Knight by a circuitous path. Descend from **(13)**, and go inside the building at the base of the ladder. You might want to stop and kill the foe wielding a crossbow outside, as he sometimes moves far enough to shoot at you while you're indoors.

The main room there has a patrolling Lothric Knight armed with a spear and a greatshield, but you don't need to fight that yet. Instead, explore the side room you see as you enter the building. There are four weaker enemies in there. None of them are a serious threat, but their positions make them a little tricky.

One is inside the room, whereas another has a crossbow with an elevated position. A third is behind some pots to your left, and a fourth is hiding in an adjoining chamber. Keep a shield ready to minimize damage from these weaker targets. Search everything to find some minor loot, some **Undead Hunter Charms**, a small soul and a **Titanite Shard**.

After you're done, return to the main room and fight the Lothric Knight. It's alone, but that won't make it an easy battle. Bait the enemy's attacks, let it finish a combo as you back away or dodge as needed, and then come forward with a short combo of your own. Don't get greedy! Remember that Lothric Knights have high Poise and can attack you if you try for too many hits in your combos.

17 The next room in the larger building is complicated. The upper ledges have a **Broadsword** and some **Green Blossoms**, so search slowly and well as you get everything. The main route along the upper ledges has a small ambush. A Hollow Soldier is waiting in a side room and will charge out after you. Either block it with a shield, or dodge away from its strike and kill it. Loot that side room and then backtrack a moment.

Break through some stacked barrels and crates to discover a somewhat hidden side passage. Go to the end of that, and drop down to a middle walkway. You find a chest below you, containing the **Astora Straight Sword**. This is a solid lightweight Straight Sword, but take note of the 12 Faith requirement, it can't be used without a little stat investment on some characters.

If you go down by the main route, you find another chest there, containing the **Silver Eagle Kite Shield**.

THE SILVER EAGLE KITE SHIELD

Despite its early location and fairly humble elemental defenses, this is one of the best medium shields in the game for a lot of character builds.

It has a nice low 5.0 weight, only requires 11 Str to use, and blocks 100% of incoming Physical damage.

On top of that, it has the Weapon Skill ability, which allows you to use the Weapon Skill of your equipped weapon *while* you have your shield up and ready.

Pair this shield with the Deep Battle Axe or an infusion on the nearby Broadsword and you have an excellent early game setup for melee combat.

Make sure to kill a Hollow Soldier that has Fire Bombs on the mid level. Otherwise, the creep bombs you constantly when you're trying to clear the lower area.

The bottom of the room has all the serious fighting, and this is a great place to practice pulling individuals to fight. If you hop down and start fighting, the two Starved Hounds, one Hollow Soldier, and two Large Hollow Soldiers are likely to overwhelm you. You're much better off pulling at least the first two or three enemies up to the staircase. Alternately, you can be evil and shoot them from the middle walkway, as there isn't a way for them to reach that area. That technique requires more arrows, but that's better than dying!

Clear the lower floor and search everything. Down a tiny ramp, you get the **Cell Key**. This unlocks Greirat, an NPC in the dungeon that you passed earlier, at **(22)**.

Don't miss the **Estus Shard** in this room, located on a small Altar! It can be used to increase the number of charges your Estus Flask carries, an extremely useful upgrade. Acquiring these as you explore every part of Lothric is very important for increasing your ability to stay out in the field away from a Bonfire.

You can now return to your Bonfire, or jump off of a balcony outside to get down to **(15)**.

18   The street that adjoins the Winged Knight's courtyard is well protected. If you descend to the main thoroughfare, you must worry about patrolling Lothric Knights. There are more on the side paths that split off from the road, so no matter where you go, your destination is going to be risky.

(LUCERNE) HAMMER TIME

Up on the top right ledge, you can find a **Lucerne**, your first Halberd class weapon. This weapon, like most Halberds, has an awkward combat style with slow swings. However, in exchange, you gain additional reach, giving you a mix of long thrusting stabs and sweeping strikes.

The Lucerne's Weapon Skill, Spin Strike, is also your first multi-stage skill. If you trigger the Spin Strike, you can press Strong Attack near the end of the animation to perform a powerful continuation of the move that continues spinning and then performs a powerful smash at the end.

You may find the Lucerne too awkward to use at this stage in the game (not least because it requires 15 Str and 13 Dex to use), but experiment with it at some point, just to get a feel for a different weapon than the basic one handers that you have seen up to this point.

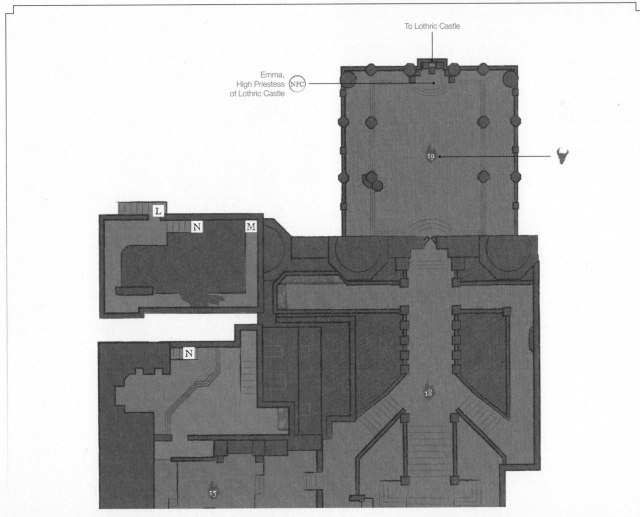

To Lothric Castle

Emma,
High Priestess
of Lothric Castle
NPC

19

18

L

N   M

N

15

One particular side path goes up instead of down. You should explore this area first because it unlocks a major shortcut through this region. Proceed to **(20)** to learn more.

BEWARE THE RED EYED KNIGHT!

In the northwest corner of this area, up a short flight of steps, is a hollowed knight clad in blue and wielding an ornate sword and a medium shield.

It is facing away from you, but if you look from the right angle, you can see its eyes glowing red.

This type of foe is a special, rare, and dangerous enemy. The glowing red eyes are a warning that you may not want to tangle with this foe just yet.

If you decide to ignore the warning and engage anyway, take advantage of the knight's position with its back toward you to sneak up slowly and land a devastating backstab.

Defeating it awards a **Refined Gem**, which allows you to infuse a weapon to gain bonus scaling from Str *and* Dex. Refined weapons require high levels of both Str and Dex to be worth using over other options, so only use this infusion if you plan on wielding weapons with demanding levels of Str and Dex both.

Otherwise, pull the two patrolling Lothric Knights up to your area and kill them individually. The other ones won't patrol into your path, so they're optional. Go up the road to **(19)**, and look inside the church.

MAJOR BATTLE

This nearly empty church has one remaining congregant. Talk to Emma, High Priestess of Lothric Castle several times. She'll give you the **Small Lothric Banner**, and give you the **Way of Blue** Covenant item and explain what you need to do next. Take the banner down to the boss' lair at **(21)**, and defeat it. You can then place the banner nearby, opening the way to the Undead Settlement.

Much later in the game, you need to return to this church. This is also a route to get to Lothric Castle and to the Consumed King's Garden. To access this area, you must return much later, having acquired the Souls of the great lords. You'll learn more about when to do this later.

However, if you're bold and cruel, you can trigger access to these areas at any time by killing this woman. When she dies, it triggers a boss fight that you would have faced later on anyway. The **Chalice of Vows** is yours if you succeed, and you'll be able to unlock the ladder that leads up to Lothric Castle.

DANCER OF THE BOREAL VALLEY

STAGE I

For a character who is just starting out, this battle is grueling. Only very experienced players would have any chance of winning here without multiple weapon upgrades.

Unless you're trying to do something creative, like looting a few advanced areas prematurely, you should have high-end equipment by the time you take this enemy on.

The Dancer has attacks that deal extremely high damage. In particular, watch out for the grab that she makes. If you see the Dancer's right hand come out wide, then wait a moment and dodge left, through the grab. Dodging right feels more intuitive, but it's more likely to get you caught (and the damage you take is ugly).

The overhead strike is much easier to avoid, and you can simply sidestep it some of the time. However, don't try that with the sweeping attacks. Roll through those, and hit the Dancer hard while she recovers.

STAGE II

The pause mid-battle is usually a good time to lay on the damage, and this is somewhat the case here. Capitalize on the Dancer's transition into the second phase. When this happens, you'll see a burst of gray smoke. Get your attacks in fast, but save enough Stamina to run away as she starts to move again. She'll go straight into a long spinning combo.

Dodge back from these combos—they continue for up to seven attacks' worth of damage. You can't take that on the chin, nor can you block your way through it. The only wise method is to dodge until you're temporarily out of range, and then sprint until you're truly safe. Regenerate your Stamina, and come back just after the brief whirlwind that ends the combination.

Continue to dodge around and then get behind the Dancer when she isn't making those huge combos. That's the way to score most of your damage. Execute at least two hits each time, unless you're using a very slow weapon.

Dispatch the Dancer. With this done, you can climb up the ladder that is revealed. Above is a path to the left, letting you reach the Consumed King's Garden. Ahead is Lothric Castle.

Dancer of the Boreal Valley

The upper path leads you away from the Lothric Knights and the church. You can clear the balcony that overlooks the Winged Knight's courtyard to get a large soul, and then jump to reach the ring on the awning nearby.

JUMP!

One of the items here looks inaccessible, though you can drop to it from above. Another way to reach it is by sprinting and jumping from the nearby ledge.

In general, you rarely need to perform acrobatic feats to reach items throughout the game, but this early one is teaching you that it is possible to do so!

In this case, your reward is a rare **Ring of Sacrifice**. This is an unusual ring that has a one-shot effect—if you die while wearing it, it preserves all of your Souls on death!

This is a neat item, but don't feel that it is so rare and precious that you can't use it, or that you *need* to have such an item around to explore safely.

If you're spending your Souls regularly each time you revisit Firelink Shrine, you should rarely have to worry about losing many even if you do die in an unrecoverable location.

Still, an insurance policy is always nice…

Continuing up the path, you reach a small yard. Though almost empty at first, it fills with the undead as you approach the far side. Aggressively wade into this group as the foes arrive. If you have a weapon with a wide, sweeping moveset, equip that beforehand to make your work even easier.

Attack the lone enemy that waits at the end of the yard, and kill off all of his friends as they climb over the wall. You can often defeat the entire group without a blow coming your way, if you're quick about it.

The tower behind the undead has a lift. Take that to the top, and unlock the door you discover. This is the shortcut all the way back to **(3)** that you passed a while ago. With this open, you can get to the boss without having to fight more than a handful of targets, using the first Bonfire in the area.

Grab the **Green Blossoms** in the corner of this room. These consumables temporarily boost your Stamina regen rate, a very useful boon when facing very dangerous foes. Typically you only want to bother using these when fighting bosses, but they can be worth keeping on your toolbelt for nastier foes like Dark Spirits (whether NPC or player invaders!), or tough mini-boss style enemies.

MAJOR BATTLE

Opposite the church, you see a foggy room that looks ominous at the base of the large stairs. The floor is damaged, and you can feel the tension in the air. There has to be a boss here. And indeed, as you step farther into the room, your dire opponent is revealed.

20   Homeward Bone   4303

Estus Flask 3   7537
21

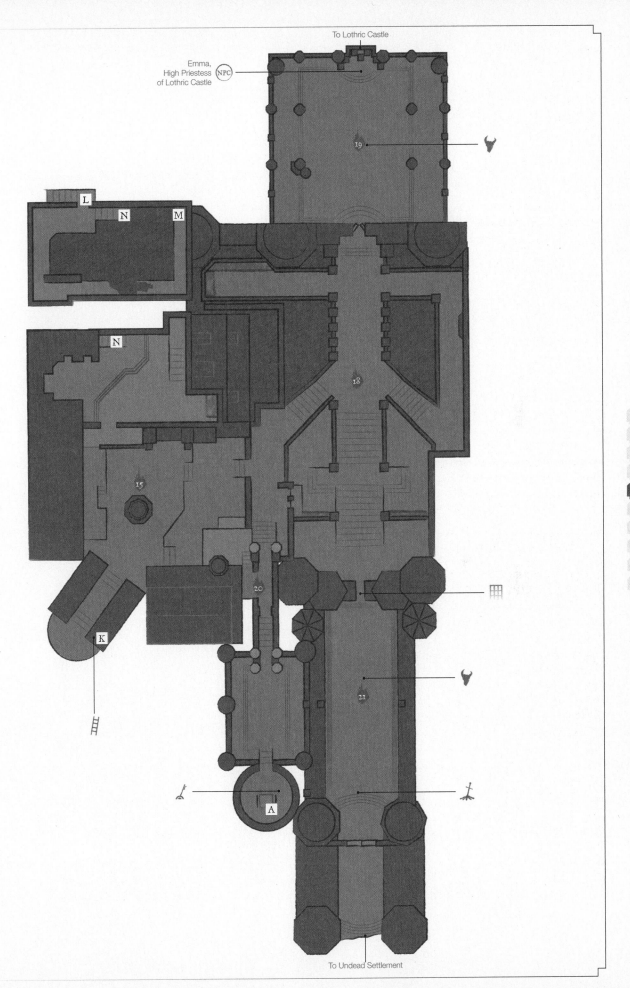

To Lothric Castle

Emma,
High Priestess (NPC)
of Lothric Castle

L

N

M

N

19

18

15

N

20

K

21

A

To Undead Settlement

VORDT OF BOREAL VALLEY

STAGE I

Vordt spends the first half of the fight making sweeping attacks and overhead strikes. These are well telegraphed, so you usually have quite a bit of time to get out of the way. As with many bosses, you should avoid using a shield because you lose so much Stamina if you take an actual hit. Instead, stay out of range when you can, and dodge at the last moment when an attack is too close for comfort.

Perform your attacks in small bursts of two or three strikes. Always keep enough Stamina free for one or two dodges so that you can get back to long range after your last swing.

Fill your Stamina gauge as fully as time allows between these series of strikes. It's very wasteful to begin these attacks when you only have partial Stamina. Also, spending time waiting for Stamina when you're within the boss' striking distance is incredibly dangerous.

Though Vordt can't close gaps instantly, he is still capable of charging over open terrain. If you see him lower and fix on your position, be ready to roll. You won't be able to outsprint him during these charges, so stand still and put all of your attention into the coming dodge. When he passes, turn and walk after him so that you have full Stamina when you get to his new position.

STAGE II

At very close to half health, Vordt glows with a strange fog. Get free shots while you can during this brief transition, and then back off to range once again. Vordt has more attacks during this portion of the fight, including several small, faster strikes. If you aren't comfortable with your health pool and/or your dodging techniques, you may want to go back to a shield so that you can block the smaller blows (while still relying on dodge for the bigger windups).

Often, rolling directly underneath Vordt works well for avoiding his big attacks. He'll flop onto you if you stay down there long, but as a short-term solution, it's very effective.

It's too early in the game to have much gear for high Resistances, but in future New Game Plus runs through *Dark Souls III*, you should keep your Frost Resistance as high as possible when killing Vordt. This prevents you from getting frostbite.

Kill Vordt. Once he is dispatched, you can use the banner that you received in the church. Take the banner to the far end of the road. Interact with the road when you've gone far enough, and watch a short scene as you are taken to Undead Settlement. This is the next step in your journey.

GREIRAT

After you've cleared this region by killing Vordt, warp to the Tower on the Wall Bonfire again. Descend to the bottom of that tower. Fight through smaller groups of undead as you look for a tiny dungeon cell at the end of this area.

The Cell Key (from **17**) unlocks it, and you meet Greirat. He'll give you a quest to find a woman named Loretta. (You'll learn more about this in the Undead Settlement.) Suffice to say that you receive a **Blue Tearstone Ring** right now. Additionally, Greirat goes to the Firelink Shrine and becomes a vendor there. He sells higher-quality arrows and bolts compared to the Shrine Handmaid, and his selection varies from hers. There is also a locked door that requires the Lift Chamber Key to open. It's at the bottom of the tower. This is part of a quest that takes you to kill the Darkwraith below the tower. Doing so earns you the **Red Eye Orb**, allowing you to invade other worlds as frequently as you wish. You get the key from Ringfinger Leonhard, an NPC that shows up occasionally in the Firelink Shrine.

UNDEAD SETTLEMENT

MAJOR ITEMS

1	Small Leather Shield
2	Loretta's Bone
3	Estus Shard
4	Warrior of Sunlight
5	Whip
6	Worker Garb
7	Reinforced Club
8	Undead Bone Shard
9	Mortician's Ashes
10	Cleric Armor (full set), Blue Wooden Shield
11	Great Scythe
12	Flame Stoneplate Ring
13	Caduceus Round Shield
14	Flame Clutch Ring
15	Hand Axe
16	Caestus
17	Bloodbite Ring (on Large Hound-rat)
18	Loincloth
19	Red Hilted Halberd
20	Saint's Talisman
21	Large Club
22	Northern Armor (full set)
23	Flynn's Ring
24	Mirrah Vest, Gloves and Trousers, Chloranthy Ring
25	Irithyll Straight Sword
26	Wargod Wooden Shield
27	Partizan
28	Blessed Red and White Shield +1
29	Life Ring+1 (New Game +1)
30	Poisonbite Ring+1 (New Game +1)
31	Covetous Silver Serpent Ring+2 (New Game +2)

ENEMIES

Starved Hound
Peasant Hollow
Hollow Slave
Cathedral Evangelist
Cage Spider
Hollow Manservant
Skeleton
Hound-rat
Large Hound-rat
Boreal Outrider Knight
Demon
Curse-rotted Greatwood

BONFIRES LOCATED HERE

Foot of the High Wall
Undead Settlement
Cliff Underside
Dilapidated Bridge
Pit of Hollows (Boss)

KEY DISCOVERIES

Yoel of Londor
Cornyx, the Pyromancer
Irina of Carim
Eygon, Knight of Carim
Siegward of Catarina

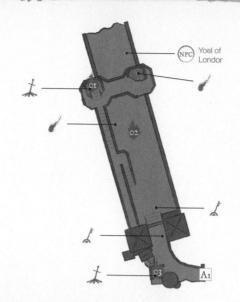

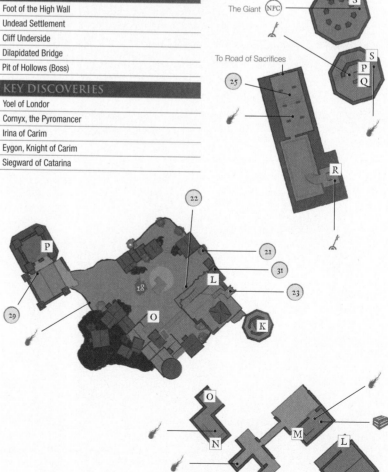

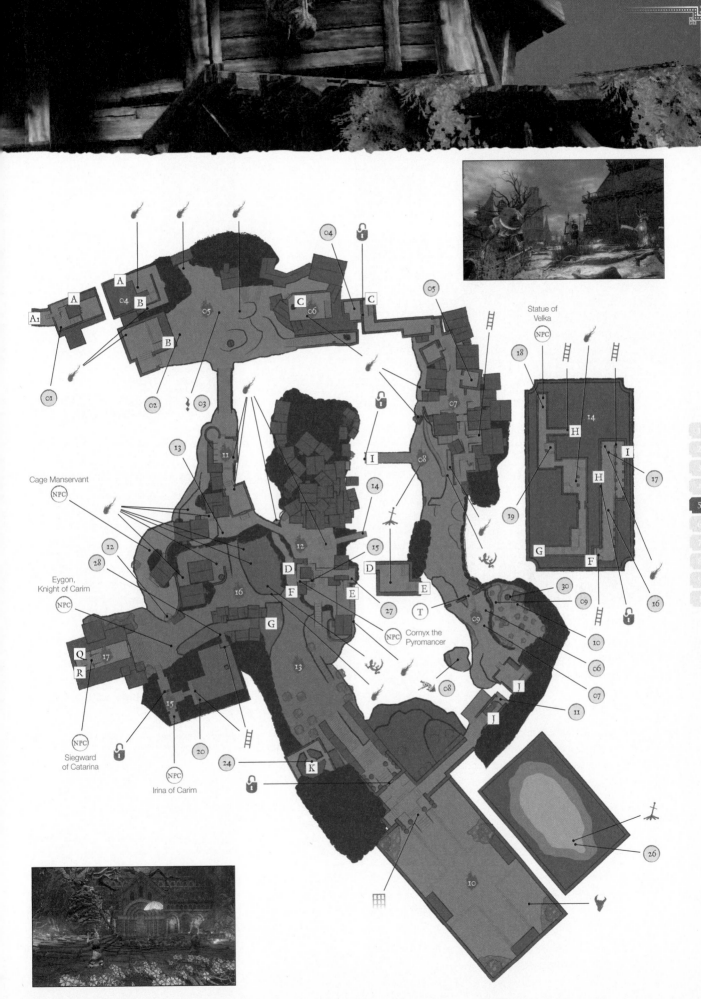

Cage Manservant

NPC

Eygon,
Knight of Carim

NPC

Q

R

NPC

Siegward
of Catarina

NPC

Irina of Carim

Statue of
Velka

NPC

Cornyx the
Pyromancer

NPC

BONFIRE—FOOT OF THE HIGH WALL

You are taken to a Bonfire far below Lothric Castle, in the settlement of undead below. Light the fire (Foot of the High Wall), and start to explore

this new area. There aren't any monsters nearby, so you're safe for now. Make your way over to the other tower to find a Soul before descending the stairs.

YOEL OF LONDOR

A long stairway leads to a road where Starved Hounds unleashed by a group of Peasant Hollows are slaughtering many weaker undead. Use the confusion as a way to sneak in a few attacks against the Starved Hounds before they finish off their prey and turn on you. They're much more of a threat than the basic, unarmed undead souls that are milling about.

Kill the pack of enemies, but don't go toward the closed gate ahead yet. Instead, follow the street in the opposite direction. Watch out as more Starved Hounds try to surprise you at the other end of the road, hiding behind a fallen carriage.

They are guarding a pair of **Alluring Skulls**, a consumable item that can be used to create a distraction—when dropped, the skulls attract nearby undead foes, allowing you to sprint past unhindered, or score free critical attacks.

In the area beyond, you meet an NPC. Yoel of Londor is crying amongst a horde of his fallen comrades, on the right side of the road. Talk to him and agree to take him into your service. He'll travel to the Firelink Shrine and serve as a dealer of spells there. Yoel also serves as a link to one of the endings to the game, so he is an important NPC despite his early appearance. See the NPC chapter for more details on the full questline involving him.

After you've finished exploring, use a lever near the large portcullis. This opens the way for you to enter the Undead Settlement proper.

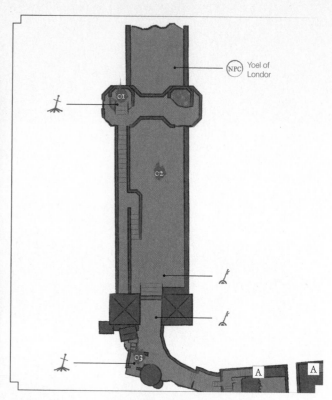

NPC Yoel of Londor

BONFIRE—UNDEAD SETTLEMENT

Light a new Bonfire (Undead Settlement) inside a cabin as you proceed. You can use another lever to close the portcullis and make it harder for the Starved Hounds to bother you in the future, but it isn't particularly important as long as you don't go near these monsters after resting. The only other monsters are a couple of Peasant Hollows guarding a building ahead.

Get used to these foes because they are a staple of this area. Though very slow to attack, they have decent damage and good range, and they can stagger you easily if they land a blow. Pulling them out singularly helps you thin their ranks and ensures that you won't become overwhelmed by numbers. It's also useful to attack early and aggressively. Don't bait them, though—it takes too long and actually leaves you more exposed because there are often multiple enemies surrounding you.

The house here has a few Hollow Slaves, which attack from dark places. Sometimes, they'll drop from a ceiling and land behind you, so listen carefully as you walk around. Keep your eyes peeled, and charge any of the Hollow Slaves that appear.

Unlike many other enemies, these foes have ranged and melee attacks. It's always faster and safer to engage these enemies directly and score your kills. Hollow Slaves don't have much health, so one or two attacks are usually enough to end the fight.

You find the **Bones of Loretta** close to this location. Her body is tied up on the outside balcony of the building. Cut her down, and collect the bones from the ground below. Bring those back to Greirat, if you've unlocked him from his cell in the High Wall of Lothric.

You can pick up a **Small Leather Shield** inside by cutting down a corpse, and some **Repair Powder** out on a ledge past Loretta's body. Repair Powder fully repairs your equipped gear, but as your gear is repaired every time you visit a bonfire, this is rarely needed unless you are making heavy use of a weapon with extremely low durability (generally only weapons in the Katana class, with a few exceptions).

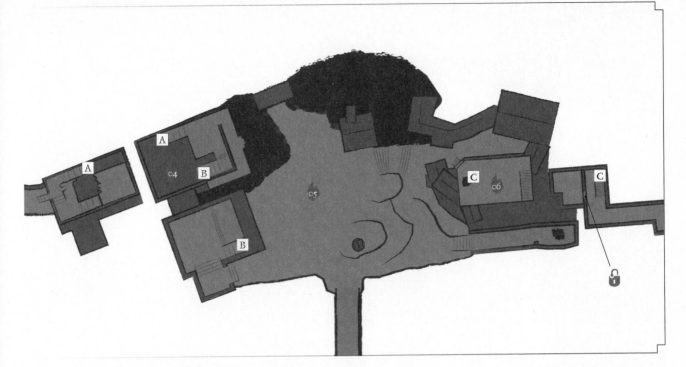

You also find a pair of **Charcoal Pine Bundles** inside, these allow you to *quickly* apply a Fire element attack to your right hand weapon. Unlike the Resin, this effect is extremely quick, fast enough to use during battle. Remember that you cannot apply an element to a weapon that is already inherently elemental (say if you have the Deep Battle Axe from the High Wall area, you can't use the bundle on it, because it already has a Dark element attack).

05 The fight outside of the cabin is draining. You're likely to use some of your Estus Flask, so you should only run this fight the first time you come through. That way, you can get all of the loot, rest afterward, and avoid the fight in the future.

There are about a dozen Peasant Hollows praying, with an Evangelist leading them. Kill as many of the Peasant Hollows as you can without drawing the attention of the entire horde. Once they realize that you're there, things get tougher. Evangelists have ranged spells that track, and their melee attacks are wicked. Don't try to interrupt them, as you likely won't be able to stagger them before you get pounded. Instead, dart in, strike, dodge back, and retreat. Don't try to perform multiple blows or long combos. Both tactics just lead to trading damage, and that isn't what you want.

Don't miss the **Estus Shard** here, it's worth dealing with the giant pack of enemies at least once to secure, the Ember and Soul nearby are less critical.

There is a split in the path here. Both routes are filled with treasure that's worth your time, and both directions lead to important locations. This walkthrough discusses the straight path first **(6)**, and then talks about the one to the right, over the bridge.

06 Fight through a few Peasant Hollows to get into a large building. You can get into the structure through either a hole on the right or a door to the left. The door route is better for treasure purposes. Go through it, and kill another new type of enemy. These Cage Spiders aren't always alive, so try to lock on to them as you approach. If you lock on, the monster is alive and can attack you. If nothing locks on, you're probably fine. These enemies can't move much. Kill them at range if you want to be safe, or wade in if you don't mind minor damage. These foes are more of a nuisance and only rip you up when there are groups of them to contend with.

Search the initial room for some **Charcoal Pine Resin**, and then drop through a hole in the floor. Below is a cauldron with Estus Soup, as well as a **Warrior of Sunlight Insignia**. This emblem is a Covenant item, allowing you to join the Covenant of jolly cooperation. If you enjoy co-op play, this is the Covenant for you. The door out of this room is locked from the outside, but you can open it from within if you dropped down from above.

NPC Cornyx the
Pyromancer

Estus Flask

07

6899

ESTUS SOUP

You occasionally find these soups out in the wild. They'll heal you as soon as you use them, and each time you rest at a Bonfire, they'll be restored. Use them as a way to conserve on using your own Estus Flask when you know that some soup is in the area.

There are more Cage Spiders and Hollow Slaves on the way out of the building. They'll be joined by an undead with red eyes that stalks you in the darkness. Watch for attacks from the walls of the corridor, and from the room above it. Back up and take the fights slowly if you need more space and want to be sure that your flanks are safe.

Be wary of the red eyed undead that awaits at the end of the hall leading towards (7). It can be a nasty fight in close quarters, so make sure the hall is clear of other foes before you engage. Try to initiate the combat using some of your Charcoal weapon enhancers, Firebombs, or ranged attacks to get in some damage before it can close with you.

A hill leads down toward more buildings, but the fighting here is very dangerous. A Peasant Hollow and a Hollow Slave wait behind a breakable door on the left, more Peasant Hollows line the road itself, and an Evangelist is off in the distance standing on an overpass above the street.

You have to dodge spells from the Evangelist while fighting off your other targets. Don't hesitate to pull the enemies here farther back up the hill, out of sight of the spell bombardment.

Once all of these enemies are dead, shoot the Evangelist, or pass underneath it and use a ladder to climb up to the walkway where your adversary stands. If the Evangelist hops down as you climb, you can use a Plunging Attack to deal heavy damage from above. She's guarding a **Titanite Shard** on the walkway with her, and there's a second located closer to the canyon edge just to the west.

You can pick up a **Whip** from the side ambush room, a Dex focused weapon that is generally not a great choice as a primary weapon, but its skill, Impact, has some interesting applications as a PvP tool, allowing you to bypass shields and slow Stamina regen. You can also use it against shielded enemies of course!

The building just past the Evangelist holds a lone Peasant Hollow armed with a two handed hammer, but you can bypass it entirely by going over the rooftops to (8) instead if you choose.

BONFIRE—DILAPIDATED BRIDGE

Before you proceed farther, you can go over the rooftops on the west edge, allowing you to get above a wooden walkway below. Make a running jump to pick up some **Rusted Coins**. These consumables temporarily boost your Item Discovery, a stat that gives you a better chance of finding items on defeated foes.

More importantly, below is a Crystal Lizard. Sprint and try to slay it quickly, because there is a Hollow Manservant waiting ahead, a dangerous foe. Don't get too close, if you feel threatened at all, run for the nearby Bonfire first! You can come back for the **Sharp Gem** it drops. This gem type allows you to infuse a weapon to become Dex focused. So it is good for fencing style characters.

The first of the Hollow Manservant you encounter here is an unpleasant sample of others waiting elsewhere in the settlement. These larger enemies have high health and long combos, and they are very hard to interrupt. Don't try to burn them down at your own expense. Use ranged weapons to pull them, bait out their combos, and take one or two hits during their recovery. When you're still getting used to them, single hits are preferable because overstaying with your combos can leave you badly injured.

Drop off the hill on the right side to find a Bonfire (Dilapidated Bridge). This is a welcome sight—your Estus Flasks might be running low by now. The door to the west of here is locked from this side, you need to approach it via the other route from **(5)**.

09 Now that you're rested, proceed ahead. You start to approach an area with many gigantic arrows stuck into the ground. That's a warning if you've ever seen one! This is a place that wants to kill you.

The branches that you collect from the pale tree in this area can be given to the Giant Slave who is shooting at everyone. Take one when you go through this area so that you have it later when you meet the Giant Slave.

To get out of there, go into the cabin that's directly across from where you entered. It's filled with even more enemies, which will ambush you in the cabin. Lure them back into the arrow strikes, or roll past them and fight inside the cabin, where you're safe from the big arrows. Be careful if you choose to enter the cabin however, as a Peasant Hollow with a two handed hammer and a dangerous red eyed assassin lurk within.

On the second level of the cabin, make a jump across a ruined gap in the floor to find a **Great Scythe**. This weapon requires moderate Str and Dex to use (14 of each). It has broad sweeping strikes, as well as a powerful critical swing as its skill, and inflicts the bleed effect.

The path through the Cabin leads up to the boss of this area. Before engaging the boss, be sure to open the large double doors that lead out onto the stairs of this temple, they only open from this side. You may also wish to reach the Bonfire at **(12)**, though it's about an equal sprint there or the one at **(8)**.

MAJOR BATTLE

10 Many Peasant Hollows are praying inside an open courtyard. If you approach them, a wicked-looking tree in the far corner starts to move. This quickly becomes a battle for survival as the Peasant Hollows approach you and their sylvan ally creeps closer.

Curse-rotted Greatwood

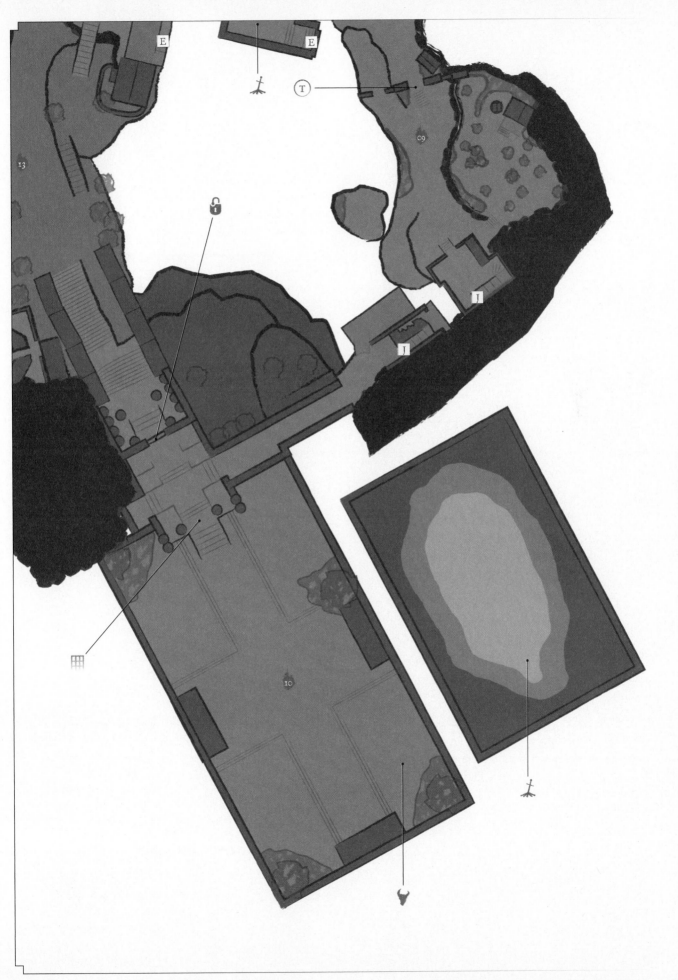

CURSE-ROTTED GREATWOOD

Curse-rotted Greatwood   110

STAGE I

Initially, you must worry about a huge number of targets. This stage of the fight ends as soon as you do any serious damage to the tree, so it's sensible to get that done quickly and avoid a lengthy battle against the congregating Peasant Hollows. The boss spawns more of them throughout this portion of the fight, so you can't even eliminate these targets completely; you can only thin their ranks.

Basically, kill any Peasant Hollows that you must eliminate when they approach you, but put your focus on the tree.

The Curse-rotted Greatwood does not take any damage from your standard attacks. Instead, you have to kill it by destroying the tumors that have grown on various parts of its body. Having a superior weapon makes each tumor burst more quickly, but you only inflict a set amount of damage when the tumor explodes. As such, you must kill a set number of these tumors to win the fight.

Because this stage can go bad so easily, you should go after the easiest possible tumor immediately. That would be the belly tumor. A few swipes destroy it, and then the boss breaks through the floor and sends everyone tumbling down to a lower chamber. This aspect of the fight gets rid of your Peasant Hollow problem very quickly.

STAGE II

The Curse-rotted Greatwood is fairly easy to dodge. At short range, it'll swipe at you, try to grab you, hop up, and try to slam you. If you get to long range, it'll walk toward you or roll in your direction.

It's better to stick close to it, since these attacks are easier to avoid. Also, it's very hard to hit the tumors at range because you need to stay mobile.

Go after all of the tumors that you can hit. Here are their locations (all are melee-accessible, in one way or another):

-Belly

-Back

-Its left side

-Its right side

-Its right ankle

-Its left hand

-Its right elbow

-High up on its right thigh

-Higher up on its body

Get all of the easier targets first. It doesn't take long if you focus on the tumors and move quickly. Once you're used to it, this becomes an easy boss fight. However, spotting the tumors and executing your attacks properly is tricky at first.

As rewards, you receive a **Transposition Kiln** and the **Soul of the Rotted Greatwood**. Take the kiln back to the Firelink Shrine and give it to Ludleth. He'll then be able to transform various boss' Souls into powerful equipment for you!

A Bonfire is down here (Pit of Hollows). Before you leave, worship at the shrine of bones near the bonfire to acquire the **Mound-Makers** Covenant item. The Mound-Makers are a dueling PvP Covenant, allowing you to place your sign anywhere and be summoned to fight, similar to the Red Soapstone, but winning fights earns you Vertebrae that you can turn in for rewards at this Covenant shrine.

You can grab some Homeward Bones and a **Wargod Wooden Shield** on the ground just in front of the shrine.

To get the most experience, practice, and treasure for this region, return to the Undead Settlement Bonfire. You should take the bridge as you continue, because there are very nice items along that path.

This bridge splits off from the Evangelist's fire. Take that to a building with more Peasant Hollows and Hollow Slaves. Don't trust your back, though—the Hollow Slaves climb up the cliffs and drop from the rafters to try to get an advantage over you. Walk slowly, be paranoid, and turn around often. Though these opponents are not very lethal, the fighting here easily saps the uses of your Estus Flasks and makes it difficult to progress if you let them drain your health.

On the outer edges to the west, you can find more Hollow Slaves, some lurking on rooftops picking away at you with their blowdarts. If you go over the rooftops there, and past a Hollow Manservant, you can find a corpse hanging out over the village floor far below. Knock it down to acquire the **Flame Stoneplate Ring**, a ring that boosts your defense against Fire damage. Tucked behind one of the houses is the somewhat less exciting **Plank Shield**.

The Hollow Manservant here has a big secret, if you can sneak up behind him and press Use on his cage from behind, he'll transport you beneath the Rotted Greatwood, where you can meet *Holy Knight Hodrick*. However, you must do this before killing the Greatwood, or the collapsing floor kills Hodrick.

Once you make your way through the barn filled with Peasant Hollows and Hollow Slaves here, you can open a door leading out to **(12)**, and pick up a **Caduceus Round Shield** just outside the door to the right.

BONFIRE—CLIFF UNDERSIDE

The Peasant Hollows have set up a good killzone. They have height over anyone who comes close, and it's fairly hard to get up to them. Either sprint through this part of town, or back off and take potshots to eliminate the ranged enemies. Be particularly careful near the barrels. They're explosive, and the firebombs tossed by the Peasant Hollows can detonate them.

There is a soul under the gallows, and a wooden dock behind this location provides the area-appropriate **Fire Clutch Ring**, a potent ring that boosts Fire attack at the cost of taking increased physical damage. A useful tool for budding Pyromancers. Either sprint over to get these items, or explore that spot after you've killed the Peasant Hollows.

Also, you can find a hidden Bonfire nearby. Stand on the stone bridge that takes you into this section of town, and look over the right edge after you kill the Peasant Hollows that are throwing Fire Bombs at you. The drop to the small ledge below is quite survivable. It's worth it to go for this Bonfire before tackling the Hollow Manservant here, as well as the other Peasant Hollows.

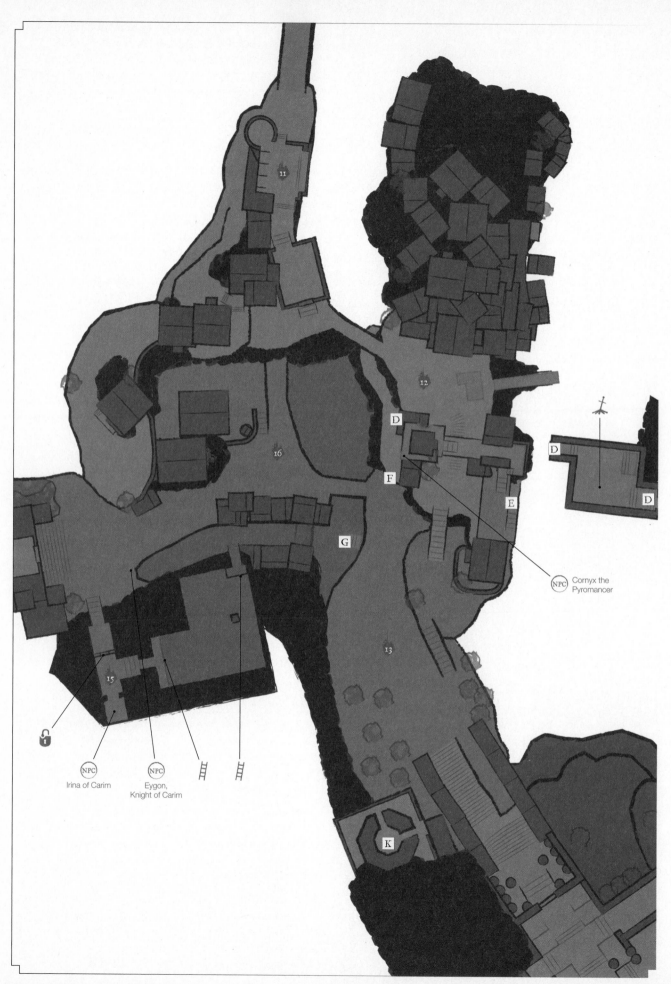

D

D

D

D

F

E

G

11

12

16

13

15

K

NPC Cornyx the Pyromancer

NPC Irina of Carim

NPC Eygon, Knight of Carim

Jump down, and kill a couple of more enemies. Then, follow the path into the next building and rest at the Cliff Underside Bonfire. This is a very nice discovery, but you're not done. The other side of the building gets you onto the rooftops. Climb them all the way up to the ranged enemies' walkway. Explore that to locate Cornyx, the Pyromancer. Talk to him to learn this new art, and he'll travel to the Firelink Shrine, where you can buy things from him in the future.

Grab the **Hand Axe** on the ground near Cornyx. A common starting weapon for Pyromancers, this is a lightweight and wieldy weapon that provides the Warcry skill, giving you a damage boost for a short time after activation.

13 This is another road that leads toward the Curse-rotted Greatwood, and it also goes deeper into the village. As you descend the stairs, you can walk left to reach the boss (if you haven't already killed it), or you can turn right to keep moving through the Undead Settlement.

There are Starved Hounds by the tree ahead. Pull them with a ranged weapon for extra safety, or sprint over there and kill them before the patrolling Evangelist arrives with her Peasant Hollow buddies.

If you're patient and want to avoid combat, wait for the Evangelist to pass with her group in tow, and simply slip down the road when they're not looking.

14 The sewers connect the Dilapidated Bridge Bonfire with the far side of the map, saving you time in future traversals. It's locked from the Bonfire side, but it can be unlocked as you explore the sewers.

You can pick up a pair of **Caestus** in the sewer channel when you first enter from the west. These melee weapons are one of the first weapons you find that are inherently dual-wieldable. Tap the two-hand button to equip a Caestus on each hand to deliver a close range melee beatdown.

The sewers have Hound-rats and a Large Hound-rat. Keep a shield up to deal with these fast foes, and dispatch them. The Large Hound-rat has a **Bloodbite Ring** that makes it easier to deal with enemies that make you bleed.

If you have the Vault Key, there is another passage that splits off from the sewers. You can obtain the Vault Key by taking Mortician's Ashes from the graveyard (where the giant arrows strike) back to the Firelink Shrine. Give them to the Shrine Handmaid, and she'll sell you the **Grave Key**. Use it to unlock the deeper passage under the sewers.

Go through there to find a Statue of Velka, the Goddess of Sin and a **Loincloth**. Praying here lets you request Absolution if you have sinned. Attacking and killing the characters in the Ashen Shrine is a common cause for this. If your Blacksmith won't offer you his services anymore, this is where you need to go.

Make your way down the passage to the south to find a **Red Hilted Halberd**. Unlike the Lucerne Halberd found in the High Wall, this Halberd has a straight thrusting attack as its basic swing, leaning more towards the spear side of the Halberd family than the hammer/axe side. It shares the Perseverence skill with the Caestus you found earlier, both boosting your Poise and slightly lowering damage output while active.

Fight some Skeletons, and then walk through a few short tunnels to get back outside. You're in a gully far beneath the main passage through the Undead Settlement. There is a Crystal Lizard to your right (it drops a **Heavy** Gem) and a pair of **Titanite Shards** on corpses ahead, but be careful, picking up the items is likely to cause a Hollow Manservant to fall on you from above!

Irina of Carim

After the gully, you reach an area with a few more Hound-rats. Kill them, and grab the **Saint's Talisman** here, then climb a ladder to get back toward the surface and reconnect with the main path. If you're not playing a character that began with a Talisman, this is your first chance to make use of a Miracle Catalyst, though this one has a bit higher Faith requirement than the regular Talisman.

On the way out, you meet two NPCs, a woman in a cell and her apparent guardian, a knight standing outside. The more important one is a woman who wanted to come here and be a Fire Keeper. She has failed, but that doesn't mean that she can't help others. Show her some warmth, and she'll teach you the Prayer gesture.

Talk to her again and agree to accept her as a follower, and she'll travel to the Firelink Shrine. There, she teaches miracles. You soon find out that she is named Irina. Unlock the door to escape from this makeshift prison, and then talk to the guard outside. He'll also come along, but he's not quite as pleasant of a person. His name is Eygon, Knight of Carim. As long as you don't harm Irina, he'll be fine. Should you decide to kill her, you can expect this knight to come calling.

The door outside of her cell only opens from this side, so you need to make the trip through the sewers to free Irina and open the door.

This is the lower route to **(17)**, and you're now at your destination. The top route is covered at **(16)**.

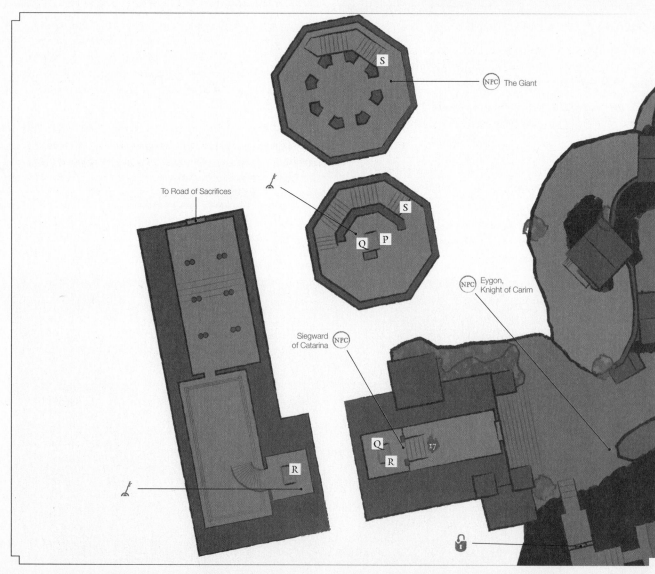

To Road of Sacrifices

The Giant (NPC)

Eygon, Knight of Carim (NPC)

Siegward of Catarina (NPC)

To leave the Undead Settlement, you need to either go through the sewers or take a small bridge and fight through a tough community of Hollow Manservants. There are Starved Hounds here, too, giving you a frightening mix of both fast and slow attackers.

Use a ranged weapon to pull the Starved Hounds and fight them far away from the larger enemies. Once they're dead, shoot one Hollow Manservant from across the bridge, and kill it while it's isolated. Do this for all of the enemies unless you're very well geared and want the challenge of a dangerous battle.

There's some minor loot up on the hill, a Soul and some Alluring Skulls.

SIEGWARD OF CATARINA

Open the large doors to a fort at the top of a hill. A lift is inside, which can take you up or down. If you trigger the lift and quickly get off of it, you switch which direction it will take you on your next trip. There are a few things to note here.

For one, you meet an NPC as he rides up on the lift the first time you arrive. This is Siegward of Catarina. He's a nifty fellow. Talk to him twice to find out what he's doing here.

MAKING THE WHITE BIRCH SAFER

Ride up on the lift to stop the massive arrows that strike the earlier portion of this region, where you saw a large white birch. Kill the Giant Slave up top to end the rain of arrows and collect a **Hawk Ring** that is very useful for range-based characters, boosting the Range stat of any bow you use.

Alternately, talk to the Giant Slave and be friendly with him. Give him a branch from the white birch, and he'll turn out to be a fairly nice guy. As long as you don't attack him after that or cause trouble for the guy, he'll stop shooting his arrows down into the valley. You won't get his ring, but this is a much more peaceful solution.

The view from the top here is pretty spectacular. You can see the whole of the Undead Settlement stretched out below you, the Cathedral of the Deep, the Road of Sacrifices, Farron Keep, Lothric Castle above, and far in the distance? Perhaps a familiar sight to *Dark Souls* veterans.

The lift also takes you to the bottom of the fort, where a Boreal Outrider Knight is waiting. This particular opponent has almost boss-like difficulty because of its strong frost effect and high damage. You must get the most that you can out of ranged attacks, thrown weapons, and evasive maneuvers.

Defeating the Boreal Outrider Knight rewards you with an **Irithyll Straight Sword**. This unusual weapon is one of the few weapons in the game that deals Frost damage, causing the frostbite status effect. Unfortunately, being a unique weapon, it requires Twinkling Titanite to upgrade, and cannot be infused with Gems.

Why Fight Fair?

Though it's mean-spirited, you can use your Longbow (or another ranged weapon) to get a perfect kill here. Hit the Boreal Outrider Knight from range, and back off once it starts getting close to you. Retreat to the previous chamber and get onto the stairs where you came in. Repeat your attacks. This can put the enemy well below half health during its approach. Dodge aside when it charges, and run to the other side of the room. Keep sniping this vicious enemy until it is dead. Melee attacks are tough to use in this match, so why not be underhanded instead.

After you win, open the doors that lead outside. You've reached the Road of Sacrifices, and a Bonfire is only a few feet away (on the right as you exit).

Estus Flask+1

There's a village that's close to the keep, but you won't easily see it until you get there. When taking the lift at **(17)**, roll off of it during your ascent to get onto a ledge. You meet Siegward here again, but there's much more to it than that.

Go outside, jump onto a rooftop, and then descend into a town that a massive demon is patrolling. As you attack, Siegward comes to your aid (if he is still alive). He'll assist in the battle, making it much safer. Play defensively and dodge the Demon's slower axe swipes. If the demon looks like it's about to breathe, sprint away—its fire attack has a decent area of effect and is easier to avoid by strafing than dodging.

Long combos are very effective because the Demon has a considerable recovery time after his attacks. You can afford to get three or even four blows with a faster weapon. Though somewhat risky, this reduces the length of the fight and makes you expend fewer resources in the long run. Also, this enemy is a special encounter, so you only have to defeat it once.

Defeating the Demon earns you a **Fire Gem**. Once you have defeated the boss of the Undead Settlement, you can make use of the Demon Soul back at the Firelink Shrine—talk to Ludleth up on his throne, he'll know what to do with it.

The Fire Gem on the other hand, can be used to infuse a weapon into a very useful Fire weapon. If you didn't take the Fire Gem as your burial gift, this is your chance to craft a weapon now. Fire weapons are very useful for characters not investing heavily in Str or Dex, but are also useful in general just due to the number of enemies weak to Fire damage.

Talk to Siegward a few times after the battle. He'll give you Siegbrau and teach you the Toast gesture. Then, he'll teach you the Sleep gesture, as well.

Check near where you fought the demon to find a **Large Club**. This brutish weapon is a powerful two handed weapon for pure Str focused characters. Cut down a corpse hanging from the building nearby to find a full set of **Northern Armor**. A sturdy set of gear for any mid weight character.

There are a pair of Evangelists, quite a few Cage Spider and a few Starved Hounds in the buildings nearby, take your time to clear them out and loot the area. You can find some **Red Bug Pellets**, a consumable that boosts Fire resistance, and more Alluring Skulls upstairs from those.

Across the walkway from where you found the skulls, a pair of Starved Hounds guard a chest containing **Human Pine Resin**, and an ambush from two more Cage Spider that drop and attack when you open the chest.

The stables have stairs that lead up and through the insides of the village structures. There are several nice items along the way here, but **Flynn's Ring** is the best of the lot, boosting your attack based on how light your equipment load is. Good for most characters, excellent for light Dex or caster focused characters. Find it on the highest roof when you leave the building.

Before returning home, look around the back side of the roof for a gray tower. You can jump over to it and then fall down the open hole in the center of that tower. Jump carefully to reach a ledge just before the bottom to avoid taking too much fall damage.

At the bottom you can find most of the **Lucatiel Mirrah** armor set, and hidden in a box nearby that you can smash, the exceptionally useful **Chloranthy Ring**, a ring that speeds your Stamina regeneration rate!

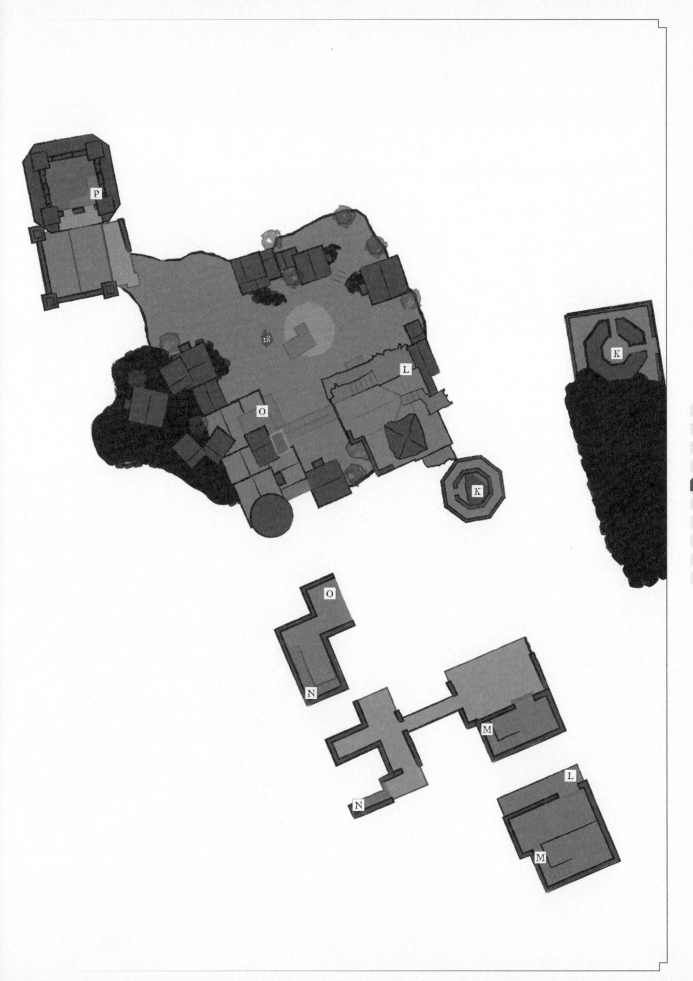

ROAD OF SACRIFICES

BONFIRES LOCATED HERE

Road of Sacrifices

Halfway Fortress

Crucifixion Woods

Crystal Sage (Boss)

Farron Keep Perimeter

ENEMIES

Corvian

Corvian Storyteller

Starved Hound

Lycanthrope Hunter

Lesser Crab

Great Crab

Lycanthrope

Black Knight

Poisonhorn Bug

Sage's Devout

Crystal Sage

KEY DISCOVERIES

Anri and Horace

Orbeck

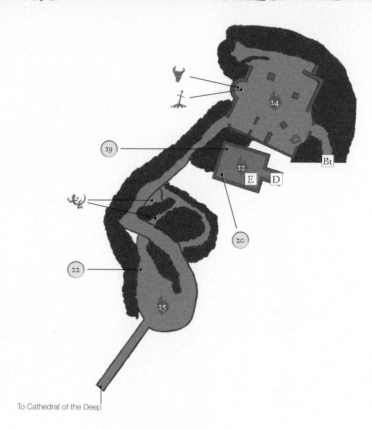

To Cathedral of the Deep

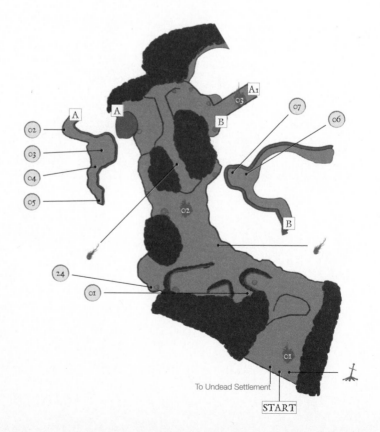

To Undead Settlement

START

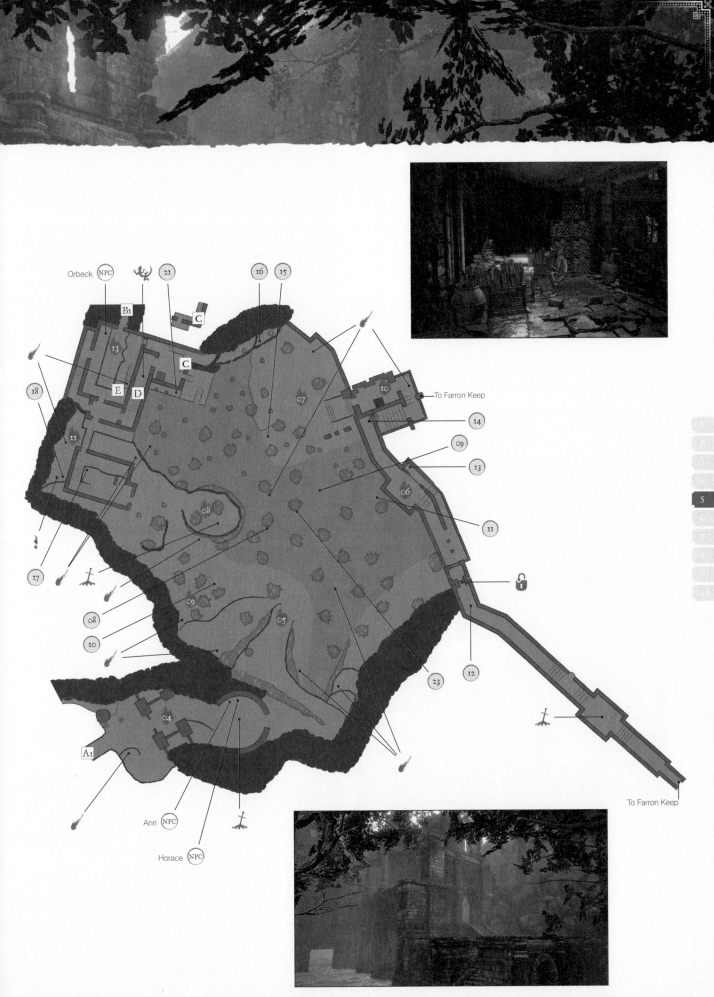

Orbeck (NPC)

B1

13

E D

C

18

11

17

c8

10

21

C

C

16 15

c7

10   To Farron Keep

14

09

13

c6

11

c8

09

c5

c4

A1

Anri (NPC)

Horace (NPC)

23

12

To Farron Keep

1
2
3
4
5
6
7
8
9
10

BONFIRE—ROAD OF SACRIFICES

In the early portion of this new area, you meet new enemies: Corvians and Corvian Storytellers. The former are rank-and-file foes that pose little threat by themselves but are often grouped together for protection. Attack them quickly to seize advantage, and kill them before they gather momentum. If you take too long, wings split out of their bodies, and they'll enter a frenzy. If that happens, they gain decent damage potential and start attacking aggressively.

The Corvian Storytellers are best vanquished with melee attacks because they have powerful spells at range. When you see them, sprint toward them so that you can kill the Corvian Storytellers before they're able to start casting.

Pick up the **Shriving Stone** tucked away in a small nook as you make your way through here.

The second group of Corvians isn't far away. Kill their leader and the followers, but regain your health and Stamina before looking around the cliff path behind the group. Another Unkindled is back there, and she's quick to attack you.

Bait this woman into making her heavy attacks. She'll leap forward and give you attacks that are easy to dodge or simply back away from. Step back, let her miss, and advance for free hits. You can kill her very safely this way. Collect the **Butcher Knife** from her body, and go about your business.

Grab the **Brigand Axe** on the path here, the full suit of **Brigand Armor** behind the Unkindled woman, and finally the **Brigand Twindaggers** at the end of the path, completing your set of Brigand gear!

After crossing a stone bridge, kill the third group of Corvian. Their caster is on top of a large boulder and takes a moment to reach. Fight through his first protector, kill the Corvian Storyteller above, and then turn around to make a Plunging Attack on the others that are approaching. It's a lovely fight.

A ledge underneath the bridge is worth mentioning. Go back to your original side of the bridge, and look over the ridge edge. Drop to the ledge below, fight two Starved Hounds, and get the treasure there. Remember to have your shield out before you turn the corner to face the Starved Hounds.

You can pick up a **Titanite Shard** and an **Ember** on the paths above, and down below by the dogs, the Miracle boosting **Morne's Ring**, and the **Braille Divine Tome of Carim**, granting you access to more Miracles when you return it to Irina in the shrine.

BONFIRE—HALFWAY FORTRESS

This Bonfire (Halfway Fortress) is in the middle of the path as you continue through the woods. It's impossible to miss, and it serves as a strong rallying point for your attacks into the tougher area below.

Here, you meet two more NPCs: Anri and Horace. Talk to Horace to receive the **Blue Sentinels Covenant** Insignia. Anri comes up many times as you play through the game, so look through the chapter at the end of this book on NPC quests to learn how this relates to your own story.

Make a point of opening up the Bonfire's at **(8)** and **(10)** as quickly as possible, a bit of sprinting should let you get both without much trouble, and with all of the Bonfires in the area lit, you can explore the swamp at your leisure.

As you approach Crucifixion Woods, you find Lycanthrope Hunters here and there. They're light on health and can be easy to kill when you get the drop on them. Dodge to the side if they charge, since they have extensive range and reach with their poles.

> **Want Some Weapon Materials?**
>
> Lycanthrope Hunters have a small chance to drop Heavy Gems. There is also a **Farron Coal** in this region. The Farron Coal lets you make your weapons scale incredibly well with Strength. Heavy Gems are the requirement for this modification. If you are playing a Strength-based character, this is the first time that you can really start pushing your weaponry to the next level of slaughter.

As you explore farther ahead, you meet many other new enemies.

Lesser Crabs are small scuttlers that are found in the marsh. They don't get you many Souls, nor are they very powerful. Kill them as targets of opportunity at best.

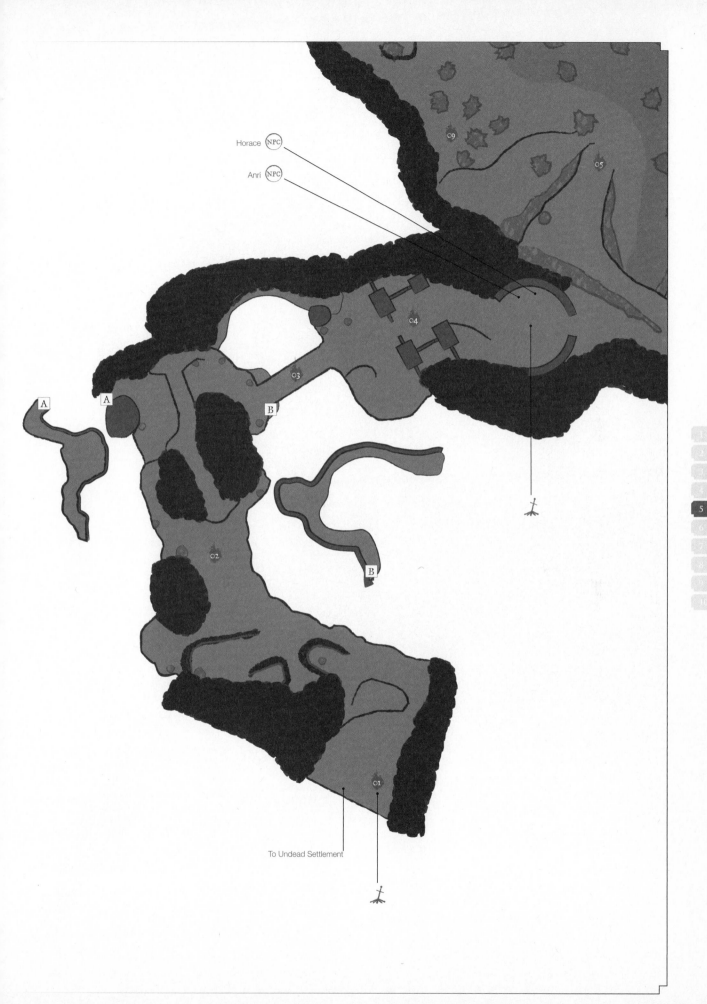

Horace (NPC)

Anri (NPC)

A

A

B

B

O9

O5

O4

O3

O2

O1

To Undead Settlement

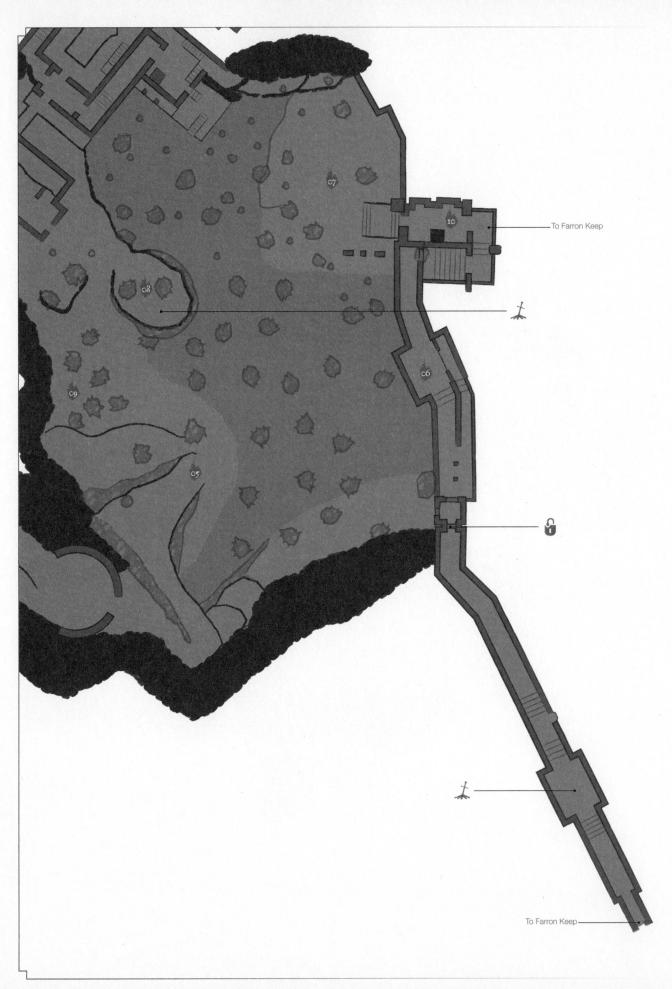

To Farron Keep

To Farron Keep

Great Crabs are rarer. They're very large and have piles of health. Even worse, you usually face them in the water. That means that you can't sprint or dodge as easily. Use long-ranged attacks or spells to fight these enemies when you have to. Because you see them at long range, it's better to avoid them and get your treasure hunting done without wasting too much time fighting in the swamp.

One of the Great Crabs out in the water is guaranteed to drop the **Great Swamp Ring**, a ring similar to Morne's Ring, but boosting Pyromancies instead of Miracles. Definitely worth going crab-hunting to track this down if you plan on using Pyromancy.

Lycanthropes stay on dry land, and they're often alone. Get the jump on them to snag a few free hits before these heavier attackers get up and enter the battle properly. Lycanthropes swing each of their arms, allowing them to cover a wider area than you'd think. If you're struck early in a combo, roll away because you can still avoid most of their attacks. If you're hit at the tail end of their frenzies, start swinging back, and make the trade count.

Out in the swamp, you can also find a full set of **Conjurator Armor**, as well as the **Great Swamp Pyromancy Tome**, unlocking more Pyromancies when given to Cornyx back at the shrine.

06 The eastern side of the swamp takes you to a long locked passage. You can't access the passage until you come up from the depths of Farron Keep, but some of the building is available for exploration immediately. Be careful on the approach, there are several Poisonhorn Bugs that aren't a threat, but the red-eyed Lycanthrope definitely is. With a non red-eyed twin nearby, try to pull them apart and deal with them separately.

Use ranged attacks to wound the Black Knight that guards that building. Up close, he can deal massive damage with heavy, single strikes. Dodge, make single attacks, and back away for the early fight. As he weakens, you can likely risk a heavier combo to secure the kill. If you're lucky, he might drop his **Black Knight Greatsword**. Search both floors of the building for multiple items; a full set of **Sellsword Armor**, a pair of **Sellsworrd Twinblades**, and the **Farron Coal** (for the Blacksmith).

Later when you come down this passage from Farron Keep, you can find **Great Magic Weapon** just on the other side of the one way door—mind the Ravenous Crystal Lizard guarding it!

07 This field has a proving ground for great fighters. There are two Unkindled here with good moves to show off. Approach slowly to avoid drawing both of them at the same time. Pull the first one you see, and try to land extra damage before it gets into melee range with you.

Both of these enemies can dodge and combo well. Bait and punish their attacks; if you try to trade blows, they'll knock you down with their heavier swings. The foe with a sword has a combo with two whirlwinds and a final strike. Force yourself to be patient and hang back until the strike is done. Otherwise, you get thrown around and lose your opportunity.

The other fighter has a Great Club. His attacks are even heavier, but his recovery is awful. Bait him, too, and use a long combo and cut him in half before he's able to return fire. If he dodges away, bait him again and repeat the trick.

You can pick up a full set of **Fallen Knight Armor** at the edge of this field. If you approach from the ledges that extend from the ruined keep area to the west, you can pick up the **Golden Falcon Shield** on a ledge at the northern end of the field. Finally both knights here can potentially drop their weapons, the **Great Club** and **Exile Greatsword**.

BONFIRE—CRUCIFIXION WOODS

08 This is the Crucifixion Woods Bonfire. It's easy to miss because you won't always spot this dry hill if you're hugging the borders of the swamp. Make sure to ignite this Bonfire so that you have a place to restore your Estus Flasks.

Be wary of an invasion by the Dark Spirit Yellowfinger Heysel while exploring the swamp near here. The exceptionally useful **Grass Crest Shield** is in the swamp nearby, granting enhanced Stamina regeneration (at the cost of some physical damage absorption %, so it's not a perfect blocking shield…).

Also located nearby is the **Twin Dragon Greatshield**, though it bears the unfortunate distinction of being the only Greatshield without 100% physical absorption. It is the lightest Greatshield, and still has excellent Stability.

The southern part of the woods is filled with monsters and has only light treasure, a few Souls and Shards. You have to fight Starved Hounds, many Poisonhorn Bugs, and a Lycanthrope as you weave around the tight paths of trees and hills. If you go there, use a shield to help with the Starved Hounds, and consider taking anything that raises your Poison Resistance in case the Poisonhorn Bugs spray you. They're slow-moving and don't attack often, so you're better off killing a few of them and sprinting away, even if there are a few left.

BONFIRE—FARRON KEEP PERIMETER

The ladder here leads down into Farron Keep, which will be covered soon enough. Even if you're not ready to look down there extensively, take a minute to climb down the ladder and get the Farron Keep Bonfire.

Kill the Lycanthrope Hunters around the side and rear of the main castle. They're easy targets and won't pose much trouble, but there is a tougher fight by a campfire. Two Lycanthropes are there, both infused with red-eyed hatred, and a Sage's Devout is on the wall above them.

Kill the caster at range before the others know to come after you. Once the Sage's Devout is dead, the others can be killed one at a time and without nearly as much risk.

Don't miss the **Estus Shard** tucked away in the corner of the rocks near the Lycanthropes!

One oddity is located here, near the southwest of the keep, there is a *purple* summon sign on the ground. Unless you've joined the Mound-Makers Covenant already and used their summoning sign, this may be the first you've seen. In this case, this is an NPC phantom. Summon Holy Knight Hodrick only if you wish to face a tough fight!

Inside the nearby keep via a crack in the wall is a large group of Hollows, along with a lantern bearer who can waken them all to attack you. Fend them off and you can find a **Heretic's Staff** tucked in the corner. Be wary of fighting on the ground floor if the Sage's Devout above is still alive, bombarding you with spells. Lure them out of the keep to fight safely, if necessary.

This room is at the waterline; follow a small passage into it. A red-eyed Lycanthrope guards the loot in this room; the spellcasting speed boosting **Sage Ring**, and a full set of **Sorcerer Armor**. You're not far from the Bonfire, so you can top off your Estus Flasks afterward if you have any trouble.

ORBECK

There are many ways into the castle, but Corvians and Sage's Devouts guard all of them. These paths come together in a pillared room with several targets. Use the pillars for cover from the caster's fire, and kill off his allies one by one until you get him, too.

A side path from that room gets you up and around to the top level. You find a studious-looking mage up there, named Orbeck. You can invite him back to the Ashen Shrine, your nice, safe sanctuary. The place where your vulnerable allies are keeping the home fires burning.

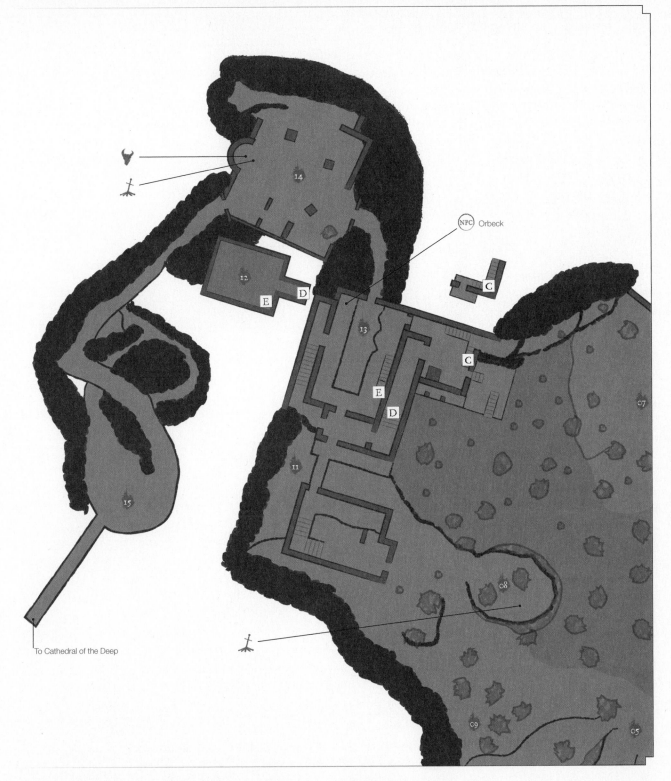

To Cathedral of the Deep

NPC Orbeck

Explore the halls above to find a Crystal Lizard that drops an area appropriate **Crystal Gem**, which can be used to infuse your weapons to scale off of Int, useful for spell-caster focused characters. Not far past the little lizard is a ledge that you can drop down from to find a second **Ring of Sacrifice** (assuming you picked up the first in High Wall!).

If you have befriended Irina and not angered Eygon, his summon sign appears in the hall below Orbeck, allowing you to gain a companion for clearing the area and battling the boss.

MAJOR BATTLE

Without much preamble, a mystic boss attacks. For this fight, you should get as much Magic Resistance as possible, and load your equipment with the best items for raw damage. The Crystal Sage does not have much health, but it can cast hateful spells at you all day long. When you close the gap with this boss, you want to put out the best damage per second that you can manage!

CRYSTAL SAGE

STAGE I

Initially, the Crystal Sage appears in front of you and uses a handful of spells to attack from range. Although many of these spells can track, skillful dodging is still 100 percent effective in avoiding the attacks.

Sprint forward to close the distance, and dodge only when you have to. Walk the last few feet to start regenerating Stamina before your big combo, and unload on the Crystal Sage. If you've kept up with your weapon upgrades, you can cut off half of the boss' health with one combo.

It's okay if you haven't been pushing a really superior damage build. If that's the case, get several attacks on the boss, and then run back to one of the stone pillars so that you can get your Stamina while maintaining some level of safety. Then, repeat your glorious charge to finish Stage I.

STAGE II

The Crystal Sage gets much smarter for the second half of the battle. It disappears at first and throws a few crystals around the arena. Stay mobile and be watchful.

When the mage returns, it will come up in multiple areas. Most of the images you see are fake, but they can still cast spells. For a crude solution, hit each image once to see if the Crystal Sage takes actual damage. If it does, you're dealing with the real one. Murder it! If not, then the image disappears, and you have one less target to worry about.

The faster way to tell which boss is real is to look for the proper color. The fake bosses use only blue spells. The real Crystal Sage casts purple spells, so it's fairly easy to see where everything is coming from. Track the spells back to their source, and beat this fight quickly.

Do not tarry. This is a fight that gets very difficult if you try to finesse it. Sprint to targets, attack, and either move on if they're fake or kill the Crystal Sage when you find it. Be a brute!

After the fight, use the new Bonfire. Your fire burns stronger with each victory.

A path leads out from the Crystal Sage's arena. The path winds here and there, and only a few enemies guard it, two Hollow Manservant and an Evangelist.

There are two Crystal Lizards here, on ledges below you as you leave the Crystal Sage's room, though defeating them before they run away can be tricky.

Remember you can port out and back (or quit and continue) to make them reappear. Both drop **Twinkling Titanite**, which can be used to upgrade unique soulbound weapons (that is, weapons that are neither normal mundane weaponry nor soul-transposed weapons from Ludleth).

The **Herald's Armor** Set is on your way. You find it just before reaching the Cathedral of the Deep. Get the Bonfire for that new region, and check on a ledge just below the Bonfire for the **Paladin's Ashes**, but consider returning to Farron Keep to clear that area before you move on formally into the cathedral.

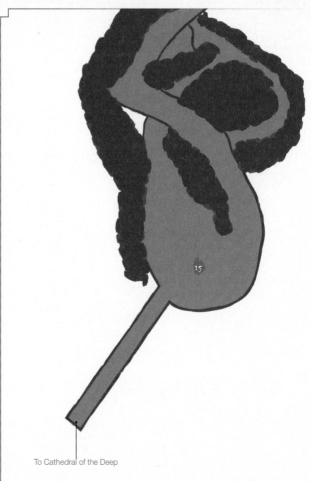

To Cathedral of the Deep

FARRON KEEP

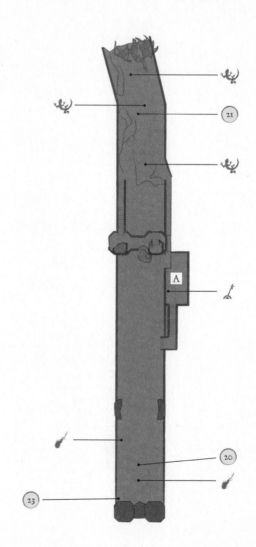

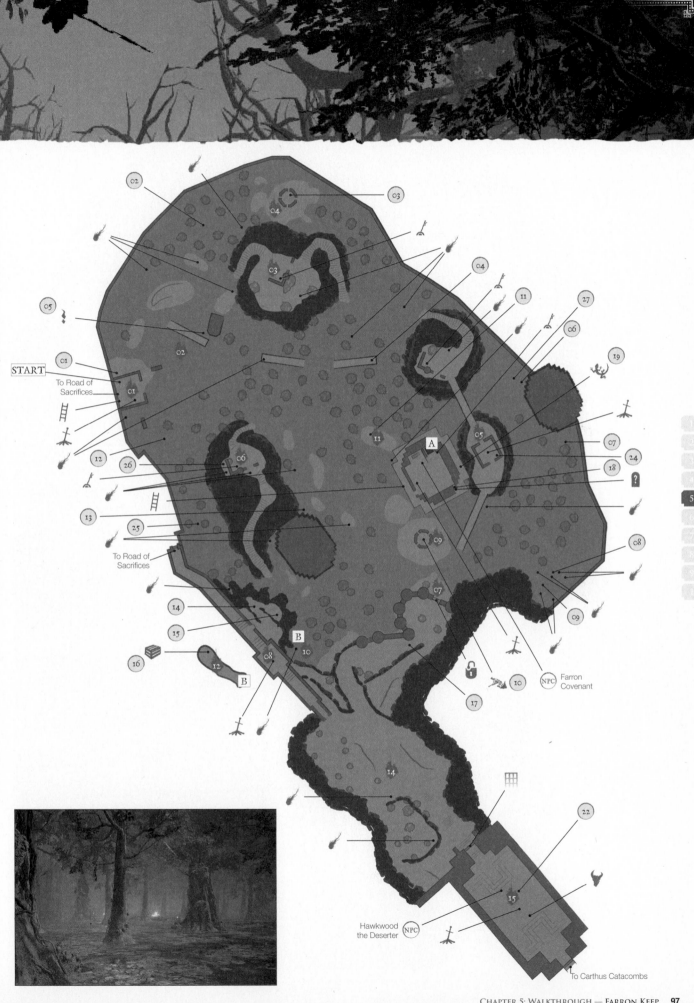

START

To Road of
Sacrifices

To Road of
Sacrifices

A

B

B

Farron
Covenant

Hawkwood
the Deserter

To Carthus Catacombs

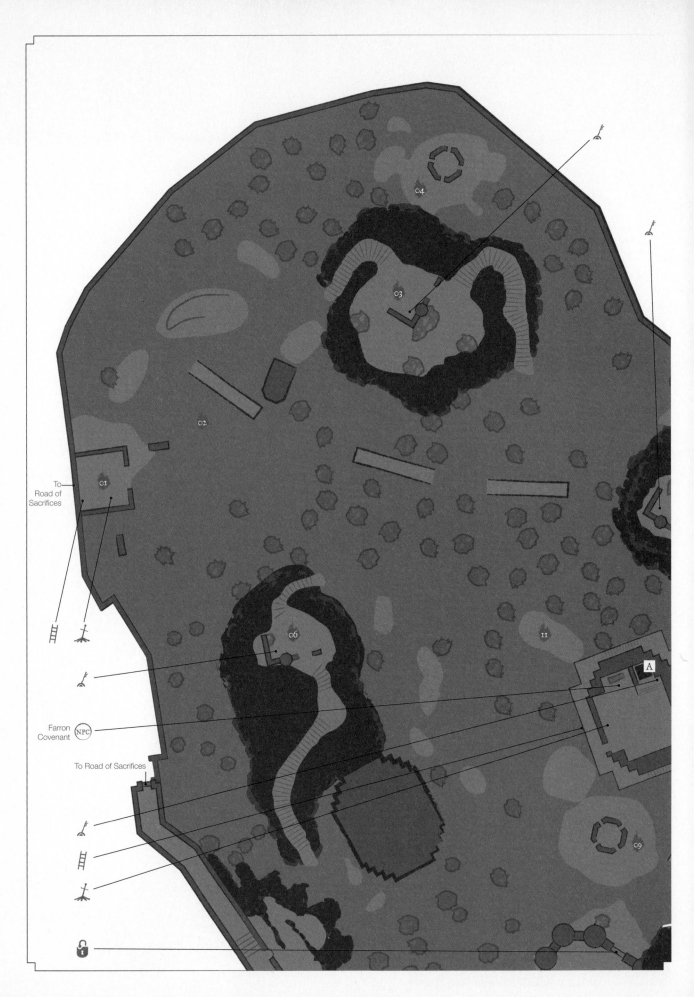

To
Road of
Sacrifices

O1

O2

O3

O4

O6

Farron
Covenant NPC

To Road of Sacrifices

11

A

O9

Bonfire—Farron Keep

This is the beginning of Farron Keep, the area beneath the Road of Sacrifices. The ladder down from that previous area takes you here. This Bonfire is on the western side of the map. Stop to examine the map for a few minutes before moving out. This is one of the easiest places to get lost or confused in the game. The lighting is dim, and the swamp is hard to move around in.

HOW TO ADVANCE

To unlock the southern exit, you must extinguish three fires in the swamp. All of them are located on raised hills, with ramps and stairways that let you access them. You can spot all three on this guide's map almost instantly.

To move through the swamp quickly, get onto those hills, put out the small flames at their altars, and then head to the large southern gateway to flee this moist wasteland.

However, you miss many useful items if you do this. The best decision is to slowly, carefully loot the swamp. Bring anything with Poison Resistance, because you're going to need it.

The Rotten Slugs in the area are some of the weakest enemies in this region. They're easy to pull and dispatch. Get them onto dry land so that you

don't have to build up even more poison while you're fighting, or pick them off with a ranged weapon. By now you should have access to several additional types of ammo, so even a basic ranged weapon can deal enough damage to eliminate them easily.

SAFE GROUND AND POISON

Fighting in the swamp is extremely unpleasant both because of the poisoning that occurs, and the slowing effect on your movement. In some areas, the swamp is deeper, and the effect on your movement is even more pronounced.

If you haven't been using pulling techniques with a ranged weapon up to this point, now is a good time to start—you can use a bow, spell, or even thrown weapon to initiate combat and drag a chosen enemy onto high ground.

Such terrain is limited in the swamp, so make use of what there is.

As far as the poisoning goes, you are going to get poisoned… but that's ok. Bring some **Purple Moss Clumps** with you, use these items to cure your poison occasionally.

Finally, wearing armor with as much Poison Resist as possible helps to slow the buildup of poison in the first place

The northern fire is on a hill, with two staircases leading up to it. There aren't any monsters to stop you, so climb the steps and extinguish the flame at your leisure.

04

Estus Flask+1

9129

A tower sits alone along the northern edge of the swamp. It's guarded by a Darkwraith. Fight this vicious foe on solid ground, you don't want to deal with slowing or poison while facing it.

UNDERSTANDING THE CURSE EFFECT

If your curse bar fills up, you die. Resistance to this effect certainly helps keep you alive, but careful maneuvering is even more important. Attack the Basilisks when they're outside of their gas, and sprint away when they breathe. Even if you have to run through the poisoned areas during the fight, it's better than dying.

Inside the northern tower is the **Elder Coal**. Take that back to the Blacksmith as soon as you can!

BONFIRE—KEEP RUINS

05 Two tall hills are connected on the eastern side of the map. This is one of the most important areas to examine as early on as you can. Not only do you find another one of the fires to extinguish there. You also discover another Bonfire (Keep Ruins)! A small group of Ghru guard the central bridge, so exercise caution if you approach the Bonfire from the north.

06 Once you put out the third fire, the southern doors unlock. You can reach the next boss as soon as you're done exploring the swamp. You may face the Dark Spirit Yellowfinger Heysel here for a second time. Defeating him rewards the **Heysel Pick** and the **Xanthous Crown**. Yellowfinger's moniker alludes to his allegiance to Rosaria's Fingers, a Covenant you encounter later in the game. Not a friendly Covenant…

05

Estus Flask+1

12572

06

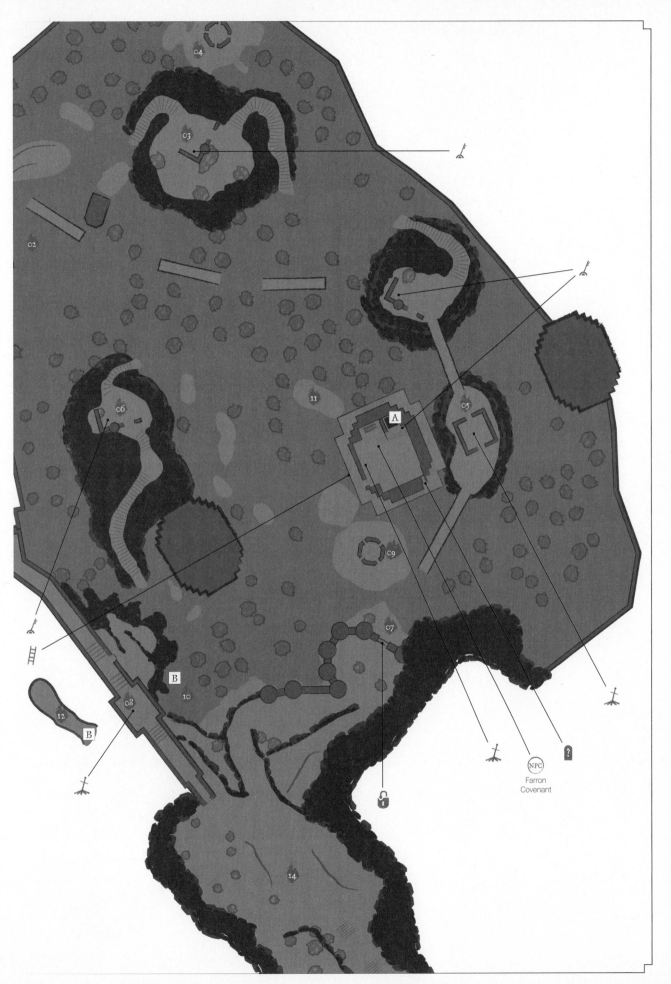

NPC
Farron
Covenant

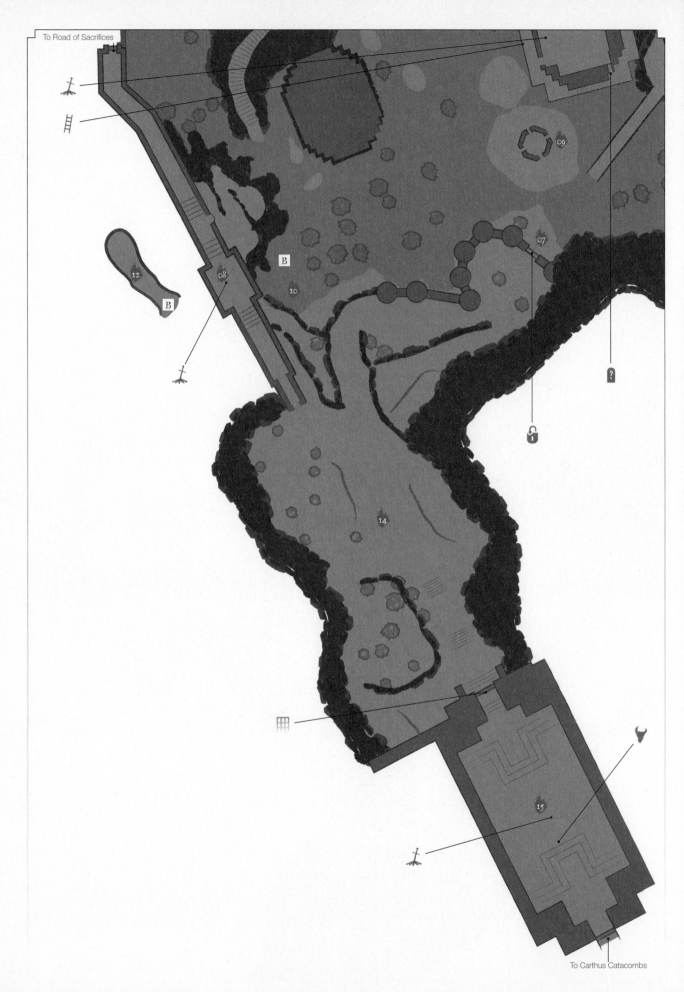

To Road of Sacrifices

C9

B

C7

12

B

C8

10

B

14

🔒
1

❓

15

To Carthus Catacombs

The tower near the southern doors is filled with Rotten Slugs. Go in there carefully, but roll back out of the archway when the enemies start falling from the ceiling. Don't let yourself get surrounded by them; fight outside of the small building to avoid trouble. Duck in and out to get easy kills, and then loot the area.

The southwestern swamp has piles of treasure, but it's guarded by Basilisks. These enemies have a Curse effect that spreads whenever they breathe their foul gas. There aren't many safe places nearby to fight them. Accept the poisoning that's going to happen, and stay mobile despite the deeper water here. It makes movement slow, but you can still roll to get distance when the Basilisks try to breathe on you.

A small rise has a pot of Estus Soup, and you find a **Sunlight Talisman** there, as well. Both of them are a welcome discovery in this troubled place.

A tiny western cave has several pieces of equipment inside of it. Look out for the Rotten Slugs outside the entrance; they'll help you to know that you're in the right area!

Nothing special protects the southern doors. They'll open once your work with the fires is done, and after that point you can travel freely back and forth between the swamp and the keep. However, *beyond* the door, a pair of Darkwraiths await. You can attempt to lure them down, or, if you choose, bypass them for now to sprint for the Bonfire ahead.

The path leads up, out of the swamp. The southern portion of it sends you toward the next boss. A small western diversion takes you toward another Bonfire and a shortcut that connects Farron Keep and the Road of Sacrifices with much more convenience.

Bonfire—Farron Keep Perimeter

The Farron Keep Perimeter has a few interesting features. From this side of it, you can unlock the door that goes back to the Road of Sacrifices. Travel between the two areas is going to be faster and safer in the future.

Corvian guard the corridor here, but they're spread out, and you can dispatch them quite easily. A Ravenous Crystal Lizard waits in that hallway. Make sure to get this one-time creature for its **Titanite Scale** before leaving.

If you look on the eastern side of the hallway, you should spot a break in the walls. After you've opened the shortcut, jump down from there to collect a few more items off of a hill that can't be accessed from the swamp.

OLD WOLF OF FARRON

A Covenant leader lives here, but you wouldn't know it unless you have very good eyes. Start from the southern doors, and look for a massive tower to the north. Its walls are almost featureless, so you might not think much about it. However, there is a ladder on the wall of that tower. A lantern attached to the ladder makes it much easier to see once you're in the correct area. Climb that ladder all the way to the top.

Walk around the parapets to find a Crystal Lizard, and go inside the upper tower to meet the Old Wolf of Farron. Talk to it to learn Legion Etiquette. If you want, you can also join its Covenant and get the **Watchdogs of Farron** item.

The outer walls have a secret door. Strike when you're close to one of the tower's corners that looks a bit off, and find the way to a small alcove. This spot has the **Ashes of a Dreamchaser** inside it. Take that to the Shrine Handmaid for a major improvement to her selection. Among other things, Titanite Shards are now available for sale, so getting your secondary weapons up to speed is a piece of cake.

A lift inside that tower takes you way up to the walls around Lothric. Remember finding Yoel back in the beginning of Undead Settlement, where there was a dragon's body and a long wall off in the distance? Well, this is it! An optional boss fight is here. You face off against another huge demon, like the one near the end of Undead Settlement.

This is a Demon. You can only kill it here once per playthrough. Dodge inside its attacks and swing at the creature from point-blank range using extended combos. The monster's time between attacks is very high, so switch to two-handed attacks for maximum damage and let loose. Avoid getting close to the edges: this monster can grab and throw you, and it's a very, very long way down.

Loot the minor items from the Demon's lair. However, you're not done yet. Go to the opposite gate, and look over the edge of the wall to locate a small walkway below you. Hop down and go to the end of that walkway. This gets you to a much better field of loot, by the dead dragon. Multiple Crystal Lizards are there.

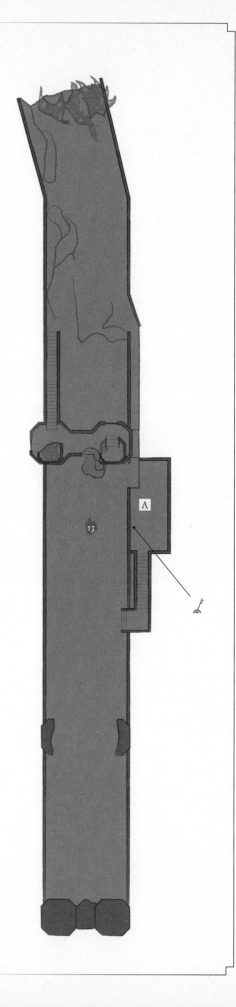

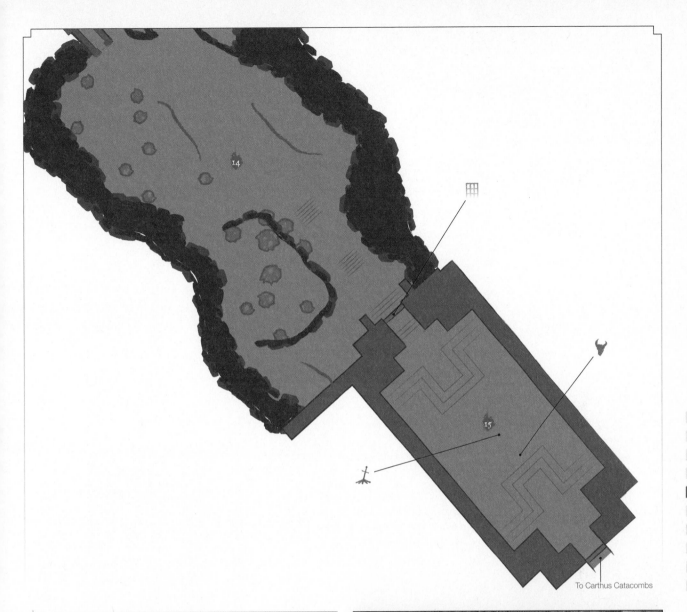

To Carthus Catacombs

14 A line of torches and enemies leads you to the next boss. Stay along the sides of the path to avoid most of the fighting, or rush up the center if you're farming extra Souls or love the combat.

The Corvians and Corvian Storytellers that are here are familiar enemies, though they appear in substantial numbers if you try to take them all on at once. Weapons with sweeping attacks are superior for battling against this large group.

There are also a couple of Darkwraith-styled enemies here, though you can kill them permanently. Do this to ensure that your future movements are unhindered. Don't fight near the Corvians because having them add to the encounter is too much to handle. Instead, pull these guys down the hill, where it's safer to fight.

MAJOR BATTLE

15 At the end of the southern road, open the doors and go into the next boss' arena. This fight is an interesting one because it has beautiful moves, multiple targets, and the usual amount of pressing danger.

This is the realm of the Abyss Watchers.

ABYSS WATCHERS

STAGE I

The first portion of this fight is a bit of a battle royale against multiple Abyss Watchers. Only one attacks initially, but more of them rise from their slumber throughout the fight. The bad news is that you can be surrounded and overwhelmed, but the good news is that the Abyss Watchers don't play favorites. They'll even attack each other if they can.

Your safest bet is to position the one you're fighting so that it has its back to the majority of the room. That dramatically increases the chance that the other combatants will focus on your enemy instead of on you.

In terms of attacks, the Abyss Watchers have wide sweeps and good lunges. Dodge multiple times when you're avoiding their short-range combo slashes, or make one late dodge when they charge forward to reach you.

This stage lasts for the Abyss Watchers' entire health bar.

STAGE II

After you defeat the main horde, a single foe rises. This one is going to be much tougher than the foes you were already attacking. Its sword is alight with flame, and the boss can backstep quite well to keep your combos from being as effective.

Bait the boss' long-range attacks because they're easier to dodge. Use this to get distance, dodge, and heal whenever you need a sip from your Estus Flask. Don't try to heal when you're up close, as it won't end in your favor. Even doing this at range is reckless if the boss hasn't already missed because it can approach you very quickly.

Long combinations aren't very doable. Let the boss have its dodges. Move in close afterward, and get one or two hits (which is all you can really hope for).

The biggest problem in this stage is the fire trail that the boss leaves behind. If you move anywhere that the boss has recently been during its attacks, you are going to take damage. Always move or roll to the side to avoid getting hit. The fire can even interrupt your attacks, so it's a massive problem.

Finish the battle, and catch your breath. You've just defeated one of the Lords of Cinder!

Use the Bonfire that appears. It looks like you've reached a dead end, but that isn't the case. When you walk over to the altar at the end of the room, it shifts. In moments, a path is revealed that leads down into the Catacombs of Carthus.

DECISIONS, DECISIONS

It's fine to go to either the Cathedral of the Deep now or the Catacombs of Carthus. This walkthrough discusses the Cathedral first because it's the slightly easier route of the two. Regardless, you can't get to Irithyll without beating both of these areas.

CATHEDRAL OF THE DEEP

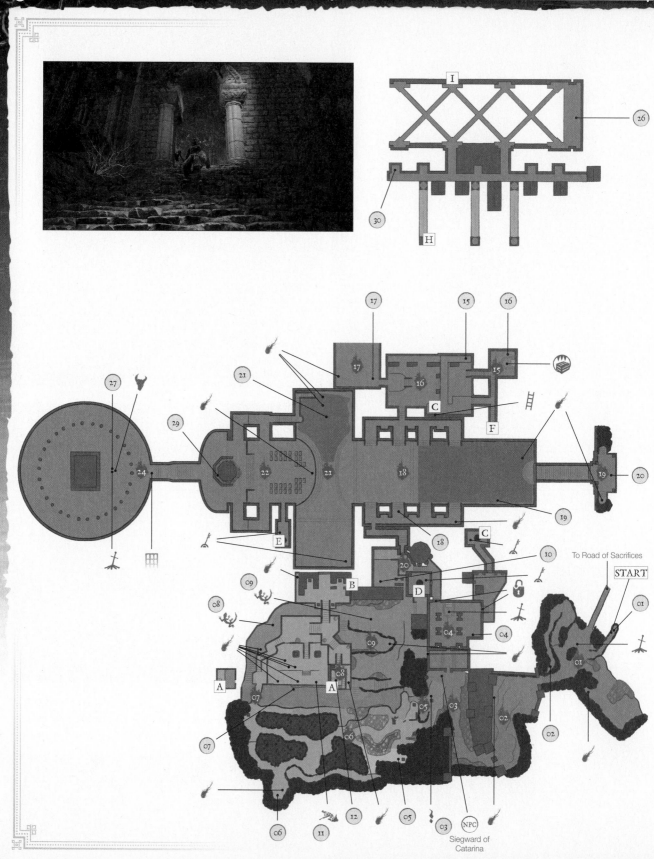

To Road of Sacrifices

START

Siegward of
Catarina

BONFIRES LOCATED HERE

- Cathedral of the Deep
- Cleansing Chapel
- Deacons of the Deep (Boss)
- Rosaria's Bed Chamber

ENEMIES

- Starved Hound
- Devout of the Deep
- Devout Bombers
- Reanimated Corpse
- Infested Corpse
- Corpse-grub
- Cathedral Grave Warden
- Ravenous Crystal Lizard
- Writhing Rotten Flesh
- Knight of the Deep
- Deep Accursed
- Giant Slave
- Deacon of the Deep
- Cathedral Evangelist
- Mimic
- Man-grub
- Deacons of the Deep

KEY DISCOVERIES

- Rosaria (Covenant NPC)
- Unbreakable Patches

MAJOR ITEMS

1	Paladin's Ashes
2	Crest Shield
3	Estus Shard
4	Notched Whip
5	Astora Greatsword
6	Executioner's Greatsword
7	Saint-tree Bellvine
8	Twinkling Titanite
9	Twinkling Titanite
10	Poisonbite Ring
11	Undead Bone Shard
12	Curse Ward Greatshield
13	Deep Gem
14	Lloyd's Sword Ring
15	Seek Guidance
16	Deep Braille Divine Tome
17	Aldrich's Sapphire (on Deep Accursed)
18	Barbed Straight Sword, Spiked Shield (Dark Spirit Longfinger Kirk)
19	Maiden Armor (full set)
20	Saint Bident
21	Drang Shoes, Drang Gauntlets, Drang Armor (under Giant Slaves feet), Drang Hammers (under stairs)
22	Red Sign Soapstone (on Man-grub)
23	Armor of Thorns (full set)
24	Deep Ring (on Deacon of the Deep)
25	Arbalest
26	Blessed Gem
27	Small Doll (from Deacons of the Deep), Archdeacon Armor (full set, from Archdeacon)
28	Black Eye Orb
29	Ring of the Evil Eye+1 (New Game +1)
30	Ring of Favor+2 (New Game +2)

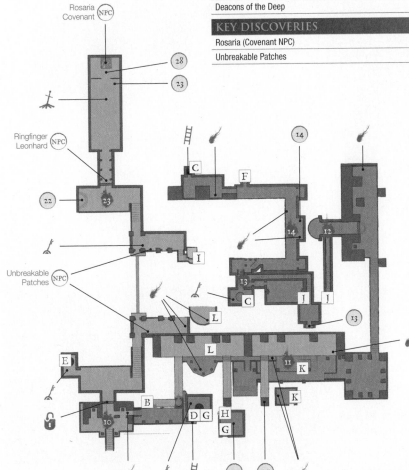

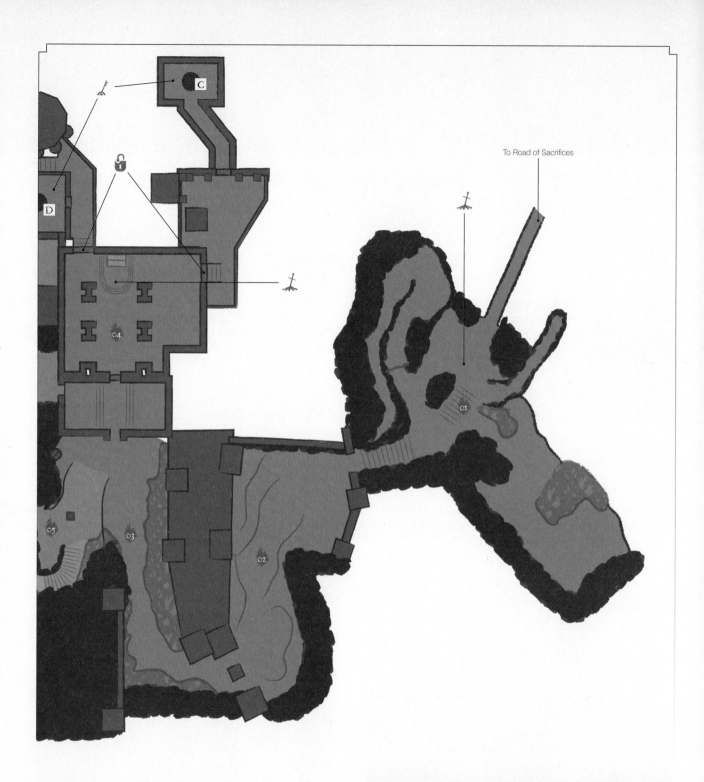

To Road of Sacrifices

BONFIRE—CATHEDRAL OF THE DEEP

01 The Cathedral of the Deep Bonfire starts at the base of several major staircases that are cut onto the side of a hill. You're in the southeastern portion of the map, and there aren't many enemies nearby.

A single powerful opponent waits for you at the top of the second set of stairs. This foe has a distinct shield and quite a bit of health. Once you engage this Unkindled, another one sneaks out of the shadows and comes at you from behind. Be ready to roll back down the stairs so that you get both of them on one side of yourself. After that, retreat, attack gently, and keep giving ground so that you aren't outflanked again.

You only have to defeat them once, so use all of your resources if you have any problems. Then, hit the Bonfire to restore yourself afterward.

The next yard has Devout of the Deep and Starved Hounds all over the place. The undead have crossbows and harass you at range, while the Starved Hounds rush in for melee. This is an area where your shield can help a great deal. All of the attacks are low damage, but they're somewhat hard to avoid.

There are many more undead in the following area, as you approach the first cathedral building. The undead with flaming swords are Devout Bombers. They'll immolate themselves and rush forward to leap on top of you; don't let them do that. Sprint away to avoid their suicidal attacks, or kill them quickly to eliminate this threat.

BONFIRE—CLEANSING CHAPEL

The small building here is a hub that you return to frequently. Not only does the small chapel have a Bonfire (Cleansing Chapel), but it's also a place that connects you to three different parts of the map. Once you unlock two shortcuts, this chapel can take you very deep into the cathedral without wasting any time.

For now, search the chapel, use the Bonfire, and take a breather.

As you leave the chapel, the path splits. A small break in the cliffs lets you drop into a creek to the west. The more obvious path trends upward. For treasure, take the southern route first and clear it completely. In the future, take the break in the hill west to get into the cathedral area a bit faster.

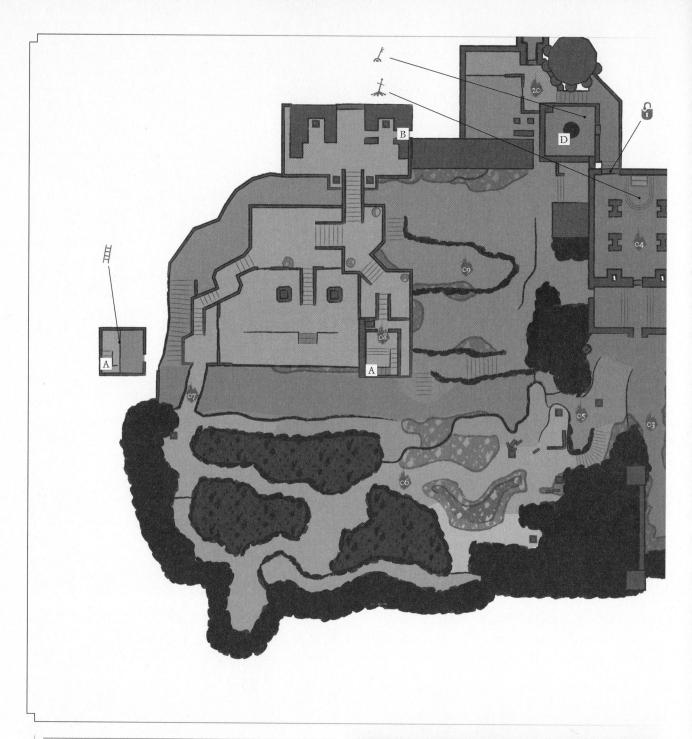

The graveyard along the southern edge of the map is filled with Reanimated Corpses. These undead are easy to kill, but they'll come back again and again if you wait for them to rise. Sprint past them, or slay them and move on before they return.

On the western edge of the graveyard, you start to encounter Infested Corpses mixed in with their weaker cousins. These foes look like Reanimated Corpses at first, but they'll have extra limbs burst out of them when you get close. Infested Corpses have more health, better attacks, and a vicious ability to make you bleed. This does horrible damage over time, so anything that raises your Bleed Resistance or cures Bleed is useful here.

Infested Corpses can land their bleeding attacks against you even if you have your shield out. To kill them safely, bait their heavier attacks. They have a substantial recovery time on their double-handed swings, and you can dispatch them easily during that time.

07 A bridge on the western edge of the map takes you toward the cathedral proper. There are more of the graveyard's enemies here, and they'll be bolstered by Cathedral Grave Wardens, as well. Use a shield to block these dual-wielders, and punish them for their aggressive attacks.

Clear out the northern stairways so that you can search for treasure. But don't take the northern stairs up to the main cathedral the first time you arrive. Instead, look for a smaller building at **(8)**. Go inside and kick down a ladder. This is now a modest shortcut, and you can take the western split from **(5)** and climb up here without facing more than a couple of enemies.

08 A small tower connects the creek in the valley with the stairways near the cathedral entrance. Once you examine the ladder at the top of this tower, it is possible to travel freely up or down through it. This makes the route between the Cleansing Chapel and the north much faster.

09 The creek has three Corpse-grubs guarding it. Bait their heavy attacks, and whittle them down in between these strikes. Be patient—these enemies combo for a bit longer than you'd expect, and it's easy to be drawn in after their third swing, only to take the fourth shot directly in the face.

You never want to fight a few of these enemies at the same time, as they interrupt you very easily and have solid damage potential. Use ranged weapons to pull them away from each other, and slaughter them individually if you must. Because they're not directly in your path, it's possible to avoid the entire group. Killing them is only necessary a single time to get the treasure along the creek bed.

The area here in the valley is filled with upgrade materials. A Ravenous Crystal Lizard is on the northern side of the tower at **(7)**. There are also a couple of Crystal Lizards to be found.

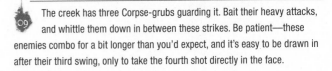

10 The front door of the cathedral is locked, and you cannot open it until you've cleared most of the region. To get inside, travel east along the rooftops of the cathedral's walkways. There are many enemies, but none of them is new. The problem is that you have to worry about ranged attackers, Hollow Slaves that climb up or drop behind you, and the sheer number of foes in this place.

Advance slowly, use ranged attacks to kill adversaries that you spot ahead of time, and retreat as needed. It's easy to die if you haven't been here before and gotten used to the rather complex enemy placement.

The worst fight in this stretch is halfway along the roof. There are undead with crossbows on a lower ledge. Kill them at range. Approaching them puts you into a fight with melee attackers, as well (in an area where you can't dodge as comfortably).

Estus Flask+2

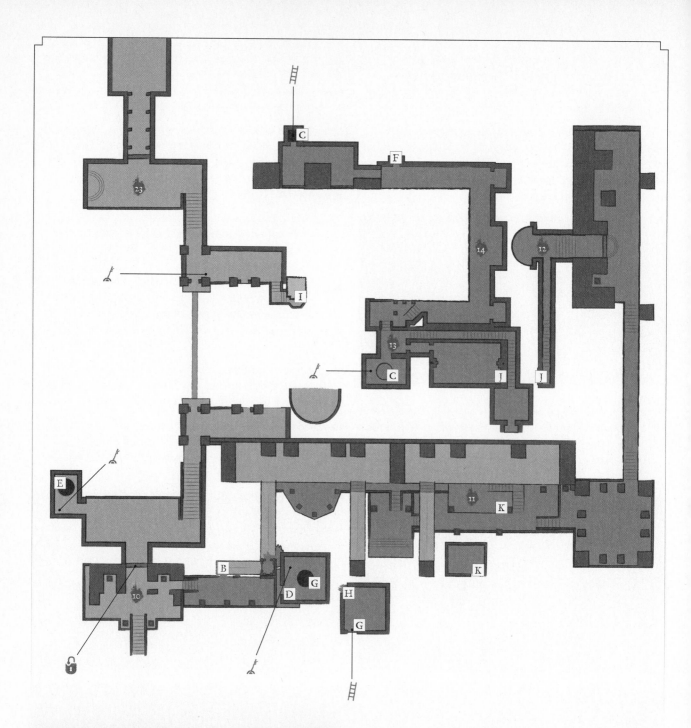

The eastern edge of the roof isn't quite as bad. You have better footing and a clean view of your opponents, and there aren't many ranged attackers. Clear your way to the large door on the right side of the map and open it; it's your way inside the cathedral.

A couple of Grave Wardens are in the corner as you turn toward the eastern door, and they're the worst of the lot. Keep a shield ready to block their fast attacks, and roll out of any combos that start to find purchase against you.

12 A small hallway takes you from the eastern vault entrance down into the upper level of the cathedral. Watch the ceilings for Writhing Rotten Flesh. They have massive Physical Resistance, so it takes quite a few hits to kill them. However, they're easy to interrupt and can't hurt you much as long as you don't let any of them fall on top of you. Use ranged weapons to knock them down as needed, or sprint underneath them to avoid the fights.

POISON ABOUNDS

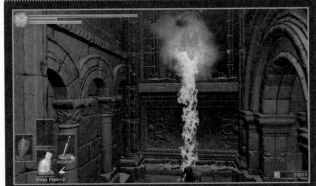

You should watch the statues throughout the cathedral carefully. Many of them dispense poison that lingers in the area for a few moments. Sprint through these clouds to minimize your exposure.

13 Do not miss the shortcut that is unlocked from the upper hallway. As you go into the cathedral, you pass through a room with a couple of Deacons of the Deep. On the other side, there is a lift on the left. Descend, and then open a gate at the bottom. This takes you quickly to a door that leads into the Cleansing Chapel. You now have a very useful shortcut between your Bonfire and the cathedral.

14 A Giant Slave is on the eastern side of the cathedral, and it can attack anyone on the ledges who might try to pass by. As soon as you see this massive foe, back into a hallway and use ranged attacks against the Giant Slave's head to kill it. The Giant Slave ducks to try to avoid this, and you might not want to waste the time it takes to slay it safely. If not, simply sprint along the upper walkway. Roll to avoid the Giant Slave's hits, and make it into the archway on the far side of the cathedral.

Once it's dead, though, you have a much easier time getting around. You can come back here later to search more if you end up killing the Giant Slave from the ground floor (which is much easier).

13

14

15 Along the northern side of the upper vault, you face an Evangelist and his ally with a crossbow. Kill these attackers, and then take a ramp down one level. Alternately, sprint past them and go into the archway; the enemies won't follow for long.

15

Going into the archway, the path descends. A side branch opens, and this takes you through the rafters of the lower level. Search the rafters, and use a ladder to climb back to the upper vault. Another Evangelist is there.

The lower part of the ramp takes you into a couple more rooms. The first looks unguarded; there is only a chest in that room. However, it's not the type of chest that you should open normally.

TREASURE THAT BITES

If you try to open this chest, it attacks you and deals high damage. This foe is a Mimic. Swing at the chest to damage it and get the drop on the nasty creature.

16 A Knight of the Deep is in a modest room here. Shoot the knight to draw him over to your location. For an easier time, fight him on his own. These knights have great stats, so you need to master some standoff tactics. These enemies try to use miracles to buff themselves if you back off. Bait this by retreating, and then charge the Knight of the Deep to gain the advantage while he's still casting.

17 The last of the northern rooms has a Greataxe sitting out in the open. Take this, but be ready for a deadly encounter after you do so. A brutal monster falls from the ceiling, blocking your retreat.

The Deep Accursed can only take a few hits, but it's mobile and inflicts high damage. Switch to two-handed attacks, bait the monster's first strike, and roll underneath its arms. Attack from almost inside the monster to kill it as quickly as possible.

18 The cathedral's main floor is littered with Hollow Slaves. Kill the Giant Slave to the east, if you haven't done so already. Do the same with the western Giant Slave as soon as you can. Both guard plentiful treasure and are simple to dispatch. Get under their feet, attack violently, and only dodge if you're about to get stepped on. The Giant Slaves don't have anywhere they can move, so they're practically sitting ducks.

The hallways to the side of the main vault have poison traps and many enemies. Watch yourself there, and pull back to the northern rooms if you start to get overwhelmed by Hollow Slave attacks.

19 The doors to the east on the lower floor lead outside. There are a couple of items out there, but otherwise, it's a dead end.

Estus Flask+2

20 As soon as you get your footing on the bottom of the cathedral, look for a passage on the southwestern end of the vault. This takes you to a door that you should unlock. A bit farther, you find a door that leads into the Cleansing Chapel again. It's now a snap to move back and forth anywhere in this region.

This passage also has a lift that leads up to a tower. Search the top of the tower for a way out, and use the ladder on the outer ledge to climb even higher. A Deacon of the Deep is on the next floor; kill him to get a couple items.

WHAT ELSE CAN YOU FIND UP HERE?

The corner of the Deacon of the Deep's tower is broken. Jump off of it to get onto a sloped roof. Climb that, and clear the top walkway of enemies. You discover an entrance to the cathedral that gets you onto the arches that hold the vault together. Walk across those, killing a few foes to protect yourself. There is treasure up here.

Additionally, you can roll off of the far side to get onto the northern side of the cathedral. That's the way you reach Rosaria's Bed Chamber (with a Bonfire and an important NPC).

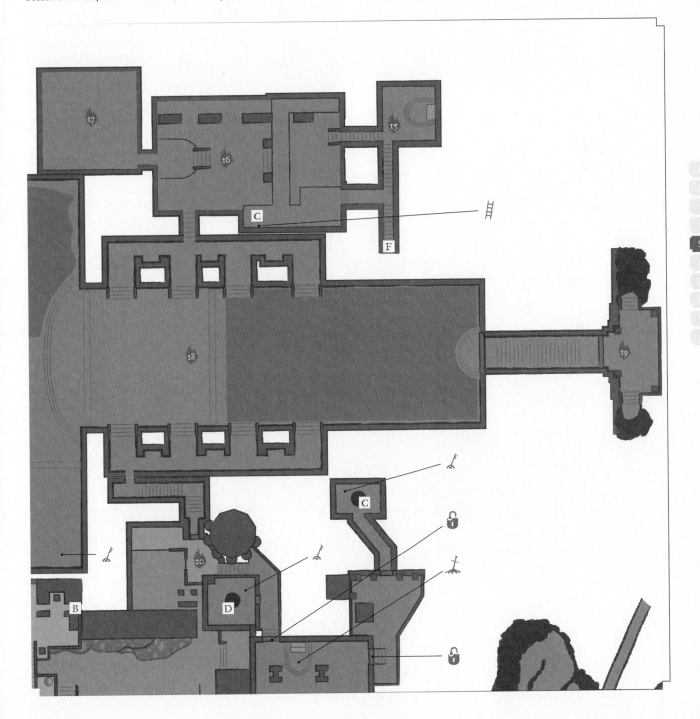

21 The levers on the floor of the cathedral raise huge gates. One of the levers is near the first Giant Slave's area, where one of the Knight of the Deep patrols. The other lever is located farther west in an open area that's south of the second Giant Slave.

Make sure to raise both of the gates. They act as walkways when you're on the upper ledges of the cathedral.

22 Many more enemies are paying respects on the western edge of the cathedral. The Deacons of the Deep have fire magic, but it's slow to track you. Stay mobile to avoid their strikes. Assassinate the praying foes, and then deal with the Deacons of the Deep.

If you need to retreat, jump off of the middle ledge. Do not retreat to the stairs that go back to the Giant Slave's area, as that location is filled with sludge and Writhing Rotten Flesh. You don't want to get bogged down while heavier enemies are chasing you.

A side passage leads to a lift that gets you up toward the front door of the cathedral. It isn't important to open it, but you can if you like.

The western route takes you to the boss.

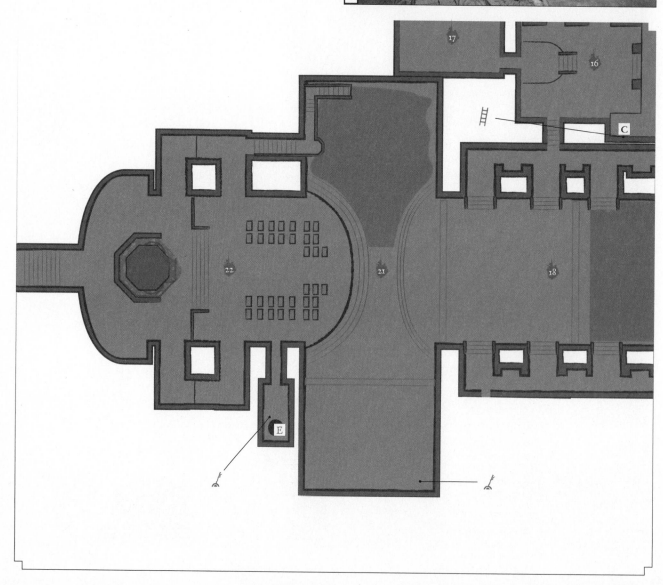

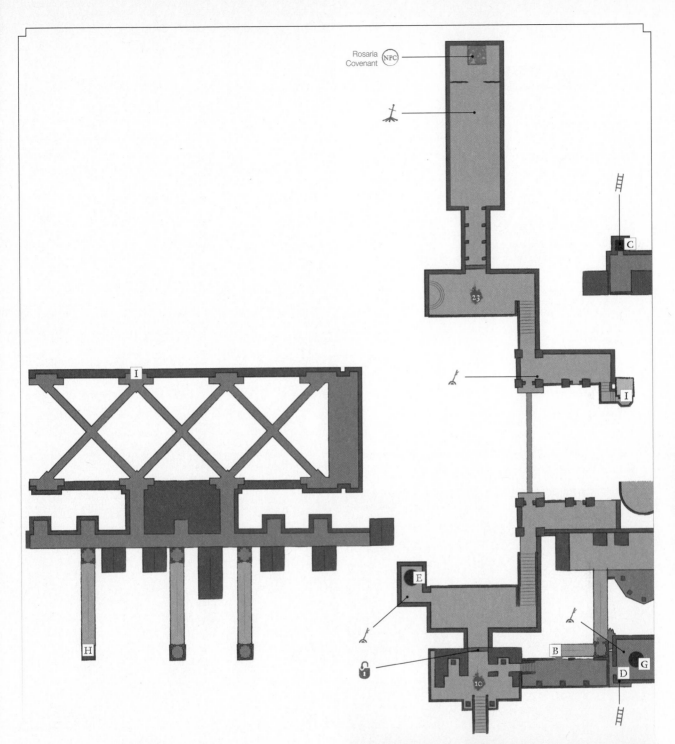

Rosaria
Covenant (NPC)

C

I

23

I

E

B
G
D

H

BONFIRE—ROSARIA'S BED CHAMBER

23 One section of the cathedral is extremely difficult to reach. However, you really should get there to find a Bonfire and to meet an important NPC, as well. Get onto the upper rafters, as described in the details for area **(20)**. From the northern rafters, you're able to delicately drop onto the ceiling of a small area below. Wiggle off of that, and explore the northwestern portion of this area.

Kill the Man-grubs you find, and look for the doors to Rosaria's chambers. Go inside and interact with her to join her Covenant, if you want. Use the Bonfire there so that you can quickly come and go as you please in the future.

The last Man-grub outside of those chambers won't normally attack you. However, you can kill it to obtain the **Red Sign Soapstone**, which is a very nice PvP item.

23

Estus Flask ×2

53772

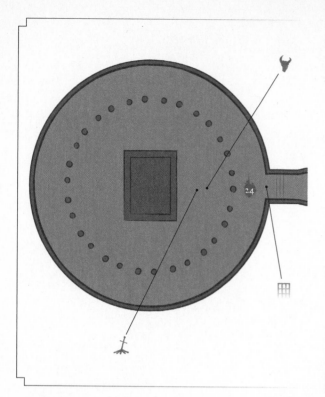

MAJOR BATTLE

24 If you're following Anri's questline, you can summon Anri and Horace before going into the boss' room. Otherwise, keep heading west until you get to the end of the cathedral. This triggers the boss fight.

DEACONS OF THE DEEP

STAGE I

The first stage of this battle becomes significantly easier once you understand its mechanics. There are a multitude of Deacons of the Deep in the area, and the "boss" doesn't take any damage when you hurt or even kill them. Instead, you have to kill the Deacon of the Deep that is glowing red to deal any permanent damage to your enemy. You can kill the other targets temporarily, but they'll return shortly.

Thus, rush for the glowing Deacon of the Deep, hack it apart, and then back off so that you can spot the red light descending on the next active Deacon of the Deep. Enemy damage output is minor, so you are going to be fine as long as you have a couple of flasks to spare throughout the fight.

STAGE II

After you get the boss to half health, the light recedes once again. It returns as a new challenger is summoned. This is the Archdeacon, and he'll be surrounded by a few tougher Deacons of the Deep in blue. As before, you can only deal lasting damage by hurting the glowing target. This time, you won't have to shift your focus. Archdeacon Royce is the real enemy, and his death ends the battle.

Use extremely long combos to deal maximum damage. These adversaries can't interrupt you very well, nor can they outdo your damage output. Make this a battle of extended trades. Combo hard, back off, heal, and repeat. This isn't a time for finesse.

Use the Bonfire that appears after the fight, and loot the Archdeacon Armor Set from a body on the floor. You're now finished in the cathedral. Proceed to the Catacombs of Carthus. If you've beaten that area already, make your way over to Irithyll instead.

CATACOMBS OF CARTHUS

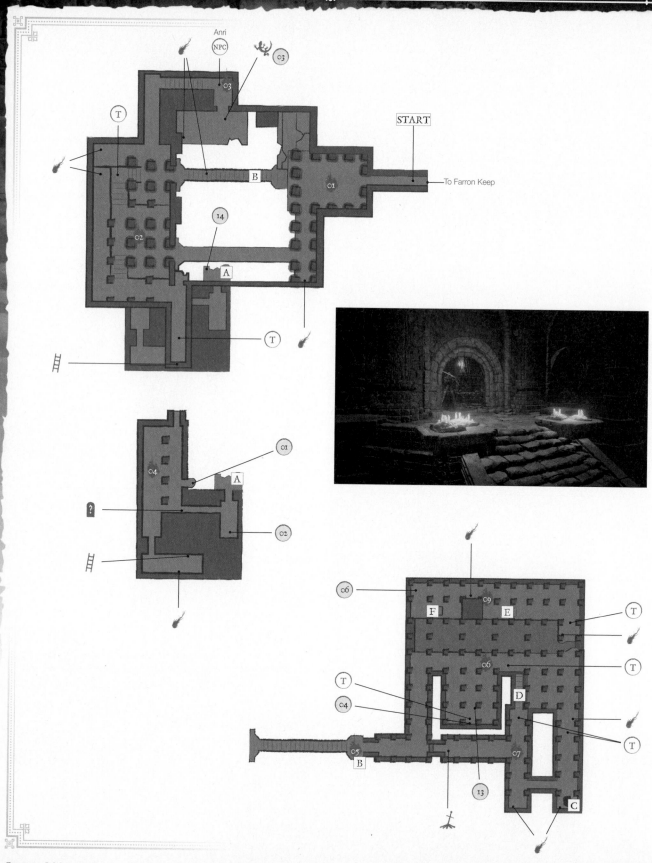

Anri
NPC
03

03

T

START

B

To Farron Keep

01

14

A

02

T

01

A

04

?

02

06

09

F

E

T

T

T

06

04

T

D

T

05

B

07

13

C

To Irithyll

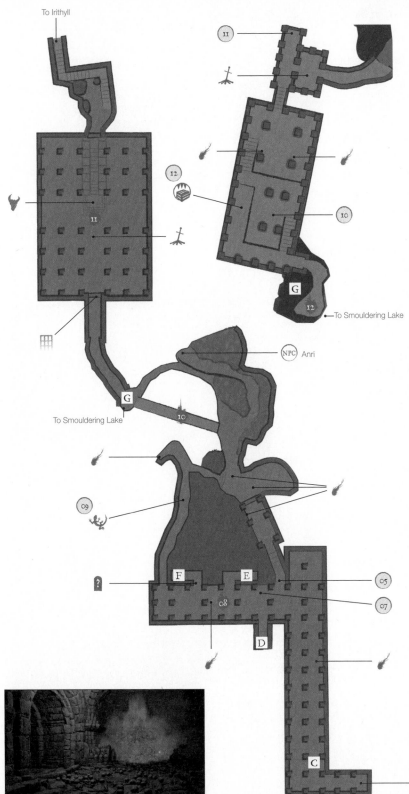

11

12

10

G

12

To Smouldering Lake

NPC Anri

G

10

To Smouldering Lake

09

F E

? 05

08 07

D

C

08

∞	MAJOR ITEMS
1	Sharp Gem
2	Carthus Pyromancy Tome
3	Twinkling Titanite
4	Carthus Milkring
5	Knight Slayer's Ring, My Thanks! Gesture (on Dark Spirit Knight Slayer Tsorig)
6	Grave Warden's Ashes
7	Dark Gem
8	Carthus Bloodring
9	Fire Gem
10	Soul of a Demon (from Demon)
11	Old Sage's Blindfold, Witch's Ring
12	Black Blade (Mimic)
13	Thunder Stoneplate Ring+1 (New Game +1)
14	Ring of Steel Protection +2 (New Game +2)

BONFIRES LOCATED HERE

Catacombs of Carthus

High Lord Wolnir (Boss)

Abandoned Tomb (Smouldering Lake)

ENEMIES

Skeleton

Skeleton Swordsman

Lesser Crab

Hound-rat

Large Hound-rat

Writhing Rotten Flesh

Skeleton Wheel

High Lord Wolnir

Demon

KEY DISCOVERIES

Anri Encounters (x2)

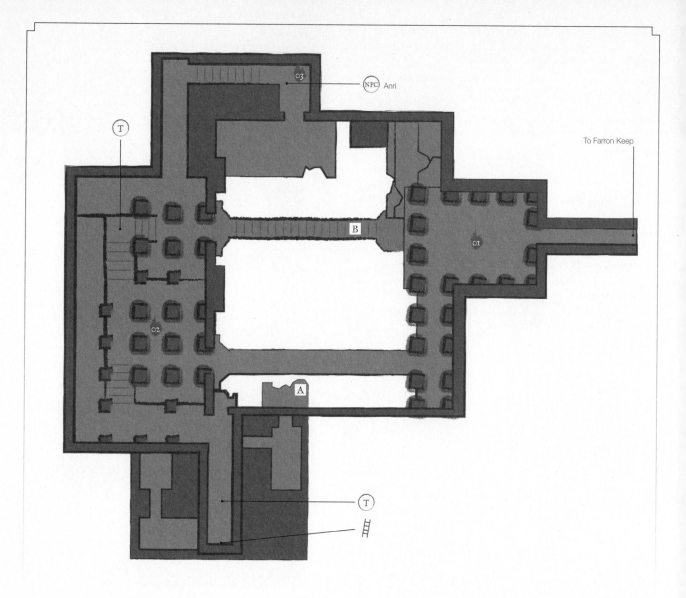

To Farron Keep

NPC Anri

Get into the catacombs by approaching the shrine in the Abyss Watchers' room. This opens a secret passage down into the catacombs. Descend, and then stop once you reach a stone bridge: enemies are going to attack you soon. The path is linear here, unless you discover the safe drop on the northern edge of the first open platform. It's possible to skip down through a section of the map by dropping over a few overhangs.

If you cross the bridge (as most players will), you're going to fight a Skeleton and then an Skeleton Swordsman. The former target is very weak. Block these enemies and eliminate them, since they're only a threat in large numbers. Skeleton Swordsmen have an aggressive, twirling charge. Ideally, put up your shield to absorb this impact, then counter quickly to dispatch them before they get to start their combos.

Skeleton Archers are positioned on ledges above and below you in this main chamber. Don't tarry here long. The best thing you can do is to move through quickly and kill these ranged foes later.

The western room has similar enemies, even though you don't have to contend with ranged attacks while you're fighting. Draw out the Skeleton Swordsmen so that they are isolated. Also, watch out for the rolling balls of skeletal limbs that glide on by.

You take a fair amount of damage if they run over you, and you also get thrown around. The balls roll back and forth along their paths, and the one that goes over the lower bridge will claim many lives from players who don't manage to avoid it. Enemies here attack quickly, so they'll punish heavy casting or ranged attacks unless you're starting a fight before they see you.

Some of the fights nearby have groups of Skeletons. In this situation, they're more than a nuisance. If you can, equip a weapon with longer reach and/or a wide, sweeping attack. Greatswords and polearms are both good examples. They're excellent for dispatching large groups of Skeletons so that you don't get overwhelmed. Alternate between using these heavy weapons for groups and employing one-handed weapons and a shield for individuals.

03 Anri is here, if you're following his questline and have already defeated the Deacons of the Deep and talked to him (or her) back at the Firelink Shrine. Talk to Anri again to continue this storyline.

04 Most of the treasure in the upper catacombs is really minor. However, the **Carthus Pyromancy Tome** is here. It's one level down from the starting point, in the crypts south of the main bridge. Make sure to collect this before you proceed.

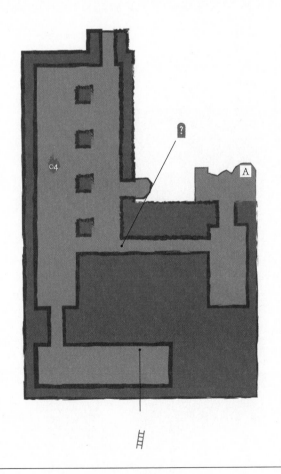

05 There are many ways to get around the upper crypts, so make sure that you don't get confused. The best way to navigate is to get onto the large staircase that leads down through the primary chamber. Use that set of stairs to keep your bearings. Once you're finished exploring, go back to this staircase.

Sprint to get down the bridge after the ball of death rolls past you. Dodge to the side at the end to make sure that you're out of the way before the next trip swings around.

If you dropped off of the ledges back at **(1)**, you will drop near the door at the bottom of **(5)**. As long as you've obtained the **Carthus Pyromancy Tome** in this area, you should feel free to take this shortcut in the future.

06 The next portion of the catacombs is divided into two levels. You start on the upper tier, but you end up traveling back and forth between the two to get everything.

SAVE YOUR STRENGTH

As you advance, arrow traps fire from various angles, triggered by pressure plates on the ground. Your shield can block most of this damage and this is essential for keeping your health up.

Be careful about destroying all of the pots that line the floors as well, some of them break open to unleash a swarm of seeking dark magic that can damage you.

BONFIRE—CATACOMBS OF CARTHUS

07 You see this Bonfire upon entering the new tier of the catacombs, but iron bars block it. To reach it, you must go all the way to the east around the level and backtrack through a few corridors. This is the Catacombs of Carthus Bonfire.

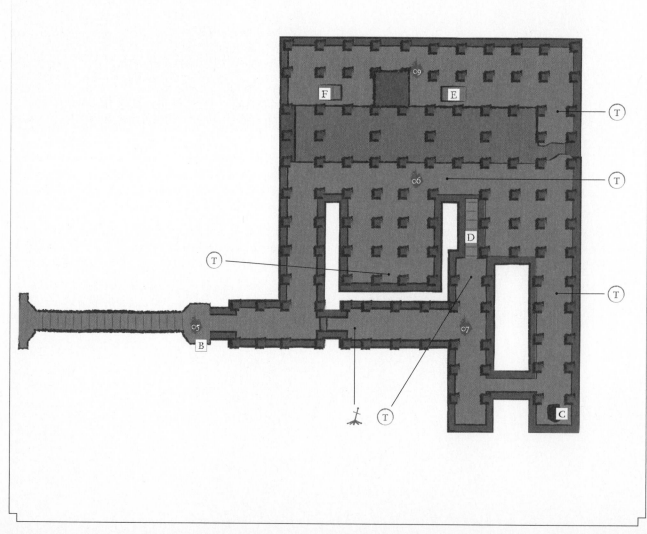

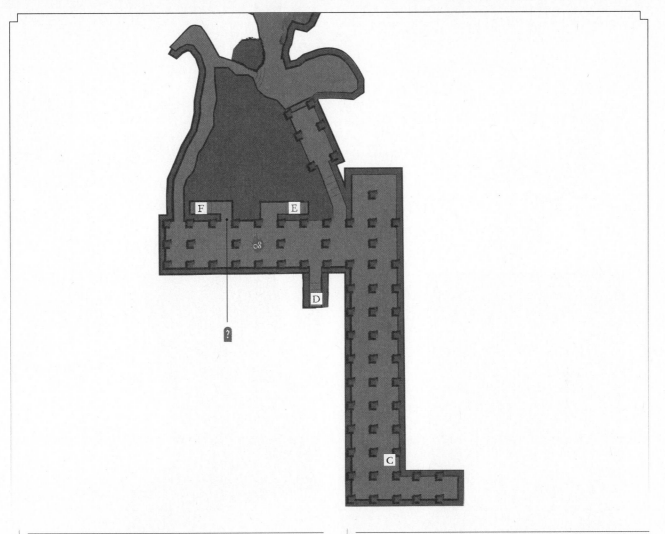

A pit in the southeast and a staircase near the Bonfire both lead down to the lower tier. This is where the worst fighting takes place. There are Hound-rats, Lesser Crabs, Large Hound-rats, Skeleton Wheels, and worse down there. It's lousy with monsters.

If you run through here and attract the attention of all of the monsters, you are likely going to die. The main room of the lower tier has so many targets. Take it slow, kill enemies a few at a time, and retreat to the stairs as often as you can.

The corridor to the southeast has a bit of treasure. You have to fight a horde to get it, so retrieve that item and then return to the Bonfire if you need to use your flasks. The primary enemies are Skeleton Wheels; they roll quickly and interrupt your attacks if they bump into you while in motion. You can either block them, or dodge and attack after they hit a wall. It takes them a couple of seconds to turn around, so they're quite vulnerable.

Stairs lead up to the northern side of the upper tier. Although this is a dangerous area and doesn't take you deeper into the catacombs, you find some interesting items.

Move very carefully as you hunt for loot. The Skeleton Swordsmen are fairly quiet, and they'll put you in bad shape if they sneak up on you. Even worse, it's possible to trigger a couple of them at a time. If that happens, run back to the stairs and make sure that all of your targets are in one direction.

Because the Skeleton Swordsmen are the nastiest enemies, you should spend the most time practicing your techniques against them. They're best to attack after they miss or get blocked during their leaping attack. If you stay defensive until after that, you can counter their attacks. When fighting a group that also has Skeleton Swordsmen, charging attacks and quick retreats are useful. Get in there, do some damage with one attack, roll backward, and flee. You don't want to fight these enemies when they have additional numbers around to interrupt you.

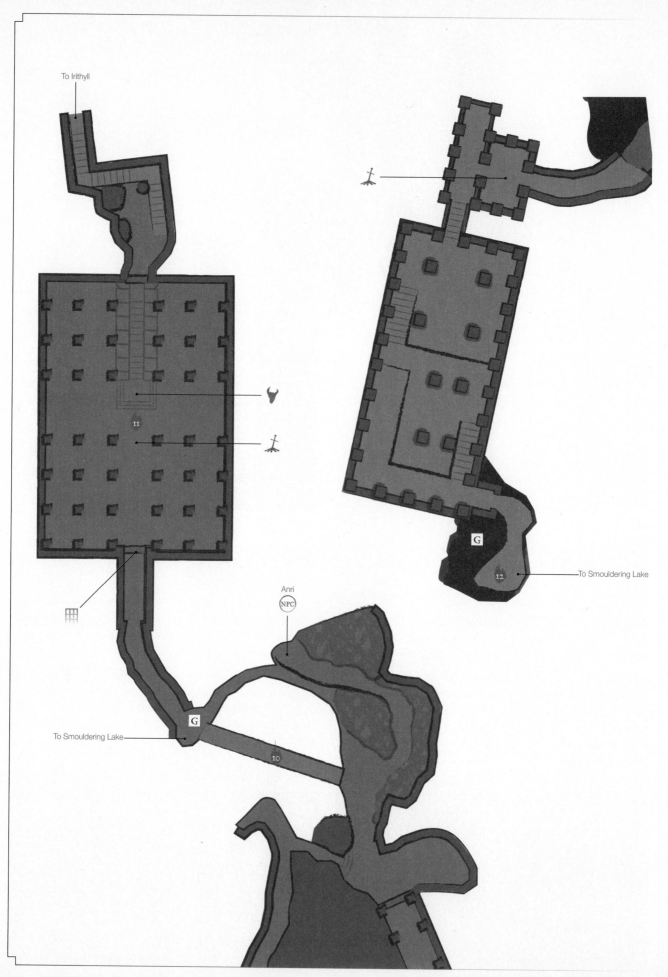

To Irithyll

Anri
(NPC)

11

To Smouldering Lake

G

To Smouldering Lake

10

G

12

To Smouldering Lake

Estus Flask+3

30163

A flimsy bridge connects the catacombs with your next boss. There is way more to this room than it initially seems. To reach it, you have to pass through a room that has a couple of Skeletons. Cross the bridge to get to your next boss fight. Or, stand on the far side and attack the bridge to break it. This drops you down into the lowest reaches of the catacombs, where there is much greater treasure (and danger, too). That route leads into the Smouldering Lake, an optional area.

WHAT IF THE BRIDGE IS OUT?

It's possible to destroy the bridge before going to see the next boss. This would prevent you from getting to the next area (and thus, the rest of the game). However, there is a side path on your right as you approach the bridge. This lets you get over the chasm even if the bridge is out.

Also, that is the area where Anri appears if you're continuing that storyline.

MAJOR BATTLE

Cross the bridge, and open the door at the end of the path. Approach the altar in the middle of the next room and interact with it. You are whisked away to a dark area, which is where you must fight.

Estus Flask+3

33595

HIGH LORD WOLNIR

To win this fight, you need to destroy Wolnir's bracelets. Wolnir has these bracelets at the end of his bony arms, and they shine with golden light. It's pretty clear what you need to hit!

Wolnir can strike you directly with his arms. He also emits a cloud of death that surrounds everything near his body. Dodge well after he raises whichever arm is closer to you. It's not too difficult to avoid these attacks.

The cloud of death is more dangerous, though, as Wolnir moves around. It's not fast, but you can still find yourself closer to the body than you expected. The damage output from this is very scary, and it's an area of effect. If you start taking damage, roll away from Wolnir, and then sprint until you're far enough away to be safe. Then, you can heal and get back into things.

Break all three bracelets, and finish the encounter. It's a quick one.

After you have destroyed the boss, you find a Bonfire and the route out to Irithyll. It's up to you whether to cut the bridge behind you and descend farther into the region, or to move forward toward Irithyll.

MAJOR BATTLE

Attack the bridge at **(10)** a single time, and wait for it to break. Make sure that your health is full so that the coming fall doesn't kill you. The bridge breaks after a few seconds, and then you have a good plunge. Stay near the halfway point of the bridge as it breaks. If you're too close to the wall, you actually end up falling farther.

You can climb up the damaged bridge from the bottom, and that is another reason why it's smart to kill the boss before coming down here (you get a Bonfire that is only a few moments from the top of the bridge).

Make sure that you are ready to tackle this area when you come back. A Demon blocks your way to the next Bonfire. It fights like the one back at the Undead Settlement, though this Demon has much more health and damage output. Fire Resistance gives you an advantage in this fight.

Roll around the large Demon to get free strikes at its flanks. Though it takes a number of hits to kill, you almost always get multiple swings every time the massive monster misses an attack. In this battle, dodging is far better than shield use.

From here, it's a dead shot into the Smouldering Lake; you can't miss it.

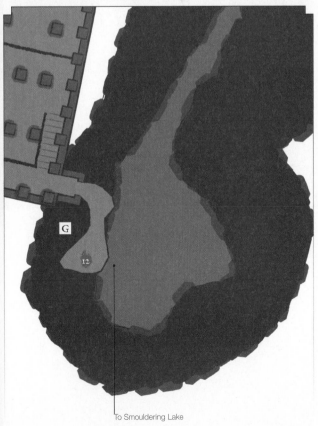

To Smouldering Lake

SMOULDERING LAKE

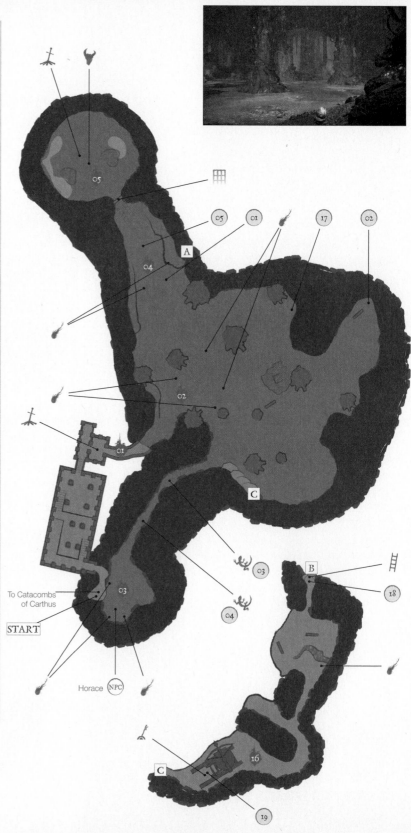

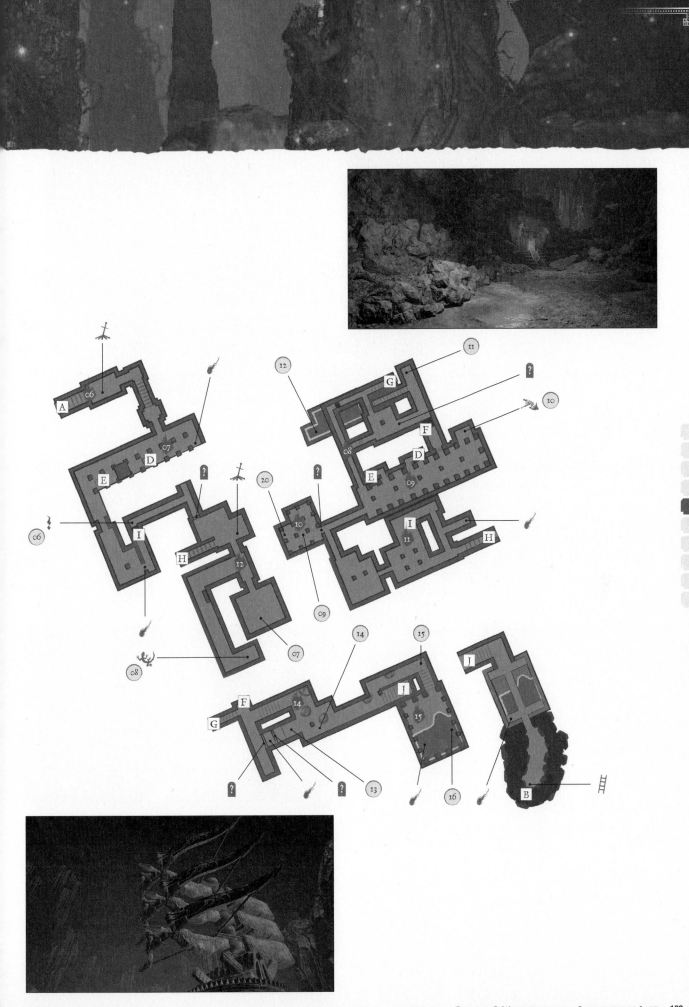

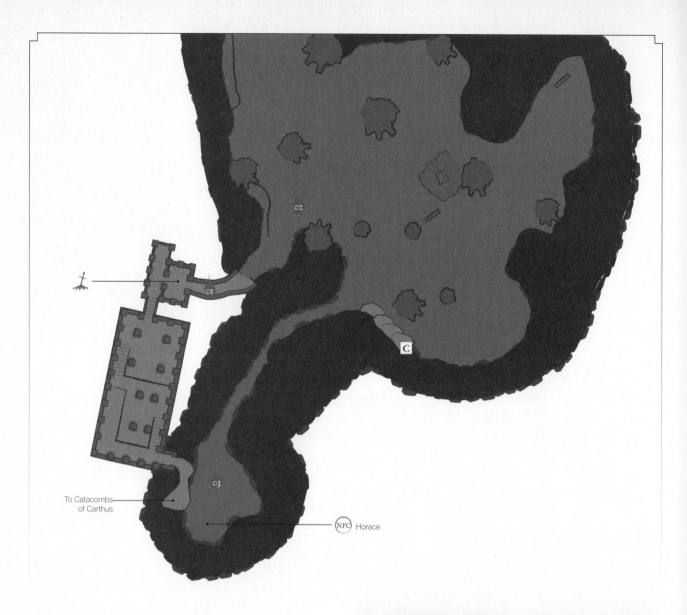

To Catacombs
of Carthus

NPC Horace

Bonfire—Abandoned Tomb

The Abandoned Tomb Bonfire is impossible to miss. It's on your way down from the Catacombs of Carthus into the Smouldering Lake region. Rest here. Things get ugly very soon. It's tough enough that players with less experience may want to run through the next area, grabbing loot without caring whether their character gets killed or not. The treasure is so powerful down there that these "suicide" runs pay for themselves in spades. You can get upgrade materials left and right, and **Large Titanite Shards** are commonplace here.

You won't get 10 steps into the lake before you realize how rough things are going to be here. The enemies are larger than life, and a humongous siege weapon has been installed on the cliffs to the south. Whenever there is a direct line of sight between you and the ballista up there, a series of shots rains down.

The shots come in waves of three, and each will knock you down if you don't roll at the correct time. Until you shut off this weapon, it's going to be a royal hassle.

Great Crabs are a common sight as you try to pick up the treasure that has been left all over the lake. Roll away from them and sprint to safety. Once the ballista is down, it's okay to fight the Great Crabs. Even then, use a ranged weapon to pull them away from each other so that you can kill them individually.

03 A narrow tunnel leaves the main room; look for this in the southwest. Along your way, kill both of the Crystal Lizards. There is more treasure in the cavern

you reach, but beware: Horace the Hushed is present. If you've been following Anri's line, this NPC will be here, attacking anyone who gets close to him. Read "A Few May Help You on Your Path" to learn more, because this NPC questline is very complex.

MAJOR BATTLE

04 The ballista attacks are bad enough, but things are even worse in the northern half of the map. Up there is a Carthus Sandworm that burrows through the ground and attacks anyone who comes near. It's extremely hard to hurt this creature with melee attacks. Although you don't need to kill it, ranged weaponry is vastly superior for doing so.

There is a ledge in the northeast that is safe from the Carthus Sandworm. If you so choose, fire from this position to kill the creature without letting it come after you. Once the Carthus Sandworm dies, you can move much more easily around the northern lake. Because the ballista can't target enemies on that ledge, you can do this at any time.

That same ledge also ushers you into another section of this region. It leads toward another Bonfire, the ballista (which can be turned off), and plenty of treasure. The path is winding and dangerous, so go here only when you're ready.

MAJOR BATTLE

05 Even if the ballista and Carthus Sandworm are both active, you can still reach a boss here in the Smouldering Lake. Sprint to the northern tip of the lake, and look for a large cave. Enter this cave to trigger the boss fight.

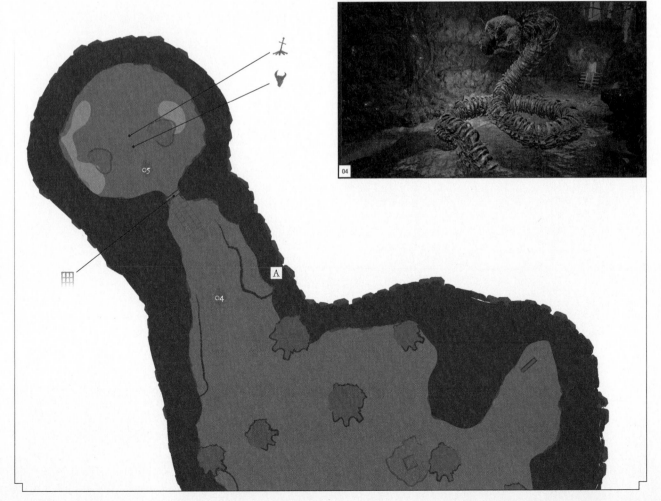

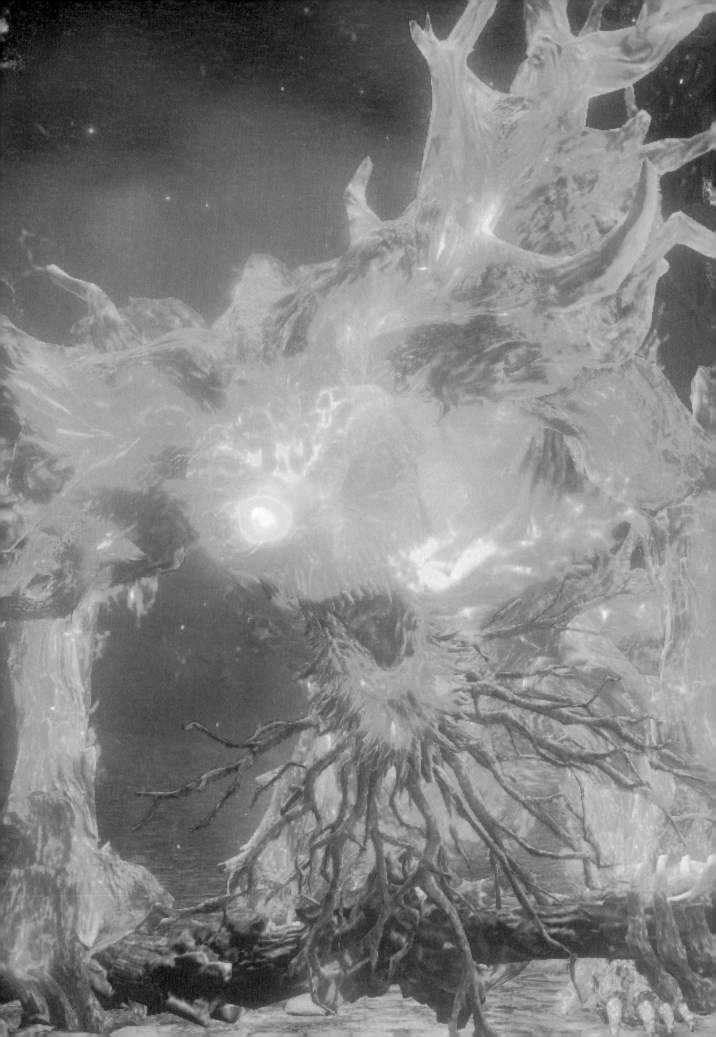

OLD DEMON KING

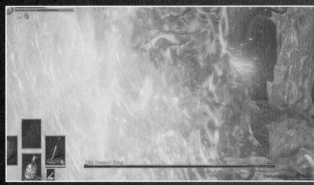

STAGE I

The Old Demon King is another fire-based enemy. Pump up your Physical and Fire Resistance as much as you can before the encounter. Use a two-handed weapon because your shield won't be of any great use; this boss employs burning attacks and heavy swings, and neither is usually safe to block.

Stay away from the creature's mouth. Its fire attacks generate there, and you can often roll under the boss or to its side to get out of the way when you see it rear back to begin a breath attack.

Hits are easy to score against the slow fiend. Its tail is quite vulnerable if you get around to the rear, but always save some of your Stamina for rolling away when it turns. Your mobility is a massive aid in this battle. The Old Demon King doesn't adjust for dodging targets as well as most bosses, so you can avoid a fair amount of damage by dodging multiple times to get some quick distance.

Make sure to keep your Equip Load as low as you can afford to. Speed is a better survival boost than raw armor here.

STAGE II

In the second half, the Old Demon King decides to use way more magic. Pyromancy spells of legendary fury and power explode around you. The damage is survivable, but you must dodge and heal often because it's very hard to totally avoid getting hit.

The careful fighting and good combos of the early fight become a frantic damage festival between the two of you. Trade blows when you can just to burn down the boss before it exhausts your supplies.

Kill the boss, and then light its Bonfire.

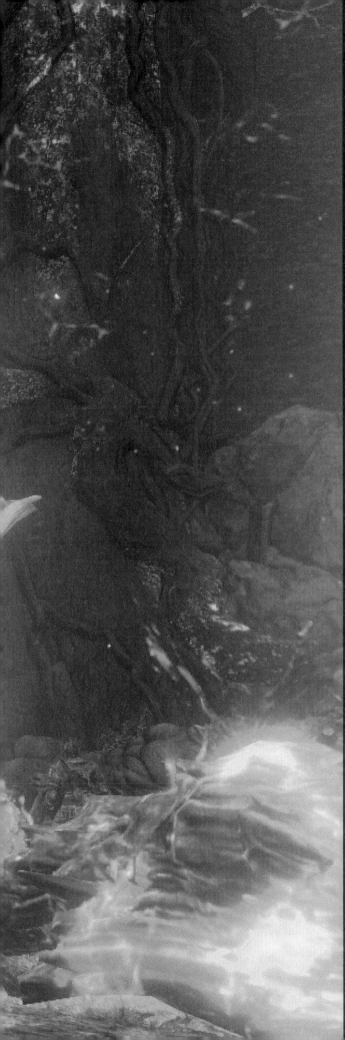

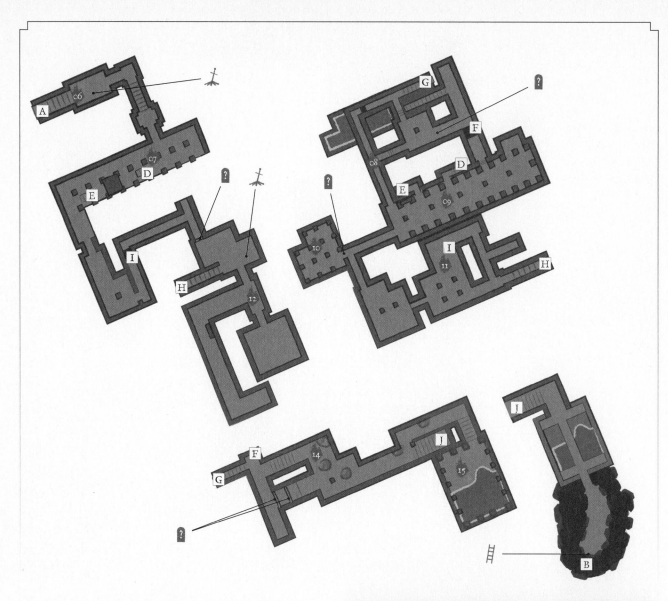

BONFIRE—OLD KING'S ANTECHAMBER

o6 Another Bonfire is inside the cave at the north end of the lake. Get this when you're prepping for the Old Demon King fight, or if you're worried about taking on the Carthus Sandworm.

o7 As you get into the northeastern dungeon, you start to encounter Demon Clerics and Smoldering Ghrus. Smoldering Ghrus have lower health and can be dispatched with a solid combo. Target them first, and lure them into side tunnels so that the Demon Clerics can't assist as well with their ranged fire attacks. Smoldering Ghrus have both toxic and poison effects, which is their real claim to fame. Run away from their clouds, even if it means giving up serious ground.

Writhing Rotten Flesh and Basilisks are on the western side of the room. Neither foe is a big threat because you've dealt with these enemies before.

If you come back toward this area from the southern side, you can score an **Estus Shard** from this section; however, that requires a long and twisting route.

This room has a secret door. Push aside some Hound-rats, and search for the door in their small chamber; it's on the eastern wall. This gets you into a hallway with the **Quelana Pyromancy Tome**. It also helps to connect the middle tier and the lower tier, where there are large pits of flame. You can't get the items from there without a massive amount of Fire Resistance. Alternately, you can always use your Estus Flask constantly, sprint, and accept that you might die on the lava anyway. If you're doing that, be sure to spend all of your Souls at the shrine before going there. Retrieving Souls from a lava run is sometimes a futile experience, even though the Souls are often closer to the entrance compared to where you died.

The open chamber has two Demon Clerics. They'll support each other with melee attacks and ranged fireballs, so they're a huge hassle. Plink away at one of them when you're at range to soften or kill it. Once isolated, the other one poses no threat. It's worth killing these two because they have very nice treasure behind their starting point.

A long hallway stops suddenly, looking more than a little suspicious. Attack the wall to open a secret door. Behind it is a room with a Black Knight and a Smoldering Ghru. Let the former kill the latter. Then, you can attack the knight with gusto. If you have trouble, retreat and use ranged attacks to wound the Black Knight. It has no response to this, though the battle takes a long time if you have to keep retreating.

Once you've beaten your adversary, search the room for the **Black Knight Sword**. Black Knight weapons deal 20% more damage against Demons, useful in this area!

Several more Smoldering Ghrus are in the south. They're spread out within their chamber, so it's not too hard to kill them individually without much risk. The staircase in the southeast gets you back up to the higher tier of the room, which lets you explore for more treasure.

BONFIRE—DEMON RUINS

12 To collect the **Estus Shard** that was mentioned earlier, you have to open another secret door. This one is in the room at the top of the staircase. Hit the northern wall to open it, and then follow the corridor around to your treasure.

Mercifully, this room also has a Bonfire. By the time you get here, you probably need a refill for your Estus Flasks.

13 Smoldering Ghrus protect this room and its treasure. Watch the sides of the room as you come in; it's easy to focus on the enemy in front of you and miss the more dangerous ones that have a flanking position.

14 There are two ways to get down to the lowest tier of the dungeon. You can drop through the pit on the eastern side of the middle tier. Or, you can take the stairs leading down at the northern end of that area. The stairs are the safer choice because you can retreat, and the initial hallway below is an ugly one.

First off, there is a multitude of Hound-rats. You can be overwhelmed and chain interrupted until you're dead if you leap down and don't have a good sweeping weapon or enough Poise to fend off the attackers. More dangerous is the pack of Basilisks below, be careful not to rush into their midst.

Look for a pair of secret doors on the eastern edge of the corridor. A chest is sandwiched inside of them, and it has a distraction inside, three **Large Titanite Shards**. The real prize is behind the second secret door, the **Izalith Staff**.

15 Another lava pool has a couple of items and Knight Slayer Tsorig. You meet this Greatsword wielder on the stairs leading down to the lava. Pull back so that you are fighting on even ground, and bait out his slower attacks. This foe has a few nice pieces of equipment, so you're well rewarded in victory!

This pool has several more items. Remember to put on your Flame Stoneplate Ring and use Flash Sweat if you're going out after these goodies.

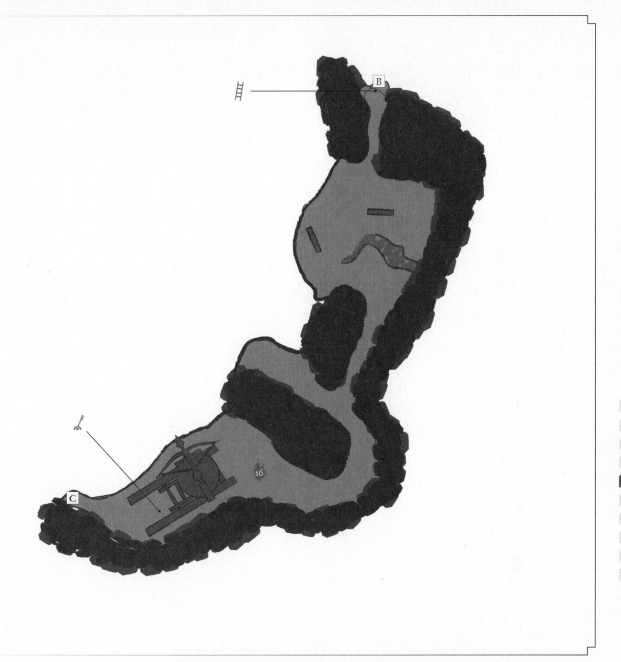

16 You finally reach the end of the dungeon. A lonely Black Knight guards the bridge that takes you out of this area. It leads to a ladder, and up toward the ballista's platform. Skeleton Wheels, Skeletons, and Skeleton Swordsmen are on the ledges above. Fight cautiously here because you're very close to your goal.

The ballista is at the very top of the hill. Use the crank beneath it to stop the weapon from firing ever again. This allows you to search the entirety of the Smouldering Lake without the constant threat of knockdowns and free damage. There is a fast way down if you hop onto a series of platforms at the edge of the cliffs, or you can use a Homeward Bone to back up without wasting time.

Remember you need the ballista activated to break the wall to the **Speckled Stoneplate Ring**, so you should try to grab this rarity before coming up here and deactivating the ballista.

IRITHYLL OF THE BOREAL VALLEY

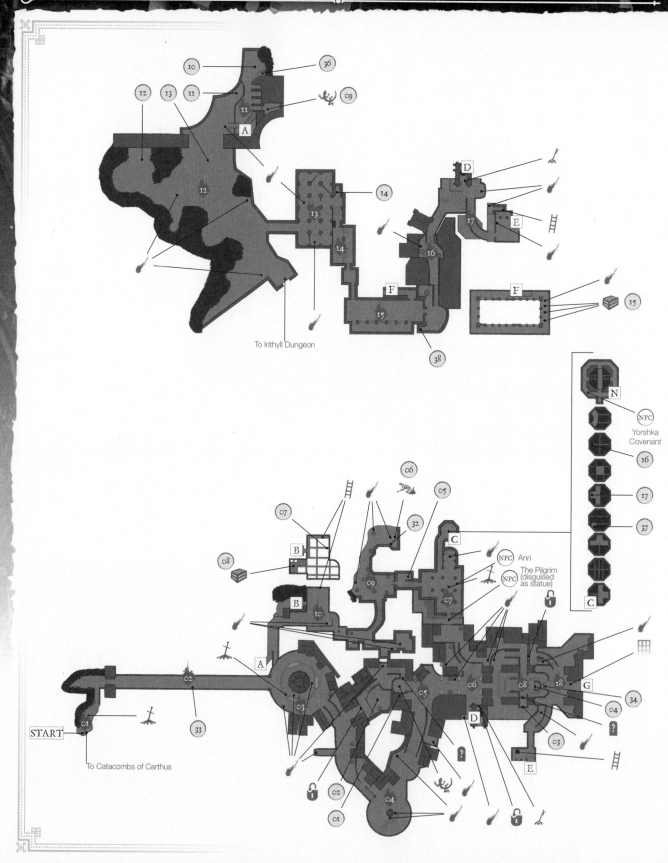

10
36
12 13 11
11
A
09
12
D
14
17
E
13
16
14
F
F
15
15
To Irithyll Dungeon
38

N
NPC
Yorshka
Covenant
16
17
37
C

06
07
05
32
C
08
NPC Anri
B
09
NPC The Pilgrim
(disguised
07 as statue)
B
10
1
A
02
06
08 18 G
03
05
34
33
D
04
START
01
02
01
04
33
E
To Catacombs of Carthus
02
01
04

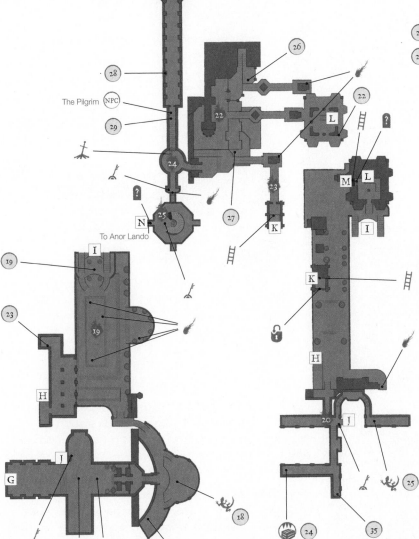

Anri (NPC)

The Pilgrim (NPC)

To Anor Londo

M

Archdeacon
McDonnell Covenant (NPC)

MAJOR ITEMS

∞	
1	Twinkling Titanite
2	Dorhys' Gnawing (on Evangelist), Witchtree Branch (on ground)
3	Magic Clutch Ring
4	Lightning Gem (ground floor), Ring of the Sun's First Born (ledge, accessible from 18)
5	Roster of Knights
6	Undead Bone Shard
7	Shriving Stone
8	Yorshka's Spear
9	Twinkling Titanite
10	Blood Gem
11	Ring of Sacrifice
12	Great Heal
13	Pontiff's Right Eye (on Sulyvahn's Beast here or from bridge entrance to Irithyll)
14	Excrement-covered Ashes
15	Smough's Great Hammer, Leo Ring (in chests)
16	Painting Guardian's Curved Sword
17	Painting Guardian's Armor (full set)
18	Twinkling Titanite
19	Drang Twinspears (on knight)
20	Deep Gem
21	Ring of Favor (on Sulyvahn's Beast)
22	Titanite Scale
23	Dark Stoneplate Ring
24	Golden Ritual Spear
25	Simple Gem
26	Easterner's Ashes
27	Dragonslayer Greatbow, Dragonslayer Greatarrow
28	Brass Armor (full set)
29	Sword of Avowel (before ceremony), Chameleon (from Pilgrim's body after Anri ceremony)
30	Anri's Straight Sword (near Anri's body after ceremony)
31	Reversal Ring
32	Dragonslayer's Axe (on Creighton, after Sirris co-op)
33	Creighton's Armor Set (after defeating Dark Spirit at Item 32)
34	Chloranthy Ring+1 (New Game +1)
35	Ring of Favor+1 (New Game +1)
36	Covetous Gold Serpent Ring+1 (New Game +1)
37	Havel's Ring +2 (New Game +2)
38	Wood Grain Ring+2 (New Game +2)

BONFIRES LOCATED HERE

Irithyll of the Boreal Valley

Central Irithyll

Church of Yorshka

Pontiff Sulyvahn

Water Reserve

Prison Tower

KEY DISCOVERIES

Archdeacon McDonnell Covenant

Anri

Company Captain Yorshka Covenant

ENEMIES

Sulyvahn's Beast

Pontiff Knight

Burning Stake Witch

Irithyllian Beast-hound

Irithyllian Slave

Crystal Lizard

Sewer Centipede

Silver Knight

Evangelist

Giant Slave

Deacon of the Deep

Pontiff Sulyvahn

BONFIRE—IRITHYLL OF THE BOREAL VALLEY

1 When you first look at the map in this book, Irithyll probably appears quite daunting. It is a fairly large area, and there are many enemies and items to uncover here. However, the map is also spread out very well, so you aren't going to be overwhelmed. Take this city in stages. Start by going after the boss, Pontiff Sulyvahn. By the time that he is slain, you have unlocked enough shortcuts to get around somewhat easily in the future, and you'll have plenty of Bonfires, as well.

02 A long bridge goes toward the city. As long as you've beaten the Deacons of the Deep, you will have the Small Doll that is required to cross that bridge and enter Irithyll. If you haven't done this, travel to the Cathedral of the Deep now and take care of that boss battle before you proceed.

As you go across this bridge, Sulyvahn's Beast attacks you. This monster only appears one time, so killing it is very important. You're close to a Bonfire, so waste as many Estus Flask uses as you need to. Sulyvahn's Beast has massive damage output. Top off your health whenever you take a hit.

BONFIRE—CENTRAL IRITHYLL

03 To celebrate your entrance into Irithyll, you get another Bonfire. Light this one (for Central Irithyll). As you go up the street from there, you start to encounter Pontiff Knights. These fast foes have lethal melee combos. It's hard to block them, it's hard to dodge away from them, and they can cut you down in seconds.

Bloody Pontiff Knights!

I have to say that these guys gave me so much trouble at first because I am such a melee brute. Their combos last for so long that I couldn't dodge and counterattack them. Though I usually favor a fast approach to kills, I suggest that players take on these enemies at range. Arrows are cheap, and dying isn't. This also ensures that you fight only one Pontiff Knight at a time. Getting two of these monsters at once is pure agony.

Another warning here: don't bait Pontiff Knights. It's better to take the initiative and hit them during their approach. Otherwise, they have a good chance of starting a combo that will deplete your Stamina, do damage, and begin the Frost effect on your character.

There are three Pontiff Knights as you go up the first street. Pull each back, isolate them, and then kill them.

A side shortcut is on the way up, but it's locked initially. You get this later, near **(5)**.

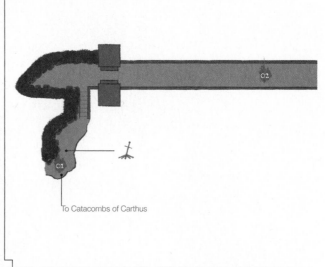

To Catacombs of Carthus

04 A fountain has a couple of Irithyllian Slaves as guardians. These are the basic foot soldiers for the area. They're low on health, only deal moderate damage, and can be killed in groups if you're prepared for them. When found in dark places, they'll be almost invisible, but you can see the few gathered here without difficulty. Dispatch them.

Nearby, another new foe is holding its ground. Burning Stake Witches fire Pyromancy spells at range, and they're able to quickly slam targets at close range, as well. You need to give them as much respect as possible. Pull enemies away from them, kill everything in the area, and then slaughter the Burning Stake Witch once it's alone. Never fight anything under the gaze of these adversaries because they'll give you constant bombardment.

On the way up to a church, you fight another Burning Stake Witch. Two patrolling Pontiff Knights are close to that street, so watch out for them while you're closing in on the Burning Stake Witch. Make sure that you don't catch their attention before their ranged ally is dealt with. If you really mess up, you're going to pull all of these enemies at once.

In the northwest, you find a modest set of stairs that seems to go almost nowhere. An empty ledge? Maybe it isn't. Try to smack the edge of the balcony up top with your weapon. A set of new stairs appears! Follow it down, and then kill an Evangelist that is praying in the yard below. You get some treasure and can open the shortcut at **(3)**. This lets you bypass quite a few monsters on the main road.

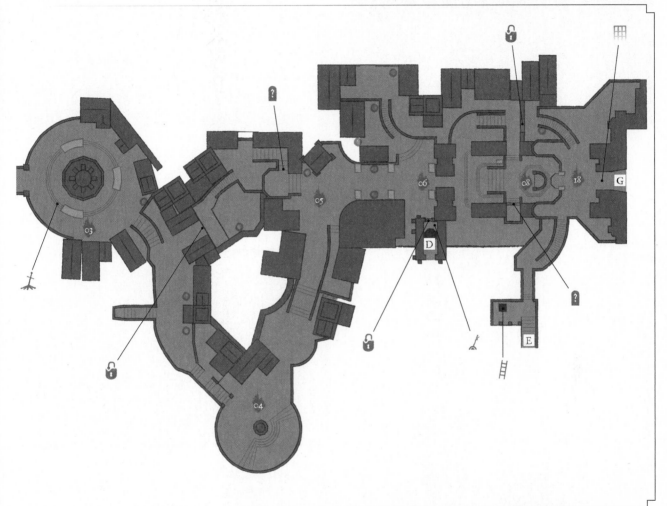

The boss, Pontiff Sulyvahn, is at the top of a building at the end of the road. You can't get in there from this part of the city without opening shortcuts. Instead, take the side path toward **(7)** to advance.

BONFIRE—CHURCH OF YORSHKA

The Church of Yorshka Bonfire makes it much easier to take out the region's boss, and it's also a critical point for exploration. The side routes away from this Bonfire let you either go after Pontiff Sulyvahn more easily or descend through the backstreets of the city. The loot improves along that route, and the path eventually takes you to the Irithyll Dungeon.

If you're going along Anri's questline, you find Anri here. Talk to Anri to continue the story. You get the **Ring of the Evil Eye** and learn the Quiet Resolve gesture.

The big building has a Burning Stake Witch and two Pontiff Knights. Pull the knights away from their support, and kill them around a corner. Look for a secret wall beside the enemies, as you find a **Magic Clutch Ring** behind it.

Once you've opened the shortcut, it's possible to go after the boss by proceeding through the large gate in this building. Otherwise, you have to go to **(7)** and take the long way around.

Stairs lead down, away from the Bonfire. They exit to a graveyard with Irithyllian Slaves here and there. Explore thoroughly, and look for an **Undead Bone Shard** behind a gravestone. Although they are easy to kill, the Irithyllian Slaves here can't be seen until you're almost on top of them. Their burning eyes appear first, but the rest of their bodies follow suit within an instant. Keep a fast weapon at the ready so that you can counter them without getting hit. At minimum, at least have a shield out so you don't get stabbed.

As you get closer to the wetlands outside of the city, many Irithyllian Slaves are hiding inside a dark basement. Hide behind your shield, and counter their attacks once they're revealed. A chest is up in the rafters of that room, and minor items are scattered below.

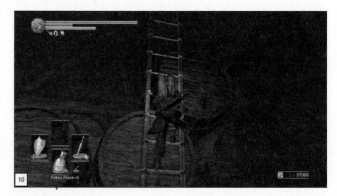

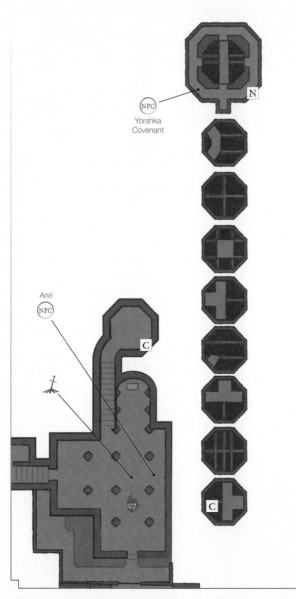

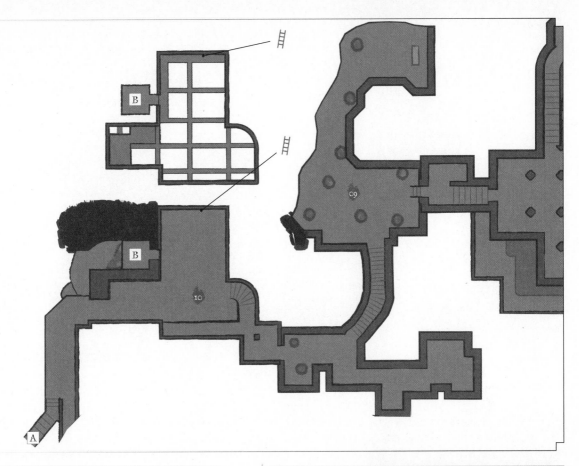

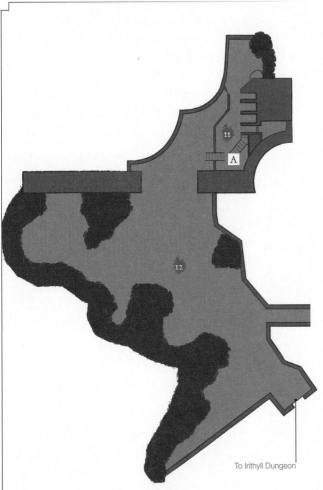

To Irithyll Dungeon

Kill the remainder of the Irithyllian Slaves on the ledges outside. The only thing that's hard to find here is a secret door that's recessed inside a brick archway. A Crystal Lizard is trapped beyond that door.

It's slow-going once you reach the water, but treasure abounds. Search all parts of the land and water to get everything that isn't nailed down. Most of the enemies here are Sewer Centipedes. They're hard to spot because they lie low in the water before they sense you, but you can still see them once you know what to look for. Ambush these foes before they rise, so you can score kills without having to really fight.

Once you arrive, you find two new ways out of the wetlands. The archway to the south takes you down into Irithyll Dungeon. There are two major regions there, and it takes a fair bit of time to clear them. There is a Bonfire called Distant Manor in that direction, and you get it without having to engage in any combat. If you're low on flasks, head over there now to restore yourself.

To the east, a sewer entrance lets you explore the remainder of Irithyll.

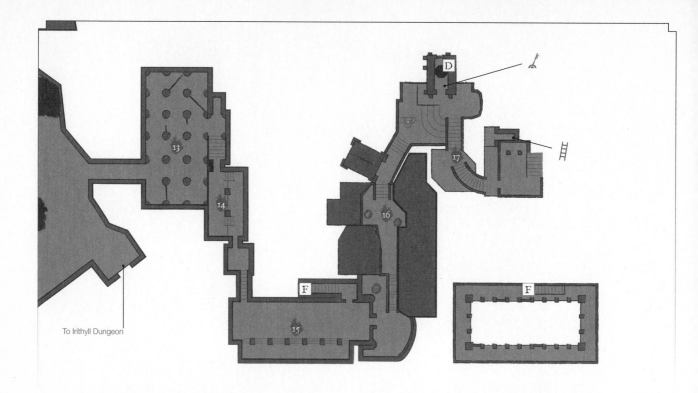

To Irithyll Dungeon

 Many Sewer Centipedes are located just inside the sewer entrance. They sometimes drop **Large Titanite Shards**, so you've found a good hunting spot if that is something that you're looking for.

Don't miss the Estus Soup that's boiling in the kitchen here. However, you may want to save this cauldron of free healing and come back to it once you deal with the Silver Knights ahead at **(15)**.

This hall has three Silver Knights. One is on the bottom floor with a sword and shield. The ones above have bows and won't let you have a moment's rest if you go too far into the chamber. Shoot the knight on the bottom level, pull him over, and kill him near the entrance wall (you can't get shot there). Silver Knights have lightning buffs for their weaponry, so blocking isn't as useful; some of the damage leaks through, even if you have a larger shield. Dodge and counter to get your kill.

Then, climb the stairs in a side hall and slay the Silver Knights above. If you push them back over the edge, it's possible to make a Plunging Attack to finish them (for extra style).

Get the three treasure chests on the upper level before you go back down.

 Irithyllian Beast-hounds try to keep you away from a shortcut and the boss' area. Go back to a shield configuration to weed these foes out.

The lift to the north gets you to a shortcut. Open this to connect with the front side of the boss' building. (You passed by there a good while earlier.)

A side lift opens a shortcut from this street to the front of the boss' area. You'll get a better shortcut in a minute or two, but open this one anyway in case you get killed before you reach the next one.

Over a half-dozen Irithyllian Slaves are at the top of the stairs when you try to approach the boss' lair. Wade through with a sweeping weapon, or retreat so that the melee Irithyllian Slaves come forward to die without getting help from their allies higher up in the chamber.

A small room with a ladder leads down to a ledge.

Do not go into Pontiff Sulyvahn's room when you first get to it. Take a staircase down on the northern side of that area. You reach a gate that is unlocked from that side. Open it and walk forward until you get back to the Church of Yorshka Bonfire at **(7)**. At this point, you've connected the entire western side of the region and won't have any issues going back and forth in the future.

Plus, you can sprint to the boss now with all of your Estus Flask uses at the ready.

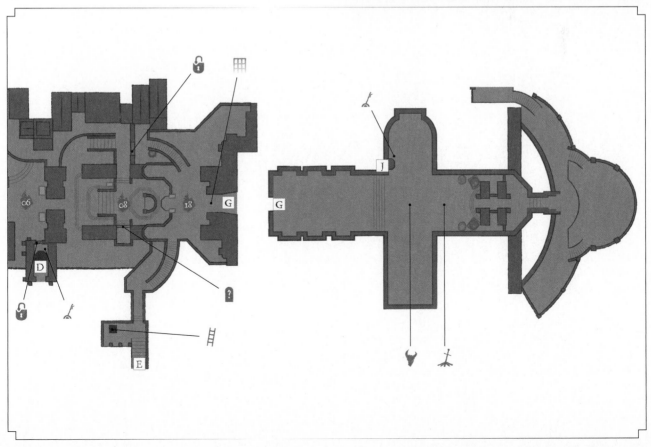

PONTIFF
SULYVAHN

STAGE I

The Pontiff is an opponent to be feared. His attack timings are fast and somewhat tricky to dodge. His ranged attacks are reliable, so you can't play too many games with him, and his damage output is fairly high. Even though you get chances to heal, this is never a fight where anything is guaranteed.

Stay close to Pontiff Sulyvahn as often as you can. He'll either cast spells at you or charge if you get too far away, so there isn't much benefit in retreating. Stick near him. His sweeping attacks cover a wide amount of territory, so dodging must be based on timing rather than position. If you roll at the wrong time, you get hit whether you're going backward, forward, or to either side.

The key to success is putting everything into raw offense. The Pontiff doesn't have that much health for a boss, and he can be brought down somewhat quickly if you hit him with a decent chain of attacks. This is especially true when he starts to transition from Stage I to Stage II.

STAGE II

The boss collapses when he starts his transition into the new phase. Do not back off here—close in, and take free shots. Get as many as you can, even if it means that you are out of Stamina when he rises again. The second stage is fairly tough, and every hit that you get now brings you that much closer to victory.

During this stage of the battle, Pontiff Sulyvahn tries to periodically summon a dark spirit to assist him. If he stands still and looks like he's charging a spell, that's what he's likely working on. Rush him and attack as much as your Stamina allows. Destroy the spirit before it's ready to come after you. Otherwise, you have to deal with two Pontiffs at once, and that's not a pleasant experience.

This is another reason not to let the boss get far away from you. The more ground you have to close, the more likely it is for Sulyvahn to finish summoning.

It's very hard to perfect this fight, but slugging your way through it doesn't take many tries. Get your health topped off frequently, and focus on Magic and Fire Resistance.

Use the new Bonfire that appears. It's now a good time to go down to the Dungeons of Irithyll. However, you can also use the exit to the east to continue exploring the rest of the city of Irithyll above. It soon leads up to Anor Londo. That's a very difficult area, but you can check it out whenever you like.

A courtyard is littered with Giant Slaves, both alive and dead. Do not go after these massive foes when you first see them. Above that yard is a balcony where there are many Deacons of the Deep. They'll hurl fire constantly while you try to engage the Giant Slaves, and it's reckless to endure that.

Instead, sprint to the western side of the yard and look for a staircase. Irithyllian Slaves are in there, but they'll pose little threat. Climb the stairs and slay the Deacons of the Deep above before you worry about the Giant Slaves.

For more excitement, finish clearing the yard, and then go toward the twin sets of stairs that lead north. When you do this, two Unkindled foes attack you. Reposition until you get a chance to strike at one of them alone. A fast combo can kill one of these dual-wielding twins before their ally arrives to complicate things. The rest of the fight is a foregone conclusion.

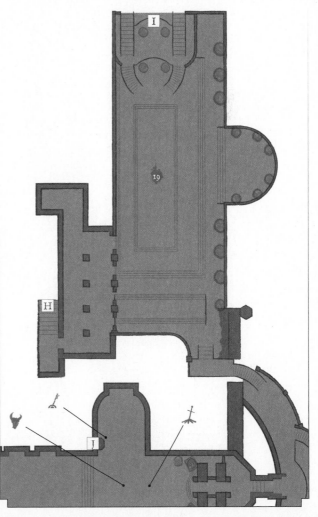

There is an upper level to Pontiff Sulyvahn's room. These upper walkways have a small platform that moves between the two tiers, so you can go back to the Bonfire and rest if you like.

Open the chest you find, and watch out for a Crystal Lizard to hunt, on the side opposite the lift.

BONFIRE—WATER RESERVE

Look for a secret door when you climb the twin staircases, and enter the next building. The first room is empty and only has a path leading up, but you know better than that. Hit the wall in the northwestern corner to open a way down. Climb the ladder but do not jump—it's a long fall!

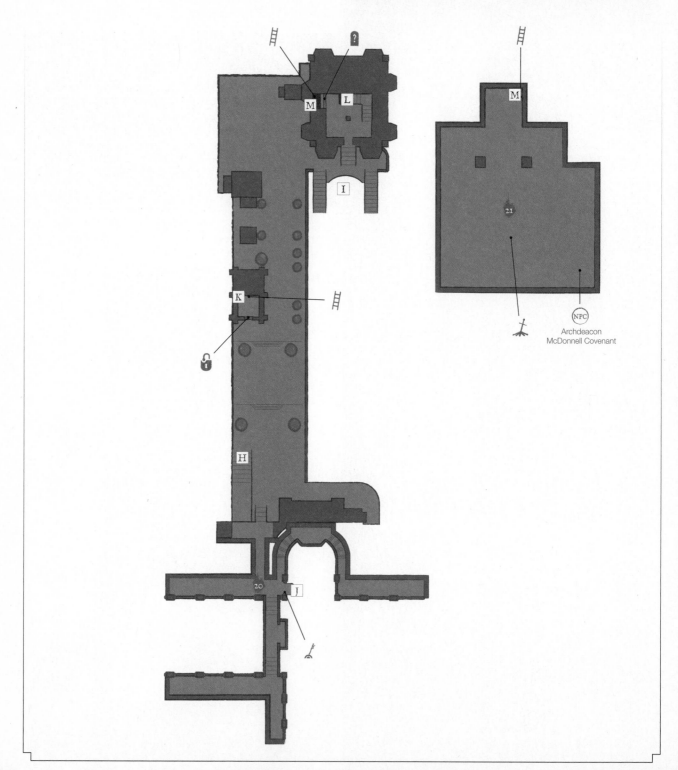

Archdeacon
McDonnell Covenant

Very Long Fall!

Jumping over a ledge without looking is a silly way to lose an Ember after killing a boss. Don't be that person. Not that I did that.

…

I totally did that.

Two of Sulyvahn's Beasts are at the bottom, in a wet reservoir. It's hard to kill them, but the entire area is a treasure trove. You get several good items, unlock a Bonfire (Water Reserve), and find Archdeacon McDonnell. The Beasts are one time-only monsters, so use everything you have and just get them down. But stick to your small entrance area while fighting the first one. If the two pair up, you're going to get chomped really hard.

When you get to the top of the stairs, sprint and run onto the rooftops. There are Silver Knights shooting from an elevated position, and anyone who has played the earlier *Dark Souls* games knows how difficult it is to rush these kinds of heavy archers on ledges like this.

It's easier than it has been in the past, and you can get to the ledge where the Silver Knights are shooting without too many problems. These archers can't see each other, so you also don't need to worry about being shot in the back while you're fighting (whew).

To the right, a small set of stairs can take you down to grab some **Easterner's Ashes**.

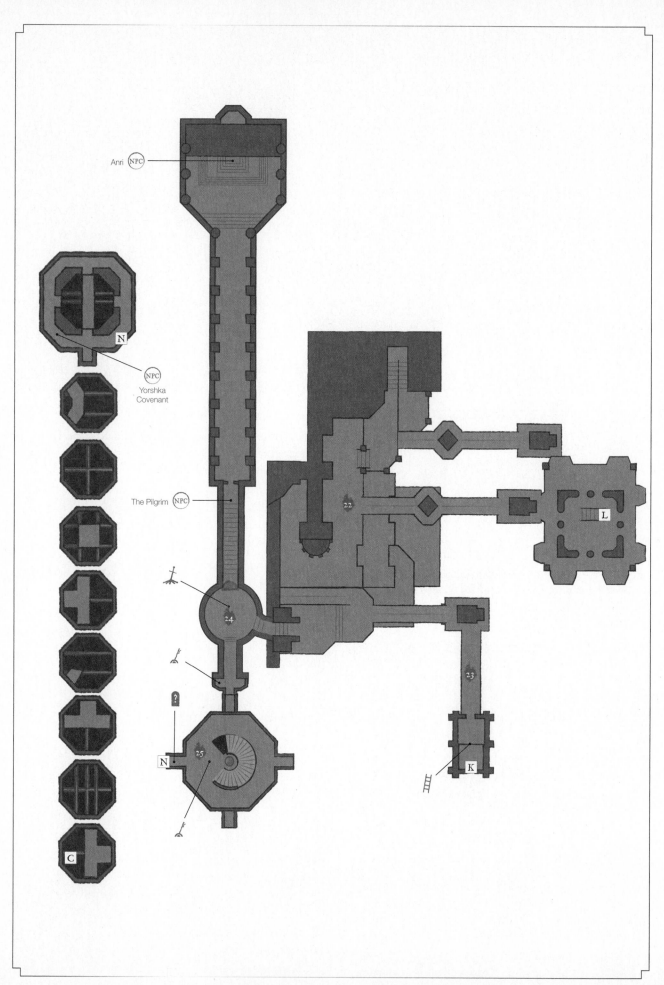

Anri NPC

N

NPC
Yorshka
Covenant

The Pilgrim NPC

22

L

24

23

?

N 25

K

C

23 Fight one more Silver Knight on a lower ledge. A sloped roof leads down toward a bridge. Take that to open a shortcut between this area and the Deacon of the Deeps at **(19)**. When you're coming back up, hop off of that sloped roof to find some equipment underneath the precarious walkway.

BONFIRE—PRISON TOWER

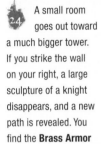

24 A small room goes out toward a much bigger tower. If you strike the wall on your right, a large sculpture of a knight disappears, and a new path is revealed. You find the **Brass Armor Set** and an intriguing room down that way.

If you've been following Anri's questline carefully up to this point, you can meet the mysterious Londor Pilgrim down the steps here, and your bride (or groom!) to be farther down the hall.

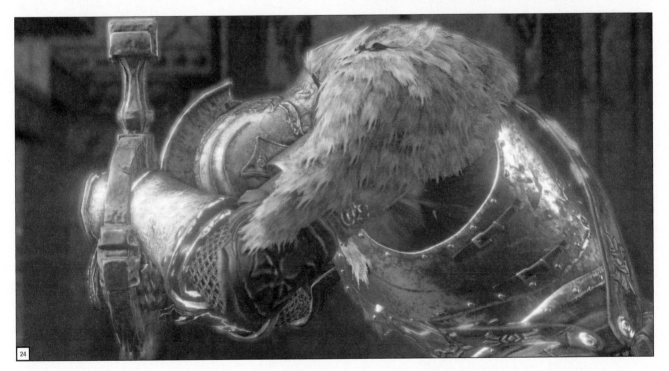

25 In the other direction, you arrive at a crank. Use that to spin the tower ahead of you. It stops, and you can then get into that tower. Climb to the top, and then use another crank to get the tower into a better position. At its highest point, the tower connects with Anor Londo. Get off of the tower bridge, and you're there. Use the Bonfire that you find.

Return to the tower, and crank it back down. From the lower tower position, walk off of the tower balcony onto thin air while looking at a tower that isn't far away.

Proceed toward the tower ahead of you, and then jump off once you're close to it. You find a Bonfire and Company Captain Yorshka, as well. From her tower, you can hop down through many ledges to get the Painted Guardian equipment and eventually land near the Church of Yorshka Bonfire at the bottom.

You can always warp back to the Anor Londo Bonfire from the bottom, so this doesn't cost you any real time.

IRITHYLL DUNGEON

∞ MAJOR ITEMS

1	Murakumo (on Dark Spirit Alva)
2	Prisoner Chief's Ashes
3	Old Sorcerer's Armor (full set)
4	Great Magic Shield (on Corpse-grub)
5	Jailbreaker's Key
6	Simple Gem
7	Titanite Scale
8	Bellowing Dragoncrest Ring
9	Estus Shard
10	Pickaxe
11	Titanite Chunk
12	Titanite Chunk (on giant), Profaned Flame (on ground)
13	Old Cell Key, Dark Clutch Ring (on Mimic)
14	Profaned Coal
15	Xanthous Ashes, Dusk Crown Ring
16	Dragon Torso Stone
17	Lightning Blade
18	Alva Armor (full set)
19	Titanite Scale x2 (Mimic)

BONFIRES LOCATED HERE

Distant Manor

Irithyll Dungeon

ENEMIES

Pontiff Knight

Peasant Hollow

Jailer

Corpse-grub

Cage Spider

Wretch

Giant Slave

Crystal Lizard

Hound-rat

Basilisk

Large Hound-rat

Lycanthrope

KEY DISCOVERIES

Siegward's Story Continues Here

Karla is Locked in a Cell

Entrance to Archdragon Peak

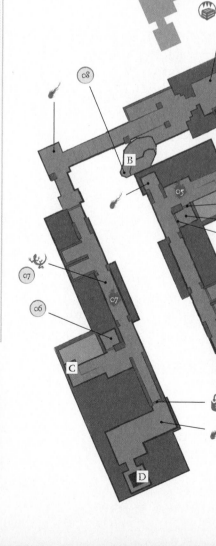

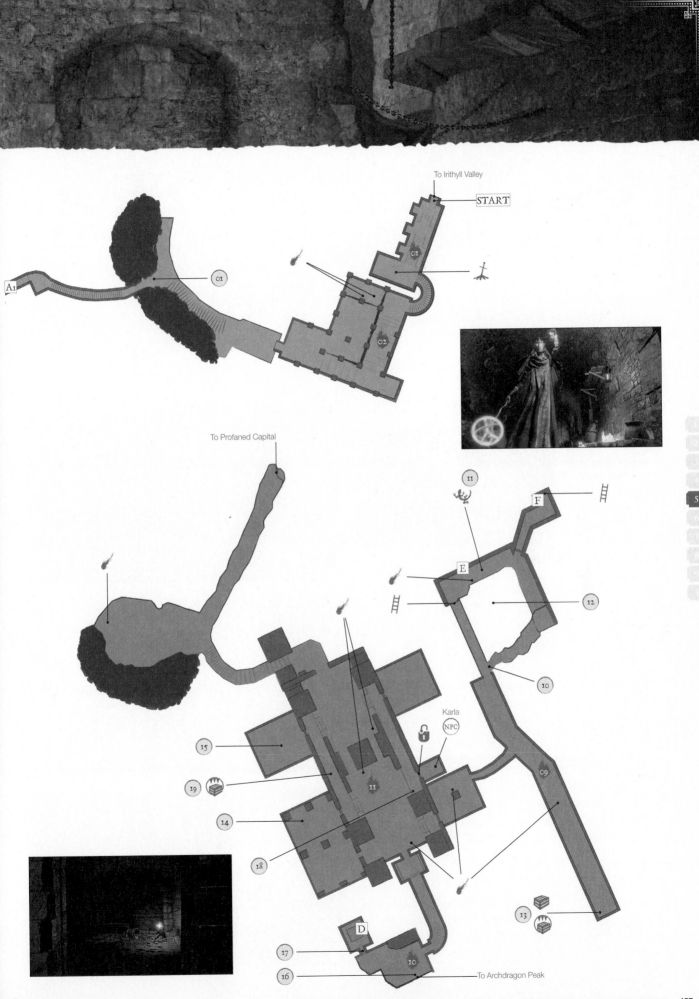

To Irithyll Valley

START

A₁

O₁

O₁

O₂

To Profaned Capital

11

F

E

12

10

Karla

NPC

C9

15

19

14

11

18

D

13

17

10

16

To Archdragon Peak

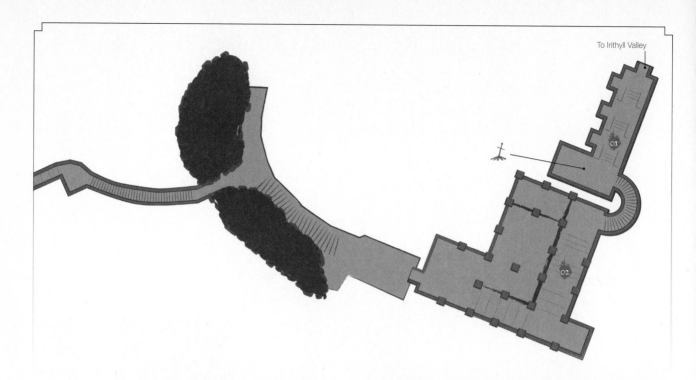

To Irithyll Valley

BONFIRE—DISTANT MANOR

01 The Distant Manor Bonfire is very close to the edge of Irithyll. Take the route through the wetlands of the city, and proceed down into the dungeon in the south. You find the Bonfire there. Light the flame!

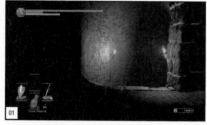

02 A Pontiff Knight is patrolling in a dark room. Use a ranged weapon to hit him, and then kill him higher on the stairs. Another one is hiding farther down, hoping that you get close enough for an ambush.

BONFIRE—IRITHYLL DUNGEON

03 There aren't any other substantial fights on the way to the next Bonfire, but it formally starts Irithyll Dungeon. It has a shortcut on the right that goes all the way down into the Profaned Capital. You won't be able to open that passage until you've gone almost to the end of this region.

The only other way to go is forward. Bleed and Curse Resistances are both useful in this area. Ranged weaponry is weaker, mostly due to the tight corridors.

04 There are six cells in this chamber. Peasant Hollows inhabit a couple of them. They'll offer only a little resistance while you search for treasure, but they attack if you give them a chance. Kill them to release the prisoners from their burden, and take what you can from their cells.

A single cell is locked, and you get the key to it quite a bit later. Luckily, you'll be able to open a shortcut by then, so it's simple to get back to this area.

One central hallway connects the cellblock, and a Jailer patrols it. These enemies Curse you simply by staying within your line of sight as they approach. They also release a gas that causes Curse to build if you stay within it. They're very bad news. Shoot at the one patrolling in the main hall, and bring it back into the previous area to deal with it. It's always good to use corners to break line of sight so that Jailers can't debuff you from afar.

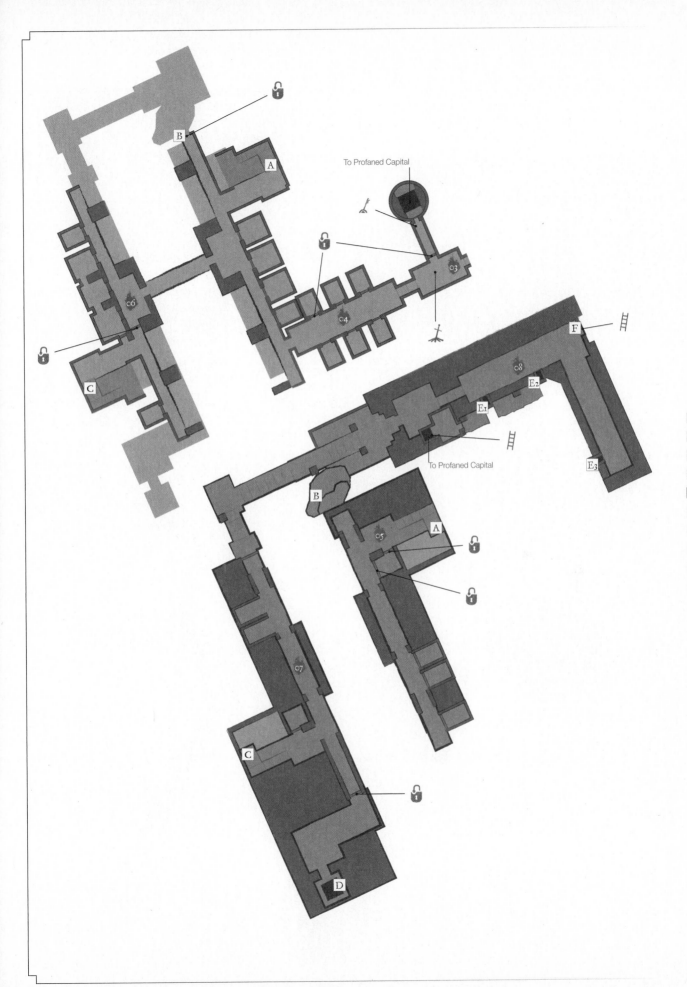

To Profaned Capital

To Profaned Capital

05 This side of the lower tier has **Ashes of the Prisoner Chief** and similar foes to fight. Attack the Jailer as you descend, and watch out for Cage Spider while you move forward. There are quite a few of them, and they become nuisances if you don't spot them before they attack.

Another Corpse-grub is in a cell farther down, but it's distracted, and you can attack it from behind.

06 If you're complacent, the far side of the upper tier gets you killed. Most of the cells have such weak monsters in them that you might dash straight into each one for the easy kills. A Jailer is in the northwestern cell. Go in carefully so that you don't breathe in a faceful of gas.

You also encounter Wretches. They're weak and slow to react, but they blend in well with the dark cells. You should spot and kill them before they have time to wake up and come after you.

The **Jailbreaker's Key** is in the southern cell on this tier. Get that, and then unlock the door in the northeast. You collect a ring and can use that as a shortcut to get down to the Profaned Capital even faster.

07 This side of the bottom tier has one patrolling Jailer and more Wretches trapped in their cells. Another shortcut is here, but it won't be opened until a little bit

later, when you're wrapping around from the basement. A lift gets you to the other side of this door, and that's where you open it.

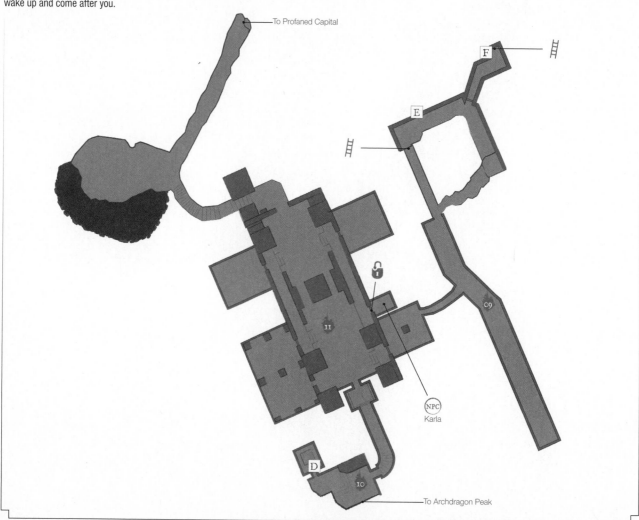

08 As you leave the cell block and try to find the areas deeper into the dungeon, many Peasant Hollows get in your way. With the proper gear, these enemies are one-shot kills, making it safe for you to wade through them. If you're a bit behind in upgrades, take the passages with a bit more care, and use your shield to block their modest attacks.

Soon, you hear loud snoring coming from an area beneath the main Peasant Hollows room. Don't jump down the holes in there; instead, use the ladder in the upper-right corner to descend safely. Open the door at the bottom to get a good view of a sleeping Giant Slave. From the safety of that hallway, you should shoot the Giant Slave to eliminate it.

A Crystal Lizard and an **Old Cell Key** are on the ledge that the Giant Slave was using for a headrest. Get what you want before climbing down a wooden ladder onto a bridge below. You can now open the locked cells in the upper ward.

There are hordes of Hound-rats at the base of the chamber, and they'll keep coming if you drop down to them. However, the loot below is worth the risk. You haven't collected many **Titanite Chunks** yet, and each one really counts. You get a **Profaned Coal**, too.

To leave this massive room, you have several choices. From the bottom, the northern exit leads to a Mimic and a ladder that returns you to the top of the Giant Slave's chamber. The other tunnel on the bottom goes to a lift that rises back to the original cellblock. Unlock the door that you reach, and connect this area with the Irithyll Dungeon Bonfire.

Finally, the stone bridge is your key to finding the Profaned Capital. Once you've looted everything and opened your new shortcut, get onto the bridge and walk south.

09 A long corridor of Hound-rats and Basilisks is south from the bridge. These are petty creatures, and you've cleared them out before from several areas. A treasure chest and a Mimic are at the top of the tunnel.

A break in the western wall lets you continue. Fight two Large Hound-rats on your way into the next room in that direction.

10 When you get to this lower cellblock, look around carefully. You can turn north or south here. The southern route has two purposes: it leads to a shortcut at **(7)**, and you get a **Dragon Torso Stone** from a strange body.

THE TRIP TO ARCHDRAGON PEAK

Later, after beating the Consumed King's Garden, return to this very spot. If you use the gesture that you learned from that area, something incredible happens here. You are granted access to an optional region that has tons of treasure, a new boss, and plenty more to accomplish.

In short:

-Defeat Oceiros and explore the area behind his lair (this is where you learn the Path of the Dragon gesture).

-Return to the site here, where you find the Dragon Torso Stone.

-Use the Path of the Dragon gesture while sitting beside the strange corpse, and wait for 20 seconds or so.

The lift behind the Dragon Stone takes you up to the original cellblock. This time, it's to the door on the western side of the block. Open that, and then return to the lower part of the dungeon.

11 A coven of Jailers wanders back and forth between the two halves of this large chamber. Don't attack the entire group. Wait until they're on the far side of the central pillar, and then move out and slaughter one of them. Retreat, and kill any others that saw you. Make more hit-and-run attacks like this until the Jailers' numbers are manageable.

Once you're finished, clear all of the cells. The cell in the southeast is locked, but you should return later to open that one. It has Karla, a student of dark magic. If you free her, she'll travel to the Firelink Shrine. To get the **Jailer's Key Ring** that you need, travel to the Profaned Capital, and climb the stairs that lead out of the eastern mire. They'll take you back into the dungeon and let you kill a lone Jailer to obtain this key.

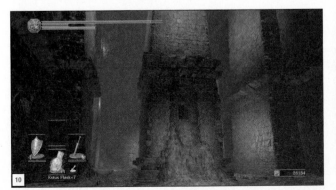

PROFANED CAPITAL

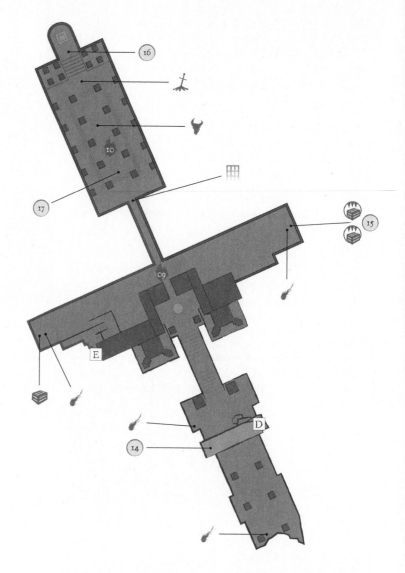

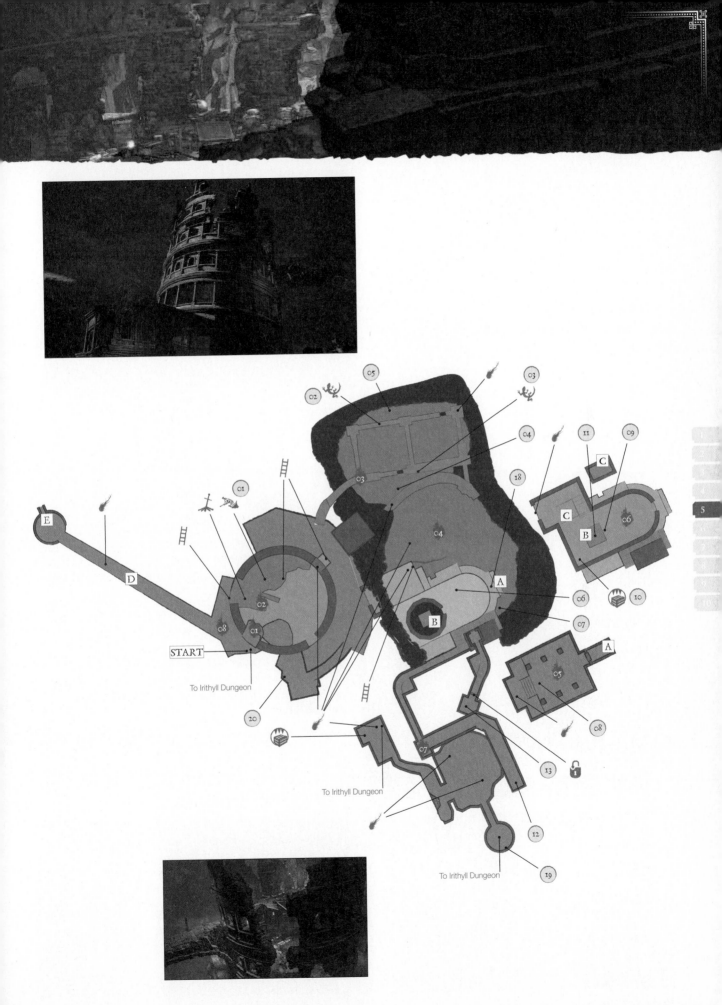

START

To Irithyll Dungeon

To Irithyll Dungeon

To Irithyll Dungeon

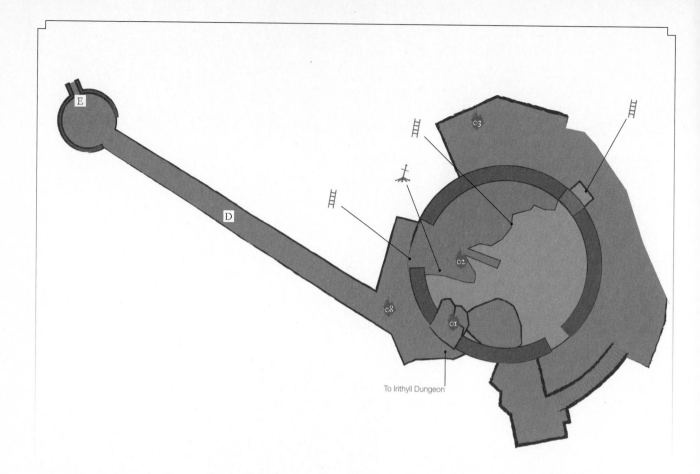

To Irithyll Dungeon

A damaged bridge connects Irithyll Dungeon and the Profaned Capital. As you try to cross it, a Headless Gargoyle attacks you. If you're confident in your footing, fight it while you're still on the bridge. Just be careful of the edges, and don't dodge unless you know where you're rolling. It's better to take a hit than fall to your death. Or you can simply dash beyond it and fight it once you reach stable footing.

BONFIRE—PROFANED CAPITAL

Go into the Profaned Capital, and climb onto a broken floor in the tower. Light a Bonfire (Profaned Capital), and then look around for an **Undead Bone Shard**. You also learn the Stretch Out gesture up here as you pick up items.

Don't try to fall down to the treasure in one of the windows. You actually get it from outside the tower, where a ladder leads up to it.

Walk out of the tower's broken wall to explore the eastern side of the capital. Though optional, there is more loot to be had over there, and some of it is quite important. You should cover that before getting everything to the west.

A small entrance to the northeast takes you into a building with narrow corridors. Though Crystal Lizards wait inside, you need to watch the floor carefully. There are gaps in the stonework, and falling causes you to drop into the mire below. If you take the path immediately to your left upon entering, you can kill both of the Crystal Lizards without plummeting into the goo.

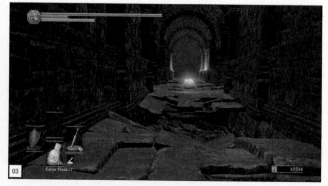

○4 The mire has Sewer Centipedes all over the place. Even worse, the water is fetid and toxic. You are going to take massive damage if you let your character suffer from its effects. Look for the small islands of dry land, and make those your refuge while you fight and explore.

Because this is toxic sludge, Purple Moss Clumps won't help you when things go too far. To explore the far edges of the mire, you're likely to take a fair amount of damage from the toxic effect, but it's still worthwhile.

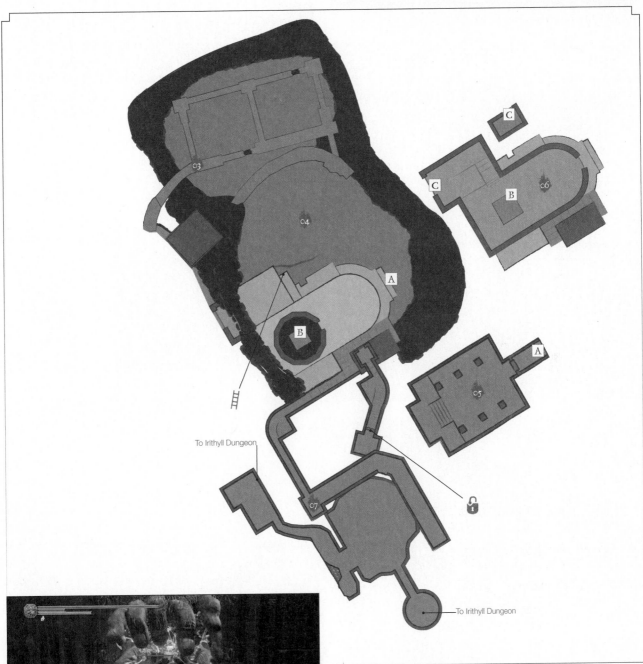

To Irithyll Dungeon

To Irithyll Dungeon

○5 The lower part of the mire temple has three Monstrosity of Sins inside of it. These thick creatures move slowly, but they can grab you or body slam you without difficulty. Let them attack first. Draw each one over, dodge its heavy slams, and then execute several hits in reprisal. Don't be greedy; back off after those hits, and repeat your run. It takes two or even three combos like this to kill each Monstrosity of Sin.

06 You access the upper section of the temple from the roof. You can use a breach in the wall, or you can drop through the ceiling from the very top of the building. There aren't many more defenders left. One more Monstrosity of Sin is inside, and a solo Unkindled is on the roof.

Dropping into the building is better because you get to pick up a **Profaned Coal** on the way, which you can take to the Blacksmith.

ANOTHER EASY TO MISS AREA

While you're on the roof, look for a small archway across a gap. It's possible to jump over to it, and you should do that when you have time. You reach a locked door but can use the Old Cell Key that you found earlier in the Irithyll Dungeon to open it.

Inside is a corpse with the **Covetous Gold Serpent Ring**. This is one of the most enjoyable items for people who farm monster drops because it raises your Item Discovery. Pair that with the Covetous Silver Serpent Ring for maximum items and Souls as you fight. Keep those both on when you're clearing levels, and then swap them out for raw power when dueling, invading, fighting bosses, etc.

07 A broken wall lets you jump back into the central area of the Profaned Capital. Otherwise, take the stairs that lead up and out of the capital. This returns you to Irithyll Dungeon, by the Giant Slave. You find a solo Jailer there with the **Jailer's Key Ring**. That's what you use to unlock Karla's cell door.

08 To clear the western side of the Profaned Capital, leave the Bonfire by climbing down a ladder; it's on the upper floor where the Bonfire is lit. A bridge down below takes you toward the boss' area, but you encounter a number of enemies along the way.

Several Jailer Handmaids are using a burning brazier below the bridge to throw fire at you. Stay in motion at all times to avoid taking damage here. While you're running, look over the right edge of the bridge. There's a pillar below you with the **Onislayer Greatbow**; dropping off of the bridge is the only way to get to it.

If you choose to stay on the bridge, you face a short fight against a Headless Gargoyle. It's much like the fight on your way into the region because you don't have much room to dodge.

Kill it as quickly as possible so that you don't take too many hits from the fire while you're engaged. Once you triumph, sprint the rest of the way across.

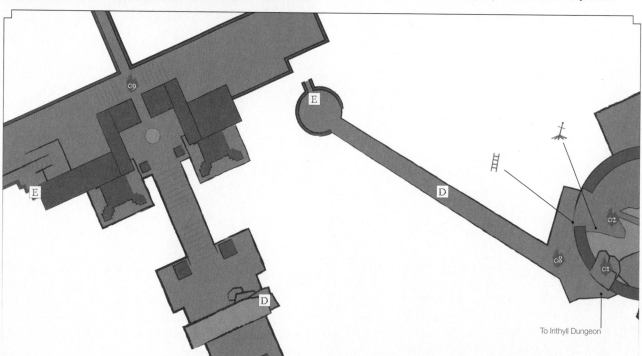

To Irithyll Dungeon

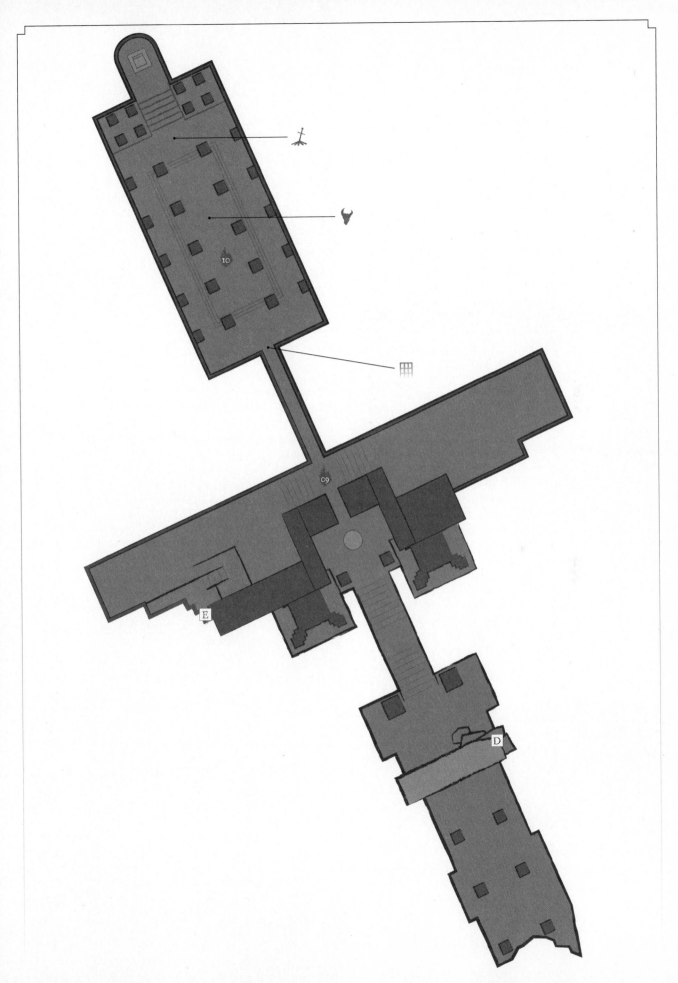

Two Headless Gargoyles and a legion of Jailer Handmaids are in the hallway that adjoins the boss' room. The fighting here is extremely tough at first, especially if you grab many targets at once.

Jailer Handmaids have slow ranged attacks. Dodge underneath their fireballs, and slice the casters apart. They are still lethal at close range if you take too long to kill each one, so roll and flee if you experience any problems. Don't bait them, and don't hesitate.

Plink away at foes from the upper doorway if you can. Or, draw the group closer to the stairs, use Plunging Attacks to burn them down, and then retreat your ambush if necessary.

If you're having trouble with the Jailer Handmaids' curse attacks, put on a Cursebite Ring to give yourself a bit more time to escape from their gas attacks. They don't use these as often as Jailers, but they are still a threat.

Don't trust the chests in this hallway—there are two Mimics directly next to each other.

Once you're prepared, go into the boss' side chamber. You can't really defeat Yhorm the Giant without using a special weapon. There is a blade called **Storm Ruler** that is meant to take this guy down. Luckily, you can find the weapon near the throne at the far side of the room. Sprint around the huge warrior to retrieve that sword as soon as possible.

If you're sane, use a Homeward Bone to port back to your Bonfire and equip the weapon while you're safe. Or, take a chance and slot that sword in during the fight. It is possible to do this without taking a hit, and even if you do get slammed, you can often recover, heal, and get back in the fight. That said, you're taking a risk, the giant can easily crush you while you're playing around in your equipment screen.

YHORM THE GIANT

Though Yhorm has two stages (like many bosses), they aren't that relevant once you understand the mechanics of the battle. Storm Ruler is the key to everything. You can't deal real damage without it, and even its regular attacks aren't of any substantial value.

Instead, you charge the weapon (see the Controlling the Game chapter for details). Wait until the wind around the blade starts to burst with energy. Then, use your charged heavy attack to bring Yhorm the Giant to his knees. It only takes a few swings like that to silence him forever.

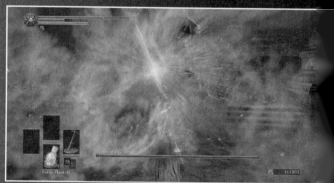

That's the short version.

But Yhorm won't take this lying down. He'll still try to rip you in half with his humongous blade. He can destroy the pillars in the room, so you can't count on them for cover. It's safer to stand in the open and use dodge to get out of the way at the last minute. Yhorm telegraphs his attacks from across the room, so you always know when one of them is coming.

It's okay to interrupt your Storm Ruler charging to dodge. In fact, it would be foolish not to. Yhorm has a long recovery time from his attacks, and he'll be very vulnerable after each one. Don't rush! This is a quick fight, even if you're defensive.

With Yhorm dead, you've finished with the Profaned Capital (and the entire Irithyll Dungeon section of the game). You should now look into Anor Londo, at the far end of Irithyll. Or, you can start clearing out Lothric Castle, which is discussed in its own chapter.

ANOR LONDO

∞ MAJOR ITEMS

1 Giant's Coal

2 Aldrich's Ruby (on Deep Accursed)

3 Sun Princess Ring (on ground),
Soul of Rosaria, Crescent Moon Sword,
Silver Mask (invading Ringfinger Leonhard
with Black Eye Orb)

4 Estus Shard

BONFIRES LOCATED HERE

Anor Londo

Aldrich, Devourer of Gods

ENEMIES

Silver Knight

Deacon of the Deep

Writhing Rotten Flesh

Deep Accursed

Aldrich, Devourer of Gods

KEY DISCOVERIES

N/A

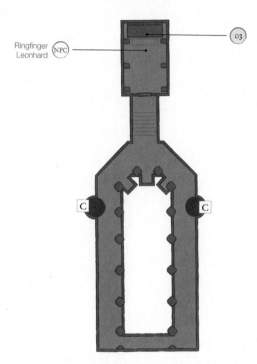

Ringfinger
Leonhard NPC

o3

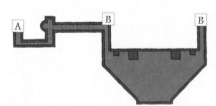

A B B

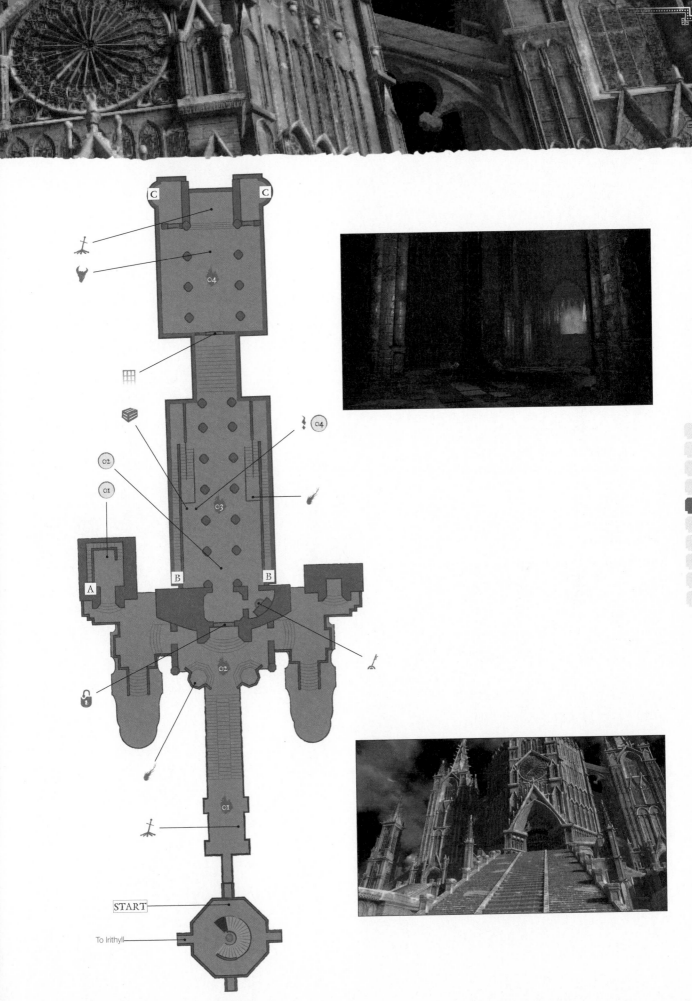

START

To Irithyll

BONFIRE—ANOR LONDO

01 Climb the towers at the far side of Irithyll to reach Anor Londo. This new area begins at the Anor Londo Bonfire, which doesn't take long to explore as long as the powerful enemies here don't kill you off again and again.

02 A Silver Knight is on the stairs as you go up. Like all of his kind, he'll use lightning to deal extra damage and wound you a bit despite the blocking you might do. Play offensively against the Silver Knights; they're hard to dodge and bait, so attack first and hit aggressively.

A second one comes down the stairs a little while after you engage his comrade. If at all possible, go crazy on the initial knight so that you can kill or badly wound him before he gets support from his ally.

To the east, there is another pair of Silver Knights. Shoot at range to soften them, and focus your damage on one of them specifically if you end up in battle with both. The sooner one goes down, the sooner this becomes a manageable fight.

You can't get into the central building initially. The path to the west wraps around the area and lets you get inside. After that, you can unlock the door and go back and forth at your leisure.

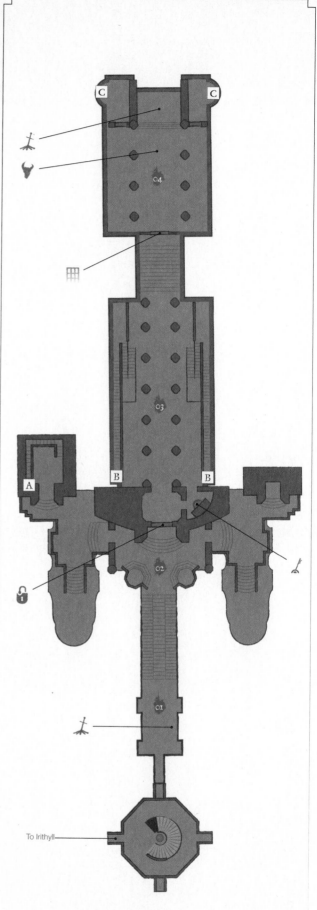

To Irithyll

A lone Silver Knight patrols the western walkways. Pull him from range, and dispatch him. The building he's guarding has the **Giant's Coal** inside, so you gain another upgrade for the Blacksmith. When you're inside, take the stairs up so that you can get into the main building.

Deacons of the Deep are on the walkways and the main floor of the central building. To have any peace, you need to kill them; otherwise, ranged Pyromancy spells fly in your direction on a constant basis. Roll under these, approach your victims, and lay them low without mercy.

There are also Writhing Rotten Flesh in the room, but they're easily avoided when you have more pressing matters to attend to. Sprint around them as you kill the Deacons of the Deep.

Use a crank to the east of the door to open it. The run from the Bonfire to the boss is now a quick one. A Deep Accursed leaps from the shadows to punish your transgression. Its blows have a Curse effect, but that won't normally be an issue as long as you dodge and counterattack aggressively. It's also a one-time spawn.

It's dark inside that building, so you might have better luck if you draw the Deep Accursed out onto the stairs. It's easier to bait the monster's attacks when you can see it clearly.

Slay the creature, and with that, you're ready. Rest if needed, and then go after Aldrich! Although it's risky, you can avoid both Silver Knights and all of the Deacons of the Deep when you're making runs from the Bonfire to the boss. Sprint quickly, and don't stop for anything. You still have to roll to avoid the Silver Knights' parting shots, but you end up saving Estus Flasks with very little practice.

The fight against Aldrich begins almost instantly, as you enter the fog gate and are beset by this dedicated spellcaster. This is what it means to face off against someone who has really mastered the ancient arts of sorcery.

ALDRICH, DEVOURER OF GODS

Killing Aldrich is the easy part; surviving Aldrich's spells long enough to finish the job is what makes your task difficult. All of Aldrich's attacks deal high damage, so it's worth pulling out your Estus Flask whenever you get hit. Beyond that, this fight is all about learning how to avoid the spells well enough so that they don't kill you outright.

The bolt that Aldrich casts is fast, has long range, and is hard to dodge. However, this spell isn't used as much if you stay at close or medium range with Aldrich. That's sensible anyway, since this is not a boss that you want to trade ranged attacks against.

It's even harder to dodge all of the small motes of Arcane energy that Aldrich summons. They'll rise as a group of eight, and then they'll individually go after you. They don't do tons of damage per hit, but you're going to waste a lot of Stamina if you want to avoid all of them. The most efficient defense is to roll under the motes and get closer to Aldrich. Absorb a couple of hits so that you arrive at the caster with most of your Stamina ready to use. As long as you're evading the majority of the motes, you should be in good shape for reprisal.

Aldrich can knock you down and do some damage if you're at point-blank range. Accept this, because that's the place where you inflict the most damage on him. He knocks you down as he's beginning to teleport to another location. That means that he won't attack for several moments, allowing you time to heal and start repositioning yourself. Aim for the farthest corner of the room, which is likely where he'll pop up again.

When in just the right mood, Aldrich charges for a big swing of his scythe and then hits everything around him. It's real damage, and you most certainly want to dodge it. The good news is that you might go an entire fight with him without seeing this bigger melee attack happen.

Unfortunately, you will see Aldrich rely on his best attack much more often. After slowly pulling out a magical bow, Aldrich summons a wave of arrows that rains down all over the field. They'll retarget often, trying to get to you. You have to stay mobile during the rain of arrows, or else you'll take cruel, unfair, and lethal damage. Run as faar away from the boss as you can before he even has the bow out, fleeing the moment that he begins his animation. If you try to trade damage with him inside the arrow rain, he'll win, and you won't feel good about it.

To win this fight, get bursts of fast damage. Use maximum Magic Resistance, extra HPs, and extra damage. You can also consider lowering your Equip Load by taking shields, ranged weapons, and other non-essential gear off of your character.

With that, you're done with Anor Londo. You are summoned back to the High Wall of Lothric. For a description of the next battle there, see the Dancer of the Boreal Valley write-up in the High Wall of Lothric portion of the walkthrough. Complete that fight to access Lothric Castle. From there, you can either wander into the Consumed King's Garden or continue through Lothric Castle.

CONSUMED KING'S GARDEN

MAJOR ITEMS

1	Estus Shard
2	Titanite Chunk
3	Ring of Sacrifice
4	Claw, Shadow Armor (full set, both underneath platform)
5	Dark Gem
6	Titanite Chunk
7	Dragonscale Ring
8	Titanite Chunk
9	Path of the Dragon gesture
10	Titanite Scale
11	Titanite Scale
12	Wood Grain Ring+1 (New Game +1)
13	Sage Ring+2 (New Game +2)
14	Magic Stoneplate Ring (on Consumed King's Knight)

BONFIRES LOCATED HERE

Oceiros, the Consumed King

ENEMIES

Rotten Slug

Pus of Man

Consumed King's Knight

Oceiros

Serpent-man

KEY DISCOVERIES

Half of the Steps for Reaching Archdragon Peak

To Untended Graves

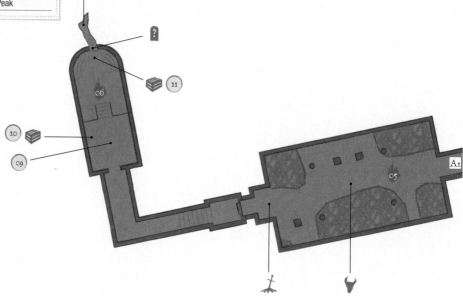

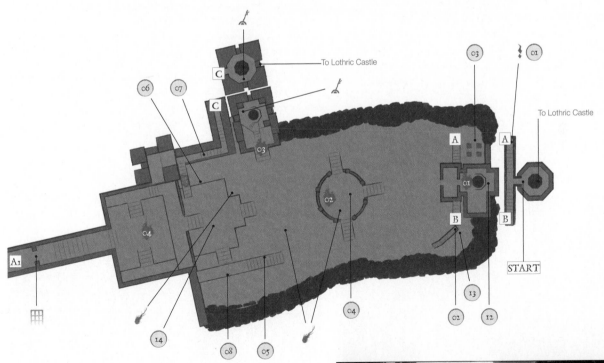

To Lothric Castle

To Lothric Castle

START

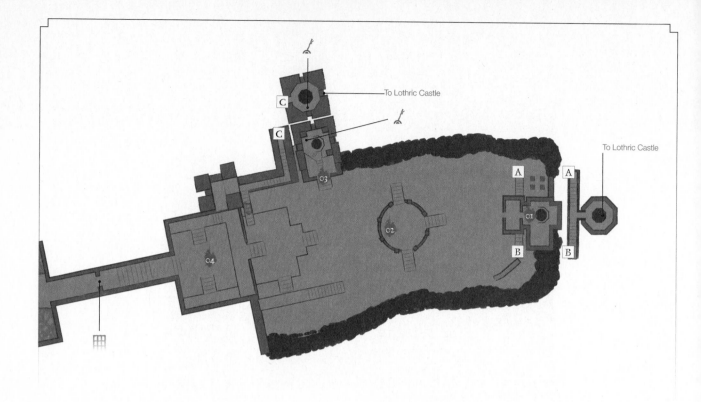

To Lothric Castle

To Lothric Castle

As soon as you reach Lothric Castle, turn south and get onto a lift at the end of that corridor. The lift takes you down into the Consumed King's Garden. You can roll off of the lift partway down, or let it go all the way to the bottom. There are Rotten Slugs at the base of the lift, but they're not really your problem. The issue is that most of this region is laden with toxins. Merely stepping on the dark patches of ground causes you to get the toxic effect.

It's safer to get off halfway down because that exit from the lift gets you onto higher ground. Even better, there are pieces of treasure up there.

The Rotten Slugs aren't tough or particularly dangerous. However, there are also Pus of Mans and Consumed King's Knights in this area. Both of those enemy types are extremely dangerous.

FREE EMBERS!

The Pus of Man are some of the best enemies in the game for dropping Embers. Even from them, Embers aren't a common drop, but get your Item Discovery up as much as possible and see if your farming pays off.

Unleash ranged attacks from the high ground, and choose your moment to descend. Either way, you are safe once you kill your foes and get onto the non-toxic ground.

Clear everything that's close to the central, raised area in the garden. Then, go after the Consumed King's Knight who is standing up there. Killing him gives you a great place to survey the garden and figure out where you're going next.

There are many small but important pieces of treasure in the surrounding area. After you've gotten everything, this place becomes a "sprint through" area. At first, though, it's useful to kill every enemy and collect each piece of treasure. This will probably take quite a few Estus Flask drinks off of your supply, but you don't need to go for a boss run just yet. Get everything you can carry, use a Homeward Bone, and then return once you're able to move through this area without having to fight all of the tougher monsters.

More items are underneath the central platform. Don't miss them! You can finally get some hardcore upgrades for your late-game weaponry. **Titanite Chunks** start showing up more often at this point.

Look for a small building along the northern wall. There is another lift inside that passes two upper floors. Jump off at the middle floor to get a **Dragonscale Ring** without putting in too much effort. Then, use the lift to reach the upper floor. Get off there, and go through a short corridor. You can find some equipment on a body a couple of rooms away, but back off as soon as you get it.

Hollow Slaves attack from higher positions in the room, and they have ranged support.

The rest of the area up top simply leads toward a barred door. Once you open that, it becomes a shortcut so that you can return from the Bonfire without having to go through the early part of the garden.

A small plaza blocks your direct route from the original lift to the boss. A serious Consumed King's Knight stands resolute on the lower floor of the area. Shoot him at range to get damage in before the real fight. If you're in the mood for cheap tactics, hop off of the wall once the knight gets close, and use the terrain to your advantage. This allows you to get more shots against him.

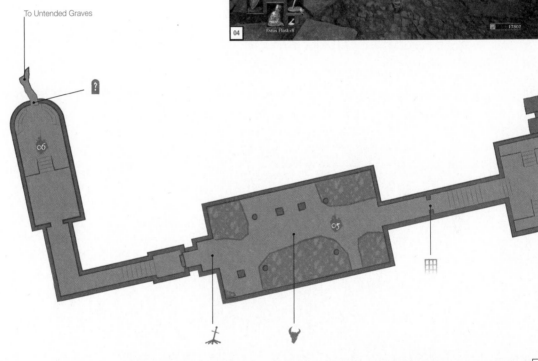

To Untended Graves

MAJOR BATTLE

The boss' room isn't far from the plaza. To save Estus Flasks for your attempt on the boss, try sprinting past as much of the garden as you can. These enemies are high-end, but they're not always so quick to chase you. Because of this, you're able to bring most or even all of your Estus Flask uses to bear against Oceiros. Rush to his fog gate, slip inside, and laugh at your pursuers.

OCEIROS, THE CONSUMED KING

STAGE I

Oceiros starts the fight with a couple of basic attacks. His staff bash comes out quickly, so dodge early if he pulls his staff arm back. The tail whip takes longer, so that's an attack you need to be patient with. Hold your dodge until the last moment to avoid the damage and still have time to pummel the boss.

Put some distance between yourself and Oceiros if he takes to the air. He'll pound the ground in just a moment. That move deals minor damage and interrupts whatever you're doing, so you can't just trade blows with him.

Oceiros also has poisonous breath, so sprint away if he breathes. This prevents you from taking poison damage throughout the fight, and it also helps to keep your vision clear. It's hard to see anything in the cloud.

Oceiros, the Consumed King

STAGE II

For the remainder of the fight, Oceiros ditches his staff and goes for claw attacks and mad dashes. His blows become more frantic and more dangerous. The single-claw swipe isn't too bad, and its timing is slightly similar to the staff bash in Stage I. Instead, it's the charge that you have to fear the most. Oceiros races forward on all fours, clawing through anything that gets in his way. Dodge repeatedly until you get to the side and are out of harm's way.

You still have to watch the tail, but that's not too bad. Use it as a way to dodge closer to the boss and gain free hits.

When you can, harp on executing head attacks. They're risky, but enough damage can stun Oceiros briefly, giving you a second to heal or attack as you see fit.

Oceiros, the Consumed King

You get a Bonfire, as usual. This time, you also get to explore a small area behind the boss' lair. It doesn't lead to a new region (not directly, at least), but there are secrets to uncover.

C6 Open the door behind Oceiros' room and descend. At the end of the tunnel, you meet a Serpent-man, which is a lesser form of dragonkin. You will encounter many more of them on Archdragon Peak. This one is alone, and you can kill it quite easily.

The corpse on the floor teaches you the Path of the Dragon gesture. A chest behind the Serpent-man contains a **Titanite Scale**, as well. The wall behind the rear chest is a secret door, so slash the wall to open it.

PATH OF THE DRAGON

This gesture has serious importance. With this, you can access an optional region of the game: Archdragon Peak. Return to Irithyll Dungeon, and go to the spot where you found the Dragon Torso Stone. Stand next to the dragon statue in that spot and use the Path of the Dragon gesture.

You've finished the Consumed King's Garden. You can return to Lothric Castle, and continue clearing it, or advance ahead into the Untended Graves, located behind the secret door in this room.

UNTENDED GRAVES

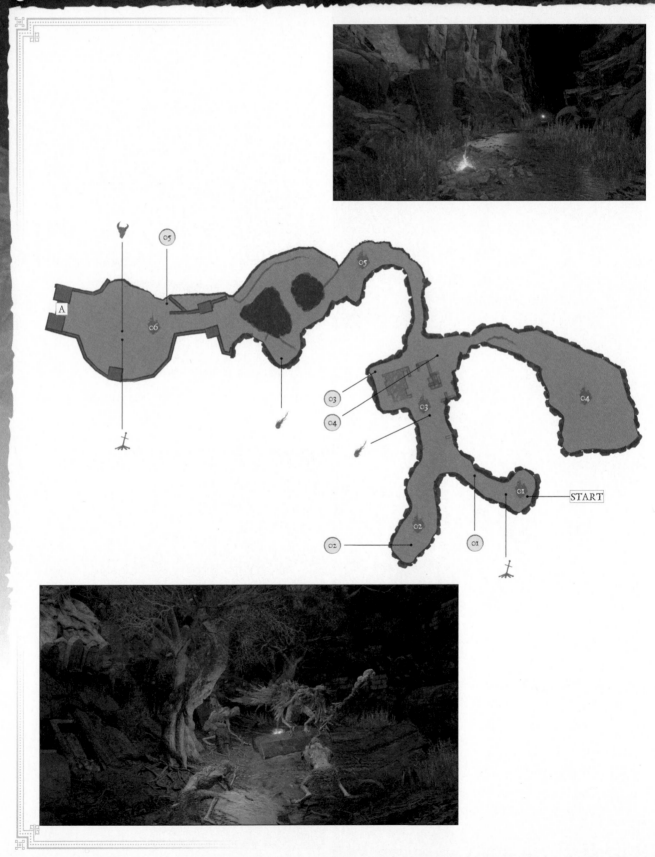

MAJOR ITEMS

1	Shriving Stone
2	Ashen Estus Ring
3	Titanite Chunk
4	Titanite Chunk
5	Black Knight Glaive
6	Chaos Blade
7	Hornet Ring
8	Coiled Sword Fragment
9	Blacksmith Hammer
10	Eyes of a Fire Keeper
11	Ring of Steel Protection+1 (New Game +1)
12	Life Ring+3 (New Game +2)

BONFIRES LOCATED HERE

Untended Graves

ENEMIES

Corvian Storyteller

Corvian

Grave Warden

Starved Hound

Ravenous Crystal Lizard

Champion Gundyr

Black Knight

KEY DISCOVERIES

N/A

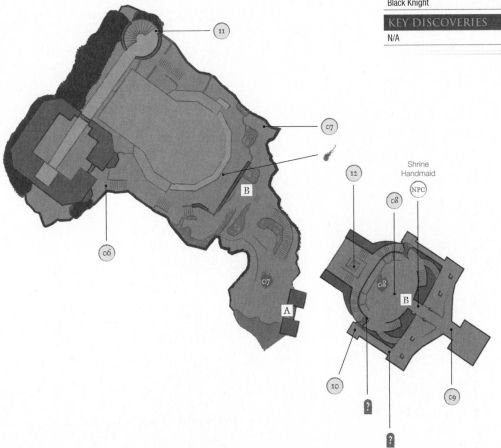

BONFIRE—UNTENDED GRAVES

You reach this dark version of the starting area by going through a secret door at the end of Consumed King's Garden. The Bonfire is at the base of the first hill.

Corvians and a Corvian Storyteller are clustered together by the grave where you first rose. This area is very dark, and new items are available. The location is essentially a copy of the Ashen Shrine, but it has worse monsters and far better treasure.

Kill these foes to get yourself the **Ashen Estus Ring**.

You find Grave Wardens and Starved Hounds in small groups toward the far side of the area. There isn't anything new or particularly dangerous about these encounters.

Two Ravenous Crystal Lizards are in the area where only one of them lived the first time you went through this region. You can pull them separately, making these fights very manageable. You obtain more **Titanite Scales** from this encounter, and **Titanite Chunks** are littered around the general map. These items are great for topping off extra equipment.

As you approach the next Bonfire, watch out for any invasions. If you have to contend with anything here, be wary of the narrow ledges. Don't roll off or let any enemies fight you with your back to the cliff's edge.

Note that there isn't a Bonfire in the old spot; you must continue using the Untended Graves Bonfire if you need any rest.

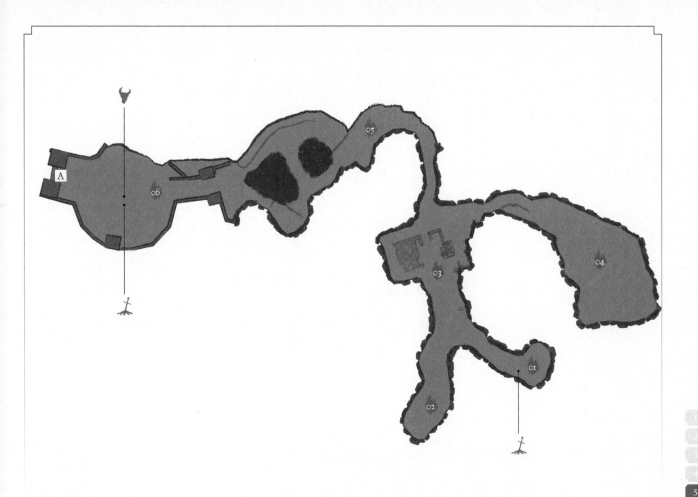

MAJOR BATTLE

 Iudex Gundyr is gone, so you probably don't expect a boss to be here. But there is, and this isn't the original boss. This is Champion Gundyr, with much more health, faster moves, a deadlier set of attacks, and an arena that is dark. These factors make the fight much more dangerous than it was originally.

Homeward Bone

136573

CHAMPION GUNDYR

Though Champion Gundyr doesn't transform, he makes use of everything that he has. His combinations are harder to dodge because they start slow but unleash very quickly. He also has a couple of hand-to-hand attacks that are brutal mix-ups. He has a shoulder charge that comes out of nowhere when it adds to a combo, and his high kick is infuriatingly tough to avoid when you're getting used to it.

The good news is that you're late enough in the game to face this version of Gundyr with a huge reserve of Estus Flask uses. As long as you don't let Champion Gundyr take you from 100-0, you're going to be in good shape. You always have the option to dodge backward, dodge again if you need even more space, and then heal. Let that be your bulwark against his upgrades.

You don't need to race him or take him down quickly. He doesn't get any nastier during the battle, so settle in and take potshots to diminish his health over time. Avoid long combos or desperate measures.

After you win the fight, the Champion Gundyr Bonfire appears.

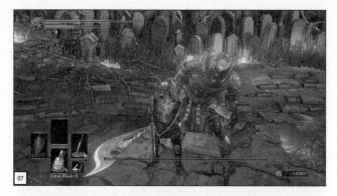

07 Open the doors to get into the Firelink Shrine yards, and start exploring them. There are Black Knights on the path, and they're tough adversaries. However, they're individuals, so you can pull them away and fight them anywhere you want.

08 There are many important things to do inside the Firelink Shrine's dark version. First, you get a **Coiled Sword Fragment** from the area where the Bonfire is supposed to be. This item acts as a permanent Homeward Bone, so that saves you some Souls in the future.

A secret door hides the **Fire Keeper's Eyes**, back in the spot where Irina normally stays. These items are vital for unlocking one of the endings to the game, see the NPC chapter for more details.

Another version of the Shrine Handmaid is here, she sells the **Wolf Knight's** armor set and the **Priestess Ring**.

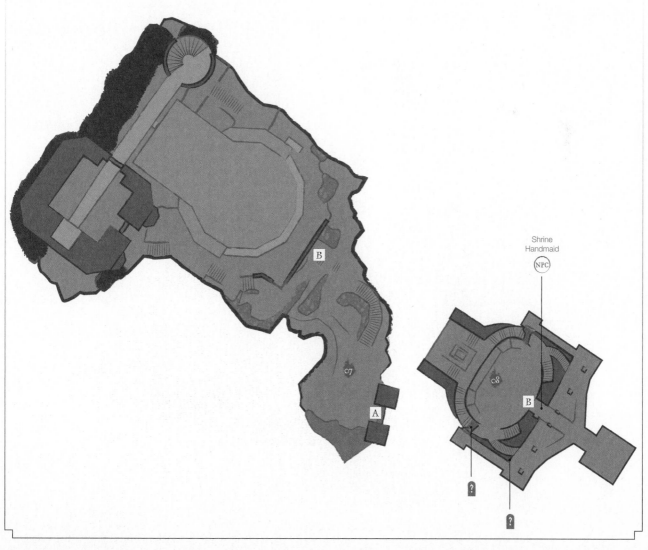

LOTHRIC CASTLE

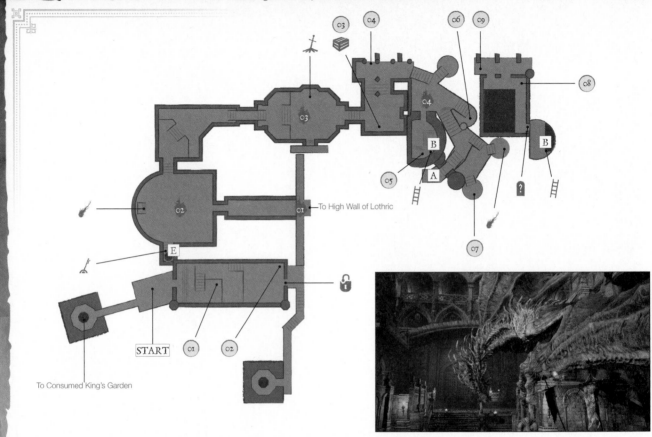

START

To Consumed King's Garden

To High Wall of Lothric

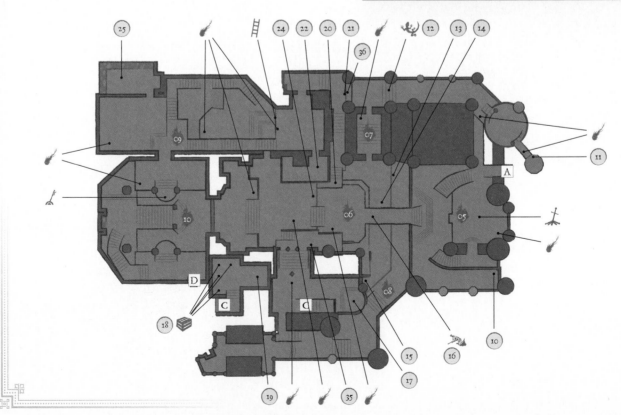

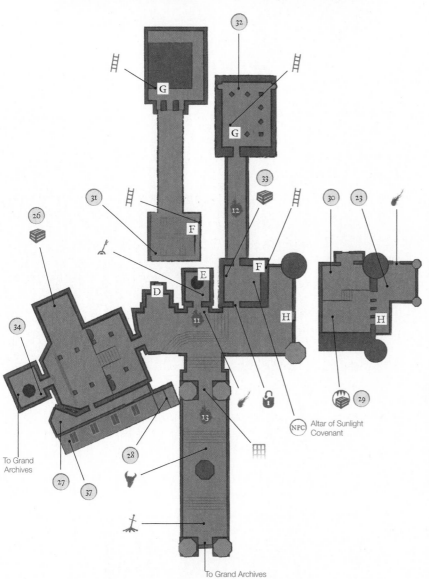

MAJOR ITEMS

1	Titanite Scale
2	Titanite Chunk
3	Armor of Prayer (full set)
4	Titanite Chunk
5	Twinkling Titanite
6	Titanite Chunk
7	Titanite Chunk x2
8	Winged Knight armor (full set)
9	Sacred Bloom Shield
10	Greatlance
11	Sniper Crossbow
12	Twinkling Titanite x2
13	Titanite Chunk
14	Titanite Chunk x2 (under bridge)
15	Twinkling Titanite x2
16	Undead Bone Shard (under bridge on ledge)
17	Raw Gem
18	Spirit Tree Crest Shield, Titanite Scale, Twinkling Titanite x3 (in chests)
19	Irithyll Rapier (on Boreal Outrider Knight)
20	Titanite Scale
21	Titanite Chunk
22	Titanite Chunk x2, Ember x2 (right Dragon)
23	Titanite Chunk x2, Ember x2 (left Dragon)
24	Refined Gem
25	Titanite Scale
26	Titanite Scale
27	Red Tearstone Ring
28	Caitha's Charm
29	Sunlight Straight Sword (on Mimic)
30	Braille Divine Tome of Lothric
31	Titanite Chunk
32	Knight's Ring
33	Titanite Scale x3
34	Titanite Slab (at bottom of lift shaft)
35	Dark Stoneplate Ring+1 (New Game +1)
36	Life Ring+2 (New Game +1)
37	Thunder Stoneplate Ring+2 (New Game +2)

BONFIRES LOCATED HERE

Lothric Castle

Dragon Barracks

Dragonslayer Armor

ENEMIES

Lothric Knight

Devout of the Deep

Hollow Soldier

Winged Knight

Lothric Wyverns

Boreal Outrider Knight

Pus of Man

Dragonslayer Armour

KEY DISCOVERIES

Altar of Sunlight Covenant

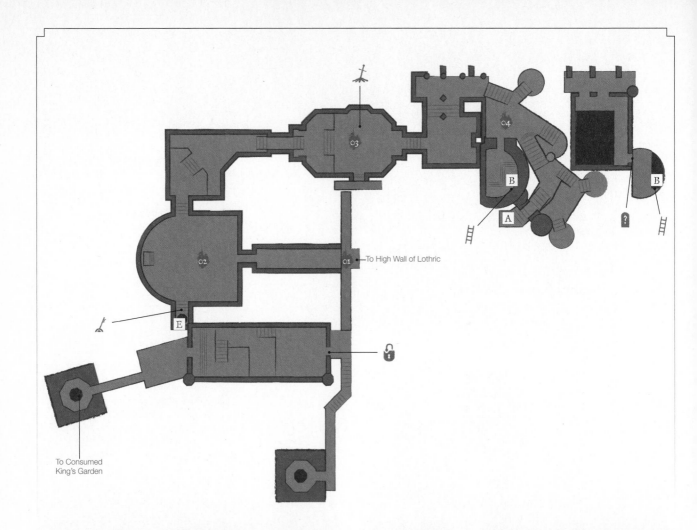

To High Wall of Lothric

To Consumed
King's Garden

01 Coiled Sword Fragment   209007

02 Estus Flask+8   209007

---

01 Your starting point in this map is near the upper-left side of the region. You climb up a ladder from the Dancer of the Boreal Valley Bonfire. A path south leads toward the Consumed King's Garden. Heading west takes you deeper into this area instead.

02 A Lothric Knight and a Devout of the Deep are in here. Roll past the knight and kill his companion first to ensure that you won't be distracted while fighting the heavier target. Then, settle in for a long fight against the Lothric Knight. He's hard as nails, so it takes many hits to drop him.

BONFIRE—LOTHRIC CASTLE

03 Two more Lothric Knights and a couple of passive Devout of the Deep are in the hallway. The Devout of the Deep won't add to your fight, so they're not a concern this time. Shoot the first knight you see, and lure him down the stairs to fight him alone if possible. Getting both is doable, too, but make sure to focus fire on the first Lothric Knight so that you get the fight down to a one-on-one level quickly.

03

Farther down the hallway, you find a Bonfire (Lothric Castle). Now you don't have to climb that ladder every time you want to come in here!

04 Climb the outer steps on the north side, which get you around to the main portion of the castle. A few Hollow Soldiers are here; they're weak targets. The ones here have adequate health, but they use simple weapons and combos, so they're only a threat when they show up in force.

Much more impressive is the Winged Knight inside a nearby guard tower. Pull him out into the yard after clearing the Hollow Soldiers. This way, you have much more room to maneuver, and that favors you in this skirmish.

Climb a short ladder inside that tower, and smack a wall up top. It fades, and you get some treasure for your efforts.

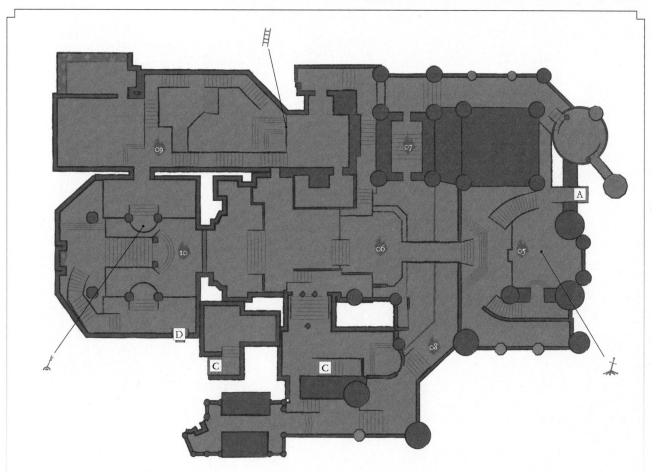

BONFIRE—DRAGON BARRACKS

05 You get another Bonfire (Dragon Barracks) without having to go far into Lothric Castle. Several more fights slow you down, but they're still against smaller groups of lesser undead. This place is trying to get you to lower your guard, but don't. It's going to get rough very soon.

Major Battle

06 The Dragon Barracks area is well named, as two dragons guard it. They're practically pinned to their perches, not far from the Bonfire. As you approach them, take shelter behind a stone statue of a knight just beside a bridge. That's your cover for the dragon's fire. Once you're safe, use a ranged weapon to kill the dragon on the left. Try to hit high on its neck so that you can target each shot easily but still get maximum damage. Body shots or wing hits deal far less damage, so experiment until you get high damage without having to expose yourself by poking too far out of cover.

Remember to bring a full complement of arrows or bolts; you'll need them.

07 After looting the area around the dragons, take a moment to search in a few directions. This place is fairly open, so you have multiple choices for where to go next. It's best not to fall off of the bridge. There is loot down there, but you can reach it by going south. Falling into the middle of the enemies is very risky, so stay on the beaten path as you explore.

08 The area south of the dragons has several targets. At first, you face a variety of Hollow Soldiers. Kill their ranged members first, and then deal with the heavier members of the group. Remember that these guys are easily staggered, so you can interrupt and slay even their best fighters with long combos.

Down in the gully, there are two Praying Hollow Soldiers. Kill them quickly if you don't want them to turn into Pus of Man. Alternately, let them change if you're farming for Souls or loot. A building north of the Pus of Man lets you climb onto the upper walkways that overlook the area. Though it's an optional place to visit, this spot has a bit of extra treasure and another Winged Knight to kill.

The fight to be most careful of while exploring is down in a basement. A simple set of stairs that's south of the dragons leads down into this basement, which is filled with upgrade materials. However, there is a Boreal Outrider Knight waiting for you. In dark and cramped quarters, this enemy is a nightmare.

Focus entirely on dodging. Get one hit every time you avoid the enemy's combos, and only risk a second strike if you've gotten into a perfect position after the large foe has missed one of its slower, heavier swings. Get used to the one-two swing that it favors most of the time, and also look for the slower single hit that it winds up to perform.

Frost Resistance is a major bonus for this fight, and it's worth equipping gear specifically for this. The Boreal Outrider Knight, as usual, is practically a boss unto himself.

09 The area northwest of the bridge is the way to go when you're trying to proceed. There are two ways in—a lower entrance near the main gate, and an upper one that leads you up a staircase that hugs the northern building. Both enter the same room, a large chamber with many weaker undead.

A Pus of Man is guarding the fallen dragon's body. Don't try to approach it. It vomits horrible material at you, causing a curse effect. Hang back and shoot it with arrows until it's dead. You get a decent amount of material for the kill, and the dragon's body disappears.

Although there aren't any other super nasty enemies in the room, you have to be careful. The sheer volume of undead ensures that it's possible to be overwhelmed and torn apart. Fight each target as you see it, and be thorough. Kill everything, or a simple battle can suddenly turn sour as you back into foes that you ignored earlier.

The end of the chamber leads you into a small balcony with a lever. Pull that to open the main gate outside.

10 Lothric Knights and Devout of the Deep are inside the main gate. Pull them out into the open and fight them safely so that you only get one knight at a time.

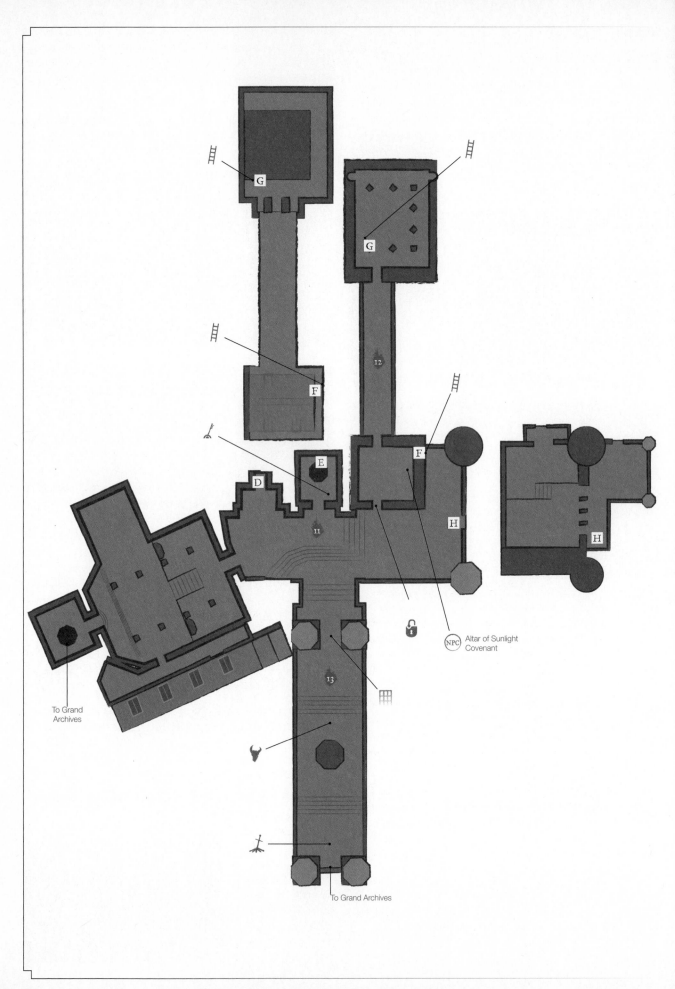

To Grand
Archives

Altar of Sunlight
Covenant

To Grand Archives

Large stairs lead to the higher tiers of the castle. The path splits when you get to the top, so check your map carefully as you consider your options. A boss' fog gate is ahead of you. To the east, you can jump off of this level and hop down to the other dragon's corpse. A second brutal Pus of Man is there, with just as much loot as the first.

The building to the west has no enemies. Take its treasure, and notice a lift. This becomes a shortcut to the Grand Archives boss once you've unlocked it from the upper level.

If you have remained friendly with Eygon of Carim, you can find his summon sign just inside in the western building, bring him along to help with the boss!

And speaking of shortcuts, the closer lift unlocks a route between this spot and the beginning of Lothric Castle. Take that down to the bottom to make sure that it's open. Now, you can get up to the boss from the Lothric Castle Bonfire without spending too much time.

ALTAR OF SUNLIGHT

A locked door blocks your way into another building near the boss. To get inside, climb a ladder around the right side of the building. Cross the rooftops while dealing with two Hollow Soldiers with crossbows and an axe-wielding buddy of theirs. If you're having trouble, shoot the weaker crossbowmen before the big guy comes out onto the roof.

Inside the building, you find a bit of loot, along with the **Altar of Sunlight**. You offer Sunlight Medals here to improve your Covenant faction. There's only a single Lothric Knight on the way to unlock the door, so getting out of there isn't too bad.

MAJOR BATTLE

After you've unlocked the lower shortcut and explored this area, hit the boss' lair. The Dragonslayer Armour does a good job of killing you the first couple of times you face it, so assume that this is going to be rough. Try to get here with a full group of flasks. The path from the Lothric Castle Bonfire still has a few Lothric Knights in your way, but you can sprint around them to get to the lift.

Remember to send the lift back down once you reach the top. Otherwise, this "run to the lift" method won't work so well the next time you try it!

DRAGONSLAYER ARMOUR

STAGE I

The first half of the battle is fairly easy after a try or two. The Dragonslayer Armour only has a few moves at this time. The axe swings are very easy to dodge, since they take a lot of time to prepare. You just need to dodge multiple times for the one-two combo that the boss enjoys. Dodge late for his overhead attacks because that takes more time to charge and inflicts way more damage if you eat it.

It's trickier to get the timing for the two types of shield punches that the Dragonslayer Armour uses. One is very quick, and the other is super slow and has a gap closer that really nails you if you dodge early, even if you roll away from the boss. Unless you have the timings down pat, always assume that the slower shield punch is the one that you're dodging. Do this because the quick punch is very minor on damage and doesn't lay you out. If you're going to err, err on the side of dodging the move that rips you apart!

The worst move for the Dragonslayer Armour in this phase is a charged lightning strike. You can get a shot in while he raises the axe over his head. Then, dodge the attack while staying close to the boss so that you can hit him even more as he recovers. It's a very good move to watch for and exploit.

When you've depleted almost half of his life, the Dragonslayer Armour takes a knee for a moment. Get one or two hits in, but stop quickly. As Stage II begins, the boss attacks you with a painful smash. If you get greedy, you're going to take that shot in the face.

STAGE II

The second stage is much harder. The undead dragon that's watching the battle breathes onto the bridge occasionally, although this isn't too bad. Still, back off if you're in the middle of it.

The real problem is the Dragonslayer Armour's superior moveset. Everything deals tremendous damage, so you must heal whenever you take a hit. Unfortunately, there isn't much time to heal. Backing away doesn't earn you much because the boss now closes quickly with most of his moves. You can only afford to drink your Estus after getting a good dodge.

Stay away from the broken side of the bridge. The Dragonslayer Armour can throw you around with his hits, and it is possible to get tossed off the bridge.

Even though this boss has a massive shield, it doesn't absorb as much as you'd think. Take occasional potshots while he's in between moves. Obviously, don't do this if you see an attack coming, but there are free moments when the Dragonslayer Armour is walking around and won't get to counterattack you if you take one of these free shots.

Practice makes perfect. This isn't a fight that's heavy on theory: move

Get the Dragonslayer Armour Bonfire. The area behind the boss takes you into the

GRAND ARCHIVES

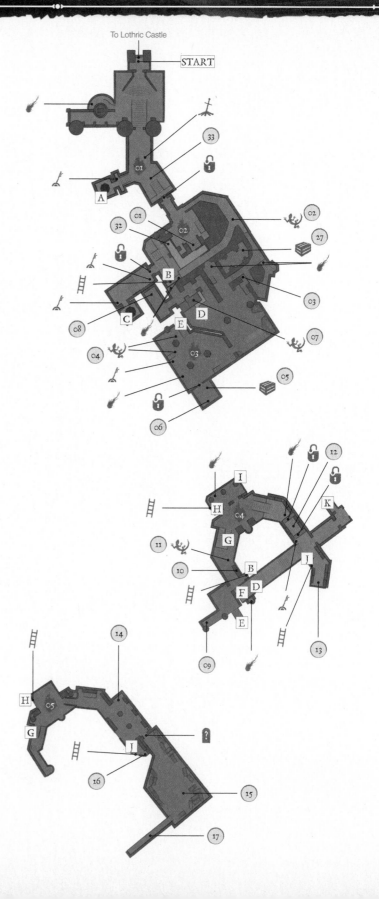

To Lothric Castle

START

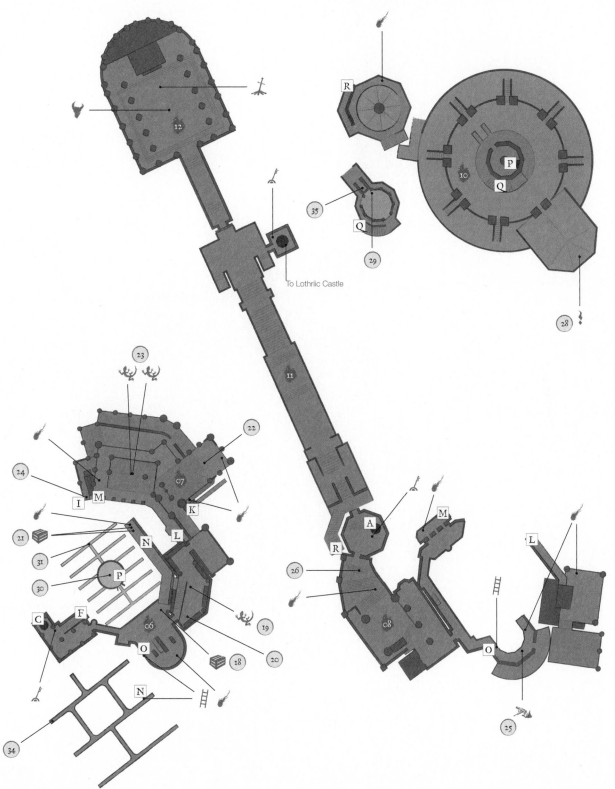

To Lothriic Castle

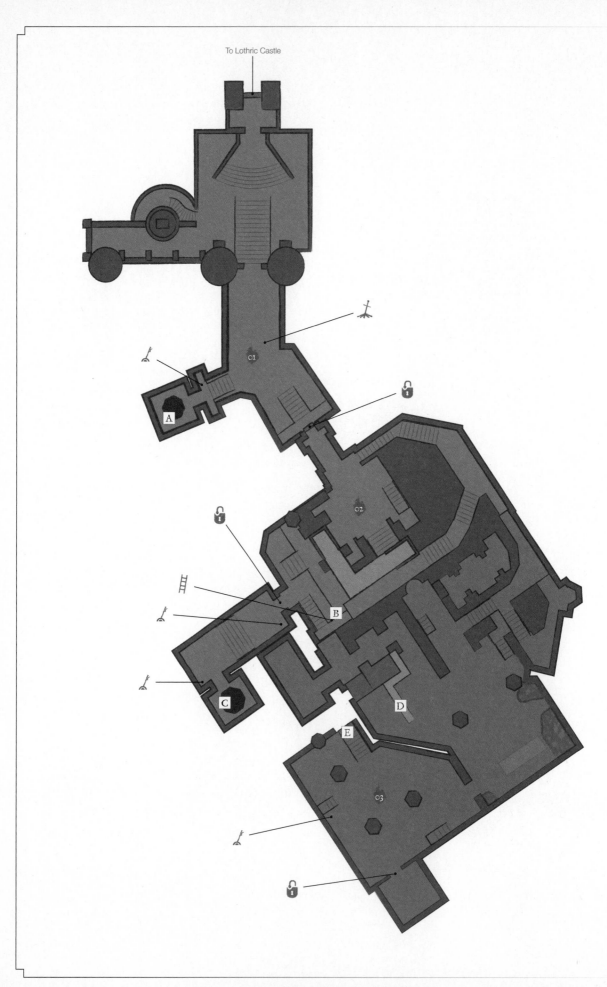

To Lothric Castle

A

B

C

D

E

o1

o2

o3

Because Titanite Chunks are becoming (relatively) common in the final areas, they are now being marked as a 'common' item on the maps like smaller Titanite pieces were in earlier areas. Anything larger is still listed as an individual item on the item key.

There are a *lot* of Titanite Scales in this area, if you've been holding off on upgrading Soul-transposed weaponry, use the resources from this area to do it.

BONFIRE—GRAND ARCHIVES

You get another Bonfire (Grand Archives) when coming into this area from the end of Lothric Castle. A body nearby has the key to the front doors of the area. A lift nearby isn't currently functional, but it will later allow you to transport yourself up toward the boss.

You're in the northwestern part of this map. It's a tough area to parse because so much of it is vertical. There is no way to make it really digestible until you've explored and gotten a feel for the layout.

01

The first major room of the archives is a doozy. There is a Crystal Sage that bombards you from range. Attack it at close range to force the powerful caster away. However, you must seek it out and do this several times throughout the chamber to finish the job.

There are also multiple Hollow Slaves, Grand Archives Scholars, and rare Lothric Knights. Treasure is everywhere, and by now, you should be able to have a +9 weapon. Titanite Chunks are becoming commonplace, so make sure that your favorite gear is at its best.

Even though the path splits immediately, all of the separate branches combine as you rise to the middle tier of the room.

A pool of hot wax is on the side of the room. After killing the Grand Archives Scholars near it, you can dunk your head in the wax. Grand Archives Scholars are very low on health, so fast weapons cut them apart in very little time.

Coating your head in wax protects you from the Curse effect of the spectral arms that reach from the books around the library. If you need to explore near any of the bookshelves, be sure to get coated first!

The Grand Archives Scholars spray wax all over the area if they have time to prepare. Avoid this at all costs. It slows your movement, prevents dodging, and causes a vulnerable animation if you even try to dodge while you're affected.

If you get hit with wax, walk out of the region, let it fade, and then come back when you're ready to fight again.

Later, there is a lift that comes down along the western edge of this room. You get to use that to slide open a bookcase and gain a shortcut to the upper reaches of the chamber. That's a godsend because there aren't any other Bonfires until you find and kill the boss.

The dark room near the wax pool has dangerous bookcases. Avoid getting too close to them: the arms that come out can cause Curse. Instead, race after the Crystal Lizards in the room to get what you can out of them.

Search for a lever, and then pull it to reveal a secret treasure area on the side of the room. Get everything inside of it.

Stairs lead up to the third tier of the room.

03

02

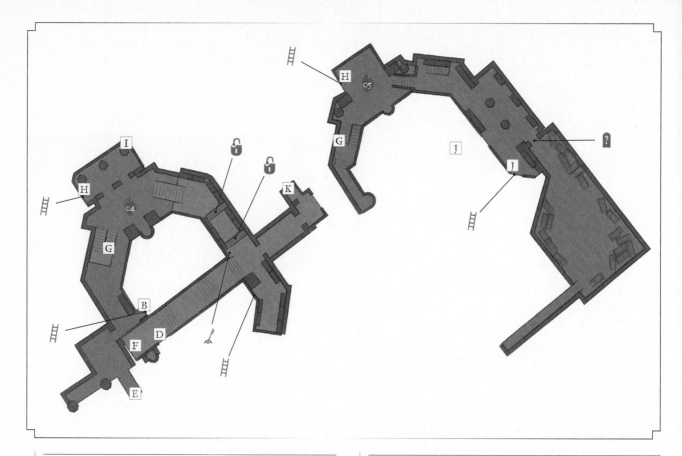

04   Throughout most of this short section, you're very exposed. The Crystal Sage is firing from above, and there are a few targets around the hallway, as well. Try to move quickly, and watch your back for any Hollow Slaves that are in pursuit.

Pull the lever opposite the outer balcony to open a path to the **Titanite Slab** chest back on the first floor. Then, look outside. Climb a ladder on that balcony and get behind the Crystal Sage. Use this surprise to deal fast damage and push the cursed caster even higher into the archives.

05   Whether you reach the next Crystal Sage tier by climbing the ladder or taking the stairs, you must contend with plenty of problems. Hollow Slaves are everywhere, and the Crystal Sage continues firing from above once you chase him up there. It's ruthless. Even though Hollow Slaves are not normally a major threat, they're very difficult to deal with here. Due to enhanced weaponry, they deal enough damage to almost combo you to death. Add ranged attacks, and death is very likely if you let them get any purchase.

Keep a shield out to block the Hollow Slaves' attacks, and kill them while they're staggered.

There is a secret door on the eastern side of this floor with a Boreal Outrider Knight inside it. You should probably hold off on fighting this one until you've unlocked a shortcut that isn't too far away. When you're ready, ambush the Boreal Outrider Knight from behind. Get a huge charged attack to start the encounter. After that, use the same techniques that have worked before. Dodge, counter with one strike (two at most), and stay defensive.

To get that shortcut, climb down a ladder near the secret door. Cross the bridge that's nearby, and look for a lift in the rooms ahead. Go down that lift, and open the secret bookcase that leads into the first room. This is a major timesaver for future efforts. Go after the Boreal Outrider Knight now that you aren't risking as much.

Another minor shortcut is by the ladder that was previously mentioned. When you climb down, look for a lever. This opens another bookcase.

After you get control of the bridge, deal with the Crystal Sage. You have access to all of the places where the mage can teleport, so it's a matter of time, patience, and healing in between each encounter.

19
Estus Flask+8

209007

05

06   Another stairway leads up and away from the major shortcut lift. Take that to go even higher in the archives. You enter a room with too many bookcases to be comfortable. You can't go anywhere near the southern side of the room without the arms harassing you.

Several Grand Archive Scholars are here. Shoot them from range so that the arms don't hurt you while you're fighting. Get a chest in the northeast corner of the room before leaving.

07

07   For a time, you end up outside. Climb down a short ladder and explore the rooftops. Several Headless Gargoyles are out there, but you have a great deal of room to fight. Stay away from the edge of the roof to avoid falling off, but otherwise, you should be completely fine. Go treasure hunting as long as you like. There are a few items below you that are from earlier parts of the level but couldn't be reached. Dropping to those doesn't help you proceed.

To get out of here, take the roof all the way north, then west, and then wrap back around the other side to the south. At the end, you drop off the ledge onto an outer balcony. Go inside, kill a lone knight, and be happy to get back on solid ground.

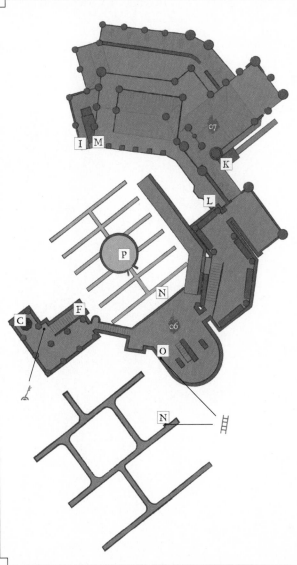

08 You're entering a large path that leads up to the boss. Three Unkindled attempt to stop you as you walk toward some impressive steps that lead north out of the room. Stop as soon as you see them. The first two usually come together, but the third one is farther back and can be fought later. For this reason, it's best if you lead the melee attacker back while you kill him. Then, charge the caster second. Their heavier buddy isn't a threat if he's alone, so this makes the fight extremely safe.

Watch the caster while you're engaged. Make sure to dodge aside when his spells are reaching completion. Otherwise, he'll nail you and give his ally an easy opening for free damage.

09 Thankfully, you find a lift after beating the trio. Take this down for a much easier route between here and the lower levels.

10 A staircase to the west is something you might miss. Take it to get onto these higher rooftops. Though it takes a lot of exploration to find everything, the rooftops lead to a central building that can't be reached any other way. You get very nice treasure on the roof over there, as well as inside the building.

You can get these items by running through, but you get even more out of the area if you beat the three Gertrude's Knights that guard the tower. This won't be as easy as you would think, though. All three are like Winged Knights with superior combo abilities. They can fly, leading to improved mobility. And one of the three patrols around the tower instead of loitering around. That gives him a substantial chance to attack while you're still engaged with one of his brothers.

For your best chance, pull the twin-axe Gertrude's Knight toward the back of the building. With him dead, the patrol isn't an issue.

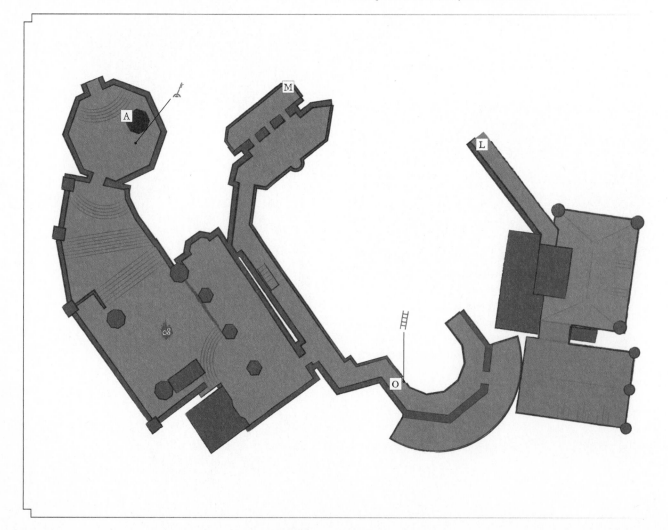

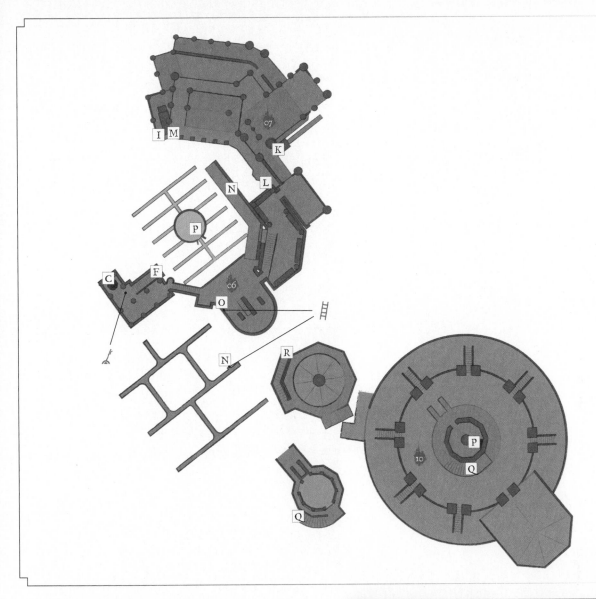

All three require very skilled dodge timing. There isn't an easy trick to beating them; it's just skill and patience. But you get a **Titanite Slab** for finishing them off, and that's one heck of a prize.

11   The long walkway toward the boss' room is amazing. Barricades are in place like the whole area is preparing for a siege. And, well, they should be: you're here to destroy them.

Cut through the Hollow Soldiers like chaff. Make sure to look around each barricade so that you don't leave any crossbowmen at your back. They're pests, but their damage adds up if you ignore them.

The real fight begins toward the end, where there is a series of Gertrude's Knights. They don't have any new attacks or weaponry to show off, but you can end up fighting them with multiple targets running around. Use ranged weapons to isolate and pull your most worrisome enemies, and run back as far down the walkway as you need to so that nothing overwhelms you.

On the right, you get to a lift that descends into Lothric Castle (near the Dragonslayer Armour Bonfire). You should definitely get this before you take on the boss.

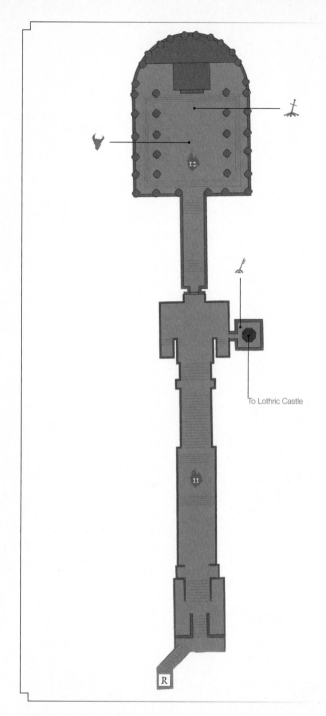

MAJOR BATTLE

Run up to the fog gate, and enter the throne room. A short scene plays as you're introduced to the two princes. And then, the battle commences.

LORIAN AND LOTHRIC

STAGE I

Lorian, the elder prince, is the one who fights you first. He's a large warrior. Lacking mobility on his own, he'll teleport to unleash his most dangerous strikes. Dodging his normal attacks isn't too hard, but when he glows white, you have to quickly see where he's teleporting and figure out when to dodge his returning strike. It's very tricky.

Stay up close with this boss, and get your attacks in after each of his swings. Although his major strikes are fairly dangerous, he doesn't do a good job of retaliating, which lets you score heavy damage throughout the encounter.

Fire Resistance is good, but Magic Resistance is also important (or it will be in just a moment).

STAGE II

Don't celebrate when you take Lorian down. His brother resurrects him and then gets onto Lorian's back. That can't bode well.

The second stage is very similar in terms of Lorian's tactics, but Lothric adds ranged magical damage to the fight. This starts something like a race, as the two combined are almost guaranteed to get damage on you. Can you kill them before your Estus Flasks run out?

For this reason, you have to attack very aggressively whenever you get a proper dodge and can hit Lorian. Side and rear attacks are the best because they'll deal damage to both twins. As soon as Lorian falls, Lothric collapses and tries to resurrect him again, but this time, you're free to cut the weaker brother in half. As long as you landed some damage against Lothric during this phase, you should be able to kill him before he succeeds.

If you're comfortable with this idea, try doing the fight without locking on to Lorian. His teleports really make life hard when you're locked on. Controlling the camera directly can be easier in the long run because you don't get as distracted when he disappears. Try things both ways, and see which one suits your playstyle.

After the fight, get the Bonfire. If you want, you can read through Archdragon Peak to go after that optional area. Or, proceed to the write-up for Kiln of the First Flame. You can end the game here and now!

ARCHDRAGON PEAK

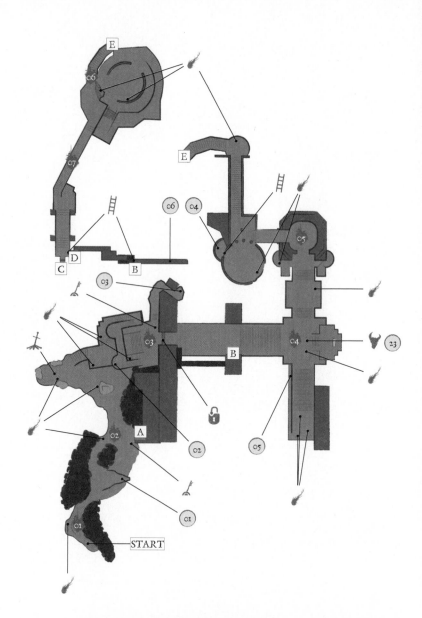

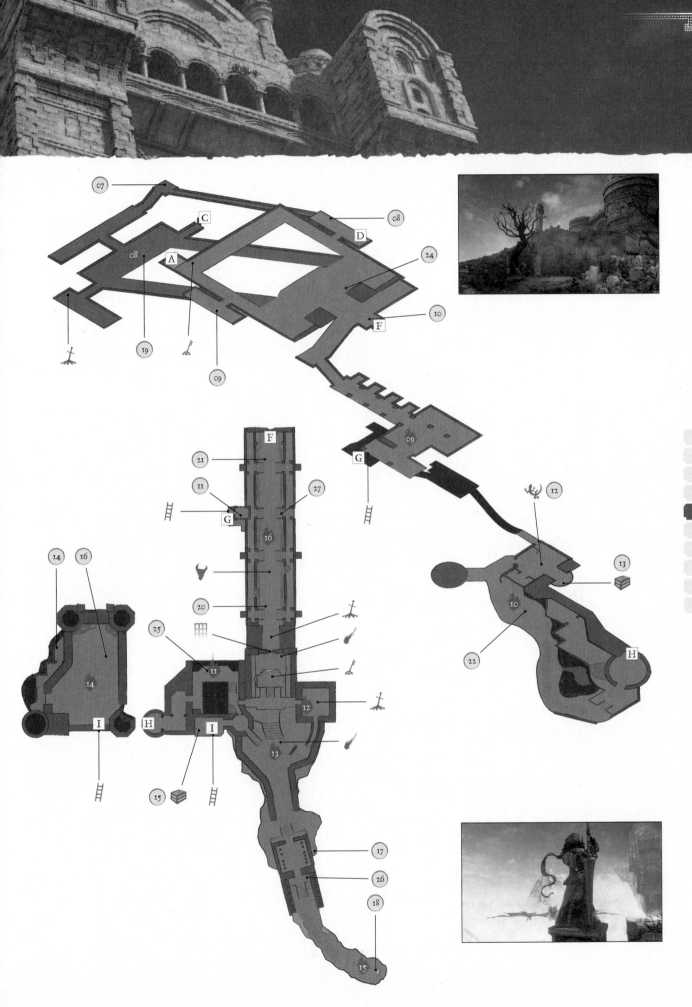

01 Use Path of the Dragon in the lower ledge of Irithyll Dungeon to teleport to this new region. You appear on the southern edge of the map. The loot is minor at first, but there aren't too many enemies, either. A couple of Serpent-men attack you on the first slope. They have more reach than it might seem, but otherwise, they're minor targets.

BONFIRE—ARCHDRAGON PEAK

02 A lift is broken as you get to the top of the hill. (It's accessible later.)

Four more Serpent-men are north of there, guarding the first Bonfire of the region. It's very hard to get initiative on these guys, and the rear attackers sit back and spit fire to make your life much more difficult. Use ranged weapons to lure the mobile ones over and to kill the ranged attackers later. Charging them is tough, unless you're impatient.

When you arrive, light the Archdragon Peak Bonfire. If you don't have a full quiver of arrows/bolts, zip down to the shrine and get those now.

03 Look around the front gate: a Serpent-man and a Large Serpent-man are above it. The Large Serpent-men have way more health. Give them heavy combos after their attacks, but always save Stamina for your retreat. You aren't going to 100-0 them in one combo.

Use the lever at the main gate to open it.

MAJOR BATTLE

04 A few steps into the new area, and the skies darken. The boss of the area has found you!

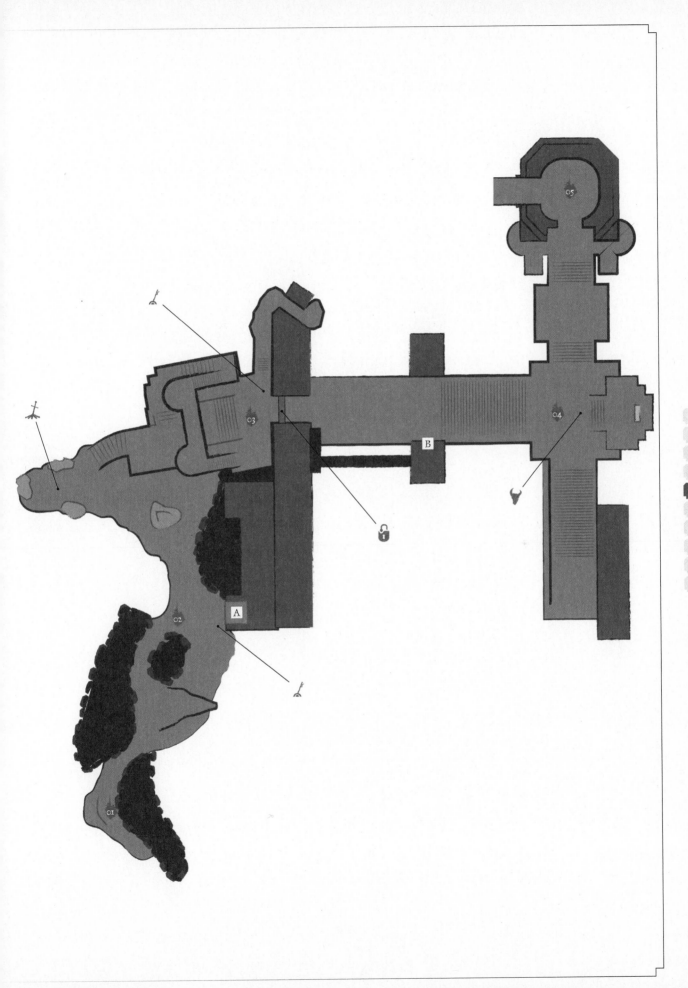

ANCIENT WYVERN

Although it's possible to defeat the wyvern from down on the ground, it takes forever and is risky. You get stepped on a lot, and trying to hit the head (which takes far more damage than the feet) is maddeningly difficult.

For a better fight, run! Turn left, and dash into the building over there. Don't fight the Serpent-men inside. You get cooked if you tarry for too long, and the Serpent-men are a pain when you're distracted.

Sprint past, following the only route around and up through the area. Dodge past a Large Serpent-man at the top, and sprint toward a ladder at the end of the route. This gets you onto a ledge where the Ancient Wyvern's fire won't hit. Get onto the stone ledge below there, and fire at the boss from above. You can kill it in total safety, or try a Plunging Attack for a very epic moment. Either way, that ledge turns a long, rough fight into an easy win.

In victory, you're teleported to the Dragon-Kin Mausoleum, deeper into the region. It's okay to warp to the previous Bonfire and grab treasure that you missed while running away from the Ancient Wyvern.

05 Three Serpent-men attack in this small room. Draw them back toward the boss' starting spot to give yourself more room to fight.

06 As you go up a curving set of stairs, you meet more Serpent-men. Be on the lookout for one that rushes from a side corridor in an attempt to ambush you.

A side area has another Large Serpent-man and additional Serpent-men. It seems like a smart place to bypass as you explore. However, the Serpent-men shoot fire from the upper ledge, harassing you as you cross the next walkway. You're better off killing them so that the way forward is clear of fire support.

07 Except for minor loot, the walkway over the boss' area isn't useful once the Ancient Wyvern is dead.

Bonfire—Dragon-Kin Mausoleum

08 The doorway near the ladder leads into the same large chamber that also connects to the Dragon-Kin Mausoleum Bonfire. Therefore, you know where you are, regardless of how you got there. This complex room has two levels. You need to move through it quickly at first because a Serpent-man Summoner on the upper level brings Unkindled into the area to fight you. It won't stop until you kill the Serpent-man Summoner, so get to the top level as soon as you can.

A lift takes you down to the starting portion of the area. Once unlocked, this is a shortcut for anyone trying to get inside from the first Bonfire.

Near the bonfire, you can find a small altar. Use the Path of the Dragon gesture next to it and wait for a moment to receive the **Calamity Ring**.

The outer ledges of the room have some treasure, but watch out for any extra Unkindled that are still there. Also, be wary of a Rock Lizard; these enemies don't do much damage, but they're hardy and can push you around. Stay away from the edge of the balcony when you're fighting one.

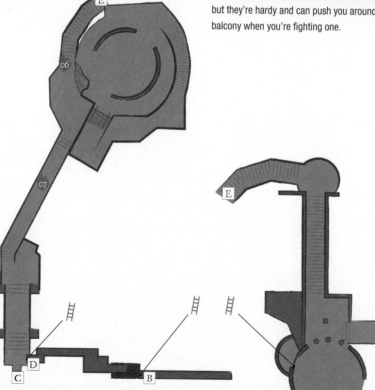

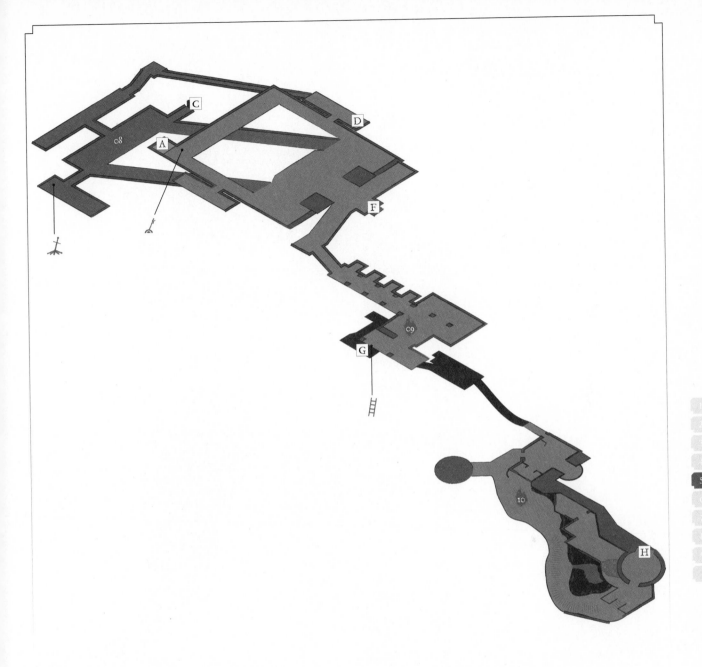

After a long hallway of Serpent-men, you face off against one more of their ilk with a Large Serpent-man ally. Back off until you can kill the Serpent-man safely, by any means. The Large Serpent-man is too dangerous of a foe to face with any level of support.

This area has a ladder that leads up to a small tower. Search for treasure up there, and then hop back down.

Another Ancient Wyvern attacks you here. It's resting on top of a tower, but it comes down as soon as you get into range. This one has less armor, so it's easier to kill by far. Try to hit the tail as often as possible, which takes much more damage than the feet. If you stand between the feet, you can often hit the tail with most of your attacks.

Dodge when the Ancient Wyvern lifts its feet, and run away if it takes off to breathe.

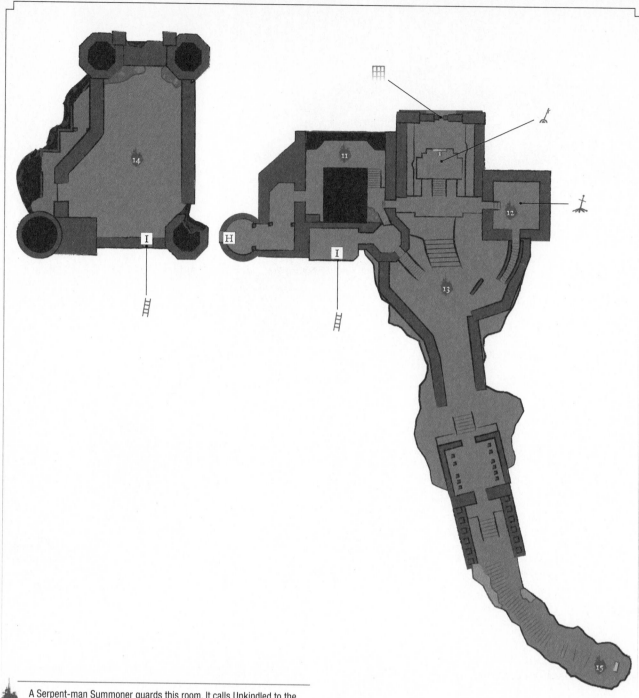

A Serpent-man Summoner guards this room. It calls Unkindled to the lower floor, where you enter. You can silence this enemy using ranged weaponry from the doorway. Or, you can sprint past the Unkindled that rise, and kill the Serpent-man Summoner quickly with melee attacks. After that, it's not too bad to defeat one Unkindled instead of an infinite supply of them.

BONFIRE—GREAT BELFRY

Rest at the Great Belfry Bonfire. A great bell is nearby, but you're warned not to ring it if you want to travel the path of the dragon.

The Bonfire leads out to a courtyard with Rock Lizards and Serpent-men. The lowest path goes down to a gate, but this won't open unless you ring the great bell.

The upper path goes through waves of Serpent-men and Large Serpent-men. There aren't any new challenges, but the fighting is still intense.

Take a side branch from the courtyard, and climb a ladder. You arrive at a large platform with a dead dragon on top of it. A dangerous Unkindled is there, wielding a heavy club and wonderful armor. Dodge or walk backward to avoid the enemy's slow attacks, and launch extended combos to punish its poor recovery time. As long as you're patient, this is an easy fight.

Follow the path all the way to the top, and use the Path of the Dragon gesture in front of an altar. You receive the Twinkling Dragon Torso Stone.

MAJOR BATTLE

Return to the Great Belfry and use the bell to darken the skies of Archdragon Peak. Don't do this until you've taken care of all your other looting in the area. The entire region gets very dark when you do this, and a fog gate appears close to the bell. Jump onto the fog that suffuses the area, and walk through the gate when you're ready for an extremely wonderful boss fight. This is way tougher than the end boss of the game. You do not need to defeat the opponents ahead, and the only reason to do so is because they're there. And they have treasure.

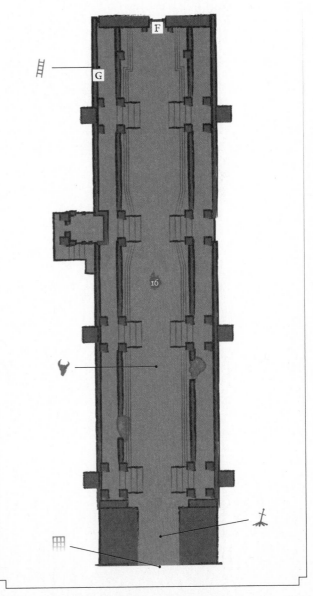

THE NAMELESS KING

STAGE I

The first stage of the fight is against The Nameless King and the King of the Storm. You need as much Fire Resistance as possible, and heavy armor wouldn't hurt. The enemies have massive damage output. In this stage, the dragon is your primary opponent. It hits you with its head and body, but only rarely. More commonly is breathes Fire onto you, and positions The Nameless King to strike at you from above.

The dragon's physical blows are often minor and unimportant. If it's going to kill you outright, it will be through the fire breath. From above, this does incredible damage and will nail you twice in a row. You must roll out of the way to avoid the second hit if you won't want to die instantly.

Running away when the dragon takes flight might let you avoid both blasts of flame, but it's harder than it sounds to pull off. The area of effect for the fire is gigantic.

Sometimes the King of the Storm breathes while it's still on the ground. This is a gift! Sprint around to the back side of its head and go to town with free hits. You do massive damage and can shorten the fight considerably. Never waste this, as it's your prime damage opportunity in Stage I.

The other recovery period that is in your favor comes when The Nameless King charges a Lightning strike and misses at close range. The targets are slow to get up from that, so you get decent hits.

The other way to survive is to master the brutal timings of the boss' 1-2 swing, and his alternate 1-2-3 combo. In both cases, the early hit(s) are quick and easy to dodge. The final shot is slow and deceptive. You're going to eat those several times before you learn to slow down and hold your dodge. Mastering this final dodge gets you a long way toward winning this match.

You can't do anything at long range. The Nameless King has two wind attacks to disrupt you, and a couple of charges. All close the gap quickly, making it dangerous to back up and heal. You have to wait until you score a dodge before drinking, most of the time.

The wide wind attack gets used early in the fight. You have to roll into the wind to avoid the damage. You can roll in almost any direction against the narrow wind strike.

Always try to roll closer to the boss. You have little time to make your counters, and you lose all of that if you have to sprint over to him. Come up from your rolls and hit him immediately, or accept that you missed your chance. Don't rush right into his spear when you're hoping to get a shot of your own.

STAGE III

After reaching half health, The Nameless King begins casting way more Lightning spells. They're slow and specific in their timing. All of these attacks can be dodged if you're good, but that takes practice. Unfortunately, this fight will take a lot of trial and error to get the timing right to avoid these repeated attacks.

Be especially watchful for his Lightning Bomb. It can hit you on the way out, and then explode after a few seconds to do even more damage.

He also has a slow spell that does so much damage that it can kill you from almost full health, depending on your build. There aren't any tricks. You have to learn to dodge it. If you're close when he starts this slow casting, punish him with several strikes. You might get lucky and stagger him. This won't happen often, but it's so sweet when it does.

To work on your timings, listen for the different crackles that the Lightning attacks make (in all three stages). These audible cues are one of your few assets as you learn to avoid everything.

Always go for the dragon's head and neck. Foot shots are very weak, and you can't afford to prolong this stage of the combat. There are two more stages to go afterward.

Don't use lock on unless you have to. It's hard to see what The Nameless King is doing, and his spear attacks come out of nowhere unless you can keep the camera on him manually.

The worst news: this is the easy stage.

STAGE II

When the King of the Storm dies, The Nameless King dismounts. Now he's mad.

The next two stages are very similar. You need to kill The Nameless King. He only has one life bar, but that's still quite a bit of health to chop through. You want a relatively quick weapon if at all possible. There are only rare moments when you get serious combo time, and this boss punishes greedy swings. One extra shot is going to cost you half of your health.

Lightning Resistance is your lifesaver for Stages II and III. Keep it as high as you can.

KILN OF THE FIRST FLAME

To reach the final boss of the game, place the remnants of the Lords of Cinder on top of their thrones in the Firelink Shrine. With this done, talk to the Fire Keeper, and then kneel by the Bonfire.

This takes you to the Flameless Shrine. Light it, and then leave the shrine. Light another Bonfire outside (the Kiln of the First Flame), and then approach the field at the top of the hill. This is where the final confrontation takes place.

The Soul of Cinder deals heavy fire and physical damage, with other damage types coming into play randomly (so you can't really count on them). Make sure that your Resistance is high toward the big two, and start this fight.

Buffing your own weapon damage is good, but this isn't going to be a quick skirmish. Anything that you use is going to wear off before the end of the battle, so keep your items on the hotbar, and refresh them between Stage I and Stage II.

It's okay to train for a few runs without worrying about Embers, but once you're really trying to win this fight, go ahead and use them. Some players like to hoard them, but this is the fight that you're hoarding them to beat. It's fine to lose one or two while you're perfecting your techniques.

ALL POSSIBLE ENDINGS (SPOILER WARNING)

There are four endings in the game. Let's talk about how to access each of them.

1. THE SIMPLE ENDING

The easiest ending is to defeat the Soul of Cinder without having eight Dark Sigils. Simply beat the boss and light the Bonfire. This is what most new players will encounter without specifically trying to get another ending.

2. THE TRUE ENDING

Get the Eyes of a Fire Keeper from the Untended Graves area (as noted earlier in this walkthrough). Give these to the Fire Keeper. Defeat the Soul of Cinder and then summon the Fire Keeper from a white sign on the ground nearby. She'll take you into the second ending from there.

3. USURPING THE FIRE

Get the Eyes of a Fire Keeper from the Untended Graves area (earlier in this walkthrough). Give these to the Fire Keeper. Defeat the Soul of Cinder and then summon the Fire Keeper from a white sign on the ground nearby. Instead of letting her complete her ritual, attack her. There is a very small window of opportunity to do this.

Wait for the cutscene to end, as the Fire Keeper starts to let the flame die in her hands. When the light is almost gone, you regain control of your character briefly. Attack the Fire Keeper immediately. Tap on the normal attack button if you need to, to make sure that this works.

This is not a kind or gentle ending.

4. LORD OF HOLLOWS ENDING

❖ This is the hardest ending to achieve, because it has many steps.

❖ Use Yoel to Draw Out True Strength 5 times in the early game.

❖ Make sure to recruit Yoel, and then kill yourself repeatedly to raise your Hollowing so that you can keep Drawing Out your power. Make sure to do this five times! Each one gets you a Dark Sigil, and this ending isn't possible if Yoel dies before you have all five of them that he has to offer.

❖ Yuria arrives in the shrine soon after. Don't worry if Yoel collapses and dies afterward. He's played his part in this already.

❖ Speak with Anri twice when you meet on the Road of Sacrifices.

❖ Defeat the Deacons of the Deep and then speak with Anri at the Firelink Shrine.

❖ Meet Anri in the Catacombs of Carthus and do not say where Horace is located. You can go back and kill Horace later, after you've seen Anri in Irithyll (but you don't need to).

❖ Speak with Anri again in Irithyll, in the Church of Yorshka (near the Bonfire).

❖ Defeat Pontiff Sulyvahn.

❖ Return to the Firelink Shrine and talk to Yuria. Talk until you've exhausted her conversation options. You're told that the wedding preparations are complete.

❖ Talk to the Pilgrim toward the end of Irithyll, on the eastern side of the map. The room is down a side hallway when you're about to enter the tower that takes you up to Anor Londo. The Pilgrim gives you the Sword of Avowal.

❖ Execute the Rite of Avowal with Anri in the rear of Gwydolin's chamber. This gets you three Dark Sigils. You now have all eight!

❖ Do not let the Fire Keeper heal your Dark Sigil at any time.

❖ Now complete the game by defeating the Soul of Cinder. If you have all eight Sigils, you get this special ending. It's pretty wicked!

SOUL OF CINDER

STAGE I

The Soul of Cinder has very reliable melee combos, and he'll mix these with a huge variety of optional attacks. You could see poison clouds, Arcane spells of several types, fire buffs and attacks, lightning spells, etc.

But you're mostly going to be okay as long as you master the timing on the central melee combos. With those perfected, you can safely heal between swings and keep yourself going throughout the engagement.

This stage lasts for the entire health bar. You need to be most concerned if the boss goes into his Arcane phase. That gives him his spells (and he'll glow with Arcane power, so you know what's coming). At that point, stick to him like glue. Any distance from the boss is going to get you hurt badly.

Offensively, Stamina is king. You have to dodge before you get any of your openings to strike, and long combos are sometimes necessary for your best damage. You rarely get to wind the Soul of Cinder, and he'll go to his knees. Use everything on him at that point. More hits, more damage, every ring that you can stack to give you extra Stamina and damage is likely to pay off.

STAGE II

When the Soul of Cinder loses his first health bar, back off and heal. He explodes when regenerating, and you shouldn't need to take any damage.

There are more mix-ups in the second half of the battle, so dodging becomes much harder. However, the core mechanic is similar. Heal only after a good dodge. Strike lightly most of the time, and then unload if you ever stagger the boss. Save your Stamina for these big frenzies. Your normal setup should be dodge, dodge again (if you need to), take a free hit or two, and then get out of range quickly.

And that's basically all there is to it. This boss doesn't rely on gimmicks, cheap shots, or invulnerabilities. He fights fair; you just need to keep on him for a few straight minutes without dying. It's harder than it sounds, but it's also insanely fun.

MULTIPLAYER AND COVENANTS

Multiplayer in *Dark Souls III* is unusual and structured differently than most online games. You can choose to play offline (and if invasions really bother you, this is one way to skip them), but if you are connected, you are always online… if not necessarily walking around in the world with other players constantly.

Instead, *Dark Souls III* uses a system where you can interact with other players by leaving messages on the ground and joining or being joined by other players (sometimes forcibly!).

Note that even if you do play offline, there are still some messages (and AI invaders) placed by the developers to help you out in a few spots and give you trouble in others.

MULTIPLAYER BASICS

Multiplayer messages can help guide you in tricky areas or alert you to traps or items nearby. If you're following this guide meticulously, you may not need these messages quite as much, but it's handy to have a visible warning on screen when you approach a dangerous area.

PvP gameplay is possible in several ways. You can join other players to aid them, request aid for yourself, or invade other players directly.

PvP is often forced and freeform (that is, someone is invading someone else, the host player may or may not have co-op help, the fight occurs wherever the host happens to be). It can be structured, and there is a dedicated community of PvP players who often look for straight duels (rather than "ganking" random players). If you simply enjoy PvP combat, period, keep an eye on online forums so you can find the level ranges and locations where intentional PvP tends to occur.

Finally, Covenants are an in-game system designed to support both PvP and co-op play. They provide in-game rewards of equipment, and they give some basic structure to PvP combat. Covenants can be joined freely once discovered on a playthrough. The early Covenants focus on PvP protection for new players, PvP hunting for slightly more experienced players, and co-operative play. Most of the Covenants accessed later in the game are focused on PvP in one form or another. They either simply actively hunt other players for trophies, or they "defend" a specific area in the game against interlopers in a location that the Covenant values.

Covenants (and indeed, the entire PvP and co-op system) are completely optional. You can play through the entire game without outside interference if you choose, but if you are interested, participating in co-op and PvP gameplay can be rewarding and entertaining.

ENGAGING IN MULTIPLAYER

Multiplayer in *Dark Souls* is a good time. While it isn't really structured to play co-operatively the whole way through the game (with the co-op player departing after a boss is slain), it is a great way to get help on a difficult boss, to help other players, and to earn handy rewards while doing so.

Finishing a boss fight successfully restores your Ember, making co-op play often a very easy means of restoring yourself to life before a boss fight of your own, and you get a hefty Soul reward for doing so. Spend a few hours helping to defeat a popular early or difficult boss, and you can gain quite a few Soul Levels or buy a mountain of consumables.

PvP, on the other hand, is almost its own game within a game. For some people, invaders are a source of stress and fear, but for a good chunk of people, PvP is just another way to have fun with the game, competing in duels, hunting hosts, and fighting multiplayer groups while solo.

If you find yourself stuck on a boss fight, bringing in a co-op partner can help you clear it, and having another player around can help in areas that are inherently dangerous (always nice to have backup in the swamp), or aid you against PvP invaders.

If you're really having a bad time with invaders or Covenant protectors of a specific area, you can always go offline temporarily—do what is most fun for you!

HELPING, SURVIVING, AND HUNTING OTHER PLAYERS

If you're online and have the Strength of Fire, you can join others co-operatively, summon them to aid you, or be invaded by sinister enemies. This chapter tells you all about the online aspects of *Dark Souls III* so that you know what to be ready for. **You cannot see other summon signs if you do not have your Ember intact.** Even NPC white summon signs while offline!

PLAYING OFFLINE

First things first. If you want to avoid the online system, it's entirely possible to stay offline. Go into the Network settings for the game and select the "Play Offline" Launch Setting. This launches your game in offline mode. You won't be able to get help from others or aid them, but you won't get invaded, either.

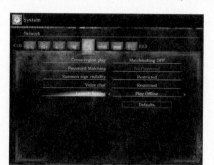

This mode isn't recommended because the online features of the game are extremely interesting. However, it's your choice, and you should play the way that you want.

With that said, it's time to delve into the online features.

MESSAGES

When you're online, you see way more messages on the ground. This is because other players can leave these messages in their worlds and have them propagate into others. The messages tip you off about dangers ahead, treasure, and so forth.

Whenever you see a message, look around carefully. You might find interesting things or avoid trouble that would otherwise have come your way without warning.

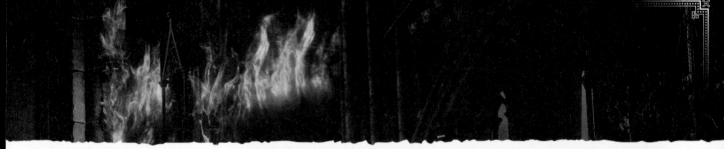

BLOODSTAINS

When you're playing online, you can see other players' bloodstains. This is incredibly useful because it shows you that an area is dangerous. Interact with the bloodstain to reveal a ghost of that player's last 10 seconds of life. Doing this is very effective for showing you what can go wrong in the area you are currently in.

HELPING OTHER PLAYERS

Using the White Sign Soapstone, you allow yourself to be summoned to other players' worlds. You get to help them defeat bosses that are giving them trouble, and in return, you gain the Strength of Fire just as if you'd beaten the boss normally or used an Ember. This is a great way to keep yourself at full strength, practice your techniques against bosses, and help others all at the same time.

There are few downsides to this. You still run the risk of being attacked by invaders, or you might lose to the boss. However, these are risks that you take all the time in your own game. It's nothing new, and the punishment for failure is no worse.

While in another person's world, you are considered a Phantom. Red Phantom invaders come to harm the host of the world, while White, Blue, and Gold Phantoms are there to help.

While you're waiting to be summoned, stay away from boss areas. Going into one of them causes your summon sign to disappear from other worlds. The same is true if you leave the greater area where you placed your sign, so don't wander too far off.

Killing a boss immediately sends you home, but fighting regular monsters does not. Feel free to attack your host's enemies.

For the best chance of being summoned, leave your sign near critical areas, boss rooms, and well-traveled portions of each region. If you're hoping to be summoned by someone on your friends list, choose an obscure location instead. This lowers the chance that a random person will summon you before your buddy finds the symbol.

THE NETWORK OF SOULS

Not all players are going to see everyone else's signs, as this would be total anarchy. Instead, the game groups people into clusters. Your contacts are given higher priority for this, which is why they have a decent chance of finding your summoning signs.

CALLING FOR AID FROM OTHER PLAYERS

When you're having trouble with a boss or simply looking to play with allies, search for summoning symbols on the ground. These are the key for bringing friends into your world. You do not need to have the Strength of Fire to place your symbol and go and help others, but you must have the Strength of Fire to summon someone like this.

As such, you must have an Ember or already be filled with the Strength of Fire to even see the symbols. You can find Embers or purchase them in limited quantities from some merchants. You can gain the Strength of Fire by helping others or killing the host during an invasion.

Once you have the Strength of Fire, scout around the outside of boss areas for the best chance of finding a summoning symbol. The main thoroughfares through each area are also likely to have these symbols from time to time.

Your Phantom allies can stay and help you fight regular monsters, invaders, and bosses. Once a boss is defeated, your friends are returned to their worlds and rewarded for their efforts. You get the advantage of surviving greater battles with less threat of defeat.

TYPES OF PHANTOMS

ENTITIES IN MP SESSIONS	HOW TO BECOME THIS ENTITY	SESSION ENDS WHEN	REWARDS
Host	Use a White Sign or Red Sign, or be Invaded	Boss is defeated, Host dies, Invader dies, or player leaves the region	Varied
White Phantom	Host uses a White Sign that someone else has placed	Boss is defeated	Host receives rewards for defeating the Boss, White Phantom Gets Sunlight Medal
Red Sign Phantom	Host uses the Red Sign that another player has placed (Red Soapstone Required)	Host or Invader is slain	Ember for the Invader, Pale Tongue
Invading Phantom	Host is Invaded without taking any action (Red Orb Required)	Host or Invader is slain, A Boss fight begins, or the Host leaves the region	Ember for the Invader, Pale Tongue
Blue Rescue Phantom	Host has to be Invaded, Blue Phantom has to have the Way of Blue or Blade of Darkmoon Insignias, Host Needs to be Way of Blue	Host or Invader is slain	Proof on Concord Kept when Invader dies or boss slain
Guardian Phantom	Host is Invaded while in Farron Keep or Irithyll Valley. The Invader has to be either in the Watchdogs of Farron or the Aldrich Faithful	Host or Invader is slain	Wolf's Blood Swordgrass for Watchdogs, Human Dregs for Aldrich Faithful

INVASIONS

Searching for another world to invade...

Invasions are launched by anyone who has a Red Sign Soapstone, A Red Eye Orb, or a Cracked Red Eye Orb.

Red Eye Orbs are permanent invasion items that are used to invade targets who have the Strength of Fire. The invader attempts to kill the host (the person that they are invading) and will gain the Strength of Fire if they succeed. Cracked Red Eye Orbs accomplish the same thing, but they're one-use items that are expended in the invasion.

RED EYE ORB

The NPC Leonhard gives you this key eventually. Take a lift down, and fight a Darkwraith there to receive the Red Eye Orb. You can now invade others at will!

Red Sign Soapstones are similar in intent, but they place an invasion sign in target worlds until someone accepts this invitation. This leads to the invader facing other players who are prepared and excited to fight. Red Eye Orbs are for unsolicited PvP, whereas Red Sign Soapstones are a way of asking permission. It's like a duel request in an MMORPG. If players don't want to fight or aren't in a good spot for it, they'll ignore the sign and move on.

RED SIGN SOAPSTONE

To get this powerful item, travel to the Cathedral of the Deep. Up high inside the cathedral, you cross bridges that lead to the chamber of Rosaria. Slay a Man-grub just outside of her room to get the Red Sign Soapstone.

Invaders are not normally influenced by the enemies in the area. They'll ghost right by, drawing little attention. This makes it easier to avoid trouble and wait for the best spots to ambush your victims. It's also easier to flee because you can race through areas with undefeated targets so that your enemy can't recklessly follow.

Invasions don't occur if you lack the Strength of Fire, so it's safer to go around in this state. However, you lose the 30% health bonus, which means that regular monsters are more of a threat.

SOUL VALUE OF VICTIMS IN PVP

Players are worth differing amounts of experience, depending on their Soul Level and the role that you and they are playing when slain.

The number of Souls you receive from a kill is 1% to 5% of the amount of Souls it would take for that player to gain their most recent level. Thus, killing a level 50 player character would take the value of going from level 49 to level 50, and multiply it by somewhere from .01 to .05.

Here is a quick table to see which roles are worth the most.

Host	Red Phantoms (2%)
White or Gold Phantom	Red Phantoms (5%)
Red Phantom	All Targets (1%)
Blue Phantom	Red Phantoms (5%)
Map Guardian	Host, White, Gold, and Blue Phantoms (4%)

HOW TO SURVIVE AGAINST INVADERS

As soon as you get the invasion notice, back away from unexplored areas, traps, and monsters. Find a location that is easy to watch so that no one can get above you or behind you, and get yourself to full health as long as you have the Estus Flasks to do so. Quickly ready your spells and tools to prepare the best possible offense for the fight ahead.

If you have a loadout of equipment that is ideal for PvP, get that ready. Some items are specifically made to assist with battles against real people. There are rings that obscure your dodging, limit your profile at long range, and so forth.

When you're being invaded, it's better to be the one to hide and ambush. The other player can hide among monsters, and they're the ones who are excited about the battle ahead. You might be, too, but they're really itching for it. Make them wait and make them search. This encourages them to be impatient and reckless, and both of those things tip the encounter in your favor.

Some invaders are polite and may emote respectfully before engaging in combat. It's up to you how to respond. As long as you feel safe and they're keeping their distance, you can respond in kind. If they get close to you before doing this, trust them a little bit less. It's not worth dying for honor, especially when you're dealing with people who invade and murder player characters for fun.

Stay as calm as you possibly can. PvP is heavily determined by control over your emotions. If you get scared or overly invested, it's easy to mess up your timings, run when you should have attacked, or swing poorly and waste your Stamina. Relax; this is just a smarter monster to contend with. Kill it, and move on.

If you have a Seed of a Giant Tree, you can use this item to force monsters to attack your invaders. This is a fun trick when opposing players are trying to hide among nastier beasts.

HOW TO SUCCEED AS AN INVADER

As an invader, you should decide from the beginning how brutal you want to be. Are you trying to ambush and massacre any hosts before they know where you are, or are you hoping to meet them, gesture kindly, and then have a proper duel? If you want to play fair, make sure that you stay in the open so that your targets can get a good view of you. Flee if they switch to ranged weaponry and start shooting at you, but otherwise, hold your ground and gesture when they appear at long range. This gives them time to see that you're here to duel and not to get a cheap kill.

Although you cannot use your flasks when invading, your host can. Remember that, and stay close to your targets. You have to punish them if they resort to healing because it puts you at a great disadvantage. A number of hosts won't do this because it's considered bad form, but everyone makes their own decisions on what they consider honorable. So, bow if you want to try engaging in a "fair" duel. Hope that your targets don't resort to healing, but accept whatever happens.

Invasions end up against targets that are within a fairly modest level range, so the fights are going to be somewhat fair. However, you can stack the odds in your favor by crafting a character that is much more powerful than their Soul Level suggests. Do this by going for high-end weapons and gear without putting many Souls into your leveling. If you have just enough Souls to properly wield the equipment you like, you're going to face easier opposition than you will if you level like crazy.

Matchmaking does take into account weapon reinforcement (among many other factors), so you can only push this edge but so far.

DRIED FINGERS

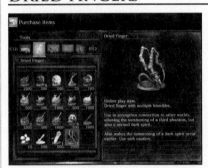

For extra insanity, use Dried Fingers to increase the number of Phantoms and invaders that can appear in your world by one each. You can end up with three Phantoms trying to help you, and two invaders trying to destroy you. It's the potential for madness that makes *Dark Souls III* even more of a thrill, although you should expect there to be quite a few casualties as a result; try to make sure that you're not one of them.

COVENANTS! WHO WILL YOU SERVE?

Part of *Dark Soul III*'s unusual multiplayer experience, Covenants allow you to pledge your allegiance to a faction within the game.

Covenants are largely focused on actual multiplayer gameplay, whether co-op or PvP (aggressively or defensively). If you greatly enjoy the multiplayer aspect of *Dark Souls*, Covenants offer rewards for your services—defending new players from invaders, aiding other players with tough boss fights, or ruthlessly hunting down others to steal their Embers for your own.

WHAT ARE COVENANTS?

You acquire Covenants simply by finding the "master" of that particular Covenant, located somewhere out in the world. The earliest accessible Covenants are focused on co-operative play and defensive PvP, while the later Covenants give you a means of joining a "defensive" PvP group that fights over specific zones in the game. Two of the Covenants offer rewards for pure offensive PvP, hunting other players for proof of victory to claim your rewards.

Remember, **you can freely join and leave Covenants**, so don't hesitate to pick up each Covenant as you travel through the game. Simply changing your equipped Covenant item is enough to change your allegiance.

EARNING COVENANT REWARDS

Each Covenant has a different reward item, earned in multiplayer play by performing actions that align with that Covenant's philosophy.

Generally, this means defending another player in PvP, hunting another player, or assisting in defeating bosses in co-op.

Turning in these reward items to the Covenant master grants **actual** rewards in the form of equipment for your character.

The Blade of the Darkmoon and Rosaria's Fingers Covenants can both earn a special reward item that counts as two for the purposes of earning gear: the Blades by slaying Aldrich Faithful and Rosaria's Fingers by hunting helpful blue spirits.

OFFLINE COVENANT REWARDS

You can acquire some Covenant rewards even while playing offline.

Some enemies occasionally drop Covenant reward items, so it is possible to farm regular foes and obtain at least some early Covenant items.

These drops are pretty rare, however. It's definitely faster to acquire rewards by playing online, if you can manage it.

ALDRICH FAITHFUL

You can join the Aldrich Faithful by finding a secret waterway beneath the Irithyll Cathedral (near Pontiff Sulyvahn's area). After defeating the boss of the cathedral, search behind it for a small tower that two dual-wielding warriors guard. Smack the walls inside to reveal an illusory wall, and then climb down a long ladder to find the Covenant and a hidden Bonfire.

Once unlocked, you can join their cult to defend the cathedral from interlopers.

While you have their Covenant equipped, you are automatically summoned to attack any non-Faithful that trespass on forbidden ground in Irithyll.

Success earns you Human Dregs that you can exchange for rewards from the Covenant master.

ALDRICH FAITHFUL REWARDS

DREGS OFFERED	REWARD
10	Great Deep Soul
30	Archdeacon's Great Staff

Human Dreg NPC Drops: Deacon of the Deep

BLADE OF THE DARKMOON

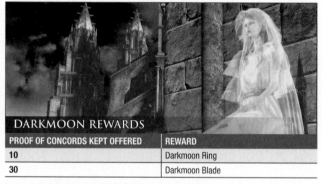

The Blade of the Darkmoon act as righteous enforcers, hunting red spirits that have transgressed repeatedly by invading and slaying other players. Like the Blue Sentinels, you are automatically summoned to defend those in the Way of Blue Covenant if they are invaded by hostile Red Phantoms.

The Blade of the Darkmoon is essentially an 'upgrade' to the Blue Sentinels Covenant, with the same reward item and same leader. The only key difference is defeating hated Aldrich Faithful rewards Proof of a Concord Well Kept, a double reward item. You still earn Proof of a Concord Kept by defeating red spirit invaders.

You can find Yorshka, the Covenant leader, by taking a leap of faith off a high tower in Anor Londo. An invisible bridge leads to her isolated tower, located above the small church in Irithyll.

DARKMOON REWARDS

PROOF OF CONCORDS KEPT OFFERED	REWARD
10	Darkmoon Ring
30	Darkmoon Blade

Proof of a Concord Kept NPC Drops: Silver Knight

BLUE SENTINELS

The Blue Sentinels are a defensive Covenant formed to protect members of the Way of Blue Covenant—in practice, this means almost every new player in the game.

You unlock the Blue Sentinels by speaking with Anri and Horace once you reach the Road of Sacrifices area, not too far into the game.

If you choose to take up their cause, you will be summoned automatically into a Way of Blue member's game if a hostile player is attacking them. Defeating hostile Red Phantoms earns you the Proof of a Concord Kept, which can be turned in later in the game at the Darkmoon Covenant leader for rewards. You can also earn these by successfully escorting the host to a boss battle.

MOUND-MAKERS

Crazed mad spirits, Mound-Makers appear as purple signs and phantoms to other players. Whether their sign is red or white, they can freely attack any phantom in the Host players game, allowing Mound-Makers to engage in voluntary PvP duels with a white sign, or to invade with a red sign, but turn against other red spirits instead of the Host…

The Mound-Maker defeating the Host or enough other phantoms or the player defeating the Mound-Maker earns a Vertebra Shackle, the Mound-Makers reward item. When invading, Mound-Makers automatically prioritize games with many players in them, the better to sow chaos.

The shrine of the Mound-Makers can be found in the Pit of Hollows, beneath the Rotted-greatwood boss in the Undead Settlement. It is possible to reach it without killing the boss in a very roundabout manner, see the NPCs chapter if you don't mind spoiling the route.

MOUND-MAKERS REWARDS

VERTEBRA SHACKLES OFFERED	REWARD
10	Bloodlust
30	Warmth

Vertebra Shackle NPC Drops: Skeleton Swordsman

ROSARIA'S FINGERS

Rosaria's Fingers is a hostile PvP faction, dedicated entirely to hunting and killing other players for their Embers. Defeat hosts to earn Pale Tongues, or defeat blue spirit defenders to earn Forked Pale Tongues, a double reward item.

You access the Rosaria's Fingers Covenant within the Cathedral of the Deep. Tucked away high in the cathedral, you can find Rosaria and pledge allegiance.

Rosaria has the special ability to change your attributes or your appearance, each up to five times per playthrough. Either change costs one Pale Tongue.

ROSARIA'S REWARDS

PALE TONGUES OFFERED	REWARD
10	Obscuring Ring
30	Man-Grub's Staff

Pale Tongue NPC Drops: Darkwraith

WARRIOR OF SUNLIGHT

Focused on jolly co-operation, the Warriors of Sunlight appear as gleaming golden spirits, beacons of light and a welcome sign for players who need aid against tough bosses.

Placing your summon sign as a Warrior of Sunlight causes the sign to show up in bright gold, and players are often keen to summon Warriors of Sunlight to aid them in co-operative battle. Defeat bosses as a White-Gold Phantom or defeat hosts as a Red-Gold Phantom to earn Sunlight Medals. You can join the Warriors of Sunlight by locating their emblem early in the game, not too far into the Undead Settlement. Their shrine is not found until much later in the game in Lothric Castle.

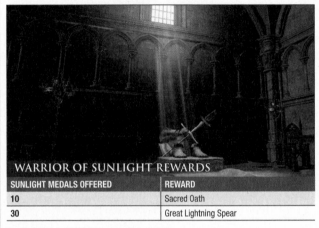

WARRIOR OF SUNLIGHT REWARDS

SUNLIGHT MEDALS OFFERED	REWARD
10	Sacred Oath
30	Great Lightning Spear

Sunlight Medal NPC Drops: Lothric Knight

WATCHDOGS OF FARRON

The Watchdogs of Farron are similar to the Aldrich Faithful in that they exist to defend a specific area in the game, located around Farron Keep.

Defeating interlopers in this region in PvP battles earns Wolf's Blood Swordgrass.

To join the Watchdogs, speak with the Old Wolf, located high in the tower above the swamp near Farron Keep.

WATCHDOGS OF FARRON REWARDS

WOLF'S BLOOD SWORDGRASS OFFERED	REWARD
10	Old Wolf Curved Sword
30	Wolf Knight's Greatshield
30	Wolf Ring

Wolf's Blood Swordgrass NPC Drops: Ghru

WAY OF BLUE

The earliest Covenant in the game, the Way of Blue is a special Covenant designed for new players. As long as you are in this Covenant, members of the Blue Sentinels and Darkmoon Blades (the "blue cops") will join and aid you should a hostile red spirit invade you.

This is basically your "default" Covenant if you aren't especially interested in the other PvP or co-op factions, and it provides you with a bit of help against hostile players.

Don't assume that being in the Way of Blue will always save you from an invader, though. You still need to defend yourself, but this Covenant can give you an edge in battle. More friends are always better, especially if you aren't confident in your PvP skills.

You join the Way of Blue early in the game by speaking to Emma, the Priestess in the High Wall of Lothric chapel.

WEAPONS, ARMOR, MAGIC, AND TOOLS

One of the great joys of exploring the world of *Dark Souls* is discovering the mountains of *loot*. Your gear defines your build as much as your stats do, and experimenting with the options available to you is great fun.

There are a *lot* of different items to be found, a wide range of weapons, many suits of armor, a range of spells, and useful tools to aid your travels.

Loot also ties into New Game Plus play, where you can carry all of your gear forward into a fresh world, with tougher foes.

On top of that, because a great many items are only accessible late in the game, if you want to enjoy a full playthrough with an interesting set of weapons and spells, you need to do so on New Game Plus to fully experience them.

One of the coolest aspects of *Dark Souls* is that virtually *any* loadout can be successful. You can take a dagger and a suit of leather armor through the entire game if you want to. It's going to be a lot harder in some places, but it is doable.

Dark Souls relies on tradeoffs to keep gearing decisions interesting—while there are certainly powerful weapons, strong suits of armor, tough shields, and hard hitting spells, they are often balanced by very high stat requirements, slow casting times, high weight or defensive deficiencies.

The result of this is you can experiment and mix and match almost endlessly with different loadouts, *and* you can choose your favorite weapons based on their moveset, without worrying that they'll be completely obsoleted by a later discovery.

Properly upgraded, a simple Broadsword or Battle Axe can take you from the start to the end of the game comfortably.

Experiment and enjoy, there's a lot to find and play with!

WEAPON SKILLS

A new feature in *Dark Souls III*, Weapon Skills are special moves granted by weapons that consume FP to produce a special effect. In previous *Souls* games, some of these moves would have been specific to certain weapons, with normal weapons having no unique ability, but in *Dark Souls III*, *all* weapons have been given a skill of some sort. In fact, every usable piece of equipment in the game has a skill, including Catalysts, Ranged Weapons, and Shields.

Some are basic maneuvers (such as Parrying with a light shield), others are almost (or entirely!) magical in nature.

Weapon Skills usually don't define most weapons, as a weapon's moveset and overall ability still tends to be its most important traits. Weapon Skills do add a lot of flavor, and in some cases, they fill some very useful niches (such as breaking shield guard cheaply and easily).

Keep in mind that some shared skills that appear on multiple weapons have slightly different FP costs, depending on the weapon in question. Check the full equipment charts for specifics.

A great many Weapon Skills are specific to unique weapons, be they Soul-transposed weapons created from boss Souls, or Soulbound weapons.

WEAPON SKILL	APPEARS ON	DESCRIPTION
Blind Spot	Corvian Greatknife, Handmaid's Daggerr	Use against shielded foes to break through their guard by attacking from the side.
Bloodlust	Blood Lust	Stain blade with one's own blood to temporarily grant uncanny sharpness.
Chain Spin	Winged Knight Twinaxes, Winged Knight Halberd	Sweep foes in a large spinning motion and use strong attack to continue the motion until stamina is exhausted.
Chained Dance	Painting Guardian's Curved Sword	Execute relentless consecutive attacks while tracing a circle in a unique dance of deadly grace.
Champion's Charge	Gundyr's Halberd	Hold spear at waist and charge at foe, and use momentum to transition into sweeping strong attack.
Charge	Astora Greatsword, Spears, Pikes, Halberd	Hold sword at waist and charge at foe. Use strong attack while charging to extend the length of the charge.
Combustion	Pyromancy Flame, White Hair Talisman	Creates a powerful flame in the wielder's hand. One of the most basic pyromancies, and for this very reason, the flame created is fierce. Works while equipped in either hand.
Crescent Blade	Crescent Moon Sword	Assume a broad stance and fire off crescent moon blades.
Dancer's Grace	Dancer's Enchanted Swords	Unleash the fury of both blades in a dancing spin motion and use strong attack to continue the performance until stamina is exhausted.
Darkdrift	Darkdrift	Aim carefully, and pierce with a large forward lunge.
Darkmoon Arrow	Darkmoon Longbow	Infuse a readied arrow with Darkmoon essence, granting it magic damage and the ability to pierce shields.
Demonic Flare	Demon's Great Axe	Briefly cause flame within to flare, and smash it upon earth and foes.
Ember	Firelink Greatsword	The fading flame momentarily illuminates and launches itself forward.
Falling Bolt	Dragonslayer Great Axe, Dragonslayer Swordspear	Hold axe high in air to gather fierce lightning, and smash ground to whip the bolts to the ground.
Feast Bell	Eleonora	Hold up axe and wave to emit a solemn chime to temporarily make weapons lacerating, and to restore HP for each hit.
Flame of Lorian	Lorian's Greatsword	Lunge forward to transform smolder into flame, and follow with strong attack to launch flame across ground.
Flame Whip	Witch's Locks	Temporarily coat the whip in fire.
Flame Whirlwind	Demon's Fist	Spin through opponents with abandon, flaming fists outstretched. Using a strong attack while spinning utilizes your momentum to slam the ground with both fists.

WEAPON SKILL	APPEARS ON	DESCRIPTION
Frost	Pontiff Knight Great Scythe	Create a bone-chilling frost with each swing of the greatscythe that causes a temporary frost effect.
Frost Blade	Pontiff Knight Curved Sword	Execute large spinning motion to imbue blade with frost, and follow through with a strong attack that slashes with a giant blade made of frost.
Galvanize	Warpick, Pickaxe	Temporarily boost stamina recovery speed.
Gentle Prayer	Talismans	Recovers HP for a period of time, albeit extremely slowly. Works while equipped in either hand.
Guiding Light	Scholar's Candlestick, Cleric's Candlestick	A candle provides a temporary source of light which reveals additional guidance. Acts as the Seek Guidance spell.
Hold	Katanas	Assume a holding stance to rapidly execute a lunging slash with normal attack, or a deflecting parry with strong attack.
Impact	Whips	Strike from the left to evade shields and deal a stinging blow that temporarily slows stamina recovery.
Kindled Charge	Gargoyle Flame Spear	Hold spear at waist and charge at foe, and use momentum to transition to a fiery strong attack.
Kindled Flurry	Gargoyle Flame Hammer	Anchor weapon in earth and use strong attack to launch successive volleys of fire from the tip of the hammer.
Leaping Slash	Claw	Perform a forward leaping slash at the opponent's head. When successful, functions as a head shot, inflicting heavy damage.
Lifedrain	Dark Hand	Embrace the victim and steal their HP. Can only be used against humans.
Lightning Charge	Dragonslayer Spear	Charge with spear at waist to enwreathe with lightning, then release bolts with final thrust.
Moan	Moaning Shield	Offer a gentle prayer to the shield, causing the woman's face to give out a low moan and attract enemies.
Molten Perseverance	Old King's Great Hammer	Anchor weapon in earth to temporarily boost poise, and use strong attack to repeatedly stab earth to trigger molten explosions.
Moonlight Vortex	Moonlight Greatsword	Draw sword back and thrust to unleash torrential moonlight.
Morne's Rage	Morne's Great Hammer	Stick weapon into earth and emit a powerful shockwave. Also, similar to Perseverance, temporarily boosts poise and reduces damage received.
Neck Swipe	Reapers	This attack aims for the scruff of a foe's neck, and when successful, functions as a head shot, inflicting heavy damage.
Oath of Sunlight	Sunlight Straight Sword	Raise the sword aloft when praising the sun to boost attack and damage absorption for self and allies in vicinity.

WEAPON SKILL	APPEARS ON	DESCRIPTION
Onislayer	Onikiri and Obadachi	Leap forward and slash mercilessly with both blades, cutting open foes.
Pacify	Yorshka's Spear	With a prayer and an offering of this spear, temporarily wear down enemy FP.
Parry	Parrying Dagger, Farron Greatsword, Light Shields, Medium Shields	Deflect an attack when timed properly and follow up with a critical hit.
Perseverance	Black Knight Sword, Hammers, Great Hammers, Red Hilted Halberd, Caestus	Temporarily boost Poise. Damage reduced while active.
Pharis Triple-shot	Black Bow of Pharis	Swiftly nocks three arrows with finesse after drawing the bow, firing them simultaneously.
Profaned Flame	Profaned Greatsword	Temporarily summon the Profaned Flame. Lunge forward and use strong attack to enshroud blade in flame.
Puncturing Arrow	Greatbows	Masterfully fires off a great arrow that pierces through all enemies in its path, inflicting damage.
Punitive Flame	Immolation Tinder	Punish foes with a flame that blankets the ground.
Quickstep	Daggers, Thrall Axe, Manikin Claws	Instantly step behind or around the side of foes. Especially effective when locked on to target.
Rapid Fire	Composite Bow, Short Bow	Swiftly nocks arrows with finesse after drawing the bow, allowing for consecutive shots.
Ricard's Lunge and Press	Ricard's Rapier	Assume a quick stance, lunge forward, and execute a stunning chain attack. Sustain offensive with strong attack.
Sacred Light and Flame	Twin Princes' Greatsword	While in stance, use normal attack to cast Sacred Lothric Light, and strong attack to cast Flame of Lorian.
Sacred Lothric Light	Lothric's Holy Sword	Assume stance to imbue sword with sacred light, and use strong attack to release light together with a great thrust of the sword.
Sharpen	Butcher Knife, Great Machete	Sharpening the blade increases HP restored with each successful hit.
Shield Bash	All Shields	Without lowering your guard, strike the enemy with the shield to knock them back or stagger them. Works while equipped in either hand.
Shield Splitter	Mail Breaker, Estoc, Irithyll Rapier, Arstor's Spear, Spear	Aim carefully, and attack in a large forward lunge to pierce through enemy shields and inflict damage directly.
Spin Slash	Gotthard Twinswords, Curved Swords, Curved Greatswords	Slice into foes with a large spinning motion, and continue spinning to transition into strong attack.
Spin Sweep	Partizan, Halberds	Sweep foes in a large spinning motion, and utilize momentum to transition into an overhanded strong attack smash.

WEAPON SKILL	APPEARS ON	DESCRIPTION
Stance	Straight Swords and Greatswords, Crystal Sage's Rapier and Rapier	While in stance, use normal attack to break a foe's guard from below, and strong attack to slash upwards with a forward lunge.
Stance of Judgment	Greatsword of Judgment	Assume stance to unleash dark magic. Use normal attack for a lunging thrust, and strong attack to emit side-sweeping wave.
Steady Chant	Heysel Pick, Golden Ritual Spear, Staffs	For a short moment, boost the strength of sorceries.
Stomp	Dark Sword, Greatswords and Ultra Greatswords	Use one's weight to lunge forward with a low stance and increased poise, and follow with strong attack for a spinning slash.
Stone Flesh	Havel's Greatshield	Raise the shield in silent prayer, turning the user's body into a solid mass of stone.
Storm King	Storm Ruler	Assume stance to imbue sword with storm. Most effective when facing giants.
Tackle	Crossbows	Lunge into a shoulder tackle, pushing back enemies to create distance.
Tornado	Storm Curved Sword	Imbue blade with the wrath of storm in a spinning motion, and follow with a strong attack to bear that wrath upon foes.
Unfaltering Prayer	Talismans	Temporarily increases poise while casting miracles, preventing enemy attacks from interrupting prayer. Works while equipped in either hand.
Unleash Dragon	Tailbone Shortsword, Tailbone Spear	Thrust the spear to unleash the strength of dragons, similar to an ancient dragon weapon, only with its power tragically faded.
Warcry	Axes, Greataxes, Hammers, Great Hammers, Crescent Axe	Let out a spirited warcry that temporarily boosts attack, and enables a crushing strong attack.
Weapon Skill	All Shields	Equipping this shield in the left hand allows one to perform the Skill of the right hand weapon.
Wheel of Fate	Bonewheel Shield	Thrust out the wheel and give it a good spin, shredding enemies with the outer lining of spikes.
Wolf Leap	Old Wolf Curved Sword	Slice into foes with a large spinning motion, then leap out of harm's way and follow with strong attack.
Wolf Sword	Wolf Knight's Greatsword	While in stance, use normal attack for a low spinning slash, or strong attack to leap forward in a vertically-slashing somersault.
Wrath of the Gods	Wolnir's Holy Sword	Thrust weapon into earth to emit powerful shockwave.

TOOLS

Tools are usable items, and an indispensable part of your arsenal. The majority of basic consumable items in the game can be purchased from vendors in Firelink Shrine (typically the Shrine Handmaid, occasionally Greirat after he has unlocked some additional items). There are a few special purpose reusable items with various unique effects as well. All of these items are extremely useful for your survival, giving you the ability to protect and recover from the untender ministrations of Lothric's unwholesome denizens. Tools are accessible as the bottom part of your toolbelt, and you can store ten items on there, and another five on your main inventory status window for less commonly used items. Be careful about jamming your toolbelt too full of items you rarely use, it's usually a good idea to keep your Estus Flasks and a few consumables that are useful for the specific area you're exploring equipped. Otherwise you can find yourself fumbling for your flask in combat at a bad time!

CRITICAL ITEMS

These vital items are crucial for your survival. The Estus and Ashen Estus Flasks allow you to restore your HP and FP, while Embers restore you to full health should you perish, restoring your lost HP.

Estus Shards and Undead Bone Shards are rare items that upgrade your Estus Flasks, giving you more uses, and more powerful uses respectively. Keep an eye out for these on the maps throughout the walkthrough. If you can sneak ahead to pick these up even if you aren't prepared for another area fully yet, do so!

ESTUS FLASK
Fill with Estus at bonfire. Restores HP.

The Undead treasure these dull green flasks.

Fill with Estus at bonfires, and drink to restore HP.

The journey of an Undead has always traced the bonfires, and no journey of import has been made without an Estus Flask.

EMBER
Gain strength of flame, boosting HP until death.

No Unkindled can ever truly claim the embers that burn within a champion's bosom, which is precisely what makes their yearning for warmth so keen.

Gain the strength of flame and increased max HP until death.

With the strength of fire, the summoning signs of Unkindled become visible, and seekers of embers can be summoned to join in co-operation. But beware, the embers may also attract invaders.

Effect: Gain 30% HP and can use White Phantom signs, and host co-op or be invaded in multiplayer.

ASHEN ESTUS FLASK
Fill with Ash Estus at bonfire. Restores FP

Undead treasure these dull ashen flasks.

Fill with Estus at bonfires, and drink to restore FP.

Quite befitting of an Unkindled, an Ashen Estus Flask turns a bonfire's heat cold.

ESTUS SHARD
Increases usages of Estus Flask

A shard soaked in Estus.

Give to the blacksmith at the shrine to increases usages of the Estus Flask.

In the old days, it was rare to see an Estus Flask far from its owner, but this shard offers hope, however shattered.

UNDEAD BONE SHARD
Burn in shrine bonfire to increase Estus recovery

Undead bones that yet burn.

Cast it into the shrine bonfire to boost the recovery provided by the Estus Flask.

The bonfire's cinders are the bones of Undead, and a bone that still burns is a fresh cinder indeed. Before feeding upon death, one must first pray to it.

TYPICAL CONSUMABLES

Basic consumable items, these are mostly focused on curing and protecting against enemy status effects, but there are also very useful buffing items to temporarily enhance your performance offensively or defensively. The throwing weapons here are very useful early in the game, and because they scale with your stats, they do improve slightly as your character's strength grows. For the elemental weapon buffing items, keep in mind that a weapon that already has an element on it (such as a Fire Longsword) cannot have another element applied. This is one benefit to using weapon infusions with no element, as you can apply temporary buffs to grant them more total damage output than a pure elemental weapon.

DIVINE BLESSING
Fully restore HP and cures ailments

Holy water blessed by the Queen of Lothric.

Fully restores HP and cures ailments.

The Queen of Lothric, married to the former King Oceiros, was initially revered as a goddess of fertility and bounty. After giving birth to Ocelotte, her youngest, she quietly disappeared.

SIEGBRÄU
Restores HP and boosts frost resist

Special brew of Siegward of Catarina.

Perfect for travel in its jolly barrel mug.

Restores HP and temporarily boosts frost resistance.

Leave it to Siegward to discover a drink that even an Undead can enjoy. Perhaps his long years spent Undead have left him wanting to drain a cup or two and revel as if he were still among the living.

Effect: Restores 20% of maximum HP + 100 HP. Gives +150 frost resist for 60 seconds.

HIDDEN BLESSING
Fully restore FP

Holy water blessed by the Queen of Lothric.

Fully restores FP.

There is a grave in Lothric that sees no visitors, a dark place where rootless warriors rest. The Queen of Lothric alone cared to wish the poor souls good fortune.

GREEN BLOSSOM
Temporary boost to stamina recovery speed

Green weed, shaped like a flower.

Temporary boost to stamina recovery speed.

The Undead Legion of Farron is remembered for using this annual plant, normally found near clear water, to swing their mighty swords with abandon.

Effect: +5 stamina recovery/second for 60 seconds.

BUDDING GREEN BLOSSOM

Large temporary boost to stamina recovery speed

Green flower-shaped weed with small white blooms.

Large temporary boost to stamina recovery speed.

Flowers of the Green Blossom are ethereal, blossoming only on the surface of chilled, but not frozen, water.

Effect: +9 stamina recovery/second for 60 seconds.

BLUE BUG PELLET

Temporarily boosts magic damage absorption

Medicinal pellet made from crushed insects.

The blue type temporarily boosts magic damage absorption.

The Boreal Valley is infested with moon bugs, meaning ingredients are never far from hand for the Irithyllian slaves who concoct this medicine.

Effect: Magic damage absorption is boosted by 15% for 60 seconds.

YELLOW BUG PELLET

Temporarily boosts lightning damage absorption

Medicinal pellet made from crushed insects.

The yellow type temporarily boosts lightning damage absorption.

The grave wardens of Carthus used these to repel a great sand worm. The worm tumbled into the catacombs, and proceeded to dominate its new home in the Smoldering Lake.

Effect: Lightning damage absorption is boosted by 15% for 60 seconds.

MOSSFRUIT

Temporarily boosts all resistances

A small clump of mossfruit.

Temporarily boosts bleed, poison, frost, and curse resistance.

All mossfruit is the same regardless of its color, and has the effects of moss of all colors.

Effect: Adds +80 to all resistances for 60 seconds.

PURPLE MOSS CLUMP

Reduce poison build-up. Cure poison.

Medicinal purple moss clump.

Reduces poison build-up. Cures poison.

Poison builds up in the body, and when it breaks out, it causes gradual damage over a period of time.

Poison can be exasperating, so be sure to carry sufficient moss clumps when traveling to a blighted area.

RIME-BLUE MOSS CLUMP

Reduces frost buildup, cures frostbite status

Moss clump radiating gentle heat and light.

Reduces frost build-up. Cures frostbite status.

Frost accumulates in the body causing frostbite, which saps one's health, lowers absorption, and slows stamina recovery.

Weapons imbued with frost are a rare thing indeed, most of them originating in the Boreal Valley.

THROWING KNIFE

Throw at foes to inflict damage

Small throwing knife.

Throw at enemies to inflict damage.

Most items choose their wielder, and only experience can improve their effectiveness. True strength can be gained in no other way.

Scaling: Strength B, Dexterity A

KUKRI

Throwing knife. Causes bleed damage.

Small throwing machete.

Throw at enemies to cause bleeding damage.

A unique weapon originally used by swordsmen of Carthus, but now popular among bandits and thieves.

Scaling: Strength A, Dexterity S

REPAIR POWDER

Repairs equipped weapons and armor

Lightly enchanted golden powder.

Repairs equipped weapons and armor, as long as they haven't already broken.

Use of a weapon depletes its durability, eventually causing it to break.

As long as a weapon is not broken, its durability can be restored at a bonfire, but for distant journeys, one may wish to prepare ahead.

RED BUG PELLET

Temporarily boosts fire damage absorption

Medicinal pellet made from crushed insects.

The red type temporarily boosts fire damage absorption.

Prepared in the Cathedral of the Deep by evangelists, who dole them out to followers to ease their suffering when they burn.

Effect: Fire damage absorption is boosted by 15% for 60 seconds.

BLACK BUG PELLET

Temporarily boosts dark damage absorption

Medicinal pellet made from crushed insects.

The black type temporarily boosts Dark damage absorption.

At all times, the Abyss Watchers of the Undead Legion keep a supply of these concoctions, prepared by the acolytes. Rumor has it their Ghru descendants still make these concoctions.

Effect: Dark damage absorption is boosted by 15% for 60 seconds.

BLOODRED MOSS CLUMP

Reduce bleeding build-up

Red moss clump used as maggot repellent.

Reduces bleeding build-up.

Bleeding builds up when attacked by sharp blades or spikes, and once triggered causes severe damage. Use this moss clump before it reaches that point.

BLOOMING PURPLE MOSS CLUMP

Reduce poison and toxin. Cures status.

Potently medicinal moss clump with a flower.

Reduces poison and toxin. Cures ailments.

A toxin is a more vicious form of poison which quickly leads to death.

Moss clumps without blooms are useless against toxin, and those who neglect to carry this flowered variety are simply courting an early demise.

PURGING STONE

Reduces undead curse build-up and cures hollowing

Ash-colored stone encasing a skull.

Reduces undead curse build-up and cures hollowing.

Inhabitants of Londor, the land of Hollows, use this secret treasure to feign normalcy.

Occasionally, a Hollow fools even himself, and turns on his own kind.

Effect: Removes Hollowing gained from deaths while carrying Dark Sigils. Does not remove Dark Sigils.

POISON THROWING KNIFE

Throw at foes to inflict damage and poison

A throwing knife dipped in poison.

Throw at enemies to inflict poison damage.

Used by assassins of Londor, land of Hollows. The poison is jokingly known as Hollow's blood.

Scaling: Strength D, Dexterity B

FIREBOMB

Explodes, inflicting fire damage

Bisque urn filled with black powder.

Explodes, inflicting fire damage.

Fire damage, which differs from physical damage, is highly effective against creatures of flesh, beasts, and other foes that might naturally have cause to fear the flame.

Scaling: Strength A, Dexterity C

ROPE FIREBOMB

Thrown behind, explodes inflicting fire damage

Bisque urn attached to a string and filled with black powder. Thrown behind and explodes, inflicting fire damage.

No different to a firebomb, save for the direction in which it is thrown. Enables a different fighting style, and flexibility in adjusting to one's circumstances.

Scaling: Strength A, Dexterity C

ROPE BLACK FIREBOMB

Thrown behind, explodes inflicting high fire damage

Black bisque urn attached to a string and filled with black powder. Thrown behind and explodes, inflicting fire damage.

No different to a black firebomb, save for the direction in which it is thrown. Enables a different fighting style, and flexibility in adjusting to one's circumstances.

Scaling: Strength A, Dexterity C

DUNG PIE

Turns enemy toxic, but also affects player

Dried fecal waste material, moist on the inside.

Throw at enemy to inflict toxin build-up, but also ups your own toxicity.

Though the stench makes it difficult to carry on one's person, inflicting toxins on an enemy yields high damage over time. Perhaps some Undead have fond memories of waste. Or, perhaps not.

CHARCOAL PINE RESIN

Apply fire to right-hand weapon

Black charcoal-like pine resin.

Temporarily applies fire to right-hand weapon.

Used in the Undead Settlement to preserve Undead bodies after dissection, and to bury them.

Effect: Applies +85 fire damage to right-hand weapon for 60 seconds.

GOLD PINE RESIN

Apply lightning to right-hand weapon

Rare pine resin which emits golden sparks.

Chunks of it are even rarer.

Temporarily applies lightning to right-hand weapon.

Its origins are unknown, although some have speculated that it may in fact be a type of fungal resin.

Effect: Applies +95 lightning damage to right-hand weapon for 60 seconds.

PALE PINE RESIN

Apply magic to right-hand weapon

Pale pine resin that faintly glimmers.

Temporarily applies magic to right-hand weapon.

The blood red substance sometimes found within suggests there is more to this so-called resin than meets the eye.

Effect: Adds +90 magic damage to right-hand weapon for 60 seconds.

ROTTEN PINE RESIN

Apply poison to right-hand weapon

Pine resin that has rotted and turned poisonous.

Likely rotten from the start.

Temporarily applies poison to right-hand weapon.

Farron Keep was swallowed by the rotted wood, where the blunt-horned Ghrus concoct this resin.

Effect: Applies +45 poison effect to right-hand weapon for 60 seconds.

ALLURING SKULL

Attract certain types of enemies

A skull resplendent in the scent of souls. Prepared by evangelists of the Cathedral of the Deep.

Throw to shatter, spreading souls which attract enemies. Not effective for all foes.

Effect: The residual sign from summoning a Mound-Makers phantom has an identical effect. The Bestiary lists enemies that are affected by this item.

BLACK FIREBOMB

Explodes, inflicting fire damage

More powerful bisque urn filled with special black powder. Explodes, inflicting great fire damage.

Fire damage, which differs from physical damage, is highly effective against creatures of flesh, beasts, and other foes that might naturally have cause to fear the flame.

Scaling: Strength A, Dexterity C

LIGHTNING URN

Explodes, inflicting lightning damage

Dragon-hunting tool used by Lothric knights.

Explodes upon contact, inflicting lightning damage.

The knights of Lothric have since tamed dragons, but were once hunters of dragons themselves.

This explains their special hunting gear, and why they worshipped the sun.

Scaling: Faith S

STALK DUNG PIE

Turns enemy toxic, but also affects player

Dried fecal waste material, marked by a long plant stalk that was not properly digested.

Throw behind at enemies to inflict toxin build-up, but also ups your own toxicity.

Strictly speaking, this consists of different material than the dung pie, but waste is waste, no sense in splitting hairs.

CHARCOAL PINE BUNDLE

Apply fire to right-hand weapon

A small bundle of charcoal pine resin.

Quickly applies fire to right-hand weapon.

Does not last for long, but can be used in inventive ways, such as applying it in the middle of a series of blows.

Effect: Applies +110 fire damage to right-hand weapon for 7 seconds.

GOLD PINE BUNDLE

Apply lightning to right-hand weapon

Rare pine resin which emits golden sparks.

Collected in a small bundle.

Quickly applies lightning to right-hand weapon.

Does not last for long, but can be used in inventive ways, such as applying it in the middle of a series of blows.

Effect: Applies +120 lightning damage to right-hand weapon for 7 seconds.

HUMAN PINE RESIN

Apply dark to right-hand weapon

Charcoal pine resin rotted with human body fluids.

Temporarily applies dark to right-hand weapon.

Normally used in the Undead Settlement for preservation and burials, but can mature into this state, becoming a valuable substance, used in a certain ceremony. Often seen for trade at exorbitant prices.

Effect: Applies +95 dark damage to right-hand weapon for 60 seconds.

CARTHUS ROUGE

Add lacerating effect to right-hand weapon

Highly viscous scarlet plant secretions.

Temporarily applies bleeding effect to right-hand weapon.

Associated with the warriors of Carthus, whose blades take on the scarlet hues of both this sanguine substance and the spatters of their victims' blood.

Effect: Applies +45 bleed effect to right-hand weapon for 60 seconds.

UNDEAD HUNTER CHARM

Prevent Estus recovery within a limited area

Tool used to hunt down the Undead.

Blocks Estus recovery within a limited area.

Used long ago by Lloyd's cleric knights on their Undead hunts. Although Allfather Lloyd is long forgotten by the Way of White, his hunts have lived on, and this charm allows one to challenge Undead without fear of tenacious healing.

Effect: Prevents the target it hits from using Estus Flasks for 25 seconds. Can also put mimics (Avaricious Beings) to sleep.

DUEL CHARM

Temporarily disables special effects in vicinity

Tool used in duels of judgment. Nulls effects of special area effects for a short time.

Allfather Lloyd's knights lived in fear of his duels of judgment, in which verdicts were carried out by his Sword of Law.

Effect: Dispels beneficial effects from the target it hits. Some beneficial effects cannot be dispelled.

RUSTED GOLD COIN

Crush to temporarily greatly boost item discovery

A rusty old gold coin that surely has no currency.

Crushing the coin gives a large, if temporary, boost to item discovery.

A rich man lost his fortune, but it returned to him twofold. He was swift to squander his retrieved fortune, smugly confident that it was bound to double once again.

Effect: Item discovery is multiplied by 2 for 60 seconds.

RUBBISH

Rubbish of no value, and certainly no avail

Rubbish with no value.

Who in their right mind would bother carrying this around? Perhaps you need help.

HOMEWARD BONE

Return to last bonfire rested at, or to shrine

Bone fragment reduced to white ash.

Return to last bonfire used for resting, or to the shrine bonfire.

Bonfires are sustained by bones of the Undead.

In rare cases, their previous owner's strong urge to seek bonfires enchants their bones with a homeward instinct.

RUSTED COIN

Crush to temporarily boost item discovery

An old rusted copper coin.

Crushing the coin boosts item discovery.

Those who have lost their fortunes rely upon this superstitious practice, hoping to retrieve what was once theirs, and more.

Effect: Item discovery is multiplied by 1.5 for 60 seconds.

YOUNG WHITE BRANCH

Transform, blending into environment

A young white branch.

Use to transform into something which blends into the surroundings.

Little Dusk's first sorcerer's staff eventually became a seedling, and then three white birch saplings. The young branch is said to still contain echoes of little Dusk's capriciousness.

Effect: Giant Sniper in Undead Settlement will not target you while carrying one (including initial burial gift).

PRISM STONE

Mark path by placing on ground

Warm pebble emitting a beautiful phasing aura of seven colors, with a very rare eighth.

The prism stone does nothing special, but can serve as a path marker, or perhaps dropped off a cliff to judge height by the sound of its descent.

If a loud noise is heard upon its landing, then a fall from the ledge is surely lethal.

PERMANENT ITEMS

Permanent items are re-usable items with specific special effects. The Darksign is a special permanent 'item' (really a cursed brand on your body!) that allows you to instantly return to a Bonfire, at the cost of losing all of your Souls. Generally you should be carrying a decent sized stack of Homeward Bone items for this purpose, until you acquire the Coiled Sword Fragment later in the game. The Dragon Torso and Head stones can only be used while not wearing armor.

COILED SWORD FRAGMENT

Return to last bonfire rested at, or to shrine

Fragment of the coiled sword of a bonfire which served its purpose long ago.

Returns caster to last bonfire used for resting, or to the bonfire in Firelink Shrine. Can be used repeatedly.

Bonfires are linked to one another irreversibly, retaining their affinity long after their purpose is exhausted.

LORETTA'S BONE

Old human bone with several holes bored into it

Old, discolored human bone with several holes bored into it.

A woman's corpse in the Undead Settlement was found clutching this bone. Her name was Loretta.

DRAGON TORSO STONE

Gain dragon torso and roar like a dragon

Stone imbued with the power of the everlasting dragons, used in a secret rite by dragon worshippers.

Gain the torso of a dragon and a dragon's roar, a transformation that is irreversible until death.

From ancient times, the path of dragon worship was walked by warriors. It is said they envision Archdragon Peak in the depths of their meditation, and at times, they even hear the distant sound of the great bell at the peak.

Effect: Shockwave can repel some projectiles. Boosts weapon damage by 10% for 7 seconds.

BINOCULARS

Use to peer at distant scenery

Binoculars made of brass.

Use to peer at distant scenery.

Their utility is singular, but applications many. The value of these specs depends greatly on the imagination of their owner.

DRAGON HEAD STONE

Gain dragon head and emit dragon breath

Stone imbued with the power of the everlasting dragons, used in a secret rite by dragon worshippers.

Gain the head of a dragon and emit dragon breath, a transformation that is irreversible until death.

Those who choose the path of the dragon strive for perfect imitation, and the dragon head rite is the first step in this grand process.

Scaling: Intelligence D, Faith C

TWINKLING DRAGON HEAD STONE

Gain dragon head and breathe until death

Stone imbued with the power of the everlasting dragons, the second of its kind, offered to a towering dragon.

Gain the head of a dragon and emit breath alongside an archdragon mirage. The transformation is irreversible until death.

The illusion achieved was the first case of a human imitating the form of an ancient dragon, and it revealed the smallness of human existence. The road to the old dragons is long and arduous, and only one can complete the journey.

Effect: Stronger than Dragon Head, drains more Stamina. Scaling: Intelligence D, Faith C

TWINKLING DRAGON TORSO STONE

Gain dragon torso and roar until death

Stone imbued with the power of the everlasting dragons, offered to a towering dragon. This stone shows signs of a nascent light.

Gain the torso of a dragon and roar alongside an archdragon mirage. The transformation is irreversible until death.

Yet true imitation will require a dragon head, as well.

Effect: Does not repel projectiles like Dragon Torso. Boosts weapon damage by 10% for 7 seconds.

HELLO CARVING

Smash on ground to say "Hello"

A strange head of unknown origin carved from archtree. It speaks when thrown on the ground.

This head says "Hello". Have another look. Do you sense the amicability in its eyes?

THANK YOU CARVING

Smash on ground to say "Thank you"

A strange head of unknown origin carved from archtree. It speaks when thrown on the ground.

This head says "Thank you". Have another look. Is this not a face of gratitude?

VERY GOOD! CARVING

Smash on ground to say "Very good!"

A strange head of unknown origin carved from archtree. It speaks when thrown on the ground.

This head says "Very good!" Have another look. Does it not appear rather jovial?

I'M SORRY CARVING

Smash on ground to say "I'm sorry"

A strange head of unknown origin carved from archtree. It speaks when thrown on the ground.

This head says "I'm sorry". Have another look. Isn't it quite the expression of atonement?

HELP ME! CARVING

Smash on ground to say "Help me!"

A strange head of unknown origin carved from archtree. It speaks when thrown on the ground.

This head says "Help me!" Look again. Can you hear the desperation of its plea?

DARKSIGN

Lose souls and return to bonfire

The Darksign is the sign of an accursed Undead.

The Darksign returns its bearer to the last bonfire rested at, or the bonfire at Firelink Shrine, but at the cost of all souls held.

Carriers of the Darksign are reborn after death, and eventually lose their minds, turning Hollow. And so it is they are driven from their homelands.

BASIC CONSUMABLE SOULS

Found throughout the lands of Lothric, these condensed souls can be used to gain a quantity of Souls, useful for 'storing' Souls. Because they are items, they are not lost on death, so you can carry these and use them when necessary. A good time to use them is when you are just short of gaining a level. Using a few soul items at a time to completely drain your Soul pool before going out exploring again is a good practice.

FADING SOUL

Use to acquire a smidgen of souls

The fading soul of a corpse.

Use to gain a smattering of souls.

Let the Fire Keeper transform this sovereignless soul into a source of strength, for to be Unkindled is to be a vessel for souls.

Souls: Obtain 50 souls.

SOUL OF A DESERTED CORPSE

Use to acquire souls

Soul found in a deserted corpse.

Use to acquire souls.

Let the Fire Keeper transform this sovereignless soul into a source of strength, for to be Unkindled is to be a vessel for souls.

Souls: Obtain 200 souls.

LARGE SOUL OF A DESERTED CORPSE

Use to acquire souls

Large soul found in a deserted corpse.

Use to acquire souls.

Let the Fire Keeper transform this sovereignless soul into a source of strength, for to be Unkindled is to be a vessel for souls.

Souls: Obtain 400 souls.

SOUL OF AN UNKNOWN TRAVELER

Use to acquire souls

Soul found in the corpse of an unknown traveler.

Use to acquire souls.

Let the Fire Keeper transform this sovereignless soul into a source of strength, for to be Unkindled is to be a vessel for souls.

Souls: Obtain 800 souls.

LARGE SOUL OF AN UNKNOWN TRAVELER

Use to acquire souls

A large soul found in the corpse of an unknown traveler.

Use to acquire souls.

Let the Fire Keeper transform this sovereignless soul into a source of strength, for to be Unkindled is to be a vessel for souls.

Souls: Obtain 1,000 souls.

SOUL OF A NAMELESS SOLDIER

Use to acquire souls

Soul found in the corpse of a nameless soldier.

Use to acquire souls.

Let the Fire Keeper transform this sovereignless soul into a source of strength, for to be Unkindled is to be a vessel for souls.

Souls: Obtain 2,000 souls.

LARGE SOUL OF A NAMELESS SOLDIER

Use to acquire souls

Large soul found in the corpse of a nameless soldier.

Use to acquire souls.

Let the Fire Keeper transform this sovereignless soul into a source of strength, for to be Unkindled is to be a vessel for souls.

Souls: Obtain 3,000 souls.

SOUL OF A WEARY WARRIOR

Use to acquire many souls

Soul found in the corpse of a battle-weary warrior.

Use to acquire a large amount of souls.

Let the Fire Keeper transform this sovereignless soul into a source of strength, for to be Unkindled is to be a vessel for souls.

Souls: Obtain 5,000 souls.

LARGE SOUL OF A WEARY WARRIOR

Use to acquire many souls

Large soul found in the corpse of a battle-weary warrior.

Use to acquire a large amount of souls.

Let the Fire Keeper transform this sovereignless soul into a source of strength, for to be Unkindled is to be a vessel for souls.

Souls: Obtain 8,000 souls.

SOUL OF A CRESTFALLEN KNIGHT

Use to acquire many souls

Soul found in the corpse of a crestfallen knight.

Use to acquire a large amount of souls.

Let the Fire Keeper transform this sovereignless soul into a source of strength, for to be Unkindled is to be a vessel for souls.

Souls: Obtain 10,000 souls.

LARGE SOUL OF A CRESTFALLEN KNIGHT

Use to acquire many souls

Large soul found in the corpse of a crestfallen knight.

Use to acquire a large amount of souls.

Let the Fire Keeper transform this sovereignless soul into a source of strength, for to be Unkindled is to be a vessel for souls.

Souls: Obtain 20,000 souls.

SOUL OF A PROUD PALADIN

Use to acquire many souls

Soul found in the corpse of a proud paladin.

Use to acquire many souls.

Let the Fire Keeper transform this sovereignless soul into a source of strength, for to be Unkindled is to be a vessel for souls.

Souls: Obtain 500 souls.

LARGE SOUL OF A PROUD PALADIN

Use to acquire many souls

Large soul found in the corpse of a proud paladin.

Use to acquire many souls.

Let the Fire Keeper transform this sovereignless soul into a source of strength, for to be Unkindled is to be a vessel for souls.

Souls: Obtain 1,000 souls.

SOUL OF AN INTREPID HERO

Use to acquire numerous souls

Soul found in the corpse of an intrepid hero.

Use to acquire a great helping of souls.

Let the Fire Keeper transform this sovereignless soul into a source of strength, for to be Unkindled is to be a vessel for souls.

Souls: Obtain 2,000 souls.

LARGE SOUL OF AN INTREPID HERO

Use to acquire numerous souls

Large soul found in the corpse of an intrepid hero.

Use to acquire a great helping of souls.

Let the Fire Keeper transform this sovereignless soul into a source of strength, for to be Unkindled is to be a vessel for souls.

Souls: Obtain 2,500 souls.

SOUL OF A SEASONED WARRIOR

Use to acquire numerous souls

Soul found in the corpse of a seasoned warrior.

Use to acquire a great helping of souls.

Let the Fire Keeper transform this sovereignless soul into a source of strength, for to be Unkindled is to be a vessel for souls.

Souls: Obtain 5,000 souls.

LARGE SOUL OF A SEASONED WARRIOR

Use to acquire numerous souls

Large soul found in the corpse of a seasoned warrior.

Use to acquire a great helping of souls.

Let the Fire Keeper transform this sovereignless soul into a source of strength, for to be Unkindled is to be a vessel for souls.

Souls: Obtain 7,500 souls.

SOUL OF AN OLD HAND

Use to acquire innumerable souls

Soul found in the corpse of an old hand at war.

Use to acquire innumerable souls.

Let the Fire Keeper transform this sovereignless soul into a source of strength, for to be Unkindled is to be a vessel for souls.

Souls: Obtain 12,500 souls.

SOUL OF A VENERABLE OLD HAND

Use to acquire innumerable souls

Large soul found in the corpse of an old hand at war.

Use to acquire innumerable souls.

Let the Fire Keeper transform this sovereignless soul into a source of strength, for to be Unkindled is to be a vessel for souls.

Souls: Obtain 20,000 souls.

SOUL OF A CHAMPION

Use to acquire enough souls to sate a lord

Soul found in the corpse of a champion of legend.

Use to acquire enough souls to sate a lord.

Let the Fire Keeper transform this sovereignless soul into a source of strength, for to be Unkindled is to be a vessel for souls.

Souls: Obtain 25,000 souls.

SOUL OF A GREAT CHAMPION

Use to acquire enough souls to sate a lord

Large soul found in the corpse of a champion of legend.

Use to acquire enough souls to sate a lord.

Let the Fire Keeper transform this sovereignless soul into a source of strength, for to be Unkindled is to be a vessel for souls.

Souls: Obtain 50,000 souls.

BOSS SOULS

Powerful souls, typically found by defeating the powerful bosses in the game. After defeating the Cursed Greatwood in the Undead Settlement, you find the Transposition Kiln. Given to Ludleth in the Firelink Shrine, this allows him to create Soul-transposed weapons and equipment from these great souls. Each great soul can be transposed into two different items, usually weapons, but sometimes spells or rings. You can also use these souls to gain Souls, but doing so is usually a waste unless you are far into multiple playthroughs and no longer need the weapons or spells! One special note here, the Twin Princes souls provide two different swords that can be combined by Ludleth... which means the only way to do this is complete the game twice to acquire both blades!

SOUL OF ROSARIA

Soul of Rosaria, Mother of Rebirth

The soul of Rosaria, Mother of Rebirth, stolen by Ringfinger Leonhard.
Return this to her extant corpse, and mother Rosaria will spring back to life.
As if nothing had ever happened.

Souls: Obtain 5,000 souls.

SOUL OF BOREAL VALLEY VORDT

One of the twisted souls, steeped in strength

Soul of Vordt of the Boreal Valley. One of the twisted souls, steeped in strength.
Use to acquire many souls, or transpose to extract its true strength.
Vordt served as an outrider knight, never far from the fleeting dancer.

Transmute to Weapons: Vordt's Great Hammer or Pontiff's Left Eye

Souls: Obtain 2,000 souls.

SOUL OF THE ROTTED GREATWOOD

One of the twisted souls, steeped in strength

Soul of the Curse-rotted Greatwood. One of the twisted souls, steeped in strength.
Use to acquire many souls, or transpose to extract its true strength.

Ever since its establishment, all manner of curses have managed to seep into the Undead Settlement. The worst of them were sealed away inside a spirit tree, but eventually the curses took their toll.

Transmute to Weapons: Hollowslayer Greatsword or Arstor's Spear

Souls: Obtain 3,000 souls.

SOUL OF A CRYSTAL SAGE

One of the twisted souls, steeped in strength

Soul of a Crystal Sage. One of the twisted souls, steeped in strength.
Use to acquire many souls, or transpose to extract its true strength.

The twin Crystal Sages once served as spiritual guides to the scholars of the Grand Archives, and one went on to ally with the Undead Legion.

Transmute to Weapons: Crystal Sage's Rapier or Crystal Hail

Souls: Obtain 3,000 souls.

SOUL OF THE DEACONS OF THE DEEP

One of the twisted souls, steeped in strength

Soul of the Deacons of the Deep. One of the twisted souls, steeped in strength.
Use to acquire many souls, or transpose to extract its true strength.

After Aldrich left for the Boreal valley, Archdeacon Royce remained in the cathedral with the high priests, to keep eternal watch over their master's coffin.

Transmute to Weapons: Deep Soul or Cleric's Candlestick

Souls: Obtain 20,000 souls.

SOUL OF HIGH LORD WOLNIR

One of the twisted souls, steeped in strength

Soul of the High Lord Wolnir. One of the twisted souls, steeped in strength.
Use to acquire many souls, or transpose to extract its true strength.

Lord Wornir of Carthus sentenced countless souls to gruesome deaths, keen to outlive them all.

Transmute to Weapons: Black Serpent or Wolnir's Holy Sword

Souls: Obtain 10,000 souls.

SOUL OF PONTIFF SULYVAHN

One of the twisted souls, steeped in strength

Soul of Pontiff Sulyvahn. One of the twisted souls, steeped in strength.
Use to acquire many souls, or transpose to extract its true strength.

Pontiff Sulyvahn of Irithyll imprisoned a god of the old royalty in the abandoned cathedral, to be fed to the devourer.

Transmute to Weapons: Greatsword of Judgment or Profaned Greatsword

Souls: Obtain 12,000 souls.

SOUL OF THE DANCER

One of the twisted souls, steeped in strength

Soul of the dancer. One of the twisted souls, steeped in strength.
Use to acquire many souls, or transpose to extract its true strength.

The Pontiff Sulyvahn bestowed a double-slashing sword upon a distant daughter of the formal royal family, ordering her to serve first as a dancer, and then as an outrider knight, the equivalent to exile.

Transmute to Weapons: Dancer's Enchanted Swords or Soothing Sunlight

Souls: Obtain 10,000 souls.

SOUL OF DRAGONSLAYER ARMOUR

One of the twisted souls, steeped in strength

Soul of the Dragonslayer Armour. One of the twisted souls, steeped in strength.
Use to acquire many souls, or transpose to extract its true strength.

The Dragonslayer Armour, controlled by the Pilgrim Butterfly, lost its master long ago, but still remembers their sporting hunts.

Transmute to Weapons: Dragonslayer Greataxe or Dragonslayer Greatshield

Souls: Obtain 15,000 souls.

SOUL OF A DEMON

One of the twisted souls, steeped in strength

Soul of a demon. One of the twisted souls, steeped in strength.
Use to acquire numerous souls, or transpose to extract its true strength.

Demons were born of the Chaos Flame, but the flame has not survived, and the demons are a dying race.

Transmute to Weapons: Demon's Greataxe or Demon's Fist

Souls: Obtain 20,000 souls.

SOUL OF A STRAY DEMON

One of the twisted souls, steeped in strength

Soul of the Stray Demon. One of the twisted souls, steeped in strength.
Use to acquire numerous souls, or transpose to extract its true strength.

The Stray Demon, now lacking even a trace of flame, was once the gatekeeper of Lothric.

Transmute to Weapons: Heavy Boulder or Havel's Ring

Souls: Obtain 20,000 souls.

SOUL OF THE OLD DEMON KING

One of the twisted souls, steeped in strength

Soul of the Old Demon King. One of the twisted souls, steeped in strength.
Use to acquire many souls, or transpose to extract its true strength.

The shriveled Old Demon King is now like a clump of burnt ash, but he is the last living witness of the Chaos of Izalith.

Transmute to Weapons: Old King's Great Hammer or Chaos Bed Vestiges

Souls: Obtain 10,000 souls.

SOUL OF CONSUMED OCEIROS

One of the twisted souls, steeped in strength

Soul of Oceiros, the Consumed King. One of the twisted souls, steeped in strength.

Use to acquire numerous souls, or transpose to extract its true strength.

Oceiros went mad trying to harness his royal blood for a greater purpose, leading him to the heretics of the Grand Archives, where he discovered the twisted worship of Seath the paledrake.

Transmute to Weapons: Moonlight Greatsword or White Dragon Breath

Souls: Obtain 12,000 souls.

SOUL OF CHAMPION GUNDYR

One of the twisted souls, steeped in strength

Soul of the champion Gundyr. One of the twisted souls, steeped in strength.

Use to acquire many souls, or transpose to extract its true strength.

Once, a champion came late to the festivities, and was greeted by a shrine without fire, and a bell that would not toll.

Transmute to Weapons: Gundyr's Halberd or Giant's Chain

Souls: Obtain 20,000 souls.

SOUL OF THE NAMELESS KING

One of the twisted souls, steeped in strength

Soul of the Nameless King. One of the twisted souls, steeped in strength.

Use to acquire many souls, or transpose to extract its true strength.

The Nameless King was once a dragon-slaying god of war, before he sacrificed everything to ally himself with the ancient dragons.

Transmute to Weapons: Dragonslayer Swordspear or Storm Curved Sword and Lightning Storm

Souls: Obtain 16,000 souls.

SOUL OF THE BLOOD OF THE WOLF

One of the twisted souls, steeped in strength

Soul of the Blood of the Wolf. One of the twisted souls, steeped in strength.

Use to acquire numerous souls, or transpose to extract its true strength.

The blood was spread amongst the Abyss Watchers, and their souls are one with the soul of the wolf blood master.

Transmute to Weapons: Farron Greatsword or Wolf Knight's Greatsword

Souls: Obtain 20,000 souls.

SOUL OF YHORM THE GIANT

One of the twisted souls, steeped in strength

Soul of Yhorm the Giant. One of the twisted souls, steeped in strength.

Use to acquire numerous souls, or transpose to extract its true strength.

Yhorm is the descendant of an ancient conqueror, but was asked by the very people once subjugated to lead them, serving as both a weighty blade and a stone-hard shield.

Transmute to Weapons: Yhorm's Greatshield or Yhorm's Great Machete

Souls: Obtain 20,000 souls.

SOUL OF ALDRICH

One of the twisted souls, steeped in strength

Soul of Aldrich. One of the twisted souls, steeped in strength.

Use to acquire many souls, or transpose to extract its true strength.

When Aldrich ruminated on the fading of the fire, it inspired visions of a coming age of the deep sea. He knew the path would be arduous, but he had no fear. He would devour the gods himself.

Transmute to Weapons: Lifehunt Scythe or Darkmoon Longbow

Souls: Obtain 15,000 souls.

SOUL OF THE TWIN PRINCES

One of the twisted souls, steeped in strength

Soul of the Twin Princes. One of the twisted souls, steeped in strength.

Use to acquire numerous souls, or transpose to extract its true strength.

The two princes rejected their duty to become Lords of Cinder, and settled down far, far away to watch the fire fade from a distance. A curse makes their souls nearly inseparable.

Transmute to Weapons: Lorian's Greatsword or Lothric's Holy Sword

Souls: Obtain 20,000 souls.

SOUL OF THE LORDS

One of the twisted souls, steeped in strength

Soul of the Lords. One of the twisted souls, steeped in strength.

Use to acquire numerous souls, or transpose to extract its true strength.

Since Lord Gwyn, the first Lord of Cinder, many exalted lords have linked the First Flame, and it is their very souls that have manifested themselves as defender of the flame.

Transmute to Weapons: Firelink Greatsword or Sunlight Spear

Souls: Obtain 20,000 souls.

COVENANT ITEMS

Items specific to the various multiplayer Covenants in the game, turning these in to their respective Covenant leaders allows you to acquire special rewards. These are earned by completing multiplayer tasks that suit your Covenant, whether cooperative boss defeats, defending against invading red spirits, winning duels, or slaying hosts or blue spirits.

SUNLIGHT MEDAL
Medal received for victory in co-op
A medal received by members of the Warrior of Sunlight covenant for victory over the final foe when summoned. The summoner also gains the same medal.

The medal, engraved with the holy symbol of the sun, is slightly warm, and reminds one of the great honor of a shared victory.

PROOF OF A CONCORD KEPT
Proof a dark spirit was felled by a Blue Sentinel
Blood-drained, shrunken ear. Souvenir taken for subduing the guilty.

The knights called the Blades of the Darkmoon punish the guilt-soaked offenders of the Gods and take this as proof of their conquest. The earless corpses of the guilty will be left behind as a warning to others, inspiring both fear and respect for the Gods. Such is the eternal mandate of the Dark Sun.

PROOF OF A CONCORD WELL KEPT
Proof a dark spirit was felled by a Blue Sentinel
Distinguished proof that one has hunted the enemies of the gods, as per the ancient accord with the Way of Blue.

The layered ear of a dark spirit is the mark of a particularly guilty offender, one who has flagrantly violated one god or another.

Only acquired by defeating an Aldrich Faithful as a Blue Phantom. Use to acquire two Proofs of a Concord Kept.

PALE TONGUE
Proof of invader's victory over a Host of Embers
Proof of a red orb invader's victory over a Host of Embers.

Claiming tongues as trophies was originally the practice of an infamous troupe of invaders, who offered them to their speechless goddess.

FORKED PALE TONGUE
Proves a blue spirit has been fended off
Proof that a red eye orb invader successfully fended off a blue spirit.

Those who hunt dark spirits take the names of gods in ancient accord with the Way of Blue, a deception exemplified by their forked tongues.

Use to acquire two Pale Tongues.

VERTEBRA SHACKLE
Special bone found by killing in other worlds
A special bone collected by members of the covenant of Mound-makers, discovered in the corpses of their victims.

Only one such bone is found in the vertebrae, and the Mound-makers believe it to be a shackle of the gods. In their minds, each victim is another connection, an addition to the family.

WOLF'S BLOOD SWORDGRASS
Proves a Watchdog of Farron has met their duty
A leaf signifying a duty fulfilled by the Watchdogs of Farron, who stand beside the old wolf to ensure the serenity of those at rest. Depicts a swordgrass leaf stained with dried blood.

Long ago, the swordgrass leaf quietly identified members of the Undead Legion. In the rotted forest rest the spirits of warriors past, their acceptance of and gratitude toward their guardians is expressed eloquently by the humble leaf.

HUMAN DREGS
Proves an Aldrich Faithful has met their duty
Proof of a duty fulfilled by the Aldrich Faithful, who patiently await the Devourer of Gods' return.

Dregs are the heaviest things within the human body, and will sink to the lowest depths imaginable, where they become the shackles that bind this world.

SPECIAL ITEMS

A handful of special items, mostly focused on multiplayer interactions. The White and Red Soapstones allow you to engage in cooperative or voluntary PvP play, while the Red Eye Orbs allow for PvP invasions. The Seed of a Giant Tree is a special item that can help to defend against invaders, by causing all monsters in the area to react to the invading phantom and attack it! You can find these Seeds dropped by the Giant Tree just outside the Firelink Shrine every now and then. And no, there is no special use for the Pendant, long time *Souls* veterans may remember similarly charming accessories in previous games...

WHITE SIGN SOAPSTONE
Leave white co-op summon sign
Online play item. Create a co-op summon sign.

Be summoned to another world as a phantom through your sign, and defeat the area boss to gain the strength of flame.

The nature of Lothric is murky, unclear. The White Sign Soapstone allows Unkindled to assist one another.

RED SIGN SOAPSTONE
Leave red antagonising invasion sign
Online play item. Create a hostile red invasion sign.

Be summoned to another world as a dark spirit, and defeat the Host of Embers to gain the strength of fire.

Not all dark spirits are unsporting, or they wouldn't make use of this soapstone.

BLACK SEPARATION CRYSTAL
Banish visiting phantom, or return home
A charm of farewell granted to banished Undead. The crystal sends phantoms back to their homes, or you back to yours.

Beware of fickle use of this item if you intend to nurture relations.

CRACKED RED EYE ORB
Consume to invade another world
Online play item. Allows a single invasion of another world.

Defeat the Host of Embers of the world you have invaded to gain the strength of fire.

The Cracked Red Orb is far from perfect, it seems, as Ringfinger Leonhard knows all too well.

RED EYE ORB

Invade other worlds at will

Online play item. Invade other worlds at will.

Defeat the Host of Embers of the world you have invaded to gain the strength of fire.

The Red Eye Orb is rooted in a tiny land swallowed by darkness long ago. Some choose to put the orb to other uses. To embark on this path, enter the service of Rosaria in the Cathedral of the Deep.

DRIED FINGER

Should only be used with the greatest of caution

Online play item. Dried finger with multiple knuckles.

Use to strengthen connection to other worlds, allowing the summoning of a third phantom, but also a second dark spirit.

Also makes the summoning of a dark spirit occur earlier. Use with caution.

WAY OF WHITE CIRCLET

Restore the link to other worlds

Online play item. Restore the connection to other worlds.

Those who engage in unjust deeds when in contact with other worlds will lose their connection to them.

Way of White Circlets assume such sin as their own, but are found few and far between. Acting without honor will never be without risk.

Repeatedly disconnecting from online sessions blocks you from using online play. Use this item to restore your connectivity. A new one only reappears about twice a day, so don't abuse disconnects!

PENDANT

No effect

This faintly warm medal, engraved with the symbol of the Sun, is the ultimate honor, awarded to show who summon the Warrior of Sunlight and complete a goal.

The symbol represents Lord Gwyn's firstborn, who lost his deity status and was expunged from the annals. But the old God of War still watches closely over his warriors.

BLACK EYE ORB

Invade the world of Rosalia's killer

Arcane orb left on Rosalia's corpse.

Have faith her soul can be retrieved, by invading the world of her killer, and returning victorious.

The Black Eye is proof of vengeance, but often appears serene as it casts its gaze toward Irithyll.

SEED OF A GIANT TREE

Enemies react to invaders

Makes enemies react to invaders.

The giant trees were also known as watcher trees, and their seeds unmask invaders.

When used effectively, these seeds will help counter dark spirits.

KNIGHT REGISTER

Displays online list of Darkmoon Knights

Online play item. A roster of knights of the Darkmoon who have served since the age of the old Royals.

Use to discover the names of Darkmoon Knights, an order of elite knights shrouded in shadows.

MATERIALS

Materials are used to improve your weapons at the Blacksmith. There are two types of upgrades you can do, **Enhancement**, which increases their stats (up to +5 for special weapons, up to +10 for normal ones), and **Infusion**, which allows you to apply a special Gem that grants unique effects to the weapon.

ENHANCEMENT

Enhancement is done with one of three different materials: pure Titanite (Shards, Large Shards, and Chunks), Twinkling Titanite (for unique weapons), and Titanite Scales (for special weapons created from powerful Souls). To reach the maximum level on *any* item requires a rare Titanite Slab.

It takes 12 basic Titanite for each set of +3 levels, finishing with a Titanite Slab for a total of 36 Titanite of three tiers to reach +9. Twinkling and Scale weapons require 15 of their respective type to reach +4. All weapons require a Titanite Slab to reach max level, be it +10 or +5.

Because Twinkling and Scale weapons are so expensive to upgrade to +4 with a rare material, consider upgrading a few that you enjoy using to +3 instead, and saving the +4 and +5 upgrades for a single weapon you really enjoy using.

Reinforcing a shield has little impact on its defensive attributes, *except* for Stability, which gains about a point per level. This isn't a great amount, but in a lot of cases, you're going to be using your shield for the majority of the game, so there's no reason not to squeeze every little bit of defensive utility out of it as you can. When you have the Titanite to spare, upgrade your shield to boost its Stability.

NORMAL ITEM LEVEL	TITANITE REQUIRED
+1	2 Titanite Shards
+2	4 Titanite Shards
+3	6 Titanite Shards
+4	2 Large Titanite Shards
+5	4 Large Titanite Shards
+6	6 Large Titanite Shards
+7	2 Titanite Chunks
+8	4 Titanite Chunks
+9	6 Titanite Chunks
+10	Titanite Slab

SOUL-TRANSPOSED ITEM LEVEL	TITANITE SCALES REQUIRED
+1	1 Titanite Scale
+2	2 Titanite Scales
+3	4 Titanite Scales
+4	8 Titanite Scales
+5	Titanite Slab

SOULBOUND ITEM LEVEL	TWINKLING TITANITE REQUIRED
+1	1 Twinkling Titanite
+2	2 Twinkling Titanite
+3	4 Twinkling Titanite
+4	8 Twinkling Titanite
+5	Titanite Slab

INFUSION

Infusion uses one of fifteen different special Gems to imbue a mundane weapon with a special attribute. The effects vary from enhancing the attribute scaling on a weapon (how much benefit they get from a high level of Str or Dex for example) to adding elemental damage, or even Poison or Bleed.

There is also a special Gem that can be used to *remove* an infusion from a weapon—infusions are separate from enhancement, you can have a +7 Blessed weapon, remove the Blessed infusion and you will still have a +7 weapon. This allows you to change your infusions based on need, or simply to experiment with other options on a favored weapon.

Infusing Shields has an odd impact on their stats, you can *very* slightly boost one elemental resist, at the cost of weakening all other defenses. This is rarely worth it, barring very rare cases where you want to block one specific high damage attack (likely from a boss).

Infusing a shield with a Blessed or Simple Gem can be useful, as you regen HP or FP even with the shield on your back, nice for two handed setups.

BLESSED GEM

Infuse to create blessed weapon

A gem of infused titanite. Commonly known as a charm kept by saints.

Used in infusion to create blessed weapons.

Special blessed weapons gradually restore HP and heavily damage reanimated foes.

Gains Faith scaling, deals 20% greater damage to reanimated undead (Skeletons and the like), and heals HP slowly over time.

It's worthwhile to make at least one Blessed weapon for the Catacombs of Carthus, and the HP regen ability isn't bad either. If you're exceptionally patient you can keep a backup un-upgraded Blessed weapon around solely to use as a source of HP regen, but there are very few situations so dire you actually need to use such a tactic to survive. In most cases you'd be better off simply using a Homeward Bone if you're that tapped out!

BLOOD GEM

Infuse to create lacerating weapon

A gem of infused titanite. Slurped by Irithyll slaves.

Used in infusion to create lacerating weapons.

Such weapons inflict lacerating damage. Most effective with sharp or spiked weapons.

Adds a Bleed effect to a weapon. If the weapon already has a Bleed attribute, slightly enhances the Bleed intensity.

Like other status effects, Bleeding effects are generally best on nimble weapons that you can strike with repeatedly, to build up the Bleed quickly and cause it to trigger before it falls off.

Bleed and Poison both are slightly enhanced by the Luck attribute, though the effect is small without a heavy investment in the stat.

CHAOS GEM

Infuse to create chaos weapon

A gem of infused titanite. Relics of lands scorched by the Chaos Flame.

Used in infusion to create chaos weapons.

Chaos weapons inflict fire damage, and scale with intelligence and faith.

Adds Fire damage and gives the weapon Int and Faith scaling. Unlike the Fire Gem, which removes all scaling, this gem is worth using if you are planning on investing heavily in Pyromancy (or all types of magic), and thus raising your Int and Faith considerably.

CRYSTAL GEM

Infuse to create crystal weapon

A gem of infused titanite. Introduced to Lothric by the Crystal Sages.

Used in infusion to create crystal weapons.

Crystal weapons inflict magic damage, and scale effectively with intelligence.

Adds Magic damage and Int scaling to a weapon. Ideal for casters focusing on Sorceries. A backup Magic damage weapon isn't a bad idea for places where you are dealing with Fire resistant foes (such as the fire demons in the Smouldering Lake).

DARK GEM

Infuse to create dark weapon

A gem of infused titanite. Born of disembodied humanity.

Used in infusion to create dark weapons.

Dark weapons inflict dark damage, and scale with faith.

Adds Dark damage and lets the weapon scale with Faith. Essentially the Miracle caster analog of the Crystal Gem, this gives you a scaling elemental weapon if you plan to invest heavily in Faith.

DEEP GEM

Infuse to create deep weapon

A gem of infused titanite. Found in the dregs of the Cathedral of the Deep.

Used in infusion to create deep weapons.

Deep weapons inflict dark damage, but lose scaling effects.

There is a darkness that lies beyond human ken.

A flat non-scaling Dark damage addition, weapons infused with a Deep Gem lose scaling effects, but gain a good amount of flat damage, making them suitable for characters not investing heavily in Str or Dex.

FIRE GEM

Infuse to create fire weapon

A gem of infused titanite. Found in rare cases inside demons.

Used in infusion to create fire weapons.

Fire weapons inflict fire damage, but lose scaling effects.

Identical to Deep Gems, but adding Fire instead of Dark damage. Quite a few enemies are vulnerable to Fire damage, making this a safe early choice for a solid weapon to upgrade.

Even if you plan on investing into Str, Dex, or both, a Fire (or Deep) weapon can often eclipse their scaling damage until your stat levels are raised quite a bit. This makes Fire and Deep weapons ideal early in the game before your stat scaling kicks in heavily.

Both types of weapon are strong enough to go all the way to the end of a normal playthrough, though you may wish to move to scaling weapons for NG+ playthroughs.

HEAVY GEM

Infuse to create heavy weapon

A gem of infused titanite. Famously used to forge Farron greatswords.

Used in infusion to create heavy weapons.

A warrior can appreciate a heavy weapon, for they scale effectively with strength.

Removes other scaling to boost (or provide) strong Str scaling.

Ideal for a brute force melee character, a Heavy Str weapon can be boosted to significant levels of physical damage fairly early in the game.

HOLLOW GEM

Infuse to create Hollow weapon

A gem of infused titanite. A stone plentiful in Londor, land of Hollows.

Used in infusion to create Hollow weapons.

Hollow weapons are said to peer into the essence of its wielder, whose luck boosts attack.

An unusual infusion, the Hollow Gem gives a weapon enhanced scaling with Luck. As this is generally not a stat you can afford to raise early in a character's life, this puts the Hollow Gem in a limited niche for characters making use of Poison or Bleed effects (which slightly benefit from Luck as well).

LARGE TITANITE SHARD

Reinforce weapon to +6

Titanite shard for weapon reinforcement. A larger shard that reinforces weapons to +6.

Titanite shards are fragments of the Legendary Slabs. Titanite is etched into weapons to reinforce.

Medium strength reinforcement, Large Titanite Shards let you get your weapons up to scratch with enemies throughout the mid game. Once you can purchase these, it's well worth upgrading several weapons to +6 to have different elemental options open.

LIGHTNING GEM

Infuse to create lightning weapon

A gem of infused titanite. Found in the aftermath of dragon hunts.

Used in infusion to create lightning weapons.

Lightning weapons inflict lightning damage, and scale with faith.

Adds Lightning damage and grants Faith scaling. Miracle users are already specialists in dealing Lightning damage with spells, this infusion lets you benefit from the Faith investment on your weapon as well.

REFINED GEM

Infuse to create refined weapon

A gem of infused titanite. Forged the weapons of Lothric knights.

Used in infusion to create refined weapons.

Refined weapons are difficult to wield properly, and scale effectively with strength and dexterity.

Provides a weapon with enhanced Str and Dex scaling. Because it requires both, this infusion is weaker than Heavy or Sharp (and sometimes even Raw) unless both of your stats are raised to a high level.

If you are planning on making use of certain weapons with naturally high base Str and Dex requirements, this can be a useful infusion, and you gain the benefit of good ranged weapon potential as well, but this is the most demanding of the physically oriented infusions.

POISON GEM

Infuse to create poison weapon

A gem of infused titanite. Discovered in the rotted forest of Farron.

Used in infusion to create poison weapons.

Such weapons inflict poison-laced damage that gradually eats away at foes.

Adds a Poison effect to a weapon, or slightly enhances an existing one. Otherwise functions identically to the Blood Gem, simply enhancing Poison instead.

Like Bleed, Poison also benefits slightly from enhanced Luck.

RAW GEM

Infuse to create raw weapon

A gem of infused titanite. Forged the weapons of Lothric foot soldiers.

Used in infusion to create raw weapons.

Raw weapons are easily wielded and have higher attack, but lose scaling effects.

Raw weapons lose all scaling, but gain enhanced physical damage in exchange. This is essentially the raw physical version of the Fire or Deep gems, giving you flat damage at the cost of scaling.

As with the other two, Raw weapons are useful for characters not planning to invest heavily in Str or Dex, and without an element attached to the weapon, this leaves you free to use elemental enchantments, either from consumable items or spells, and you don't need to worry about Fire or Dark resistant enemies.

SHARP GEM

Infuse to create sharp weapon

A gem of infused titanite. Forged the unique curved swords of Carthus.

Used in infusion to create sharp weapons.

A swordsman can appreciate a sharp weapon, for they scale effectively with dexterity.

Similar but not identical to the Heavy Gem, the Sharp Gem boosts Dex scaling, making it ideal for Fencer archetype characters interested in focusing on Dex based weapons and bows.

SHRIVING STONE

Undo weapon infusion

A gem of infused titanite. Also known as stark stone.

Reverses weapon infusion.

Has the benefit of undoing the effects of infusion without reducing the reinforcement level.

The Shriving Stone is a special type of gem that allows you to remove an infusion from a weapon—but removing the infusion does not affect the reinforcement level, so a +4 weapon stays +4, it simply loses whatever gem effect you had applied. This is useful for 'redoing' a weapon if you decide you want to change its infusion type.

SIMPLE GEM

Infuse to create simple weapon

A gem of infused titanite, said to be an object of infatuation for victims of stunted development.

Used in infusion to create simple weapons.

Simple weapons inflict magic damage and restore FP very gradually, to help even a simpleton muster some mettle.

Simple weapons add Magic damage, benefit from Int scaling, and provide slight FP regeneration. This effect is small, but over the course of a lengthy expedition away from a Bonfire, it can add up to a decent amount of free FP, giving you some extra uses of your weapon skills and spells.

Compared to Crystal weapons, they have better physical damage bonuses, and slightly less Magic damage, but you gain the FP regen in exchange.

TITANITE CHUNK

Reinforce weapon to +9

Titanite chunk for weapon reinforcement. Reinforces weapons to +9.

Few records of chunks exist, and once one was discovered in Lothric, the race to locate Legendary Slabs began, but there have been no reports of success.

The high-tier Titanite material, these are relatively rare until later in the game, and are required to boost your weapons to penultimate level.

TITANITE SCALE

Reinforce soul-transposed weapon to +4

Titanite altered by a soul. Reinforces soul-transposed weapons to +4.

Weapons forged by soul transposition can only be reinforced by titanite of the same kind.

In rare cases, crystal lizards devour souls, growing to monstrous proportion and leaving these great scales.

Weapons created from powerful Souls by Ludleth using the Transposition Kiln can only be reinforced using these rare scales. Typically only found on Ravenous Crystal Lizards, you need to be choosy about which soul-transposed weapons you decide to improve on any given playthrough due to their rarity.

TITANITE SHARD

Reinforce weapon to +3

Titanite shard for weapon reinforcement. Reinforces weapons to +3.

Titanite shards are fragments of the Legendary Slabs. Titanite is etched into weapons to reinforce.

The basic upgrade material, Titanite Shards can enhance your mundane equipment up to +3, giving you a slight edge early in the game.

As these become quite common (and buyable) not too far into the game, don't hesitate to upgrade your less frequently used gear to +3—ranged weapons if you only use them occasionally, your shield, alternate weapons and the like.

TITANITE SLAB

Reinforce weapon to highest level

Titanite slab for weapon reinforcement, said to once belong to the gods. Reinforces weapons to their highest level.

Titanite slabs are smithing materials of the gods, and weapons reinforced with slabs will be admired no less than their precious legendary weapons.

Rare and powerful, complete slabs of Titanite are necessary to infuse any type of weapon to its maximum level.

Because these are so rare, and because you only gain comparatively slight benefits for the jump to the final level, don't sweat having multiple weapons 'stuck' at +9. Save the Slabs for your absolute favorite weapons, particularly if you plan on venturing into NG+ with them.

TWINKLING TITANITE

Reinforce soulbound weapon to +4

Twinkling titanite for weapon reinforcement. Reinforces soulbound weapons to +4.

Soulbound weapons cannot be reinforced with ordinary titanite, nor can they be infused.

Unless one uses this twinkling titanite, which reinforces these weapons without reversing their bolstered strength.

Twinkling Titanite is necessary to upgrade unique soulbound weapons. These are weapons that are not soul-transposed (created by Ludleth from powerful Souls), and not mundane weapons found or purchased.

Twinkling Titanite is fairly rare, though not quite so much as Titanite Scales. Experiment with unique equipment before you decide to use your Twinkling Titanite on it, you want to get the most value from your limited supply.

WEAPON ENHANCEMENT AND INFUSION EXAMPLES

To demonstrate the effect of Infusions on a weapons statline, we've included this chart of a simple Long Sword, imbued with every different Gem in the game at minimum (+0) and maximum enhancement (+10), and at four different stat levels – 10 in every stat, 20, 40, and finally 99.

This should give you a feel for the impact of enhancement, infusion, and attributes on a common weapon. Because weapon scaling improves as a weapon is leveled up, this can result in some cases where at one combination of enhancement level and character attributes, an infusion pulls ahead or falls behind where it was at the previous attribute level.

In general, the non-scaling and single attribute infusions are best in your first playthrough, while the more demanding scaling and multi-attribute infusions work best at the tail end of a playthrough, or when you venture into New Game Plus territory.

Weapons that have different beginning scaling attributes respond slightly differently to the infusions that affect attribute scaling, but the general principles outlined in this table apply across all weapons in the game.

KEY: **p** = Physical damage, **m** = Magic damage, **f** = Fire damage, **d** = Dark damage, **l** = Lightning damage

WEAPON	ATTACK POWER AT LEVEL 0	ATTRIBUTE BONUS AT ALL 10S	ATTRIBUTE BONUS AT ALL 20S	ATTRIBUTE BONUS AT ALL 40S	ATTRIBUTE BONUS AT ALL 99S	STR/DEX/INT/FTH SCALING
Long Sword	110p	+10p	+28p	+70p	+93p	D/D/-/-
Heavy Longsword	107p	+16p	+36p	+64p	+86p	D/-/-/-
Sharp Longsword	104p	+17p	+42p	+81p	+108p	D/D/-/-
Refined Longsword	99p	+17p	+43p	+90p	+128p	C/C/-/-
Crystal Longsword	82p/82m	+4p/+7m	+10p/+19m	+26p/47m	+35p/63m	D/D/B/-
Simple Longsword	82p/82m	+5p/+4m	+14p/+10m	+36p/26m	+49p/35m	D/D/B/-
Fire Longsword	99p/99f	-	-	-	-	D/D/-/-
Chaos Longsword	88p/88f	+2p/+9f	+6/+24f	+16p/60f	+22p/80f	D/D/B/B
Lightning Longsword	82p/82l	+4p/+7l	+10p/+19l	+26p+47l	+35p/63l	D/D/-/B
Deep Longsword	99p/99d	-	-	-	-	D/D/-/-
Dark Longsword	88p/88d	+2p/+9d	+6p/+24d	+16p/60d	+22p/80d	D/D/B/B
*Poison Longsword	99p	+8p	+23p	+56	+75	D/D/-/-
*Blood Longsword	99p	+8p	+23p	+56	+75	D/D/-/-
Raw Longsword	143p	-	-	-	-	D/D/-/-
Blessed Longsword	88p	+14p	+38p	+95	+127p	D/D/-/B
Hollow Longsword	104p	+12p	+32p	+79	+106p	D/D/-/-

WEAPON	ATTACK POWER AT LEVEL 10	ATTRIBUTE BONUS AT ALL 10S	ATTRIBUTE BONUS AT ALL 20S	ATTRIBUTE BONUS AT ALL 40S	ATTRIBUTE BONUS AT ALL 99S	STR/DEX/INT/FTH SCALING
Long Sword	220p	+30p	+79p	+196p	+261p	C/D/-/-
Heavy Longsword	203p	+40p	+91p	+160p	+213p	A/-/-/-
Sharp Longsword	203p	+45p	+109p	+212p	+282p	C/B/-/-
Refined Longsword	198p	+44p	+111p	+230p	+329p	B/B/-/-
Crystal Longsword	104p/143m	+10p/+23m	+27p/60m	+66p/150m	+88p/200m	D/D/A/-
Simple Longsword	110p/126m	+14p/17m	+36p/45m	+91p/112m	+121p/150m	C/D/A/-
Fire Longsword	181p/181f	-	-	-	-	-/-/-/-
Chaos Longsword	110p/143f	+13p/31f	+34p/81f	+84p/200f	+112p/267f	C/D/B/B
Lightning Longsword	104p/143l	+10p/23l	+27p/60l	+66p/150l	+88p/200l	D/D/-/A
Deep Longsword	181p/181d	-	-	-	-	-/-/-/-
Dark Longsword	110p/143d	+13p/31d	+34p/81d	+84p/200d	+112p/267d	C/D/B/B
*Poison Longsword	170p	+23p	+61p	+152p	+202p	C/D/-/-
*Blood Longsword	170p	+23p	+61p	+152p	+202p	C/D/-/-
Raw Longsword	275p	-	-	-	-	-/-/-/-
Blessed Longsword	143p	+33p	+88p	+218p	+291p	C/D/-/A
Hollow Longsword	209p	+38p	+99p	+245p	+327p	C/D/-/-

* Poison Longsword has 33 Poison effect.
* Blood Longsword has 33 Bleed effect.

KEY ITEMS

Key Items are special items, often required for story advancement. There are also keys for unlocking doors, and some of these items can be turned in to NPCs. The Tomes and Scrolls are used to unlock additional spells from Orbeck, Karla, Cornyx, and Irina, while the Ashes can be turned in to the Shrine Handmaid to unlock new items to purchase. Coals should be delivered to the Blacksmith, granting new Infusions for your weapons. Finally you may notice that some of the Ashes are NPC ashes... the only way to acquire these is by being especially dastardly and killing the NPC in question!

BASIN OF VOWS
Place basin at a statue of a beheading knight
Chalice used in old ceremony in which Lothric knights take their vows.
It is only a formality now, but it remains as an empty practice.
Place this basin at a statue of a beheading knight.

BRAILLE DIVINE SUNLIGHT TOME
Learn miracles of the sun
A sacred braille tome of sunlight, written for warriors of the sun covenant.
Give it to a storyteller to learn sun miracles.
Knights of the sunlight covenant are brilliantly beaming co-operators who volley lightning, and hand out medals before disappearing into the sunset.

BRAILLE DIVINE TOME OF CARIM
Learn high miracles of Carim
A sacred braille tome from Carim, filled with advanced miracles.
Give to a storyteller to learn advanced Carim miracles.
In the Way of White, there is a tradition of placing great faith in the words of the blind, and braille tomes are not unusual.

BRAILLE DIVINE TOME OF LOTHRIC
Learn miracles of Lothric
A sacred braille tome from Lothric, filled with miracles for use by knights.
Give to a storyteller to learn Lothric miracles.
It is said that no paladin inside Lothric castle could fall, owing to the divine protection they enjoyed.

CARTHUS PYROMANCY TOME
Learn pyromancies of Carthus
A pyromancy tome from Carthus containing pyromancies crafted for battle.
Give to the old master pyromancer to learn advanced pyromancies of the Great Swamp.
Carthus pyromancies developed in isolation from other forms, explaining their divergent evolution.

GRAVE KEY
Key to a door in the Undead Settlement sewer
Key to a door in the Undead Settlement sewer.
The grave, which no longer receives visitors, was once the site of a statue of Velka, Goddess of Sin, and was believed to pardon wrongdoing, and lift curses.

CINDERS OF A LORD
Cinders of lord left by the Abyss Watchers
Cinders of a lord left by the Abyss Watchers.
If the lords will not return to their thrones themselves, let them return as cinders.
The Watchers of the Abyss swore upon their shared wolf's blood, which also served as their mandate as lords.

CINDERS OF A LORD
Cinders of a lord left by the God Devourer Aldrich
Cinders of a lord left by Aldrich, Devourer of Gods.
If the lords will not return to their thrones themselves, let them return as cinders.
Aldrich became a lord by devouring men, but was disillusioned with his throne, and so took to devouring gods instead.

CINDERS OF A LORD
Cinders of a lord left by the Giant Yhorm
Cinders of a lord left by Yhorm the Giant.
If the lords will not return to their thrones themselves, let them return as cinders.
Lonely Yhorm became a Lord of Cinder to put the Profaned Flame to rest, knowing full well that those who spoke of him as lord were quite insincere.

CINDERS OF A LORD
Cinders of a lord left by Prince Lothric
Cinders of a lord left by Prince Lothric.
If the lords will not return to their thrones themselves, let them return as cinders.
The Lothric bloodline was obsessed with creating a worthy heir, and when this proved impossible, resorted to unspeakable means. Suffice it to say, the path to linking the fire is a cursed one indeed.

COILED SWORD
Thrust in shrine bonfire to activate bonfire warp
Sword missing from the shrine bonfire.
Cannot be equipped as a weapon.
Thrust into the shrine bonfire to restore its power and enable travel between bonfires.
This sword is only bequeathed to chosen ash, as judged by the ludex, who awaits the arrival of ash as a scabbard.

CORNYX'S ASHES
Shrine handmaid will prepare new items
Umbral ash of Cornyx of the Great Swamp. With this, the shrine handmaid will prepare new items.
Cornyx was tired and defeated until he discovered one final pupil, like so many pyromancers before him.

CRYSTAL SCROLL
Learn crystal sorceries
Secret crystal scroll of the Grand Archives of Lothric.
Give to a sorcerer to learn crystal sorceries.
These sorceries are the work of the paledrake, Seath the Scaleless, whom Logan is said to have met, a branch of sorcery that has been carried on by the Crystal Sages.

DARK SIGIL
Accumulates Curse
A black, gaping hole in the flesh that resembles the brand of an Undead.
The darkness of humanity seeps from this bottomless pitch-black hole, the gap filled by the accumulation of the curse.
This Dark Sigil will never heal, but there is a tale told of a Fire Keeper who returned from the Abyss, and brought great comfort to a bearer of the curse.
Gain 1 Dark Sigil each time you level up with Yoel of Londor. Dying with a Dark Sigil raises Hollowing by 1 per Dark Sigil held. Hollowing can be removed with a Purging Stone, but the Dark Sigil can only be removed by the Fire Keeper after giving her the Fire Keeper's Soul, at a cost of next Soul Level x Number of Dark Sigils held.

DEEP BRAILLE DIVINE TOME

Learn miracles of the Deep

A braille divine tome of the Deep, belonging to the deacons of the cathedral.
Give this to a storyteller to learn miracles of the Deep.
Intended to teach divine protection to the deacons of the deep, but later, dark tales
were added to its pages, such that it is now considered a thing profane.
**Can be given to Irina or Karla. Giving to Irina can have consquences
(see NPC chapter).**

DREAMCHASER'S ASHES

Shrine handmaid will prepare new items

Umbral ash of one who dreamt of joining the Undead Legion. With this, the shrine
handmaid will prepare new items.
In the end, the dream chasers who wandered aimlessly in the rotted forest found
a sense of fulfillment.

EASTERNER'S ASHES

Shrine handmaid prepares new item

Umbral ash of an armor merchant from an eastern land. Surely the handmaid of
Firelink Shrine can turn this into a few new things.
The merchant, the captain of a clan of hunters, was fascinated with weaponry.

EYES OF A FIRE KEEPER

Reveals horrors to the sightless Fire Keeper

A pair of dark eyes.
Said to be the eyes of the first Fire Keeper, and the light that was lost by all Fire
Keepers to come.
It reveals to the sightless Fire Keepers things that they should never see.
Giving these to the Fire Keeper unlocks two possible alternate endings.

FIRE KEEPER SOUL

Soul of a Fire Keeper who returned from the Abyss

Soul of a Fire Keeper who is said to have returned from the Abyss.
This Fire Keeper preserves the bonfire, and serves its champion. She is said to
have soothed and accepted the dark sigil, which has tainted her soul.
And yet, her soul will one day embed itself in the bosom of another Fire Keeper.
**Allows the Fire Keeper to remove Dark Sigils, at a cost in Souls. Angers
Yuria of Londor if you do so, and removes one possible ending.**

GOLDEN SCROLL

Learn sorceries of Oolacile

A golden scroll chronicling the vast research of the xanthous scholars.
Give to a sorcerer to learn the arts of Oolacile.
In the lost land of Oolacile, the sorceries orchestrated light, and were said to shine
in golden hues.

GRAVE KEY

Key to a door in Undead settlement sewer

Ring of keys to the Irithyll dungeon held by the jailer.
Opens most cell doors.
On what grounds do they remain imprisoned, considering that by now they are
mindless Hollows, or unrealized, gibbering fools?

GRAVE WARDEN'S ASHES

Shrine handmaid will prepare new items

Umbral ash of the grave warden of the catacombs of Carthus. With this, the shrine
handmaid will prepare new items.
The old man began as a squire, carrying his master's accoutrements. He ended
his days a grave warden, and carried them still.

DRAGON CHASER'S ASHES

Shrine handmaid prepares new item

Umbral ash of the fallen warrior who chose the path of the ancient dragons. With
this, the shrine handmaid will prepare new items.
Whatever it is, it is sure to grant strength to the most unrelenting warriors.

CELL KEY

Key to a cell holding thieves and the like

Key to a cell holding thieves and the like.
There is no shortage of brash thieves in Lothric, and these particular thieves likely
scaled the wall from the Undead Settlement.
But they are only willing to practice their thievery on the High Wall, for their fear of
Lothric castle, rumored to devour men, keeps them clear of its grounds.

EXCREMENT-COVERED ASHES

Shrine handmaiden prepares new item, perhaps

Unclean umbral ash coated with excrement.
Perhaps it's possible the handmaid of Firelink Shrine could turn this into a few
new things...
Oh to savor the sweet pungency but once more...

FARRON COAL

Enable heavy, sharp, and poison infusion

Coal used for weapon infusion.
Long ago, used to forge the greatswords of the Undead Legion of Farron.
Give to the blacksmith in the shrine to allow the use of gems for heavy, sharp, and
poison infusion.

GIANT'S COAL

Enable lightning, simple, and chaos infusion

Coal used for weapon infusion.
It is said that the giant blacksmith of Anor Londo was once the blacksmith of the
gods.
Give to the blacksmith in the shrine to allow the use of gems for lightning, simple,
and chaos infusion.

GRAND ARCHIVES KEY

Key to the main door of Lothric's Grand Archives

Key to the main entrance to the Grand Archives of Lothric.
With the fire fading, and the spreading pus of man tainting the castle, the Grand
Archives closed its doors for good.
Today, only a few of its keys remain. This one likely belonged to Gotthard, one of
the king's Black Hands, who fled the castle.

GRAVE WARDEN PYROMANCY TOME

Learn black flame pyromancies

A pyromancy tome of the grave warden, from the Carthus catacombs.
Give to the pyromancer master to learn black flame sorceries.
High Lord Wolnir of Carthus succumbed to the Abyss, but the pyromancer later
became a grave warden, and discovered the black flame.

GREAT SWAMP PYROMANCY TOME

Learn high pyromancies of the Great Swamp

Pyromancy tome from the Great Swamp containing advanced pyromancies.
Give to the old master pyromancer to learn advanced pyromancies of the Great
Swamp.
Spells of the Great Swamp are passed down from master to pupil. Without a
master, there is no pupil, but without a pupil, there is also no master.

GREIRAT'S ASHES

Shrine handmaid will prepare new items

Umbral ash of Greirat of the Undead Settlement. With this, the shrine handmaid will prepare new items.
Greirat was a thief who fancied himself a martyr for the poor, which is what drove him to climb the wall.

HAWKWOOD'S SWORDGRASS

Message from Hawkwood kept by the blacksmith

Blood-stained swordgrass of Hawkwood, deserter of the Undead Legion.
Traditionally, the Undead Legion of Farron sends the gravest of messages using swordgrass.
Come to the mausoleum in Farron. Only one can take the path of ancient dragons.
Given by the Blacksmith to issue a challenge from Hawkwood, after you acquire the Twinkling Dragon Torso Stone.

HOLLOW'S ASHES

Shrine handmaid prepares new item

Umbral ash of a Hollow who faithfully served a woman, only to become separated from her. With this, the shrine handmaid will prepare new items.
It takes but a brief glance at this thing to easily envision Londor, the foreboding land of Hollows.

IRINA'S ASHES

Shrine handmaid will prepare new items

Umbral ash of Irina of Carim. With this, the shrine handmaid will prepare new items.
Irina was a frail woman. This frailty led to her becoming a saint of Carim, and to her grand treachery.

IZALITH PYROMANCY TOME

Learn chaos pyromancies of Izalith

A pyromancy tome from Izalith containing pyromancies of the witches.
Give to the old master pyromancer to learn chaos pyromancies of Izalith.
Chaos pyromancies manipulate lava, and birthed all later forms of pyromancy.

JAILBREAKER'S KEY

Key to the barred window of Irithyll dungeon

Small silverwork doll depicting a young squire.
In the legendary old city of Irithyll situated in the Boreal Valley, the Pontiff Sulyvahn gave this doll to valued subjects, so that they might use it to cross the barrier when they return home.
Listen carefully, and you can hear it say, Wherever you go, the moon still sets in Irithyll. Wherever you may be, Irithyll is your home.

JAILER'S KEY RING

Irithyllian Jailer's ring, filled with many keys

Key to the barred window in the Irithyll dungeon. But the window only leads to a bottomless black pit below, and above, a paltry view of the ruined Profaned Capital.
The very architecture appears to be a cruel joke the jailers played on would-be escapees.

KARLA'S ASHES

Shrine handmaid will prepare new items

Umbral ash of Karla. With this, the shrine handmaid will prepare new items.
The spurned child of the Abyss never dies, but phases in and out of its fringes.
Only, there is no one to search for her any longer.

LIFT CHAMBER KEY

Key to the underground lift

Key to the room of the lift that descends to the deepest dungeon in Lothric.
A surviving Darkwraith, from the land swallowed by darkness, is said to be held there.
Given by Ringfinger Leonhard in Firelink Shrine after talking with him several times.

LOGAN'S SCROLL

Learn Logan's sorceries

Secret scroll of the Profaned Capital court sorcerers, containing sorceries of Logan.
Give to a sorcerer to learn Logan's sorceries.
The court sorcerers used this scroll to claim heirship to Logan's legacy, though how that claim stands up to closer scrutiny is another story.

LONDOR BRAILLE DIVINE TOME

Learn Londor miracles

A braille tome of Londor, first spoken by Liliane of the Sable Church.
Give this to a storyteller to learn miracles of Londor.
This is a forbidden tome, as it offers salvation to all Hollows, and conversely curses all things living.
Can be given to Irina or Karla. Giving to Irina can have consquences (see NPC chapter).

MORTICIAN'S ASHES

Shrine handmaid will prepare new items

Umbral ash of a resident of the Undead Settlement who made a living burying corpses.
With this, the shrine handmaid will prepare new items.

OLD CELL KEY

Key to the oldest cell in all of Irithyll dungeon

Key to the oldest cell in the Irithyll dungeon.
The first prisoner of the dungeon was a lone giant. Cells for men were built at his feet.

ORBECK'S ASHES

Shrine handmaid will prepare new items

Umbral ash of Orbeck of Vinheim. With this, the shrine handmaid will prepare new items.
Orbeck was fascinated with sorcery but without means, so offered to serve as an assassin in exchange for acceptance into the Dragon Academy, believing that one day he could reinvent himself as a sorcerer.

PALADIN'S ASHES

Shrine handmaid will prepare new items

Umbral ash of a worn-out paladin who sought the Cathedral of the Deep. With this, the shrine handmaid will prepare new items.
This paladin paid quite a price for his headstrong justice.

PATCHES' ASHES

Shrine handmaid prepares new items

Umbral ash of Unbreakable Patches. With this, the shrine handmaid will prepare new items.
Patches never lost heart, and never looked back. He marched in one direction, and that direction was dead ahead. Did you see him passing by?

PRISONER CHIEF'S ASHES

Shrine handmaid prepares new item

Umbral ash of the prisoner chief of the catacombs.
With this, the shrine handmaid will prepare new items.
The prisoner chief used his clout to hoard all manner of things, but died without putting them to use.

QUELANA PYROMANCY TOME

Learn Quelana pyromancies

A pyromancy tome of Quelana containing her unique spells. These pyromancies can only be taught by a female master.
Give to a female pyromancy master to learn Quelana's pyromancies.
Quelana, the sole surviving witch of Izalith, once accepted a human pupil, but after the pupil moved on, she never took another.

SAGE'S SCROLL

Learn sorceries of the Crystal Sages

Scroll containing sorceries of the Crystal Sages.
Give to a sorcerer to learn sorceries of the Sages.
As any sorcerer knows, sorcery is a talent, and these sorceries were refined to nurture a very special talent.

SMALL LOTHRIC BANNER

Hold up outside the main castle gate to be taken

Small banner held by Lothric messengers.
Hold up outside the main castle gate to be greeted by an escort.
When the High Wall appeared, the path to the Undead Settlement was blocked, and messengers came bearing this banner. They were sent out with a duty, but had no way of returning.

TOWER KEY

Key to the dilapidated tower behind the shrine

Key to the decrepit tower behind Firelink Shrine which leads to the Bell Tower.
The Bell Tower is the grave of Fire Keepers past. When a Fire Keeper has served her purpose, she is led to true darkness, where she enjoys a long-deserved sleep.

XANTHOUS ASHES

Shrine handmaid will prepare new items

Umbral ash of a sorcerer who explored the golden sorceries of a long-lost land.
With this, the shrine handmaid will prepare new items.
They were called xanthous scholars, but some foolishly imitate them by simply dressing in yellow.

PROFANED COAL

Enable dark, lacerating, and Hollow infusion

Coal used for weapon infusion.
Remnants of the fire that burned down the Profaned Capital, preserved in an icy skull.
Give to the blacksmith in the shrine to allow the use of gems for dark, blood, and Hollow infusion.

SAGE'S COAL

Enable crystal, blessed, and deep infusion

Coal used for weapon infusion.
The white magic flame produced by this coal was given to the Undead Legion long ago by one of the Crystal Sage twins.
Give to the blacksmith in the shrine to allow the use of gems for crystal, blessed, and dark infusion.

SMALL DOLL

Silverwork doll depicting a young squire

Crest opening the way to Fort Faran, home to the Undead Corps.
Passed down to cursed undead warriors, the stench of death still lingers.
Perhaps Freise of Vinheim will have some use for it...

SWORD OF AVOWAL

Rite of wedlock gives birth to a true Hollow Lord

Ceremonial sword of Londor.
Cannot be equipped as a weapon.
It is said that a rite of wedlock will presage a true Hollow lord.
Your spouse's name is Anri, who patiently awaits a rightful lord, deep within the mausoleum.

TRANSPOSING KILN

Make soul tranposition possible

An old transposing kiln from Courland, crafted with stitched crystal lizard hide.
Give to Ludleth, Lord of Cinder, to conduct soul transposition.
This kiln can transpose twisted souls to craft special items with their concentrated essence. Deemed forbidden by those unable to make proper use of it.

YURIA'S ASHES

Shrine handmaid will prepare new items

Umbral ash of Yuria of Londor. With this, the shrine handmaid will prepare new items.
Having three founders of the Black Church ensured Yuria's legacy would survive. Her two sisters could carry the torch, making certain their lord claims the flame, for the sake of all Hollows.

SPELLS

Magic is an entirely optional part of the game, but it is very useful, and even melee focused characters can get a lot of return out of a few points put towards Int, Faith, or both.

Unless you're intentionally challenging yourself with a specific character concept, it's a good idea to make use of as many spells as you are able—while straight offensive magic tends to be less useful without a lot of points invested, supportive and healing magic is extremely helpful for any character.

Just because you're a brute with 40 Strength doesn't mean you can't heal up between fights with a bit of magic!

Using spells is as simple as equipping a proper Catalyst and attuning spells at a Bonfire. Staffs are used for Sorcery, the Pyromancy Flame for Pyromancy, and a Talisman for Miracles.

You can equip a Catalyst in one of your secondary slots and swap to it as needed. If you are playing an actual combat caster, you probably want to keep it in your main hand so you can still use a shield. If you're mostly using out of combat support magic, it's usually safe to swap out your shield or one-hand your giant weapon for a moment.

You do add on a bit of extra weight to use a Catalyst, but it's a small price to pay for the benefits. Much like ranged combat, spells are another facet of your character's power that you would do well to take full advantage of!

UNLOCKING MAGIC

If you begin the game as a background with a magical history, you start with access to a Catalyst for your respective magic type and a basic spell.

Otherwise, you gain access to all three types of magic when you reach the Undead Settlement, not far into the game.

There are three NPCs there that offer to join and serve you, and if you accept, all three appear in the Firelink Shrine.

Each teaches a different type of magic, and as you explore the world, you can find special items that unlock new spells.

There are a few other spell trainers in the game, one found in the Road of Sacrifices, one in the Irithyll Dungeon, and one who appears in Firelink Shrine if you use Draw Out True Strength five times from Yoel of Londor.

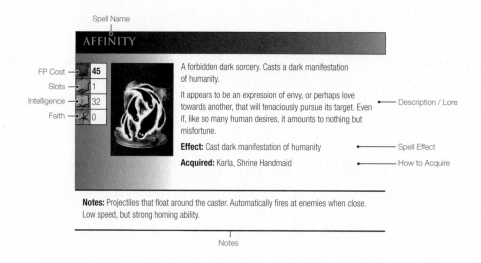

SORCERY

Raw Magical damage and spells that attack primarily with single target focused bolts of energy. Some humanity focused Sorceries dabble in projecting dark damage. Sorcery also has quite a few useful utility spells. Sorcery uses pure Intelligence and your equipped Catalyst's spell bonus to determine spell power.

SORCERY	EFFECT	FP	SLOTS	REQUIREMENTS
Affinity	Cast dark manifestation of humanity	45	1	32/0
Aural Decoy	Distract foes with a distant sound	15	1	18/0
Cast Light	Cast a light to illuminate surroundings	20	1	15/0
Chameleon	Transform into something inconspicuous	20	1	12/0
Crystal Hail	Cast cascade of small crystal soulmasses from sky	25	1	18/0
Crystal Magic Weapon	Reinforce right weapon with crystal	50	1	30/0

SORCERY	EFFECT	FP	SLOTS	REQUIREMENTS
Crystal Soul Spear	Fire piercing crystal soul spear	55	1	48/0
Dark Edge	Strike with blade formed of humanity's darkness	33	1	30/0
Deep Soul	Fire darkened soul sediment	7	1	12/0
Farron Dart	Fire soul dart	3	1	8/0
Farron Flashsword	Attack with a sword formed from souls	5	1	23/0
Farron Hail	Fire cascade of soul darts	2	1	28/0
Great Deep Soul	Fire more powerful darkened soul sediment	11	1	20/0

SORCERY	EFFECT	FP	SLOTS	REQUIREMENTS
Great Farron Dart	Fire more powerful soul dart	4	1	23/0
Great Heavy Soul Arrow	Fire more powerful heavy soul arrow	14	1	18/0
Great Magic Shield	Greatly reinforce left shield with magic	45	1	18/0
Great Magic Weapon	Greatly reinforce right weapon with magic	35	1	15/0
Great Soul Arrow	Fire more powerful soul arrow	11	1	15/0
Heavy Soul Arrow	Fire heavy soul arrow	11	1	13/0
Hidden Body	Turn body nearly invisible	15	1	15/0
Hidden Weapon	Turn right weapon invisible	25	1	12/0
Homing Crystal Soulmass	Release homing crystal soulmass	53	1	30/0
Homing Soulmass	Release homing soulmass	20	1	20/0
Magic Shield	Reinforce left shield with magic	30	1	10/0

SORCERY	EFFECT	FP	SLOTS	REQUIREMENTS
Magic Weapon	Reinforce right weapon with magic	25	1	10/0
Pestilent Mercury	Release mercury that eats away at HP	17	1	30/0
Repair	Repair equipped weapons and armor	20	1	15/0
Soul Arrow	Fire soul arrow	7	1	10/0
Soul Greatsword	Attack with a greatsword formed from souls	28	1	22/0
Soul Spear	Fire soul spear	40	1	32/0
Soul Stream	Fire torrential volley of souls	60	2	45/0
Spook	Mask noises of caster and prevent fall damage	15	1	10/0
Twisted Wall of Light	Distort light in order to deflect magic	10	1	27/0
White Dragon Breath	Emit crystal breath of Seath the Scaleless	30	1	50/0

AFFINITY

| 45 |
| 1 |
| 32 |
| 0 |

A forbidden dark sorcery. Casts a dark manifestation of humanity.

It appears to be an expression of envy, or perhaps love towards another, that will tenaciously pursue its target. Even if, like so many human desires, it amounts to nothing but misfortune.

Effect: Cast dark manifestation of humanity

Acquired: Karla, Shrine Handmaid

Notes: Projectiles that float around the caster. Automatically fires at enemies when close. Low speed, but strong homing ability.

AURAL DECOY

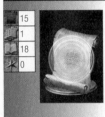

| 15 |
| 1 |
| 18 |
| 0 |

Sorcery developed by a certain surreptitious sorcerer at Vinheim Dragon School.

Distracts foes with a distant sound.

The sound carries with it a strangely infectious resonance that may cause one to stray from their post and expose their back.

Effect: Distract foes with a distant sound

Acquired: Orbeck, Shrine Handmaid

Notes: Attracts enemies' attention by producing a sound somewhere away from you. Effective only against enemies that are not aware of the player yet.

CAST LIGHT

| 20 |
| 1 |
| 15 |
| 0 |

Lost sorcery from Oolacile, land of ancient golden sorceries.

Casts a light to illuminate surroundings.

This light-producing magic is elementary but nonetheless demonstrates the pure nature of golden sorceries; the likes of which have not been developed even at the Dragon School.

Effect: Cast a light to illuminate surroundings

Acquired: Orbeck

Notes: Summons a light source that illuminates surroundings for 60 seconds. Light source follows player.

CHAMELEON

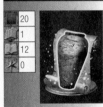

| 20 |
| 1 |
| 12 |
| 0 |

Lost sorcery from Oolacile, land of ancient golden sorceries. Transforms into something inconspicuous.

Far from formally developed, this magic was instead born from the mischief of a young girl who sought relief from the solitude of the woods at dusk.

Effect: Transform into something inconspicuous

Acquired: Irithyll of the Boreal Valley

Notes: Transforms you into an object suitable to your surroundings. Effect is removed when you take any action other than moving.

CRYSTAL HAIL

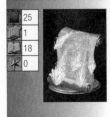

| 25 |
| 1 |
| 18 |
| 0 |

Unique sorcery developed by extraordinary preacher twins known as the Crystal Sages.

Casts a cascade of small crystal soulmasses from above. Crystal soulmasses have piercing qualities.

In a pact said to have been formed long ago, one of the Sages allied with the Undead Legion in order to train the sorcerers of Farron.

Effect: Cast cascade of small crystal soulmasses from sky

Acquired: Crystal Sage Soul

Notes: Fires an orb that breaks off into splinter-like projectiles. These projectiles have slight homing ability.

CRYSTAL MAGIC WEAPON

| 50 |
| 1 |
| 30 |
| 0 |

Further sharpens Magic Weapon via crystallization. Reinforces right weapon with crystal.

After much experimentation, Logan found the crystal medium facilitated a stronger bond between weapon and soul.

Effect: Reinforce right weapon with crystal

Acquired: Orbeck, Crystal Scroll

Notes: Enchants right-hand weapon with magic damage for 45 seconds (strong).

CRYSTAL SOUL SPEAR

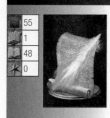

| 55 |
| 1 |
| 48 |
| 0 |

Further sharpens Soul Spear via crystallization.

Fires a piercing crystal soul spear.

According to the Crystal Sages, old Big Hat achieved enlightenment within the Regal Archives, where he came to find the quintessence of sorcery in the facets of a certain crystal.

Effect: Fire piercing crystal soul spear

Acquired: Orbeck, Crystal Scroll

Notes: Powerful projectile that fires relatively quickly. High damage, but FP cost is also high. Pierces through enemies. Stronger than Soul Spear.

DEEP SOUL

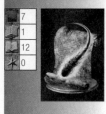

| 7 |
| 1 |
| 12 |
| 0 |

Sorcery of Archdeacon Royce and his deacons, said to have been imparted to them by McDonnell of the Boreal Valley.

Fires dark soul dregs.

Souls which swell from the deep pursue their target, drawn towards life.

Effect: Fire darkened soul sediment

Acquired: Deacons of the Deep Soul

Notes: Homing projectile that steadily accelerates. Has strong homing ability but is relatively slow.

FARRON FLASHSWORD

| 5 |
| 1 |
| 23 |
| 0 |

Alteration of Soul Greatsword developed by sorcerers of the Undead Legion of Farron.

The Legion has a tendency to emphasize speed over power, and this practical alteration of an existing sorcery is no exception.

Effect: Attack with a sword formed from souls

Acquired: Orbeck, Shrine Handmaid

Notes: Cut into enemies with a dagger made of souls. Can be used continuously to perform combo techniques similar to a close-range weapon.

GREAT DEEP SOUL

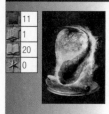

| 11 |
| 1 |
| 20 |
| 0 |

Sorcery which improves upon Deep Soul. Fires powerful darkened soul dregs.

Archdeacon McDonnell, a sorcerer himself, delighted in the cathedral's stagnating souls. For him, they represented the glorious bedrock of this world.

Effect: Fire more powerful darkened soul sediment

Acquired: Aldrich Faithful Reward

Notes: Homing projectile that steadily accelerates. Has strong homing ability but is relatively slow.

DARK EDGE

| 33 |
| 1 |
| 30 |
| 0 |

A forbidden dark sorcery. Strikes with blade formed of humanity's darkness.

Passed from mother to daughter, this blade was intended for both protection and as a means of taking one's own life. The young girl never swung it more than once.

Effect: Strike with blade formed of humanity's darkness

Acquired: Karla, Shrine Handmaid

Notes: Swing down a large sword made of souls.

FARRON DART

| 3 |
| 1 |
| 8 |
| 0 |

Variation of Soul Arrow developed by sorcerers of the Undead Legion of Farron.

Fire a soul dart.

Well known among the Farron sorceries, it is learned far and wide due to its ease of use.

Effect: Fire soul dart

Acquired: Orbeck, Shrine Handmaid

Notes: Low damage, but can fire fast projectiles quickly. Motion changes if used coming from attacking/dashing/rolling states.

FARRON HAIL

| 2 |
| 1 |
| 28 |
| 0 |

Sorcery which improves upon Farron Dart. Fires a cascade of soul darts.

Entrusted to the leader of the Legion's acolytes, and apparently a sorcery of his daughter, Heysel, that was refined by a Crystal Sage.

Effect: Fire cascade of soul darts

Acquired: Orbeck, Sage's Scroll

Notes: Fires low-damage projectiles one after the other. Hits multiple times.

GREAT FARRON DART

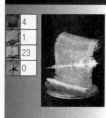

| 4 |
| 1 |
| 23 |
| 0 |

Sorcery which improves upon Farron Dart. Fires a more powerful soul dart.

Entrusted to the leader of the Legion's acolytes, and apparently a sorcery of his daughter, Heysel, that was refined by a Crystal Sage.

Effect: Fire more powerful soul dart

Acquired: Orbeck, Sage's Scroll

Notes: Low damage, but can fire fast projectiles quickly. Motion changes if used coming from attacking/dashing/rolling states.
Stronger than Farron Dart.

GREAT HEAVY SOUL ARROW

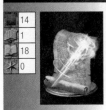

14
1
18
0

Sorcery which improves upon Heavy Soul Arrow. Fires a more powerful heavy soul arrow.

Sorceries are a logical discipline; their strength influenced by the caster's intelligence.

Effect: Fire more powerful heavy soul arrow

Acquired: Orbeck, Shrine Handmaid

Notes: Fires projectile that takes time to cast, but has high damage for its FP cost. Has slight homing ability. Stronger than Heavy Soul Arrow.

GREAT MAGIC WEAPON

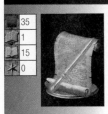

35
1
15
0

Sorcery which improves upon Magic Weapon. Greatly reinforces right weapon with magic.

Only sorcerer-swordsmen with special duties are permitted the use of this spell. The azure blade is said to cut down heavily armored knights with ease.

Effect: Greatly reinforce right weapon with magic

Acquired: Road of Sacrifices

Notes: Enchants right-hand weapon with magic damage for 60 seconds (moderate).

HEAVY SOUL ARROW

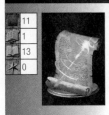

11
1
13
0

Elementary, yet practical sorcery from long ago. Fires a heavy soul arrow.

Offers greater power but slower casting time, entailing a vulnerability that makes this sorcery trickier to handle.

Effect: Fire heavy soul arrow

Acquired: Orbeck, Shrine Handmaid, Yuria

Notes: Fires projectile that takes time to cast, but has high damage for its FP cost. Has slight homing.

HIDDEN WEAPON

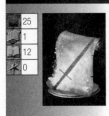

25
1
12
0

Lost sorcery from Oolacile, land of ancient golden sorceries. Turns right weapon invisible.

The weapon itself undergoes no inherent changes. Effective use of this, like any tool, perhaps, is reliant upon the ingenuity of its caster.

Effect: Turn right weapon invisible

Acquired: Orbeck, Golden Scroll

Notes: Makes right-hand weapon transparent for 45 seconds.

GREAT MAGIC SHIELD

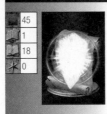

45
1
18
0

Sorcery which improves upon Magic Shield. Greatly reinforces left shield with magic.

Only sorcerer-swordsmen with special duties are permitted the use of this spell, which temporarily grants even the smallest of shields fortitude more akin to that of a greatshield.

Effect: Greatly reinforce left shield with magic

Acquired: Irithyll Dungeon

Notes: Increases damage absorption of left-hand shield to 100% when successfully guarding, and grants x1.5 stability effect. Effect lasts for 30 seconds.

GREAT SOUL ARROW

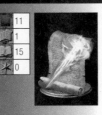

11
1
15
0

Sorcery which improves upon Soul Arrow. Fires a more powerful soul arrow.

Many sorceries inflict magic damage, making them effective against iron armor, tough scales, and other physically resilient materials.

Effect: Fire more powerful soul arrow

Acquired: Orbeck, Shrine Handmaid

Notes: Fires projectile with slight homing ability. Basic attack sorcery. Stronger than Soul Arrow.

HIDDEN BODY

15
1
15
0

Lost sorcery from Oolacile, land of ancient golden sorceries. Turns body nigh on invisible.

Although perfect invisibility is unachievable due to the risk of dissipation, the caster need only stand still for a moment to blend in to environs with astounding camouflage.

Effect: Turn body nearly invisible

Acquired: Orbeck, Golden Scroll

Notes: Makes your body semi-transparent for 20-seconds, reducing range at which enemies spot you to 10%.

HOMING CRYSTAL SOULMASS

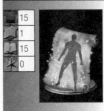

53
1
30
0

Sharpens Homing Soulmass via crystallization.

Releases a homing crystal soulmass. Crystal soulmass has piercing qualities.

According to the Crystal Sages, old Big Hat achieved enlightenment within the Regal Archives, where he came to find the quintessence of sorcery in the facets of a certain crystal.

Effect: Release homing crystal soulmass

Acquired: Orbeck, Crystal Scroll

Notes: Projectiles that float around the caster. Automatically fires at enemies when close. High damage, but FP cost is also high. Pierces through enemies.

HOMING SOULMASS

	20
	1
	20
	0

Sorcery developed by Big Hat Logan, the great sorcerer who left the Dragon School in an age long past.

Releases a homing soulmass.

This sorcery may offer a clue as to what Logan sought, but further investigation suggests its attraction to living things mirrors the nature of the dark.

Effect: Release homing soulmass

Acquired: Orbeck, Logan's Scroll

Notes: Projectiles that float around the caster. Automatically fires at enemies when close. Low damage, but FP cost is also low.

MAGIC WEAPON

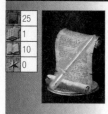

	25
	1
	10
	0

Sorcery for casters who wield swords. Reinforces right weapon with magic.

The power of the sorcerer-swordsmen of Vinheim is predicated upon this and Magic Shield. Many warriors learn sorcery just for this enchantment.

Effect: Reinforce right weapon with magic

Acquired: Orbeck, Shrine Handmaid, Yuria

Notes: Enchants right-hand weapon with magic damage for 90 seconds (weak).

REPAIR

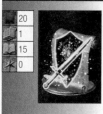

	20
	1
	15
	0

Lost sorcery from Oolacile, land of ancient golden sorceries.

Repairs equipped weapons and armor. Includes weapons with exhausted durability.

While the effects of this spell are rather subtle, its foundations are a well-guarded secret. Light is time, and the reversal of its effects is a forbidden art.

Effect: Repair equipped weapons and armor

Acquired: Orbeck, Golden Scroll

Notes: Restores durability of equipment you are currently wearing by 10. Will also affect broken equipment (durability 0).

SOUL GREATSWORD

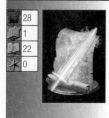

	28
	1
	22
	0

Sorcery developed primarily for sorcerer-swordsmen. Attacks with a greatsword formed from souls.

The ephemeral blade only exists as an extension of the caster, but its power is said to rival that of physical greatswords. Even the most obstinate magic purists may resort to this spell in times of crisis.

Effect: Attack with a greatsword formed from souls

Acquired: Orbeck, Shrine Handmaid, Yuria

Notes: Sweeping attack with a large sword made of souls. Cannot be deflected by enemy shields or walls.

MAGIC SHIELD

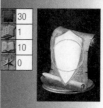

	30
	1
	10
	0

Sorcery for casters who wield swords. Reinforces left shield with magic.

Shields augmented by magic have higher stability and damage absorption. Even the smallest of shields can be toughened considerably with the use of this spell.

Effect: Reinforce left shield with magic

Acquired: Orbeck, Shrine Handmaid, Yuria

Notes: Gives left-hand shield a 30% boost to damage absorption (70% for magic only), and grants a x1.2 stability effect. Lasts for 60 seconds.

PESTILENT MERCURY

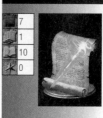

	17
	1
	30
	0

Highly dangerous sorcery employed by Dragon School spooks. Only taught to trusted members.

Releases mercury that eats away at HP. Beware, as the caster is not immune to its effect.

A body caught in the silent mercury cloud lies still, while the face twists in a tortured scream. The names of these learned sorcerers became feared for this gruesome spectacle.

Effect: Release mercury that eats away at HP

Acquired: Orbeck, Sage's Scroll

Notes: Produces a mist in front of you that inflicts continuous damage. Damage ignores absorption rates. Affects both you and enemies (does not affect allies).

SOUL ARROW

	7
	1
	10
	0

Elementary sorcery. Fires a soul arrow.

To use sorceries, equip a staff and attune a sorcery at a bonfire.

Effect: Fire soul arrow

Acquired: Orbeck, Shrine Handmaid, Yuria

Notes: Fires projectile with slight homing ability. Basic attack sorcery.

SOUL SPEAR

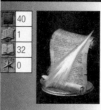

	40
	1
	32
	0

Sorcery developed by Big Hat Logan, the great sorcerer who left the Dragon School in an age long past.

Fires a soul spear.

The spear boasts superior penetrating power, and is testament to Logan's strength in battle.

Effect: Fire soul spear

Acquired: Orbeck, Logan's Scroll

Notes: Powerful projectile that fires relatively quickly. High damage, but FP cost is also high. Pierces through enemies.

SOUL STREAM

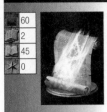

60	
2	
45	
0	

Sorcery imparted by the first of the Scholars, when Lothric and the Grand Archives were but young.

Fires a torrential volley of souls.

The first of the Scholars doubted the linking of the fire, and was alleged to be a private mentor to the Royal Prince.

Effect: Fire torrential volley of souls

Acquired: Grand Archives

Notes: Fires a powerful beam. Casting takes an extremely long time, but has high damage.

SPOOK

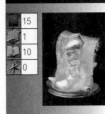

15	
1	
10	
0	

Sorcery developed by a certain surreptitious sorcerer at Vinheim Dragon School.

Masks noises of the caster and prevents fall damage.

Their mastery of this sorcery alone allows Vinheim spooks to demand handsome payment for their services.

Effect: Mask noises of caster and prevent fall damage

Acquired: Orbeck, Shrine Handmaid

Notes: Silences sounds produced by player moving, making it harder to be identified by enemies unless you attack. Prevents fall damage (except for instant death when falling for a distance of 20 metres or higher).

TWISTED WALL OF LIGHT

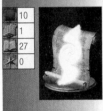

10	
1	
27	
0	

Lost sorcery from Oolacile, land of ancient golden sorceries. Distorts light in order to deflect magic.

A closely-guarded light manipulation spell that contorts the very fabric of fundamental laws, negating magic by denying its claim to physicality.

Effect: Distort light in order to deflect magic

Acquired: Orbeck, Golden Scroll

Notes: Creates a field around yourself that dissolves spell projectiles. Lasts for 2 seconds.

WHITE DRAGON BREATH

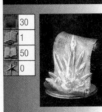

30	
1	
50	
0	

Sorcery of the deluded Consumed King Oceiros.

Emits crystal breath of Seath the Scaleless. Crystal breath has piercing qualities.

Seath's research seemed to strike a chord with old Big Hat who, in his mad, disrobed state, made divine works such as this, his own. Oceiros was no doubt edified by this.

Effect: Emit crystal breath of Seath the Scaleless

Acquired: Oceiros, Consumed King Soul

Notes: Emit crystal breath. Crystals travel across the ground.

PYROMANCY

Pure fire damage, though darker Pyromancies dabble in actual Dark damage. Pyromancies use a mix of Intelligence and Faith for their power, but a substantial Spell Buff bonus comes from leveling your Pyromancy Flame at the trainer.

Pyromancies tend to be area of effect damage and usually a bit slower to cast than Sorcery. Because so much of the spell power is tied to the Pyromancy Flame, Pyromancy makes a good offensive spellcasting adjunct for characters without a heavy investment in Intelligence or Faith.

Some Pyromancies require pure Intelligence or pure Faith, so there are options if you are specialized.

PYROMANCY	EFFECT	FP	SLOTS	REQUIREMENTS
Acid Surge	Emit acid which corrodes weapons and armor	30	1	0/13
Black Fire Orb	Hurl a black fireball	22	1	20/20
Black Flame	Create giant, black flame in hand	28	1	15/15
Black Serpent	Release undulating black flame that runs along the ground	19	1	15/15
Boulder Heave	Spew a boulder from one's mouth	17	1	8/12
Bursting Fireball	Hurl a bursting fireball	14	1	18/12
Carthus Beacon	Damage increases with consecutive attacks	35	2	12/12
Carthus Flame Arc	Reinforce right weapon with flame	30	1	10/10
Chaos Bed Vestiges	Hurl chaos flame that scorches vicinity	35	2	20/10
Chaos Storm	Erect multiple chaos fire pillars in vicinity	3	2	0/0
Fire Orb	Hurl giant fire orb	15	1	8/8
Fire Surge	Emit a constant stream of fire	2	1	6/0
Fire Whip	Sweep foes with fire whip	2	1	13/8
Fireball	Hurl fireball	11	1	6/6
Firestorm	Erect multiple fire pillars in vicinity	2	1	18/0

PYROMANCY	EFFECT	FP	SLOTS	REQUIREMENTS
Flash Sweat	Intense sweating increases fire damage absorption	20	1	6/6
Great Chaos Fire Orb	Hurl giant chaos fire orb	25	2	0/0
Great Combustion	Create powerful, giant flame in hand	20	1	10/10
Iron Flesh	Boost absorption/resistances, but increase weight	45	1	8/0
Poison Mist	Create poison mist	20	1	0/10
Power Within	Temporarily boost attack, but gradually lose HP	30	1	10/10
Profaned Flame	Engulf foes at range and burn them to ashes	30	1	25/0
Profuse Sweat	Profuse sweating temporarily boosts all resistances	20	1	6/6
Rapport	Charm the enemy, making them a temporary ally	30	1	15/0
Sacred Flame	Flame burrows inside foes and ignites	25	1	8/8
Toxic Mist	Create intense poison mist	30	1	0/15
Warmth	Create a gentle flame that restores HP on touch	50	2	0/25

ACID SURGE

	30
	1
	0
	13

Pyromancy of Carthus of the Sands. Emits an acid which corrodes weapons and armor.

Carthus' swordsmen attached great value to victory, and would not shun the use of such pyromancies. For where is the honor in death and scoured bones?

Effect: Emit acid which corrodes weapons and armor

Acquired: Cornyx, Carthus Pyromancy Tome

Notes: Produces an acidic mist that wears down equipment. Reduces durability of equipment worn by enemies standing within it.

BLACK FLAME

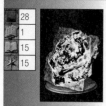

	28
	1
	15
	15

Pyromancy discovered by grave wardens after High Lord Wolnir fell to the Abyss.

Creates a giant, black flame in hand

Black flames born from the Abyss bear no shadow. They are said to be the impenetrable fires of humanity.

Effect: Create giant, black flame in hand

Acquired: Karla, Grave Warden Pyromancy Tome

Notes: Produces a large, powerful blast of black fire from your hand. Has a short range, but activates quickly. Can heavily reduce opponents' stamina.

BOULDER HEAVE

	17
	1
	8
	12

Art of a stray demon of stifled flame.

Spews a boulder from one's mouth.

The boulder is heavy, but shatters easily.

Effect: Spew a boulder from one's mouth

Acquired: Stray Demon Soul

Notes: Summon a great boulder and throw it at foes. Can heavily reduce opponents' stamina.

CARTHUS BEACON

	35
	2
	12
	12

The most obscure pyromancy developed in Carthus of the Sands.

Damage increases with consecutive attacks.

Carthus's aggression has been likened to an uncontrollable fire, and since ancient times its beacon has been used as a signal for war.

Effect: Damage increases with consecutive attacks

Acquired: Cornyx, Carthus Pyromancy Tome

Notes: For 30 seconds, gain increased attack (up to a maximum of x1.15) the more you hit enemies. The effect will wear off if you do not continue to land attacks.

BLACK FIRE ORB

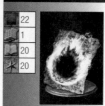

	22
	1
	20
	20

Pyromancy discovered by grave wardens after High Lord Wolnir fell to the Abyss.

Hurls a black fireball.

The black flame inflicts dark damage, striking targets with weighty force.

Effect: Hurl a black fireball

Acquired: Karla, Grave Warden Pyromancy Tome

Notes: Throw a fire projectile. Has a blast radius (area damage) on impact. Can heavily reduce opponents' stamina.

BLACK SERPENT

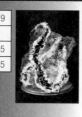

	19
	1
	15
	15

Pyromancy discovered from the Abyss by High Lord Wolnir that inspired the black arts of the grave wardens.

Releases undulating black flames that trace the ground.

Be it sorcery or pyromancy, all techniques that infringe on humanity lead to the same place. That is to say, they all seek a will of their own.

Effect: Release undulating black flame that runs along the ground

Acquired: High Lord Wolnir's Soul

Notes: Summons flames that travel across the ground. Advances forwards at random trajectories.

BURSTING FIREBALL

	14
	1
	18
	12

Pyromancy of old restored by Cornyx. One of the Great Swamp's more advanced spells.

Hurls an exploding fireball.

A rare technique that undergoes change after leaving the caster's hand, making this a spell renowned for its difficulty.

Effect: Hurl a bursting fireball

Acquired: Cornyx, Great Swamp Pyromancy Tome

Notes: Throw a fireball that bursts into several projectiles. Hits multiple times.

CARTHUS FLAME ARC

	30
	1
	10
	10

Pyromancy of Carthus of the Sands. Reinforces right weapon with flame.

Warriors of Carthus favored supplemental pyromancies such as this, which was used to enhance the curved blades of its swordsmen.

Effect: Reinforce right weapon with flame

Acquired: Cornyx, Carthus Pyromancy Tome

Notes: Enchants right-hand weapon with fire damage for 90 seconds (weak).

CHAOS BED VESTIGES

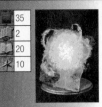

| 35 |
| 2 |
| 20 |
| 10 |

Traces of the tumultuous seedbed that birthed the beings known as Demons.

Hurls chaos flame that scorches vicinity.

Demons born from fire bore its smoldering essence and perished soon after. Man shares this rapport with the flames to this day.

Effect: Hurl chaos flame that scorches vicinity

Acquired: Old Demon King Soul

Notes: Produces a fire projectile that travels in a straight line. The projectile scatters small projectiles around it as it travels.

CHAOS STORM

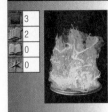

| 3 |
| 2 |
| 0 |
| 0 |

Art of the Flame of Chaos, from Ancient Izalith. Erects multiple chaos fire pillars in vicinity.

Chaotic flame melts even great boulders, and creates a brief surge of molten lava on impact.

The all-engulfing Chaos Flame eventually formed a tumultuous seedbed, which birthed the twisted things known as Demons.

Effect: Erect multiple chaos fire pillars in vicinity

Acquired: Cornyx, Izalith Pyromancy Tome

Notes: Summons several pillars of fire from the ground at random locations centred around the player. These pillars of fire leave behind molten lava.

FIRE ORB

| 15 |
| 1 |
| 8 |
| 8 |

The signature flame-manipulating spell common to pyromancers. Hurls a giant fire orb.

The blazing fire orb explodes on impact, dealing fire damage to the surrounding area.

They say that once a pyromancer learns this spell, their understanding of the flame deepens, together with a yearning for it.

Effect: Hurl giant fire orb

Acquired: Cornyx, Great Swamp Pyromancy Tome

Notes: Throw a fire projectile. Has a blast radius (area damage) on impact. Stronger than Fireball.

FIRE SURGE

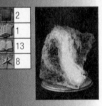

| 2 |
| 1 |
| 6 |
| 0 |

Pyromancy of Cornyx of the Great Swamp. Emits a constant stream of fire.

Cornyx is a venerable pyromancer of an older mold, said to have restored a number of spells lost to the past, amongst which this is the most well-known.

Effect: Emit a constant stream of fire

Acquired: Cornyx, Shrine Handmaid

Notes: Produces a jet of fire in front of you from your hand. Has a short range, but can continue to produce fire as long as you hold the button down. Can be used while moving.

FIRE WHIP

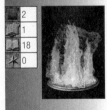

| 2 |
| 1 |
| 13 |
| 8 |

Primal pyromancy taught by Quelana, daughter of the Witch of Izalith.

Sweeps foes with a fire whip.

The caster manipulates the flames at will, making this an extremely difficult spell to use.

Pyromancy is at once the knowledge of controlling flame, and the knowledge that control is impossible.

Effect: Sweep foes with fire whip

Acquired: Karla, Quelana Pyromancy Tome

Notes: Swing a whip of fire.

FIREBALL

| 11 |
| 1 |
| 6 |
| 6 |

Elementary pyromancy that is often the first learned. Hurls a fireball.

To use pyromancies, equip a pyromancy flame and attune a pyromancy at a bonfire.

Effect: Hurl fireball

Acquired: Cornyx, Shrine Handmaid

Notes: Throw a fire projectile. Has a blast radius (area damage) on impact.

FIRESTORM

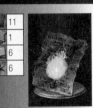

| 2 |
| 1 |
| 18 |
| 0 |

Primal pyromancy taught by Quelana, a daughter of the Witch of Izalith.

Surrounds the caster with multiple pillars of flame.

The raging storm is indiscriminate; such is the intrinsic horror of the flame.

Effect: Erect multiple fire pillars in vicinity

Acquired: Karla, Quelana Pyromancy Tome

Notes: Summons several pillars of fire from the ground at random locations centred around the player.

FLASH SWEAT

| 20 |
| 1 |
| 6 |
| 6 |

Unique pyromancy of the Great Swamp associated with Carmina.

Intense sweating increases fire damage absorption.

An influential pyromancy that internalizes flame, likely forming the foundation for many subsequent spells.

Effect: Intense sweating increases fire damage absorption

Acquired: Cornyx, Shrine Handmaid

Notes: Boosts fire damage absorption by 30% for 30 seconds.

GREAT CHAOS FIRE ORB

	25
	2
	0
	0

Art of the Flame of Chaos, from Ancient Izalith. Hurls a great chaos fire orb.

Chaotic flame melts even great boulders, and creates a brief surge of molten lava on impact.

The Witch of Izalith and her daughters birthed the Flame of Chaos, but it devoured them along with their home.

Effect: Hurl giant chaos fire orb

Acquired: Cornyx, Izalith Pyromancy Tome

Notes: Throw a fire projectile. Leaves molten lava with a damaging effect on impact. Stronger than Fire Orb.

GREAT COMBUSTION

	20
	1
	10
	10

Pyromancy which improves upon Combustion. Creates a powerful, giant flame in hand.

A very powerful, yet simple spell to use.

Pyromancy is to at once know fear and longing, the resultant power of which depends on both the caster's intelligence and faith.

Effect: Create powerful, giant flame in hand

Acquired: Cornyx, Shrine Handmaid

Notes: Produces a large, powerful blast of fire from your hand. Has a short range, but activates quickly.

IRON FLESH

	45
	1
	8
	0

Pyromancy that internalizes flame.

Iron flesh boosts damage absorption and resistance, but significantly increases weight.

Not advisable for walking in marshlands, perhaps resulting in its obsolescence in the Great Swamp.

Effect: Boost absorption/resistances, but increase weight

Acquired: Farron Keep

Notes: For 17 seconds, boosts physical damage absorption by 40%, reduces lightning damage absorption by 60%, and grants +45 for all resistances. Increases your ability to deflect attacks (deflects enemies who attack you with weak weapons). Has a super armor effect (prevents you from staggering on taking damage and reduces staggering animation).

POISON MIST

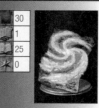

	20
	1
	0
	10

Unique pyromancy crafted by Eingyi, a heretic inhabiting the Great Swamp long ago. Creates a poison mist.

Eingyi was driven from the Great Swamp, however his pyromancy continues to succeed him.

Perhaps dwellers of the Great Swamp were reminded that their very existence is one rooted in heresy.

Effect: Create poison mist

Acquired: Cornyx, Great Swamp Pyromancy Tome, Shrine Handmaid

Notes: Produces a poisonous mist. Enemies standing within it take poison damage.

POWER WITHIN

	30
	1
	10
	10

Forbidden pyromancy amongst those who internalize flame.

Temporarily boosts attack, but gradually lose HP.

A pyromancer fears the flame. However, this fear subsides once it is accepted as a substitute for strength.

Effect: Temporarily boost attack, but gradually lose HP

Acquired: Grand Archives

Notes: Grants attack x1.2 and +30 stamina recovery per second, but inflicts damage equivalent to 1% of your maximum HP every 0.5 seconds. Effect lasts for 15 seconds.

PROFANED FLAME

	30
	1
	25
	0

Pyromancy deriving from the Profaned Flame.

Engulfs foes at range and burns them to ashes.

The Profaned Capital was consumed by fire after Yhorm the Giant became a Lord of Cinder. The fire, born of the sky, is said to have incinerated naught but human flesh.

Effect: Engulf foes at range and burn them to ashes

Acquired: Irithyll Dungeon

Notes: Produces an explosion near the target location. There is a time delay before it activates.

PROFUSE SWEAT

	20
	1
	6
	6

Advanced pyromancy that internalizes flame, associated with Carmina.

Profuse sweating temporarily boosts resistance to bleeding, poison, frost and curses.

The yellowish sweat cures all kinds of ailments.

Effect: Profuse sweating temporarily boosts all resistances

Acquired: Cornyx, Great Swamp Pyromancy Tome

Notes: Grants +80 to all resistances for 60 seconds.

RAPPORT

	30
	1
	15
	0

Advanced pyromancy of Quelana, a daughter of the Witch of Izalith.

Charms the enemy, making them a temporary ally.

The living are lured by flame, and this tendency is elemental to the art of pyromancy.

Effect: Charm the enemy, making them a temporary ally

Acquired: Karla, Quelana Pyromancy Tome

Notes: Undead-type enemies become friendly for 30 seconds. Cannot be used as a red phantom or when invading.

SACRED FLAME

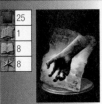

25	
1	
8	
8	

Pyromancy taught amongst savages. Flame burrows inside foes and ignites.

Originally used in a ceremony for cleansing sacrificial impurities, thereby lending the spell its name.

As barbaric as it seems, this may in fact be quite fitting for the savage pyromancers who consider themselves servants of the divine.

Effect: Flame burrows inside foes and ignites

Acquired: Smouldering Lake

Notes: Grab an enemy and perform a burning attack. Some enemies cannot be grabbed.

WARMTH

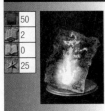

50	
2	
0	
25	

Peculiar pyromancy of the Mound-makers. Creates a gentle flame that restores HP on touch.

They feared separation from the gods and sought a familial bond, perhaps leading to the creation of this flame of harmony.

Effect: Create a gentle flame that restores HP on touch

Acquired: Mound-Makers Reward

Notes: Place an area-of-effect heal that lasts for 30 seconds. All characters near the location you place it (whether friend or foe) recover HP.

TOXIC MIST

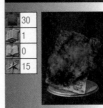

30	
1	
0	
15	

Unique pyromancy of Eingyi that never gained currency in the Great Swamp.

Creates an intense poison mist.

Driven from the Great Swamp, they say that at the end of his journey, Eingyi happened upon a virulent poison and a young lady.

Effect: Create intense poison mist

Acquired: Smouldering Lake

Notes: Produces a toxic mist. Enemies standing within it take toxic damage.

MIRACLES

Primarily healing and supportive magic, Miracles do specialize in Lightning damage with spells that can lob thunderbolts at your foes. Miracles require Faith almost exclusively, with a single spell demanding Intelligence.

MIRACLES	EFFECT	FP	SLOTS	REQUIREMENTS
Atonement	Attract more attention from foes	15	1	0/18
Blessed Weapon	Bless right weapon	35	1	0/15
Bountiful Light	Gradually restore high HP	45	1	0/25
Bountiful Sunlight	Gradually restore high HP for self and broad area	70	2	0/35
Caressing Tears	Cure ailments for self and vicinity	14	1	0/12
Dark Blade	Reinforce right weapon with dark	35	1	0/25
Darkmoon Blade	Reinforce right weapon with Darkmoon light	50	1	0/30
Dead Again	Bless corpses, transforming them into traps	45	1	15/23
Deep Protection	Some extra ATK/absorption/resist/stamina recovery	25	1	0/20
Divine Pillars of Light	Bring down multiple pillars of light in vicinity	3	1	0/30
Dorhys' Gnaw	Summon great insect swarm to feast on foes	24	1	0/25
Emit Force	Release shockwave in front	20	1	0/18
Force	Create shockwave	26	1	0/12
Gnaw	Summon insect swarm to feast on foes	18	1	0/18
Great Heal	Restore high HP	65	1	0/25
Great Lightning Spear	Hurl giant lightning spear	45	1	0/30
Great Magic Barrier	Greatly increase magic damage absoroption with coating	45	2	0/25
Heal	Restore HP for self and vicinity	45	1	0/12

MIRACLES	EFFECT	FP	SLOTS	REQUIREMENTS
Heal Aid	Slightly restore HP	27	1	0/8
Homeward	Return caster to last bonfire rested at, or to shrine	30	1	0/18
Lifehunt Scythe	Steal HP of foes using an illusory scythe	25	1	0/22
Lightning Blade	Reinforce right weapon with lightning	50	1	0/30
Lightning Spear	Hurl lightning spear	30	1	0/20
Lightning Stake	Strike with a stake of lightning	50	2	0/35
Lightning Storm	Call forth furious bolts of lightning	50	2	0/45
Magic Barrier	Increase magic damage absorption with coating	30	1	0/15
Med Heal	Restore moderate HP for self and vicinity	55	1	0/15
Replenishment	Gradually restore HP	30	1	0/15
Sacred Oath	Boost ATK/DMG absorption for self and vicinity	65	2	0/28
Seek Guidance	Reveal more help, and signs without using ember	15	1	0/12
Soothing Sunlight	Restore high HP for self and broad area	80	1	0/45
Sunlight Spear	Hurl sunlight spear	70	1	0/40
Tears of Denial	Grant one chance to endure when HP reaches 0	100	2	0/15
Vow of Silence	Prevent spells in vicinity, including one's own	35	2	0/30
Wrath of the Gods	Create powerful shockwave	40	2	0/30

ATONEMENT

	15
	1
	0
✴	18

Miracle given to those cast out from the Sable Church of Londor.

Attracts more attention from foes.

This is the only tale known by the exiles, who believe it carries words of forgiveness. Cursed journeys, too, must ultimately come to an end.

Effect: Attract more attention from foes

Acquired: Farron Keep

Notes: Makes enemies target you for 30 seconds.

BOUNTIFUL LIGHT

	45
	1
	0
✴	25

Miracle taught to knights by Gertrude, holy maiden to the Queen.

Gradually restores a large amount of HP.

The Heavenly Daughter is said to be the Queen's child.

Effect: Gradually restore high HP

Acquired: Irina, Braille Divine Tome of Lothric

Notes: Continually regain HP over 60 seconds (moderate effect).

CARESSING TEARS

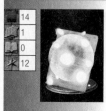

	14
	1
	0
✴	12

Miracle taught by Morne, the Archbishop's apostle.

Cures bleeding, poison and frost for self and those in the vicinity.

Caressing Tears is a tale of the many deaths surrounding the goddess Caitha, of whom Morne was a known follower.

Effect: Cure ailments for self and vicinity

Acquired: Irina, Shrine Handmaid

Notes: Removes status ailments other than curse and clear ailment build-up gauges.

DARKMOON BLADE

	50
	1
	0
✴	30

Miracle of those who devoted themselves to the Darkmoon covenant.

Reinforces right weapon with Darkmoon light.

Miracles of the Darkmoon are tales of revenge, but Captain Yorshka recites only for the sake of remembering her brother, without knowledge of its meaning.

Perhaps this is better, as revenge is better left to the Blades.

Effect: Reinforce right weapon with Darkmoon light

Acquired: Blade of the Darkmoon Reward

Notes: Enchants right-hand weapon with magic damage for 60 seconds (moderate).

BLESSED WEAPON

	35
	1
	0
✴	15

Miracle taught to Lothric Knights.

Blesses right weapon, increasing attack power, as well as gradually restoring HP.

The Knight is one of the Three Pillars of Lothric, said to have strengthened ties with the High Priestess after the Scholars acquired the Grand Archives.

Effect: Bless right weapon

Acquired: Irina, Braille Divine Tome of Lothric

Notes: Boosts physical attack of right-hand weapon and significantly increases damage against Hollows. Effect lasts for 45 seconds. During the effect, you continuously recover HP.

SOOTHING SUNLIGHT

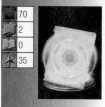

	70
	2
	0
✴	35

Special miracle granted by the Princess of Sunlight.

Gradually restores a large amount of HP for self and those in the vicinity.

The miracles of Gwynevere, loved as both mother and wife bestow their blessing on a great many warriors.

Effect: Gradually restore high HP for self and broad area

Acquired: Soul of the Dancer

Notes: Continual HP regeneration for you and nearby allies over 60 seconds (high effect).

DARK BLADE

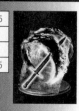

	35
	1
	0
✴	25

Miracle of the Sable Church of Londor.

Reinforces right weapon with dark.

The third daughter Liliane, one of the founders of the Sable Church, is said to recount tales that portray the suffering and conflict of Hollows.

Effect: Reinforce right weapon with dark

Acquired: Irina or Karla, Londor Braille Divine Tome

Notes: Enchants right-hand weapon with dark damage for 60 seconds (moderate).

DEAD AGAIN

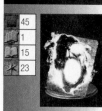

	45
	1
	15
✴	23

Sacrilegious miracle of the Sable Church of Londor.

Bless corpses, transforming them into traps.

Londor, the Hollow Realm, is a society of undead, comprised of the corpses and shades of those who led unsavory lives. Is such blessing really something one must ponder?

Effect: Bless corpses, transforming them into traps

Acquired: Irina or Karla, Londor Braille Divine Tome

Notes: Causes nearby enemy corpses to explode, dealing dark damage to nearby enemies.

DEEP PROTECTION

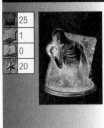

25
1
0
20

Miracle taught to inaugurated deacons of the Cathedral of the Deep.

Slightly boosts attack, damage absorption and resistance, while also increasing stamina recovery speed.

The Deep was originally a peaceful and sacred place, but became the final rest for many abhorrent things. This tale of the Deep offers protection for those who worship amidst those horrors.

Effect: Some extra ATK/absorption/resist/stamina recovery

Acquired: Irina or Karla, Deep Braille Divine Tome

Notes: For 60 seconds, grants attack x1.05, +5% to all damage absorption types, +3 stamina recovery per second, and +20 to all resistances.

DORHYS' GNAW

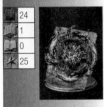

24
1
0
25

Miracle of Dorhys the deranged evangelist.

Summons great insect swarm to feast on foes.

Those who linger too long on the brink of the Deep will often slip. Dorhys is sure to have wallowed in this darkness, intoxicated by its peril.

Effect: Summon great insect swarm to feast on foes

Acquired: Irithyll of the Boreal Valley

Notes: Throw projectile that inflicts dark damage and bleed damage on enemies. Has slight homing ability. Stronger than Gnaw.

FORCE

26
1
0
12

Elementary miracle among clerics. Creates a shockwave.

While it inflicts no direct damage, this miracle propels foes back, staggering them. Can also defend against incoming arrows.

Effect: Create shockwave

Acquired: Irina, Braille Divine Tome of Lothric

Notes: Blows away nearby enemies with a shockwave. Has no damage effect. Can deflect weak physical projectiles like arrows.

GREAT HEAL

65
1
0
25

Glorious miracle used by high-ranking clerics. Restores a large amount of HP for self and those in the vicinity.

Only a select few have learned to recite this epic tale in its entirety, but those who do are amply rewarded.

Effect: Restore high HP

Acquired: Irithyll of the Boreal Valley

Notes: Restores your HP (high effect). Restores HP of nearby allies (moderate effect).

DIVINE PILLARS OF LIGHT

3
1
0
30

Miracle of Gertrude, the Heavenly Daughter.

Brings down multiple pillars of light in vicinity.

The Queen's holy maiden Gertrude was visited by an angel, who revealed this tale to her.

Despite losing both her sight and her voice, she was determined to record the tale. Ordinary men cannot decipher her fragmentary scrawl, nor comprehend how it became the foundation of the Angelic faith of Lothric.

Effect: Bring down multiple pillars of light in vicinity

Acquired: Grand Archives

Notes: Summons several pillars of light from the ground at random locations centred around the player.

EMIT FORCE

20
1
0
18

Traditional miracle of Catarina. Releases a shockwave in front.

The people of lands known for festivity and drink are typically outspoken. One can be sure that they will not bottle their emotions, instead venting anger and the like with confidence.

Effect: Release shockwave in front

Acquired: Gifted by Siegward of Catarina during his questline

Notes: Emits a shockwave that knocks back enemies. Produces an area-of-effect shockwave on impact.

GNAW

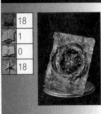

18
1
0
18

Dark miracle taught in the Cathedral of the Deep.

Summons insect swarm to feast on foes.

These insects which lurk in the Deep have tiny jaws lined with fangs to tear open the skin and burrow into the flesh in the blink of an eye, causing intense bleeding.

Effect: Summon insect swarm to feast on foes

Acquired: Irina or Karla, Deep Braille Divine Tome

Notes: Throw projectile that inflicts dark damage and bleed damage on enemies. Has slight homing ability.

GREAT LIGHTNING SPEAR

45
1
0
30

Primal account of Lightning Spear, which tells of an ancestral dragonslayer.

Hurls a giant lightning spear.

Gwyn, the First Lord, slew dragons with his sunlight spear, a tradition upheld by his firstborn and the greatspear he wielded.

Much of this resplendent tale of father and son, while epic, remains tragically untold.

Effect: Hurl giant lightning spear

Acquired: Warrior of Sunlight Reward

Notes: Throws a high-speed projectile at enemies that travels in a straight line. Inflicts additional damage if you land a hit at point-blank range. Stronger than Lightning Spear.

GREAT MAGIC BARRIER

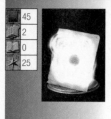

| 45 |
| 2 |
| 0 |
| 25 |

The tale which was later interpreted as Magic Barrier.

Greatly increases magic damage absorption by covering the body in a strong white protective coating.

Said to be a tale of Havel the Rock, arch enemy of Seath the Scaleless. Havel despised magic, and was never complacent in preparing means to counter it.

Effect: Greatly increase magic damage absorption with coating

Acquired: Archdragon Peak

Notes: Boosts magic damage absorption by 50% for 20 seconds.

HEAL

| 45 |
| 1 |
| 0 |
| 12 |

Elementary miracle cast by clerics.

Restores HP for self and those in the vicinity.

To use miracles, equip a talisman or sacred chime and attune a miracle at a bonfire.

Effect: Restore HP for self and vicinity

Acquired: Irina, Shrine Handmaid

Notes: Restores your HP (small effect). Restores HP of nearby allies (very small effect).

HEAL AID

| 27 |
| 1 |
| 0 |
| 8 |

Miracle imparted as charity to those of little faith. A show of tolerance from the Way of White.

Slightly restores HP.

To use miracles, equip a talisman or sacred chime and attune a miracle at a bonfire.

Effect: Slightly restore HP

Acquired: Shrine Handmaid

Notes: Restores your HP (very small effect).

HOMEWARD

| 30 |
| 1 |
| 0 |
| 18 |

Miracle taught to traveling clerics. Returns caster to the last bonfire used for resting, or to the bonfire in the shrine.

It would normally link to one's homeland, only the curse of the Undead has twisted its power, redirecting casters to a bonfire. Perhaps for Undead, the bonfire serves as home.

Effect: Return caster to last bonfire rested at, or to shrine

Acquired: Irina, Shrine Handmaid

Notes: Return to the last bonfire rested at, or the shrine. Cannot be used as a phantom.

LIFEHUNT SCYTHE

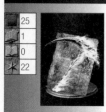

| 25 |
| 1 |
| 0 |
| 22 |

Miracle of Aldrich, Devourer of Gods.

Steals HP of foes using an illusory scythe.

Aldrich dreamt as he slowly devoured the God of the Darkmoon. In this dream, he perceived the form of a young, pale girl in hiding.

Effect: Steal HP of foes using an illusory scythe

Acquired: Aldrich Soul

Notes: Perform a sweeping attack with a phantom scythe. Land hits on enemies to inflict damage and regain some of your HP.

LIGHTNING BLADE

| 50 |
| 1 |
| 0 |
| 30 |

Miracle allegedly wielded by a certain dragonslayer knight in the Age of Gods.

Reinforces right weapon with lightning.

Tales of dragonslayers are now a rare thing, told only in fragments and whispers in remote regions.

Effect: Reinforce right weapon with lightning

Acquired: Irithyll Dungeon

Notes: Enchants right-hand weapon with lightning damage for 60 seconds (moderate).

LIGHTNING SPEAR

| 30 |
| 1 |
| 0 |
| 20 |

Miracle allegedly used by Warriors of Sunlight.

Hurls a lightning spear.

The spears inflict lightning damage, providing an effective counter to magic or fire. Especially powerful against metal armor and dragons.

Effect: Hurl lightning spear

Acquired: Farron Keep

Notes: Throws a high-speed projectile at enemies that travels in a straight line. Inflicts additional damage if you land a hit at point-blank range.

LIGHTNING STAKE

| 50 |
| 2 |
| 0 |
| 35 |

A lost dragonslaying miracle.

Strikes with a stake of lightning.

This tale describes the lost practices of ancient dragonslayers, who found that in order to pierce dragonscale, lightning should not be hurled as a bolt, but rather be thrust as a stake directly into the dragon's hide, to be truly effective.

Effect: Strike with a stake of lightning

Acquired: Smouldering Lake

Notes: Drive a lightning stake into enemies in front of you. Short range magic that does not produce a projectile, but has high damage.

LIGHTNING STORM

| 50 |
| 2 |
| 0 |
| 45 |

Miracle of the Nameless King, ally to the ancient dragons.

Calls forth furious bolts of lightning.

Once a slayer of dragons, the former king and wargod tamed a Stormdrake, on which he led a lifetime of battle. This miracle is likely a tale of their bond.

Effect: Call forth furious bolts of lightning

Acquired: Nameless King Soul

Notes: Electrocutes surroundings by bringing down bolts of lightning centered around you.

MAGIC BARRIER

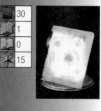

| 30 |
| 1 |
| 0 |
| 15 |

Miracle of clerics who wield weapons.

Increases magic damage absorption by covering the body in a white protective coating.

There was a short period in history where clerics and sorcerers opposed one another. Thus it became necessary for even simple clerics to have some means of opposing magic.

Effect: Increase magic damage absorption with coating

Acquired: Irina, Braille Divine Tome of Lothric

Notes: Boosts magic damage absorption by 25% for 30 seconds.

MED HEAL

55
1
0
15

Miracle superior to Heal. Restores moderate HP for self and those in the vicinity.

Miracles are fruit of the study of divine tales, a blessing received from the gods through acts of prayer. Miracle strength depends on the caster's faith.

Effect: Restore moderate HP for self and vicinity

Acquired: Irina, Braille Divine Tome of Carim

Notes: Restores your HP (moderate effect). Restores HP of nearby allies (small effect).

SACRED OATH

65
2
0
28

Miracle of those chosen by the Sunlight covenant.

Temporarily boosts attack and damage absorption for self and those in the vicinity.

This is the tale of the Sun's firstborn, his faithful first knight, and the brave dragonslayer who served them both.

Effect: Boost ATK/DMG absorption for self and vicinity

Acquired: Warrior of Sunlight Reward

Notes: Grants you and nearby allies x1.1 attack and x1.1 damage absorption for all types. Effect lasts for 60 seconds.

SOOTHING SUNLIGHT

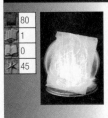

80
1
0
45

Special miracle granted to the maidens of the Princess of Sunlight.

Restores a large amount of HP for self and those in the general area.

The miracles of Gwynevere, the princess cherished by all, bestow their blessing on a great many warriors.

Effect: Restore high HP for self and broad area

Acquired: Dancer of the Boreal Valley Soul

Notes: Restores your HP (very high effect). Restores HP of nearby allies (very high effect).

TEARS OF DENIAL

100
2
0
15

Miracle taught by Morne, the Archbishop's apostle.

Grants one chance to endure when HP reaches 0

Intended to grant the dying a few moments for a final farewell. Tears are shed for the sake of the living, more so than the deceased.

Effect: Grant one chance to endure when HP reaches 0

Acquired: Irina, Braille Divine Tome of Carim

Notes: Evade death only once and survive with 1 HP.

WRATH OF THE GODS

40
2
0
30

Primal form of Force. Creates a powerful shockwave.

Wrath of the Gods is an epic tale, while Force is but a woefully incomplete version of that yarn.

This primal account of profound fury emits a shockwave that also inflicts damage.

Effect: Create powerful shockwave

Acquired: Profaned Capital

Notes: Blows away nearby enemies with a shockwave. Takes a long time to cast, but has high damage. Can deflect weak physical projectiles like arrows.

REPLENISHMENT

30
1
0
15

Miracle once cherished by cleric knights. Gradually restores HP.

Replenishment is a relic of the old Lloyd faith, whose cleric knights were unfaltering in battle.

Effect: Gradually restore HP

Acquired: Irina, Shrine Handmaid

Notes: Continually regain HP over 60 seconds (small effect).

SEEK GUIDANCE

15
1
0
12

Miracle of stray souls. Displays more help from other worlds and reveals summon signs without using an ember.

Faith serves as a guide for clerics, meaning they should have no need for secondhand wisdom.

Be that as it may, this miracle has been passed down from soul to soul, providing a tiny ray of hope for the lost.

Effect: Reveal more help, and signs without using ember

Acquired: Cathedral of the Deep

Notes: Increases amount of messages displayed. Allows you to see summon signs even when not a Host of Embers (but you cannot pick them up unless you are a Host of Embers).

SUNLIGHT SPEAR

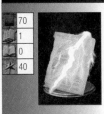

70
1
0
40

Miracle of Gwyn, the First Lord. Hurls a sunlight spear.

The tales of Gwyn's Archdragon hunts describe the inception of the Age of Fire.

Effect: Hurl sunlight spear

Acquired: Soul of the Lords

Notes: Throws a high-speed projectile at enemies that travels in a straight line. Inflicts additional damage if you land a hit at point-blank range. Stronger than Great Lightning Spear.

VOW OF SILENCE

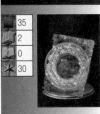

35
2
0
30

Miracle of the Sable Church of Londor.

Prevents spells in vicinity, including one's own.

Members of the Sable Church are all trained swordsmen, each sworn only to their weapons as they bear the leaden silence of Londor.

Effect: Prevent spells in vicinity, including one's own

Acquired: Irina, Karla, Londor Braille Divine Tome

Notes: Prevents you and all nearby enemies from using any kind of spell for 10 seconds. Can also work on enemy characters in some cases.

EQUIPMENT

This section guides you through the massive variety of arms and armor to be found in the realm of Lothric.
Prepare yourself for battle.

MELEE WEAPONS

Your faithful companion from start to finish, a good solid melee weapon is vital to success in *Dark Souls III*. There are a huge number of weapons to be discovered out in the world. Some can be found while exploring, some come from enemies, others can be created using Soul Transposition, a special process of creating items from powerful Souls by the NPC Ludleth in the Firelink Shrine.

The Blacksmith in town is also important for your weapons, as he can upgrade their power, and for mundane weapons, infuse them with special Gems to give them new abilities.

The majority of melee weapons require some level of Str or Dex to equip and use effectively, though there are are also weapons that require Int or Faith (sometimes 3 or even all 4 attributes!).

At the beginning of each weapon category is a chart showing a breakdown of every weapon in the game in that category. You can see a weapon's name, it's damage type, what skill it possesses and how much that skill costs to use in FP, and its weight.

The Power column shows you the base power of a weapon, with short abbreviations in the comparison table for damage type, **p** for Physical, **m** for Magic, **f** for Fire, **l** for Lightning, **d** for Dark, and finally for weapons that have a non standard Critical value above 100, **c** for Critical. For the few weapons that can act as Catalysts for spells and have the Spell Buff stat, this is also shown as **sb**.

The Additional Effect column indicates if a weapon has any Bleed, Poison, or the rare Frost damage (**b, po, f r**), while the Scaling and Requirements columns are both ordered as Str/Dex/Int/Faith. Scaling indicates how much a weapon benefits from a high attribute level, ranked from E on the low end to S at the highest. Weapon scaling improves as you enhance a weapon at the Blacksmith.

Finally the Material column shows what type of Titanite a weapon requires to be enhanced. Normal mundane weapons only require 'normal' Titanite, and reach reach an enhancement level of +10, while unique Soulbound weaponry requires rare Twinkling Titanite, and Soul-transposed weaponry requires even rarer Titanite Scales, both upgradable to +5. Neither Soulbound nor Soul-transposed weapons can be infused by the Blacksmith, the price you pay for their inherent power.

WEAPON BONUS DAMAGE

A rare few weapons deal bonus damage to certain enemy types, summarized in this table.

WEAPON	BONUS DAMAGE VS. DEMONS	BONUS DAMAGE VS. REANIMATED	BONUS DAMAGE VS. HOLLOWS	BONUS DAMAGE VS. ABYSSAL FOES
Black Knight Greatsword	20%	0	0	0
Black Knight Sword	20%	0	0	0
Black Knight Greataxe	20%	0	0	0
Black Knight Glaive	20%	0	0	0
Anri's Straight Sword	0	10%	0	0
Any Blessed Weapon	0	20%	0	0
Hollowslayer Greatsword	0	0	50%	0
Farron Greatsword	0	0	0	20%
Wolf Knight's Greatsword	0	0	0	20%

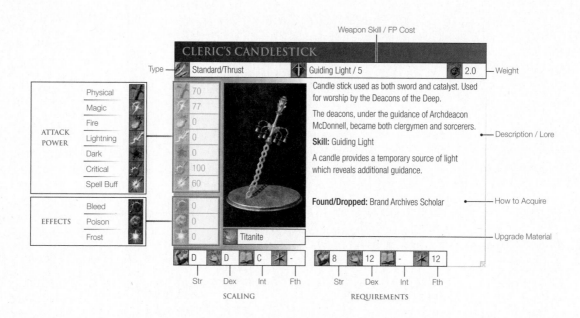

Weapon Skill / FP Cost

CLERIC'S CANDLESTICK

Type — Standard/Thrust | Guiding Light / 5 | 2.0 — Weight

ATTACK POWER
- Physical — 70
- Magic — 77
- Fire — 0
- Lightning — 0
- Dark — 0
- Critical — 100
- Spell Buff — 60

EFFECTS
- Bleed — 0
- Poison — 0
- Frost — 0

Candle stick used as both sword and catalyst. Used for worship by the Deacons of the Deep.

The deacons, under the guidance of Archdeacon McDonnell, became both clergymen and sorcerers. — Description / Lore

Skill: Guiding Light

A candle provides a temporary source of light which reveals additional guidance.

Found/Dropped: Brand Archives Scholar — How to Acquire

Titanite — Upgrade Material

D	D	C	-		8	12	-	12
Str	Dex	Int	Fth		Str	Dex	Int	Fth

SCALING | REQUIREMENTS

DAGGERS

Nimble weapons, Daggers are lightweight and quick, requiring minimal Stamina for attacks. The majority of Daggers have low-cost weapon skills focused on evasion or defeating opposing shield usage, useful against NPC humanoid foes, and some players in PvP as well.

Most Daggers have enhanced Critical damage above 100, granting boosted damage for parry-ripostes and backstabs. Daggers are largely Dex focused, both in requirements and scaling. With their rapid strikes, they are ideal for interrupting slower attacks and inflicting status damage buildup.

On the downside, Daggers have little reach, and don't hit hard per swing, which can make them difficult to use against the truly massive enemies out in the world. If you are playing a Dex focused character, you may want to keep a Dagger around for fighting humanoids, and switch to a different Dex weapon with a bit more punch for larger foes that cannot be backstabbed and shrug off weak hits.

DAGGERS	TYPE	ART/COST	WEIGHT	POWER	ADD. EFFECT	SCALING	REQUIREMENTS	MATERIAL
Bandit's Knife	Slash/Thrust	Quickstep/5	1.5	66p/110c	33bl	D/D/-/-	6/12/0/0	Titanite
Brigand Dual Shortsword	Slash/Thrust	Quickstep/5	2.5	55p/110c	-	D/D/-/-	10/18/0/0	Titanite
Corvian Greatknife	Slash/Thrust	Blind Spot/10	2.5	83p/110c	-	E/E/-/-	12/16/0/0	Titanite
Dagger	Slash/Thrust	Quickstep/5	1.5	55p/130c	-	E/C/-/-	5/9/0/0	Titanite
Handmaid's Dagger	Slash/Thrust	Blind Spot/10	0.5	72p/110c	-	E/E/-/-	4/8/0/0	Titanite
Harpe	Slash/Thrust	Quickstep/5	1.5	52p	-	E/C/-/-	8/10/0/0	Titanite
Mail Breaker	Slash/Thrust	Shield Splitter/12	1.5	75p/130c	-	E/D/-/-	7/12/0/0	Titanite
Parrying Dagger	Slash/Thrust	Parry/-	1.0	50p/110c	-	E/C/-/-	5/14/0/0	Titanite
Rotten Ghru Dagger	Slash/Thrust	Quickstep/5	2.0	54p	33po	E/C/-/-	10/8/0/0	Titanite
Scholar's Candle Stick	Slash/Thrust	Guiding Light/5	1.5	58p/110c	-	E/C/-/-	7/0/0/0	Titanite
Tailbone Short Sword	Slash/Thrust	Unleash Dragon/25	2.0	90p/110c	-	E/E/-/-	8/14/0/0	Titanite Scale

BANDIT'S KNIFE

Slash/Thrust | Quickstep / 5 | 1.5

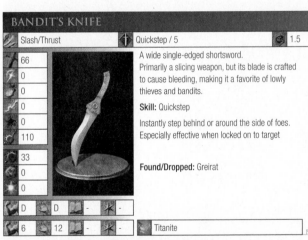

| 66 |
| 0 |
| 0 |
| 0 |
| 0 |
| 110 |
| 33 |
| 0 |
| 0 |

| D | D | - | - |
| 6 | 12 | - | - | Titanite |

A wide single-edged shortsword.
Primarily a slicing weapon, but its blade is crafted to cause bleeding, making it a favorite of lowly thieves and bandits.

Skill: Quickstep

Instantly step behind or around the side of foes. Especially effective when locked on to target

Found/Dropped: Greirat

BRIGAND TWINDAGGERS

Slash/Thrust | Quickstep / 5 | 2.5

| 55 |
| 0 |
| 0 |
| 0 |
| 0 |
| 110 |
| 0 |
| 0 |
| 0 |

| D | D | - | - |
| 10 | 18 | - | - | Titanite |

These paired daggers are the preferred weapons of the brigands of a distant land.

When two-handed, the wielder holds a blade in each hand, allowing for divergent attacks that include left-handed moves.

Skill: Quickstep

Instantly step behind or around the side of foes. Especially effective when locked on to target.

Found/Dropped: Road of Sacrifices

CORVIAN GREATKNIFE

Slash/Thrust | Blind Spot / 10 | 2.5

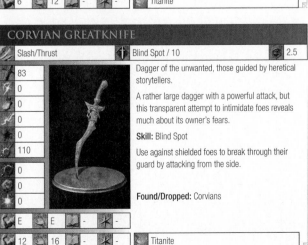

| 83 |
| 0 |
| 0 |
| 0 |
| 0 |
| 110 |
| 0 |
| 0 |
| 0 |

| E | E | - | - |
| 12 | 16 | - | - | Titanite |

Dagger of the unwanted, those guided by heretical storytellers.

A rather large dagger with a powerful attack, but this transparent attempt to intimidate foes reveals much about its owner's fears.

Skill: Blind Spot

Use against shielded foes to break through their guard by attacking from the side.

Found/Dropped: Corvians

DAGGER

Slash/Thrust | Quickstep / 5 | 1.5

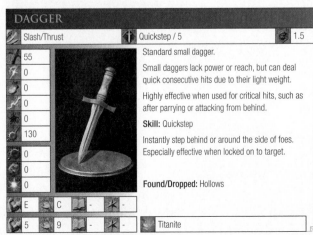

| 55 |
| 0 |
| 0 |
| 0 |
| 0 |
| 130 |
| 0 |
| 0 |
| 0 |

| E | C | - | - |
| 5 | 9 | - | - | Titanite |

Standard small dagger.

Small daggers lack power or reach, but can deal quick consecutive hits due to their light weight.

Highly effective when used for critical hits, such as after parrying or attacking from behind.

Skill: Quickstep

Instantly step behind or around the side of foes. Especially effective when locked on to target.

Found/Dropped: Hollows

HANDMAID'S DAGGER

Slash/Thrust		Blind Spot / 10			0.5

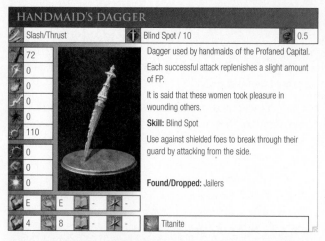

	72
	0
	0
	0
	0
	110
	0
	0
	0

Dagger used by handmaids of the Profaned Capital.

Each successful attack replenishes a slight amount of FP.

It is said that these women took pleasure in wounding others.

Skill: Blind Spot

Use against shielded foes to break through their guard by attacking from the side.

Found/Dropped: Jailers

	E		E		-		-
	4		8		-		-

Titanite

MAIL BREAKER

Slash/Thrust		Shield Splitter / 12			1.5

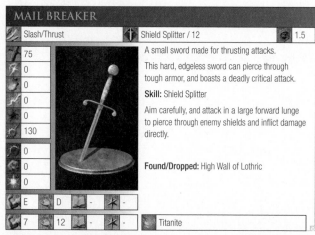

	75
	0
	0
	0
	0
	130
	0
	0
	0

A small sword made for thrusting attacks.

This hard, edgeless sword can pierce through tough armor, and boasts a deadly critical attack.

Skill: Shield Splitter

Aim carefully, and attack in a large forward lunge to pierce through enemy shields and inflict damage directly.

Found/Dropped: High Wall of Lothric

	E		D		-		-
	7		12		-		-

Titanite

ROTTEN GHRU DAGGER

Slash/Thrust		Quickstep / 5			2.0

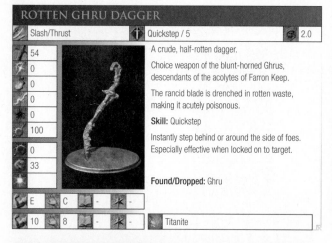

	54
	0
	0
	0
	0
	100
	0
	33
	0

A crude, half-rotten dagger.

Choice weapon of the blunt-horned Ghrus, descendants of the acolytes of Farron Keep.

The rancid blade is drenched in rotten waste, making it acutely poisonous.

Skill: Quickstep

Instantly step behind or around the side of foes. Especially effective when locked on to target.

Found/Dropped: Ghru

	E		C		-		-
	10		8		-		-

Titanite

TAILBONE SHORT SWORD

Slash/Thrust		Unleash Dragon / 25			2.0

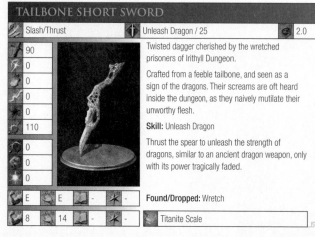

	90
	0
	0
	0
	0
	110
	0
	0
	0

Twisted dagger cherished by the wretched prisoners of Irithyll Dungeon.

Crafted from a feeble tailbone, and seen as a sign of the dragons. Their screams are oft heard inside the dungeon, as they naively mutilate their unworthy flesh.

Skill: Unleash Dragon

Thrust the spear to unleash the strength of dragons, similar to an ancient dragon weapon, only with its power tragically faded.

Found/Dropped: Wretch

	E		E		-		-
	8		14		-		-

Titanite Scale

HARPE

Slash/Thrust		Quickstep / 5			1.5

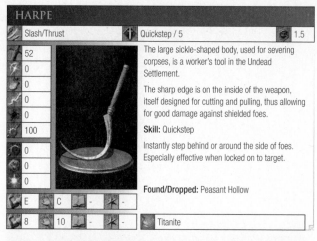

	52
	0
	0
	0
	0
	100
	0
	0
	0

The large sickle-shaped body, used for severing corpses, is a worker's tool in the Undead Settlement.

The sharp edge is on the inside of the weapon, itself designed for cutting and pulling, thus allowing for good damage against shielded foes.

Skill: Quickstep

Instantly step behind or around the side of foes. Especially effective when locked on to target.

Found/Dropped: Peasant Hollow

	E		C		-		-
	8		10		-		-

Titanite

PARRYING DAGGER

Slash/Thrust		Parry / 0			1.0

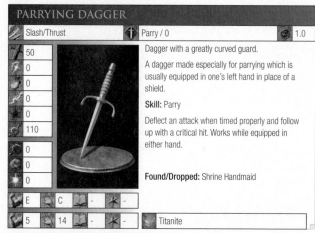

	50
	0
	0
	0
	0
	110
	0
	0
	0

Dagger with a greatly curved guard.

A dagger made especially for parrying which is usually equipped in one's left hand in place of a shield.

Skill: Parry

Deflect an attack when timed properly and follow up with a critical hit. Works while equipped in either hand.

Found/Dropped: Shrine Handmaid

	E		C		-		-
	5		14		-		-

Titanite

SCHOLAR'S CANDLE STICK

Slash/Thrust		Guiding Light / 5			1.5

	58
	0
	0
	0
	0
	110
	0
	0
	0

A candlestick covered in ivory scales once used by the Scholars of the Great Archives.

This served as their guiding light, as well as a tool of self-restraint. Even today, wielders of this weapon benefit from the resulting sorcery-strengthening properties.

Skill: Guiding Light

A candle provides a temporary source of light which reveals additional guidance.

Found/Dropped: Grand Archives Scholar

	E		C		-		-
	7		-		-		-

Titanite

STRAIGHT SWORDS

If there's a 'standard' weapon in *Dark Souls,* a Straight Sword is probably it. With a balance of speed and damage, Straight Swords are easy to use and quite effective, useful in almost all situations. Be warned that in PvP, veteran opponents tend to be very familiar with Straight Sword move sets, so you are usually at an increased risk of being parried.

Most Straight Swords have the Stance skill, a two-part skill that allows you to assume a stance and then lash out with a rising swing or a lunging strike. You can use this to break through an opponent's shield block, or close distance quickly.

An upgraded Straight Sword can work well from start to finish, but be sure to experiment with the individual variants as you explore Lothric, you may find slight differences in move set that appeal to you more like, Broadsword vs. the Long Sword.

STRAIGHT SWORDS	TYPE	ART/COST	WEIGHT	POWER	ADD. EFFECT	SCALING	REQUIREMENTS	MATERIAL
Anri's Straight Sword	Standard/Thrust	Stance/17/20	3.0	117p	-	D/E/-/E	10/10/0/0	Twinkling Titanite
Astora Straight Sword	Standard/Thrust	Stance/17/20	3.0	129p	-	D/E/-/-	10/10/0/12	Titanite
Barbed Straight Sword	Standard/Thrust	Stance/17/20	3.0	111p	33bl	D/D/-/-	11/11/0/0	Titanite
Broadsword	Standard	Stance/17/20	3.0	117p	-	C/D/-/-	10/10/0/0	Titanite
Broken Straight Sword	Standard	Stance/17/20	1.0	70p	-	D/D/-/-	8/8/0/0	Titanite
Cleric's Candlestick	Standard/Thrust	Guiding Light/5	2.0	70p/77m/60sb	-	D/D/C/-	8/12/0/12	Titanite
Dark Sword	Standard/Thrust	Stomp/13/13	4.5	115p	-	C/D/-/-	16/15/0/0	Titanite
Gotthard Twinswords	Standard/Thrust	Spin Slash/5/17	6.5	100p	-	D/D/-/-	12/18/0/0	Titanite
Irithyll Straight Sword	Standard/Thrust	Stance/17/20	4.0	124p	35fr	D/D/-/-	12/14/0/0	Twinkling Titanite
Long Sword	Standard/Thrust	Stance/17/20	3.0	110p	-	D/D/-/-	10/10/0/0	Titanite
Lothric Knight Sword	Standard/Thrust	Stance/17/20	4.0	103p/110c	-	D/D/-/-	11/18/0/0	Titanite
Lothric's Holy Sword	Standard/Thrust	Sacred Lothric Light/17/22	4.0	107p	-	D/D/-/-	10/18/0/14	Titanite Scale
Morion Blade	Standard/Thrust	Stance/17/20	4.0	131p	33bl	D/D/-/-	12/17/0/0	Twinkling Titanite
Shortsword	Standard/Thrust	Stance/17/20	2.0	99p/110c	-	D/C/-/-	8/10/0/0	Titanite
Sunlight Straight Sword	Standard/Thrust	Oath of Sunlight/40	3.0	112p	-	C/C/-/-	12/12/0/16	Twinkling Titanite

1
2
3
4
5
6
7
8
9
10

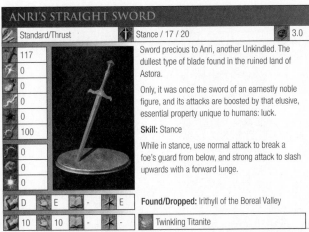

ANRI'S STRAIGHT SWORD

Standard/Thrust   Stance / 17 / 20   3.0

117	
0	
0	
0	
0	
100	
0	
0	
0	

Sword precious to Anri, another Unkindled. The dullest type of blade found in the ruined land of Astora.

Only, it was once the sword of an earnestly noble figure, and its attacks are boosted by that elusive, essential property unique to humans: luck.

Skill: Stance

While in stance, use normal attack to break a foe's guard from below, and strong attack to slash upwards with a forward lunge.

D	E	-	E
10	10	-	-

Found/Dropped: Irithyll of the Boreal Valley

Twinkling Titanite

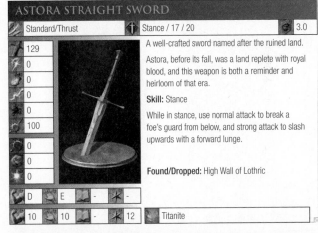

ASTORA STRAIGHT SWORD

Standard/Thrust   Stance / 17 / 20   3.0

129	
0	
0	
0	
0	
100	
0	
0	
0	

A well-crafted sword named after the ruined land.

Astora, before its fall, was a land replete with royal blood, and this weapon is both a reminder and heirloom of that era.

Skill: Stance

While in stance, use normal attack to break a foe's guard from below, and strong attack to slash upwards with a forward lunge.

Found/Dropped: High Wall of Lothric

D	E	-	-
10	10	-	12

Titanite

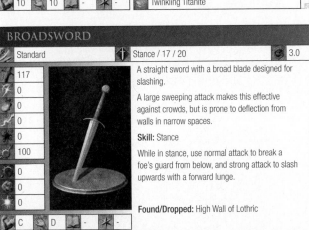

BROADSWORD

Standard   Stance / 17 / 20   3.0

117	
0	
0	
0	
0	
100	
0	
0	
0	

A straight sword with a broad blade designed for slashing.

A large sweeping attack makes this effective against crowds, but is prone to deflection from walls in narrow spaces.

Skill: Stance

While in stance, use normal attack to break a foe's guard from below, and strong attack to slash upwards with a forward lunge.

Found/Dropped: High Wall of Lothric

C	D	-	-
10	10	-	-

Titanite

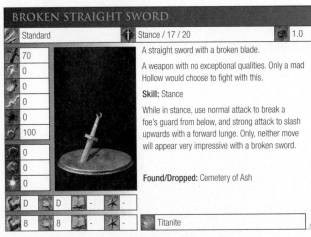

BROKEN STRAIGHT SWORD

Standard   Stance / 17 / 20   1.0

70	
0	
0	
0	
0	
100	
0	

A straight sword with a broken blade.

A weapon with no exceptional qualities. Only a mad Hollow would choose to fight with this.

Skill: Stance

While in stance, use normal attack to break a foe's guard from below, and strong attack to slash upwards with a forward lunge. Only, neither move will appear very impressive with a broken sword.

Found/Dropped: Cemetery of Ash

D	D	-	-
8	8	-	-

Titanite

CLERIC'S CANDLESTICK

Standard/Thrust | Guiding Light / 5 | 2.0

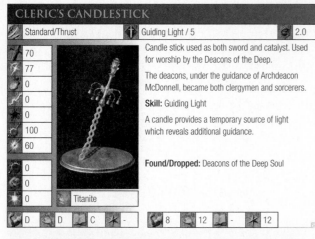

70	
77	
0	
0	
0	
100	
60	
0	
0	
0	Titanite

D	D	C	-	-
8	12	-	12	

Candle stick used as both sword and catalyst. Used for worship by the Deacons of the Deep.

The deacons, under the guidance of Archdeacon McDonnell, became both clergymen and sorcerers.

Skill: Guiding Light

A candle provides a temporary source of light which reveals additional guidance.

Found/Dropped: Deacons of the Deep Soul

DARK SWORD

Standard/Thrust | Stomp / 13 / 13 | 4.5

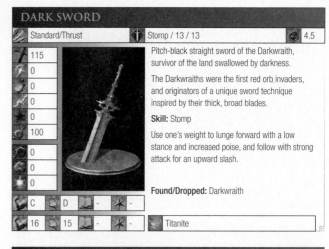

115	
0	
0	
0	
0	
100	
0	
0	
0	

C	D	-	-
16	15	-	-

Titanite

Pitch-black straight sword of the Darkwraith, survivor of the land swallowed by darkness.

The Darkwraiths were the first red orb invaders, and originators of a unique sword technique inspired by their thick, broad blades.

Skill: Stomp

Use one's weight to lunge forward with a low stance and increased poise, and follow with strong attack for an upward slash.

Found/Dropped: Darkwraith

GOTTHARD TWINSWORDS

Standard/Thrust | Spin Slash / 5 / 17 | 6.5

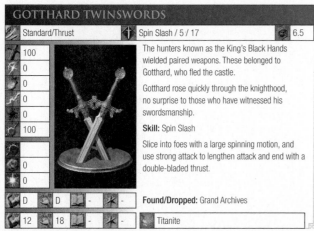

100	
0	
0	
0	
0	
100	
0	
0	

D	D	-	-
12	18	-	-

Titanite

The hunters known as the King's Black Hands wielded paired weapons. These belonged to Gotthard, who fled the castle.

Gotthard rose quickly through the knighthood, no surprise to those who have witnessed his swordsmanship.

Skill: Spin Slash

Slice into foes with a large spinning motion, and use strong attack to lengthen attack and end with a double-bladed thrust.

Found/Dropped: Grand Archives

IRITHYLL STRAIGHT SWORD

Standard/Thrust | Stance / 17 / 20 | 4.0

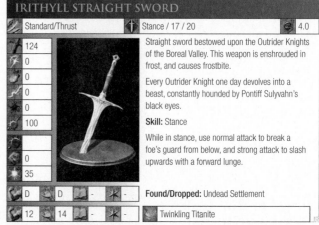

124	
0	
0	
0	
0	
100	
0	
35	

D	D	-	-
12	14	-	-

Twinkling Titanite

Straight sword bestowed upon the Outrider Knights of the Boreal Valley. This weapon is enshrouded in frost, and causes frostbite.

Every Outrider Knight one day devolves into a beast, constantly hounded by Pontiff Sulyvahn's black eyes.

Skill: Stance

While in stance, use normal attack to break a foe's guard from below, and strong attack to slash upwards with a forward lunge.

Found/Dropped: Undead Settlement

LONG SWORD

Standard/Thrust | Stance / 17 / 20 | 3.0

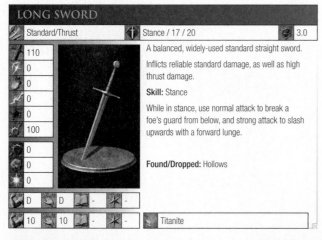

110	
0	
0	
0	
0	
100	
0	
0	
0	

D	D	-	-
10	10	-	-

Titanite

A balanced, widely-used standard straight sword.

Inflicts reliable standard damage, as well as high thrust damage.

Skill: Stance

While in stance, use normal attack to break a foe's guard from below, and strong attack to slash upwards with a forward lunge.

Found/Dropped: Hollows

LOTHRIC KNIGHT SWORD

Standard/Thrust | Stance / 17 / 20 | 4.0

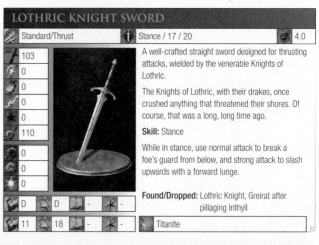

103	
0	
0	
0	
0	
110	
0	
0	
0	

D	D	-	-
11	18	-	-

Titanite

A well-crafted straight sword designed for thrusting attacks, wielded by the venerable Knights of Lothric.

The Knights of Lothric, with their drakes, once crushed anything that threatened their shores. Of course, that was a long, long time ago.

Skill: Stance

While in stance, use normal attack to break a foe's guard from below, and strong attack to slash upwards with a forward lunge.

Found/Dropped: Lothric Knight, Greirat after pillaging Irithyll

LOTHRIC'S HOLY SWORD

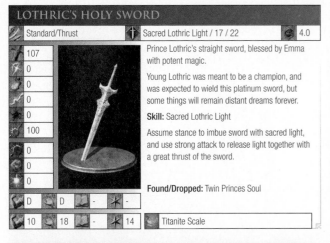

Standard/Thrust		Sacred Lothric Light / 17 / 22		4.0

107	
0	
0	
0	
0	
100	
0	
0	
0	

Prince Lothric's straight sword, blessed by Emma with potent magic.

Young Lothric was meant to be a champion, and was expected to wield this platinum sword, but some things will remain distant dreams forever.

Skill: Sacred Lothric Light

Assume stance to imbue sword with sacred light, and use strong attack to release light together with a great thrust of the sword.

Found/Dropped: Twin Princes Soul

D		D		-		-
10		18		-		14

Titanite Scale

MORION BLADE

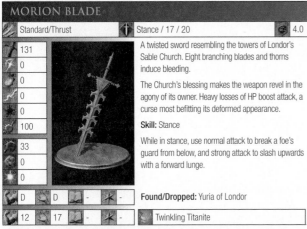

Standard/Thrust		Stance / 17 / 20		4.0

131	
0	
0	
0	
0	
100	
33	
0	
0	

A twisted sword resembling the towers of Londor's Sable Church. Eight branching blades and thorns induce bleeding.

The Church's blessing makes the weapon revel in the agony of its owner. Heavy losses of HP boost attack, a curse most befitting its deformed appearance.

Skill: Stance

While in stance, use normal attack to break a foe's guard from below, and strong attack to slash upwards with a forward lunge.

Found/Dropped: Yuria of Londor

D		D		-		-
12		17		-		-

Twinkling Titanite

SHORTSWORD

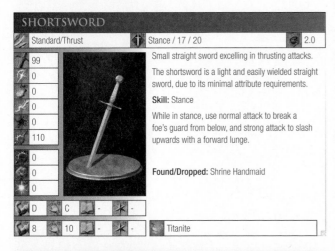

Standard/Thrust		Stance / 17 / 20		2.0

99	
0	
0	
0	
0	
110	
0	
0	
0	

Small straight sword excelling in thrusting attacks.

The shortsword is a light and easily wielded straight sword, due to its minimal attribute requirements.

Skill: Stance

While in stance, use normal attack to break a foe's guard from below, and strong attack to slash upwards with a forward lunge.

Found/Dropped: Shrine Handmaid

D		C		-		-
8		10		-		-

Titanite

SUNLIGHT STRAIGHT SWORD

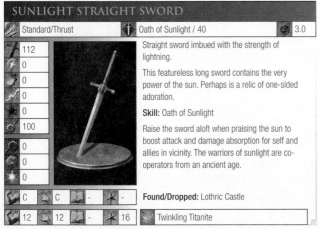

Standard/Thrust		Oath of Sunlight / 40		3.0

112	
0	
0	
0	
0	
100	
0	
0	
0	

Straight sword imbued with the strength of lightning.

This featureless long sword contains the very power of the sun. Perhaps is a relic of one-sided adoration.

Skill: Oath of Sunlight

Raise the sword aloft when praising the sun to boost attack and damage absorption for self and allies in vicinity. The warriors of sunlight are co-operators from an ancient age.

Found/Dropped: Lothric Castle

C		C		-		-
12		12		-		16

Twinkling Titanite

GREATSWORDS

The first of the large weapon classes, Greatswords strike a balance between the monstrous hitting power of the Great Hammers and Ultra Greatswords, and the faster and lighter weaponry.

Most Greatswords require moderate levels of both Str and Dex, so they are usually hard to use very early in the game, but you can find a few blades with lower requirements in the mix. Greatswords have a fairly large variety of weapon skills, from the more common Stance and Stomp, to the completely unique, with most weapons in this category requiring Titanite Scales to upgrade.

Greatswords can be used one-handed reasonably effectively, but like all large weapons, they are made to be wielded two handed, to deal heavy crushing hits that stagger your opposition and down them quickly. Like other large weapons, be careful about how you attack with them in PvP, their slower swings can telegraph your intent against skilled opponents.

GREATSWORDS	TYPE	ART/COST	WEIGHT	POWER	ADD. EFFECT	SCALING	REQUIREMENTS	MATERIAL
Bastard Sword	Standard	Stomp/12/15	8.0	125p	-	D/D/-/-	16/10/0/0	Titanite
Black Knight Sword	Standard/Thrust	Perseverance/10	10.0	156p	-	D/D/-/-	20/18/0/0	Twinkling Titanite
Claymore	Standard/Thrust	Stance/17/20	9.0	125p	-	D/D/-/-	16/13/0/0	Titanite
Drakeblood Greatsword	Standard/Thrust	Stance/17/20	6.0	83p/65m/65l	-	D/D/-/-	18/16/0/0	Titanite
Executioner's Greatsword	Strike	Stomp/12/17	9.0	119p	-	C/E/-/-	19/13/0/0	Titanite
Firelink Greatsword	Standard	Ember/25	9.0	119p/80f	-	D/D/-/-	20/10/10/10	Titanite Scale
Flamberge	Slash	Stance/17/20	8.5	144p	33bl	D/D/-/-	15/14/0/0	Titanite
Greatsword of Judgement	Standard	Stance of Judgment/19/22	9.0	101p/78m	-	D/D/C/-	17/15/12/0	Titanite Scale
Hollowslayer Greatsword	Standard/Thrust	Stance/17/20	8.5	130p	-	D/C/-/-	14/18/0/0	Titanite Scale
Moonlight Greatsword	Standard	Moonlight Vortex/18	10.5	79p/110m	-	E/E/D/-	16/11/26/0	Titanite Scale
Storm Ruler	Standard	Storm King/20/20	8.0	110p	-	D/D/-/-	0/0/0/0	Titanite Scale
Twin Princes' Greatsword	Standard	Sacred Light and Flame/22/22	9.5	118p/73f	-	D/D/D/D	22/14/0/0	Titanite Scale
Wolf Knight's Greatsword	Standard/Thrust	Wolf Sword/19/23	11.5	126p	-	C/D/-/-	24/18/0/0	Titanite Scale
Wolnir's Holy Sword	Standard	Wrath of the Gods/30	7.5	137p	-	D/D/-/-	13/13/0/13	Titanite Scale

BASTARD SWORD

Standard	Stomp / 12 / 15	8.0

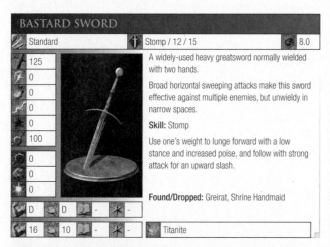

| 125 |
| 0 |
| 0 |
| 0 |
| 0 |
| 100 |
| 0 |
| 0 |
| 0 |

A widely-used heavy greatsword normally wielded with two hands.

Broad horizontal sweeping attacks make this sword effective against multiple enemies, but unwieldy in narrow spaces.

Skill: Stomp

Use one's weight to lunge forward with a low stance and increased poise, and follow with strong attack for an upward slash.

Found/Dropped: Greirat, Shrine Handmaid

D	D	-	* -
16	10	-	* -

Titanite

BLACK KNIGHT SWORD

Standard/Thrust	Perseverance / 10	10.0

| 156 |
| 0 |
| 0 |
| 0 |
| 0 |
| 100 |
| 0 |
| 0 |
| 0 |

Greatsword wielded by the Black Knights who wander the lands. Designed to face chaos demons.

The Black Knights constantly faced foes larger than themselves, and this sword's unique attack greatly reduces enemy poise.

Skill: Perseverance

Raise sword in the name of the First Lord to temporarily boost poise. Damage reduced while activated.

Found/Dropped: Smouldering Lake

D	D	-	* -
20	18	-	* -

Twinkling Titanite

CLAYMORE

Standard/Thrust	Stance / 17 / 20	9.0

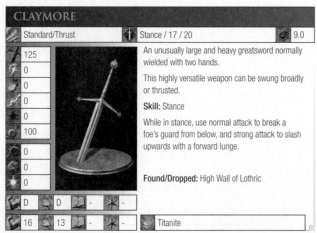

| 125 |
| 0 |
| 0 |
| 0 |
| 0 |
| 100 |
| 0 |
| 0 |
| 0 |

An unusually large and heavy greatsword normally wielded with two hands.

This highly versatile weapon can be swung broadly or thrusted.

Skill: Stance

While in stance, use normal attack to break a foe's guard from below, and strong attack to slash upwards with a forward lunge.

Found/Dropped: High Wall of Lothric

D	D	-	* -
16	13	-	* -

Titanite

DRAKEBLOOD GREATSWORD

Standard/Thrust	Stance / 17 / 20	6.0

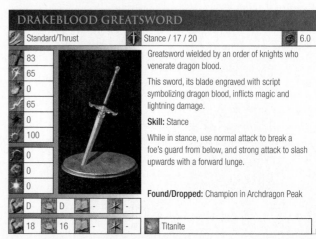

| 83 |
| 65 |
| 0 |
| 65 |
| 0 |
| 100 |
| 0 |
| 0 |
| 0 |

Greatsword wielded by an order of knights who venerate dragon blood.

This sword, its blade engraved with script symbolizing dragon blood, inflicts magic and lightning damage.

Skill: Stance

While in stance, use normal attack to break a foe's guard from below, and strong attack to slash upwards with a forward lunge.

Found/Dropped: Champion in Archdragon Peak

D	D	-	* -
18	16	-	* -

Titanite

EXECUTIONER'S GREATSWORD

Strike	Stomp / 12 / 17	9.0

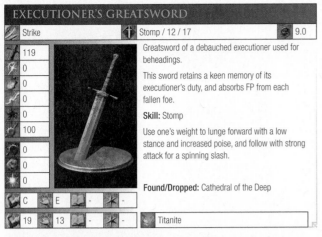

119	
0	
0	
0	
0	
100	
0	
0	
0	

Greatsword of a debauched executioner used for beheadings.

This sword retains a keen memory of its executioner's duty, and absorbs FP from each fallen foe.

Skill: Stomp

Use one's weight to lunge forward with a low stance and increased poise, and follow with strong attack for a spinning slash.

Found/Dropped: Cathedral of the Deep

C	E	-	-
19	13	-	-

Titanite

FIRELINK GREATSWORD

Standard	Ember / 25	9.0

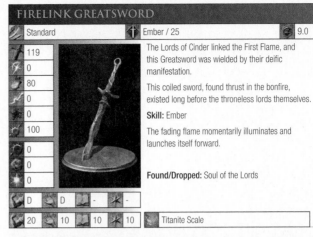

119	
0	
80	
0	
0	
100	
0	
0	
0	

The Lords of Cinder linked the First Flame, and this Greatsword was wielded by their deific manifestation.

This coiled sword, found thrust in the bonfire, existed long before the throneless lords themselves.

Skill: Ember

The fading flame momentarily illuminates and launches itself forward.

Found/Dropped: Soul of the Lords

D	D	-	-
20	10	10	10

Titanite Scale

FLAMBERGE

Slash	Stance / 17 / 20	8.5

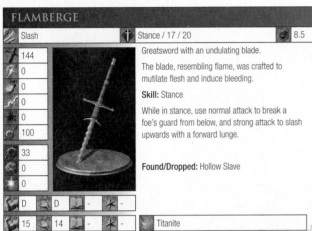

144	
0	
0	
0	
0	
100	
33	
0	
0	

Greatsword with an undulating blade.

The blade, resembling flame, was crafted to mutilate flesh and induce bleeding.

Skill: Stance

While in stance, use normal attack to break a foe's guard from below, and strong attack to slash upwards with a forward lunge.

Found/Dropped: Hollow Slave

D	D	-	-
15	14	-	-

Titanite

GREATSWORD OF JUDGEMENT

Standard	Stance of Judgment / 19 / 22	9.0

101	
78	
0	
0	
0	
100	
0	
0	
0	

A ceremonial sword, held in Pontiff Sulyvahn's left hand, representing the judgment of the moon, but with magic far closer to sorcery than any existing lunar power. Its dark blue hues, deeper than the darkest moon, reflect sorcerer Sulyvahn's true nature.

Skill: Stance of Judgment

Assume stance to unleash dark magic. Use normal attack for a lunging thrust, and strong attack to emit side-sweeping wave.

Found/Dropped: Soul of Sulyvahn

D	D	C	-
17	15	12	-

Titanite Scale

HOLLOWSLAYER GREATSWORD

Standard/Thrust	Stance / 17 / 20	8.5

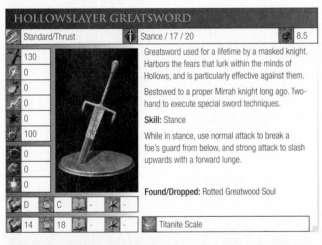

130	
0	
0	
0	
0	
100	
0	
0	
0	

Greatsword used for a lifetime by a masked knight. Harbors the fears that lurk within the minds of Hollows, and is particularly effective against them.

Bestowed to a proper Mirrah knight long ago. Two-hand to execute special sword techniques.

Skill: Stance

While in stance, use normal attack to break a foe's guard from below, and strong attack to slash upwards with a forward lunge.

Found/Dropped: Rotted Greatwood Soul

D	C	-	-
14	18	-	-

Titanite Scale

MOONLIGHT GREATSWORD

Standard	Moonlight Vortex / 18	10.5

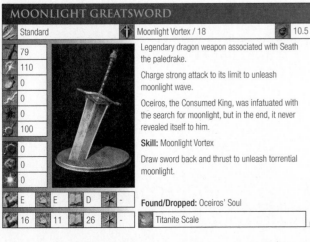

79	
110	
0	
0	
0	
100	
0	
0	
0	

Legendary dragon weapon associated with Seath the paledrake.

Charge strong attack to its limit to unleash moonlight wave.

Oceiros, the Consumed King, was infatuated with the search for moonlight, but in the end, it never revealed itself to him.

Skill: Moonlight Vortex

Draw sword back and thrust to unleash torrential moonlight.

Found/Dropped: Oceiros' Soul

E	E	D	-
16	11	26	-

Titanite Scale

STORM RULER

Standard	Storm King / 20 / 20	8.0

⚔	110
	0
	0
	0
	0
	100
	0
	0
	0

D	D	-	✸	-
-	-	-	✸	-

Titanite Scale

Greatsword with a broken blade, also known as the Giantslayer for the residual strength of storm that brings giants to their knees.

Yhorm the Giant once held two of these, but gave one to the humans who doubted him, and left the other to a dear friend before facing his fate as a Lord of Cinder.

Skill: Storm King

Assume stance to imbue sword with storm. Most effective when facing giants.

Found/Dropped: Profaned Capital, Siegward of Catarina

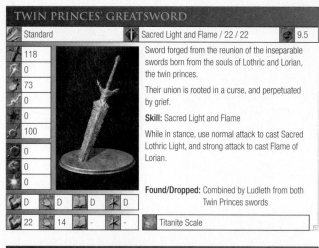

TWIN PRINCES' GREATSWORD

Standard	Sacred Light and Flame / 22 / 22	9.5

⚔	118
	0
	73
	0
	0
	100
	0
	0
	0

D	D	D	✸	D
22	14	-	✸	-

Titanite Scale

Sword forged from the reunion of the inseparable swords born from the souls of Lothric and Lorian, the twin princes.

Their union is rooted in a curse, and perpetuated by grief.

Skill: Sacred Light and Flame

While in stance, use normal attack to cast Sacred Lothric Light, and strong attack to cast Flame of Lorian.

Found/Dropped: Combined by Ludleth from both Twin Princes swords

WOLF KNIGHT'S GREATSWORD

Standard/Thrust	Wolf Sword / 19 / 23	11.5

⚔	126
	0
	0
	0
	0
	100
	0
	0
	0

C	D	-	✸	-
24	18	-	✸	-

Titanite Scale

Greatsword of a knight tainted by the dark of the Abyss, and master of the wolf's blood of Farron.

The wolf knight was the first Abyss Watcher, and his sword is more punishing against creations of the abyss.

Skill: Wolf Sword

While in stance, use normal attack for a low spinning slash, or strong attack to leap forward in a vertically-slashing somersault.

Found/Dropped: Blood of the Wolf Soul

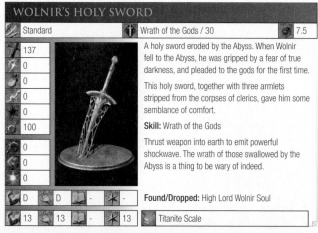

WOLNIR'S HOLY SWORD

Standard	Wrath of the Gods / 30	7.5

⚔	137
	0
	0
	0
	0
	100
	0
	0
	0

D	D	-	✸	-
13	13	-	✸	13

Titanite Scale

A holy sword eroded by the Abyss. When Wolnir fell to the Abyss, he was gripped by a fear of true darkness, and pleaded to the gods for the first time.

This holy sword, together with three armlets stripped from the corpses of clerics, gave him some semblance of comfort.

Skill: Wrath of the Gods

Thrust weapon into earth to emit powerful shockwave. The wrath of those swallowed by the Abyss is a thing to be wary of indeed.

Found/Dropped: High Lord Wolnir Soul

ULTRA GREATSWORDS

Sharing the podium for heaviest weapon class with Great Hammers, Ultra Greatswords are massive weapons, more slabs of metal than elegant blades.

Ultra Greatswords are heavy and have high stat requirements (right up to the incredibly demanding 50 Str for the Fume), but in exchange they offer crushing hitting power, delivering hits hard enough to down weaker enemies in a single strike, and deal impressive damage even to bosses in a few hits.

They pay for this power with their huge weight requirements and sluggish handling, and between the weight and the stat requirements, most Ultra Greatswords remain unusable until later in a playthrough, when you have enough stat muscle to properly wield these beasts.

Appropriately, most Ultra Greatswords have the Stomp skill, though there are a few others mixed in as well. The Farron Greatsword is particularly notable for possessing an offhand light blade that can be used to Parry!

ULTRA GREATSWORDS	TYPE	ART/COST	WEIGHT	POWER	ADD. EFFECT	SCALING	REQUIREMENTS	MATERIAL
Astora Greatsword	Standard/Thrust	Charge/13/13	8.0	122p	-	D/C/-/-	16/18/0/0	Titanite
Black Knight Greatsword	Standard/Thrust	Stomp/10/16	16.0	185p	-	C/D/-/-	30/18/0/0	Twinkling Titanite
Cathedral Knight Greatsword	Strike/Thrust	Stomp/10/20	15.0	149p	-	C/E/-/-	26/10/0/0	Titanite
Farron Greatsword	Standard/Thrust	Parry/-	12.5	125p	-	D/C/-/-	18/20/0/0	Titanite Scale
Fume Ultra Greatsword	Strike	Stomp/10/18	25.5	189p	-	A/E/-/-	50/10/0/0	Twinkling Titanite
Greatsword	Standard	Stomp/10/20	20.0	159p	-	D/D/-/-	28/10/0/0	Titanite
Lorian's Greatsword	Standard/Thrust	Flame of Lorian/10/18	14.0	151p/79f	-	D/D/D/D	26/10/0/0	Titanite Scale
Lothric Knight Greatsword	Standard/Thrust	Stomp/10/15	16.5	131p/87l	-	D/D/-/-	24/16/0/0	Titanite
Profaned Greatsword	Standard/Thrust	Profaned Flame/10/17	13.5	161p	-	C/D/-/-	22/10/0/0	Titanite Scale
Zweihander	Standard/Thrust	Stomp/10/15	10.0	140p	-	D/D/-/-	19/11/0/0	Titanite

ASTORA GREATSWORD

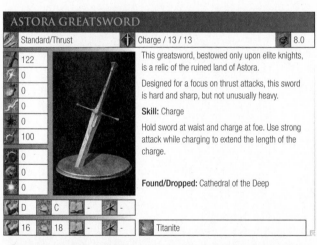

Standard/Thrust | Charge / 13 / 13 | 8.0

| 122 |
| 0 |
| 0 |
| 0 |
| 0 |
| 100 |
| 0 |
| 0 |
| 0 |

This greatsword, bestowed only upon elite knights, is a relic of the ruined land of Astora.

Designed for a focus on thrust attacks, this sword is hard and sharp, but not unusually heavy.

Skill: Charge

Hold sword at waist and charge at foe. Use strong attack while charging to extend the length of the charge.

Found/Dropped: Cathedral of the Deep

| D | C | - | - |
| 16 | 18 | - | - |

Titanite

BLACK KNIGHT GREATSWORD

Standard/Thrust | Stomp / 10 / 16 | 16.0

| 185 |
| 0 |
| 0 |
| 0 |
| 0 |
| 100 |
| 0 |
| 0 |
| 0 |

Ultra greatsword wielded by the Black Knights who wander the lands.

Designed to face chaos demons.

The Black Knights constantly faced foes larger than themselves, and this sword's unique attack greatly reduces enemy poise.

Skill: Stomp

Use one's weight to lunge forward with a low stance and increased poise, and follow with a crushing strong attack.

Found/Dropped: Black Knight

| C | D | - | - |
| 30 | 18 | - | - |

Twinkling Titanite

CATHEDRAL KNIGHT GREATSWORD

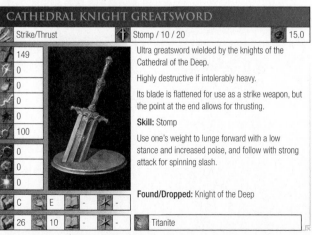

Strike/Thrust | Stomp / 10 / 20 | 15.0

| 149 |
| 0 |
| 0 |
| 0 |
| 0 |
| 100 |
| 0 |
| 0 |
| 0 |

Ultra greatsword wielded by the knights of the Cathedral of the Deep.

Highly destructive if intolerably heavy.

Its blade is flattened for use as a strike weapon, but the point at the end allows for thrusting.

Skill: Stomp

Use one's weight to lunge forward with a low stance and increased poise, and follow with strong attack for spinning slash.

Found/Dropped: Knight of the Deep

| C | E | - | - |
| 26 | 10 | - | - |

Titanite

FARRON GREATSWORD

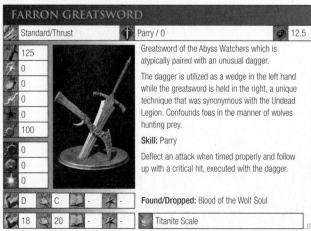

Standard/Thrust | Parry / 0 | 12.5

| 125 |
| 0 |
| 0 |
| 0 |
| 0 |
| 100 |
| 0 |
| 0 |
| 0 |

Greatsword of the Abyss Watchers which is atypically paired with an unusual dagger.

The dagger is utilized as a wedge in the left hand while the greatsword is held in the right, a unique technique that was synonymous with the Undead Legion. Confounds foes in the manner of wolves hunting prey.

Skill: Parry

Deflect an attack when timed properly and follow up with a critical hit, executed with the dagger.

Found/Dropped: Blood of the Wolf Soul

| D | C | - | - |
| 18 | 20 | - | - |

Titanite Scale

FUME ULTRA GREATSWORD

Strike	Stomp / 10 / 18	25.5

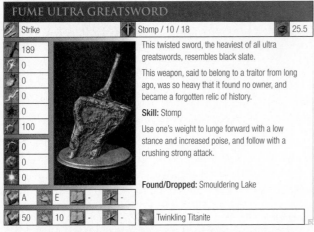

	189
	0
	0
	0
	0
	100
	0
	0
	0

This twisted sword, the heaviest of all ultra greatswords, resembles black slate.

This weapon, said to belong to a traitor from long ago, was so heavy that it found no owner, and became a forgotten relic of history.

Skill: Stomp

Use one's weight to lunge forward with a low stance and increased poise, and follow with a crushing strong attack.

Found/Dropped: Smouldering Lake

A	E	-	-
50	10	-	-

Twinkling Titanite

GREATSWORD

Standard	Stomp / 10 / 20	20.0

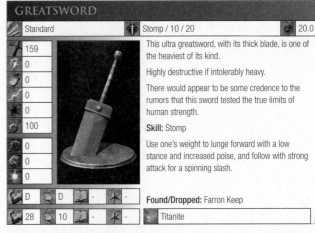

	159
	0
	0
	0
	0
	100
	0
	0
	0

This ultra greatsword, with its thick blade, is one of the heaviest of its kind.

Highly destructive if intolerably heavy.

There would appear to be some credence to the rumors that this sword tested the true limits of human strength.

Skill: Stomp

Use one's weight to lunge forward with a low stance and increased poise, and follow with strong attack for a spinning slash.

Found/Dropped: Farron Keep

D	D	-	-
28	10	-	-

Titanite

LORIAN'S GREATSWORD

Standard/Thrust	Flame of Lorian / 10 / 18	14.0

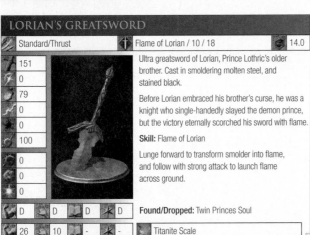

	151
	0
	79
	0
	0
	100
	0
	0
	0

Ultra greatsword of Lorian, Prince Lothric's older brother. Cast in smoldering molten steel, and stained black.

Before Lorian embraced his brother's curse, he was a knight who single-handedly slayed the demon prince, but the victory eternally scorched his sword with flame.

Skill: Flame of Lorian

Lunge forward to transform smolder into flame, and follow with strong attack to launch flame across ground.

Found/Dropped: Twin Princes Soul

D	D	D	D
26	10	-	-

Titanite Scale

LOTHRIC KNIGHT GREATSWORD

Standard/Thrust	Stomp / 10 / 15	16.5

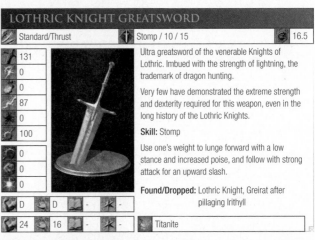

	131
	0
	0
	87
	0
	100
	0
	0
	0

Ultra greatsword of the venerable Knights of Lothric. Imbued with the strength of lightning, the trademark of dragon hunting.

Very few have demonstrated the extreme strength and dexterity required for this weapon, even in the long history of the Lothric Knights.

Skill: Stomp

Use one's weight to lunge forward with a low stance and increased poise, and follow with strong attack for an upward slash.

Found/Dropped: Lothric Knight, Greirat after pillaging Irithyll

D	D	-	-
24	16	-	-

Titanite

PROFANED GREATSWORD

Standard/Thrust	Profaned Flame / 10 / 17	13.5

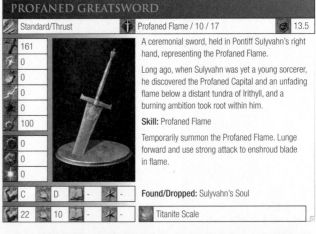

	161
	0
	0
	0
	0
	100
	0
	0
	0

A ceremonial sword, held in Pontiff Sulyvahn's right hand, representing the Profaned Flame.

Long ago, when Sulyvahn was yet a young sorcerer, he discovered the Profaned Capital and an unfading flame below a distant tundra of Irithyll, and a burning ambition took root within him.

Skill: Profaned Flame

Temporarily summon the Profaned Flame. Lunge forward and use strong attack to enshroud blade in flame.

Found/Dropped: Sulyvahn's Soul

C	D	-	-
22	10	-	-

Titanite Scale

ZWEIHANDER

Standard/Thrust	Stomp / 10 / 15	10.0

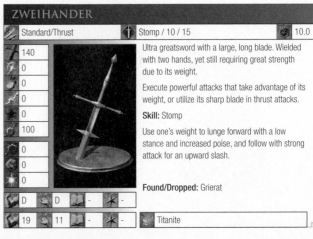

	140
	0
	0
	0
	0
	100
	0
	0
	0

Ultra greatsword with a large, long blade. Wielded with two hands, yet still requiring great strength due to its weight.

Execute powerful attacks that take advantage of its weight, or utilize its sharp blade in thrust attacks.

Skill: Stomp

Use one's weight to lunge forward with a low stance and increased poise, and follow with strong attack for an upward slash.

Found/Dropped: Greirat

D	D	-	-
19	11	-	-

Titanite

CURVED SWORDS

Graceful weapons, Curved Swords have a flowing combat style that lets them smoothly link one swing into the next with little delay. The dancer's version of a Straight Sword (indeed, there are a pair of twinned blades from the Dancer), Curved Swords let you get in, deal a series of rapid blows, and back off quickly.

Curved Sword skills focus on mobile combat, with Spin Slash giving you the ability to move and strike repeatedly at the same time, and the other unique skills have similar behavior.

Curved Swords are primarily Dex focused, and a good number of them have inherent Bleed, giving you the ability to sap your opponents health even further after landing a series of blows. Their requirements vary, with some of them being usable early in the game, and others requiring a decent investment in Dex to handle.

CURVED SWORDS	TYPE	ART/COST	WEIGHT	POWER	ADD. EFFECT	SCALING	REQUIREMENTS	MATERIAL
Carthus Curved Sword	Slash	Spin Slash/6/12	5.5	115p	33bl	D/D/-/-	15/18/0/0	Titanite
Carthus Shotel	Slash	Spin Slash/5/12	3.0	106p	33bl	E/C/-/-	12/19/0/0	Titanite
Crescent Moon Sword	Slash	Crescent Blade/15	2.5	78p/78m	-	E/C/-/-	10/16/0/0	Titanite Scale
Dancer's Enchanted Swords	Slash	Dancer's Grace/6/17	8.5	79p/62m/62f	-	D/D/D/D	12/20/9/9	Titanite Scale
Falchion	Slash	Spin Slash/6/12	4.0	117p	-	D/D/-/-	9/13/0/0	Titanite
Painting Guardian's Curved Sword	Slash	Chained Dance/5/15	1.5	88p	33bl	E/B/-/-	7/19/0/0	Titanite
Pontiff Knight Curved Sword	Slash	Frost Blade/8/14	3.5	123	-	D/D/10/0	12/18/10/0	Twinkling Titanite
Rotten Ghru Curved Sword	Slash	Spin Slash/6/12	2.0	103p	33po	E/C/-/-	10/13/0/0	Titanite
Scimitar	Slash	Spin Slash/4/12	2.5	90p	-	E/C/-/-	7/13/0/0	Titanite
Sellsword Twinblades	Slash	Spin Slash/4/12	5.5	99p	-	E/C/-/-	10/16/0/0	Titanite
Shotel	Slash	Spin Slash/5/12	2.5	104p	-	E/C/-/-	9/14/0/0	Titanite
Storm Curved Sword	Slash	Tornado/7/15	5.0	110p	-	D/C/-/-	14/20/0/0	Titanite Scale
Warden Twinblades	Slash	Spin Slash/7/9	6.5	93p	33bl	D/D/-/-	10/18/0/0	Titanite

CARTHUS CURVED SWORD

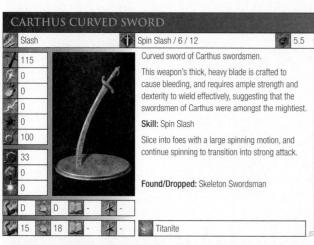

Slash		Spin Slash / 6 / 12		5.5

| 115 |
| 0 |
| 0 |
| 0 |
| 0 |
| 100 |
| 33 |
| 0 |
| 0 |

Curved sword of Carthus swordsmen.

This weapon's thick, heavy blade is crafted to cause bleeding, and requires ample strength and dexterity to wield effectively, suggesting that the swordsmen of Carthus were amongst the mightiest.

Skill: Spin Slash

Slice into foes with a large spinning motion, and continue spinning to transition into strong attack.

Found/Dropped: Skeleton Swordsman

| D | D | - | - |
| 15 | 18 | - | - | Titanite |

CARTHUS SHOTEL

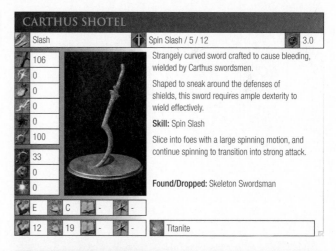

Slash		Spin Slash / 5 / 12		3.0

| 106 |
| 0 |
| 0 |
| 0 |
| 0 |
| 100 |
| 33 |
| 0 |
| 0 |

Strangely curved sword crafted to cause bleeding, wielded by Carthus swordsmen.

Shaped to sneak around the defenses of shields, this sword requires ample dexterity to wield effectively.

Skill: Spin Slash

Slice into foes with a large spinning motion, and continue spinning to transition into strong attack.

Found/Dropped: Skeleton Swordsman

| E | C | - | - |
| 12 | 19 | - | - | Titanite |

CRESCENT MOON SWORD

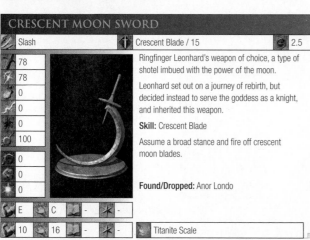

Slash		Crescent Blade / 15		2.5

| 78 |
| 78 |
| 0 |
| 0 |
| 0 |
| 100 |
| 0 |
| 0 |
| 0 |

Ringfinger Leonhard's weapon of choice, a type of shotel imbued with the power of the moon.

Leonhard set out on a journey of rebirth, but decided instead to serve the goddess as a knight, and inherited this weapon.

Skill: Crescent Blade

Assume a broad stance and fire off crescent moon blades.

Found/Dropped: Anor Londo

| E | C | - | - |
| 10 | 16 | - | - | Titanite Scale |

DANCER'S ENCHANTED SWORDS

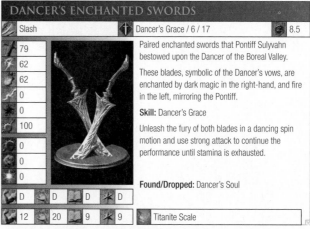

Slash		Dancer's Grace / 6 / 17		8.5

| 79 |
| 62 |
| 62 |
| 0 |
| 0 |
| 100 |
| 0 |
| 0 |
| 0 |

Paired enchanted swords that Pontiff Sulyvahn bestowed upon the Dancer of the Boreal Valley.

These blades, symbolic of the Dancer's vows, are enchanted by dark magic in the right-hand, and fire in the left, mirroring the Pontiff.

Skill: Dancer's Grace

Unleash the fury of both blades in a dancing spin motion and use strong attack to continue the performance until stamina is exhausted.

Found/Dropped: Dancer's Soul

| D | D | D | D |
| 12 | 20 | 9 | 9 | Titanite Scale |

FALCHION

| Slash | | Spin Slash / 6 / 12 | | 4.0 |

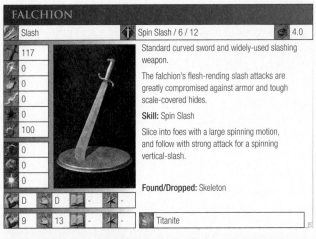

| 117 |
| 0 |
| 0 |
| 0 |
| 0 |
| 100 |
| 0 |
| 0 |
| 0 |

Standard curved sword and widely-used slashing weapon.

The falchion's flesh-rending slash attacks are greatly compromised against armor and tough scale-covered hides.

Skill: Spin Slash

Slice into foes with a large spinning motion, and follow with strong attack for a spinning vertical-slash.

Found/Dropped: Skeleton

| D | D | - | - |
| 9 | 13 | - | - | Titanite |

PONTIFF KNIGHT CURVED SWORD

| Slash | | Frost Blade / 8 / 14 | | 3.5 |

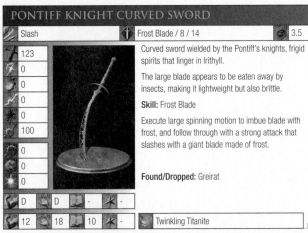

| 123 |
| 0 |
| 0 |
| 0 |
| 0 |
| 100 |
| 0 |
| 0 |
| 0 |

Curved sword wielded by the Pontiff's knights, frigid spirits that linger in Irithyll.

The large blade appears to be eaten away by insects, making it lightweight but also brittle.

Skill: Frost Blade

Execute large spinning motion to imbue blade with frost, and follow through with a strong attack that slashes with a giant blade made of frost.

Found/Dropped: Greirat

| D | D | - | - |
| 12 | 18 | 10 | - | Twinkling Titanite |

PAINTING GUARDIAN'S CURVED SWORD

| Slash | | Chained Dance / 5 / 15 | | 1.5 |

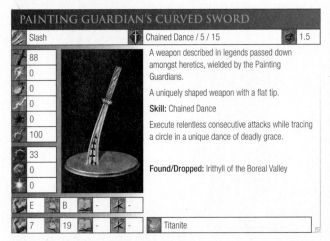

| 88 |
| 0 |
| 0 |
| 0 |
| 0 |
| 100 |
| 33 |
| 0 |
| 0 |

A weapon described in legends passed down amongst heretics, wielded by the Painting Guardians.

A uniquely shaped weapon with a flat tip.

Skill: Chained Dance

Execute relentless consecutive attacks while tracing a circle in a unique dance of deadly grace.

Found/Dropped: Irithyll of the Boreal Valley

| E | B | - | - |
| 7 | 19 | - | - | Titanite |

ROTTEN GHRU CURVED SWORD

| Slash | | Spin Slash / 6 / 12 | | 2.0 |

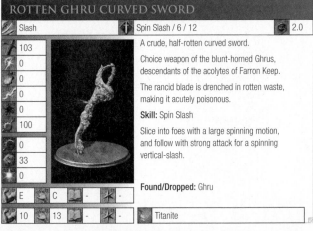

| 103 |
| 0 |
| 0 |
| 0 |
| 0 |
| 100 |
| 0 |
| 33 |
| 0 |

A crude, half-rotten curved sword.

Choice weapon of the blunt-horned Ghrus, descendants of the acolytes of Farron Keep.

The rancid blade is drenched in rotten waste, making it acutely poisonous.

Skill: Spin Slash

Slice into foes with a large spinning motion, and follow with strong attack for a spinning vertical-slash.

Found/Dropped: Ghru

| E | C | - | - |
| 10 | 13 | - | - | Titanite |

SCIMITAR

| Slash | | Spin Slash / 4 / 12 | | 2.5 |

| 90 |
| 0 |
| 0 |
| 0 |
| 0 |
| 100 |
| 0 |
| 0 |
| 0 |

Small curved sword that excels in swift movements and consecutive attacks.

The scimitar's flesh-rending slash attacks are greatly compromised against armor and tough scale-covered hides.

Skill: Spin Slash

Slice into foes with a large spinning motion, and follow with strong attack for a spinning vertical-slash.

Found/Dropped: Shrine Handmaid

| E | C | - | - |
| 7 | 13 | - | - | Titanite |

SELLSWORD TWINBLADES

| Slash | | Spin Slash / 4 / 12 | | 5.5 |

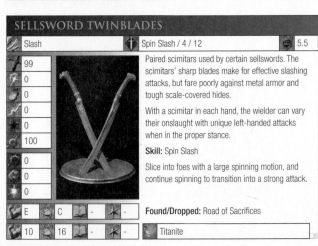

| 99 |
| 0 |
| 0 |
| 0 |
| 0 |
| 100 |
| 0 |
| 0 |
| 0 |

Paired scimitars used by certain sellswords. The scimitars' sharp blades make for effective slashing attacks, but fare poorly against metal armor and tough scale-covered hides.

With a scimitar in each hand, the wielder can vary their onslaught with unique left-handed attacks when in the proper stance.

Skill: Spin Slash

Slice into foes with a large spinning motion, and continue spinning to transition into a strong attack.

Found/Dropped: Road of Sacrifices

| E | C | - | - |
| 10 | 16 | - | - | Titanite |

SHOTEL

	Slash		Spin Slash / 5 / 12			2.5

104	
0	
0	
0	
0	
100	
0	
0	
0	

E		C		-	-	-
9		14		-	-	Titanite

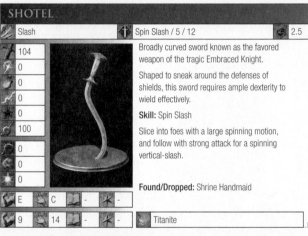

Broadly curved sword known as the favored weapon of the tragic Embraced Knight.

Shaped to sneak around the defenses of shields, this sword requires ample dexterity to wield effectively.

Skill: Spin Slash

Slice into foes with a large spinning motion, and follow with strong attack for a spinning vertical-slash.

Found/Dropped: Shrine Handmaid

STORM CURVED SWORD

	Slash		Tornado / 7 / 15			5.0

110	
0	
0	
0	
0	
100	
0	
0	
0	

D		C		-	-	-
14		20		-	-	Titanite Scale

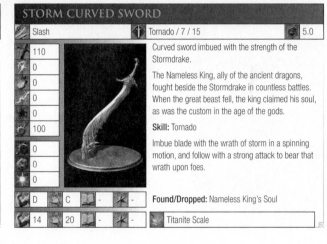

Curved sword imbued with the strength of the Stormdrake.

The Nameless King, ally of the ancient dragons, fought beside the Stormdrake in countless battles. When the great beast fell, the king claimed his soul, as was the custom in the age of the gods.

Skill: Tornado

Imbue blade with the wrath of storm in a spinning motion, and follow with a strong attack to bear that wrath upon foes.

Found/Dropped: Nameless King's Soul

WARDEN TWINBLADES

	Slash		Spin Slash / 7 / 9			6.5

93	
0	
0	
0	
0	
100	
33	
0	
0	

D		D		-	-	-
10		18		-	-	Titanite

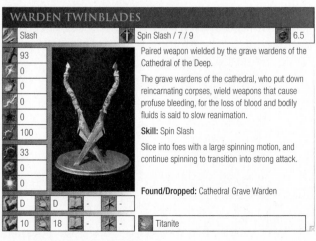

Paired weapon wielded by the grave wardens of the Cathedral of the Deep.

The grave wardens of the cathedral, who put down reincarnating corpses, wield weapons that cause profuse bleeding, for the loss of blood and bodily fluids is said to slow reanimation.

Skill: Spin Slash

Slice into foes with a large spinning motion, and continue spinning to transition into strong attack.

Found/Dropped: Cathedral Grave Warden

CURVED GREATSWORDS

A rare weapon category, there are only four such weapons in the game. While Greatswords and Ultra Greatswords have significantly different movesets from their Straight Sword children, Curved Greatswords retain a significant amount of the grace of their smaller versions.

Curved Greatswords still require a healthy attribute investment however, demanding both Str and Dex to use, and with moderate weight requirements. Three of them share the Spin Slash skill, while the fourth makes use of a leaping strike that emulates the Abyss Watcher's graceful fighting style.

If you want a larger weapon but don't enjoy the movesets on Greatswords, try a Curved Greatsword and see if it suits your playstyle.

CURVED GREATSWORDS	TYPE	ART/COST	WEIGHT	POWER	ADD. EFFECT	SCALING	REQUIREMENTS	MATERIAL
Carthus Curved Greatsword	Slash	Spin Slash/9/13	10.5	132p	33bl	D/C/-/-	18/22/0/0	Titanite
Exile Greatsword	Slash	Spin Slash/12/13	17.0	157p	-	D/D/-/-	24/16/0/0	Titanite
Murakumo	Slash	Spin Slash/9/15	11.0	135p	-	D/C/-/-	20/18/0/0	Titanite
Old Wolf Curved Sword	Slash	Wolf Leap/10/15	13.0	151p/79f	-	D/C/-/-	19/25/0/0	Twinkling Titanite

CARTHUS CURVED GREATSWORD

	Slash		Spin Slash / 9 / 13		10.5

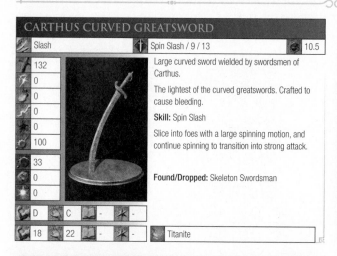

| 132 |
| 0 |
| 0 |
| 0 |
| 0 |
| 100 |
| 33 |
| 0 |
| 0 |

| D | C | - | - |
| 18 | 22 | - | - |

Large curved sword wielded by swordsmen of Carthus.

The lightest of the curved greatswords. Crafted to cause bleeding.

Skill: Spin Slash

Slice into foes with a large spinning motion, and continue spinning to transition into strong attack.

Found/Dropped: Skeleton Swordsman

Titanite

EXILE GREATSWORD

	Slash		Spin Slash / 12 / 13		17.0

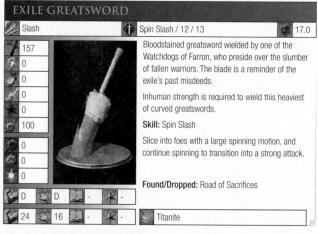

| 157 |
| 0 |
| 0 |
| 0 |
| 0 |
| 100 |
| 0 |
| 0 |
| 0 |

| D | D | - | - |
| 24 | 16 | - | - |

Bloodstained greatsword wielded by one of the Watchdogs of Farron, who preside over the slumber of fallen warriors. The blade is a reminder of the exile's past misdeeds.

Inhuman strength is required to wield this heaviest of curved greatswords.

Skill: Spin Slash

Slice into foes with a large spinning motion, and continue spinning to transition into a strong attack.

Found/Dropped: Road of Sacrifices

Titanite

MURAKUMO

	Slash		Spin Slash / 9 / 15		11.0

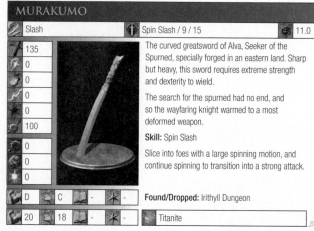

| 135 |
| 0 |
| 0 |
| 0 |
| 0 |
| 100 |
| 0 |
| 0 |
| 0 |

| D | C | - | - |
| 20 | 18 | - | - |

The curved greatsword of Alva, Seeker of the Spurned, specially forged in an eastern land. Sharp but heavy, this sword requires extreme strength and dexterity to wield.

The search for the spurned had no end, and so the wayfaring knight warmed to a most deformed weapon.

Skill: Spin Slash

Slice into foes with a large spinning motion, and continue spinning to transition into a strong attack.

Found/Dropped: Irithyll Dungeon

Titanite

OLD WOLF CURVED SWORD

	Slash		Wolf Leap / 10 / 15		13.0

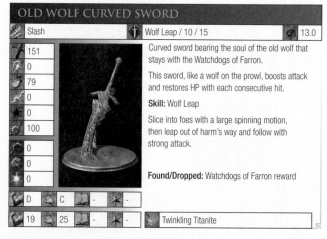

| 151 |
| 0 |
| 79 |
| 0 |
| 0 |
| 100 |
| 0 |
| 0 |
| 0 |

| D | C | - | - |
| 19 | 25 | - | - |

Curved sword bearing the soul of the old wolf that stays with the Watchdogs of Farron.

This sword, like a wolf on the prowl, boosts attack and restores HP with each consecutive hit.

Skill: Wolf Leap

Slice into foes with a large spinning motion, then leap out of harm's way and follow with strong attack.

Found/Dropped: Watchdogs of Farron reward

Twinkling Titanite

THRUSTING SWORDS

Dedicated fencer's weapons, Thrusting Swords focus on rapid piercing strikes. Almost a dagger in sword form, these are fast, lightweight weapons. They mix skills from Daggers and Straight Swords, giving you access to Stance and Shield Splitter both, granting an easy way around shielded opponents.

Ricard's Rapier is notable for having a unique skill that attacks with a very rapid flurry of blows. Enchant it with powders or enchantment spells to deal heavy elemental burst damage.

If you favor Dagger's speed but want a bit more punch on each hit, try a Thrusting Sword.

THRUSTING SWORDS	TYPE	ART/COST	WEIGHT	POWER	ADD. EFFECT	SCALING	REQUIREMENTS	MATERIAL
Crystal Sage's Rapier	Thrust	Stance/15/15	2.5	55p/82m	-	E/E/C/-	13/18/0/0	Titanite Scale
Estoc	Standard/Thrust	Shield Splitter/14	3.5	105p	-	D/D/-/-	10/12/0/0	Titanite
Irithyll Rapier	Thrust	Shield Splitter/14	3.0	116p/110c	35fr	D/D/-/-	10/16/0/0	Twinkling Titanite
Rapier	Thrust	Stance/15/15	2.0	95p/110c	-	E/C/-/-	7/12/0/0	Titanite
Ricard's Rapier	Thrust	Ricard's Lunge and Press	2.5	97p	-	D/C/-/-	8/20/0/0	Titanite

CRYSTAL SAGE'S RAPIER

Thrust | Stance / 15 / 15 | 2.5

| 55 |
| 82 |
| 0 |
| 0 |
| 0 |
| 100 |
| 0 |
| 0 |
| 0 |

Thrusting sword with tiny crystals scattered across its blade, used by the Crystal Sages for self-defense.

The crystals boost the magic damage inflicted by the sword, and the item discovery of its wielder, fruits of the lifetime of research conducted by the sages.

Skill: Stance

From stance, use normal attack to back step and execute a surprise attack, or strong attack for consecutive thrusting.

Found/Dropped: Crystal Sage's Soul

| E | E | C | - |

| 13 | 18 | - | - | Titanite Scale |

ESTOC

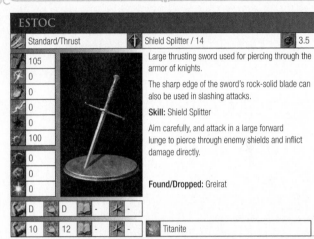

Standard/Thrust | Shield Splitter / 14 | 3.5

| 105 |
| 0 |
| 0 |
| 0 |
| 0 |
| 100 |
| 0 |
| 0 |
| 0 |

Large thrusting sword used for piercing through the armor of knights.

The sharp edge of the sword's rock-solid blade can also be used in slashing attacks.

Skill: Shield Splitter

Aim carefully, and attack in a large forward lunge to pierce through enemy shields and inflict damage directly.

Found/Dropped: Greirat

| D | D | - | - |

| 10 | 12 | - | - | Titanite |

IRITHYLL RAPIER

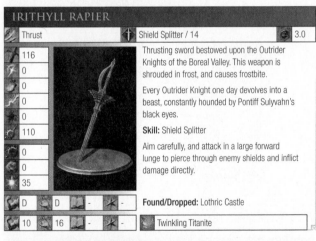

Thrust | Shield Splitter / 14 | 3.0

| 116 |
| 0 |
| 0 |
| 0 |
| 0 |
| 110 |
| 0 |
| 0 |
| 35 |

Thrusting sword bestowed upon the Outrider Knights of the Boreal Valley. This weapon is shrouded in frost, and causes frostbite.

Every Outrider Knight one day devolves into a beast, constantly hounded by Pontiff Sulyvahn's black eyes.

Skill: Shield Splitter

Aim carefully, and attack in a large forward lunge to pierce through enemy shields and inflict damage directly.

Found/Dropped: Lothric Castle

| D | D | - | - |

| 10 | 16 | - | - | Twinkling Titanite |

RAPIER

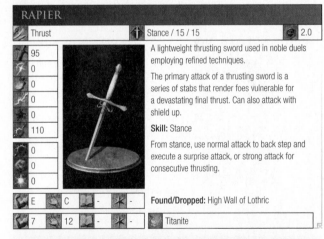

Thrust | Stance / 15 / 15 | 2.0

| 95 |
| 0 |
| 0 |
| 0 |
| 0 |
| 110 |
| 0 |
| 0 |
| 0 |

A lightweight thrusting sword used in noble duels employing refined techniques.

The primary attack of a thrusting sword is a series of stabs that render foes vulnerable for a devastating final thrust. Can also attack with shield up.

Skill: Stance

From stance, use normal attack to back step and execute a surprise attack, or strong attack for consecutive thrusting.

Found/Dropped: High Wall of Lothric

| E | C | - | - |

| 7 | 12 | - | - | Titanite |

RICARD'S RAPIER

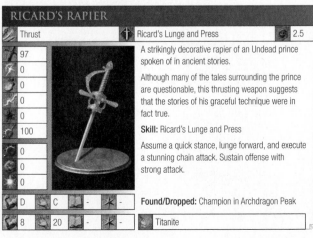

Thrust | Ricard's Lunge and Press | 2.5

| 97 |
| 0 |
| 0 |
| 0 |
| 0 |
| 100 |
| 0 |
| 0 |
| 0 |

A strikingly decorative rapier of an Undead prince spoken of in ancient stories.

Although many of the tales surrounding the prince are questionable, this thrusting weapon suggests that the stories of his graceful technique were in fact true.

Skill: Ricard's Lunge and Press

Assume a quick stance, lunge forward, and execute a stunning chain attack. Sustain offense with strong attack.

Found/Dropped: Champion in Archdragon Peak

| D | C | - | - |

| 8 | 20 | - | - | Titanite |

KATANAS

Unique blades, Katanas posses their own distinct fighting style, both in moveset and in weapon skills. They fall somewhere between Straight Swords and Curved Swords in style. You can acquire the Uchigatana early in the game by defeating the nearly naked Hollow just outside Firelink Shrine. Try it out and see if you like their style.

Katanas make use of wide arcing blows, great for dealing with multiple opponents or fighting in the open, harder to use in confined quarters. Every single Katana cuts deep enough to possess a Bleed attribute, giving these blades a little extra damage potential against most enemies.

Katanas are also notable for being one of the few weapon categories that have durability levels low enough that you can potentially drain their durability on a single outing from a Bonfire. Carry a backup weapon, some Repair Powder, the Repair spell, or some Homeward Bones to return to a Bonfire should this prove to be an issue.

KATANAS	TYPE	ART/COST	WEIGHT	POWER	ADD. EFFECT	SCALING	REQUIREMENTS	MATERIAL
Black Blade	Slash/Thrust	Hold/17/5	6.5	122p	33bl	D/D/-/-	18/18/0/0	Titanite
Bloodlust	Slash/Thrust	Bloodlust/10	5.0	105p	34bl	E/C/-/-	11/24/0/0	Twinkling Titanite
Chaos Blade	Slash/Thrust	Hold/17/5	6.0	103p	34bl	E/A/-/-	16/14/0/0	Twinkling Titanite
Darkdrift	Slash/Thrust	Darkdrift/20	3.5	129p	33bl	E/D/-/-	10/28/0/0	Twinkling Titanite
Onikiri and Ubadachi	Slash/Thrust	Onislayer/20	8.5	104p	33bl	D/C/-/-	13/25/0/0	Titanite
Uchigatana	Slash/Thrust	Hold/17/5	5.5	115p	33bl	E/D/-/-	11/16/0/0	Titanite
Washing Pole	Slash/Thrust	Hold/22/8	8.5	126p	33bl	D/D/-/-	18/20/0/0	Titanite

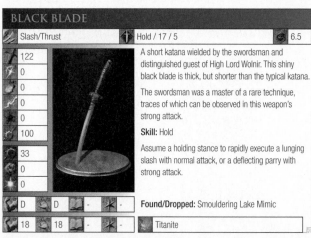

BLACK BLADE

Slash/Thrust   Hold / 17 / 5   6.5

122	
0	
0	
0	
0	
100	
33	
0	
0	

D	D	-	-
18	18	-	-

Titanite

A short katana wielded by the swordsman and distinguished guest of High Lord Wolnir. This shiny black blade is thick, but shorter than the typical katana.

The swordsman was a master of a rare technique, traces of which can be observed in this weapon's strong attack.

Skill: Hold

Assume a holding stance to rapidly execute a lunging slash with normal attack, or a deflecting parry with strong attack.

Found/Dropped: Smouldering Lake Mimic

BLOODLUST

Slash/Thrust   Bloodlust / 10   5.0

105	
0	
0	
0	
0	
100	
34	
0	
0	

E	C	-	-
11	24	-	-

Twinkling Titanite

Katana of the old Mound-maker.

The Mound-maker piled sacrifices upon the altar, but became the final offering himself, leaving this single-swing katana as a gift for his dear family.

Skill: Bloodlust

Stain blade with one's own blood to temporarily grant uncanny sharpness. For one driven by bloodlust, nothing deserves to remain standing.

Found/Dropped: Mound-Makers

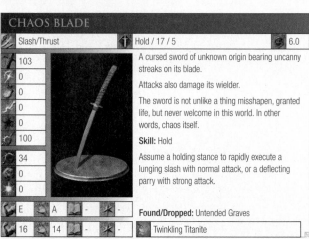

CHAOS BLADE

Slash/Thrust   Hold / 17 / 5   6.0

103	
0	
0	
0	
0	
100	
34	
0	
0	

E	A	-	-
16	14	-	-

Twinkling Titanite

A cursed sword of unknown origin bearing uncanny streaks on its blade.

Attacks also damage its wielder.

The sword is not unlike a thing misshapen, granted life, but never welcome in this world. In other words, chaos itself.

Skill: Hold

Assume a holding stance to rapidly execute a lunging slash with normal attack, or a deflecting parry with strong attack.

Found/Dropped: Untended Graves

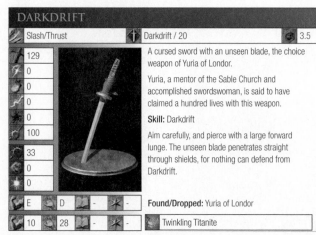

DARKDRIFT

Slash/Thrust   Darkdrift / 20   3.5

129	
0	
0	
0	
0	
100	
33	
0	
0	

E	D	-	-
10	28	-	-

Twinkling Titanite

A cursed sword with an unseen blade, the choice weapon of Yuria of Londor.

Yuria, a mentor of the Sable Church and accomplished swordswoman, is said to have claimed a hundred lives with this weapon.

Skill: Darkdrift

Aim carefully, and pierce with a large forward lunge. The unseen blade penetrates straight through shields, for nothing can defend from Darkdrift.

Found/Dropped: Yuria of Londor

ONIKIRI AND UBADACHI

Slash/Thrust		Onislayer / 20		8.5

⚔	104
⚡	0
🔥	0
✦	0
✴	0
🛡	100
🛡	33
	0
	0

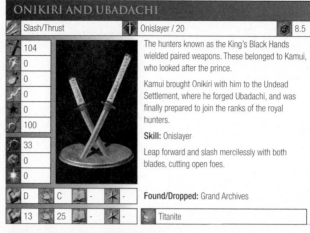

The hunters known as the King's Black Hands wielded paired weapons. These belonged to Kamui, who looked after the prince.

Kamui brought Onikiri with him to the Undead Settlement, where he forged Ubadachi, and was finally prepared to join the ranks of the royal hunters.

Skill: Onislayer

Leap forward and slash mercilessly with both blades, cutting open foes.

Found/Dropped: Grand Archives

D	C	-	⚡ -	
13	25	-	✴ -	Titanite

UCHIGATANA

Slash/Thrust		Hold / 17 / 5		5.5

⚔	115
⚡	0
🔥	0
✦	0
✴	0
🛡	100
🛡	33
	0
	0

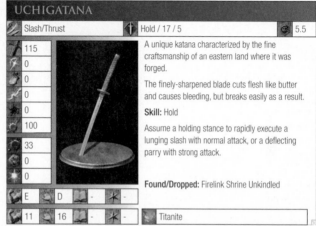

A unique katana characterized by the fine craftsmanship of an eastern land where it was forged.

The finely-sharpened blade cuts flesh like butter and causes bleeding, but breaks easily as a result.

Skill: Hold

Assume a holding stance to rapidly execute a lunging slash with normal attack, or a deflecting parry with strong attack.

Found/Dropped: Firelink Shrine Unkindled

E	D	-	⚡ -	
11	16	-	✴ -	Titanite

WASHING POLE

Slash/Thrust		Hold / 22 / 8		8.5

⚔	126
⚡	0
🔥	0
✦	0
✴	0
🛡	100
🛡	33
	0
	0

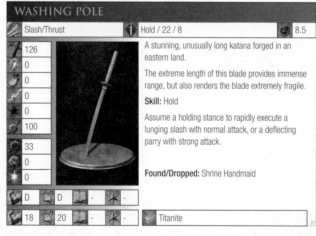

A stunning, unusually long katana forged in an eastern land.

The extreme length of this blade provides immense range, but also renders the blade extremely fragile.

Skill: Hold

Assume a holding stance to rapidly execute a lunging slash with normal attack, or a deflecting parry with strong attack.

Found/Dropped: Shrine Handmaid

D	D	-	⚡ -	
18	20	-	✴ -	Titanite

AXES

Sturdy Strength based weapons with frequent access to the damage boosting Warcry skill, Axes are straightforward weapons with an easy to use move set and a solid mix of damage and speed.

Compared to Straight Swords, they lean a little more towards Str and a little more towards power over speed, but they don't totally give up the ability to stick and move, unlike slower, heavier versions.

Axes are another good candidate for an all-purpose weapon, experiment with one early in the game and see if you prefer an axe and shield mix over a sword and shield.

AXES	TYPE	ART/COST	WEIGHT	POWER	ADD. EFFECT	SCALING	REQUIREMENTS	MATERIAL
Battle Axe	Standard	Warcry/20	4.0	125p	-	D/D/-/-	12/8/0/0	Titanite
Brigand Axe	Standard	Warcry/20	3.0	124p	-	D/D/-/-	14/8/0/0	Titanite
Butcher Knife	Slash	Sharpen/18	7.0	95p	-	A/-/-/-	24/0/0/0	Titanite
Dragonslayer's Axe	Standard	Warcry/20	4.0	90p/90l	-	D/E/-/-	18/14/0/0	Titanite
Eleonora	Standard	Feast Bell/24	6.5	156p	-	D/E/-/-	20/8/0/0	Titanite Scale
Hand Axe	Standard	Warcry/20	2.5	110p	-	D/D/-/-	9/8/0/0	Titanite
Man Serpent Hatchet	Standard	Warcry/20	4.0	125p	-	D/D/-/-	16/13/0/0	Titanite
Thrall Axe	Standard	Quickstep/5	1.5	104p	-	D/D/-/-	8/8/0/0	Titanite
Winged Knight Twinaxes	Standard	Chain Spin/8/17	8.5	122p	-	D/D/-/-	20/12/0/0	Titanite

BATTLE AXE

Standard	Warcry / 20	4.0

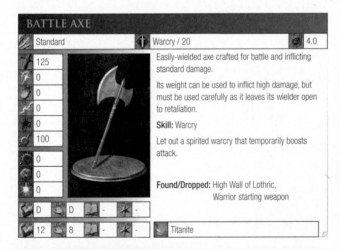

| 125 |
| 0 |
| 0 |
| 0 |
| 0 |
| 100 |
| 0 |
| 0 |
| 0 |

Easily-wielded axe crafted for battle and inflicting standard damage.

Its weight can be used to inflict high damage, but must be used carefully as it leaves its wielder open to retaliation.

Skill: Warcry

Let out a spirited warcry that temporarily boosts attack.

Found/Dropped: High Wall of Lothric, Warrior starting weapon

| D | D | - | - | - |
| 12 | 8 | - | - | - | Titanite |

BRIGAND AXE

Standard	Warcry / 20	3.0

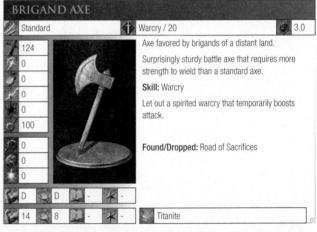

| 124 |
| 0 |
| 0 |
| 0 |
| 0 |
| 100 |
| 0 |
| 0 |
| 0 |

Axe favored by brigands of a distant land.

Surprisingly sturdy battle axe that requires more strength to wield than a standard axe.

Skill: Warcry

Let out a spirited warcry that temporarily boosts attack.

Found/Dropped: Road of Sacrifices

| D | D | - | - | - |
| 14 | 8 | - | - | - | Titanite |

BUTCHER KNIFE

Slash	Sharpen / 18	7.0

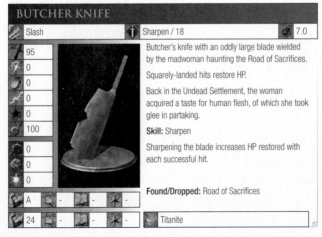

| 95 |
| 0 |
| 0 |
| 0 |
| 0 |
| 100 |
| 0 |
| 0 |
| 0 |

Butcher's knife with an oddly large blade wielded by the madwoman haunting the Road of Sacrifices.

Squarely-landed hits restore HP.

Back in the Undead Settlement, the woman acquired a taste for human flesh, of which she took glee in partaking.

Skill: Sharpen

Sharpening the blade increases HP restored with each successful hit.

Found/Dropped: Road of Sacrifices

| A | - | - | - | - |
| 24 | - | - | - | - | Titanite |

DRAGONSLAYER'S AXE

Standard	Warcry / 20	4.0

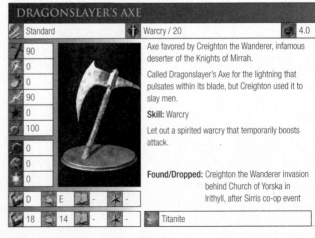

| 90 |
| 0 |
| 0 |
| 0 |
| 90 |
| 0 |
| 100 |
| 0 |
| 0 |
| 0 |

Axe favored by Creighton the Wanderer, infamous deserter of the Knights of Mirrah.

Called Dragonslayer's Axe for the lightning that pulsates within its blade, but Creighton used it to slay men.

Skill: Warcry

Let out a spirited warcry that temporarily boosts attack.

Found/Dropped: Creighton the Wanderer invasion behind Church of Yorska in Irithyll, after Sirris co-op event

| D | E | - | - | - |
| 18 | 14 | - | - | - | Titanite |

ELEONORA

Standard	Feast Bell / 24		6.5

⚔	156
	0
	0
	0
	0
	100
	0
	0
	0

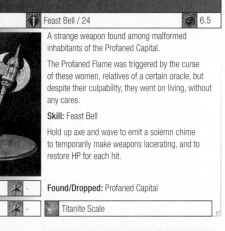

A strange weapon found among malformed inhabitants of the Profaned Capital.

The Profaned Flame was triggered by the curse of these women, relatives of a certain oracle, but despite their culpability, they went on living, without any cares.

Skill: Feast Bell

Hold up axe and wave to emit a solemn chime to temporarily make weapons lacerating, and to restore HP for each hit.

Found/Dropped: Profaned Capital

	D		E		-		-
	20		8		-		-

Titanite Scale

HAND AXE

Standard	Warcry / 20		2.5

⚔	110
	0
	0
	0
	0
	100
	0
	0
	0

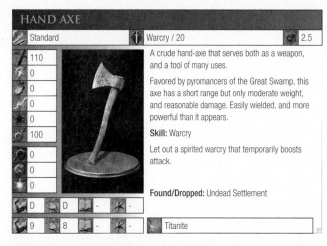

A crude hand-axe that serves both as a weapon, and a tool of many uses.

Favored by pyromancers of the Great Swamp, this axe has a short range but only moderate weight, and reasonable damage. Easily wielded, and more powerful than it appears.

Skill: Warcry

Let out a spirited warcry that temporarily boosts attack.

Found/Dropped: Undead Settlement

	D		D		-		-
	9		8		-		-

Titanite

MAN SERPENT HATCHET

Standard	Warcry / 20		4.0

⚔	125
	0
	0
	0
	0
	100
	0
	0
	0

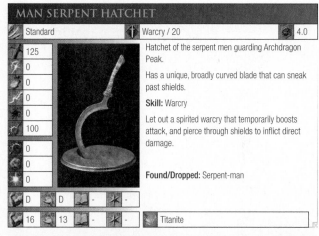

Hatchet of the serpent men guarding Archdragon Peak.

Has a unique, broadly curved blade that can sneak past shields.

Skill: Warcry

Let out a spirited warcry that temporarily boosts attack, and pierce through shields to inflict direct damage.

Found/Dropped: Serpent-man

	D		D		-		-
	16		13		-		-

Titanite

THRALL AXE

Standard	Quickstep / 5		1.5

⚔	104
	0
	0
	0
	0
	100
	0
	0
	0

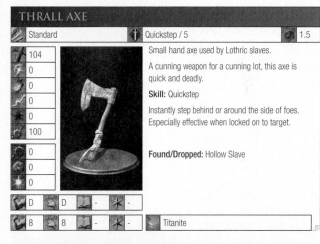

Small hand axe used by Lothric slaves.

A cunning weapon for a cunning lot, this axe is quick and deadly.

Skill: Quickstep

Instantly step behind or around the side of foes. Especially effective when locked on to target.

Found/Dropped: Hollow Slave

	D		D		-		-
	8		8		-		-

Titanite

WINGED KNIGHT TWINAXES

Standard	Chain Spin / 8 / 17		8.5

⚔	122
	0
	0
	0
	0
	100
	0
	0
	0

Paired beheading axes wielded by the Winged Knights, who swore themselves to the Angels.

These axes, more befitting of an executioner than a knight, are indented to fit the human body.

Technique: Chain Spin

Sweep foes in a large spinning motion and use strong attack to continue the motion until stamina is exhausted.

Found/Dropped: Winged Knight/Gertrude's Knight

	D		D		-		-
	20		12		-		-

Titanite

GREATAXES

Heavy and powerful, Greataxes have intense Str requirements to even wield them, on top of hefty weights that demand even more attribute investment to use them effectively.

With common access to Warcry, these weapons can potentially hit even harder than a Greatsword of equivalent upgrade level, if you can handle their attribute demands and ponderous combat style.

GREATAXES	TYPE	ART/COST	WEIGHT	POWER	ADD. EFFECT	SCALING	REQUIREMENTS	MATERIAL
Black Knight Greataxe	Standard	Warcry/20	19.5	216p	-	C/D/-/-	36/18/0/0	Twinkling Titanite
Demon's Great Axe	Standard	Demonic Flare/35	14.5	157p/88f	-	C/E/D/D	28/0/12/12	Titanite Scale
Dragonslayer Greataxe	Standard	Falling Bolt/35	20.0	203p/74l	-	D/E/-/-	40/0/0/0	Titanite Scale
Great Machete	Slash	Sharpen/20	14.0	167p	-	D/E/-/-	24/10/0/0	Titanite
Greataxe	Standard	Warcry/20	16.0	188p	-	D/E/-/-	32/8/0/0	Titanite
Yhorm's Great Machete	Standard	Warcry/20	19.0	185p	-	C/-/-/-	38/10/0/0	Titanite Scale

BLACK KNIGHT GREATAXE

Standard	Warcry / 20	19.5

| 216 |
| 0 |
| 0 |
| 0 |
| 0 |
| 100 |
| 0 |
| 0 |
| 0 |

Greataxe of the black knights who wander the lands. Used to face chaos demons.

The unique attack of this axe greatly reduces enemy poise, reflecting the tremendous size of the enemies that the knights have fearlessly faced.

Skill: Warcry

Let out a spirited warcry that temporarily boosts attack, and enables a special consecutive strong attack.

Found/Dropped: Black Knight

C	D	-	-
36	18	-	-
Twinkling Titanite			

DEMON'S GREAT AXE

Standard	Demonic Flare / 35	14.5

| 157 |
| 0 |
| 88 |
| 0 |
| 0 |
| 100 |
| 0 |
| 0 |
| 0 |

This greataxe, a favorite among demons, contains the strength of fire.

The demons, born of Chaos, harbor fire, and yet they are twisted and malformed, such that they were never meant to be.

Skill: Demonic Flare

Briefly cause flame within to flare, and smash it upon earth and foes.

Found/Dropped: Demon Soul

C	E	D	D
28	-	12	12
Titanite Scale			

DRAGONSLAYER GREATAXE

Standard	Falling Bolt / 35	20.0

| 203 |
| 0 |
| 0 |
| 74 |
| 0 |
| 100 |
| 0 |
| 0 |
| 0 |

Melted iron greataxe that once formed part of the Dragonslayer Armour.

Thickly imbued with the power of lightning. Use skill to draw upon the techniques used to slay the archdragons.

Skill: Falling Bolt

Hold axe high in air to gather fierce lightning, and smash ground to whip the bolts to the ground.

Found/Dropped: Dragonslayer Armour Soul

D	E	-	-
40	-	-	-
Titanite Scale			

GREAT MACHETE

Slash	Sharpen / 20	14.0

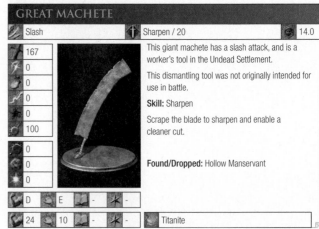

| 167 |
| 0 |
| 0 |
| 0 |
| 0 |
| 100 |
| 0 |
| 0 |
| 0 |

This giant machete has a slash attack, and is a worker's tool in the Undead Settlement.

This dismantling tool was not originally intended for use in battle.

Skill: Sharpen

Scrape the blade to sharpen and enable a cleaner cut.

Found/Dropped: Hollow Manservant

D	E	-	-
24	10	-	-
Titanite			

GREATAXE

Standard	Warcry / 20	16.0

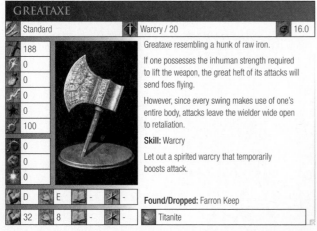

| 188 |
| 0 |
| 0 |
| 0 |
| 0 |
| 100 |
| 0 |
| 0 |
| 0 |

Greataxe resembling a hunk of raw iron.

If one possesses the inhuman strength required to lift the weapon, the great heft of its attacks will send foes flying.

However, since every swing makes use of one's entire body, attacks leave the wielder wide open to retaliation.

Skill: Warcry

Let out a spirited warcry that temporarily boosts attack.

Found/Dropped: Farron Keep

D	E	-	-
32	8	-	-
Titanite			

YHORM'S GREAT MACHETE

Standard	Warcry / 20	19.0

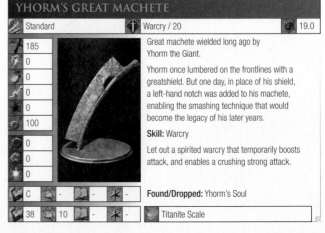

| 185 |
| 0 |
| 0 |
| 0 |
| 0 |
| 100 |
| 0 |
| 0 |
| 0 |

Great machete wielded long ago by Yhorm the Giant.

Yhorm once lumbered on the frontlines with a greatshield. But one day, in place of his shield, a left-hand notch was added to his machete, enabling the smashing technique that would become the legacy of his later years.

Skill: Warcry

Let out a spirited warcry that temporarily boosts attack, and enables a crushing strong attack.

Found/Dropped: Yhorm's Soul

C	-	-	-
38	10	-	-
Titanite Scale			

HAMMERS

The simplest form of weapon, Hammers can be literally no more than a stout stick, perhaps with some metal banding attached. Elegance and sophistication are not to be found here, but heavy hitting weapons with mild attribute requirements and good Str scaling are.

Primarily dealing Strike damage, Hammers fare well against armored foes, and with a common mix of access to the Warcry and Perseverence skills, you can choose between damage boosting or Poise boosting.

Like Straight Swords and Axes, Hammers are another potential choice for a one handed and shield mix. You can easily find a Club or Mace early in the game, so experiment with them to see if they suit your tastes.

HAMMERS	TYPE	ART/COST	WEIGHT	POWER	ADD. EFFECT	SCALING	REQUIREMENTS	MATERIAL
Blacksmith Hammer	Strike	Perseverance/9	5.0	105p	-	C/-/-/-	13/13/0/0	Titanite
Club	Strike	Warcry/20	2.5	108p	-	C/-/-/-	10/0/0/0	Titanite
Drang Hammers	Strike	Spin Bash/7/15	9.0	110p	-	C/E/-/-	18/16/0/0	Titanite
Heysel Pick	Thrust	Steady Chant/9	4.5	93p/70m/60sb	-	D/E/C/-	12/10/19/0	Twinkling Titanite
Mace	Strike	Perseverance/9	5.0	115p	-	C/E/-/-	12/7/0/0	Titanite
Morning Star	Strike	Perseverance/9	5.0	122p	33bl	D/E/-/-	11/9/0/0	Titanite
Reinforced Club	Strike	Warcry/20	4.0	110p	33bl	C/-/-/-	12/0/0/0	Titanite
Warpick	Thrust	Galvanize/9	4.5	113p	-	C/E/-/-	12/10/0/0	Titanite

BLACKSMITH HAMMER

Strike	Perseverance / 9	5.0

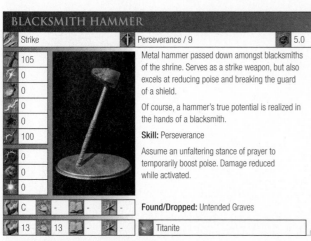

| 105 |
| 0 |
| 0 |
| 0 |
| 0 |
| 100 |
| 0 |
| 0 |
| 0 |

| C | - | - | ✳ - |
| 13 | 13 | - | ✳ - | Titanite |

Metal hammer passed down amongst blacksmiths of the shrine. Serves as a strike weapon, but also excels at reducing poise and breaking the guard of a shield.

Of course, a hammer's true potential is realized in the hands of a blacksmith.

Skill: Perseverance

Assume an unfaltering stance of prayer to temporarily boost poise. Damage reduced while activated.

Found/Dropped: Untended Graves

CLUB

Strike	Warcry / 20	2.5

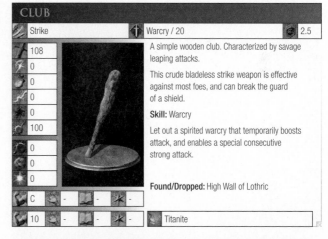

| 108 |
| 0 |
| 0 |
| 0 |
| 0 |
| 100 |
| 0 |
| 0 |
| 0 |

| C | - | - | ✳ - |
| 10 | - | - | ✳ - | Titanite |

A simple wooden club. Characterized by savage leaping attacks.

This crude bladeless strike weapon is effective against most foes, and can break the guard of a shield.

Skill: Warcry

Let out a spirited warcry that temporarily boosts attack, and enables a special consecutive strong attack.

Found/Dropped: High Wall of Lothric

DRANG HAMMERS

Strike	Spin Bash / 7 / 15	9.0

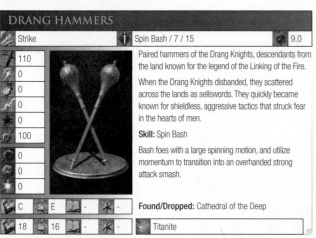

| 110 |
| 0 |
| 0 |
| 0 |
| 0 |
| 100 |
| 0 |
| 0 |
| 0 |

| C | E | - | ✳ - |
| 18 | 16 | - | ✳ - | Titanite |

Paired hammers of the Drang Knights, descendants from the land known for the legend of the Linking of the Fire.

When the Drang Knights disbanded, they scattered across the lands as sellswords. They quickly became known for shieldless, aggressive tactics that struck fear in the hearts of men.

Skill: Spin Bash

Bash foes with a large spinning motion, and utilize momentum to transition into an overhanded strong attack smash.

Found/Dropped: Cathedral of the Deep

HEYSEL PICK

Thrust	Steady Chant / 9	4.5

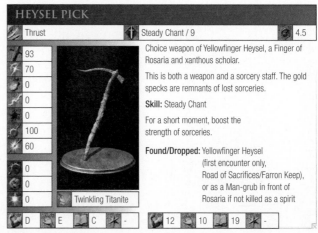

| 93 |
| 70 |
| 0 |
| 0 |
| 100 |
| 60 |
| 0 |
| 0 |
| 0 | Twinkling Titanite |

| D | E | | C | ✳ - |
| 12 | 10 | 19 | ✳ - |

Choice weapon of Yellowfinger Heysel, a Finger of Rosaria and xanthous scholar.

This is both a weapon and a sorcery staff. The gold specks are remnants of lost sorceries.

Skill: Steady Chant

For a short moment, boost the strength of sorceries.

Found/Dropped: Yellowfinger Heysel
(first encounter only, Road of Sacrifices/Farron Keep), or as a Man-grub in front of Rosaria if not killed as a spirit

MACE

Strike		Perseverance / 9		5.0

115		Iron hammer designed for use in battle. A common weapon for clerics.
0		This bladeless strike weapon is effective against most foes, and can break the guard of a shield.
0		**Skill:** Perseverance
0		Assume an unfaltering stance of prayer to temporarily boost poise. Damage reduced while activated.
0		
100		
0		
0		**Found/Dropped:** Greirat
0		

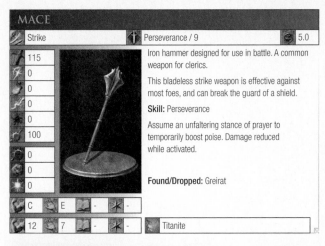

C	E	-	-
12	7	-	-	Titanite

MORNING STAR

Strike		Perseverance / 9		5.0

122		Hammer with a sharp spike on its pommel. One of the more barbaric cleric weapons.
0		The sharp thorns allow this strike weapon to induce bleeding.
0		**Skill:** Perseverance
0		Assume an unfaltering stance of prayer to temporarily boost poise. Damage reduced while activated.
0		
100		
33		
0		**Found/Dropped:** Shrine Handmaid
0		

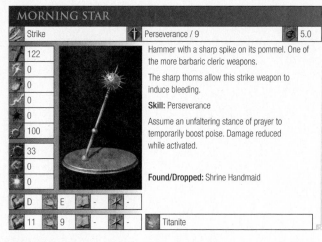

D	E	-	-
11	9	-	-	Titanite

WARPICK

Thrust		Galvanize / 9		4.5

113		A war hammer with a hard pronged head. Was originally a pickaxe, but was refitted for battle.
0		This simple but deadly weapon hits heavily with thrust damage, easily puncturing metal armor.
0		**Skill:** Galvanize
0		Temporarily boost stamina recovery speed by sheer force of will, or perhaps as a channeling of the original owner's industrious efforts.
0		
100		
0		
0		**Found/Dropped:** Greirat
0		

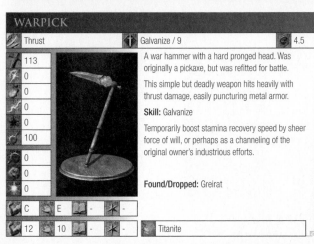

C	E	-	-
12	10	-	-	Titanite

REINFORCED CLUB

Strike		Warcry / 20		4.0

110		A club made more deadly by the attachment of numerous nails to its head.
0		The nails allow this strike weapon to be lacerating, but the damage caused by their insertion has reduced its durability, making the weapon fragile.
0		**Skill:** Warcry
0		Let out a spirited warcry that temporarily boosts attack, and enables a special consecutive strong attack.
0		
100		
33		
0		
0		**Found/Dropped:** Undead Settlement

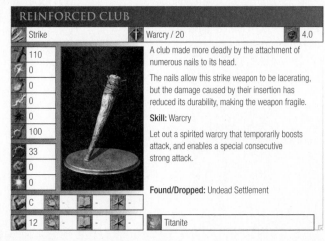

C		-	-
12	-	-	-	Titanite

GREAT HAMMERS

Even more brutish than Great Axes, Great Hammers abandon all subtlety in favor of raw damage output and crushing moves.

Like other great weaponry, most of them have demanding attribute requirements, though there are a number of Great Hammers that have relatively mild weight, giving you the option of using a hefty two handed weapon earlier in the game.

Great Hammers mix common access to Perseverance with a few Warcry enabled weapons, so this gives you the option of enhancing their already formidable damage output, or boosting your poise to ensure those swings reach their mark. The few with the Spin Bash skill give you a useful area clearing attack for smashing weaker foes en masse.

GREAT HAMMERS	TYPE	ART/COST	WEIGHT	POWER	ADD. EFFECT	SCALING	REQUIREMENTS	MATERIAL
Dragon Tooth	Strike	Perseverance/12	21.0	188	-	C/-/-/-	40/0/0/0	Titanite Scale
Gargoyle Flame Hammer	Strike	Kindled Flurry/12/15	11.0	122p/100f	-	D/-/E/E	22/0/9/9	Titanite
Great Club	Strike	Warcry/20	12.0	152p	-	C/-/-/-	28/0/0/0	Titanite
Great Mace	Strike	Perseverance/12	18.0	173p	-	D/-/-/-	32/0/0/0	Titanite
Great Wooden Hammer	Strike	Spin Bash/13/10	6.0	103p	-	C/-/-/-	18/0/0/0	Titanite
Large Club	Strike	Warcry/20	10.0	148p	-	C/-/-/-	22/0/0/0	Titanite
Morne's Great Hammer	Strike	Morne's Rage/50	24.0	200p	-	C/-/-/-	50/0/0/30	Twinkling Titanite
Old King's Great Hammer	Strike	Molten Perseverance/12/15	18.5	180p/69f	-	D/-/D/D	30/0/10/10	Titanite Scale
Pickaxe	Thrust	Galvanize/11	8.0	140p	-	C/-/-/-	18/9/0/0	Titanite
Smough's Great Hammer	Strike	Perseverance/12	24.0	205p	-	C/-/-/-	45/0/0/0	Twinkling Titanite
Spiked Mace	Strike	Spin Bash/13/10	16.0	149p	33bl	C/-/-/-	21/13/0/0	Titanite
Vordt's Great Hammer	Strike	Perseverance/12	17.0	176p	50fr	C/-/-/-	30/0/0/0	Titanite Scale

DRAGON TOOTH

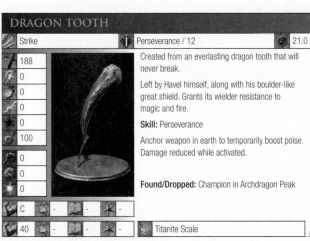

| Strike | Perseverance / 12 | 21.0 |

| 188 |
| 0 |
| 0 |
| 0 |
| 0 |
| 100 |
| 0 |
| 0 |
| 0 |

Created from an everlasting dragon tooth that will never break.

Left by Havel himself, along with his boulder-like great shield. Grants its wielder resistance to magic and fire.

Skill: Perseverance

Anchor weapon in earth to temporarily boost poise. Damage reduced while activated.

Found/Dropped: Champion in Archdragon Peak

| C | - | - | - |
| 40 | - | - | - | Titanite Scale |

GARGOYLE FLAME HAMMER

| Strike | Kindled Flurry / 12 / 15 | 11.0 |

| 122 |
| 0 |
| 100 |
| 0 |
| 0 |
| 100 |
| 0 |
| 0 |
| 0 |

Stone torch hammer wielded by gargoyles of the Profaned Capital.

The Profaned Flame, which never goes out, imbues this weapon with a fire attack.

Skill: Kindled Flurry

Anchor weapon in earth and use strong attack to launch successive volleys of fire from the tip of the hammer.

Found/Dropped: Headless Gargoyle

| D | - | E | E |
| 22 | - | 9 | 9 | Titanite |

GREAT CLUB

| Strike | Warcry / 20 | 12.0 |

| 152 |
| 0 |
| 0 |
| 0 |
| 0 |
| 100 |
| 0 |
| 0 |
| 0 |

Wood club fashioned from the branch of a giant tree. Requires considerable strength to wield.

A hard, durable weapon. Its weight makes it easier to break the guard of shields.

Skill: Warcry

Let out a spirited warcry that temporarily boosts attack, and enables special consecutive strong attack.

Found/Dropped: Road of Sacrifices

| C | - | - | - |
| 28 | - | - | - | Titanite |

GREAT MACE

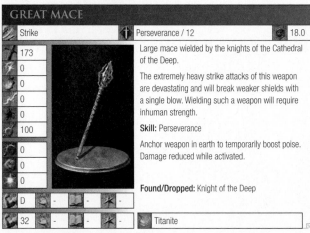

| Strike | Perseverance / 12 | 18.0 |

| 173 |
| 0 |
| 0 |
| 0 |
| 0 |
| 100 |
| 0 |
| 0 |
| 0 |

Large mace wielded by the knights of the Cathedral of the Deep.

The extremely heavy strike attacks of this weapon are devastating and will break weaker shields with a single blow. Wielding such a weapon will require inhuman strength.

Skill: Perseverance

Anchor weapon in earth to temporarily boost poise. Damage reduced while activated.

Found/Dropped: Knight of the Deep

| D | - | - | - |
| 32 | - | - | - | Titanite |

GREAT WOODEN HAMMER

Strike		Spin Bash / 13 / 10		6.0

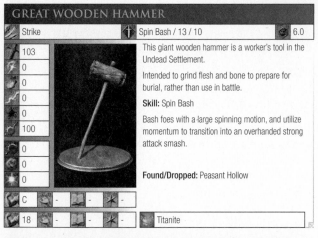

	103
	0
	0
	0
	0
	100
	0
	0
	0

	C	-	-	-
	18	-	-	-

Titanite

This giant wooden hammer is a worker's tool in the Undead Settlement.

Intended to grind flesh and bone to prepare for burial, rather than use in battle.

Skill: Spin Bash

Bash foes with a large spinning motion, and utilize momentum to transition into an overhanded strong attack smash.

Found/Dropped: Peasant Hollow

LARGE CLUB

Strike		Warcry / 20		10.0

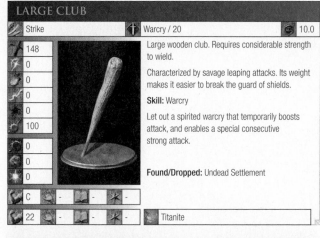

	148
	0
	0
	0
	0
	100
	0
	0
	0

	C	-	-	-
	22	-	-	-

Titanite

Large wooden club. Requires considerable strength to wield.

Characterized by savage leaping attacks. Its weight makes it easier to break the guard of shields.

Skill: Warcry

Let out a spirited warcry that temporarily boosts attack, and enables a special consecutive strong attack.

Found/Dropped: Undead Settlement

MORNE'S GREAT HAMMER

Strike		Morne's Rage / 50		24.0

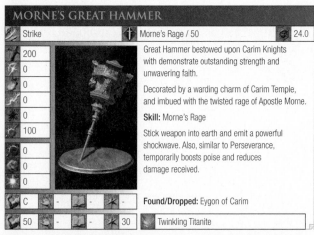

	200
	0
	0
	0
	0
	100
	0
	0
	0

	C	-	-	-
	50	-	-	30

Twinkling Titanite

Great Hammer bestowed upon Carim Knights with demonstrate outstanding strength and unwavering faith.

Decorated by a warding charm of Carim Temple, and imbued with the twisted rage of Apostle Morne.

Skill: Morne's Rage

Stick weapon into earth and emit a powerful shockwave. Also, similar to Perseverance, temporarily boosts poise and reduces damage received.

Found/Dropped: Eygon of Carim

OLD KING'S GREAT HAMMER

Strike		Molten Perseverance / 12 / 15		18.5

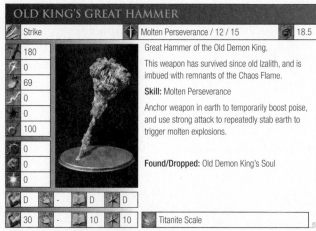

	180
	0
	69
	0
	0
	100
	0
	0
	0

	D	-	D	D
	30	-	10	10

Titanite Scale

Great Hammer of the Old Demon King.

This weapon has survived since old Izalith, and is imbued with remnants of the Chaos Flame.

Skill: Molten Perseverance

Anchor weapon in earth to temporarily boost poise, and use strong attack to repeatedly stab earth to trigger molten explosions.

Found/Dropped: Old Demon King's Soul

PICKAXE

Thrust		Galvanize / 11		8.0

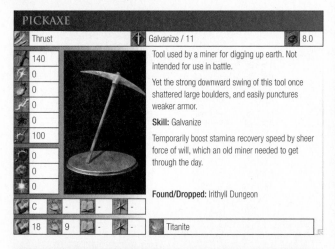

	140
	0
	0
	0
	0
	100
	0
	0
	0

	C	-	-	-
	18	9	-	-

Titanite

Tool used by a miner for digging up earth. Not intended for use in battle.

Yet the strong downward swing of this tool once shattered large boulders, and easily punctures weaker armor.

Skill: Galvanize

Temporarily boost stamina recovery speed by sheer force of will, which an old miner needed to get through the day.

Found/Dropped: Irithyll Dungeon

SMOUGH'S GREAT HAMMER

Strike		Perseverance / 12		24.0

	205
	0
	0
	0
	0
	100
	0
	0
	0

	C	-	-	-
	45	-	-	-

Twinkling Titanite

Twisted great Hammer associated with Smough, the last knight to remain at his post, guarding the ruined cathedral.

Restore HP while attacking, a carryover from Smough's past as an executioner.

Skill: Perseverance

Anchor weapon in earth to temporarily boost poise. Damage reduced while activated.

Found/Dropped: Irithyll of the Boreal Valley

SPIKED MACE

Strike		Spin Bash / 13 / 10		16.0

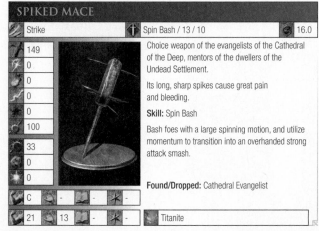

	149
	0
	0
	0
	0
	100
	33
	0
	0

	C	-	-	-
	21	13	-	-

Titanite

Choice weapon of the evangelists of the Cathedral of the Deep, mentors of the dwellers of the Undead Settlement.

Its long, sharp spikes cause great pain and bleeding.

Skill: Spin Bash

Bash foes with a large spinning motion, and utilize momentum to transition into an overhanded strong attack smash.

Found/Dropped: Cathedral Evangelist

VORDT'S GREAT HAMMER

Strike		Perseverance / 12		17.0

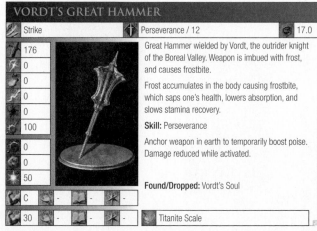

	176
	0
	0
	0
	0
	100
	0
	0
	50

	C	-	-	-
	30	-	-	-

Titanite Scale

Great Hammer wielded by Vordt, the outrider knight of the Boreal Valley. Weapon is imbued with frost, and causes frostbite.

Frost accumulates in the body causing frostbite, which saps one's health, lowers absorption, and slows stamina recovery.

Skill: Perseverance

Anchor weapon in earth to temporarily boost poise. Damage reduced while activated.

Found/Dropped: Vordt's Soul

SPEARS

A very friendly weapon class for players new to *Dark Souls*, Spears allow you to attack while blocking with a shield, making them ideal weapons for a very cautious playstyle.

That isn't to say Spears are purely defensive however, with common access to the aggressive Charge move and great reach, Spears are also good for striking enemies at long range and fading away from retaliation.

Spears are notable for being fairly difficult to parry due to their tough to read jabbing strikes. Though not as difficult as a Thrusting Sword, it's something to keep in mind for PvP (and when facing humanoid foes armed with Spears).

Spears generally favor Dex, with most having relatively mild attribute requirements, though they do tend to skew a bit high in the weight department, so keep that in mind if you favor lightweight loadouts.

SPEARS	TYPE	ART/COST	WEIGHT	POWER	ADD. EFFECT	SCALING	REQUIREMENTS	MATERIAL
Arstor's Spear	Thrust	Shield Splitter/16	6.5	118	33po	D/C/-/-	11/19/0/0	Titanite Scale
Dragonslayer Spear	Thrust	Lightning Charge/17/12	9.5	113p/70l	-	D/C/-/D	20/20/0/0	Twinkling Titanite
Dragonslayer Swordspear	Standard/Thrust	Falling Bolt/20	14.5	128p/34l	-	D/D/-/D	16/22/0/18	Titanite Scale
Drang Twinspears	Standard/Thrust	Charge/13/9	8.0	100	-	D/D/-/-	14/20/0/0	Titanite
Four-Pronged Plow	Thrust	Charge/13/9	6.5	105p	-	D/D/-/-	13/11/0/0	Titanite
Gargoyle Flame Spear	Thrust	Kindled Charge/13/15	9.5	103p/90f	-	E/D/E/E	15/18/9/9	Titanite
Golden Ritual Spear	Thrust	Steady Chant/9	3.0	73p/77m/20sb	-	E/D/-/B	10/10/18/14	Twinkling Titanite
Partizan	Standard/Thrust	Spin Sweep/11/11	6.5	108p	-	D/D/-/-	14/12/0/0	Titanite
Rotten Ghru Spear	Thrust	Charge/13/9	5.5	104p	33po	D/D/-/-	10/12/0/0	Titanite
Saint Bident	Thrust	Charge/13/9	8.5	98p	-	E/E/-/D	12/12/0/16	Titanite
Soldering Iron	Standard	Charge/13/9	5.0	39p/96f	-	D/D/-/-	10/12/0/0	Titanite
Spear	Thrust	Shield Splitter/16	4.5	104p	-	D/C/-/-	11/10/0/0	Titanite
Tailbone Spear	Thrust	Unleash Dragon/25	4.5	118p	-	E/D/-/-	13/15/0/0	Titanite Scale
Winged Spear	Thrust	Charge/13/9	6.0	95p	-	D/C/-/-	12/15/0/0	Titanite
Yorshka's Spear	Strike/Thrust	Pacify/25	6.5	98p	-	D/C/-/-	18/14/0/13	Twinkling Titanite

ARSTOR'S SPEAR

Thrust		Shield Splitter / 16		6.5

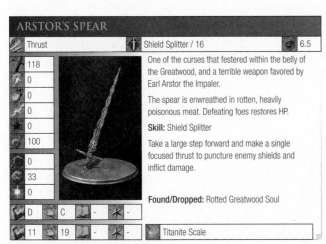

| 118 |
| 0 |
| 0 |
| 0 |
| 0 |
| 100 |
| 0 |
| 33 |
| 0 |

One of the curses that festered within the belly of the Greatwood, and a terrible weapon favored by Earl Arstor the Impaler.

The spear is enwreathed in rotten, heavily poisonous meat. Defeating foes restores HP.

Skill: Shield Splitter

Take a large step forward and make a single focused thrust to puncture enemy shields and inflict damage.

Found/Dropped: Rotted Greatwood Soul

| D | C | - | - |
| 11 | 19 | - | - |

Titanite Scale

DRAGONSLAYER SPEAR

Thrust		Lightning Charge / 17 / 12		9.5

| 113 |
| 0 |
| 0 |
| 70 |
| 0 |
| 100 |
| 0 |
| 0 |
| 0 |

Cross spear associated with Ornstein the Dragonslayer. A weapon of the gods imbued with the strength of lightning.

Two-handed thrust utilizes the support of the cross and requires great might, but can pierce deep into the flesh of dragons, and send mere men flying.

Skill: Lightning Charge

Charge with spear at waist to enwreathe with lightning, then release bolts with final thrust.

Found/Dropped: Archdragon Peak

| D | C | - | D |
| 20 | 20 | - | - |

Twinkling Titanite

DRAGONSLAYER SWORDSPEAR

Standard/Thrust		Falling Bolt / 20		14.5

| 128 |
| 0 |
| 0 |
| 34 |
| 0 |
| 100 |
| 0 |
| 0 |
| 0 |

A dragon hunting weapon from the age of the gods. The earliest form of the cross spear, serving as both sword and spear.

Its owner was the Nameless King and deific hunter of dragons. The swordspear is imbued with lightning, of which he was the heir.

Skill: Falling Bolt

Hold swordspear high in the air to summon fierce lightning that descends upon distant foes.

Found/Dropped: Nameless King's Soul

| D | D | - | D |
| 16 | 22 | - | 18 |

Titanite Scale

DRANG TWINSPEARS

Standard/Thrust		Charge / 13 / 9		8.0

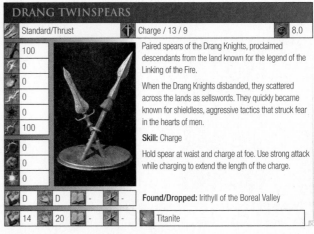

| 100 |
| 0 |
| 0 |
| 0 |
| 0 |
| 100 |
| 0 |
| 0 |
| 0 |

Paired spears of the Drang Knights, proclaimed descendants from the land known for the legend of the Linking of the Fire.

When the Drang Knights disbanded, they scattered across the lands as sellswords. They quickly became known for shieldless, aggressive tactics that struck fear in the hearts of men.

Skill: Charge

Hold spear at waist and charge at foe. Use strong attack while charging to extend the length of the charge.

Found/Dropped: Irithyll of the Boreal Valley

| D | D | - | - |
| 14 | 20 | - | - |

Titanite

FOUR-PRONGED PLOW

Thrust		Charge / 13 / 9		6.5

105	This four-pronged plow is shaped like a fist, and is a worker's tool in the Undead Settlement.
0	Not originally intended for battle, but serves as a deadly weapon owing to its sharp points.
0	
0	**Skill:** Charge
0	
100	Hold spear at waist and charge at foe. Only, it is important to have good footing.
0	
0	
0	**Found/Dropped:** Peasant Hollow

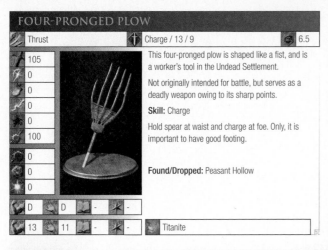

D	D	-	-	
13	11	-	-	Titanite

GARGOYLE FLAME SPEAR

Thrust		Kindled Charge / 13 / 15		9.5

103	Stone torch spear wielded by gargoyles of the Profaned Capital.
0	The Profaned Flame, which never goes out, imbues this weapon with a fire attack.
90	
0	**Skill:** Kindled Charge
0	
100	Hold spear at waist and charge at foe, and use momentum to transition to a fiery strong attack.
0	
0	
0	**Found/Dropped:** Headless Gargoyle

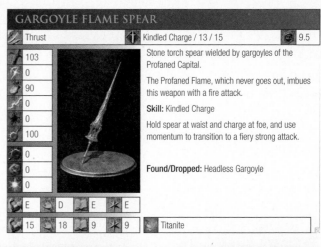

E	D	E	E	
15	18	9	9	Titanite

GOLDEN RITUAL SPEAR

Thrust		Steady Chant / 9		3.0

73	A ritual spear presented to Darkmoon Knights before Sulyvahn claimed the title of Pontiff.
77	
0	Can also be used as a staff. Sorceries cast using this weapon channel the wielder's faith.
0	
0	**Skill:** Steady Chant
100	
20	Boost the strength of sorceries for a very short period.
0	
0	
0	**Found/Dropped:** Irithyll of the Boreal Valley

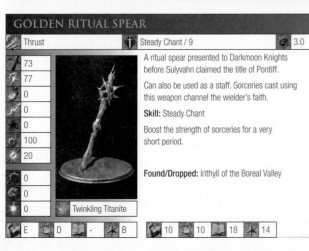

Twinkling Titanite

E	D	-	B	10	10	18	14	

PARTIZAN

Standard/Thrust		Spin Sweep / 11 / 11		6.5

108	Spear with blade attached to broad point. Long reach, and can be used with shield up.
0	
0	This weapon can utilize its blade for slicing attacks, and is generally adaptable to many situations, but in cramped quarters, its slices ricochet off walls.
0	
0	
100	**Skill:** Spin Sweep
0	
0	Sweep foes in a large spinning motion, and utilize momentum to transition into an overhanded strong attack smash.
0	

Found/Dropped: Undead Settlement

D	D	-	-	
14	12	-	-	Titanite

ROTTEN GHRU SPEAR

Thrust		Charge / 13 / 9		5.5

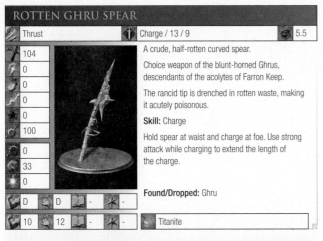

104
0
0
0
0
100
0
33
0

A crude, half-rotten curved spear.

Choice weapon of the blunt-horned Ghrus, descendants of the acolytes of Farron Keep.

The rancid tip is drenched in rotten waste, making it acutely poisonous.

Skill: Charge

Hold spear at waist and charge at foe. Use strong attack while charging to extend the length of the charge.

Found/Dropped: Ghru

D		D		-		-
10		12		-		-

Titanite

SOLDERING IRON

Standard		Charge / 13 / 9		5.0

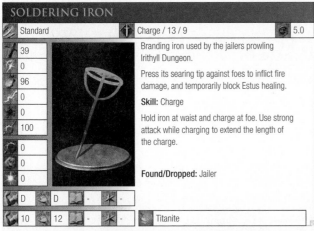

39
0
96
0
0
100
0
0
0

Branding iron used by the jailers prowling Irithyll Dungeon.

Press its searing tip against foes to inflict fire damage, and temporarily block Estus healing.

Skill: Charge

Hold iron at waist and charge at foe. Use strong attack while charging to extend the length of the charge.

Found/Dropped: Jailer

D		D		-		-
10		12		-		-

Titanite

TAILBONE SPEAR

Thrust		Unleash Dragon / 25		4.5

118
0
0
0
0
100
0
0
0

Twisted spear cherished by the wretched, failed prisoners of Irithyll Dungeon.

Crafted from a feeble tailbone, and seen as a sign of the dragons. Their screams are oft heard inside the dungeon, as they naively mutilate their unworthy flesh.

Skill: Unleash Dragon

Thrust the spear to unleash the strength of dragons, similar to an ancient dragon weapon, only with its power tragically faded.

Found/Dropped: Wretch

E		D		-		-
13		15		-		-

Titanite Scale

YORSHKA'S SPEAR

Strike/Thrust		Pacify / 25		6.5

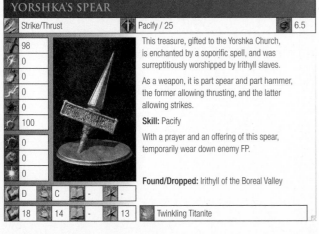

98
0
0
0
0
100
0
0
0

This treasure, gifted to the Yorshka Church, is enchanted by a soporific spell, and was surreptitiously worshipped by Irithyll slaves.

As a weapon, it is part spear and part hammer, the former allowing thrusting, and the latter allowing strikes.

Skill: Pacify

With a prayer and an offering of this spear, temporarily wear down enemy FP.

Found/Dropped: Irithyll of the Boreal Valley

D		C		-		-
18		14		-		13

Twinkling Titanite

SAINT BIDENT

Thrust		Charge / 13 / 9		8.5

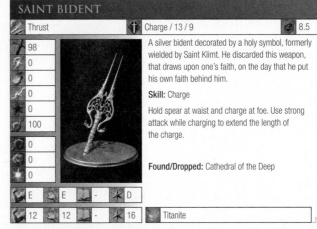

98
0
0
0
0
100
0
0
0

A silver bident decorated by a holy symbol, formerly wielded by Saint Klimt. He discarded this weapon, that draws upon one's faith, on the day that he put his own faith behind him.

Skill: Charge

Hold spear at waist and charge at foe. Use strong attack while charging to extend the length of the charge.

Found/Dropped: Cathedral of the Deep

E		E		-		D
12		12		-		16

Titanite

SPEAR

Thrust		Shield Splitter / 16		4.5

104
0
0
0
0
100
0
0
0

Common short spear that allows attacking with shield up.

Spear attacks are centered on thrusting, but can inflict high damage when timed with the end of an enemy's swing.

Skill: Shield Splitter

Take a large step forward and make a single focused thrust to puncture enemy shields and inflict damage.

Found/Dropped: Greirat

D		C		-		-
11		10		-		-

Titanite

WINGED SPEAR

Thrust		Charge / 13 / 9		6.0

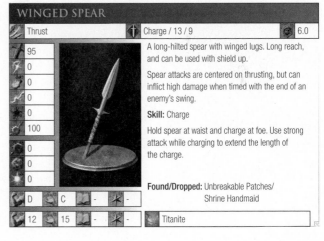

95
0
0
0
0
100
0
0
0

A long-hilted spear with winged lugs. Long reach, and can be used with shield up.

Spear attacks are centered on thrusting, but can inflict high damage when timed with the end of an enemy's swing.

Skill: Charge

Hold spear at waist and charge at foe. Use strong attack while charging to extend the length of the charge.

Found/Dropped: Unbreakable Patches/
Shrine Handmaid

D		C		-		-
12		15		-		-

Titanite

PIKES

Spears taken to the extreme, Pikes have the greatest reach in the game, with suitably increased attribute requirements and weight.

All three have the Charge skill, and all three can be used to poke and stab your enemies from long range. If you really enjoy the keepaway style of play that Spears promote, give Pikes a try once you have the attributes to use them effectively.

PIKES	TYPE	ART/COST	WEIGHT	POWER	ADD. EFFECT	SCALING	REQUIREMENTS	MATERIAL
Greatlance	Thrust	Charge/15/15	10.5	129p	-	D/D/-/-	21/16/0/0	Titanite
Lothric Knight Long Spear	Thrust	Charge/13/9	8.0	112p	-	D/D/-/-	14/20/0/0	Titanite
Pike	Thrust	Charge/13/9	7.5	105p	-	D/C/-/-	18/14/0/0	Titanite

GREATLANCE

Thrust		Charge / 15 / 15		10.5

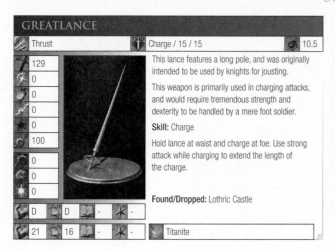

	129
	0
	0
	0
	0
	100
	0
	0
	0

This lance features a long pole, and was originally intended to be used by knights for jousting.

This weapon is primarily used in charging attacks, and would require tremendous strength and dexterity to be handled by a mere foot soldier.

Skill: Charge

Hold lance at waist and charge at foe. Use strong attack while charging to extend the length of the charge.

Found/Dropped: Lothric Castle

D	D	-	-	-
21	16	-	-	Titanite

LOTHRIC KNIGHT LONG SPEAR

Thrust		Charge / 13 / 9		8.0

	112
	0
	0
	0
	0
	100
	0
	0
	0

Long spear wielded by the proud Lothric Knights. Designed for long-range thrusting.

Lothric spear knights are known for their steadfastness, and this spear boosts the poise of its wielder.

Skill: Charge

Hold spear at waist and charge at foe. Use strong attack while charging to extend the length of the charge.

Found/Dropped: Lothric Knight, Greirat after pillaging Irithyll

D	D	-	-	-
14	20	-	-	Titanite

PIKE

Thrust		Charge / 13 / 9		7.5

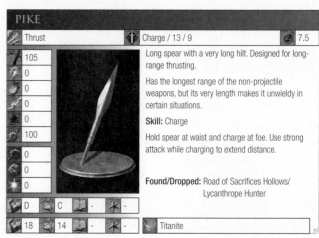

	105
	0
	0
	0
	0
	100
	0
	0
	0

Long spear with a very long hilt. Designed for long-range thrusting.

Has the longest range of the non-projectile weapons, but its very length makes it unwieldy in certain situations.

Skill: Charge

Hold spear at waist and charge at foe. Use strong attack while charging to extend distance.

Found/Dropped: Road of Sacrifices Hollows/ Lycanthrope Hunter

D	C	-	-	-
18	14	-	-	Titanite

HALBERDS

Probably the most unusual class of weapons in the game, Halberds mix the reach of a Spear with the striking and slashing motions of Axes or Hammers.

Halberds tend to have fairly demanding attribute requirements, moderate weights, and an awkward move set, all of which makes them relatively unfriendly to new players.

However, they do offer a mix of reach and sweeping area blows that few other weapons can match, and while they are ungainly weapons to use, they still have reasonably good speed for the moves that they offer. Halberds are also fairly easy to use against very large enemies, where their swing patterns are all but guaranteed to connect with ease.

Appropriate for their mixed heritage, they offer a wide range of weapon skills, taking a little from Hammers, Spears, and Axes.

HALBERDS	TYPE	ART/COST	WEIGHT	POWER	ADD. EFFECT	SCALING	REQUIREMENTS	MATERIAL
Black Knight Glaive	Standard	Spin Sweep/8/14	9.0	159p	-	D/D/-/-	28/18/0/0	Twinkling Titanite
Crescent Axe	Standard	Warcry/20	6.0	129p	-	D/D/-/-	14/12/0/0	Titanite
Glaive	Slash	Spin Sweep/8/14	11.0	141p	-	D/E/-/-	17/11/0/0	Titanite
Gundyr's Halberd	Standard	Champion's Charge/15/15	13.0	145p	-	C/E/-/-	30/15/0/0	Titanite Scale
Halberd	Standard/Thrust	Charge/15/13	8.0	125p	-	D/D/-/-	16/12/0/0	Titanite
Immolation Tinder	Thrust	Punitive Flame/20	10.0	118p/75f/20sb	-	D/D/B/-	18/18/12/12	Twinkling Titanite
Lucerne	Thrust	Spin Sweep/8/14	7.5	126p	-	D/D/-/-	15/13/0/0	Titanite
Red Hilted Halberd	Standard/Thrust	Perseverance/11	8.0	130p	-	D/D/-/-	14/14/0/0	Titanite
Winged Knight Halberd	Standard	Chain Spin/10/18	14.0	145p	-	D/E/-/-	26/16/0/0	Titanite

BLACK KNIGHT GLAIVE

Standard	Spin Sweep / 8 / 14	9.0

| 159 |
| 0 |
| 0 |
| 0 |
| 0 |
| 100 |
| 0 |
| 0 |
| 0 |

Glaive of the black knights who wander the lands. Used to face chaos demons.

The unique attack of this axe greatly reduces enemy poise, reflecting the tremendous size of the enemies that the knights have fearlessly faced.

Skill: Spin Sweep

Sweep foes in a large spinning motion, and utilize momentum to transition into an overhanded strong attack smash.

Found/Dropped: Untended Graves

D	D	-	-
28	18	-	-

Twinkling Titanite

CRESCENT AXE

Standard	Warcry / 20	6.0

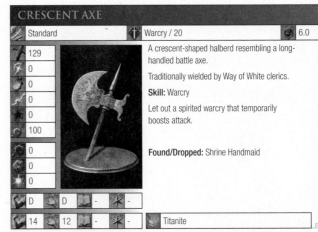

| 129 |
| 0 |
| 0 |
| 0 |
| 0 |
| 100 |
| 0 |
| 0 |
| 0 |

A crescent-shaped halberd resembling a long-handled battle axe.

Traditionally wielded by Way of White clerics.

Skill: Warcry

Let out a spirited warcry that temporarily boosts attack.

Found/Dropped: Shrine Handmaid

D	D	-	-
14	12	-	-

Titanite

GLAIVE

Slash	Spin Sweep / 8 / 14	11.0

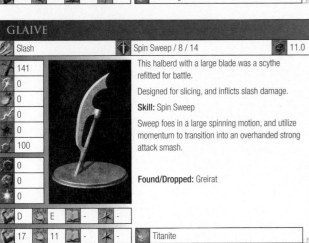

| 141 |
| 0 |
| 0 |
| 0 |
| 0 |
| 100 |
| 0 |
| 0 |
| 0 |

This halberd with a large blade was a scythe refitted for battle.

Designed for slicing, and inflicts slash damage.

Skill: Spin Sweep

Sweep foes in a large spinning motion, and utilize momentum to transition into an overhanded strong attack smash.

Found/Dropped: Greirat

D	E	-	-
17	11	-	-

Titanite

GUNDYR'S HALBERD

Standard	Champion's Charge / 15 / 15	13.0

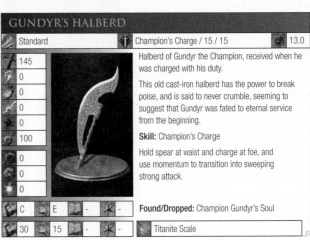

| 145 |
| 0 |
| 0 |
| 0 |
| 0 |
| 100 |
| 0 |
| 0 |
| 0 |

Halberd of Gundyr the Champion, received when he was charged with his duty.

This old cast-iron halberd has the power to break poise, and is said to never crumble, seeming to suggest that Gundyr was fated to eternal service from the beginning.

Skill: Champion's Charge

Hold spear at waist and charge at foe, and use momentum to transition into sweeping strong attack.

Found/Dropped: Champion Gundyr's Soul

C	E	-	-
30	15	-	-

Titanite Scale

HALBERD

Standard/Thrust	Charge / 15 / 13	8.0

125	This long-hilted weapon mixing spear and axe is difficult to handle, requiring both strength and dexterity.
0	
0	Can be thrust like a spear or swept sideways like an axe, making it a versatile weapon effective against multiple foes.
0	
0	
100	**Skill:** Charge
0	Hold spear at waist and charge at foe. Use strong attack while charging to extend the length of the charge.
0	
0	

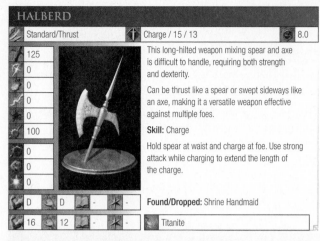

D	D	-	-

Found/Dropped: Shrine Handmaid

16	12	-	-	Titanite

IMMOLATION TINDER

Thrust	Punitive Flame / 20	10.0

118	Profaned Flame wielded by the Irithyllian witches, frigid spirits roaming the Boreal Valley.
0	
75	This torch, both a weapon and a staff, is enshrouded in an everlasting flame.
0	
0	**Skill:** Punitive Flame
100	Punish foes with a flame that blankets the ground.
20	
0	**Found/Dropped:** Burning Stake Witch
0	
0	Twinkling Titanite

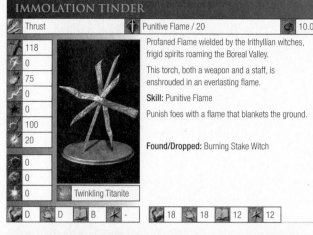

D	D	B	-

18	18	12	12

LUCERNE

Thrust	Spin Sweep / 8 / 14	7.5

126	A polearm with a sharp, hard pronged head that inflicts thrust attacks.
0	
0	The Lucerne is wielded overhand like a hammer, or can be swung from the side to break through shields.
0	
0	
100	**Skill:** Spin Sweep
0	Sweep foes in a large spinning motion, and utilize momentum to transition into an overhanded strong attack smash.
0	
0	

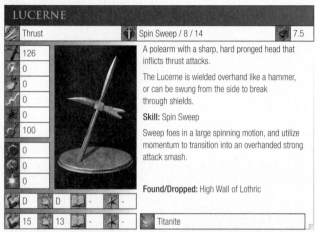

D	D	-	-

Found/Dropped: High Wall of Lothric

15	13	-	-	Titanite

RED HILTED HALBERD

Standard/Thrust	Perseverance / 11	8.0

130	Long-hilted weapon mixing spear and axe. The red-hilted halberd is associated with clerics.
0	
0	Can be thrust like a spear or swept sideways like an axe, making it a versatile weapon effective against multiple foes.
0	
0	
100	**Skill:** Perseverance
0	Assume an unfaltering stance of prayer to temporarily boost poise. Damage reduced while activated.
0	
0	

D	D	-	-

Found/Dropped: Undead Settlement

14	14	-	-	Titanite

WINGED KNIGHT HALBERD

Standard	Chain Spin / 10 / 18	14.0

145	Halberd wielded by the Winged Knights, who swore themselves to the Angels.
0	
0	The thick, heavy, bloodstained blade can only be swung by one with inhuman strength.
0	
0	**Skill:** Chain Spin
100	Sweep foes in a large spinning motion and use strong attack to continue the motion until stamina is exhausted.
0	
0	
0	**Found/Dropped:** Winged Knight

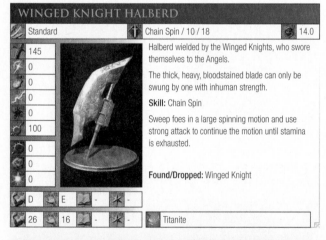

D	E	-	-

26	16	-	-	Titanite

REAPERS

The rare Reaper weapons offer the best mix of reach and sweeping, area of effect swings. Appropriately, they are ideal for scything down weaker foes in groups.

Reapers take a decent level of both Str and Dex to use and are midweight weapons that can be tough to use in enclosed spaces, so they aren't a great early-game choice, but as a mid or late-game tool, they can be useful as an alternate weapon to deal with certain areas and enemy combinations. Their Neck Swipe skill is a hard hitting and fairly low cost move, and you can dish out either Bleed or Frost status effects.

REAPERS	TYPE	ART/COST	WEIGHT	POWER	ADD. EFFECT	SCALING	REQUIREMENTS	MATERIAL
Great Scythe	Slash	Neck Swipe/13	7.0	105p	33bl	E/C/-/-	14/14/0/0	Titanite
Pontiff Knight Great Scythe	Slash	Frost/15	7.5	100p	-	E/A/-/-	14/19/0/12	Twinkling Titanite
Storyteller's Great Scythe	Slash	Neck Swipe/13	9.0	97p	36bl	D/C/-/-	16/18/0/0	Titanite

GREAT SCYTHE

Slash	Neck Swipe / 13	7.0

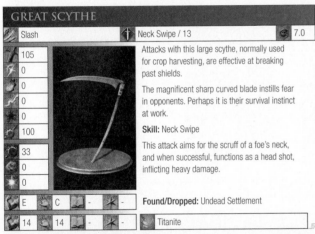

| 105 |
| 0 |
| 0 |
| 0 |
| 0 |
| 100 |
| 33 |
| 0 |
| 0 |

E	C	-	-
14	14	-	-

Attacks with this large scythe, normally used for crop harvesting, are effective at breaking past shields.

The magnificent sharp curved blade instills fear in opponents. Perhaps it is their survival instinct at work.

Skill: Neck Swipe

This attack aims for the scruff of a foe's neck, and when successful, functions as a head shot, inflicting heavy damage.

Found/Dropped: Undead Settlement

Titanite

PONTIFF KNIGHT GREAT SCYTHE

Slash	Frost / 15	7.5

| 100 |
| 0 |
| 0 |
| 0 |
| 0 |
| 100 |
| 0 |
| 0 |
| 0 |

E	A	-	-
14	19	-	12

Great scythe wielded by the Pontiff's knights, frigid spirits that linger in Irithyll.

The large blade appears to be eaten away by insects, making it lightweight but also brittle.

Skill: Frost

Create a bone-chilling frost with each swing of the greatscythe that causes a temporary frost effect.

Found/Dropped: Pontiff Knight

Twinkling Titanite

STORYTELLER'S GREAT SCYTHE

Slash	Neck Swipe / 13	9.0

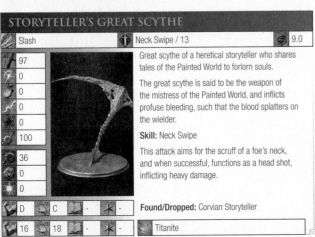

| 97 |
| 0 |
| 0 |
| 0 |
| 0 |
| 100 |
| 36 |
| 0 |
| 0 |

D	C	-	-
16	18	-	-

Great scythe of a heretical storyteller who shares tales of the Painted World to forlorn souls.

The great scythe is said to be the weapon of the mistress of the Painted World, and inflicts profuse bleeding, such that the blood splatters on the wielder.

Skill: Neck Swipe

This attack aims for the scruff of a foe's neck, and when successful, functions as a head shot, inflicting heavy damage.

Found/Dropped: Corvian Storyteller

Titanite

WHIPS

Unusual weapons all around, Whips require high Dex to use, but have light weight and quick strikes. They can also deal Bleed or Poison damage, and the Impact move gives them a means of bypassing shields and damaging Stamina recovery.

This makes Whips an interesting choice for PvP players, and they can be a viable alternative to Daggers, Curved Swords, or Thrusting Swords if none of those suit your Dex build tastes.

WHIPS	TYPE	ART/COST	WEIGHT	POWER	ADD. EFFECT	SCALING	REQUIREMENTS	MATERIAL
Notched Whip	Slash	Impact/14	2.0	95p	33bl	-/D/-/-	6/19/0/0	Titanite
Spotted Whip	Slash	Impact/14	2.5	102p	33po	-/D/-/-	9/20/0/0	Titanite
Whip	Slash	Impact/14	2.0	90p	-	-/C/-/-	6/14/0/0	Titanite
Witch's Locks	Slash	Flame Whip/18	3.0	77p/80f	-	-/D/C/C	9/17/12/12	Twinkling Titanite

NOTCHED WHIP

Slash		Impact / 14		2.0

| 95 |
| 0 |
| 0 |
| 0 |
| 0 |
| 100 |
| 33 |
| 0 |
| 0 |

| - | | D | | - | | - |
| 6 | | 19 | | - | | - |
Titanite

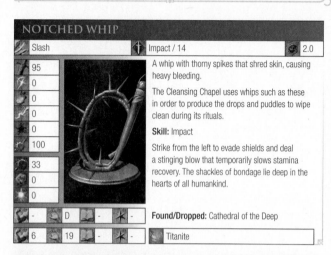

A whip with thorny spikes that shred skin, causing heavy bleeding.

The Cleansing Chapel uses whips such as these in order to produce the drops and puddles to wipe clean during its rituals.

Skill: Impact

Strike from the left to evade shields and deal a stinging blow that temporarily slows stamina recovery. The shackles of bondage lie deep in the hearts of all humankind.

Found/Dropped: Cathedral of the Deep

SPOTTED WHIP

Slash		Impact / 14		2.5

| 102 |
| 0 |
| 0 |
| 0 |
| 100 |
| 0 |
| 33 |
| 0 |

| - | | D | | - | | - |
| 9 | | 20 | | - | | - |
Titanite

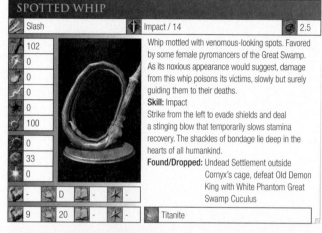

Whip mottled with venomous-looking spots. Favored by some female pyromancers of the Great Swamp. As its noxious appearance would suggest, damage from this whip poisons its victims, slowly but surely guiding them to their deaths.

Skill: Impact

Strike from the left to evade shields and deal a stinging blow that temporarily slows stamina recovery. The shackles of bondage lie deep in the hearts of all humankind.

Found/Dropped: Undead Settlement outside Cornyx's cage, defeat Old Demon King with White Phantom Great Swamp Cuculus

WHIP

Slash		Impact / 14		2.0

| 90 |
| 0 |
| 0 |
| 0 |
| 0 |
| 100 |
| 0 |
| 0 |
| 0 |

| - | | C | | - | | - |
| 6 | | 14 | | - | | - |
Titanite

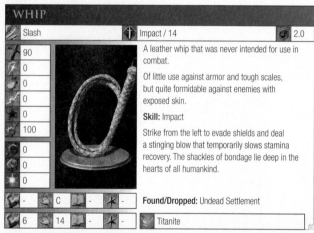

A leather whip that was never intended for use in combat.

Of little use against armor and tough scales, but quite formidable against enemies with exposed skin.

Skill: Impact

Strike from the left to evade shields and deal a stinging blow that temporarily slows stamina recovery. The shackles of bondage lie deep in the hearts of all humankind.

Found/Dropped: Undead Settlement

WITCH'S LOCKS

Slash		Flame Whip / 18		3.0

| 77 |
| 0 |
| 80 |
| 0 |
| 0 |
| 100 |
| 0 |
| 0 |
| 0 |

| - | | D | | C | | C |
| 9 | | 17 | | 12 | | 12 |
Twinkling Titanite

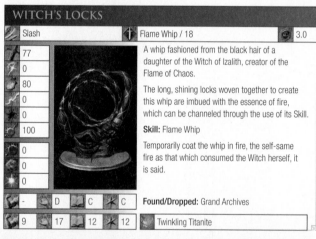

A whip fashioned from the black hair of a daughter of the Witch of Izalith, creator of the Flame of Chaos.

The long, shining locks woven together to create this whip are imbued with the essence of fire, which can be channeled through the use of its Skill.

Skill: Flame Whip

Temporarily coat the whip in fire, the self-same fire as that which consumed the Witch herself, it is said.

Found/Dropped: Grand Archives

FISTS

For when you really want to get up close and personal, Fist weapons give you some extra pounding power on your hands. Fists are all inherently dual-wieldable weapons, giving you a weapon in each hand and a dual wield attack moveset.

Fists have extremely limited reach, but they do have the benefit of low weight and rapid strikes, making them a viable option against smaller enemies and humanoid foes. They can be considerably harder to use against truly massive enemies or bosses that are extremely dangerous to stay in close proximity with.

FISTS	TYPE	ART/COST	WEIGHT	POWER	ADD. EFFECT	SCALING	REQUIREMENTS	MATERIAL
Caestus	Strike	Perseverance/7	0.5	80p	-	D/D/-/-	5/8/0/0	Titanite
Dark Hand	Strike	Lifedrain/18	0.0	77p/150d	-	E/E/C/C	0/0/0/0	Titanite
Demon's Fist	Strike	Flame Whirlwind/10/10	8.0	93p/77f	-	D/-/E/E	20/8/9/9	Titanite Scale

CAESTUS

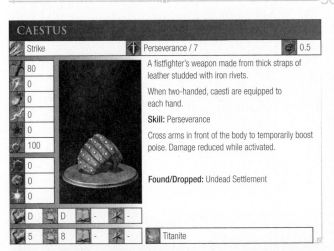

Strike	Perseverance / 7
	0.5

	80
	0
	0
	0
	0
	100
	0
	0
	0

| D | D | - | - |
| 5 | 8 | - | - |

Titanite

A fistfighter's weapon made from thick straps of leather studded with iron rivets.

When two-handed, caesti are equipped to each hand.

Skill: Perseverance

Cross arms in front of the body to temporarily boost poise. Damage reduced while activated.

Found/Dropped: Undead Settlement

DARK HAND

Strike	Lifedrain / 18
	0.0

	77
	0
	0
	0
	150
	100
	0
	0
	0

E	E	C	C

Titanite

Weapon that allows its wielder to evoke an art unique to Londor, the land of the Hollow. It is also said to be an ancient relic of a Primordial Serpent.

The Dark Hand mercilessly saps the essence of its victims, and can also double as a special shield.

Cannot be used two-handed.

Skill: Lifedrain

Embrace the victim and steal their HP. Can only be used against humans.

Found/Dropped: Yuria of Londor

DEMON'S FIST

Strike	Flame Whirlwind / 10 / 10
	8.0

	93
	0
	77
	0
	0
	100
	0
	0
	0

| D | - | E | E |
| 20 | 8 | 9 | 9 |

Titanite Scale

A demonic fist that burns with fiery essence. Its wielder can release this power through use of its Skill.

When two-handed, fists are equipped to each hand.

Skill: Flame Whirlwind

Spin through opponents with abandon, flaming fists outstretched. Using a strong attack while spinning utilizes your momentum to slam the ground with both fists.

Found/Dropped: Demon Soul

CLAWS

Similar to Fists in that they are both dual-wieldable weapons, Claws give an edge to your close quarters combat strikes. They require fairly high Dex to use, but both offer Bleed effects and skills that give rapid mobility in combat.

If you're really dead set on a fisticuffs concept character, you can go with Fists with a Str focus, or Claws if you're leaning towards Dex.

CLAWS	TYPE	ART/COST	WEIGHT	POWER	ADD. EFFECT	SCALING	REQUIREMENTS	MATERIAL
Claw	Slash/Thrust	Leaping Slash/10	1.5	75p/110c	33bl	E/C/-/-	6/14/0/0	Titanite
Manikin Claws	Slash/Thrust	Quickstep/4	2.0	79p/110c	33bl	E/C/-/-	8/18/0/0	Titanite

CLAW

	Slash/Thrust		Leaping Slash / 10		1.5

	75
	0
	0
	0
	0
	110
	33
	0
	0

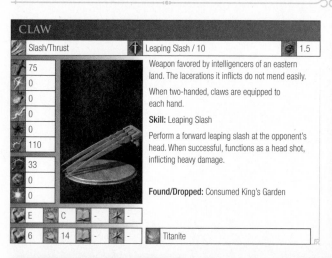

Weapon favored by intelligencers of an eastern land. The lacerations it inflicts do not mend easily.

When two-handed, claws are equipped to each hand.

Skill: Leaping Slash

Perform a forward leaping slash at the opponent's head. When successful, functions as a head shot, inflicting heavy damage.

Found/Dropped: Consumed King's Garden

	E		C		-		-
	6		14		-		-

Titanite

MANIKIN CLAWS

	Slash/Thrust		Quickstep / 4		2.0

	79
	0
	0
	0
	0
	110
	33
	0
	0

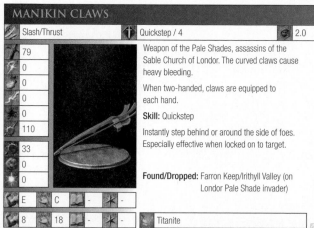

Weapon of the Pale Shades, assassins of the Sable Church of Londor. The curved claws cause heavy bleeding.

When two-handed, claws are equipped to each hand.

Skill: Quickstep

Instantly step behind or around the side of foes. Especially effective when locked on to target.

Found/Dropped: Farron Keep/Irithyll Valley (on Londor Pale Shade invader)

	E		C		-		-
	8		18		-		-

Titanite

RANGED WEAPONS

Ranged Weapons comprise Bows and Crossbows, with the special Greatbows mixed in.

Ranged weaponry gives your character the ability to strike foes from a distance, and this is extremely useful and powerful in many parts of the game. It is very easy to neglect ranged weapons, skipping them entirely or rarely using them. Don't do this if you're a new player!

Pulling enemies apart with a bow can make tough encounters manageable, and some difficult encounters or enemies can be outright defeated without ever engaging them with sufficient arrows.

Very early in the game, you can buy an unlimited amount of arrows or bolts cheaply. Take advantage of this. As you progress, you unlock new and more powerful types of ammunition, and combined with the right stats and an upgraded bow, this can allow you to inflict considerable damage from a distance.

For veteran players, some of the bow skills may be of interest, giving bows an extra option in combat.

BOWS

Basic bows require a light investment in stats, with the Short Bow, Composite Bow, and Longbow all being reasonable options early in the game. The rarer bows require a heavier investment in Dex or Str to be used, making them more suitable for builds already planning on raising those attributes.

For veteran players, the Rapid Fire skill on the Composite and Short Bows may be of particular interest. It allows you to unleash a hail of shots quickly, giving you the option to mix in quick ranged attacks while still fighting in melee range. This has PvP implications, but also gives you the real option of fighting with a bow in close quarters combat alongside your melee weapon, which can be very handy against some enemy types.

BOWS	ART/COST	WEIGHT	POWER	RANGE	SCALING	REQUIREMENTS	MATERIAL
Black Bow of Pharis	Pharis Triple-shot/7	3.0	67p	50	E/C/-/-	9/18/0/0	Titanite
Composite Bow	Rapid Fire/4	3.5	73p	42	D/D/-/-	12/12/0/0	Titanite
Darkmoon Long Bow	Darkmoon Arrow/10	4.5	36p/55m	50	-/E/C/-	7/16/10/0	Titanite Scale
Dragonrider Bow	Puncture/9	6.5	110p	50	D/E/-/-	19/15/0/0	Titanite Scale
Longbow	Puncture/9	4.0	82p	50	E/D/-/-	9/14/0/0	Titanite
Short Bow	Rapid Fire/4	2.0	77p	42	E/D/-/-	7/12/0/0	Titanite

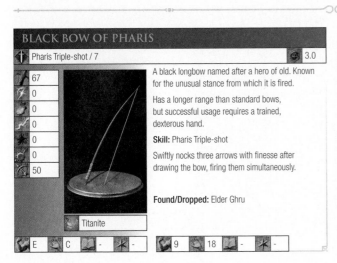

BLACK BOW OF PHARIS

Pharis Triple-shot / 7   3.0

67
0
0
0
0
0
50

A black longbow named after a hero of old. Known for the unusual stance from which it is fired.

Has a longer range than standard bows, but successful usage requires a trained, dexterous hand.

Skill: Pharis Triple-shot

Swiftly nocks three arrows with finesse after drawing the bow, firing them simultaneously.

Found/Dropped: Elder Ghru

Titanite

E   C   -   *-   9   18   -   *-

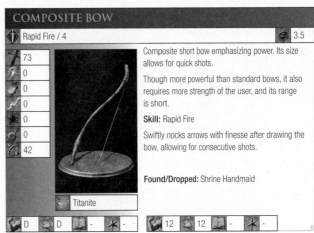

COMPOSITE BOW

Rapid Fire / 4   3.5

73
0
0
0
0
0
42

Composite short bow emphasizing power. Its size allows for quick shots.

Though more powerful than standard bows, it also requires more strength of the user, and its range is short.

Skill: Rapid Fire

Swiftly nocks arrows with finesse after drawing the bow, allowing for consecutive shots.

Found/Dropped: Shrine Handmaid

Titanite

D   D   -   *-   12   12   -   *-

DARKMOON LONG BOW

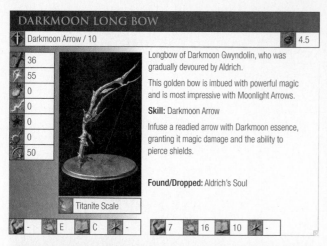

| Darkmoon Arrow / 10 | 4.5 |

| 36 |
| 55 |
| 0 |
| 0 |
| 0 |
| 0 |
| 50 |

Longbow of Darkmoon Gwyndolin, who was gradually devoured by Aldrich.

This golden bow is imbued with powerful magic and is most impressive with Moonlight Arrows.

Skill: Darkmoon Arrow

Infuse a readied arrow with Darkmoon essence, granting it magic damage and the ability to pierce shields.

Found/Dropped: Aldrich's Soul

Titanite Scale

| - | E | C | - | 7 | 16 | 10 | - |

DRAGONRIDER BOW

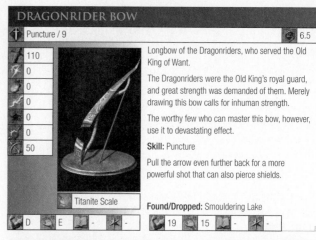

| Puncture / 9 | 6.5 |

| 110 |
| 0 |
| 0 |
| 0 |
| 0 |
| 0 |
| 50 |

Longbow of the Dragonriders, who served the Old King of Want.

The Dragonriders were the Old King's royal guard, and great strength was demanded of them. Merely drawing this bow calls for inhuman strength.

The worthy few who can master this bow, however, use it to devastating effect.

Skill: Puncture

Pull the arrow even further back for a more powerful shot that can also pierce shields.

Found/Dropped: Smouldering Lake

Titanite Scale

| D | E | - | - | 19 | 15 | - | - |

LONGBOW

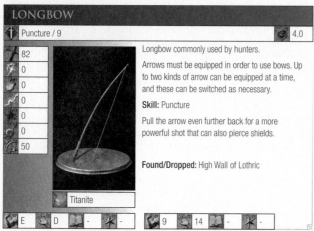

| Puncture / 9 | 4.0 |

| 82 |
| 0 |
| 0 |
| 0 |
| 0 |
| 0 |
| 50 |

Longbow commonly used by hunters.

Arrows must be equipped in order to use bows. Up to two kinds of arrow can be equipped at a time, and these can be switched as necessary.

Skill: Puncture

Pull the arrow even further back for a more powerful shot that can also pierce shields.

Found/Dropped: High Wall of Lothric

Titanite

| E | D | - | - | 9 | 14 | - | - |

SHORT BOW

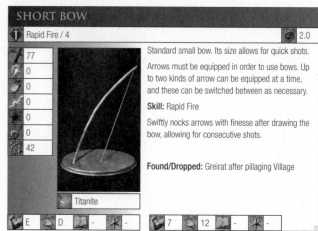

| Rapid Fire / 4 | 2.0 |

| 77 |
| 0 |
| 0 |
| 0 |
| 0 |
| 0 |
| 42 |

Standard small bow. Its size allows for quick shots.

Arrows must be equipped in order to use bows. Up to two kinds of arrow can be equipped at a time, and these can be switched between as necessary.

Skill: Rapid Fire

Swiftly nocks arrows with finesse after drawing the bow, allowing for consecutive shots.

Found/Dropped: Greirat after pillaging Village

Titanite

| E | D | - | - | 7 | 12 | - | - |

GREATBOWS

Massive, heavy bows with demanding attribute requirements, Greatbows typically cannot be used until later in a playthrough.

They require specialized ammunition, and are slow to wield and fire. Best used as an alpha strike against distant foes, or for landing hits on truly massive targets while they are disengaged from you, Greatbows are a poor choice for general combat, but they can come in handy against certain big game targets.

GREATBOWS	ART/COST	WEIGHT	POWER	RANGE	SCALING	REQUIREMENTS	MATERIAL
Dragonslayer Greatbow	Puncturing Arrow/20	10.0	126p	50	D/D/-/-	20/20/0/0	Twinkling Titanite
Onislayer Greatbow	Puncturing Arrow/17	7.5	111p	63	E/C/-/-	18/24/0/0	Twinkling Titanite

DRAGONSLAYER GREATBOW

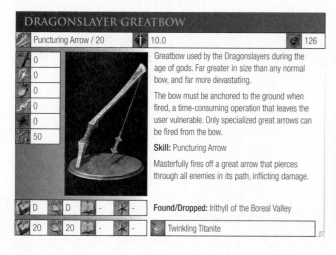

| Puncturing Arrow / 20 | 10.0 | 126 |

| 0 |
| 0 |
| 0 |
| 0 |
| 0 |
| 50 |

Greatbow used by the Dragonslayers during the age of gods. Far greater in size than any normal bow, and far more devastating.

The bow must be anchored to the ground when fired, a time-consuming operation that leaves the user vulnerable. Only specialized great arrows can be fired from the bow.

Skill: Puncturing Arrow

Masterfully fires off a great arrow that pierces through all enemies in its path, inflicting damage.

Found/Dropped: Irithyll of the Boreal Valley

| D | D | - | - |
| 20 | 20 | - | - |

Twinkling Titanite

ONISLAYER GREATBOW

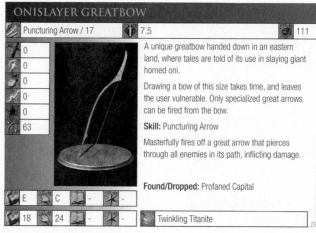

| Puncturing Arrow / 17 | 7.5 | 111 |

| 0 |
| 0 |
| 0 |
| 0 |
| 0 |
| 63 |

A unique greatbow handed down in an eastern land, where tales are told of its use in slaying giant horned oni.

Drawing a bow of this size takes time, and leaves the user vulnerable. Only specialized great arrows can be fired from the bow.

Skill: Puncturing Arrow

Masterfully fires off a great arrow that pierces through all enemies in its path, inflicting damage.

Found/Dropped: Profaned Capital

| E | C | - | - |
| 18 | 24 | - | - |

Twinkling Titanite

CROSSBOWS

Crossbows offer a ranged option for characters uninterested in heavily investing in Dex, as they have no inherent stat scaling, and can be used to quickly fire offhand shots.

This makes them a good choice for using while in-combat to pepper enemies with attacks even when they back off, and for interrupting spellcasting (or item usage, in the case of other players or NPC phantoms trying to drink Estus).

Crossbows only have a basic Tackle skill, lacking the dedicated ranged skills of the other bows.

CROSSBOWS	ART/COST	WEIGHT	POWER	RANGE	SCALING	REQUIREMENTS	MATERIAL
Arbalest	Tackle/7	6.0	78p	50	-/-/-/-	18/8/0/0	Titanite
Avelyn	Tackle/7	7.5	64p	35	-/-/-/-	16/14/0/0	Titanite
Heavy Crossbow	Tackle/7	7.5	72p	50	-/-/-/-	14/8/0/0	Titanite
Knight's Crossbow	Tackle/7	4.0	40p/40l	42	-/-/-/-	12/8/0/0	Titanite
Light Crossbow	Tackle/7	3.0	64p	42	-/-/-/-	10/8/0/0	Titanite
Sniper Crossbow	Tackle/7	4.5	70p	59	-/-/-/-	18/16/0/0	Titanite

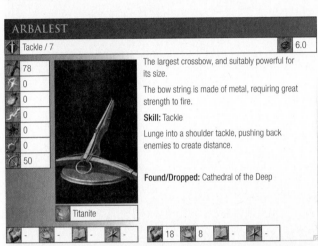

ARBALEST

Tackle / 7 — 6.0

	78
	0
	0
	0
	0
	0
	50

The largest crossbow, and suitably powerful for its size.

The bow string is made of metal, requiring great strength to fire.

Skill: Tackle

Lunge into a shoulder tackle, pushing back enemies to create distance.

Found/Dropped: Cathedral of the Deep

Titanite

18 8 - -

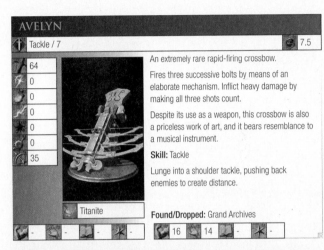

AVELYN

Tackle / 7 — 7.5

	64
	0
	0
	0
	0
	0
	35

An extremely rare rapid-firing crossbow.

Fires three successive bolts by means of an elaborate mechanism. Inflict heavy damage by making all three shots count.

Despite its use as a weapon, this crossbow is also a priceless work of art, and it bears resemblance to a musical instrument.

Skill: Tackle

Lunge into a shoulder tackle, pushing back enemies to create distance.

Found/Dropped: Grand Archives

Titanite

16 14 - -

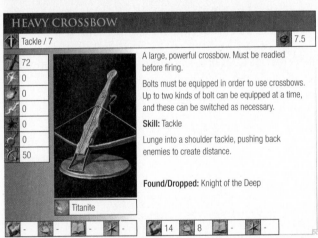

HEAVY CROSSBOW

Tackle / 7 — 7.5

	72
	0
	0
	0
	0
	0
	50

A large, powerful crossbow. Must be readied before firing.

Bolts must be equipped in order to use crossbows. Up to two kinds of bolt can be equipped at a time, and these can be switched as necessary.

Skill: Tackle

Lunge into a shoulder tackle, pushing back enemies to create distance.

Found/Dropped: Knight of the Deep

Titanite

14 8 - -

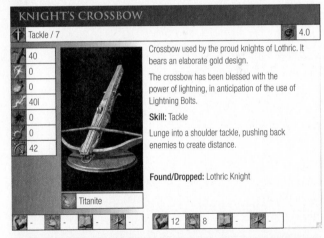

KNIGHT'S CROSSBOW

Tackle / 7 — 4.0

	40
	0
	0
	40l
	0
	0
	42

Crossbow used by the proud knights of Lothric. It bears an elaborate gold design.

The crossbow has been blessed with the power of lightning, in anticipation of the use of Lightning Bolts.

Skill: Tackle

Lunge into a shoulder tackle, pushing back enemies to create distance.

Found/Dropped: Lothric Knight

Titanite

12 8 - -

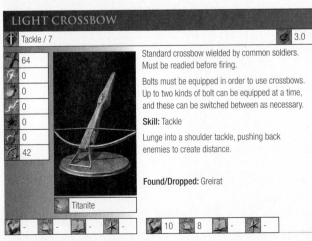

LIGHT CROSSBOW

Tackle / 7 — 3.0

	64
	0
	0
	0
	0
	0
	42

Standard crossbow wielded by common soldiers. Must be readied before firing.

Bolts must be equipped in order to use crossbows. Up to two kinds of bolt can be equipped at a time, and these can be switched between as necessary.

Skill: Tackle

Lunge into a shoulder tackle, pushing back enemies to create distance.

Found/Dropped: Greirat

Titanite

10 8 - -

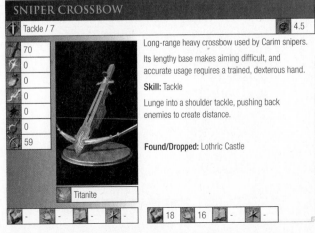

SNIPER CROSSBOW

Tackle / 7 — 4.5

	70
	0
	0
	0
	0
	0
	59

Long-range heavy crossbow used by Carim snipers.

Its lengthy base makes aiming difficult, and accurate usage requires a trained, dexterous hand.

Skill: Tackle

Lunge into a shoulder tackle, pushing back enemies to create distance.

Found/Dropped: Lothric Castle

Titanite

18 16 - -

CATALYSTS

Catalysts are required for spellcasting, with Staffs used for Sorceries, Talismans for Miracles, and the Pyromancy Flame for Pyromancies.

Catalysts give a Spell Buff stat, boosting your spell damage or healing output. Different catalysts offer different types of attribute scaling, and different base levels of Spell Buff (there are a few rare weapons that act as Catalysts, see the melee weapons for more info on those).

STAFFS

Necessary for Sorcery casting, all but one Staff offers the Steady Chant skill, which boosts your Sorcery damage output temporarily after activation.

Staff selection largely comes down to picking one that has a special effect that most suits your particular build and tastes, with effects ranging from gaining added stat scaling from Luck to increasing the speed of your casts.

STAFFS	TYPE	ART/COST	WEIGHT	POWER	SPELL BUFF	SCALING	REQUIREMENTS	MATERIAL
Archdeacon's Great Staff	Strike	Steady Chant/7	2.5	89p	20	D/-/-/A	8/0/12/12	Twinkling Titanite
Court Sorcerer's Staff	Strike	Steady Chant/15	2.0	60p	60	E/-/A/-	6/0/14/0	Titanite
Heretic's Staff	Strike	Steady Chant/7	3.0	63p	60	D/-/B/-	8/0/16/0	Titanite
Izalith Staff	Strike	Steady Chant/7	3.0	120p	20	D/D/B/C	12/0/14/10	Twinkling Titanite
Man-grub's Staff	Strike	Steady Chant/7	3.0	90p	60	D/-/-/-	9/0/18/0	Twinkling Titanite
Mendicant's Staff	Strike	Steady Chant/7	2.5	60p	60	D/-/B/-	7/0/18/0	Titanite
Sage's Crystal Staff	Strike	Steady Chant/30	2.5	84p	60	E/-/B/-	7/0/24/0	Titanite Scale
Sorcerer's Staff	Strike	Steady Chant/7	2.0	60p	60	E/-/B/-	6/0/10/0	Titanite
Storyteller's Staff	Strike	Poison Spores/20	2.5	60p	60	E/-/B/-	6/0/12/0	Titanite
Witchtree Branch	Strike	Steady Chant/7	2.0	57p	60	E/-/C/-	7/0/18/0	Titanite

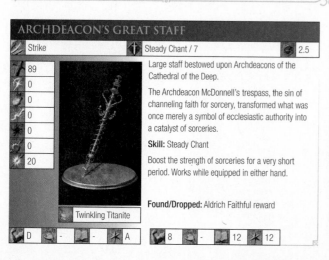

ARCHDEACON'S GREAT STAFF

Strike — Steady Chant / 7 — 2.5

89 / 0 / 0 / 0 / 0 / 0 / 20

Large staff bestowed upon Archdeacons of the Cathedral of the Deep.

The Archdeacon McDonnell's trespass, the sin of channeling faith for sorcery, transformed what was once merely a symbol of ecclesiastic authority into a catalyst of sorceries.

Skill: Steady Chant

Boost the strength of sorceries for a very short period. Works while equipped in either hand.

Found/Dropped: Aldrich Faithful reward

Twinkling Titanite

D - - A — 8 - 12 12

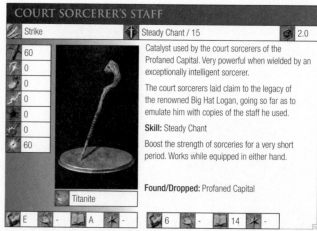

COURT SORCERER'S STAFF

Strike — Steady Chant / 15 — 2.0

60 / 0 / 0 / 0 / 0 / 0 / 60

Catalyst used by the court sorcerers of the Profaned Capital. Very powerful when wielded by an exceptionally intelligent sorcerer.

The court sorcerers laid claim to the legacy of the renowned Big Hat Logan, going so far as to emulate him with copies of the staff he used.

Skill: Steady Chant

Boost the strength of sorceries for a very short period. Works while equipped in either hand.

Found/Dropped: Profaned Capital

Titanite

E - - A - — 6 - 14 -

HERETIC'S STAFF

Strike	Steady Chant / 7	3.0

⚔	63
	0
	0
	0
	0
	0
✸	60

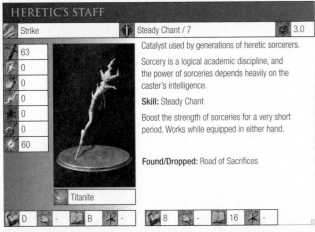

Titanite

Catalyst used by generations of heretic sorcerers.

Sorcery is a logical academic discipline, and the power of sorceries depends heavily on the caster's intelligence.

Skill: Steady Chant

Boost the strength of sorceries for a very short period. Works while equipped in either hand.

Found/Dropped: Road of Sacrifices

D	-	B	✱	-		8	-	16	✱	-

IZALITH STAFF

Strike	Steady Chant / 7	3.0

⚔	120
	0
	0
	0
	0
	0
✸	20

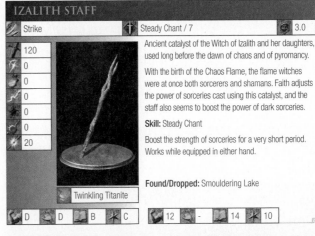

Twinkling Titanite

Ancient catalyst of the Witch of Izalith and her daughters, used long before the dawn of chaos and of pyromancy.

With the birth of the Chaos Flame, the flame witches were at once both sorcerers and shamans. Faith adjusts the power of sorceries cast using this catalyst, and the staff also seems to boost the power of dark sorceries.

Skill: Steady Chant

Boost the strength of sorceries for a very short period. Works while equipped in either hand.

Found/Dropped: Smouldering Lake

D	D	B	✱	C		12	-	14	✱	10

MAN-GRUB'S STAFF

Strike	Steady Chant / 7	3.0

⚔	90
	0
	0
	0
	0
	0
✸	60

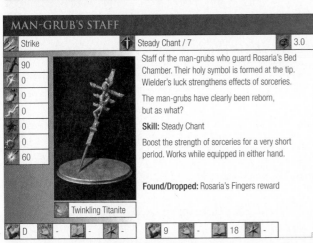

Twinkling Titanite

Staff of the man-grubs who guard Rosaria's Bed Chamber. Their holy symbol is formed at the tip. Wielder's luck strengthens effects of sorceries.

The man-grubs have clearly been reborn, but as what?

Skill: Steady Chant

Boost the strength of sorceries for a very short period. Works while equipped in either hand.

Found/Dropped: Rosaria's Fingers reward

D	-	B	✱	-		9	-	18	✱	-

MENDICANT'S STAFF

Strike	Steady Chant / 7	2.5

⚔	60
	0
	0
	0
	0
	0
✸	60

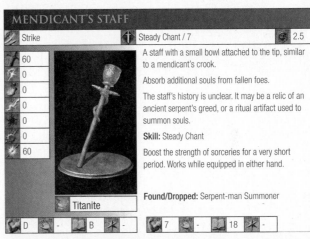

Titanite

A staff with a small bowl attached to the tip, similar to a mendicant's crook.

Absorb additional souls from fallen foes.

The staff's history is unclear. It may be a relic of an ancient serpent's greed, or a ritual artifact used to summon souls.

Skill: Steady Chant

Boost the strength of sorceries for a very short period. Works while equipped in either hand.

Found/Dropped: Serpent-man Summoner

D	-	B	✱	-		7	-	18	✱	-

SAGE'S CRYSTAL STAFF

Strike	Steady Chant / 30	2.5

⚔	84
	0
	0
	0
	0
	0
✸	60

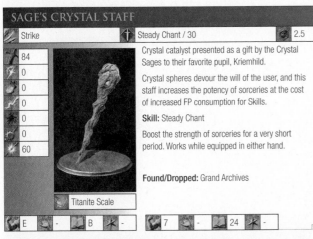

Titanite Scale

Crystal catalyst presented as a gift by the Crystal Sages to their favorite pupil, Kriemhild.

Crystal spheres devour the will of the user, and this staff increases the potency of sorceries at the cost of increased FP consumption for Skills.

Skill: Steady Chant

Boost the strength of sorceries for a very short period. Works while equipped in either hand.

Found/Dropped: Grand Archives

E	-	B	✱	-		7	-	24	✱	-

SORCERER'S STAFF

Strike	Steady Chant / 7	2.0

⚔	60
	0
	0
	0
	0
	0
✸	60

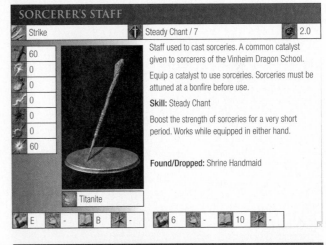

Titanite

Staff used to cast sorceries. A common catalyst given to sorcerers of the Vinheim Dragon School.

Equip a catalyst to use sorceries. Sorceries must be attuned at a bonfire before use.

Skill: Steady Chant

Boost the strength of sorceries for a very short period. Works while equipped in either hand.

Found/Dropped: Shrine Handmaid

E	-	B	✱	-		6	✱	-	10	✱	-

STORYTELLER'S STAFF

Strike	Poison Spores / 20	2.5

⚔	60
	0
	0
	0
	0
	0
✸	60

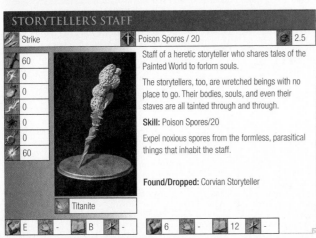

Titanite

Staff of a heretic storyteller who shares tales of the Painted World to forlorn souls.

The storytellers, too, are wretched beings with no place to go. Their bodies, souls, and even their staves are all tainted through and through.

Skill: Poison Spores/20

Expel noxious spores from the formless, parasitical things that inhabit the staff.

Found/Dropped: Corvian Storyteller

E	-	B	✱	-		6	-	12	✱	-

WITCHTREE BRANCH

Strike	Steady Chant / 7	2.0

⚔	57
	0
	0
	0
	0
	0
✸	60

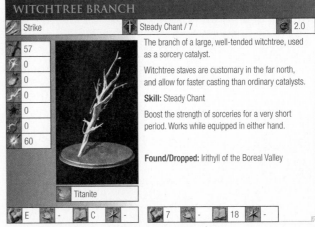

Titanite

The branch of a large, well-tended witchtree, used as a sorcery catalyst.

Witchtree staves are customary in the far north, and allow for faster casting than ordinary catalysts.

Skill: Steady Chant

Boost the strength of sorceries for a very short period. Works while equipped in either hand.

Found/Dropped: Irithyll of the Boreal Valley

E	-	C	✱	-		7	-	18	✱	-

PYROMANCY FLAME

There's only one choice for Pyromancies, but the Pyromancy Flame does have the benefit of having a naturally higher base Spell Buff level, and upgrading it at the Pyromancy trainer increases its base power even more.

This makes Pyromancies a solid choice as an offensive magic for characters who may not want to invest heavily in Int or Faith.

While you still need to raise both Int and Faith to use high powered Pyromancy spells, there are a decent number of options for even a dabbler. The Pyromancy Flame itself comes with the Combustion spell 'built-in' as its skill, a good spell for a melee fighter.

PYROMANCY FLAME	TYPE	ART/COST	WEIGHT	POWER	SPELL BUFF	SCALING	REQUIREMENTS	MATERIAL
Pyromancy Flame	Strike	Combustion/12	0.0	100f	110	-/-/C/C	0/0/0/0	Titanite

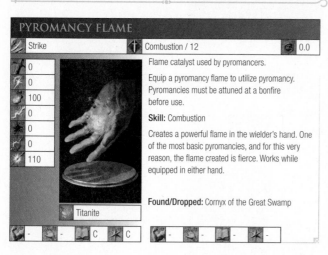

PYROMANCY FLAME

	Strike		Combustion / 12		0.0

	0
	0
	100
	0
	0
	0
	110

Titanite

-	-	C	✦ C

-	-	-	✦ -

Flame catalyst used by pyromancers.

Equip a pyromancy flame to utilize pyromancy. Pyromancies must be attuned at a bonfire before use.

Skill: Combustion

Creates a powerful flame in the wielder's hand. One of the most basic pyromancies, and for this very reason, the flame created is fierce. Works while equipped in either hand.

Found/Dropped: Cornyx of the Great Swamp

TALISMANS

Necessarily for the healing and defensive magics of Miracles, Talismans have a range of special effects like Staffs.

Many Talismans offer the Gentle Prayer skill, giving you the ability to freely heal yourself at any time. Even for a character not planning on using Miracles heavily, it is worthwhile to carry a basic Talisman for spot healing now and again.

The Unfaltering Prayer skill improves Poise, potentially useful for a more offensive focused Miracle caster.

TALISMANS	TYPE	ART/COST	WEIGHT	POWER	SPELL BUFF	SCALING	REQUIREMENTS	MATERIAL
Caitha's Chime	Strike	Gentle Prayer/13	0.5	74p	20	E/-/C/B	3/0/12/12	Twinkling Titanite
Canvas Talisman	Strike	Unfaltering Prayer/8	0.5	52p	60	D/-/-/B	4/0/0/14	Titanite
Cleric's Sacred Chime	Strike	Gentle Prayer/13	0.5	52p	60	D/-/-/A	3/0/0/14	Titanite
Crystal Chime	Strike	Gentle Prayer/13	0.5	73p	20	E/-/D/D	3/0/18/18	Twinkling Titanite
Priest's Chime	Strike	Gentle Prayer/13	0.5	52p	60	E/-/-/B	3/0/0/10	Titanite
Saint's Talisman	Strike	Unfaltering Prayer/8	0.5	53p	60	D/-/-/A	4/0/0/16	Titanite
Saint-tree Bellvine	Strike	Gentle Prayer/13	0.5	52p	60	E/-/-/C	3/0/0/18	Titanite
Sunless Talisman	Strike	Unfaltering Prayer/8	0.5	74p	60	E/-/C/B	4/0/0/24	Twinkling Titanite
Sunlight Talisman	Strike	Unfaltering Prayer/9	0.5	53p	60	D/-/-/B	4/0/0/14	Titanite
Talisman	Strike/Thrust	Unfaltering Prayer/8	0.5	52p	60	E/-/-/B	4/0/0/10	Titanite
White Hair Talisman	Strike	Combustion/12	0.5	73p/79f	20	E/-/D/D	4/0/16/20	Twinkling Titanite
Yorshka's Chime	Strike	Gentle Prayer/13	0.5	54p	60	D/-/-/A	3/0/0/30	Titanite

CAITHA'S CHIME

Strike	Gentle Prayer / 13 0.5

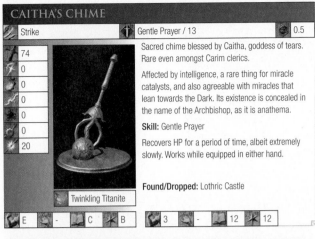

74	
0	
0	
0	
0	
0	
20	

Twinkling Titanite

E	-	C	B

3	-	12	12

Sacred chime blessed by Caitha, goddess of tears. Rare even amongst Carim clerics.

Affected by intelligence, a rare thing for miracle catalysts, and also agreeable with miracles that lean towards the Dark. Its existence is concealed in the name of the Archbishop, as it is anathema.

Skill: Gentle Prayer

Recovers HP for a period of time, albeit extremely slowly. Works while equipped in either hand.

Found/Dropped: Lothric Castle

CANVAS TALISMAN

Strike	Unfaltering Prayer / 8 0.5

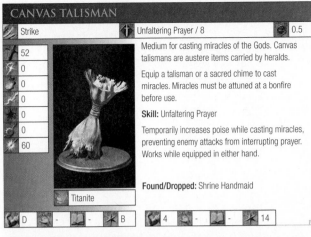

52	
0	
0	
0	
0	
0	
60	

Titanite

D	-	-	B

4	-	-	14

Medium for casting miracles of the Gods. Canvas talismans are austere items carried by heralds.

Equip a talisman or a sacred chime to cast miracles. Miracles must be attuned at a bonfire before use.

Skill: Unfaltering Prayer

Temporarily increases poise while casting miracles, preventing enemy attacks from interrupting prayer. Works while equipped in either hand.

Found/Dropped: Shrine Handmaid

CLERIC'S SACRED CHIME

Strike	Gentle Prayer / 13 0.5

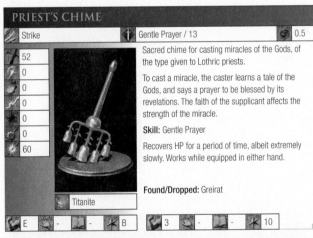

52	
0	
0	
0	
0	
0	
60	

Titanite

D	-	-	A

3	-	-	14

Sacred chime for casting miracles of the Gods. Chimes such as these are often given to clerics who become Undead.

Equip a talisman or a sacred chime to cast miracles. Miracles must be attuned at a bonfire before use.

Skill: Gentle Prayer

Recovers HP for a period of time, albeit extremely slowly. Works while equipped in either hand.

Found/Dropped: Grave Warden Cemetary of Ash/ Untended Graves

CRYSTAL CHIME

Strike	Gentle Prayer / 13 0.5

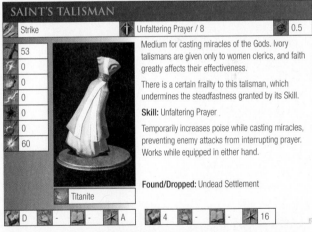

73	
0	
0	
0	
0	
0	
20	

Twinkling Titanite

E	-	D	D

3	-	18	18

A sacred chime, once the possession of Gertrude, the Heavenly Daughter, and defiled by the scholars of the Grand Archives.

The power of crystals granted the scholars a degree of success. In this case, their work enabled this chime to be suitable for casting both miracles and sorceries.

Skill: Gentle Prayer

Recovers HP for a period of time, if extremely slowly. Works while equipped in either hand.

Found/Dropped: Grand Archives

PRIEST'S CHIME

Strike	Gentle Prayer / 13 0.5

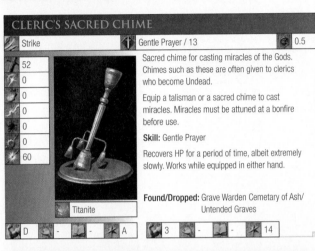

52	
0	
0	
0	
0	
0	
60	

Titanite

E	-	-	B

3	-	-	10

Sacred chime for casting miracles of the Gods, of the type given to Lothric priests.

To cast a miracle, the caster learns a tale of the Gods, and says a prayer to be blessed by its revelations. The faith of the supplicant affects the strength of the miracle.

Skill: Gentle Prayer

Recovers HP for a period of time, albeit extremely slowly. Works while equipped in either hand.

Found/Dropped: Greirat

SAINT'S TALISMAN

Strike	Unfaltering Prayer / 8 0.5

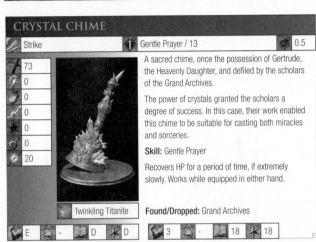

53	
0	
0	
0	
0	
0	
60	

Titanite

D	-	-	A

4	-	-	16

Medium for casting miracles of the Gods. Ivory talismans are given only to women clerics, and faith greatly affects their effectiveness.

There is a certain frailty to this talisman, which undermines the steadfastness granted by its Skill.

Skill: Unfaltering Prayer

Temporarily increases poise while casting miracles, preventing enemy attacks from interrupting prayer. Works while equipped in either hand.

Found/Dropped: Undead Settlement

SAINT-TREE BELLVINE

Strike	Gentle Prayer / 13 0.5

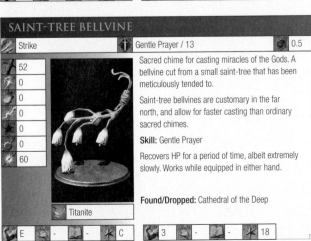

52	
0	
0	
0	
0	
0	
60	

Titanite

E	-	-	C

3	-	-	18

Sacred chime for casting miracles of the Gods. A bellvine cut from a small saint-tree that has been meticulously tended to.

Saint-tree bellvines are customary in the far north, and allow for faster casting than ordinary sacred chimes.

Skill: Gentle Prayer

Recovers HP for a period of time, albeit extremely slowly. Works while equipped in either hand.

Found/Dropped: Cathedral of the Deep

SUNLESS TALISMAN

Strike	Unfaltering Prayer / 8 0.5

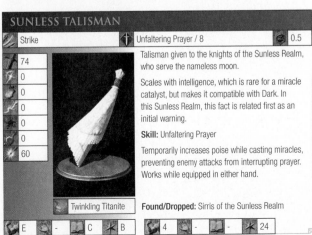

74	
0	
0	
0	
0	
0	
60	

Twinkling Titanite

E	-	C	B

4	-	-	24

Talisman given to the knights of the Sunless Realm, who serve the nameless moon.

Scales with intelligence, which is rare for a miracle catalyst, but makes it compatible with Dark. In this Sunless Realm, this fact is related first as an initial warning.

Skill: Unfaltering Prayer

Temporarily increases poise while casting miracles, preventing enemy attacks from interrupting prayer. Works while equipped in either hand.

Found/Dropped: Sirris of the Sunless Realm

SUNLIGHT TALISMAN

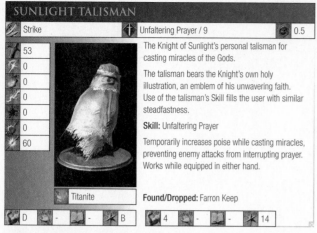

Strike	Unfaltering Prayer / 9	0.5

	53
	0
	0
	0
	0
	0
	60

The Knight of Sunlight's personal talisman for casting miracles of the Gods.

The talisman bears the Knight's own holy illustration, an emblem of his unwavering faith. Use of the talisman's Skill fills the user with similar steadfastness.

Skill: Unfaltering Prayer

Temporarily increases poise while casting miracles, preventing enemy attacks from interrupting prayer. Works while equipped in either hand.

Titanite

Found/Dropped: Farron Keep

D	-	-	B		4	-	-	14

TALISMAN

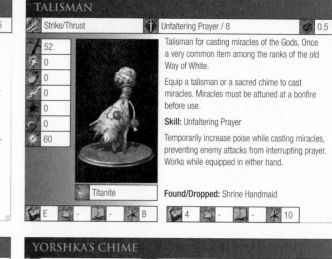

Strike/Thrust	Unfaltering Prayer / 8	0.5

	52
	0
	0
	0
	0
	0
	60

Talisman for casting miracles of the Gods. Once a very common item among the ranks of the old Way of White.

Equip a talisman or a sacred chime to cast miracles. Miracles must be attuned at a bonfire before use.

Skill: Unfaltering Prayer

Temporarily increase poise while casting miracles, preventing enemy attacks from interrupting prayer. Works while equipped in either hand.

Titanite

Found/Dropped: Shrine Handmaid

E	-	-	B		4	-	-	10

WHITE HAIR TALISMAN

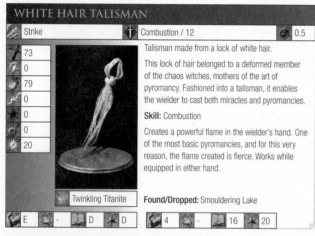

Strike	Combustion / 12	0.5

	73
	0
	79
	0
	0
	0
	20

Talisman made from a lock of white hair.

This lock of hair belonged to a deformed member of the chaos witches, mothers of the art of pyromancy. Fashioned into a talisman, it enables the wielder to cast both miracles and pyromancies.

Skill: Combustion

Creates a powerful flame in the wielder's hand. One of the most basic pyromancies, and for this very reason, the flame created is fierce. Works while equipped in either hand.

Twinkling Titanite

Found/Dropped: Smouldering Lake

E	-	D	D		4	-	16	20

YORSHKA'S CHIME

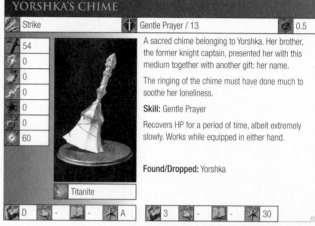

Strike	Gentle Prayer / 13	0.5

	54
	0
	0
	0
	0
	0
	60

A sacred chime belonging to Yorshka. Her brother, the former knight captain, presented her with this medium together with another gift: her name.

The ringing of the chime must have done much to soothe her loneliness.

Skill: Gentle Prayer

Recovers HP for a period of time, albeit extremely slowly. Works while equipped in either hand.

Found/Dropped: Yorshka

Titanite

D	-	-	A		3	-	-	30

SHIELDS

Shields are a vital defensive tool in *Dark Souls*. They are particularly important for new players, giving you a much needed wall to hold against the many foes that seek to take you down. As players grow in experience and master dodging (and sometimes parrying), hiding behind a shield becomes less necessary, but they still remain useful tools, trivializing many commonplace enemy encounters throughout the game, and still serving to protect you well against quite a few dangerous boss attacks. Remember that you can swap a shield on and off your back by two handing your weapon, allowing you to use large weapons, inflict some extra damage with typical one handers, or even use dual-wield weapons in concert with a shield. With some effort, it is even possible to make use of shields as weapons, using the Shield Bash skill to smack your foes in the face.

Many shields provide either the Parry or the Weapon Skill ability. Parry grants you the ability to intercept incoming attacks and counter them, and the Weapon Skill ability let you make use of the skill of your right hand weapon while retaining your ability to block with a shield. Remember that while blocking, your Stamina regen rate is lowered, so try not to keep your shield up at all times! Block when necessary, dodge roll away from truly hard hits.

Shields are defined by their defenses, and a shield with 100% physical damage block should be one of your earliest goals as a new player. High elemental resistances are rarely necessary, but they can prove useful against certain bosses who have dangerous attacks of a specific element. Finally, the Stability value on shields is important, as it determines how well you can block extremely heavy hits. As it scales almost exactly with shield weight and size, it is generally only Greatshields that have a chance of successfully blocking the hardest blows in the game. Any shield can have its Stability value (slightly) improved by enhancing it at the Blacksmith. Infusing mundane shields with an element very slightly boosts that single elemental defense, at the cost of lowering all others. Rarely a worthwhile upgrade, again barring specific use cases against certain boss attacks.

Infusing a shield with a Blessed or Simple Gem allows you to regenerate HP or FP, even while the shield is on your back!

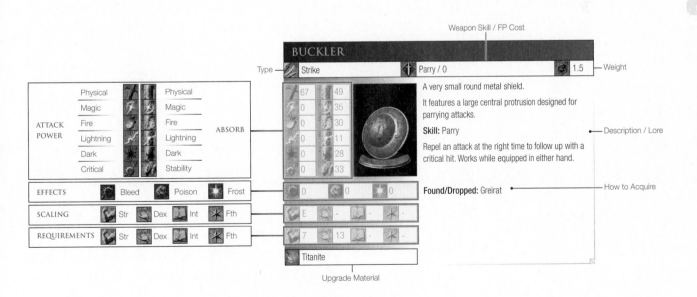

SMALL SHIELDS

Lightweight Small Shields most commonly have the Parry skill on them, and require very little in the way of attributes. This makes them ideal for Dex focused fencer style characters, and casters who aren't concerned about outright blocking all attacks.

Parrying can be very difficult as a new player, so don't feel that you need to attempt parries on every attack in the game. It's absolutely a skill worth learning though, and a vital one if you plan on participating in PvP heavily.

SMALL SHIELDS	TYPE	ART/COST	WEIGHT	POWER	SCALING	REQ.	PHYS	MAGIC	FIRE	LIGHTNING	DARK	STABILITY	MATERIAL
Buckler	Strike	Parry/-	1.5	67p	E/-/-/-	7/13/-/-	49	35	30	11	28	33	Titanite
Caduceus Round Shield	Strike	Parry/-	1.5	69p	E/-/-/-	10/0/0/0	52	63	46	36	25	39	Titanite
Crimson Parma	Strike	Parry/-	1.5	69p	E/-/-/-	7/0/0/0	52	63	40	36	39	39	Titanite
Eastern Iron Shield	Strike	Weapon Skill/-	3.0	81p	D/-/-/-	8/0/0/0	85	40	41	22	39	48	Titanite
Elkhorn Round Shield	Strike	Parry/-	1.5	69p	E/-/-/-	8/0/0/0	59	63	33	36	25	39	Titanite
Ghru Rotshield*	Strike	Shield Bash/12	1.5	78p	E/-/-/-	5/0/0/0	62	43	39	34	37	44	Titanite
Golden Falcon Shield	Strike	Parry/-	2.5	74p	D/-/-/-	10/0/0/0	59	45	39	20	37	48	Titanite
Hawkwood's Shield	Strike	Parry/-	2.0	72p	E/-/-/-	5/0/0/0	56	35	58	45	55	41	Titanite
Iron Round Shield	Strike	Parry/-	2.0	71p	E/-/-/-	5/0/0/0	67	44	38	19	36	47	Titanite
Leather Shield	Strike	Parry/-	1.5	69p	E/-/-/-	7/0/0/0	52	38	40	42	32	36	Titanite
Llewellyn Shield	Strike	Parry/-	3.0	76p	D/-/-/-	12/0/0/0	68	69	63	44	61	45	Titanite
Plank Shield	Strike	Shield Bash/12	1.0	53p	E/-/-/-	8/0/0/0	41	24	27	23	25	34	Titanite
Red and White Round Shield	Strike	Parry/-	1.5	69p	E/-/-/-	10/0/0/0	52	58	46	36	32	39	Titanite
Sacred Bloom Shield	Strike	Spell Parry/-	1.5	82p	D/-/-/-	10/0/0/0	54	81	49	44	47	38	Twinkling Titanite
Small Leather Shield	Strike	Parry/-	2.0	70p	E/-/-/-	7/0/0/0	42	42	50	38	35	35	Titanite
Target Shield	Strike	Parry/-	2.0	69p	E/-/-/-	8/11/-/-	61	36	31	12	29	36	Titanite
Torch	Strike	None	1.0	35p/80f	D/-/-/-	5/0/0/0	30	20	15	15	20	17	Titanite
Warrior's Round Shield	Strike	Weapon Skill/-	1.5	74p	E/-/-/-	10/0/0/0	62	68	45	46	36	41	Titanite

* Additional Effect: 33 Poison Damage

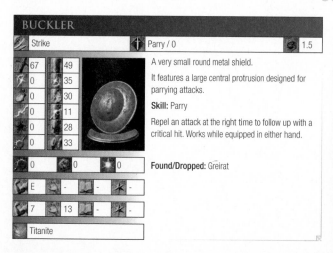

BUCKLER

Strike		Parry / 0		1.5

67		49		
0		35		
0		30		
0		11		
0		28		
0		33		

0	0	0

E	-	-
7	13	-	-

Titanite

A very small round metal shield.

It features a large central protrusion designed for parrying attacks.

Skill: Parry

Repel an attack at the right time to follow up with a critical hit. Works while equipped in either hand.

Found/Dropped: Greirat

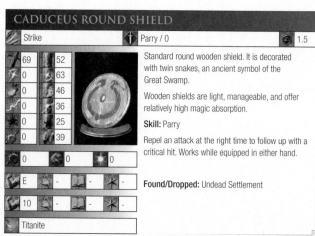

CADUCEUS ROUND SHIELD

Strike		Parry / 0		1.5

69		52		
0		63		
0		46		
0		36		
0		25		
0		39		

0	0	0

E	-	-
10	-	-	-

Titanite

Standard round wooden shield. It is decorated with twin snakes, an ancient symbol of the Great Swamp.

Wooden shields are light, manageable, and offer relatively high magic absorption.

Skill: Parry

Repel an attack at the right time to follow up with a critical hit. Works while equipped in either hand.

Found/Dropped: Undead Settlement

CRIMSON PARMA

Strike		Parry / 0			1.5

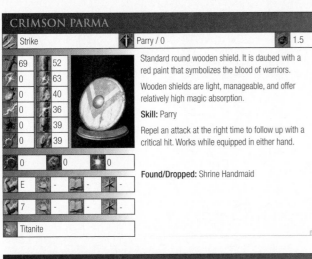

69		52	
0		63	
0		40	
0		36	
0		39	
0		39	

0	0	0

E	-	-	*	-
7	-	-	*	-

Titanite

Standard round wooden shield. It is daubed with a red paint that symbolizes the blood of warriors.

Wooden shields are light, manageable, and offer relatively high magic absorption.

Skill: Parry

Repel an attack at the right time to follow up with a critical hit. Works while equipped in either hand.

Found/Dropped: Shrine Handmaid

EASTERN IRON SHIELD

Strike		Weapon Skill / 0			3.0

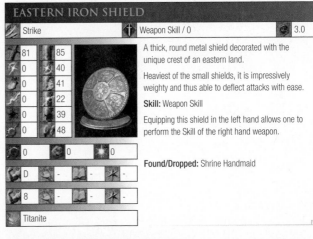

81		85	
0		40	
0		41	
0		22	
0		39	
0		48	

0	0	0

D	-	-	*	-
8	-	-	*	-

Titanite

A thick, round metal shield decorated with the unique crest of an eastern land.

Heaviest of the small shields, it is impressively weighty and thus able to deflect attacks with ease.

Skill: Weapon Skill

Equipping this shield in the left hand allows one to perform the Skill of the right hand weapon.

Found/Dropped: Shrine Handmaid

ELKHORN ROUND SHIELD

Strike		Parry / 0			1.5

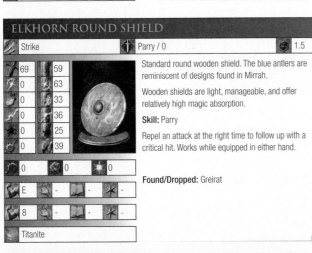

69		59	
0		63	
0		33	
0		36	
0		25	
0		39	

0	0	0

E	-	-	*	-
8	-	-	*	-

Titanite

Standard round wooden shield. The blue antlers are reminiscent of designs found in Mirrah.

Wooden shields are light, manageable, and offer relatively high magic absorption.

Skill: Parry

Repel an attack at the right time to follow up with a critical hit. Works while equipped in either hand.

Found/Dropped: Greirat

GHRU ROTSHIELD

Strike		Shield Bash / 12			1.5

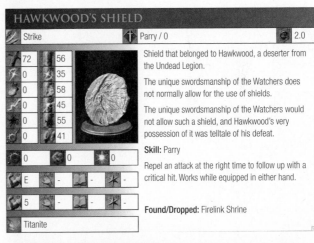

78		62	
0		43	
0		39	
0		34	
0		37	
0		44	

0	33	0

E	-	-	*	-
5	-	-	*	-

Titanite

A rotting makeshift shield scavenged by the forest-dwelling Ghrus.

Barely effective as a shield. However, its rotten state has made it poisonous, and resistant to other poisons as a result.

Skill: Shield Bash

Without lowering your guard, strike the enemy with the shield to knock them back or stagger them. Works while equipped in either hand.

Found/Dropped: Ghru

GOLDEN FALCON SHIELD

Strike		Parry / 0			2.5

74		59	
0		45	
0		39	
0		20	
0		37	
0		48	

0	0	0

D	-	-	*	-
10	-	-	*	-

Titanite

A metal shield fashioned in the form of a falcon with wings outstretched.

The golden falcon was the emblem of an ancient band of sellswords, and even to this day, many mercenaries remain who look upon it as a token of good fortune.

Skill: Parry

Repel an attack at the right time to follow up with a critical hit. Works while equipped in either hand.

Found/Dropped: Road of Sacrifices

HAWKWOOD'S SHIELD

Strike		Parry / 0			2.0

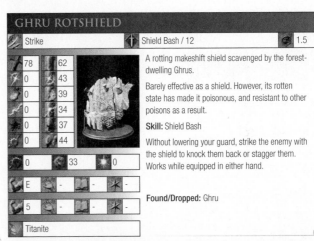

72		56	
0		35	
0		58	
0		45	
0		55	
0		41	

0	0	0

E	-	-	*	-
5	-	-	*	-

Titanite

Shield that belonged to Hawkwood, a deserter from the Undead Legion.

The unique swordsmanship of the Watchers does not normally allow for the use of shields.

The unique swordsmanship of the Watchers would not allow such a shield, and Hawkwood's very possession of it was telltale of his defeat.

Skill: Parry

Repel an attack at the right time to follow up with a critical hit. Works while equipped in either hand.

Found/Dropped: Firelink Shrine

IRON ROUND SHIELD

Strike		Parry / 0			2.0

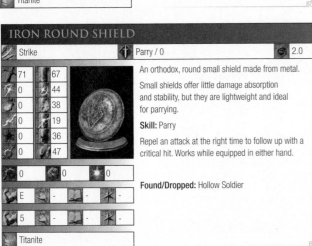

71		67	
0		44	
0		38	
0		19	
0		36	
0		47	

0	0	0

E	-	-	*	-
5	-	-	*	-

Titanite

An orthodox, round small shield made from metal.

Small shields offer little damage absorption and stability, but they are lightweight and ideal for parrying.

Skill: Parry

Repel an attack at the right time to follow up with a critical hit. Works while equipped in either hand.

Found/Dropped: Hollow Soldier

LEATHER SHIELD

Strike		Parry / 0			1.5

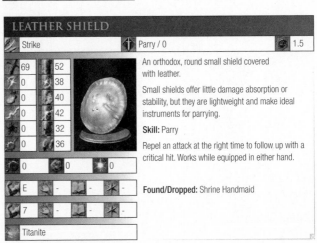

69		52	
0		38	
0		40	
0		42	
0		32	
0		36	

0	0	0

E	-	-	*	-
7	-	-	*	-

Titanite

An orthodox, round small shield covered with leather.

Small shields offer little damage absorption or stability, but they are lightweight and make ideal instruments for parrying.

Skill: Parry

Repel an attack at the right time to follow up with a critical hit. Works while equipped in either hand.

Found/Dropped: Shrine Handmaid

LLEWELLYN SHIELD

Strike	Parry / 0	3.0

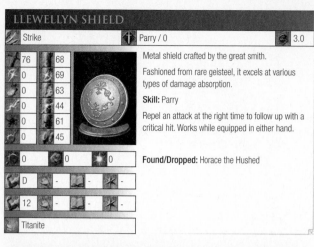

76	68		
0	69		
0	63		
0	44		
0	61		
0	45		

0	0	0

D	-	-	*	-
12				

Titanite

Metal shield crafted by the great smith.

Fashioned from rare geisteel, it excels at various types of damage absorption.

Skill: Parry

Repel an attack at the right time to follow up with a critical hit. Works while equipped in either hand.

Found/Dropped: Horace the Hushed

PLANK SHIELD

Strike	Shield Bash / 12	1.0

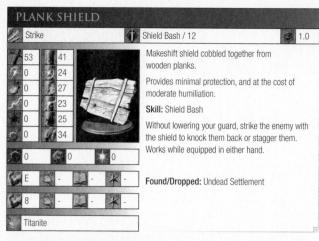

53	41		
0	24		
0	27		
0	23		
0	25		
0	34		

0	0	0

E	-	-	*	-
8				

Titanite

Makeshift shield cobbled together from wooden planks.

Provides minimal protection, and at the cost of moderate humiliation.

Skill: Shield Bash

Without lowering your guard, strike the enemy with the shield to knock them back or stagger them. Works while equipped in either hand.

Found/Dropped: Undead Settlement

RED AND WHITE ROUND SHIELD

Strike	Parry / 0	1.5

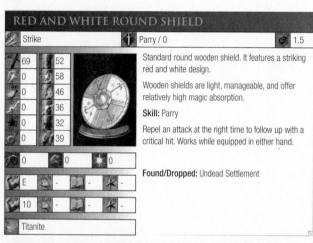

69	52		
0	58		
0	46		
0	36		
0	32		
0	39		

0	0	0

E	-	-	*	-
10				

Titanite

Standard round wooden shield. It features a striking red and white design.

Wooden shields are light, manageable, and offer relatively high magic absorption.

Skill: Parry

Repel an attack at the right time to follow up with a critical hit. Works while equipped in either hand.

Found/Dropped: Undead Settlement

SACRED BLOOM SHIELD

Strike	Spell Parry / 0	1.5

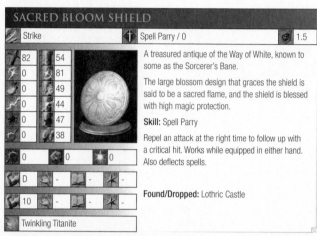

82	54		
0	81		
0	49		
0	44		
0	47		
0	38		

0	0	0

D	-	-	*	-
10				

Twinkling Titanite

A treasured antique of the Way of White, known to some as the Sorcerer's Bane.

The large blossom design that graces the shield is said to be a sacred flame, and the shield is blessed with high magic protection.

Skill: Spell Parry

Repel an attack at the right time to follow up with a critical hit. Works while equipped in either hand. Also deflects spells.

Found/Dropped: Lothric Castle

SMALL LEATHER SHIELD

Strike	Parry / 0	2.0

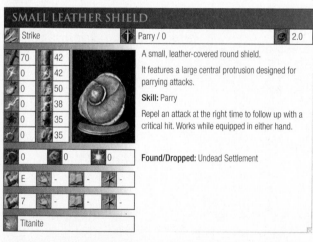

70	42		
0	42		
0	50		
0	38		
0	35		
0	35		

0	0	0

E	-	-	*	-
7				

Titanite

A small, leather-covered round shield.

It features a large central protrusion designed for parrying attacks.

Skill: Parry

Repel an attack at the right time to follow up with a critical hit. Works while equipped in either hand.

Found/Dropped: Undead Settlement

TARGET SHIELD

Strike	Parry / 0	2.0

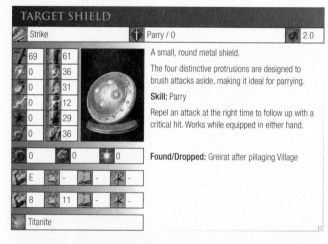

69	61		
0	36		
0	31		
0	12		
0	29		
0	36		

0	0	0

E	-	-	*	-
8	11	-	*	-

Titanite

A small, round metal shield.

The four distinctive protrusions are designed to brush attacks aside, making it ideal for parrying.

Skill: Parry

Repel an attack at the right time to follow up with a critical hit. Works while equipped in either hand.

Found/Dropped: Greirat after pillaging Village

TORCH

Strike	None	1.0

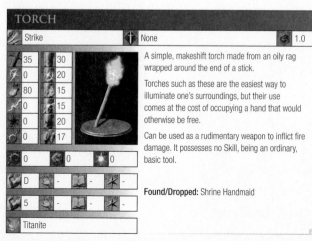

35	30		
0	20		
80	15		
0	15		
0	20		
0	17		

0	0	0

D	-	-	*	-
5				

Titanite

A simple, makeshift torch made from an oily rag wrapped around the end of a stick.

Torches such as these are the easiest way to illuminate one's surroundings, but their use comes at the cost of occupying a hand that would otherwise be free.

Can be used as a rudimentary weapon to inflict fire damage. It possesses no Skill, being an ordinary, basic tool.

Found/Dropped: Shrine Handmaid

WARRIOR'S ROUND SHIELD

Strike	Weapon Skill / 0	1.5

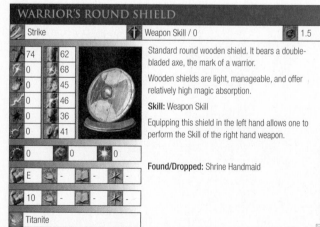

74	62		
0	68		
0	45		
0	46		
0	36		
0	41		

0	0	0

E	-	-	*	-
10				

Titanite

Standard round wooden shield. It bears a double-bladed axe, the mark of a warrior.

Wooden shields are light, manageable, and offer relatively high magic absorption.

Skill: Weapon Skill

Equipping this shield in the left hand allows one to perform the Skill of the right hand weapon.

Found/Dropped: Shrine Handmaid

SHIELDS

Mid-weight shields are the most common form of defense alongside a basic one hander for any new player in Dark Souls, and they serve this role admirably.

With moderate weight and usually low attribute requirements, they pair very well with a Straight Sword, Fencing Sword, Curved Sword, Axe, or Hammer to make a balanced offensive and defensive package.

Quite a few regular shields have 100% physical damage block, with the more demanding shields usually giving some extra Stability as a bonus. Normal shields also have common access to the Parry skill, but there are a fair number with Weapon Skill if you want to make use of your weapons arts.

SHIELDS	TYPE	ART/COST	WEIGHT	POWER	SCALING	REQ.	PHYS	MAGIC	FIRE	LIGHTNING	DARK	STABILITY	MATERIAL
Black Knight Shield	Strike	Weapon Skill/-	7.5	113p	D/-/-/-	18/0/0/0	100	65	85	52	63	60	Twinkling Titanite
Blue Wooden Shield	Strike	Parry/-	2.5	77p	D/-/-/-	8/0/0/0	56	70	54	56	39	50	Titanite
Carthus Shield	Strike	Parry/-	2.5	56p	D/-/-/-	8/0/0/0	61	45	21	56	52	45	Titanite
Crest Shield	Strike	Parry/-	5.0	95p	D/-/-/-	14/0/0/0	100	67	56	43	86	49	Twinkling Titanite
Dragon Crest Shield	Strike	Parry/-	5.0	95p	D/-/-/-	14/0/0/0	100	67	89	43	53	49	Twinkling Titanite
East-West Shield	Strike	Parry/-	2.0	76p	D/-/-/-	8/0/0/0	55	70	53	56	46	45	Titanite
Golden Wing Crest Shield	Strike	Parry/-	5.5	102p	D/-/-/-	14/0/0/0	100	75	50	57	47	50	Twinkling Titanite
Grass Crest Shield	Strike	Parry/-	4.5	92	D/-/-/-	10/0/0/0	89	43	38	33	36	50	Twinkling Titanite
Kite Shield	Strike	Parry/-	4.5	80p	D/-/-/-	12/0/0/0	100	50	52	33	50	47	Titanite
Knight Shield	Strike	Parry/-	4.5	79p	D/-/-/-	13/0/0/0	100	51	46	34	44	48	Titanite
Large Leather Shield	Strike	Parry/-	3.5	78p	D/-/-/-	8/0/0/0	85	54	56	58	48	51	Titanite
Lothric Knight Shield	Strike	Parry/-	6.0	83p	D/-/-/-	18/0/0/0	100	59	53	87	51	54	Titanite
Pierce Shield	Thrust	Shield Bash/14	3.5	87p	D/-/-/-	10/0/0/0	93	62	50	31	48	53	Titanite
Pontiff Knight Shield	Strike	Weapon Skill/-	3.5	63p	D/-/-/-	8/12/0/0	73	79	69	69	72	42	Twinkling Titanite
Porcine Shield	Strike	Shield Bash/14	4.5	85p	D/-/-/-	8/0/0/0	74	43	38	27	36	48	Titanite
Round Shield	Strike	Parry/-	3.5	79p	D/-/-/-	8/0/0/0	86	68	50	45	41	51	Titanite
Shield of Want	Strike	Weapon Skill/-	5.5	104p	D/-/-/-	18/0/0/0	100	61	63	43	61	58	Titanite Scale
Silver Eagle Kite Shield	Strike	Weapon Skill/-	5.0	88p	D/-/-/-	11/0/0/0	100	44	45	33	43	45	Titanite
Silver Knight Shield	Strike	Parry/-	6.5	98p	D/-/-/-	16/0/0/0	100	60	54	48	52	55	Twinkling Titanite
Spider Shield	Strike	Weapon Skill/-	6.0	83p	D/-/-/-	18/0/0/0	100	59	53	87	51	54	Titanite
Spiked Shield	Strike	Shield Strike/-	3.5	86p	D/-/-/-	12/12/0/0	91	49	51	32	56	48	Titanite
Spirit Tree Crest Shield	Strike	Parry/-	5.0	95p	D/-/-/-	14/0/0/0	100	67	56	83	53	49	Twinkling Titanite
Stone Parma	Strike	Weapon Skill/-	7.0	94p	D/-/-/-	17/0/0/0	100	58	52	53	57	57	Titanite
Sunlight Shield	Strike	Parry/-	5.0	82p	D/-/-/-	12/0/0/0	100	60	55	55	26	49	Titanite
Sunset Shield	Strike	Parry/-	3.5	88p	D/-/-/-	10/0/0/0	80	52	47	29	46	56	Titanite
Wargod Wooden Shield	Strike	Weapon Skill/-	4.0	88p	D/-/-/-	12/0/0/0	84	47	69	64	67	57	Titanite
Wooden Shield	Strike	Parry/-	2.5	78p	D/-/-/-	8/0/0/0	47	66	48	44	39	53	Titanite

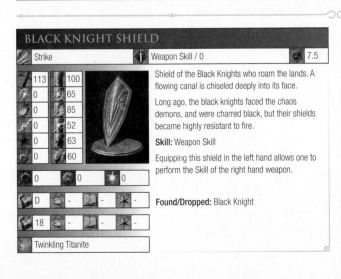

BLACK KNIGHT SHIELD

Strike		Weapon Skill / 0		7.5

113		100
0		65
0		85
0		52
0		63
0		60

0		0		0

D	-		-	-

18	-		-	-

Twinkling Titanite

Shield of the Black Knights who roam the lands. A flowing canal is chiseled deeply into its face.

Long ago, the black knights faced the chaos demons, and were charred black, but their shields became highly resistant to fire.

Skill: Weapon Skill

Equipping this shield in the left hand allows one to perform the Skill of the right hand weapon.

Found/Dropped: Black Knight

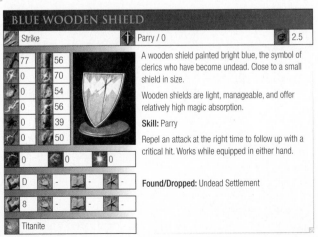

BLUE WOODEN SHIELD

Strike		Parry / 0		2.5

77		56
0		70
0		54
0		56
0		39
0		50

0		0		0

D	-		-	-

8	-		-	-

Titanite

A wooden shield painted bright blue, the symbol of clerics who have become undead. Close to a small shield in size.

Wooden shields are light, manageable, and offer relatively high magic absorption.

Skill: Parry

Repel an attack at the right time to follow up with a critical hit. Works while equipped in either hand.

Found/Dropped: Undead Settlement

CARTHUS SHIELD

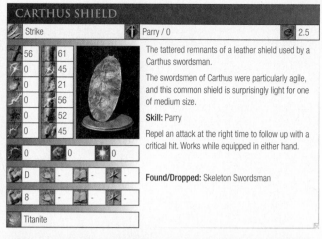

Strike		Parry / 0		2.5

56		61	
0		45	
0		21	
0		56	
0		52	
0		45	

0		0		0

D	-		-		-

8	-		-		-

Titanite

The tattered remnants of a leather shield used by a Carthus swordsman.

The swordsmen of Carthus were particularly agile, and this common shield is surprisingly light for one of medium size.

Skill: Parry

Repel an attack at the right time to follow up with a critical hit. Works while equipped in either hand.

Found/Dropped: Skeleton Swordsman

CREST SHIELD

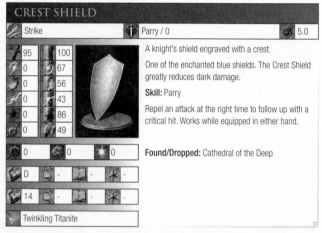

Strike		Parry / 0		5.0

95		100	
0		67	
0		56	
0		43	
0		86	
0		49	

0		0		0

D	-		-		-

14	-		-		-

Twinkling Titanite

A knight's shield engraved with a crest.

One of the enchanted blue shields. The Crest Shield greatly reduces dark damage.

Skill: Parry

Repel an attack at the right time to follow up with a critical hit. Works while equipped in either hand.

Found/Dropped: Cathedral of the Deep

DRAGON CREST SHIELD

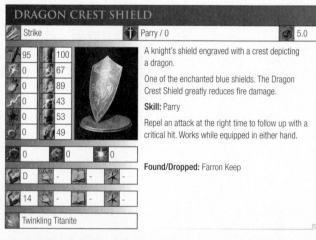

Strike		Parry / 0		5.0

95		100	
0		67	
0		89	
0		43	
0		53	
0		49	

0		0		0

D	-		-		-

14	-		-		-

Twinkling Titanite

A knight's shield engraved with a crest depicting a dragon.

One of the enchanted blue shields. The Dragon Crest Shield greatly reduces fire damage.

Skill: Parry

Repel an attack at the right time to follow up with a critical hit. Works while equipped in either hand.

Found/Dropped: Farron Keep

EAST-WEST SHIELD

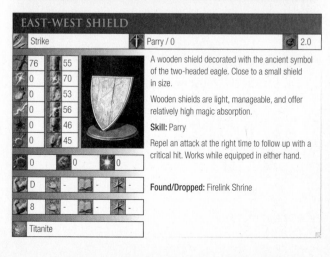

Strike		Parry / 0		2.0

76		55	
0		70	
0		53	
0		56	
0		46	
0		45	

0		0		0

D	-		-		-

8	-		-		-

Titanite

A wooden shield decorated with the ancient symbol of the two-headed eagle. Close to a small shield in size.

Wooden shields are light, manageable, and offer relatively high magic absorption.

Skill: Parry

Repel an attack at the right time to follow up with a critical hit. Works while equipped in either hand.

Found/Dropped: Firelink Shrine

GOLDEN WING CREST SHIELD

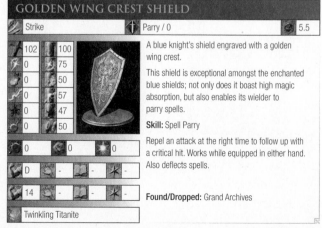

Strike		Parry / 0		5.5

102		100	
0		75	
0		50	
0		57	
0		47	
0		50	

0		0		0

D	-		-		-

14	-		-		-

Twinkling Titanite

A blue knight's shield engraved with a golden wing crest.

This shield is exceptional amongst the enchanted blue shields; not only does it boast high magic absorption, but also enables its wielder to parry spells.

Skill: Spell Parry

Repel an attack at the right time to follow up with a critical hit. Works while equipped in either hand. Also deflects spells.

Found/Dropped: Grand Archives

GRASS CREST SHIELD

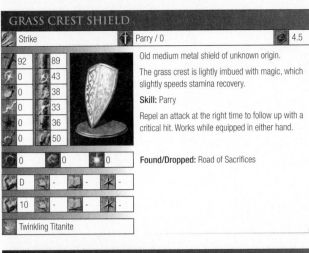

	Strike		Parry / 0		4.5

92		89	
0		43	
0		38	
0		33	
0		36	
0		50	

0	0	0

D	-	-	-
10	-	-	-

Twinkling Titanite

Old medium metal shield of unknown origin.

The grass crest is lightly imbued with magic, which slightly speeds stamina recovery.

Skill: Parry

Repel an attack at the right time to follow up with a critical hit. Works while equipped in either hand.

Found/Dropped: Road of Sacrifices

KITE SHIELD

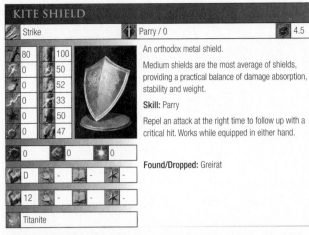

	Strike		Parry / 0		4.5

80		100	
0		50	
0		52	
0		33	
0		50	
0		47	

0	0	0

D	-	-	-
12	-	-	-

Titanite

An orthodox metal shield.

Medium shields are the most average of shields, providing a practical balance of damage absorption, stability and weight.

Skill: Parry

Repel an attack at the right time to follow up with a critical hit. Works while equipped in either hand.

Found/Dropped: Greirat

KNIGHT SHIELD

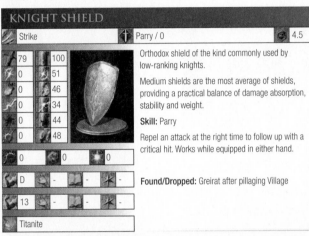

	Strike		Parry / 0		4.5

79		100	
0		51	
0		46	
0		34	
0		44	
0		48	

0	0	0

D	-	-	-
13	-	-	-

Titanite

Orthodox shield of the kind commonly used by low-ranking knights.

Medium shields are the most average of shields, providing a practical balance of damage absorption, stability and weight.

Skill: Parry

Repel an attack at the right time to follow up with a critical hit. Works while equipped in either hand.

Found/Dropped: Greirat after pillaging Village

LARGE LEATHER SHIELD

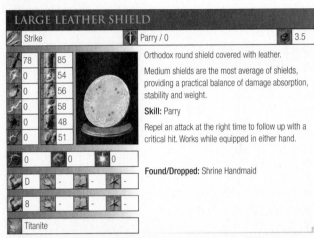

	Strike		Parry / 0		3.5

78		85	
0		54	
0		56	
0		58	
0		48	
0		51	

0	0	0

D	-	-	-
8	-	-	-

Titanite

Orthodox round shield covered with leather.

Medium shields are the most average of shields, providing a practical balance of damage absorption, stability and weight.

Skill: Parry

Repel an attack at the right time to follow up with a critical hit. Works while equipped in either hand.

Found/Dropped: Shrine Handmaid

LOTHRIC KNIGHT SHIELD

	Strike		Parry / 0		6.0

83		100	
0		59	
0		53	
0		87	
0		51	
0		54	

0	0	0

D	-	-	-
18	-	-	-

Titanite

Shield of the renowned Lothric Knights, decorated with the royal crest.

The Lothric Knights contended with dragons, and their shields have suitably high lightning absorption befitting a Dragonslayer's arms.

Skill: Parry

Repel an attack at the right time to follow up with a critical hit. Works while equipped in either hand.

Found/Dropped: Lothric Knight, Greirat after pillaging Irithyll

PIERCE SHIELD

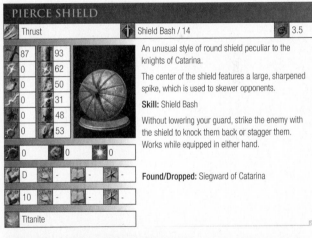

	Thrust		Shield Bash / 14		3.5

87		93	
0		62	
0		50	
0		31	
0		48	
0		53	

0	0	0

D	-	-	-
10	-	-	-

Titanite

An unusual style of round shield peculiar to the knights of Catarina.

The center of the shield features a large, sharpened spike, which is used to skewer opponents.

Skill: Shield Bash

Without lowering your guard, strike the enemy with the shield to knock them back or stagger them. Works while equipped in either hand.

Found/Dropped: Siegward of Catarina

PONTIFF KNIGHT SHIELD

	Strike		Weapon Skill / 0		3.5

63		73	
0		79	
0		69	
0		69	
0		72	
0		42	

0	0	0

D	-	-	-
8	12	-	-

Twinkling Titanite

Shield of the Pontiff's knights, frigid spirits that linger in Irithyll.

This blue-gray shield, shrouded in a thinly cold air, is light and brittle.

Skill: Weapon Skill

Equipping this shield in the left hand allows one to perform the Skill of the right hand weapon.

Found/Dropped: Grierat after pillaging Village

PORCINE SHIELD

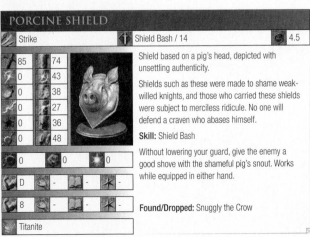

	Strike		Shield Bash / 14		4.5

85		74	
0		43	
0		38	
0		27	
0		36	
0		48	

0	0	0

D	-	-	-
8	-	-	-

Titanite

Shield based on a pig's head, depicted with unsettling authenticity.

Shields such as these were made to shame weak-willed knights, and those who carried these shields were subject to merciless ridicule. No one will defend a craven who abases himself.

Skill: Shield Bash

Without lowering your guard, give the enemy a good shove with the shameful pig's snout. Works while equipped in either hand.

Found/Dropped: Snuggly the Crow

ROUND SHIELD

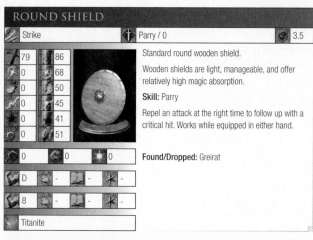

Strike		Parry / 0		3.5

79	86	
0	68	
0	50	
0	45	
0	41	
0	51	

0	0	0

D	-	-	✱ -
8	-	-	✱ -

Titanite

Standard round wooden shields.

Wooden shields are light, manageable, and offer relatively high magic absorption.

Skill: Parry

Repel an attack at the right time to follow up with a critical hit. Works while equipped in either hand.

Found/Dropped: Greirat

SILVER EAGLE KITE SHIELD

Strike		Weapon Skill / 0		5.0

88	100	
0	44	
0	45	
0	33	
0	43	
0	45	

0	0	0

D	-	-	✱ -
11	-	-	✱ -

Titanite

Orthodox metal shield engraved with a crest depicting a silver eagle.

Medium shields are the most average of shields, providing a practical balance of damage absorption, stability and weight.

Skill: Weapon Skill

Equipping this shield in the left hand allows one to perform the Skill of the right hand weapon.

Found/Dropped: High Wall of Lothric

SPIDER SHIELD

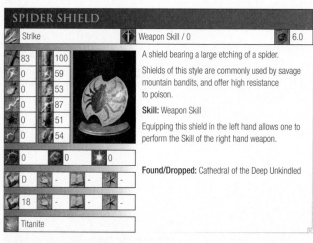

Strike		Weapon Skill / 0		6.0

83	100	
0	59	
0	53	
0	87	
0	51	
0	54	

0	0	0

D	-	-	✱ -
18	-	-	✱ -

Titanite

A shield bearing a large etching of a spider.

Shields of this style are commonly used by savage mountain bandits, and offer high resistance to poison.

Skill: Weapon Skill

Equipping this shield in the left hand allows one to perform the Skill of the right hand weapon.

Found/Dropped: Cathedral of the Deep Unkindled

SPIRIT TREE CREST SHIELD

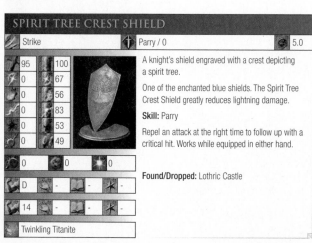

Strike		Parry / 0		5.0

95	100	
0	67	
0	56	
0	83	
0	53	
0	49	

0	0	0

D	-	-	✱ -
14	-	-	✱ -

Twinkling Titanite

A knight's shield engraved with a crest depicting a spirit tree.

One of the enchanted blue shields. The Spirit Tree Crest Shield greatly reduces lightning damage.

Skill: Parry

Repel an attack at the right time to follow up with a critical hit. Works while equipped in either hand.

Found/Dropped: Lothric Castle

SHIELD OF WANT

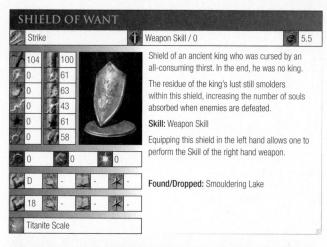

Strike		Weapon Skill / 0		5.5

104	100	
0	61	
0	63	
0	43	
0	61	
0	58	

0	0	0

D	-	-	✱ -
18	-	-	✱ -

Titanite Scale

Shield of an ancient king who was cursed by an all-consuming thirst. In the end, he was no king.

The residue of the king's lust still smolders within this shield, increasing the number of souls absorbed when enemies are defeated.

Skill: Weapon Skill

Equipping this shield in the left hand allows one to perform the Skill of the right hand weapon.

Found/Dropped: Smouldering Lake

SILVER KNIGHT SHIELD

Strike		Parry / 0		6.5

98	100	
0	60	
0	54	
0	48	
0	52	
0	55	

0	0	0

D	-	-	✱ -
16	-	-	✱ -

Twinkling Titanite

Heavy shield carried by the Silver Knights who served the old royal family. A flowing canal is chiseled deeply into its face.

The Silver Knights stayed behind to protect the humble manor and ruined cathedral. Though their goddess has long since left, her blessing upon her knights' shields remains.

Skill: Parry

Repel an attack at the right time to follow up with a critical hit. Works while equipped in either hand.

Found/Dropped: Silver Knight

SPIKED SHIELD

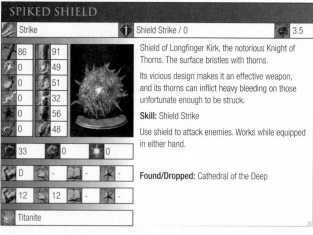

Strike		Shield Strike / 0		3.5

86	91	
0	49	
0	51	
0	32	
0	56	
0	48	

33	0	0

D	-	-	✱ -
12	12	-	✱ -

Titanite

Shield of Longfinger Kirk, the notorious Knight of Thorns. The surface bristles with thorns.

Its vicious design makes it an effective weapon, and its thorns can inflict heavy bleeding on those unfortunate enough to be struck.

Skill: Shield Strike

Use shield to attack enemies. Works while equipped in either hand.

Found/Dropped: Cathedral of the Deep

STONE PARMA

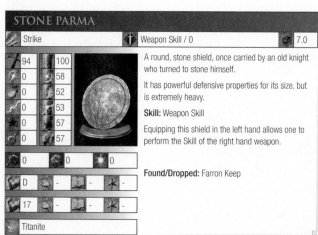

Strike		Weapon Skill / 0		7.0

94	100	
0	58	
0	52	
0	53	
0	57	
0	57	

0	0	0

D	-	-	✱ -
17	-	-	✱ -

Titanite

A round, stone shield, once carried by an old knight who turned to stone himself.

It has powerful defensive properties for its size, but is extremely heavy.

Skill: Weapon Skill

Equipping this shield in the left hand allows one to perform the Skill of the right hand weapon.

Found/Dropped: Farron Keep

SUNLIGHT SHIELD

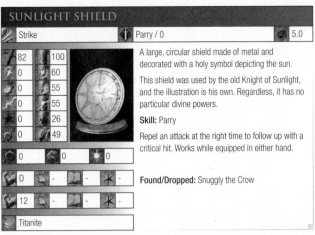

Strike | Parry / 0 | 5.0

82	100		
0	60		
0	55		
0	55		
0	26		
0	49		

0 | 0 | 0

D | - | - | - | -

12 | - | - | - | -

Titanite

A large, circular shield made of metal and decorated with a holy symbol depicting the sun.

This shield was used by the old Knight of Sunlight, and the illustration is his own. Regardless, it has no particular divine powers.

Skill: Parry

Repel an attack at the right time to follow up with a critical hit. Works while equipped in either hand.

Found/Dropped: Snuggly the Crow

SUNSET SHIELD

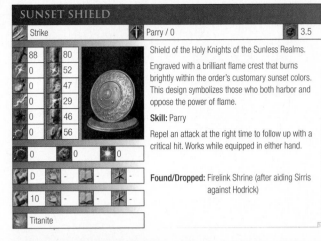

Strike | Parry / 0 | 3.5

88	80		
0	52		
0	47		
0	29		
0	46		
0	56		

0 | 0 | 0

D | - | - | - | -

10 | - | - | - | -

Titanite

Shield of the Holy Knights of the Sunless Realms.

Engraved with a brilliant flame crest that burns brightly within the order's customary sunset colors. This design symbolizes those who both harbor and oppose the power of flame.

Skill: Parry

Repel an attack at the right time to follow up with a critical hit. Works while equipped in either hand.

Found/Dropped: Firelink Shrine (after aiding Sirris against Hodrick)

WARGOD WOODEN SHIELD

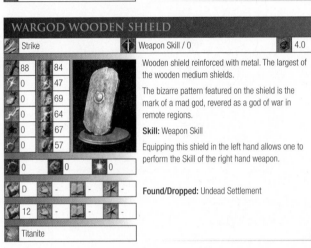

Strike | Weapon Skill / 0 | 4.0

88	84		
0	47		
0	69		
0	64		
0	67		
0	57		

0 | 0 | 0

D | - | - | - | -

12 | - | - | - | -

Titanite

Wooden shield reinforced with metal. The largest of the wooden medium shields.

The bizarre pattern featured on the shield is the mark of a mad god, revered as a god of war in remote regions.

Skill: Weapon Skill

Equipping this shield in the left hand allows one to perform the Skill of the right hand weapon.

Found/Dropped: Undead Settlement

WOODEN SHIELD

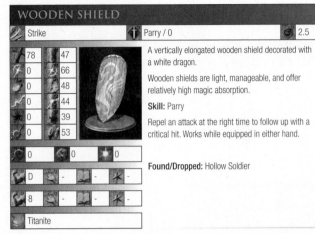

Strike | Parry / 0 | 2.5

78	47		
0	66		
0	48		
0	44		
0	39		
0	53		

0 | 0 | 0

D | - | - | - | -

8 | - | - | - | -

Titanite

A vertically elongated wooden shield decorated with a white dragon.

Wooden shields are light, manageable, and offer relatively high magic absorption.

Skill: Parry

Repel an attack at the right time to follow up with a critical hit. Works while equipped in either hand.

Found/Dropped: Hollow Soldier

GREATSHIELDS

Ponderous Greatshields are the heaviest and most stable of all shields. They have hefty attribute requirements, both in raw Str required to simply use them, and in their high weight values.

It requires a specific build to take advantage of a Greatshield's strengths, but with an appropriately sturdy set of heavy armor and a Greatshield, it is possible to block and tank attacks that would otherwise be impossible in lighter armor or with a lighter shield.

This playstyle isn't for everyone, as it tends to be very sluggish and slow, but once you have the attributes for it, it can make handling certain fights quite easy without the need to dodge most incoming attacks.

Most Greatshields use the Shield Bash skill, but there are a few with Weapon Skill, allowing you to use your one handers special abilities.

GREATSHIELDS	TYPE	ART/COST	WEIGHT	POWER	SCALING	REQ.	PHYS	MAGIC	FIRE	LIGHTNING	DARK	STABILITY	MATERIAL
Ancient Dragon Greatshield	Strike	Weapon Skill/-	6.5	87p	D/-/-/-	16/0/0/0	77	45	43	46	45	54	Twinkling Titanite
Black Iron Greatshield	Strike	Shield Bash/16	14.5	112p	D/-/-/-	32/0/0/0	100	69	83	53	69	64	Titanite
Bonewheel Shield	Strike	Wheel of Fate/14	15.0	111p	D/-/-/-	30/10/0/0	100	63	59	54	63	59	Titanite
Cathedral Knight Greatshield	Strike	Shield Bash/16	15.5	112p	D/-/-/-	32/0/0/0	100	63	60	54	83	67	Titanite
Curse Ward Greatshield	Strike	Weapon Skill/-	17.0	125p	D/-/-/-	34/0/0/0	100	75	69	63	75	66	Titanite Scale
Dragonslayer Greatshield	Strike	Shield Bash/16	26.0	134p	D/-/-/-	38/0/0/0	100	71	70	95	77	74	Titanite Scale
Greatshield of Glory	Strike	Shield Bash/16	18.5	134p	D/-/-/-	40/0/0/0	100	70	65	52	63	80	Twinkling Titanite
Havel's Greatshield	Strike	Stone Flesh/16	28.0	143	D/-/-/-	40/0/0/0	100	83	83	82	83	75	Twinkling Titanite
Lothric Knight Greatshield	Strike	Shield Bash/16	15.0	111p	D/-/-/-	36/0/0/0	100	83	66	54	63	64	Titanite
Moaning Shield	Strike	Moan/10	21.5	136p	D/-/-/-	50/0/0/0	100	81	69	76	67	77	Twinkling Titanite
Stone Greatshield	Strike	Shield Bash/16	18.0	115p	D/-/-/-	38/0/0/0	100	75	71	71	75	67	Titanite
Twin Dragon Greatshield	Strike	Shield Bash/16	7.0	106p	D/-/-/-	16/0/0/0	84	59	63	66	59	63	Titanite
Wolf Knight's Greatshield	Strike	Weapon Skill/-	11.0	124	D/-/-/-	30/0/0/0	100	68	65	52	68	67	Twinkling Titanite
Yhorm's Greatshield	Strike	Shield Bash/16	20.5	132p	D/-/-/-	40/0/0/0	100	74	76	63	74	73	Titanite Scale

ANCIENT DRAGON GREATSHIELD

Strike		Weapon Skill / 0			6.5

	87		77
	0		45
	0		43
	0		46
	0		45
	0		54

	0		0		0

D	-	-	-	✶	-

16	-	-	-	✶	-

Twinkling Titanite

A wooden shield bearing the image of an ancient dragon. Very slowly regenerates HP.

The painting is the result of an exquisite but painstaking technique.

Lingering, undying traces of the ancient dragons can still be seen in their descendants, the man-serpents, though they have fallen far from grace.

Skill: Weapon Skill

Equipping this shield in the left hand allows one to perform the Skill of the right-hand weapon.

Found/Dropped: Archdragon Peak

BLACK IRON GREATSHIELD

Strike		Shield Bash / 16			14.5

	112		100
	0		69
	0		83
	0		53
	0		69
	0		64

	0		0		0

D	-	-	-	✶	-

32	-	-	-	✶	-

Titanite

Greatshield made of black iron, deeply feared for its association with Knightslayer Tsorig.

Black iron offers high defense, and is particularly effective at warding off fire.

Skill: Shield Bash

Without lowering your guard, strike the enemy with the shield to knock them back or stagger them. Works while equipped in either hand.

Found/Dropped: Smouldering Lake

BONEWHEEL SHIELD

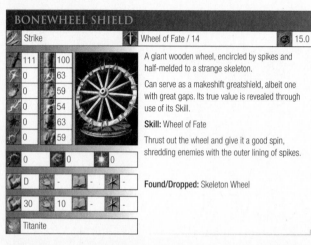

Strike		Wheel of Fate / 14			15.0

	111		100
	0		63
	0		59
	0		54
	0		63
	0		59

	0		0		0

D	-	-	-	✶	-

30	10	-	-	✶	-

Titanite

A giant wooden wheel, encircled by spikes and half-melded to a strange skeleton.

Can serve as a makeshift greatshield, albeit one with great gaps. Its true value is revealed through use of its Skill.

Skill: Wheel of Fate

Thrust out the wheel and give it a good spin, shredding enemies with the outer lining of spikes.

Found/Dropped: Skeleton Wheel

CATHEDRAL KNIGHT GREATSHIELD

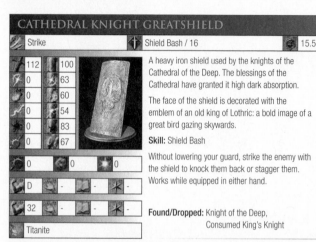

Strike		Shield Bash / 16			15.5

	112		100
	0		63
	0		60
	0		54
	0		83
	0		67

	0		0		0

D	-	-	-	✶	-

32	-	-	-	✶	-

Titanite

A heavy iron shield used by the knights of the Cathedral of the Deep. The blessings of the Cathedral have granted it high dark absorption.

The face of the shield is decorated with the emblem of an old king of Lothric: a bold image of a great bird gazing skywards.

Skill: Shield Bash

Without lowering your guard, strike the enemy with the shield to knock them back or stagger them. Works while equipped in either hand.

Found/Dropped: Knight of the Deep,
Consumed King's Knight

CURSE WARD GREATSHIELD

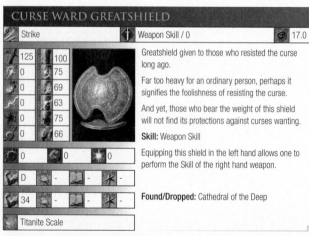

Strike		Weapon Skill / 0			17.0

	125		100
	0		75
	0		69
	0		63
	0		75
	0		66

	0		0		0

D	-	-	-	✶	-

34	-	-	-	✶	-

Titanite Scale

Greatshield given to those who resisted the curse long ago.

Far too heavy for an ordinary person, perhaps it signifies the foolishness of resisting the curse.

And yet, those who bear the weight of this shield will not find its protections against curses wanting.

Skill: Weapon Skill

Equipping this shield in the left hand allows one to perform the Skill of the right hand weapon.

Found/Dropped: Cathedral of the Deep

DRAGONSLAYER GREATSHIELD

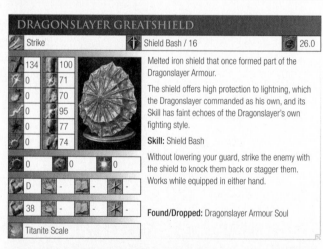

Strike		Shield Bash / 16			26.0

	134		100
	0		71
	0		70
	0		95
	0		77
	0		74

	0		0		0

D	-	-	-	✶	-

38	-	-	-	✶	-

Titanite Scale

Melted iron shield that once formed part of the Dragonslayer Armour.

The shield offers high protection to lightning, which the Dragonslayer commanded as his own, and its Skill has faint echoes of the Dragonslayer's own fighting style.

Skill: Shield Bash

Without lowering your guard, strike the enemy with the shield to knock them back or stagger them. Works while equipped in either hand.

Found/Dropped: Dragonslayer Armour Soul

GREATSHIELD OF GLORY

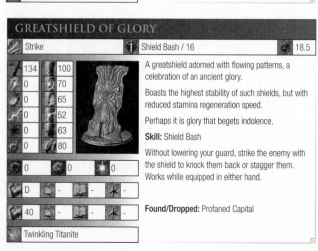

Strike		Shield Bash / 16			18.5

	134		100
	0		70
	0		65
	0		52
	0		63
	0		80

	0		0		0

D	-	-	-	✶	-

40	-	-	-	✶	-

Twinkling Titanite

A greatshield adorned with flowing patterns, a celebration of an ancient glory.

Boasts the highest stability of such shields, but with reduced stamina regeneration speed.

Perhaps it is glory that begets indolence.

Skill: Shield Bash

Without lowering your guard, strike the enemy with the shield to knock them back or stagger them. Works while equipped in either hand.

Found/Dropped: Profaned Capital

HAVEL'S GREATSHIELD

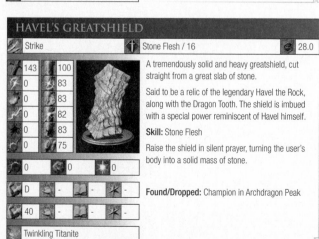

Strike		Stone Flesh / 16			28.0

	143		100
	0		83
	0		83
	0		82
	0		83
	0		75

	0		0		0

D	-	-	-	✶	-

40	-	-	-	✶	-

Twinkling Titanite

A tremendously solid and heavy greatshield, cut straight from a great slab of stone.

Said to be a relic of the legendary Havel the Rock, along with the Dragon Tooth. The shield is imbued with a special power reminiscent of Havel himself.

Skill: Stone Flesh

Raise the shield in silent prayer, turning the user's body into a solid mass of stone.

Found/Dropped: Champion in Archdragon Peak

LOTHRIC KNIGHT GREATSHIELD

Strike	Shield Bash / 16	15.0

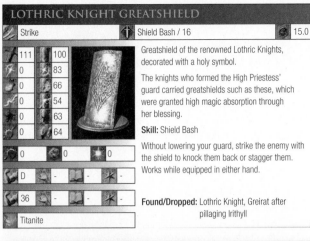

111	100
0	83
0	66
0	54
0	63
0	64

0	0	0

D	-	-	-

36	-	-	-

Titanite

Greatshield of the renowned Lothric Knights, decorated with a holy symbol.

The knights who formed the High Priestess' guard carried greatshields such as these, which were granted high magic absorption through her blessing.

Skill: Shield Bash

Without lowering your guard, strike the enemy with the shield to knock them back or stagger them. Works while equipped in either hand.

Found/Dropped: Lothric Knight, Greirat after pillaging Irithyll

STONE GREATSHIELD

Strike	Shield Bash / 16	18.0

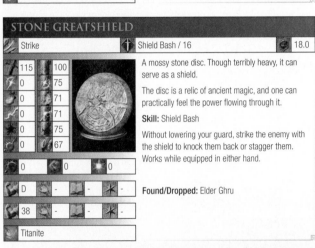

115	100
0	75
0	71
0	71
0	75
0	67

0	0	0

D	-	-	-

38	-	-	-

Titanite

A mossy stone disc. Though terribly heavy, it can serve as a shield.

The disc is a relic of ancient magic, and one can practically feel the power flowing through it.

Skill: Shield Bash

Without lowering your guard, strike the enemy with the shield to knock them back or stagger them. Works while equipped in either hand.

Found/Dropped: Elder Ghru

MOANING SHIELD

Strike	Moan / 10	21.5

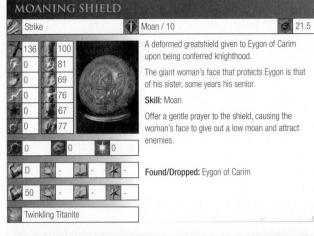

136	100
0	81
0	69
0	76
0	67
0	77

0	0	0

D	-	-	-

50	-	-	-

Twinkling Titanite

A deformed greatshield given to Eygon of Carim upon being conferred knighthood.

The giant woman's face that protects Eygon is that of his sister, some years his senior.

Skill: Moan

Offer a gentle prayer to the shield, causing the woman's face to give out a low moan and attract enemies.

Found/Dropped: Eygon of Carim

TWIN DRAGON GREATSHIELD

Strike	Shield Bash / 16	7.0

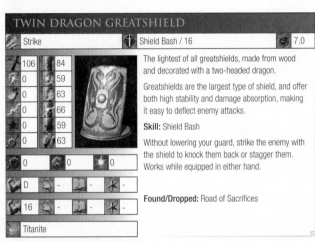

106	84
0	59
0	63
0	66
0	59
0	63

0	0	0

D	-	-	-

16	-	-	-

Titanite

The lightest of all greatshields, made from wood and decorated with a two-headed dragon.

Greatshields are the largest type of shield, and offer both high stability and damage absorption, making it easy to deflect enemy attacks.

Skill: Shield Bash

Without lowering your guard, strike the enemy with the shield to knock them back or stagger them. Works while equipped in either hand.

Found/Dropped: Road of Sacrifices

WOLF KNIGHT'S GREATSHIELD

Strike	Weapon Skill / 0	11.0

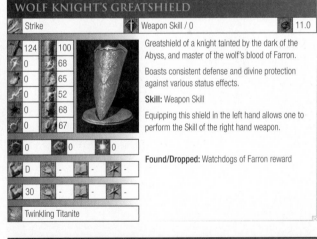

124	100
0	68
0	65
0	52
0	68
0	67

0	0	0

D	-	-	-

30	-	-	-

Twinkling Titanite

Greatshield of a knight tainted by the dark of the Abyss, and master of the wolf's blood of Farron.

Boasts consistent defense and divine protection against various status effects.

Skill: Weapon Skill

Equipping this shield in the left hand allows one to perform the Skill of the right hand weapon.

Found/Dropped: Watchdogs of Farron reward

YHORM'S GREATSHIELD

Strike	Shield Bash / 16	20.5

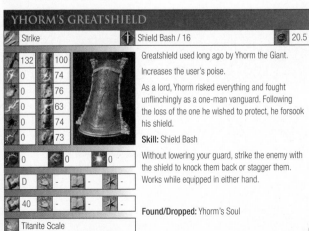

132	100
0	74
0	76
0	63
0	74
0	73

0	0	0

D	-	-	-

40	-	-	-

Titanite Scale

Greatshield used long ago by Yhorm the Giant.

Increases the user's poise.

As a lord, Yhorm risked everything and fought unflinchingly as a one-man vanguard. Following the loss of the one he wished to protect, he forsook his shield.

Skill: Shield Bash

Without lowering your guard, strike the enemy with the shield to knock them back or stagger them. Works while equipped in either hand.

Found/Dropped: Yhorm's Soul

ARMOR

Your final line of defense against the blades and fangs of this dark world, armor provides protection against physical and elemental damage, and resistance to status effects. Armor's defensive benefits stack with those provided by your personal stats, so as you level, you naturally take less damage overall, though a suit of heavy plate will always provide more raw physical reduction than a dress!

Armor in *Dark Souls* is largely about tradeoffs between weight and protection. Any suit of armor is viable throughout the game, as lightweight armor leaves you nimble enough to dodge most incoming attacks, while heavy armor lets you absorb more damage directly. The Poise value on armor is important, as it provides protection from flinching when you take damage during an attack. High Poise allows you to ignore harder hits, and Poise is particularly important for avoiding stunlocks from multiple rapid enemy attacks, and for ensuring that your slow and hard hitting swings find their target.

Because you can change armor at any time, think of your armor as a situation-specific tool to help you get through areas. Facing the poisonous swamp? Stock up on high poison resist armor. Heading into the depths of the Smouldering Lake? Fire resistance can come in handy. Up against a boss with lethal magic attacks? You know what to do. In general, lighter armor tends to have higher elemental defense, and heavier armor better physical defense, while status effect resistance varies across many armor pieces. You can usually get away with ignoring status resistance attributes, excepting Curse (which is extremely deadly in the few areas that have Curse inflicting enemies), if you bring along enough curative items. However it's usually pretty easy to find a mix of armor pieces that have similar weight to what you normally wear and provide extra resists suitable for an area, so if you're exploring an area with a lot of Bleed inflicting foes, its worth taking a few moments to swap some gear around. A rare few armor pieces (often helms) provide some unique effects, check their in-game descriptions as you acquire new armor.

There is no one single 'best' suit of armor, as much depends on the weight your stats will allow and how much speed you personally prefer, so feel free to mix and match individual pieces as you see fit. And of course, we won't judge if you choose to play a bit of Fashion Souls, looking sharp is important for the undead...

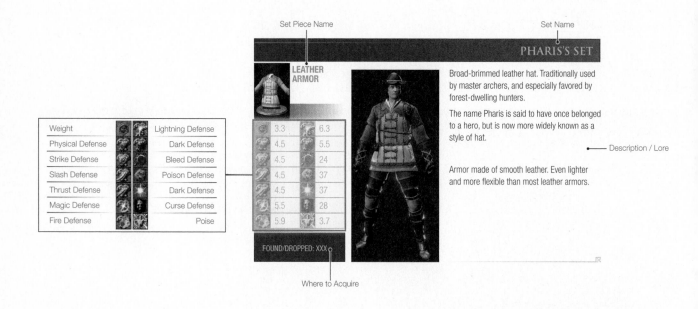

Set Piece Name

Set Name

PHARIS'S SET

LEATHER ARMOR

Broad-brimmed leather hat. Traditionally used by master archers, and especially favored by forest-dwelling hunters.

The name Pharis is said to have once belonged to a hero, but is now more widely known as a style of hat.

Description / Lore

Armor made of smooth leather. Even lighter and more flexible than most leather armors.

Weight			Lightning Defense		
Physical Defense		3.3	Dark Defense		6.3
Strike Defense		4.5	Bleed Defense		5.5
Slash Defense		4.5	Poison Defense		24
Thrust Defense		4.5	Dark Defense		37
Magic Defense		4.5	Curse Defense		37
Fire Defense		5.5	Poise		28
		5.9			3.7

FOUND/DROPPED: XXX

Where to Acquire

SPECIAL ARMOR SETS

Some full armor sets are not found or dropped anywhere in the game, instead they are sold by the Shrine Handmaid in Firelink Shrine. They are unlocked after either defeating a boss, or after completing an NPC questline. A few NPC armor sets can only be acquired by killing that specific NPC!

For special armor that is sold by the Shrine Handmaid, you must complete the conditions for her to sell it on each playthrough. If you start a New Game Plus journey, she won't sell any of the 'reward' armor until you complete the task again in that playthrough.

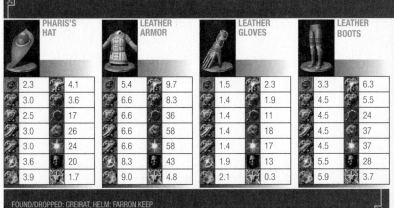

PHARIS'S HAT		LEATHER ARMOR		LEATHER GLOVES		LEATHER BOOTS	
2.3	4.1	5.4	9.7	1.5	2.3	3.3	6.3
3.0	3.6	6.6	8.3	1.4	1.9	4.5	5.5
2.5	17	6.6	36	1.4	11	4.5	24
3.0	26	6.6	58	1.4	18	4.5	37
3.0	24	6.6	58	1.4	17	4.5	37
3.6	20	8.3	43	1.9	13	5.5	28
3.9	1.7	9.0	4.8	2.1	0.3	5.9	3.7

FOUND/DROPPED: GREIRAT, HELM: FARRON KEEP

Broad-brimmed leather hat. Traditionally used by master archers, and especially favored by forest-dwelling hunters.

The name Pharis is said to have once belonged to a hero, but is now more widely known as a style of hat.

Armor made of smooth leather. Even lighter and more flexible than most leather armors.

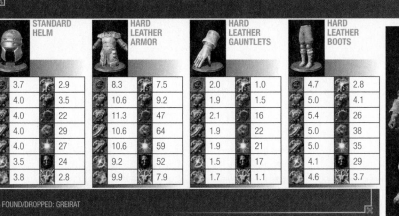

STANDARD HELM		HARD LEATHER ARMOR		HARD LEATHER GAUNTLETS		HARD LEATHER BOOTS	
3.7	2.9	8.3	7.5	2.0	1.0	4.7	2.8
4.0	3.5	10.6	9.2	1.9	1.5	5.0	4.1
4.0	22	11.3	47	2.1	16	5.4	26
4.0	29	10.6	64	1.9	22	5.0	38
4.0	27	10.6	59	1.9	21	5.0	35
3.5	24	9.2	52	1.5	17	4.1	29
3.8	2.8	9.9	7.9	1.7	1.1	4.6	3.7

FOUND/DROPPED: GREIRAT

A sturdy helm made of iron. Used by warriors of old, but one can still expect sound defense.

It is never unwise to wear a sturdy form of head protection against arrows and other somatic threats.

Armor made of thick, layered leather. Used by warriors of old, but one can still expect sound defense.

BRIGAND HOOD		BRIGAND ARMOR		BRIGAND GAUNTLETS		BRIGAND TROUSERS	
2.7	3.3	4.8	8.2	2.4	2.3	5.0	5.6
3.6	2.7	9.0	5.9	2.5	1.9	6.0	4.8
3.6	19	8.2	37	2.3	14	5.6	32
3.6	29	9.0	59	2.5	20	6.0	43
3.6	28	9.0	57	2.5	19	6.0	41
2.7	19	5.9	37	1.9	14	4.8	32
3.0	1.9	7.3	3.9	2.1	1.3	5.2	3.9

FOUND/DROPPED: ROAD OF SACRIFICES

Leather armor from a foreign land. Probably belonged to a brigand who met his match.

In foreign lands, undead were banished to send a message to populace, and when the message was not heard, they banished the living, too.

LUCATIEL'S MASK		MIRRAH VEST		MIRRAH GLOVES		MIRRAH TROUSERS	
2.9	4.8	7.0	12.8	2.1	2.5	3.5	6.4
4.0	3.8	10.6	9.9	1.9	1.7	5.0	4.6
4.0	22	10.6	54	1.9	17	5.0	29
4.0	26	8.4	64	1.3	21	3.6	37
4.0	22	8.4	54	1.3	17	3.6	29
4.0	24	10.6	60	1.9	19	5.0	32
3.8	2.1	9.9	5.7	1.7	0.4	4.6	1.8

FOUND/DROPPED: UNDEAD SETTLEMENT, HELM: SNUGGLY THE CROW

Mask attached to a ceremonial hat.

A Hollow once fought valiantly with this mask, but feared the fading of her self, and implored a comrade to remember her name.

Perhaps that is why this gentleman's mask is named after a woman.

Garb worn by Mirrah Knights sent on journeys. This hard leather vest is bestowed only upon proven knights.

Knights travel afar to fulfill their sacred duties, but few are ever able to deliver on their vows.

CHAIN SET

Chainmail armor of thin interlinking rings of steel. Popular due to its ease of crafting, respectable damage absorption, and light weight.

Knights may favor imposing armor, but for warriors on the battlefield, that which keeps them alive is armor enough.

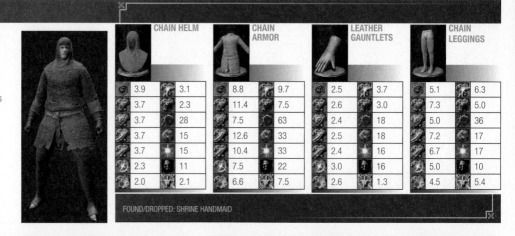

	CHAIN HELM		CHAIN ARMOR		LEATHER GAUNTLETS		CHAIN LEGGINGS	
	3.9	3.1	8.8	9.7	2.5	3.7	5.1	6.3
	3.7	2.3	11.4	7.5	2.6	3.0	7.3	5.0
	3.7	28	7.5	63	2.4	18	5.0	36
	3.7	15	12.6	33	2.5	18	7.2	17
	3.7	15	10.4	33	2.4	16	6.7	17
	2.3	11	7.5	22	3.0	16	5.0	10
	2.0	2.1	6.6	7.5	2.6	1.3	4.5	5.4

FOUND/DROPPED: SHRINE HANDMAID

NORTHERN SET

Iron armor of a stalwart northern warrior. Supported by interwoven chainmail.

Iron defensive wear grants superior absorption. Being from the north, it should also offer resistance to the cold.

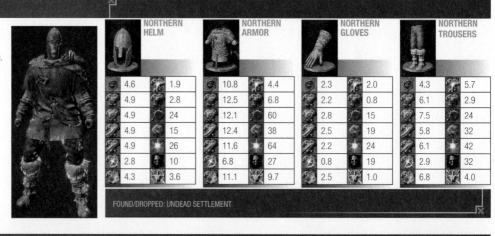

	NORTHERN HELM		NORTHERN ARMOR		NORTHERN GLOVES		NORTHERN TROUSERS	
	4.6	1.9	10.8	4.4	2.3	2.0	4.3	5.7
	4.9	2.8	12.5	6.8	2.2	0.8	6.1	2.9
	4.9	24	12.1	60	2.8	15	7.5	24
	4.9	15	12.4	38	2.5	19	5.8	32
	4.9	26	11.6	64	2.2	24	6.1	42
	2.8	10	6.8	27	0.8	19	2.9	32
	4.3	3.6	11.1	9.7	2.5	1.0	6.8	4.0

FOUND/DROPPED: UNDEAD SETTLEMENT

CREIGHTON SET

Attire of Creighton the Wanderer, a notorious deserter who fled an order of Mirrah Knights.

Despite the mask's being a symbol of a criminal sentenced to death, Creighton never removed it.

Formal attire of the honorable knights of Mirrah, featuring their heraldry, a stag set against a blue field.

Oddly, it was a dishonorable deserter who wore this attire most religiously.

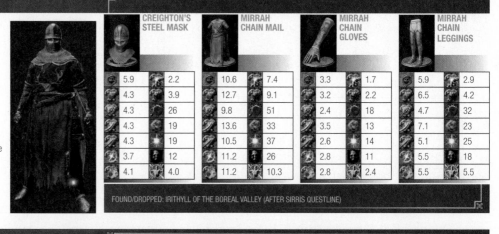

	CREIGHTON'S STEEL MASK		MIRRAH CHAIN MAIL		MIRRAH CHAIN GLOVES		MIRRAH CHAIN LEGGINGS	
	5.9	2.2	10.6	7.4	3.3	1.7	5.9	2.9
	4.3	3.9	12.7	9.1	3.2	2.2	6.5	4.2
	4.3	26	9.8	51	2.4	18	4.7	32
	4.3	19	13.6	33	3.5	13	7.1	23
	4.3	19	10.5	37	2.6	14	5.1	25
	3.7	12	11.2	26	2.8	11	5.5	18
	4.1	4.0	11.2	10.3	2.8	2.4	5.5	5.5

FOUND/DROPPED: IRITHYLL OF THE BOREAL VALLEY (AFTER SIRRIS QUESTLINE)

IRON SET

Large, durable iron helm, known as a heaume.

This helm with a red feather is said to have belonged to a Knight of Sunlight in a previous age.

The heaume has no particular powers, but is of fine quality, and appears to have been looked after with the greatest of care.

Chainmail armor and white coat featuring a large rendition of the holy symbol of the sun.

The choice attire of a singular Knight of Sunlight from a previous age. The symbol was painted by the knight himself, but the armor never bore any special power, sacred or otherwise.

	IRON HELM		ARMOR OF THE SUN		IRON BRACELETS		IRON LEGGINGS	
	6.0	4.5	8.6	9.8	2.9	2.0	5.3	5.1
	4.7	4.7	11.2	10.5	2.4	2.2	5.9	5.5
	4.7	17	8.3	34	1.6	11	4.2	21
	4.7	17	11.2	28	2.4	9	5.9	17
	4.7	17	11.2	31	2.4	10	5.9	19
	4.7	15	10.5	26	2.2	9	5.5	16
	4.7	4.0	10.5	10.3	2.2	1.9	5.5	5.8

FOUND/DROPPED: SNUGGLY THE CROW

SELLSWORD SET

SELLSWORD HELM
3.7	3.0
4.3	3.0
4.3	27
4.3	17
4.3	16
3.0	12
3.0	3.5

SELLSWORD ARMOR
10.8	7.6
12.4	10.7
12.4	59
12.4	39
12.4	35
10.7	26
9.3	10.5

SELLSWORD GAUNTLET
1.4	0.6
1.2	0.4
1.2	15
0.6	10
1.4	11
0.4	8
0.6	0.3

SELLSWORD TROUSERS
3.6	2.1
4.5	2.1
4.9	28
4.0	17
4.5	19
2.1	9
3.5	4.0

Metal armor interwoven with coarse cloth. Able to endure the hardships of battle and prolonged travel.

It is light considering the build, striking a fine balance between absorption and substance.

FOUND/DROPPED: ROAD OF SACRIFICES

DRANG SET

DRANG ARMOR
5.1	10.9
9.0	9.7
8.3	42
7.5	62
5.2	66
9.7	45
7.5	1.3

DRANG GAUNTLETS
1.7	2.3
1.8	2.0
1.6	13
1.4	19
0.9	21
2.0	14
1.4	0.4

DRANG SHOES
4.0	7.0
5.0	6.3
5.5	24
5.5	37
5.5	39
6.3	26
5.0	1.6

Armor of the Drang Knights, proclaimed descendants from the land known for the legend of the Linking of the Fire.

Fine protection that is both light and strong, having been reinforced with rare geisteel.

The Drang Knights were once feared sellswords, until treason meant descending into the abyss, and they were separated forever.

FOUND/DROPPED: CATHEDRAL OF THE DEEP

UNDEAD LEGION SET

UNDEAD LEGION HELM
4.0	4.9
3.8	4.2
3.8	19
3.8	24
3.8	29
4.7	21
4.8	2.6

UNDEAD LEGION ARMOR
7.6	13.2
10.4	10.4
10.4	39
5.7	51
9.0	65
12.6	42
13.0	6.3

UNDEAD LEGION GAUNTLET
2.4	3.0
2.3	2.3
2.3	16
1.4	20
1.9	24
2.9	17
3.0	1.1

UNDEAD LEGION LEGGINGS
4.6	7.2
5.6	5.6
5.6	27
3.2	35
4.8	43
6.9	29
7.1	3.5

Attire of the Abyss Watchers, the Undead Legion of Farron. A black-dyed leather vest worn over chainmail.

These undead warriors vowed to partake of wolf blood. They acted in the dark, seeking out any sign of the Abyss, fighting a constant war with its abominations.

FOUND/DROPPED: SHRINE HANDMAID (AFTER ABYSS WATCHERS)

HERALD SET

HERALD HELM
3.7	1.6
4.4	3.2
4.4	24
4.4	14
4.4	17
3.5	10
3.2	3.4

HERALD ARMOR
8.6	3.8
12.4	8.4
8.0	52
12.6	30
11.9	36
9.2	19
8.4	9.5

HERALD GLOVES
2.9	0.7
3.1	1.5
2.1	16
3.1	12
2.9	12
1.7	8
2.1	1.6

HERALD TROUSERS
5.3	1.8
7.1	4.1
6.5	26
6.8	20
6.5	20
4.6	11
4.6	5.1

Steel helm said to be worn by Heralds of the Way of White, who deliver commandments of duty.

Steel armor with a pure white cape, the signature of Heralds of the way of White.

Protection made of steel has excellent physical absorption, but is found lacking against blunt strikes and lightning damage.

FOUND/DROPPED: ROAD OF SACRIFICES

KNIGHT SET

Armor of a lowly knight, fashioned from solid iron.

This iron armor might be on the heftier side compared to others of its ilk, but as such offers great physical absorption in exchange for its imposing weight.

Do not think to wear it without the necessary vitality.

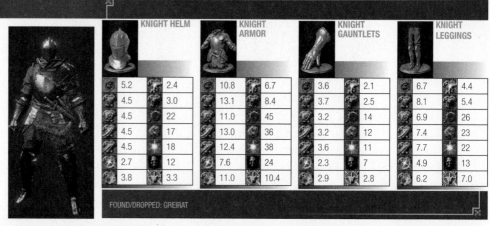

KNIGHT HELM		KNIGHT ARMOR		KNIGHT GAUNTLETS		KNIGHT LEGGINGS	
5.2	2.4	10.8	6.7	3.6	2.1	6.7	4.4
4.5	3.0	13.1	8.4	3.7	2.5	8.1	5.4
4.5	22	11.0	45	3.2	14	6.9	26
4.5	17	13.0	36	3.2	12	7.4	23
4.5	18	12.4	38	3.6	11	7.7	22
2.7	12	7.6	24	2.3	7	4.9	13
3.8	3.3	11.0	10.4	2.9	2.8	6.2	7.0

FOUND/DROPPED: GREIRAT

NAMELESS KNIGHT SET

Armor of a nameless knight.

Crafted with thin metal greatly reinforced by a grooved finish.

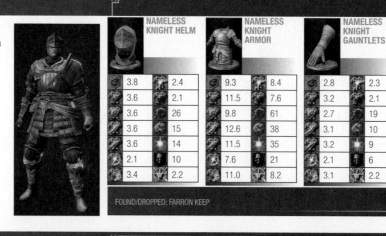

NAMELESS KNIGHT HELM		NAMELESS KNIGHT ARMOR		NAMELESS KNIGHT GAUNTLETS		NAMELESS KNIGHT LEGGINGS	
3.8	2.4	9.3	8.4	2.8	2.3	5.6	5.4
3.6	2.1	11.5	7.6	3.2	2.1	7.2	4.9
3.6	26	9.8	61	2.7	19	6.2	36
3.6	15	12.6	38	3.1	10	7.2	22
3.6	14	11.5	35	3.2	9	7.2	20
2.1	10	7.6	21	2.1	6	4.9	11
3.4	2.2	11.0	8.2	3.1	2.2	6.9	5.6

FOUND/DROPPED: FARRON KEEP

FALLEN KNIGHT SET

Armor of an order of fallen knights who disbanded and fled, but met untimely deaths.

The drab, tattered cloth conceals tough, black metal which provides dependable protection from fire. It is just possible to make out the majestic gold engravings on its surface.

FALLEN KNIGHT HELM		FALLEN KNIGHT ARMOR		FALLEN KNIGHT GAUNTLETS		FALLEN KNIGHT TROUSERS	
4.6	3.5	9.2	10.4	2.9	3.0	5.3	6.3
4.2	2.6	12.3	9.0	3.6	2.2	7.6	5.5
4.2	21	12.3	43	3.6	11	7.6	22
4.2	14	12.3	28	3.6	5	7.6	10
4.2	19	12.3	39	3.6	10	7.6	20
2.9	12	8.3	22	2.4	4	5.0	9
4.2	2.1	12.5	7.0	3.7	2.0	7.8	4.6

FOUND/DROPPED: ROAD OF SACRIFICES

ELITE KNIGHT SET

Armor said to have been given to elite knights of fallen Astora.

The mere mention of Astora invokes wistful pangs, and perhaps it was such a dream that drew Anri to this faraway home known only by name.

ELITE KNIGHT HELM		ELITE KNIGHT ARMOR		ELITE KNIGHT GAUNTLETS		ELITE KNIGHT LEGGINGS	
5.3	3.1	8.9	6.8	3.4	2.0	6.9	5.3
4.5	3.5	12.1	8.5	3.4	2.4	7.8	6.1
4.5	24	9.2	46	2.8	18	6.5	38
4.5	15	12.1	32	3.4	13	7.6	25
4.5	15	11.1	33	3.4	14	7.4	26
3.7	9	9.2	18	2.6	9	6.5	16
4.1	3.1	10.6	8.8	3.0	2.3	7.1	6.4

FOUND/DROPPED: SHRINE HANDMAID (AFTER ANRI'S DEATH)

ALVA SET

	ALVA HELM		ALVA ARMOR		ALVA GAUNTLETS		ALVA LEGGINGS	
	4.2	3.1	9.0	8.8	3.3	2.1	5.5	5.0
	4.2	3.6	11.9	10.2	2.9	2.5	6.8	5.8
	4.2	28	9.5	59	2.3	22	5.4	36
	4.2	18	11.9	35	2.9	14	6.8	21
	4.2	19	11.4	37	2.8	15	6.5	22
	3.1	12	8.8	21	2.1	10	5.0	12
	3.8	3.9	10.9	11.7	2.7	2.6	6.2	7.2

FOUND/DROPPED: IRITHYLL DUNGEON (AFTER DEFEATING ALVA INVADER)

Protection of Alva, seeker of the spurned. This steel body armor was trimmed to reduce weight.

To this day, troubadours sing of tales of the wandering knight Alva and his travels, and of his involvement with the saint and the witch. Needless to say, the songs traditionally end in tragedy.

DRAKEBLOOD SET

	DRAKEBLOOD HELM		DRAKEBLOOD ARMOR		DRAKEBLOOD GAUNTLETS		DRAKEBLOOD LEGGINGS	
	6.3	4.0	14.4	11.1	4.8	2.6	8.6	6.0
	4.9	4.0	13.3	11.1	3.1	2.6	7.3	6.0
	4.9	34	13.0	78	3.0	25	7.1	45
	4.9	19	14.0	43	3.3	13	7.7	23
	4.9	21	12.8	46	3.0	14	7.0	25
	4.8	15	13.0	33	3.0	9	7.1	17
	4.4	3.8	12.1	11.0	2.9	2.3	6.6	6.4

FOUND/DROPPED: —

Armor of the Drakeblood Knights, worshippers of the blood of dragons. The red cloth is said to symbolize their yearning for blood.

Dragon worship has captured the hearts and minds of warriors across the lands for many ages. Perhaps such warriors are attracted to doctrines of few words.

FARAAM SET

	FARAAM HELM		FARAAM ARMOR		FARAAM GAUNTLETS		FARAAM BOOTS	
	6.6	4.2	13.1	10.7	4.8	3.0	6.8	5.6
	4.8	4.2	12.9	10.7	3.3	3.0	7.3	5.6
	4.8	27	12.6	59	3.4	21	7.3	34
	4.8	22	12.6	40	3.2	16	7.3	24
	4.8	28	12.2	60	3.1	22	6.7	37
	4.0	14	10.0	27	2.9	11	5.2	15
	4.4	4.1	11.7	11.0	3.3	2.8	6.4	6.5

FOUND/DROPPED: SHRINE HANDMAID (AFTER LION KNIGHT ALBERT IN GRAND ARCHIVES)

Armor named after a god of war.

The armor of the Forossa Lion Knights was preserved even after the destruction of their homeland, and is mentioned in numerous legends, alongside the names of those who are said to have gone beyond death.

SUNSET SET

	SUNSET HELM		SUNSET ARMOR		SUNSET GAUNTLETS		SUNSET LEGGINGS	
	5.0	1.7	13.8	8.3	4.5	2.2	7.2	2.9
	4.5	3.1	13.4	10.5	3.7	2.8	6.8	4.7
	4.5	26	11.2	63	3.4	24	5.1	40
	4.5	25	13.6	58	3.6	22	7.0	35
	4.5	14	13.1	39	3.5	16	6.8	26
	2.5	15	9.1	42	2.4	17	3.7	26
	3.1	3.0	11.2	11.1	3.0	2.7	5.1	5.5

FOUND/DROPPED: UNDEAD SETTLEMENT (AFTER INVADING HODRICK DURING SIRRIS QUESTLINE)

Armor of Hodrick, holy knight of the Sunless Realms.

This light gold armor, named for its sunset hues, is now faded and wrapped in tainted rags.

The sorry fool was known to wander the battlefield as a crazed ghoul, lashing out at friend and foe alike.

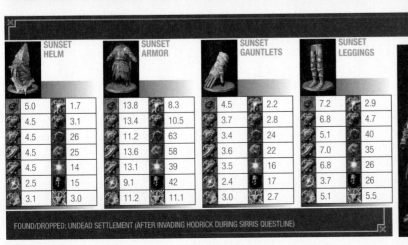

SUNLESS SET

Attire of a knight from the Sunless Realms, known for their resistance to both magic and the dark.

Metal plating and chainmail, treated with silver.

Sunless Knights serve the nameless moon, and perhaps it is for this reason the attire casts a feminine silhouette.

SUNLESS VEIL

1.8	4.9
1.7	5.3
1.7	7.0
1.7	14
1.7	14
5.2	30
4.9	0.9

SUNLESS ARMOR
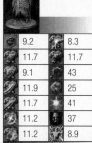

9.2	8.3
11.7	11.7
9.1	43
11.9	25
11.7	41
11.2	37
11.2	8.9

SUNLESS GAUNTLETS

3.6	1.8
2.6	2.6
2.0	13
3.1	7
2.6	12
2.5	7
2.5	1.7

SUNLESS LEGGINGS

5.7	4.2
6.2	6.2
4.7	27
6.8	18
6.2	26
5.9	18
5.9	4.9

FOUND/DROPPED: SHRINE HANDMAID (AFTER SIRRIS' DEATH)

BRASS SET

Armor of a knight once known as the Darkmoon.

It is said that this brass armor hides something hideous within.

Something about its silhouette suggests femininity.

BRASS HELM

4.7	2.3
4.5	3.4
4.5	27
4.5	15
4.5	17
4.6	13
3.4	2.9

BRASS ARMOR

10.7	6.9
12.9	10.0
10.0	60
12.6	33
11.7	36
13.3	27
10.0	9.3

BRASS GAUNTLETS

3.5	1.9
3.4	2.7
2.7	19
3.4	10
3.1	11
3.5	8
2.7	2.3

BRASS LEGGINGS
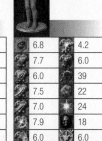

6.8	4.2
7.7	6.0
6.0	39
7.5	22
7.0	24
7.9	18
6.0	6.0

FOUND/DROPPED: IRITHYLL OF THE BOREAL VALLEY

FAVOR SET

Helm of the pitiable Embraced knight. Depicts the affection of the goddess Fina.

Adrift on a sea of isolation, only his faith in the love of his goddess remained true, and so the knight forsook all else.

Armor of the pitiable Embraced knight. Depicts the affection of the goddess Fina.

The face is crafted to depict the goddess's embrace, quite ignoring the fact that her love is in fact as fickle as the weather.

HELM OF FAVOR

5.9	2.5
4.3	3.7
4.3	30
4.3	23
4.3	25
3.5	18
3.7	3.6

EMBRACED ARMOR OF FAVOR

13.0	7.7
12.5	11.1
11.6	63
12.3	46
12.5	51
10.6	35
11.1	11.4

GAUNTLETS OF FAVOR

3.8	2.0
3.4	3.0
3.1	19
3.4	13
3.4	14
2.8	10
3.0	2.8

LEGGINGS OF FAVOR

7.7	4.3
7.4	6.5
6.8	41
7.4	29
7.5	32
6.1	24
6.5	7.2

FOUND/DROPPED: SHRINE HANDMAID

EASTERN SET

Distinctive armor made in an Eastern land.

The exquisite craftsmanship and artistic design made these prized pieces in the collection of any nobleman.

Offers excellent damage absorption, particularly from slashing attacks from katanas, which are commonly encountered threats in battles fought in the East.

EASTERN HELM

3.8	1.6
3.8	2.4
3.2	29
4.4	12
3.4	15
1.6	9
3.4	2.9

EASTERN ARMOR

11.0	6.7
12.0	8.4
10.5	78
13.4	37
11.0	43
6.7	25
11.5	9.9

EASTERN GAUNTLETS

2.9	1.8
3.3	2.3
2.9	22
3.7	9
3.1	11
1.8	7
3.1	2.5

EASTERN LEGGINGS

5.0	6.9
5.4	6.2
6.2	43
7.5	40
4.9	41
4.5	39
7.2	4.9

FOUND/DROPPED: SHRINE HANDMAID

Thorn Set

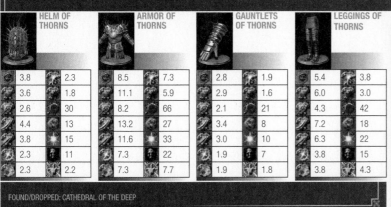

HELM OF THORNS		ARMOR OF THORNS		GAUNTLETS OF THORNS		LEGGINGS OF THORNS	
3.8	2.3	8.5	7.3	2.8	1.9	5.4	3.8
3.6	1.8	11.1	5.9	2.9	1.6	6.0	3.0
2.6	30	8.2	66	2.1	21	4.3	42
4.4	13	13.2	27	3.4	8	7.2	18
3.8	15	11.6	33	3.0	10	6.3	22
2.3	11	7.3	22	1.9	7	3.8	15
2.3	2.2	7.3	7.7	1.9	1.8	3.8	4.3

FOUND/DROPPED: CATHEDRAL OF THE DEEP

Armor of Kirk, the notorious knight of Thorns. A dense patch of thorns grows from its surface.

A fitting item for the murderous Kirk, for even the simple act of rolling can damage enemies when wearing this attire.

Special: Damage enemies while rolling.

Catarina Set

CATARINA HELM		CATARINA ARMOR		CATARINA GAUNTLETS		CATARINA LEGGINGS	
7.7	5.5	17.9	14.6	6.0	3.8	11.1	4.8
5.4	5.0	14.7	13.1	3.9	3.4	8.5	6.8
4.6	34	12.8	74	3.4	29	7.4	47
5.6	27	15.4	57	4.2	22	9.3	35
5.0	27	14.1	57	3.8	22	8.3	35
4.3	17	11.4	33	3.0	14	6.0	21
4.7	5.7	12.4	15.9	3.3	3.1	6.6	9.2

FOUND/DROPPED: UNBREAKABLE PATCHES, OR SIEGWARD AFTER YHORM BATTLE

Distinctively shaped armor worn by the Knights of Catarina.

Often ridiculed for its onion-like shape, infuriating the country's proud knights, but the masterfully forged curved design makes it very effective for deflecting blows.

Morne Set

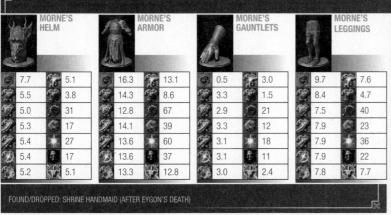

MORNE'S HELM		MORNE'S ARMOR		MORNE'S GAUNTLETS		MORNE'S LEGGINGS	
7.7	5.1	16.3	13.1	0.5	3.0	9.7	7.6
5.5	3.8	14.3	8.6	3.3	1.5	8.4	4.7
5.0	31	12.8	67	2.9	21	7.5	40
5.3	17	14.1	39	3.3	12	7.9	23
5.4	27	13.6	60	3.1	18	7.9	36
5.4	17	13.6	37	3.1	11	7.9	22
5.2	5.1	13.3	12.8	3.0	2.4	7.8	7.7

FOUND/DROPPED: SHRINE HANDMAID (AFTER EYGON'S DEATH)

Unusual helm bestowed upon knights of Carim.

Modeled on Morne, the Archbishop's apostle, the helm is of perfect likeness to the stone heads lining the cathedral.

A Carim knight will dedicate an entire career to attending a single maiden, just as Morne once served one goddess alone.

Black armor bestowed upon knights of Carim.

Modeled on Morne, the Archbishop's apostle, cast from a unique mineral resembling stone.

Lothric Knight Set

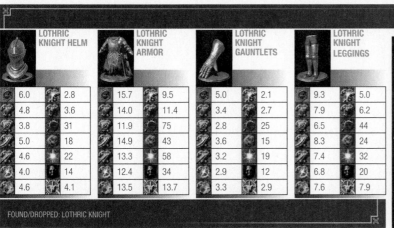

LOTHRIC KNIGHT HELM		LOTHRIC KNIGHT ARMOR		LOTHRIC KNIGHT GAUNTLETS		LOTHRIC KNIGHT LEGGINGS	
6.0	2.8	15.7	9.5	5.0	2.1	9.3	5.0
4.8	3.6	14.0	11.4	3.4	2.7	7.9	6.2
3.8	31	11.9	75	2.8	25	6.5	44
5.0	18	14.9	43	3.6	15	8.3	24
4.6	22	13.3	58	3.2	19	7.4	32
4.0	14	12.4	34	2.9	12	6.8	20
4.6	4.1	13.5	13.7	3.3	2.9	7.6	7.9

FOUND/DROPPED: LOTHRIC KNIGHT

Armor of a celebrated Lothric knight.

The coat of distinction is all but fallen apart.

The Knight has served as one of the Three Pillars since ancient times, and shares place alongside the wyverns as a symbol of Lothric.

Only those possessing a knight's resolve are fit to wear this garment.

CATHEDRAL KNIGHT SET

Massive iron armor worn by knights serving the Cathedral of the Deep.

Repulsive creatures of the deep are sure to attract the foolish, but the cathedral knights are prepared to meet such intruders head on with their more than ample might.

	CATHEDRAL KNIGHT HELM		CATHEDRAL KNIGHT ARMOR		CATHEDRAL KNIGHT GAUNTLETS		CATHEDRAL KNIGHT LEGGINGS	
	7.6	4.6	17.8	14.1	5.5	3.6	10.2	7.3
	4.9	3.9	14.8	12.2	3.8	3.0	7.7	5.9
	4.9	28	14.8	66	3.7	22	7.6	40
	4.7	26	13.3	62	3.2	21	7.3	38
	5.2	26	15.7	62	3.9	21	8.0	38
	4.7	20	14.4	47	3.6	15	7.4	26
	4.3	4.9	13.3	15.7	3.4	3.4	6.9	8.1

FOUND/DROPPED: KNIGHT OF THE DEEP/CONSUMED KING'S KNIGHT

WINGED SET

Armor of the Winged Knights, named for their appearance, who swore themselves to the Angels.

Worship of the divine messengers was viewed as heresy in Lothric and unrecognized by any of the Three Pillars of rule.

This is believed to be why Gertrude, the Heavenly Daughter, was imprisoned in the lofty cell of the Grand Archives.

	WINGED KNIGHT HELM		WINGED KNIGHT ARMOR		WINGED KNIGHT GAUNTLETS		WINGED KNIGHT LEGGINGS	
	7.4	4.5	19.0	14.6	6.3	3.7	11.0	7.4
	5.3	5.4	14.5	16.0	3.9	4.3	8.3	8.0
	4.7	31	13.0	73	3.3	22	7.4	42
	5.2	29	14.1	60	3.8	21	8.1	32
	5.0	29	13.8	68	3.5	21	7.9	39
	4.2	18	14.0	45	3.5	13	7.1	24
	4.8	4.1	13.8	16.2	3.9	3.6	6.9	9.0

FOUND/DROPPED: LOTHRIC CASTLE

OUTRIDER KNIGHT SET

Armor of an Irithyll outrider knight. Enveloped in a dimly cool air.

The knights were given the eyes of the Pontiff, but the eyes transformed them into savage, raving warriors who only knew how to serve as mindless guards.

	OUTRIDER KNIGHT HELM		OUTRIDER KNIGHT ARMOR		OUTRIDER KNIGHT GAUNTLETS		OUTRIDER KNIGHT LEGGINGS	
	3.8	2.3	12.3	9.0	2.9	2.4	6.9	5.5
	4.1	1.1	13.0	6.6	3.7	1.6	8.0	3.7
	2.6	17	9.7	50	2.6	12	5.9	32
	4.4	12	12.8	43	3.1	10	7.2	24
	4.0	32	12.5	91	3.6	25	7.8	55
	2.3	5	9.0	22	2.4	4	5.5	14
	3.1	2.6	10.9	9.8	3.0	2.6	6.7	6.6

FOUND/DROPPED: BOREAL OUTRIDER KNIGHT

PONTIFF KNIGHT SET

Crown of the Pontiff's Knights, now harrowed spirits of Irithyll.

The golden crown signifies those who report directly to Sulyvahn. The knights were his watchful eyes, and when needed, his punitive blades.

Armor of the Pontiff's Knights, now harrowed spirits of Irithyll.

This blue-gray armor, shrouded in a thinly cold air, is light and brittle.

	PONTIFF KNIGHT CROWN		PONTIFF KNIGHT ARMOR		PONTIFF KNIGHT GAUNTLETS		PONTIFF KNIGHT LEGGINGS	
	2.7	4.3	7.3	11.9	2.2	2.3	4.3	6.0
	4.1	5.0	11.4	13.3	2.2	2.7	5.7	6.8
	2.5	15	7.6	40	1.2	14	3.5	23
	4.1	12	11.4	36	2.2	13	5.7	21
	3.3	31	9.3	81	1.6	28	4.5	48
	4.7	10	12.9	29	2.6	10	6.6	16
	3.3	2.9	9.3	8.5	1.6	1.3	4.5	4.4

FOUND/DROPPED: PONTIFF KNIGHT

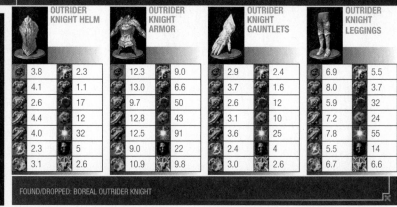

FIRE WITCH HELM

3.9		2.8	
4.7		3.9	
2.3		18	
3.7		13	
3.7		15	
4.1		11	
4.5		3.1	

FIRE WITCH ARMOR

11.1		8.5	
12.8		11.1	
7.7		47	
10.6		34	
10.6		36	
11.6		27	
12.3		9.2	

FIRE WITCH GAUNTLETS

2.6		1.4	
2.8		2.2	
1.4		15	
2.4		10	
2.2		12	
2.4		9	
2.6		1.6	

FIRE WITCH LEGGINGS

5.5		4.3	
7.4		6.1	
3.5		24	
5.7		16	
5.7		20	
6.5		13	
7.1		5.5	

FOUND/DROPPED: BURNING STAKE WITCH

Armor of witches who bore the Profaned Flame, now harrowed spirits of Irithyll.

The witches who lead the Pontiff's Knights were originally ordained as holy knights.

It was not long however, before their hearts were swallowed by the Profaned Flame.

DANCER'S CROWN

2.8		2.5	
2.8		2.8	
1.3		14	
4.2		10	
3.5		23	
2.2		7	
1.7		2.1	

DANCER'S ARMOR

7.3		9.1	
10.5		9.8	
7.4		41	
11.9		33	
11.7		55	
8.3		22	
6.0		8.3	

DANCER'S GAUNTLETS

2.4		2.4	
2.8		2.6	
2.0		15	
2.9		12	
3.1		20	
2.2		9	
1.7		2.1	

DANCER'S LEGGINGS

4.4		4.7	
5.5		5.1	
3.7		22	
6.8		17	
6.2		31	
4.2		10	
2.9		4.6	

FOUND/DROPPED: SHRINE HANDMAID (AFTER DANCER OF THE BOREAL VALLEY)

Crown worn by the Dancer of the Boreal Valley.

The mirage-like aurora veil is said to be an article of the old gods, permitted only for direct descendants of the old royal family.

Armor worn by the Dancer of the Boreal Valley.

The black eyes of the Pontiff eventually transformed the Dancer into a beastly creature, her armor fusing with her own hide.

DARK MASK

4.0		1.3	
4.3		3.1	
3.1		18	
3.9		14	
3.7		15	
3.1		7	
2.5		2.7	

DARK ARMOR

9.1		4.4	
12.5		9.2	
9.2		38	
11.6		30	
11.1		33	
9.2		14	
7.7		8.8	

DARK GAUNTLETS

3.2		1.4	
3.5		2.6	
2.6		12	
3.2		9	
3.1		10	
2.6		4	
2.2		2.3	

DARK LEGGINGS

5.8		2.9	
7.8		6.1	
5.7		26	
7.1		20	
6.8		23	
6.1		10	
5.3		6.1	

FOUND/DROPPED: DARKWRAITH

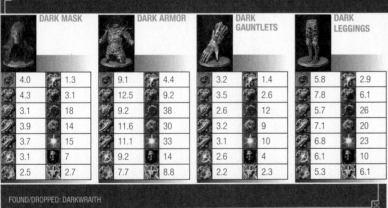

Armor of the Darkwraiths, relics of a small country that fell to the dark long ago.

Looks as if it may crumble to dust at any moment.

The Darkwraiths were the oldest of the Red Eye Invaders, and rumored to have served a Primordial Serpent.

BLACK KNIGHT HELM

5.6		3.0	
4.5		3.6	
3.6		27	
4.2		19	
4.1		19	
3.2		19	
4.5		3.0	

BLACK KNIGHT ARMOR

9.1			
		58	
		42	
		39	
		39	

BLACK KNIGHT GAUNTLETS

4.0		2.3	
3.4		2.8	
2.9		18	
3.3		12	
3.1		11	
2.5		11	
3.4		2.7	

BLACK KNIGHT LEGGINGS

8.0		5.8	
8.3		6.9	
6.9		38	
7.7		27	
7.6		26	
6.2		26	
8.3		6.7	

FOUND/DROPPED: BLACK KNIGHT

Armor of the Black Knights who roam the lands.

The knights served the First Lord Gwyn, and followed him into the flame upon its linking. They became ash, but still wander the realms to this day.

SILVER KNIGHT SET

Armor of the Silver Knights allegiant to the royals of old.

It is said that even after the family's passing, the knights continued to watch over their manor, and the ruined cathedral.

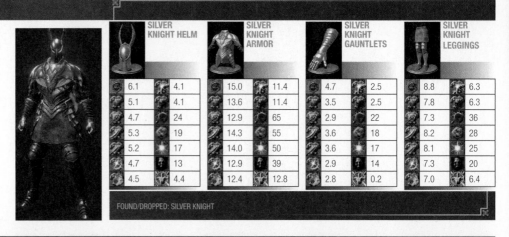

	SILVER KNIGHT HELM		SILVER KNIGHT ARMOR		SILVER KNIGHT GAUNTLETS		SILVER KNIGHT LEGGINGS	
	6.1	4.1	15.0	11.4	4.7	2.5	8.8	6.3
	5.1	4.1	13.6	11.4	3.5	2.5	7.8	6.3
	4.7	24	12.9	65	2.9	22	7.3	36
	5.3	19	14.3	55	3.6	18	8.2	28
	5.2	17	14.0	50	3.6	17	8.1	25
	4.7	13	12.9	39	2.9	14	7.3	20
	4.5	4.4	12.4	12.8	2.8	0.2	7.0	6.4

FOUND/DROPPED: SILVER KNIGHT

DRAGONSLAYER SET

Golden lion armor associated with Dragonslayer Ornstein, from the age of gods, and imbued with the strength of lightning.

In the dragonless age, this knight, who long guarded the ruined cathedral, left the land in search of the nameless king.

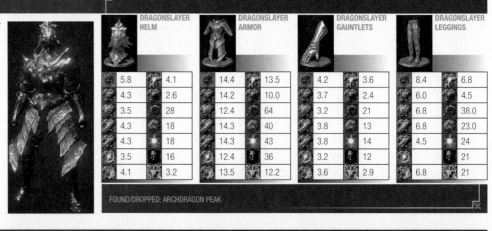

	DRAGONSLAYER HELM		DRAGONSLAYER ARMOR		DRAGONSLAYER GAUNTLETS		DRAGONSLAYER LEGGINGS	
	5.8	4.1	14.4	13.5	4.2	3.6	8.4	6.8
	4.3	2.6	14.2	10.0	3.7	2.4	6.0	4.5
	3.5	28	12.4	64	3.2	21	6.8	38.0
	4.3	18	14.3	40	3.8	13	6.8	23.0
	4.3	18	14.3	43	3.8	14	4.5	24
	3.5	16	12.4	36	3.2	12		21
	4.1	3.2	13.5	12.2	3.6	2.9	6.8	21

FOUND/DROPPED: ARCHDRAGON PEAK

WOLF KNIGHT SET

Armor of a knight tainted by the dark of the Abyss. The twilight blue cape is damp, and will ever remain so.

A vanquished knight left behind only wolf's blood, and his legacy of duty. The Undead Legion of Farron was formed to bear his torch, and the armor of these Abyss Watchers suggests their own eventual end.

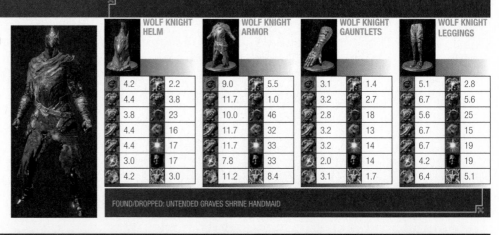

	WOLF KNIGHT HELM		WOLF KNIGHT ARMOR		WOLF KNIGHT GAUNTLETS		WOLF KNIGHT LEGGINGS	
	4.2	2.2	9.0	5.5	3.1	1.4	5.1	2.8
	4.4	3.8	11.7	1.0	3.2	2.7	6.7	5.6
	3.8	23	10.0	46	2.8	18	5.6	25
	4.4	16	11.7	32	3.2	13	6.7	15
	4.4	17	11.7	33	3.2	14	6.7	19
	3.0	17	7.8	33	2.0	14	4.2	19
	4.2	3.0	11.2	8.4	3.1	1.7	6.4	5.1

FOUND/DROPPED: UNTENDED GRAVES SHRINE HANDMAID

SMOUGH SET

Grotesque armor associated with Smough, the last knight to stand in defense of the ruined cathedral.

Boasts extremely high defense and can be donned by humans, but not without great difficulty.

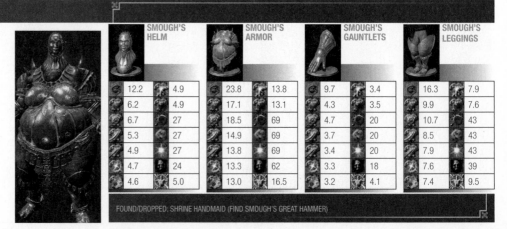

	SMOUGH'S HELM		SMOUGH'S ARMOR		SMOUGH'S GAUNTLETS		SMOUGH'S LEGGINGS	
	12.2	4.9	23.8	13.8	9.7	3.4	16.3	7.9
	6.2	4.9	17.1	13.1	4.3	3.5	9.9	7.6
	6.7	27	18.5	69	4.7	20	10.7	43
	5.3	27	14.9	69	3.7	20	8.5	43
	4.9	27	13.8	69	3.4	20	7.9	43
	4.7	24	13.3	62	3.3	18	7.6	39
	4.6	5.0	13.0	16.5	3.2	4.1	7.4	9.5

FOUND/DROPPED: SHRINE HANDMAID (FIND SMOUGH'S GREAT HAMMER)

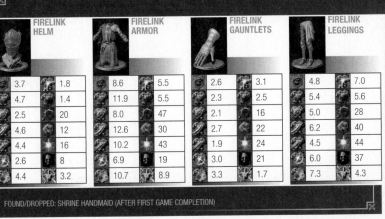

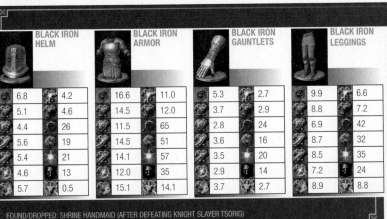

LORIAN SET

Armor of Prince Lothric's older brother Lorian.

This black-dyed brass armor was passed down to him from the royal family.

Lorian, raised as a knight, is said to have been left mute and crippled by his younger brother's curse. It is also said that Lorian, in fact, wished it so.

LORIAN'S HELM

5.6		3.3	
5.0		4.8	
3.3		24	
4.8		12	
3.6		17	
4.7		15	
3.3		3.5	

LORIAN'S ARMOR

15.3		10.7	
14.1		13.3	
9.3		67	
13.6		41	
13.3		61	
13.1		50	
10.7		11.0	

LORIAN'S GAUNTLETS

3.2		1.5	
3.0		2.9	
1.9		16	
2.9		7	
2.9		11	
2.7		10	
1.5		1.8	

LORIAN'S LEGGINGS

7.0		4.7	
7.7		7.4	
5.6		38	
7.5		21	
7.4		27	
7.3		25	
4.7		6.0	

FOUND/DROPPED: SHRINE HANDMAID (AFTER TWIN PRINCES)

GOLDEN SET

Crown of a nameless king who was ally to the ancient dragons.

This golden crown, buried amidst long strands of bristling ash, is said to closely resemble that of the First Lord.

Dragonscale armor of a nameless king who was ally to the ancient dragons.

Dragon scales are razor-sharp and cannot be burned.

Bracelets of a nameless king who was ally to the ancient dragons.

These golden bracelets, together with the golden breastplate and crown, are said to closely resemble those of the First Lord.

GOLDEN CROWN

3.5		3.8	
3.8		4.2	
3.2		21	
3.2		29	
2.4		28	
4.2		27	
4.8		2.6	

DRAGONSCALE ARMOR

12.7		6.1	
13.9		9.9	
12.3		62	
13.2		43	
12.3		46	
9.9		28	
13.4		12.7	

GOLDEN BRACELETS

1.5		1.7	
1.5		1.7	
1.7		10	
1.3		18	
0.7		16	
1.7		13	
2.3		0.4	

DRAGONSCALE WAISTCLOTH

6.3		1.8	
6.9		4.1	
5.8		31	
6.7		21	
5.8		22	
4.1		10	
6.8		6.5	

FOUND/DROPPED: SHRINE HANDMAID (AFTER NAMELESS KING DEFEATED)

FIRELINK SET

Armor of the Soul of Cinder, a deific manifestation of the Lords of Cinder, who linked the First Flame.

It resembles a knight's armor, but bears hideous burns and contortions, taking the shape of a deathly ribcage.

It exists as a symbol of the great Lords and the noble act of linking the fire, though it is no more than an empty husk.

FIRELINK HELM

3.7		1.8	
4.7		1.4	
2.5		20	
4.6		12	
4.4		16	
2.6		8	
4.4		3.2	

FIRELINK ARMOR

8.6		5.5	
11.9		5.5	
8.0		47	
12.6		30	
10.2		43	
6.9		19	
10.7		8.9	

FIRELINK GAUNTLETS

2.6		3.1	
2.3		2.5	
2.1		16	
2.7		22	
1.9		24	
3.0		21	
3.3		1.7	

FIRELINK LEGGINGS

4.8		7.0	
5.4		5.6	
5.0		28	
6.2		40	
4.5		44	
6.0		37	
7.3		4.3	

FOUND/DROPPED: SHRINE HANDMAID (AFTER FIRST GAME COMPLETION)

BLACK IRON SET

Chest piece made of black iron, from the set of armor for which Knightslayer Tsorig was infamously known.

Offers extensive and particularly effective protection from fire.

BLACK IRON HELM

6.8		4.2	
5.1		4.6	
4.4		26	
5.6		19	
5.4		21	
4.6		13	
5.7		0.5	

BLACK IRON ARMOR

16.6		11.0	
14.5		12.0	
11.5		65	
14.5		51	
14.1		57	
12.0		35	
15.1		14.1	

BLACK IRON GAUNTLETS

5.3		2.7	
3.7		2.9	
2.8		24	
3.6		16	
3.5		20	
2.9		14	
3.7		2.7	

BLACK IRON LEGGINGS

9.9		6.6	
8.8		7.2	
6.9		42	
8.7		32	
8.5		35	
7.2		24	
8.9		8.8	

FOUND/DROPPED: SHRINE HANDMAID (AFTER DEFEATING KNIGHT SLAYER TSORIG)

EXECUTIONER SET

Steel armor of Horace the Hushed, who took a liking to its cold, bulky insides.

The original owner was said to be a corrupt executioner, who was killed and stripped of his armor.

Horace is one of only two children to escape Aldrich's clutches.

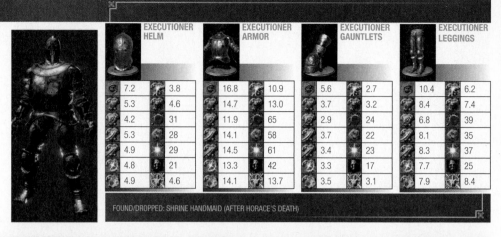

	EXECUTIONER HELM		EXECUTIONER ARMOR		EXECUTIONER GAUNTLETS		EXECUTIONER LEGGINGS	
	7.2	3.8	16.8	10.9	5.6	2.7	10.4	6.2
	5.3	4.6	14.7	13.0	3.7	3.2	8.4	7.4
	4.2	31	11.9	65	2.9	24	6.8	39
	5.3	28	14.1	58	3.7	22	8.1	35
	4.9	29	14.5	61	3.4	23	8.3	37
	4.8	21	13.3	42	3.3	17	7.7	25
	4.9	4.6	14.1	13.7	3.5	3.1	7.9	8.4

FOUND/DROPPED: SHRINE HANDMAID (AFTER HORACE'S DEATH)

EXILE SET

Armor of the watchdogs of Farron's Keep.

After the Legion's Watchers became Lords of Cinder, the wolf blood dried up, and Farron was consumed by a festering wood.

Within the wood, an emaciated old wolf commands watchdogs to defend the sanctity of sleeping warriors.

Both the exiles were surely watchdogs themselves, for Farron has always been a land of itinerants.

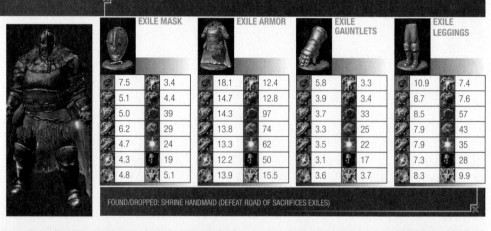

	EXILE MASK		EXILE ARMOR		EXILE GAUNTLETS		EXILE LEGGINGS	
	7.5	3.4	18.1	12.4	5.8	3.3	10.9	7.4
	5.1	4.4	14.7	12.8	3.9	3.4	8.7	7.6
	5.0	39	14.3	97	3.7	33	8.5	57
	6.2	29	13.8	74	3.3	25	7.9	43
	4.7	24	13.3	62	3.5	22	7.9	35
	4.3	19	12.2	50	3.1	17	7.3	28
	4.8	5.1	13.9	15.5	3.6	3.7	8.3	9.9

FOUND/DROPPED: SHRINE HANDMAID (DEFEAT ROAD OF SACRIFICES EXILES)

GUNDYR SET

Ancient helm of a set of cast iron armor, belonging to Champion Gundyr. Modeled after a former king.

Ancient chest piece of a set of cast iron armor, belonging to Champion Gundyr.

Gundyr, or the Belated Champion, was bested by an unknown warrior. He then became sheath to a coiled sword in the hopes that someday, the first flame would be linked once more.

	GUNDYR'S HELM		GUNDYR'S ARMOR		GUNDYR'S GAUNTLETS		GUNDYR'S LEGGINGS	
	7.6	4.3	18.0	12.8	6.1	3.3	10.3	6.9
	4.9	4.4	14.5	13.0	3.7	3.4	7.8	7.0
	4.4	35	13.0	86	3.4	29	7.0	48
	6.2	25	17.1	62	4.3	21	9.3	36
	4.6	25	13.7	62	3.5	21	7.4	36
	4.4	25	13.0	62	3.4	21	7.0	36
	4.5	5.2	13.5	16.3	3.5	3.9	7.2	9.5

FOUND/DROPPED: SHRINE HANDMAID (AFTER CHAMPION GUNDYR)

HAVEL SET

Armor as if hewn from a giant boulder. Highly protective, but excessively heavy.

The warriors who followed Havel the Rock never flinched, nor retreated from battle, crushing any foe that stood in their way.

	HAVEL'S HELM		HAVEL'S ARMOR		HAVEL'S GAUNTLETS		HAVEL'S LEGGINGS	
	11.2	4.6	22.4	12.8	9.4	3.2	15.9	7.3
	5.8	5.0	16.2	14.1	4.0	3.5	9.3	8.1
	5.2	31	14.5	72	3.6	24	8.3	45
	5.5	30	15.4	69	3.8	23	8.9	43
	5.2	30	14.5	69	3.6	23	8.3	43
	5.0	26	14.1	61	3.5	20	8.1	38
	5.9	5.8	16.3	17.0	4.1	3.9	9.4	10.5

FOUND/DROPPED: FARRON KEEP (BEHIND STRAY DEMON AFTER DEFEATING HAVEL IN ARCHDRAGON PEAK)

ASSASSIN SET

	ASSASSIN HOOD		ASSASSIN ARMOR		ASSASSIN GLOVES		ASSASSIN TROUSERS	
	1.5	3.3	6.9	10.4	2.0	1.9	4.3	5.2
	2.1	2.5	8.3	9.0	1.9	1.5	5.2	4.3
	3.0	17	9.7	40	1.2	12	3.8	29
	1.6	27	8.8	62	2.5	20	6.2	43
	2.5	20	9.0	47	1.7	13	4.8	32
	3.3	20	10.4	52	2.6	16	6.6	38
	4.3	1.7	11.4	5.6	2.7	0.6	6.9	3.0

FOUND/DROPPED: GREIRAT

Black cloth covering the face of the assassins who lurk in the shadows.

Grants much-needed protection to the head as well as cover from rain while pursuing a target on the road.

Soft leather armor worn by assassins who lurk in the shadows.

The thick leather offers reasonable absorption without creating any undesired noise. A well-crafted piece of protection.

Critical spots are reinforced with metal.

BLACK HAND SET

	BLACK HAND HAT		BLACK HAND ARMOR	
	2.5	3.3	7.8	10.4
	2.7	2.7	9.0	9.0
	2.2	19	8.2	46
	3.6	30	11.4	67
	3.0	21	9.7	51
	4.2	25	12.6	58
	4.4	1.4	12.8	6.3

FOUND/DROPPED: SHRINE HANDMAID (AFTER LOOTING GOTTHARD'S CORPSE IN GRAND ARCHIVES)

Attire of hunters known as the King's Black Hands. A black cape covers leather armor, shrouding the wearer in darkness.

Black Hand was a title established to honor hunters who served successive generations of kings. To date, no more than three such individuals have borne this distinction.

BLACK LEATHER SET

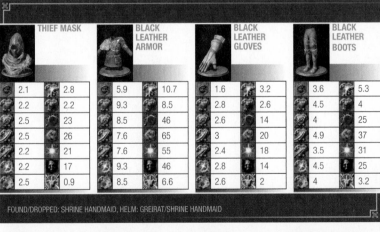

	THIEF MASK		BLACK LEATHER ARMOR		BLACK LEATHER GLOVES		BLACK LEATHER BOOTS	
	2.1	2.8	5.9	10.7	1.6	3.2	3.6	5.3
	2.2	2.2	9.3	8.5	2.8	2.6	4.5	4
	2.5	23	8.5	46	2.6	14	4	25
	2.5	26	7.6	65	3	20	4.9	37
	2.2	21	7.6	55	2.4	18	3.5	31
	2.2	17	9.3	46	2.8	14	4.5	25
	2.5	0.9	8.5	6.6	2.6	2	4	3.2

FOUND/DROPPED: SHRINE HANDMAID, HELM: GREIRAT/SHRINE HANDMAID

Mask worn by those with something to hide. Used to conceal the face, muffle the voice, and go by cover of darkness.

Black dyed leather armor. Enables its wearer to hide in the shadows with silent finesse.

The wearer of this fine attire was admired by friends and enemies alike, for his skills were unmatched, and his heart was true as gold. As its new owner, you have quite the shoes to fill.

SHADOW SET

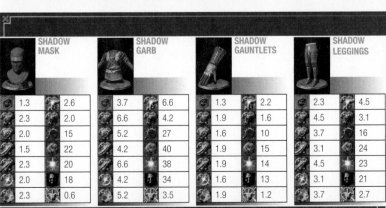

	SHADOW MASK		SHADOW GARB		SHADOW GAUNTLETS		SHADOW LEGGINGS	
	1.3	2.6	3.7	6.6	1.3	2.2	2.3	4.5
	2.3	2.0	6.6	4.2	1.9	1.6	4.5	3.1
	2.0	15	5.2	27	1.6	10	3.7	16
	1.5	22	4.2	40	1.9	15	3.1	24
	2.3	20	6.6	38	1.9	14	4.5	23
	2.0	18	4.2	34	1.6	13	3.1	21
	2.3	0.6	5.2	3.5	1.9	1.2	3.7	2.7

FOUND/DROPPED: CONSUMED KING'S GARDEN

Black cloth garb worn by spooks from an Eastern land. Sacrifices defense for greater mobility.

The late King Oceiros was obsessed by dragons, to the extent that he would later be known as the Consumed King. Countless assassins were sent to end his reign, but none returned.

LEONHARD SET

Silver mask of Ringfinger Leonhard.

In his youth, Leonhard suffered grave burns to his entire body. His face in particular, which he hid beneath his mask, was terribly scalded.

He abstained from restoring these injuries, even after becoming a Finger of Rosaria.

Garb of Ringfinger Leonhard.

Leonhard was born into royalty, which is believed to be the reason for his skill in both sorcery and swordsmanship.

Indeed, this dingy garb is in fact embroidered with gold thread, betraying its purpose as military wear designed for a noble.

	SILVER MASK		LEONHARD'S GARB		LEONHARD'S GAUNTLETS		LEONHARD'S TROUSERS	
	3.3	3.1	6.9	10.0	2.6	3.0	3.6	4.5
	3.1	2.6	10.0	8.5	2.8	2.6	4.0	3.5
	3.7	19	10.0	41	3.2	12	4.9	21
	3.6	27	8.8	55	2.5	18	4.5	28
	3.1	28	10.0	62	2.8	18	4.5	34
	3.3	27	12.4	55	3.6	18	6.0	28
	4.0	2.1	12.9	7.3	3.6	2.1	6.3	3.2

FOUND/DROPPED: SHRINE HANDMAID (AFTER DEFEATING LEONHARD, HELM: DEFEAT LEONHARD)

PALE SHADE SET

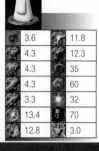

Gold mask worn by those who kill in the name of the Sable Church of Londor.

A faint, kindly smile is bound to its surface, giving them the moniker Harlots of Death.

What lies beneath that expression, however, is nothing more than the face of a darkly shriveled Hollow.

Attire worn by those who kill in the name of the Sable Church of Londor.

The Pale Shades of the Sable Church are all undying Hollows, giving rise to much fear and contempt.

Their fight is one of neither honor nor exaltation, yielding nothing but withered moans.

	SNEERING MASK		PALE SHADE ROBE		PALE SHADE GLOVES		PALE SHADE TROUSERS	
	2.1	2.4	3.6	11.8	1.0	3.1	2.2	6.1
	1.2	1.6	4.3	12.3	1.2	3.2	1.8	6.4
	1.6	35	4.3	35	1.2	9	1.8	20
	1.2	28	4.3	60	1.2	17	1.8	35
	1.0	22	3.3	32	1.1	8	1.2	18
	3.6	20	13.4	70	3.6	21	7.0	44
	4.1	0.2	12.8	3.0	3.3	0.8	6.7	1.1

FOUND/DROPPED: FIRELINK SHRINE (ANGER YURIA AND DEFEAT PALE SHADE INVADER IN FARRON KEEP AND IRITHYLL VALLEY)

BLACK SET

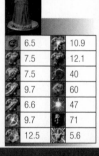

Attire of the three mentors of the Sable Church of Londor, this billed mask belongs to Yuria, the second eldest.

These maidens of a Primordial Serpent were renowned as founders of the Sable Church, which offered salvation for Hollows.

Attire of the three mentors of the Sable Church of Londor, this pitch-black dress resembles a mourning dress.

It is apparent that the women in black were highly skilled fencers, capable of founding the Sable Church between just the three of them.

	BILLED MASK		BLACK DRESS		BLACK GAUNTLETS		BLACK LEGGINGS	
	3.7	2.0	6.5	10.9	3.5	2.2	4.5	7.3
	3.7	3.7	7.5	12.1	3.4	3.4	5.5	7.8
	2.6	24	7.5	40	2.6	19	5.5	26
	4.1	16	9.7	60	3.7	13	6.7	38
	3.3	14	6.6	47	3.2	11	5.0	32
	2.6	18	9.7	71	2.6	15	6.7	46
	4.1	2.6	12.5	5.6	3.7	2.6	8.1	4.6

FOUND/DROPPED: SHRINE HANDMAID (OR FIRELINK SHRINE BY YURIA AFTER YURIA WHITE PHANTOM AIDS FINAL BATTLE)

PAINTING GUARDIAN SET

Attire of the Painting Guardians, whose forms are described in the mythology of heretics.

A smooth pale gown that deters magic.

The hunchbacked teller of ancient tales describes unwanted souls who are unwelcome across the lands, and are eventually drawn into a cold, painted world.

	PAINTING GUARDIAN HOOD		PAINTING GUARDIAN GOWN		PAINTING GUARDIAN GLOVES		PAINTING GUARDIAN WAISTCLOTH	
	1.4	2.3	3.5	5.4	1.3	1.1	4.4	2.9
	1.9	1.9	4.4	4.4	0.8	0.8	3.5	2.9
	1.5	25	3.1	59	0.5	21	2.9	42
	1.9	30	4.4	71	0.8	25	3.5	31
	1.9	15	4.4	36	0.8	13	4.8	17
	4.3	25	11.1	60	2.5	21	6.5	22
	1.9	0.6	4.4	0.8	0.8	0.2	5.3	4.8

FOUND/DROPPED: IRITHYLL OF THE BOREAL VALLEY

SORCERER SET

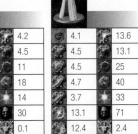

SORCERER HOOD		SORCERER ROBE		SORCERER GLOVES		SORCERER TROUSERS	
1.4	4.2	4.1	13.6	1.3	3.4	3.2	7.6
1.0	4.5	4.5	13.1	1.3	3.5	3.4	6.7
1.0	11	4.5	25	1.3	8	4.2	22
1.2	18	4.7	40	1.1	13	3.2	26
0.8	14	3.7	33	1.1	10	3.4	31
4.4	30	13.1	71	3.5	23	6.0	28
4.0	0.1	12.4	2.4	3.3	0.8	7.5	1.7

FOUND/DROPPED: ROAD OF SACRIFICES

Attire of a sorcerer from the Vinheim Dragon School. A simple hood worn inside the robes.

Represents those who have outgrown the academy, abandoning formal headwear and distancing themselves in order to continue their research in solitude.

Attire of a sorcerer from the Vinheim Dragon School. Long, ash-colored robes.

Underneath is a deep blue sorcerer's coat; conventional uniform of the academy.

CLANDESTINE SET

		CLANDESTINE COAT					
		3.0	13.1				
		4.4	13.5				
		4.4	25				
		3.9	36				
		3.9	30				
		13.5	65				
		12.9	1.6				

FOUND/DROPPED: SHRINE HANDMAID (AFTER ORBECK'S DEATH)

Traditional coat of the Vinheim Dragon School.

Normally a deep blue color, this black variation is a sign of a sorcerer engaged in surreptitious work. These were covert agents who excelled at manipulating sound.

OLD SORCERER SET

OLD SORCERER HAT		OLD SORCERER COAT		OLD SORCERER GAUNTLETS		OLD SORCERER BOOTS	
1.2	4.7	3.7	12.3	1.3	2.8	2.1	7.5
1.5	4.8	3.6	12.5	0.6	2.9	2.5	7.6
1.5	9	3.6	27	0.6	10	2.5	15
1.5	16	3.6	45	0.6	16	2.5	26
1.3	12	3.1	35	0.5	12	2.2	20
4.8	28	12.5	70	2.9	24	7.6	42
4.5	0.6	12.1	1.5	2.8	0.1	7.4	1.4

FOUND/DROPPED: IRITHYLL DUNGEON

Traditional attire worn by sorcerers of the Vinheim Dragon School.

Long ago, sorcerers were said to always dress properly, even while on distant journeys of discovery, even before such journeys were established curriculum.

COURT SORCERER SET

COURT SORCERER HOOD		COURT SORCERER ROBE		COURT SORCERER GLOVES		COURT SORCERER TROUSERS	
1.5	4.4	4.2	13.0	1.0	3.5	2.2	7.9
	4.3	3.6	13.0	1.1	3.5	2.2	7.7
	13	4.4	26	1.1	6	2.5	18
	21	3.9	46	0.8	12	1.9	29
	16	3.1	32	0.1	8	1.9	23
	33	12.3	74	3.2	21	7.4	47
3.7	0.3	11.6	2.3	3.0	0.5	6.8	1.4

FOUND/DROPPED: PROFANED CAPITAL

Robe worn by court sorcerers of the Profaned Capital.

The formal gold stitching suggests they may have also been oracles.

There are many sorcerers who claim heirship to the great sage "Big Hat" Logan, and the Profaned Capital houses one of two leading schools.

KARLA SET

Hat of the dark witch Karla.

A pointed hat is the signature of a heretical sorceress. Karla, however, always kept it close.

Coat of the dark witch Karla.

This stained coat is torn and odorous, telling of a long journey and even longer imprisonment.

It would be madness to wear such a thing.

	KARLA'S POINTED HAT		KARLA'S COAT		KARLA'S GLOVES		KARLA'S TROUSERS	
	1.5	4.9	3.6	13.8	1.2	3.4	2.6	8.1
	1.6	4.9	3.9	13.8	0.8	3.4	2.6	8.1
	1.4	9	3.9	20	0.9	7	2.6	14
	1.4	15	3.9	35	0.9	12	2.6	23
	1.2	13	2.9	31	0.9	10	1.9	21
	5.0	23	14.1	53	3.5	18	8.3	36
	4.7	0.6	13.3	1.8	3.3	0.4	7.7	1.5

FOUND/DROPPED: SHRINE HANDMAID (AFTER SAVING OR KILLING KARLA)

DUSK SET

Feathered crown bestowed upon the princess of Oolacile, land of ancient golden sorceries.

Through the guardian Elizabeth's blessing, this raises the power and effect of the wearer's magic, but damage suffered by magic attacks rises in tandem.

Dress sewn in a long-lost fashion. The elaborately embroidered, ivory-colored silk is imbued with ancient magic power.

No protection is offered by this garment, as it was never intended for battle.

Helm: Magic damage inflicted by spells x1.09
Magic damage inflicted by other sources x1.05
Magic damage absorption x0.7

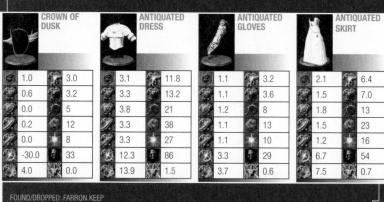

	CROWN OF DUSK		ANTIQUATED DRESS		ANTIQUATED GLOVES		ANTIQUATED SKIRT	
	1.0	3.0	3.1	11.8	1.1	3.2	2.1	6.4
	0.6	3.2	3.3	13.2	1.1	3.6	1.5	7.0
	0.0	5	3.8	21	1.2	8	1.8	13
	0.2	12	3.3	38	1.1	13	1.5	23
	0.0	8	3.3	27	1.1	10	1.2	16
	-30.0	33	12.3	86	3.3	29	6.7	54
	4.0	0.0	13.9	1.5	3.7	0.6	7.5	0.7

FOUND/DROPPED: FARRON KEEP

XANTHOUS SET

Crown supposedly made in imitation of a divine creature of Oolacile, land of ancient, golden sorceries.

Xanthous clothing is the mark of a researcher of lost sorceries, and the oversized crown is emblematic of their work.

Such a curious pursuit is surely nothing to be ashamed of.

Yellowish overcoat covering a band of brass medallions.

Xanthous clothing is the mark of a researcher of lost sorceries, and the number of medallions denotes their success.

A point of pride for the researchers, even if its significance is lost on others.

	XANTHOUS CROWN		XANTHOUS OVERCOAT		XANTHOUS GLOVES		XANTHOUS TROUSERS	
	3.0	5.0	8.6	9.8	2.0	2.7	3.6	7.6
	2.4	4.8	9.8	11.5	1.5	2.4	4.9	6.9
	2.9	21	6.7	39	1.7	15	5.4	22
	2.5	27	10.9	46	1.4	22	3.2	35
	2.4	24	9.1	33	1.5	22	4.9	35
	4.8	27	11.5	22	2.5	18	7.2	28
	2.4	1.0	5.3	7.1	1.0	0.0	3.6	1.5

FOUND/DROPPED: SHRINE HANDMAID, HELM: YELLOWFINGER HEYSEL BLACK SPIRIT OR MAN-GRUB IN ROSARIA'S CHAMBER

SCHOLAR SET

Skin shed from a sage of the Grand Archives. The ivory wax has hardened, forming a mask.

Wax protected the inquirer from exposure to the foulness that permeated the majority of the texts, preventing one's anchor of reason from being too easily washed away.

Robe of a sage from the Grand Archives, stained quite deliberately with wax.

The scholars of the Grand Archives, sorcerers by craft, tend to their candles with a reverence that exceeds the simple burden of labor. They know dangers of the Archives' store of knowledge all too well.

	SCHOLAR'S SHED SKIN		SCHOLAR'S ROBE					
	1.8	4.8	4.2	12.8				
	4.2	4.8	6.9	12.6				
	1.1	15	2.7	36				
	1.4	17	4.7	43				
	4.0	18	5.5	39				
	5.0	32	13.3	71				
	1.6	2.4	11.2	5.1				

FOUND/DROPPED: GRAND ARCHIVES SCHOLAR

SAGE'S BIG HAT

1.7		4.6	
2.5		4.6	
2.0		15	
2.0		21	
1.6		13	
5.2		26	
3.6		0.6	

Enormous hat that completely obscures the face. Belonged to twin gurus known as the Crystal Sages.

The pair are said to be successors to the great sage Logan, and this big hat is a symbol of their pedigree.

FOUND/DROPPED: SHRINE HANDMAID (AFTER CRYSTAL SAGE)

PYROMANCER CROWN

1.1	3.6
0.5	4.0
0.5	9
0.9	14
0.5	15
4.2	21
4.8	0.0

PYROMANCER GARB

4.2	12.0
4.3	14.1
3.5	22
3.9	50
3.5	43
12.0	74
13.1	1.4

PYROMANCER WRAP

1.5	3.5
1.5	3.6
1.5	6
0.9	14
1.3	11
3.5	22
3.6	1.0

PYROMANCER TROUSERS

2.6	7.5
3.0	7.8
2.6	14
2.2	43
2.6	26
7.5	47
8.1	1.5

Attire of pyromancers of the Great Swamp. Comprised of a leather crown and animal bones.

In the Great Swamp, it was thought that adorning oneself with natural fauna would provide protection from the flames of pyromancy.

Attire of pyromancers of the Great Swamp. Comprised of bronze ornamentation and animal pelt.

In the Great Swamp, bronze was used ritualistically to ward off evil spirits and keep darkness at bay.

FOUND/DROPPED: CORNYX OF THE GREAT SWAMP

OLD SAGE'S BLINDFOLD

1.0	3.8
0.7	4.2
0.7	10
0.9	14
0.7	11
4.0	28
4.4	0.0

CORNYX'S GARB

4.1	12.8
4.1	13.2
4.1	22
4.7	40
3.6	30
13.0	88
13.7	7.0

CORNYX'S WRAP

1.3	3.3
1.0	3.4
1.0	7
0.9	13
0.9	11
3.6	26
3.4	1.0

CORNYX'S SKIRT

2.0	6.6
1.7	7.0
1.7	15
1.9	24
1.4	18
6.9	48
7.1	3.0

Attire of pyromancers of the Great Swamp, particularly favored by old sages.

The large blindfold blocks out unnecessary light, allowing one to observe a pyromancy's true essence.

The flame reveals all, and obscures all.

Attire of Cornyx, pyromancer of the Great Swamp.

In the Great Swamp, it was customary to adorn oneself with articles of nature. Cornyx favored the use of raven feathers.

Ravens are said to have once been Firelink messengers, guiding the undead to the land of ancient gods.

FOUND/DROPPED: CORNYX OF THE GREAT SWAMP, UNDEAD SETTLEMENT (AFTER WHITE PHANTOM CUCULUS AIDS AGAINST OLD DEMON KING BOSS)

CONJURATOR HOOD

1.8	5.0
1.6	4.6
1.6	13
1.6	27
1.4	19
4.4	26
5.1	0.8

CONJURATOR ROBE

4.2	13.3
3.7	12.2
3.7	31
3.7	63
3.2	44
11.7	61
13.6	1.6

CONJURATOR MANCHETTES

1.4	3.1
0.7	2.9
0.7	10
0.7	21
0.6	15
2.7	20
3.2	0.2

CONJURATOR BOOTS

2.6	7.9
2.4	7.3
2.4	19
2.4	39
2.1	27
7.0	38
8.1	1.3

Attire of traveling conjurators.

Conjurators were the predecessors to pyromancers, and spent their lives roaming the lands. No wonder their attire was designed to protect them from fire, poison, and other threats of nature.

FOUND/DROPPED: ROAD OF SACRIFICES

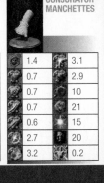

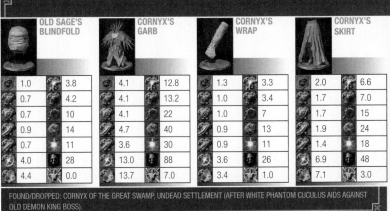

CLERIC SERIES

Hat worn by a cleric turned undead. Typical attire for blue-robed travelers.

It is said that they were entrusted with a duty, still its nature is yet to be revealed.

Garb worn by a cleric turned undead. Unmistakable vibrant blue robes.

It is said that the blue-robed travelers were entrusted with a duty. They bore large covers on their backs to ensure that they would not become seedbeds for spreading darkness.

CLERIC HAT		CLERIC BLUE ROBE		CLERIC GLOVES		CLERIC TROUSERS	
1.4	4.9	6.0	13.2	1.5	2.8	2.1	6.8
2.0	5.0	5.1	13.2	1.0	2.9	2.2	7.0
1.6	18	7.5	45	0.5	17	1.5	26
1.2	25	5.7	61	0.9	21	1.9	36
1.8	12	4.3	49	0.7	11	1.8	18
5.0	29	12.8	68	2.8	25	6.9	42
3.8	1.0	12.3	2.2	2.1	0.4	5.0	0.7

FOUND/DROPPED: UNDEAD SETTLEMENT

MAIDEN SET

White robe worn by traveling maidens. Part of their formal attire, regardless of rank.

It is soft and well-made, but ill-suited for use in battle.

MAIDEN HOOD		MAIDEN ROBE		MAIDEN GLOVES		MAIDEN SKIRT	
1.4	4.4	3.5	13.0	1.3	3.4	2.3	7.1
1.0	4.6	3.6	13.7	1.0	3.5	1.7	7.5
1.2	8	4.1	19	1.1	8	2.0	13
0.1	16	3.6	38	1.0	14	1.7	25
0.8	12	3.1	30	0.9	11	1.4	20
4.6	31	13.7	75	3.5	26	7.5	48
4.3	0.0	12.8	0.8	3.3	0.3	7.0	0.2

FOUND/DROPPED: CATHEDRAL OF THE DEEP

EVANGELIST SET

Robe of an evangelist sent from the cathedral.

These teachers, all women, came to enlighten inhabitants of the Undead Settlement and sent carriers on the path of sacrifice.

Helm: Giant Sniper will not target you while wearing the Evangelist Hat

EVANGELIST HAT		EVANGELIST ROBE		EVANGELIST GLOVES		EVANGELIST TROUSERS	
3.5	4.8	12.2	9.9	2.4	2.8	4.9	7.5
3.7	3.1	12.8	6.8	1.8	1.4	5.7	4.8
4.5	15	12.3	49	2.5	13	7.1	22
3.4	27	12.3	42	1.6	22	5.3	39
3.1	24	11.6	38	1.4	19	4.8	35
4.3	25	10.6	35	2.4	21	6.8	37
4.8	2.5	12.3	10.0	2.8	1.0	7.5	4.4

FOUND/DROPPED: CATHEDRAL EVANGELIST

DEACON SET

Robe worn by deacons of the Cathedral of the Deep. The deep red pigment denotes the blessing of fire.

In time, those dedicated to sealing away the horrors of the Deep succumbed to their very power. It seems that neither tending to the flame, nor the faith, could save them.

DEACON ROBE		DEACON SKIRT	
3.5	11.8	2.3	7.1
3.6	13.2	2.5	8.0
3.6	19	2.5	13
	40	2.6	26
	33	2.5	22
12.5	79	7.6	50
12.7	1.5	7.7	1.4

FOUND/DROPPED: DEACON OF THE DEEP

ARCHDEACON WHITE CROWN

	1.8		5.0
	1.8		5.4
	2.9		11
	1.6		19
	2.0		19
	5.0		38
	4.6		2.1

ARCHDEACON HOLY GARB

	4.2		12.4
	3.5		13.7
	6.7		18
	4.7		39
	4.3		37
	12.4		83
	11.5		4.9

ARCHDEACON SKIRT

	2.6		7.7
	2.6		8.5
	4.4		14
	2.6		27
	3.0		26
	7.7		55
	7.2		3.6

FOUND/DROPPED: CATHEDRAL OF THE DEEP (AFTER BOSS FIGHT ON GROUND)

Holy garb worn by an Archdeacon of the Cathedral of the Deep.

A sign of the Way of White's highest rank.

Of the three Archdeacons of the Deep, one stood over Aldrich's casket, with hope that he would return one day.

ARISTOCRAT'S MASK

	5.9		2.1
	5.5		3.6
	2.5		25
	5.2		17
	5.1		17
	3.9		28
	4.1		4.6

JAILER ROBE

	4.8		11.4
	8.5		13.5
	4.4		24
	8.5		37
	6.2		32
	13.5		87
	13.1		3.1

JAILER GLOVES

	1.6		2.2
	1.4		2.7
	0.4		10
	1.4		15
	0.9		13
	2.7		32
	2.6		0.1

JAILER TROUSERS

	2.8		5.7
	4.0		6.9
	1.7		12
	4.0		22
	2.7		19
	6.9		53
	6.7		1.0

FOUND/DROPPED: JAILERS

Robe worn by jailers of Irithyll Dungeon. Originally ritualistic formal wear.

The jailers were among the few survivors inhabiting the Profaned Capital, later serving under Pontiff Sulyvahn.

Perhaps the screams emanating from the cells help them forget their old home.

HOOD OF PRAYER

	1.5		3.7
	0.5		4.4
	0.5		8
	0.5		28
	1.0		13
	3.9		40
	3.5		0.2

ROBE OF PRAYER

	3.4		13.1
	3.9		14.6
	3.4		13
	3.4		61
	3.4		24
	13.5		89
	13.1		1.6

SKIRT OF PRAYER

	2.4		6.7
	1.4		7.6
	1.7		14
	1.9		39
	1.1		18
	6.9		58
	6.7		0.1

FOUND/DROPPED: LOTHRIC CASTLE

Prince Lothric's robe.

The prince, destined to be a Lord of Cinder, was cherished by the royal family, despite being born into illness, a frail and shriveled child.

His swaddling clothes were made of aged, coarse cloth used in ancient prayer, and are all that he has ever worn.

FIRE KEEPER ROBE

	5.1		8.8
	5.7		12.4
	7.1		36
	7.1		54
	8.0		49
	7.1		42
	11.9		2.6

FIRE KEEPER GLOVES

	1.3		2.9
	0.8		3.6
	0.9		9
	1.1		15
	0.7		11
	3.1		23
	3.3		0.2

FIRE KEEPER SKIRT

	2.1		6.8
	1.9		8.3
	2.6		13
	1.9		24
	1.9		18
	7.1		40
	7.6		0.6

FOUND/DROPPED: CEMETARY OF ASH

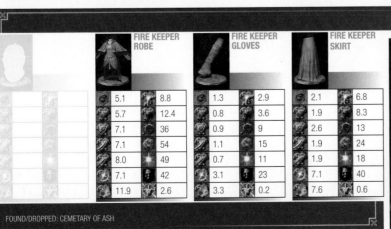

Robe worn by the guardian of the shrine.

The Fire Keepers were robbed of light, to better serve as vessels for souls.

Only those who cherish the writhing, searing darkness were given the keepers' black attire.

RAGGED SET

Rag that covers the wearer's mouth.

Likely a makeshift item that helped reduce intake of various poisonous and noxious fumes.

A terribly worn shirt.

Men are fond of weaving tales to explain the raggedness of their garb.

"My sixth sense warned me of danger, and I danced between flurries of blades, unscathed, but alas, my clothes went to tatters."

	RAGGED MASK		MASTER'S ATTIRE		MASTER'S GLOVES		LOINCLOTH	
	0.7	3.5	2.0	8.4	0.3	1.7	1.1	5.4
	1.2	3.8	2.5	9.1	0.3	1.9	2.0	5.8
	1.2	13	2.5	37	0.3	14	2.0	20
	1.2	25	2.5	62	0.3	22	2.0	35
	1.2	7	2.0	22	0.2	9	1.7	10
	3.8	29	9.1	74	1.9	26	5.8	43
	3.2	0.4	7.6	0.0	1.5	0.0	4.9	0.4

FOUND/DROPPED: CHEST, GLOVES: UNKINDLED OUTSIDE FIRELINK SHRINE. HELM: FARRON KEEP. LEGS: UNDEAD SETTLEMENT.

WORKER SET

Garb worn by inhabitants of the Undead Settlement.

Official attire for the dissection and burial of undead. Naturally, the ceremonial significance of such work is long forgotten.

Indeed, no one could continue to entertain such horrors.

Helm: Giant Sniper will not target you while wearing the Worker Hat

	WORKER HAT		WORKER GARB		WORKER GLOVES		WORKER TROUSERS	
	2.3	2.5	4.2	5.2	1.4	0.9	2.9	3.7
	2.1	4.5	4.2	10.9	0.6	2.3	3.1	7.0
	3.0	16	6.6	34	1.2	11	4.5	23
	2.5	31	5.2	68	0.9	22	3.7	44
	2.5	20	5.2	43	0.9	14	3.7	28
	3.0	27	6.6	60	1.2	19	4.5	39
	2.5	1.3	5.2	2.1	0.9	0.1	3.7	2.0

FOUND/DROPPED: PEASANT HOLLOW

GRAVE WARDEN SET

Rotting, tattered robe.

Attire of grave wardens at the Cathedral of the Deep.

Grave wardens were tasked with disposing of the ever rising corpses that plagued the cathedral.

Their clothes are utterly putrid, drenched in the blood and mucilage of their undertaking.

	GRAVE WARDEN HOOD		GRAVE WARDEN ROBE		GRAVE WARDEN WRAP		GRAVE WARDEN SKIRT	
	1.5	4.0	3.6	11.1	1.2	2.5	2.2	6.0
	1.6	1.4	4.1	3.6	0.7	0.6	2.0	1.7
	1.2	30	3.1	63	0.5	20	1.4	42
	2.8	28	8.0	59	1.9	18	4.5	40
	1.8	8	4.9	13	0.9	3	2.4	11
	3.3	25	9.0	51	1.9	16	4.8	35
	3.3	0.5	9.0	1.3	1.9	0.0	4.8	0.4

FOUND/DROPPED: CATHEDRAL GRAVE WARDEN

SOLDIER SET

Typical helm for a Lothric soldier. Iron-made, but half fallen apart.

It is never unwise to wear a sturdy form of head protection against arrows and other somatic threats.

Common soldier's armor. Its insignia is worn beyond recognition.

This musty, rusted hunk of metal befits one reduced to thievery.

	STEEL SOLDIER HELM		DESERTER ARMOR				DESERTER TROUSERS	
	4.6	2.0	8.6	4.2			3.1	5.9
	4.1	3.7	11.4	10.4			4.5	7.0
	3.3	27	9.0	50			5.0	21
	4.5	18	11.9	33			4.0	34
	3.9	18	10.9	36			4.5	28
	2.6	13	6.6	22			5.0	25
	2.9	2.8	7.5	8.6			5.0	2.7

FOUND/DROPPED: HOLLOW SOLDIER

THRALL HOOD

1.5	4.0		
2.0	4.2		
1.4	17		
1.6	28		
1.2	19		
4.2	38		
3.8	1.0		

FOUND/DROPPED: HOLLOW SLAVE

Hood used to cover the head of lesser folk who were set to work as slaves throughout Lothric.

Also occasionally used to shame and humiliate criminals.

WOLNIR'S CROWN

3.4	4.5		
3.1	4.9		
3.1	18		
3.1	29		
2.8	27		
3.9	37		
4.3	2.3		

FOUND/DROPPED: SHRINE HANDMAID

Crown of Wolnir, the Carthus conqueror.

Once upon a time, such things were bequeathed judiciously to each of the rightful lords, until Wolnir brought them to their knees, and ground their crowns to dust. Then the crowns became one, and Wolnir, the one High Lord.

SYMBOL OF AVARICE

11.0	4.8		
4.8	3.8		
4.6	27		
4.3	27		
4.1	27		
4.1	22		
3.4	5.0		

FOUND/DROPPED: AVARICIOUS BEING/MIMIC

Head of the avaricious creature that mimics treasure chests. Can be worn, if one so wishes.

Increases soul absorption from defeated enemies as well as item discovery, but the curse of the branded also drains HP.

The very form of this creature is thought to be a form of brand, a punishment for sin.

Helm: Receive x1.5 souls when defeating enemies, Item drop rate doubled, Lose 10 HP per second

DRAGON HEAD / DRAGON BODY / DRAGON ARMS / DRAGON LEGS

DRAGON HEAD		DRAGON BODY		DRAGON ARMS		DRAGON LEGS	
0.0	4.0	0.0	11.0	0.0	5.0	0.0	7.0
4.0	4.0	11.0	11.0	5.0	5.0	7.0	7.0
4.0	9	11.0	23	5.0	8	7.0	14
4.0	6	11.0	16	5.0	5	7.0	9
4.0	0	11.0	0	5.0	0	7.0	0
4.0	20	11.0	20	5.0	20	7.0	20
4.0	0.0	11.0	0.0	5.0	0.0	7.0	0.0

FOUND/DROPPED: IRITHYLL DUNGEON, ARCHDRAGON PEAK, FARRON KEEP

This special "armor" is worn by activating the Dragon Head and Dragon Torso stone items in your inventory. You must NOT be wearing armor for this to take effect.

RINGS

Rings are powerfully enchanted items that grant unique abilities. Many rings provide benefits that you cannot find on any other type of equipment or spell, and quite a few rings are incredibly useful for specific builds. By and large, the uses for most rings are pretty straightforward and obvious (Using Sorcery heavily? Equip good Sorcery boosting rings), the trick is figuring out which ones to equip as your collection grows. You can only use four, so choose wisely! The +1/2 versions of some rings are straight numeric upgrades to the earlier version (that is, a resistance ring gains more resistance, a carrying capacity ring lets you carry more, and so on). All of the upgraded rings can only be found out in the world in New Game Plus, as you go on to Journey 2, 3, and beyond.

ALDRITCH'S RUBY

Recovers HP from critical attacks

A malformed ring left by Aldrich, Saint of the Deep. Recovers HP from critical attacks.
Aldrich, infamous for his appetite for flesh, apparently had the desire to share with others his joy of imbibing the final shudders of life while luxuriating in his victim's screams.

Effect: Recover 85 HP when performing critical attacks

Acquired: Anor Londo

ASHEN ESTUS RING

Increases FP restored with Ashen Estus Flask

Gray crystalline ring crafted from shards. Increases FP restored by Ashen Estus Flask.
Once a treasure brought before Lothric's Queen, she had it enshrined in the Cemetery of Untended Graves, so that one day an Unkindled might profit from its use.

Effect: Increases FP restored by Ashen Estus Flask

Acquired: Untended Graves

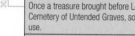

BLOODBITE RING (+1)

Increases bleed resistance

One of the bite rings native to Carim. Increases bleed resistance.
The crafting of these rings is forbidden, perhaps owing to a fear of malleable stone. Clerics, however, dabble freely in the art.

Effect: Bleed resistance +90
    +1 Bleed resistance +140

Acquired: Undead Settlement, +1 Smouldering Lake (NG+1)

CALAMITY RING

Receive double damage

A ring made from the orange eye of a calamitous dragon. Receive double damage.
This ring has no useful powers, and is merely a symbol of dragon worship, a thing quietly passed down amongst its most fervent adherents, some of whom become convinced the task has been bestowed upon them as a sacred duty.

Effect: Receive double damage

Acquired: Archdragon Peak

CARTHUS MILKRING

Slightly boosts dexterity and obscures rolling

Ring worn by warriors of the sand kingdom, Carthus. Slightly boosts dexterity and obscures the wearer while rolling.
The sword technique of Carthus allows for fluid movement with a curved sword. Masters of the technique are said to dazzle their opponents by moving as weightlessly as a grain of sand.
They live for their High Lord Wolnir, conqueror of most kingdoms known to their people.

Effect: Dexterity +3, disappear while rolling

Acquired: Catacombs of Carthus

ALDRITCH'S SAPPHIRE

Recovers FP from critical attacks

A malformed ring left by Aldrich, Saint of the Deep. Recovers FP from critical attacks.
Aldrich, infamous for his appetite for flesh, apparently had the desire to share with others his joy of imbibing the final shudders of life while luxuriating in his victim's screams.

Effect: Recover 15 FP when performing critical attacks

Acquired: Cathedral of the Deep

BELLOWING DRAGONCREST RING

Greatly boosts sorceries

A special ring given to those who are deemed fit to undertake the journey of discovery in Vinheim, home of sorcery.
Greatly boosts sorceries.
Apropos to the Dragon School, the seal depicts an everlasting dragon. A bellowing dragon symbolizes the true nature of the consummate sorcerer.

Effect: Sorcery damage +20%

Acquired: Irithyll Dungeon

BLUE TEARSTONE RING

Increases defense when HP is low

A ring set with a large rare tearstone jewel. Temporarily boosts damage absorption when HP is low.
This stone is said to be a tear of sorrow of the goddess Caitha, and of course, tears are always more beautiful near death.

Effect: Incoming damage x0.8 when HP is at 20% or lower

Acquired: Greirat

CARTHUS BLOODRING

Boosts rolling invincibility, at the cost of defense

Ring worn by warriors of the sand kingdom, Carthus. Boosts rolling invincibility, at the cost of defense.
The sword technique of Carthus allows for fluid movement with a curved sword. Masters of the technique are said to dazzle their opponents by moving as weightlessly as a grain of sand.
They live for their High Lord Wolnir, conqueror of most kingdoms known to their people.

Effect: Increases incoming damage, but extends invincibility frames during rolls

Acquired: Catacombs of Carthus

CHLORANTHY RING (+1) (+2)

Raises stamina recovery speed

This old ring is named for its decorative green blossom, but its luster is long since faded.
Raises stamina recovery speed.

Effect: Stamina recovery +7
    +1 Stamina recovery +8
    +2 Stamina recovery +9

Acquired: Undead Settlement, +1 Irithyll of the Boreal Valley (NG+1),
    +2 Road of Sacrifices (NG+2)

COVETOUS GOLD SERPENT RING (+1) (+2)

Fallen foes are more likely to drop items

A gold ring depicting a snake that could have been, but never was, a dragon.
Fallen foes are more likely to drop items.
Snakes are known as creatures of great avarice, devouring prey even larger than themselves by swallowing them whole.
If one's shackles are cause for discontent, perhaps it is time for some old-fashioned greed.

Effect: Boosts drop rate to 150%
  +1 Boosts drop rate to 175%
  +2 Boosts drop rate to 200%

Acquired: Profaned Capital, +1 Irithyll of the Boreal Valley (NG+1),
  Archdragon Peak (NG+2)

COVETOUS SILVER SERPENT RING (+1) (+2)

Fallen foes yield more souls

A silver ring depicting a snake that could have been, but never was, a dragon.
Fallen foes yield more souls.
Snakes are known as creatures of great avarice, devouring prey even larger than themselves by swallowing them whole.
If one's shackles are cause for discontent, perhaps it is time for some old-fashioned greed.

Effect: Increases amount of souls received after defeating enemies to 110%
  +1 Increases amount of souls received after defeating enemies to 120%
  +2 Increases amount of souls received after defeating enemies to 130%

Acquired: Firelink Shrine +1 Profaned Capital (NG+1),
  +2 Undead Settlement (NG+2)

CURSEBITE RING

Increases curse resistance

One of the bite rings native to Carim. Increases curse resistance.
The crafting of these rings is forbidden, perhaps owing to a fear of malleable stone. Clerics, however, dabble freely in the art.

Effect: Curse resistance +150

Acquired: Profaned Capital

DARK CLUTCH RING

Increases dark attack but reduces defense

Ring depicting a hand grasping a purple stone. Increases dark attack, but compromises damage absorption.
An old fable in Londor claims that the lure of the clutch ring reaches out to the crestfallen, who might otherwise be overcome by despair.

Effect: Dark attack x1.15, incoming physical damage x1.1

Acquired: Irithyll Dungeon

DARK STONEPLATE RING (+1) (+2)

Increases dark defense

Stoneplates are symbols of true knights, and dark purple stoneplates are granted to Undead knights.
Increases dark damage absorption.

Effect: Incoming dark damage x0.87
  +1 Incoming dark damage x0.83
  +2 Incoming dark damage x0.8

Acquired: Irithyll of the Boreal Valley, +1 Lothric Castle (NG+1),
  +2 Farron Keep (NG+2)

DARKMOON RING

Adds many slots for attunement

Ring of the moon deity Gwyndolin, youngest son of Gwyn, the First Lord.
Adds many slots for attunement.
Gwyndolin, also known as the Dark Sun, commands the Darkmoon Knights, and bestows this ring upon the best of them.

Effect: Increases FP restored by Ashen Estus Flask

Acquired: Blade of the Darkmoon reward

DEEP RING

Allows attunement of additional spells

A ring bestowed upon the Deacons of the Cathedral of the Deep. Allows attunement of additional spells.
In the Cathedral slumber things most terrible, and as such, the deacons require a grand narrative, to ensure they do not falter in their duty.
A philosophy, to ward away the madness beckoned by the grotesqueries at hand.

Effect: Attunement slots +1

Acquired: Cathedral of the Deep

DRAGONSCALE RING

Reduces damage from backstabs

Ring of Oceiros, former king of Lothric. Reduces damage from backstabs.
In his later years, Oceiros became fascinated with dragons. After going mad, he was more commonly known as the Consumed King. Many assassins were dispatched to his domain, but none returned.
The Consumed King ascribed his resilience to the divine protection of the dragon scale.

Effect: Incoming damage from backstabs x0.7

Acquired: Consumed King's Garden

DUSK CROWN RING

Reduces consumption of FP, but also lowers HP

Leaf-colored crown ring bestowed upon the princess of Oolacile, ancient land of golden sorceries.
Reduces consumption of FP, but also lowers HP.
Oolacile is synonymous for its lost sorceries, of which the xanthous sorcerers are dedicated scholars. This crown ring is a rare artifact of great magic heritage.

Effect: FP consumption of sorceries/pyromancies/miracles x0.75, but maximum HP x0.8

Acquired: Irithyll Dungeon

ESTUS RING

Increases HP restored with Estus Flask

A green ring crafted from shards. Increases HP restored by Estus Flask.
This ring was entrusted to a certain Fire Keeper, but in the end she never met her champion, and the ensuing tragic farce became a favorite tale of the masses.

Effect: Increases HP restored by Estus Flask

Acquired: Cemetery of Ash

FARRON RING

Reduces Skill FP consumption

A ring given to Undead Legion of Farron. Reduces Skill FP consumption.
The Abyss Watchers, for their hunting, required a sword technique that went beyond any existing art. Wolf's blood provided just that, and this ring further extends the effect.

Effect: Skill FP consumption x0.7

Acquired: Hawkwood the Deserter

FIRE CLUTCH RING

Increases fire attack but reduces defense

Ring depicting a hand grasping a red stone. Increases fire attack, but compromises damage absorption.
An old fable in Londor claims that the lure of the clutch ring reaches out to the crestfallen, who might otherwise be overcome by despair.

Effect: Fire attack x1.15, incoming physical damage x1.1

Acquired: Undead Settlement

FLAME STONEPLATE RING (+1) (+2)

Increases fire defense

Stoneplates are symbols of true knights, and red stoneplates are granted to those who valiantly face Chaos.
Increases fire damage absorption.

Effect: Incoming fire damage x0.87
+1 Incoming fire damage x0.83
+2 Incoming fire damage x0.8

Acquired: Smouldering Lake, +1 Profaned Capital (NG+1),
+2 Smouldering Lake (NG+2)

FLESHBITE RING (+1)

Raises poison, bleed, curse and frost resist

One of the bite rings native to Carim. Raises poison, bleed, frost and curse resist. The crafting of these rings is forbidden, perhaps owing to a fear of malleable stone. Clerics, however, dabble freely in the art.

Effect: Poison, bleed, curse, and frost resist +40
+1 Poison, bleed, curse, and frost resist +60

Acquired: Grand Archives, +1 High Wall of Lothric (NG+1)

FLYNN'S RING

Lowering equip load increases attack

Ring of Flynn, the eulogized thief. Lowering equip load increases attack power. Flynn fought with the wind on his side, and was a hero among the weak and poor, yet even his admirers knew that it was little more than an idyllic fable.

Effect: Physical attack increased the lower equip load is, up to a maximum of x1.15

Acquired: Undead Settlement

GIANT'S CHAIN

Increases VGR, END and VIT, but take more damage

Portion of a steel chain used to restrain Gundyr. Gain vigor, endurance, and vitality, but take extra damage.
A prisoner is one who has staked everything on a belief, a proclivity most apparent in the greatest of champions.

Effect: Incoming damage +10%, Vigor +5, Endurance +5, Vitality +5

Acquired: Champion Gundyr's Soul

GREAT SWAMP RING

Boosts pyromancies

Ring said to be chiseled from the bone of a flame salamander by blighted Pyromancers living in the Great Swamp.
Boosts pyromancies.
It is believed that salamanders are the descendants of demons, born of the Chaos Flame, from which Pyromancy is also said to have originated.

Effect: Pyromancy damage +12%

Acquired: Road of Sacrifices

HAVEL'S RING (+1) (+2)

Increases maximum load

A ring for warriors keen on heavy accoutrements. Increases maximum equip load. This ring was named after Havel the Rock, the battlefield compatriot of Gwyn, the First Lord.
The art of war has been a constant since ages past, and those who would follow in Havel's footsteps are no fewer now than in his own day.

Effect: Maximum load +15%
+1 Maximum load +17%
+2 Maximum load +18%

Acquired: Stray Demon Soul, +1 Archdragon Peak (NG+1),
+2 Irithyll of the Boreal Valley (NG+2)

HAWK RING

Extends the range of bows

Ring associated with Hawkeye Gough, one of the Four Knights of Gwyn, the First Lord.
Extends the range of arrows.
In his later years, the giant Gough was blinded, but this did not prevent him from striking down a calamitous dragon with his Greatbow.

Effect: Extends the range of bows

Acquired: Undead Settlement (kill Giant or collect all White Branches and Giant dies naturally)

HORNET RING

Boosts critical attacks

Ring associated with the Lord's Blade Ciaran, one of the Four Knights of Gwyn, the First Lord.
Boosts critical attacks.
The masked Ciaran was the only woman to serve in Gwyn's Four Knights, and her curved sword granted a swift death to any and all enemies of the throne.

Effect: Critical attack motion changes, thrown attack damage x1.3

Acquired: Untended Graves

HORSEHOOF RING

Boosts kick effect

An old ring with a seal depicting a horse's hoof. Boosts kick effect.
Unbreakable Patches adored this ring and the feeling that it gave it him when he kicked his marks into the depths of treacherous traps, but suffered no shortage of ridicule from his associates for relying so heavily on the tired old trick.
But who is the sorrier? The horse who knows only to kick, or the fool who approaches the old beast without thought?

Effect: Boosts damage level of kicks / Enemies lose x1.3 stamina when guarding against your kicks

Acquired: Unbreakable Patches in Cathedral of the Deep/Firelink Shrine

HUNTER'S RING

Increases dexterity

Ring engraved with a portrait of a hunter. Increases dexterity.
The hunters serve Lothric on the fringes and in the shadows. For generations, rulers of Lothric have relied especially upon the Black Hand hunters to punish enemies in ways that the king's Three Pillars cannot.

Effect: Dexterity +5

Acquired: Grand Archives

KNIGHT SLAYER'S RING

Enemies lose more stamina when guarding attacks

Ring of the savage Tsorig, more commonly known as the Knight Slayer.
Enemies lose more stamina when guarding attacks.
Long ago, Tsorig engaged the guardians of an ancient city in a bloody confrontation, and returned with their rings as his prize, still frozen on their dismembered fingers.

Effect: Enemy stamina reduction when guarding against your attacks x1.1

Acquired: Catacombs of Carthus

KNIGHT'S RING

Increases strength

Ring engraved with a portrait of a knight. Increases strength.
In Lothric, the Knight has long been considered one of the Three Pillars of the king's rule, and were thus allowed to rear dragons.

Effect: Strength +5

Acquired: Lothric Castle

LEO RING

Strengthens thrust weapon counter attacks

Ring associated with Dragon Slayer Ornstein, one of the Four Knights of Gwyn, the First Lord.
Strengthens thrust weapon counter attacks.
Ornstein was the first knight of the sun's eldest born, and his cross spear is said to have pierced scales made of stone.

Effect: Strengthens thrust weapon counter attacks (15%)

Acquired: Irithyll of the Boreal Valley

LIFE RING (+1) (+2) (+3)

Raises maximum HP

A generations-old ring set with a small red jewel. Raises maximum HP.
Rings have unique powers, and their discovery will do much to ease a wearisome journey.

Effect: HP +7%
    +1 HP +8%
    +2 HP +9%
    +3 HP +10%

Acquired: Shrine Handmaid, Burial Gift, +1 Undead Settlement (NG+1),
    +2 Lothric Castle (NG+1), +3 Untended Graves (NG+2)

LIGHTNING CLUTCH RING

Increases lightning attack but reduces defense

Ring depicting a hand grasping a yellow stone. Increases lightning attack, but compromises damage absorption.
An old fable in Londor claims that the lure of the clutch ring reaches out to the crestfallen, who might otherwise be overcome by despair.

Effect: Lightning attack x1.15, incoming physical damage x1.1

Acquired: Archdragon Peak

LINGERING DRAGONCREST RING (+1) (+2)

Extends length of spell effect

A special ring given to those who are deemed fit to undertake the journey of discovery in Vinheim, home of sorcery.
Extends length of spell effect.
Apropos to the Dragon School, the seal depicts an everlasting dragon. A lingering dragon symbolizes the true nature of the consummate sorcerer.

Effect: Extends length of spell effects (30%)
    +1 Extends length of spell effects (35%)
    +2 Extends length of spell effects (40%)

Acquired: Farron Keep, +1 Road of Sacrifices (NG+1), +2 Grand Archives (NG+2)

LLOYD'S SHIELD RING

Boosts defense when HP is full

Ring given to knights of the Way of White. Depicts Allfather Lloyd's Shield of Caste.
Boosts damage absorption when HP is full.
Much time has passed since the worship of Lloyd was common in the Way of White. The clerics of Carim had always strongly asserted that Lloyd was a derivative fraud, and that the Allfather title was self-proclaimed.

Effect: Incoming damage x0.75 when HP is full

Acquired: Shrine Handmaid

LLOYD'S SWORD RING

Boosts attacks when HP is full

Ring given to knights of the Way of White. Depicts Allfather Lloyd's Sword of Law.
Boosts attack power when HP is full.
Much time has passed since the worship of Lloyd was common in the Way of White. The clerics of Carim had always strongly asserted that Lloyd was a derivative fraud, and that the Allfather title was self-proclaimed.

Effect: Attack power x1.1 when HP is full

Acquired: Cathedral of the Deep

MAGIC CLUTCH RING

Increases magic attack but reduces defense

Ring depicting a hand grasping a blue stone. Increases magic attack, but compromises damage absorption.
An old fable in Londor claims that the lure of the clutch ring reaches out to the crestfallen, who might otherwise be overcome by despair.

Effect: Magic attack x1.15, incoming physical damage x1.1

Acquired: Irithyll of the Boreal Valley

MAGIC STONEPLATE RING (+1) (+2)

Increases magic defense

Stoneplates are symbols of true knights, and blue stoneplates are granted to the royal palace guards.
Increases magic damage absorption.

Effect: Incoming magic damage x0.87
    +1 Incoming magic damage x0.83
    +2 Incoming magic damage x0.8

Acquired: Consumed King's Garden on Consumed King's Knight,
    +1 Farron Keep (NG+1), +2 Profaned Capital (NG+2)

MORNE'S RING

Boosts miracles

A malformed ring given to knights of Carim.
Boosts miracles.
Morne served the goddess Caitha and later became an apostle of the Archbishop.
They labored together to provide comfort to the suffering.

Effect: Miracle damage +12

Acquired: Road of Sacrifices

OBSCURING RING

Obscures wearer while far away

Ring bestowed upon the Fingers of Rosaria, invaders who seek tongues for their goddess.
Hides the presence of the wearer when far away.
It is said that Rosaria, the mother of rebirth, was robbed of her tongue by her firstborn, and has been waiting for their return ever since.

Effect: Disappear from enemy's vision after moving away from them

Acquired: Rosaria's Fingers reward

POISONBITE RING (+1)

Increases poison resistance

One of the bite rings native to Carim. Increases poison resistance.
The crafting of these rings is forbidden, perhaps owing to a fear of malleable stone. Clerics, however, dabble freely in the art.

Effect: Poison resistance +90
    +1 Poison resistance +140

Acquired: Cathedral of the Deep, +1 Undead Settlement (NG+1)

PONTIFF'S LEFT EYE

Recovers HP with successive attacks

Bewitched ring that Pontiff Sulyvahn bestowed upon his knights.
Recovers HP with successive attacks.
Knights who peer into the black orb are lured into battles of death, transformed into frenzied beasts. No wonder the Pontiff only provides these rings to those dispatched to foreign lands.

Effect: Recover 60 HP after repeatedly hitting enemies. Counter resets if you stop hitting enemies for a short period of time.

Acquired: Vordt's Soul

PONTIFF'S RIGHT EYE

Boosts attacks, as long as attacking persists

Bewitched ring that Pontiff Sulyvahn bestowed upon his knights.
Boosts attacks, as long as attacking persists.
Knights who peer into the black orb are lured into battles of death, transformed into frenzied beasts. No wonder the Pontiff only provides these rings to those dispatched to foreign lands.

Effect: Boosts attack (max. x1.15) the more you continue to hit enemies. Effect wears off if you stop hitting enemies for a short period of time.

Acquired: Irithyll of the Boreal Valley

RED TEARSTONE RING

Boosts attacks when HP is low

A ring set with a large rare tearstone jewel. Temporarily boosts attack when HP is low.
This stone is said to be a tear of mourning of the goddess Caitha, and of course, tears are always more beautiful near death.

Effect: Attack damage x1.2 when HP is at 20% or lower

Acquired: Lothric Castle

RING OF FAVOR (+1) (+2)

Increases HP, stamina, and maximum equip load

A ring symbolizing the favor of the Goddess Fina, whose "fateful beauty" is mentioned in legend.
True to the fickle nature of Fina's favor, her ring increases max HP, stamina, and maximum equip load.

Effect: Increases HP (3%), stamina (10%), and maximum equip load (8%)
    +1 Increases HP (4%), stamina (11%), and maximum equip load (9%)
    +2 Increases HP (5%), stamina (12%), and maximum equip load (10%)

Acquired: Irithyll of the Boreal Valley, +1 Irithyll of the Boreal Valley (NG+1), +2 Cathedral of the Deep (NG+2)

RING OF STEEL PROTECTION (+1) (+2)

Increases physical defense

Ring of the Knight King of ancient legend. Increases physical damage absorption.
The Knight King was said to be lined with steel on the inside, such that even the talons of mighty dragons did him little harm.

Effect: Incoming physical damage x0.9
    +1 Incoming physical damage x0.87
    +2 Incoming physical damage x0.85

Acquired: Archdragon Peak, +1 Untended Graves (NG+1), +2 Catacombs of Carthus (NG+2)

RING OF THE SUN'S FIRST BORN

Greatly boosts miracles

Ring of the Sun's first born, who inherited the light of Gwyn, the First Lord.
Greatly boosts miracles.
The Sun's first born was once a god of war, until he was stripped of his stature as punishment for his foolishness. No wonder his very name has slipped from the annals of history.

Effect: Miracle damage +20%

Acquired: Irithyll of the Boreal Valley

SAINT'S RING

Allows attunement of additional spells

A ring bestowed upon a Carim saint. Allows attunement of additional spells.
In Carim, the saints give voice to the ancient tales. They memorize countless cumbersome sacred books and read them in sonorous tones, a function for which they are widely renowned.

Effect: Attunement slots +1

Acquired: Irina of Carim

PRIESTESS RING

Increases faith

A ring engraved with a portrait of the High Priestess. Increases faith.
In Lothric, the High Priestess has long been considered one of the Three Pillars of the king's rule. The High Priestess also served as the prince's wet nurse.

Effect: Faith +5

Acquired: Untended Graves Handmaid

REVERSAL RING

Males can perform female actions and vice versa

A divine ring granted to the Darkmoon Gwyndolin in his youth.
Causes males to perform female actions, and vice-versa.
Gwyndolin was raised like a daughter through the aura of the moon, and was said to behave like a sullen brooding goddess.

Effect: Males can perform female actions and vice versa

Acquired: Irithyll of the Boreal Valley

RING OF SACRIFICE

Lose nothing upon death, but ring breaks

This mystical ring was created in a sacrificial rite of Velka, the Goddess of Sin.
Its wearer will lose nothing upon death, but the ring itself breaks.
A sacrifice is only worth as much as the life it spares.

Effect: Do not lose souls on death. Ring breaks after effect activates (item is consumed)

Acquired: High Wall, Road of Sacrifices, Irithyll Valley, Consumed King's Garden, various merchants

RING OF THE EVIL EYE (+1) (+2)

Absorb HP from each defeated foe

This ring captured the foul spirit of an evil eye, a creature that ravaged Astora.
Absorb HP from each defeated foe.
The horrid spirit nearly destroyed Astora, but was eventually defeated by "the sword of one most noble."

Effect: Recover 30 HP each time you defeat an enemy
    +1 Recover 50 HP each time you defeat an enemy
    +2 Recover 70 HP each time you defeat an enemy

Acquired: Irithyll of the Boreal Valley, +1 Cathedral of the Deep (NG+1), +2 High Wall of the Lothric (NG+2)

SAGE RING (+1) (+2)

Shortens spell casting time

A ring given to Farron's Undead Legion by one of the preacher twins, known more commonly as the Crystal Sages.
Shortens spell casting time.
The sorcerers of Farron's Abyss Watchers were known to be lonesome warriors who would only rely upon more pragmatic spells.

Effect: Shortens spell casting time / "Virtual dexterity" (dexterity only regarding spell casting time) +30
    +1 Shortens spell casting time / "Virtual dexterity" (dexterity only regarding spell casting time) +35
    +2 Shortens spell casting time / "Virtual dexterity" (dexterity only regarding spell casting time) +40

Acquired: Road of Sacrifices, +1 Grand Archives (NG+1), +2 Consumed King's Garden (NG+2)

SCHOLAR RING

Increases intelligence

A ring engraved with a portrait of a scholar. Increases intelligence.
In Lothric, the Scholar has long been considered one of the Three Pillars of the king's rule, and is therefore master of the Grand Archives.

Effect: Intelligence +5

Acquired: Grand Archives

SILVERCAT RING

Prevents damage from falling

Silver ring depicting a leaping feline. Prevents damage from falling.
In the Age of Gods, or possibly just following it, an old cat was said to speak a human tongue, with the voice of an old woman, and the form of a fanciful immortal.

Effect: Prevents damage from falling (however, does not prevent instant death from falling down a distance of 20 meters or more)

Acquired: Sirris after saving her from Creighton invasion on Irithyll bridge

SLUMBERING DRAGONCREST RING

Masks the sounds of its wearer

Ring of a clandestine guild of sorcerers based in Vinheim, home of sorcery.
Masks the sound of its wearer.
The Dragon School held effective sovereignty over Vinheim, with a great many adept assassins at its disposal.

Effect: Masks the sounds of its wearer / Sound radius magnification x0

Acquired: Orbeck of Vinheim

SUN PRINCESS RING

Gradually restores HP

Ring associated with Gwynevere, princess of sunlight and eldest daughter of Gwyn, the First Lord.
The ring is vaguely warm, like a beam of sunlight, and gradually restores HP.
Gwynevere left her home with a great many other deities, and became a wife and mother, raising several heavenly children.

Effect: Gradually restores HP (2 points per second)

Acquired: Anor Londo

UNTRUE DARK RING

Retain human appearance while Hollow

One of the illusory rings worn by the Hollows of Londor.
Retain human appearance while Hollow.
The Hollows of Londor are wretchedly aged, fraught with deceit, and dubiously secretive. It is no wonder that they are deeply detested.

Effect: Retain human appearance (appear human while hollow, or in your actual form while a phantom)

Acquired: Yuria of Londor

WITCH'S RING

Greatly boosts pyromancies

The Witch of Izalith and her daughters, scorched by the Flame of Chaos, taught humans the art of pyromancy and offered them this ring.
Greatly boosts pyromancies.
Every pyromancer is familiar with the parable that tells of the witches espousing the need to fear the flame, and teaching the art of pyromancy to men in hopes that they might learn to control it.

Effect: Pyromancy damage +20%

Acquired: Catacombs of Carthus

WOOD GRAIN RING (+1) (+2)

Slows equipment degradation

This special ring crafted in an Eastern land is made of metal, but with a wood grain crest on its surface. Slows equipment degradation.
Wielders of swords originating in the same region follow a practice of inscribing special words on the blades of their swords, and are naturally drawn to this ring.

Effect: Weapon durability +20%
 +1 Weapon durability +30%
 +2 Weapon durability +40%

Acquired: Shrine Handmaid, +1 Consumed King's Garden (NG+1),
 +2 Irithyll of the Boreal Valley (NG+2)

SKULL RING

Easier to be detected by enemies

One of Courland's transposed wonders. Derived from the soul of a Soulfeeder.
Easier to be detected by enemies.
The Soulfeeder was a beast that insatiably absorbed souls to feed its own power.
Even after its accursed corpse was burned, it is said that the pungent stench of souls left the air permanently stained.

Effect: Makes it easier to be detected by enemies, changing monster targeting priority

Acquired: Ludleth

SPECKLED STONEPLATE RING (+1)

Slightly ups magic, lightning, fire and dark defense

Stoneplates are symbols of true knights, and speckled stoneplates are granted to those who face an endless journey.
Slightly increases magic, lightning, fire and dark damage absorption.

Effect: Incoming elemental damage x0.95
 +1 Incoming elemental damage x0.93

Acquired: Smouldering Lake, +1 Cemetery of Ash (NG+1)

THUNDER STONEPLATE RING (+1) (+2)

Increases lightning defense

Stoneplates are symbols of true knights, and yellow stoneplates are granted to those who would become dragons.
Increases lightning damage absorption.

Effect: Incoming lightning damage x0.87
 +1 Incoming lightning damage x0.83
 +2 Incoming lightning damage x0.8

Acquired: Archdragon Peak, +1 Catacombs of Carthus (NG+1),
 +2 Lothric Castle (NG+2)

UNTRUE WHITE RING

Take the appearance of a phantom

One of the illusory rings worn by the Hollows of Londor.
Take the appearance of a phantom.
The Hollows of Londor are wretchedly aged, fraught with deceit, and dubiously secretive. It is no wonder that they are deeply detested.

Effect: Take the appearance of a white phantom

Acquired: Yuria of Londor

WOLF RING (+1) (+2)

Increases poise

Ring associated with Abysswalker Artorias, one of the Four Knights of Gwyn, the First Lord.
Increases poise.
Artorias had an unbendable will of steel, and was unmatched with a greatsword.

Effect: Poise x1.125
 +1 Poise x1.175
 +2 Poise x1.2

Acquired: Watchdogs of Farron reward, +1 Farron Keep (NG+1),
 +2 Cemetery of Ash (NG+2)

YOUNG DRAGON RING

Boosts sorceries

Ring given in Vinheim, home of sorcery, when newly ordained as a sorcerer.
Boosts sorceries.
Apropos to the Dragon School, the seal depicts an everlasting dragon. A young dragon presages the great length of the journey to mastery.

Effect: Sorcery damage +12%

Acquired: Orbeck of Vinheim

ARROWS & BOLTS

Ammunition for your ranged weapons. You can find very small quantities out in the world as you explore. For the rest, you can purchase it from the Shrine Handmaid or Grierat. As you offer the Handmaid more Ashes and as Greirat explores the world, both unlock the ability to sell new types of ammo. A good bow and a stack of arrows can solve a lot of problems from a distance.

ARROWS

Used for all types of regular bow, the different arrow types give you access to Dark, Fire, and Magic damage, as well as ranged Poisoning capability.

ARROWS	CATEGORY	TYPE	POWER	ADD. EFFECT
Dark Arrow	Arrow	Thrust	65d	-
Feather Arrow	Arrow	Thrust	40p	-
Fire Arrow	Arrow	Thrust	25p/40f	-
Large Arrow	Arrow	Thrust	55p	-
Moonlight Arrow	Arrow	Thrust	75m	-
Poison Arrow	Arrow	Thrust	10p	30po
Standard Arrow	Arrow	Thrust	30p	-
Wood Arrow	Arrow	Thrust	30p	-

DARK ARROW

Ritual arrows said to have been used by savage hunters.

Inflict dark damage.

It is said that these arrows scrape out death from their targets, but savages are known to tell tall tales.

FEATHER ARROW

Red feathered arrows used by hunters.

Their long range makes them ideal for distant targets.

Simultaneously equip up to two types of arrows, and switch between them as needed.

FIRE ARROW

Shoot arrows with burning tips dealing fire damage.

Simultaneously equip up to two types of arrows, and switch between them as needed.

LARGE ARROW

Large, more powerful arrows with a shorter range due to their weight.

Simultaneously equip up to two types of arrows, and switch between them as needed.

MOONLIGHT ARROW

Magical arrows said to have been used by the Darkmoon Knights.

Imbued with a silver light, these arrows inflict magic damage.

It is said that long ago the God of the Darkmoon Gwyndolin wielded these arrows with a matching golden bow.

POISON ARROW

Arrows with poisoned tips.

Inflict poison damage that gradually wears down foes.

STANDARD ARROW

Standard arrows used with bows.

Simultaneously equip up to two types of arrows, and switch between them as needed.

WOOD ARROW

Inexpensive wooden arrows.

Weaker arrows that can be easily purchased in bulk.

Simultaneously equip up to two types of arrows, and switch between them as needed.

GREATARROWS

Specific to the massive Greatbows, these huge arrows are almost miniature spears.

GREATARROWS	CATEGORY	TYPE	POWER	ADD. EFFECT
Dragonslayer Greatarrow	Greatarrow	Thrust	90p	-
Dragonslayer Lightning Arrow	Greatarrow	Thrust	90l	-
Onislayer Greatarrow	Greatarrow	Thrust	60p	-

DRAGONSLAYER GREATARROW

Large spear-like arrows created by the giant blacksmith of the gods.

Can only be used with greatbows.

These large arrows were said to have been used by dragon hunters during the age of the gods. Easily pierces human flesh.

DRAGONSLAYER LIGHTNING ARROW

Large spear-like arrows enveloped in lightning created by the giant blacksmith of the gods.

Can only be used with greatbows.

Lightning has been a weapon of dragonslayers ever since the time of Gwyn, the First Lord.

ONISLAYER GREATARROW

Large arrows used to destroy giant horned oni in an eastern land.

Can only be used with greatbows.

Made from the feathers of an aged crow, it is said that these arrows fly as straight as their master.

BOLTS

Used in all types of crossbows, Bolts can deal Fire or Lightning damage, and inflict Bleeding from a distance.

BOLTS	CATEGORY	TYPE	POWER	ADD. EFFECT
Exploding Bolt	Bolt	Thrust	140f	-
Heavy Bolt	Bolt	Thrust	64p	-
Lightning Bolt	Bolt	Thrust	110l	-
Sniper Bolt	Bolt	Thrust	53p	-
Splintering Bolt	Bolt	Thrust	20p	7bl
Standard Bolt	Bolt	Thrust	48p	-
Wood Bolt	Bolt	Thrust	38p	-

EXPLODING BOLT

Bolts that explode on impact. Deals area fire damage in the immediate vicinity.

Due to the risk of detonation, the amount of bolts the user can carry is greatly limited.

These are, after all, prototypes created by the weapon craftsman Edmond. You get what you pay for.

HEAVY BOLT

Large, more powerful bolts with a shorter range due to their weight.

Simultaneously equip up to two types of bolts, and switch between them as needed.

LIGHTNING BOLT

Bolts imbued with lightning created by the giant blacksmith of the gods.

However, the gods never used crossbows.

These bolts are likely artifacts of the dragonless era, when the pact between gods and humans was upheld.

SNIPER BOLT

Red feathered bolts used by snipers of Carim.

Their long range makes them ideal for distant targets.

Though typically used with Sniper Crossbows in Carim, these arrows can still be used with any kind of crossbow.

SPLINTERING BOLT

Bolts that explode immediately after being shot.

Makes unusual shots possible, and releases splinters that cause immense bleeding.

These are, after all, prototypes created by the weapon craftsman Edmond. You get what you pay for.

STANDARD BOLT

Standard bolts used with crossbows.

Simultaneously equip up to two types of bolts, and switch between them as needed.

WOOD BOLT

Inexpensive wooden bolts.

Weaker bolts that can be easily purchased in bulk.

Simultaneously equip up to two types of bolts, and switch between them as needed.

THE
BESTIARY

A DARK WORLD, FILLED WITH GRIM FOES

While exploring the beautiful world of *Dark Souls III* is a pleasure, it is the monstrous foes you encounter that bring the pain.

From the lowliest undead dreg to the most massive boss encounters, every enemy in the game is capable of sending you to your grave time and again. Learn each foe, and you can overcome what feels like an insurmountable challenge at first.

The beasts you face are gathered in this chapter, grouped by the area that they appear in. Some enemies do reside in more than one location, and there are some variant enemies that behave in the same way, but they are simply tougher and more damaging when encountered later in the game.

Should you travel on to New Game Plus, all of the foes in the game become stronger, so make sure you are well prepared before you complete the game, if you plan to travel onward!

COMBAT NOTES

As a rule, we assume you are tackling the game your first time as a generalist—you have a one handed weapon and a shield, a ranged weapon, access to at least basic spellcasting, and some early low requirement spells.

If you are choosing to play through with a two-handed weapon or dual wielding, much of the advice still applies, but when we're discussing shield blocking tactics, you're going to be relying more on your dodge roll to avoid incoming damage.

You *can* block with a weapon, but weapons always have worse block ratings than shields, and critically, without 100% physical absorption, you're always going to take damage when you block with a weapon.

If you see no other option to avoid an incoming blow when using a two-hander (or dual wielding), go ahead and block, but otherwise, stick to dodging!

If you are choosing to play without a ranged weapon or any magic, understand you are choosing to make the game more difficult. It's certainly possible (and even enjoyable to experiment with once you're experienced), but we definitely don't recommend doing so for your first playthrough.

ENEMY DATA NOTES

Many of the enemies encountered throughout the world of *Dark Souls III* have basic variations, typically common humanoid foes wielding different weapons. Likewise, enemies may be encountered in multiple areas, and they are usually tougher when encountered later in the game (and usually drop a few more Souls in recompense).

Red-eyed versions of some foes behave identically to their normal counterparts, but they are tougher to take down.

In almost all cases, if there are variants of a humanoid foe that uses multiple weapons, it has a chance to drop whatever weapon it is wielding.

In cases where there are many variants of a common foe (such as the Hollow Soldier), we list their "most complete" drop list, and variants wearing/using less gear have less drops.

In each area, any new enemy type is described; enemies from previous areas are shown in the data table.

CEMETERY OF ASH

NAME	HP	SOULS	ITEM DROP	SPECIAL ABILITY	WEAKNESS	RESISTANT TO	INEFFECTIVE	TYPE & EFFECTIVE ITEMS
Grave Warden	88	20	Cleric's Sacred Chime/Fading Soul	None	Poison & Toxic	None	None	Hollow/Alluring Skull/Rapport
Starved Hound	110	10	None	None	Fire	None	None	Hollow/Alluring Skull
Crystal Lizard	63	0	Twinkling Titanite(Fixed)	None	None	Magic	Poison & Toxic/Bleed/Frost	None
Ravenous Crystal Lizard	1200	4000	Titanite Scale(Fixed)	Elemental Attack (Magic)	None	Magic	Poison & Toxic/Bleed/Frost	None
Iudex Gundyr	1037	3000	Coiled Sword(Fixed)	None	Frost	Dark/Bleed	Poison & Toxic	Abyssal

GRAVE WARDEN

The most basic humanoid foes in the game, these poor souls are other cursed undead who have lost all of their humanity. Most wander aimlessly, some stand idly in place. These sad souls are pitiable, but do not mistake their often passive demeanor as reason to treat them carelessly.

Roused from their stupor, they can lash out and deal heavy damage if you let them past your guard. Keep a sturdy shield between you and their attacks, or dodge when they charge and go for a fatal backstab to finish them quickly.

These undead have been carefully placed as an early game tutorial lesson in basic combat against humanoids, use the opportunity to practice if you are new to the game!

STARVED HOUND

Don't underestimate these emaciated undead hounds. They are lethally fast, and can quickly flank you and break your guard. They are often encountered in packs later in the game, and it is *very* easy to get overwhelmed and killed if you stumble into a group of them.

Starved Hound attacks don't have a lot of punch individually, so if you can keep them at bay by blocking with a shield, they're fairly easy to dispatch—just watch your flanks and don't let them surround you.

If you do get rushed, dodge roll away repeatedly and get some distance. If you can make them come at you while you're on elevated terrain, it restricts their movements, and they're a lot easier to handle.

When encountered later in the game in packs, if at all possible, try to pull them (or kill them!) from a distance with ranged attacks. You really don't want these dogs ambushing you in unfavorable terrain (or worse still, with other foes nearby).

RAVENOUS CRYSTAL LIZARD

These rare foes are apparently an evolved form of Crystal Lizards, and the only ready source of Titanite Scales in the game until much later on, when you can buy them from the Shrine Handmaid, or loot them from Rock Lizards in Archdragon Peak. Scales (and only Scales) are used to upgrade specific special weapons.

Unlike most enemies, Ravenous Crystal Lizards do not respawn after they are slain. They are the larger, angrier version of Crystal Lizards who simply flee when encountered.

Ravenous Crystal Lizards have a fairly nasty arsenal of attacks, and they are your first real encounter with a non-humanoid foe. Learning its tells can be tricky at first—if you don't mind dying a few times, it is well worth it to engage this foe and let it attack you at close range and a distance—it is good training for learning to read non-humanoid attacks, a very useful skill that will come in handy.

Ravenous Crystal Lizards move quickly and can close distance rapidly with lunging and sweeping attacks that cover a lot of ground. Blocking all of their attacks with low Stamina or a weak shield is inadvisable, and they are an excellent foe to learn dodge timing against.

Because you encounter this dangerous foe literally at the beginning of the game, don't hesitate to move on if you find it too difficult to defeat—you can always return later!

If you stock up on a few thrown weapon consumables (or you have access to offensive magic), Ravenous Crystal Lizards make good targets if you're not comfortable mixing it up in melee.

When encountered later in the game, you usually want to actively seek these out and defeat them for their material drops.

CRYSTAL LIZARD

These tiny glimmering lizards are covered in a shell of precious stones. If you manage to kill one, its load of Titanite is yours!

Crystal Lizards are a special sort of *Dark Souls* enemy—when approached, they instantly begin to flee, and if you do not defeat them quickly, they vanish entirely!

They do reappear after a reload or zone warp, so you can return to try again with a different weapon should you miss one (not an uncommon occurrence if you accidentally stumble across one unprepared).

You may want to carry around a weapon (even unequipped) that has a good sweeping downward strike. Because Crystal Lizards are so small, large slow weapons or precise weapons such as spears or thrusting swords can be really awkward to use against them.

Also be sure to try different attack types—a sprinting strong strike or standing two handed strong strike with some weapons may work best, or some quick weapons with good downward arcs can get away with sprinting at the critter and mashing weak attacks rapidly.

Crystal Lizards drop different chunks of Titanite depending on where you kill them, but they are all useful, especially early in the game. Later when you have a range of Gems for infusion, they are a luxury, but early on, they can provide you access to valuable infusions for your weapons, setting you on the path to success with a strong upgraded weapon that suits your build's stats.

NAME	HP	SOULS	ITEM DROP	SPECIAL ABILITY	WEAKNESS	RESISTANT TO	INEFFECTIVE	TYPE & EFFECTIVE ITEMS
Pus of Man	587	250	Titanite Shard(Fixed)/Dark Gem/Ember(Fixed)	None	Fire	Dark/Frost	Poison & Toxic	Abyssal/Alluring Skull/Rapport
*Hollow Soldier	167	30	Long Sword/Iron Round Shield/Steel Soldier Helm/Deserter Armor/Deserter Trousers/Firebomb/Titanite Shard/Raw Gem	Elemental Attack (Fire)	Poison & Toxic	None	None	Hollow/Alluring Skull/Rapport
Hollow Assassin	130	30	Dagger/Deserter Trousers/Throwing Knife/Titanite Shard/Raw Gem	None	Poison & Toxic	None	None	Hollow/Alluring Skull/Rapport
Hollow Soldier (Large)	357	80	Greataxe or Halberd/Titanite Shard/Raw Gem	None	Poison & Toxic	None	None	Hollow/Alluring Skull/Rapport
Lothric Knight	326	220	Lothric Knight Sword or Lothric Knight Long Spear/Knight's Crossbow/Lothric Knight Shield/Lothric Knight Helm/Lothric Knight Armor/Lothric Knight Gauntlets/Lothric Knight Leggings/Titanite Shard/Ember	None	Lightning/Frost	Bleed	None	Hollow/Alluring Skull/Rapport
Lothric Knight (Red-eyed Royal Guard)	468	1200	Lothric Knight Sword/Knight's Crossbow/Lothric Knight Shield/Lothric Knight Helm/Lothric Knight Armor/Lothric Knight Gauntlets/Lothric Knight Leggings/Titanite Shard/Ember/Refined Gem(Fixed for the first time defeated, random for the second time or later)	None	Lightning/Frost	Bleed	None	Hollow/Alluring Skull/Rapport
Winged Knight	508	300	Winged Knight Halberd/Titanite Shard/Blessed Gem	Elemental Attack (Magic)	Frost	Strike/Poison & Toxic/Bleed	None	Hollow/Rapport
*Starved Hound	147	40	None	None	Fire	None	None	Hollow/Alluring Skull
Avaricious Being	854	1500	Deep Battle Axe(Fixed)/Symbol of Avarice	None	Dark	Lightning/Poison & Toxic/Bleed/Frost	None	Alluring Skull/Rapport
Crystal Lizard	70	0	Raw Gem(Fixed)	None	None	Magic	Poison & Toxic/Bleed/Frost	None
Vordt of the Boreal Valley	1328	3000	Vordt of the Boreal Valley(Fixed)	Ailment (Frost)	Dark	Slash/Thrust	Poison & Toxic/Bleed/Frost	None
Lothric Wyvern	2723	0	Large Titanite Shard(Fixed)	Elemental Attack (Fire)	Lightning/Frost	Poison & Toxic/Bleed	None	None
Darkwraith	692	2500	Dark Sword/Dark Mask/Dark Armor/Dark Gauntlets/Dark Leggings/Pale Tongue/Red Eye Orb(Fixed when defeated for the first time)	None	None	Dark/Bleed/Frost	Poison & Toxic	Abyssal
Dancer of the Boreal Valley	5111	60000	Soul of the Dancer(Fixed)	Elemental Attack (Fire)/Elemental Attack (Magic)	Dark	Bleed	Poison & Toxic/Frost	None

*There are multiple Hollow Soldier types in High Wall (and elsewhere), this table lists the 'most complete' drop variant, the lesser equipped types have less drops.

*The Starved Hounds here are likely to engage you with other humanoid undead foes nearby. Try to pull them away and deal with them first, you really don't want them tearing at your heels while you're fighting other undead.

LARGE HOLLOW SOLDIER

Most likely, this will be your first encounter with a seriously brutish enemy that can end your life quickly. This archetype of foe is encountered with some frequency throughout the game, sometimes as a sort of "miniboss," though later in the game you can expect to find this sort of foe more commonly.

Large Hollow Soldiers hit extremely hard, but they are relatively slow, learning to punish their attacks when they overextend is a valuable lesson that carries forward to a lot of other enemies you must face.

Like most humanoid foes, Large Hollow Soldiers can wield a variety of (large!) weapons. Expect wide sweeping strikes and blows from halberds or large axes on the High Wall.

As a fresh-from-the-grave Unkindled, you are still weak this early in the game, and with low stamina (and possibly a shield that doesn't block 100% of physical damage, if you even have a shield), blocking their heavy hitting attacks repeatedly is a good way to get your guard blown out and then killed.

It's safer to roll out of the way of an incoming strike, strafe beside them, and unleash a flurry of attacks, then back off and repeat. It is possible to backstab these foes, and quickly strafing behind them after they are frozen from a heavy swing is an effective tactic.

HOLLOW SOLDIER

The most "normal" undead enemy you face, Hollow Soldiers are basic humanoid foes, armed with poorly preserved equipment and possessing some basic combat knowledge. You can expect to encounter them with single weapons, a weapon and shield, or occasionally, perched up on a ledge with a ranged weapon.

These enemies are easily dispatched with basic combat techniques, keep your shield up, block their weak hits, and retaliate. Most are very susceptible to backstabs as well, though parries can be a little tricky, as they often attack with flurries of weak swings. Avoid being surrounded and you can easily take these enemies down with a few swings even with early un-upgraded weapons.

PRAYING HOLLOW SOLDIER

More a sad commentary on the state of undead existence than actual foe, Praying Hollow Soldiers appear along the walls of Lothric and in a few other places throughout the land.

Focused on praying rather than fighting you, they can often be ignored completely, as few bother to rouse themselves from their activity to attack.

If they do attack, they behave much like the early Grave Wardens, furiously lunging with weak weaponry, with little in the way of martial discipline.

LOTHRIC KNIGHT

Your first highly trained humanoid opposition, these Lothric Knights are very dangerous, so don't be too surprised if you end up running back from a Bonfire after engaging in battle with one. Lothric Knights are challenging foes, as they mix controlled aggression with a solid defense.

Lothric Knights are armed with suits of sturdy armor, a stout shield, and a weapon with which they are considerably proficient.

Basic combat tactics of blocking and strafing around them work, but Lothric Knights are wise to your attempts to backstab them, and will quickly pivot in place while lashing out with their shield to fend you off.

On top of that, if you persist in cowering behind a shield, they can switch from using their shield to two handing their sword, and performing a lunging strike that will blow out your guard if it connects.

Lothric Knights are *very* vulnerable to parry, because their attacks are cleanly telegraphed, if you can muster up the courage to attempt a parry on their initial swings, you can punish their tells with a powerful counterattack.

Otherwise, if you are really struggling in melee, mix up your approach—bypass them entirely by running, pick them off from a distance with a bow, or bring a stack of firebombs and burn them down.

HOLLOW ASSASSIN

These foul assassins present a danger mostly because of their ambush tactics, not as much their sustained durability in combat. Typically armed with light daggers and throwing knives, they are often hidden in the shadows in room corners or shadowed alcoves. If you spot them early by moving carefully, you can nullify their greatest strength; surprise.

In combat, Hollow Assassins attack with vicious flurries of blows, but they can be defended fairly easily by blocking, and they are both fairly weak defensively, and quite vulnerable to backstabs or parries. If you try to keep your distance from them for too long, they can throw knives at you, though this is rarely a serious threat.

PUS OF MAN

Exploding from the bodies of unfortunate undead, this consuming chaos corruption manifests itself as an amorphous black blob, vaguely resembling some horrific beast in silhouette, but with no recognizable shape.

The Pus of Man moves relatively slowly until it attacks, but when it does strike, it hits hard, and has surging and sweeping melee strikes that can be hard to evade.

Very early in the game, you are best served either avoiding these entirely, or dispatching them swiftly with some spare firebombs, which they are quite vulnerable to.

It is possible to block and counter against them, but because they hit hard, you may find your stamina sapped swiftly. They can drop Titanite Shards and Embers, which makes for appealing loot, just be aware of the danger!

WINGED KNIGHT

Another lesson in the virtue of avoidance, the Winged Knight is an enemy normally encountered *much* later in the game. Tough and powerful, it can dispatch you with speed when you first encounter it.

Like the Dragon, if you do insist on engaging the Winged Knight, you are best served by attacking it from a distance and taking it down slowly but safely.

If you engage up close, you need to deal with wide sweeping swings from its halberd, a spinning attack that covers a lot of ground, crushing vertical strikes with great reach, *and* just to top it all off, blasts of magic that incinerate the area around it (and you, if you get touched by any of the white pillars it calls down).

This enemy can be defeated in a straight fight, but it's a tough battle, so make sure you have the nearby Bonfire or shortcuts unlocked before you decide to tangle with it!

DRAGON

A classic *Dark Souls* tradition, throwing a dragon in your face this early in the game seems quite cruel, but it mostly serves as a lesson in avoiding dangerous threats... and archery.

This Dragon can be dispatched by means of a bow, and a small sum of Souls spent buying arrows. If you aren't planning on dispatching it with ranged attacks, avoid it entirely!

The dragon located here coats part of the wall with flames should you attempt to venture past it, but it is possible to skip it via a side path.

If you do scare the Dragon off, you can reap the rewards, a small heap of treasure items left behind by their burnt owners, and a chest in the building beneath it.

UNDEAD SETTLEMENT

NAME	HP	SOULS	ITEM DROP	SPECIAL ABILITY	WEAKNESS	RESISTANT TO	INEFFECTIVE	TYPE & EFFECTIVE ITEMS
Undead Settlement Skeleton	148	50	Scimitar or Falchion/Human Pine Resin	None	Strike	Thrust/Lightning/Dark	Poison & Toxic/Bleed/Frost	Reanimated
Hollow	78	0	None	None	Poison & Toxic	None	None	Hollow/Alluring Skull/Rapport
Hollow Slave	144	80	Thrall Axe or Flamberge/Thrall Hood/Titanite Shard	None	Poison & Toxic	None	None	Hollow/Alluring Skull/Rapport
Cathedral Evangelist	657	380	Spiked Mace/Evangelist Hat/Evangelist Robe/Evangelist Gloves/Evangelist Trousers/Titanite Shard/Blessed Gem	Elemental Attack (Fire)	Thrust	Fire	None	Hollow/Alluring Skull/Rapport
Peasant Hollow	153	60	Harpe or Great Wooden Hammer or Four-Pronged Plow/Worker Hat/Worker Garb/Worker Gloves/Worker Trousers/Firebomb/Charcoal Pine Resin/Fire Gem/Rubbish	Elemental Attack (Fire)	Poison & Toxic		None	Hollow/Alluring Skull/Rapport
Hollow Manservant	551	320	Great Machete/Titanite Shard/Rubbish	Ailment (Bleed)	None	None	None	Hollow/Alluring Skull/Rapport
Boreal Outrider Knight	654	1600	Irithyll Straight Sword	Ailment (Frost)	Dark	Bleed	Poison & Toxic/Frost	None
Starved Hound	167	40	None	None	Fire	None	None	Hollow/Alluring Skull
Hound-rat	111	30	Soul of a Deserted Corpse	None	Slash/Fire	Poison & Toxic	None	Alluring Skull
Crystal Lizard	79	0	Sharp Gem(Fixed)/ Heavy Gem(Fixed)	None	None	Magic	Poison & Toxic/Bleed/Frost	None
Hound-rat (Large)	334	450	Bloodbite Ring(Fixed when defeated for the first time)/Large soul of a Deserted Corpse	None	Slash/Fire	Poison & Toxic	None	Alluring Skull
Giant Slave	348	1000	None	None	None	Slash/Thrust/Fire/Lightning	Poison & Toxic/Bleed/Frost	None
Demon	1390	5000	Fire Gem(Fixed)	Elemental Attack (Fire)	None	Fire/Poison & Toxic	Bleed/Frost	Demon/Alluring Skull/Rapport
Cage Spider	135	40	Fading Soul	None	Thrust/Lightning	Slash	None	Hollow/Alluring Skull/Rapport
Curse-rotted Greatwood	5405	7000	Soul of the Rotted Greatwood(Fixed)/Transposing Kiln(Fixed)	None	Slash/Thrust/Fire	None	Poison & Toxic/Bleed/Frost	Alluring Skull

PEASANT HOLLOW

The main "citizens" of the Undead Settlement. These enemies are slow to attack, so you gain a great deal by seizing initiative against them. Move forward and attack before they're ready to strike. You can engage them with a combo that is likely to score a kill without needing to dodge or block.

However, Peasant Hollows don't come alone. They're usually in small groups, but can appear in very large numbers in a few areas of the Undead Settlement. This is especially bad if they're following a Cathedral Evangelist!

Always rush to thin the Peasant Hollows numbers. Attack around the periphery of the group, get a kill or two, and fade back to regain your Stamina while any survivors start to gather. Lure solo targets away with ranged weapons, and kill them on their own if you're worried about being overwhelmed.

CATHEDRAL EVANGELIST

Cathedral Evangelists are religious leaders of the Undead Settlement. They have ranged magic and wide, sweeping melee attacks. Avoid their ranged attacks by dodging forward; the attacks track, but they can't turn around to hit you. As long as you roll away, but toward them, you're likely to avoid all of the damage.

The melee attacks are trickier. Although you see them from a mile away, it's still intimidating to dodge through these huge swings. One trick to help with this is to back away, bait the Cathedral Evangelist's spells, and then rush forward to get a free attack or two before they recover and go into melee mode.

Don't try to burn these heavier enemies down in a single go. Kill any support they have before you try to do any damage against the bigger threat, and then use hit and run combos to get free hits without exposing yourself.

HOLLOW SLAVE

Hollow Slaves would be comical if they weren't so dangerous. Tiny undead wearing masks, they lunge from the shadows with a range of weaponry, from tiny harvesting blades to massive over-large swords.

Hollow Slaves are weak defensively; their main threat comes from surprise, much like the Hollow Assassins of the High Wall. You can block their attacks fairly easily and dispatch them quickly, just be careful not to get surrounded in a confined space. Like packs of Starved Hounds, they are most dangerous in numbers and on unfavorable terrain.

At a distance, they can needle you with dart shots, which are annoying and fairly low damage, but can get you in trouble in a hurry if you're trying to fight other enemies nearby. You can block these projectiles, or sprint past them if you're far enough away.

HOLLOW MANSERVANT

Hollow Manservants are large and mean. They either attack with their heavy saws or use clay pots. Both have the ability to knock down your character, leaving you exposed to additional strikes if you don't get up with a fast roll.

Always be cautious against Hollow Manservants. Bait their combos and punish them with two hits while they're recovering from their repeated strikes. It's better to retreat early, because these foes do massive damage and can kill you very quickly if you try to trade blows with them.

If any other targets are near a Hollow Manservant, make sure to lure them away with ranged attacks. You never want to fight these enemies while anything else is around to distract you.

CAGE SPIDER

A horrific mix of undead bodies left imprisoned in a cage. The limbs dangling between the bars are used for locomotion and violent attacks.

These Cage Spiders are rarely threatening unless they manage to surprise you, since they move slowly and can be taken down quickly. Dispatch them safely from a distance, or strike with a few hard swings and back off before the monster can retaliate.

One trick to watch out for, the Cage Spiders often appear near other "dead" cages, just look at their coloration and the legs sticking out to spot the real ones, or use target-lock to acquire a target.

HOUND-RAT

Hound-rats are a trivial threat. They have speed on their side, and usually attack in small packs, but you can destroy their groups easily with even minor damage. Wide, sweeping weapons are very good against them. Anything with range is also quite powerful.

If a Hound-rat pack starts to surround you, roll back, and then sprint away. Once a pack has good positioning, they can disrupt you again and again while you try to get even a single strike back against them.

Also, keep a shield out when you're dealing with Hound-rats. They have a leaping charge that is hard to avoid unless you already have a shield held high.

LARGE HOUND-RAT

Large Hound-rats are much worse than their smaller companions. They have higher health and give you plenty of Bleed damage if you aren't careful. You can always put on items to increase your Bleed Resistance, but that's not actually necessary. You're better off ambushing and killing Large Hound-rats before they're able to get many attacks against you. One extended combo is usually enough to get the job done.

SKELETON

Skeletons are seen several times throughout the game. They're weaker targets, on their own, but tend to appear in clusters. They attack with short-range melee weaponry unless you're dealing with ones that spawn with bows. These archer Skeletons are always in the same locations, so you're able to learn where they are each time you enter a new region.

For melee Skeletons you want to back up until you find a chokepoint. Let a group of these creatures file into a bottleneck, and then you should hit them with a combo to kill the entire group simultaneously.

When there are mixed groups of ranged and melee Skeletons, look for columns or other types of cover that break line of sight. Hide and pull the melee Skeletons over to your location.

DEMON

The Demon in the Undead Settlement is another unique enemy. As long as Siegward is alive, he'll come down the hill to assist you in your battle against this mini-boss, but it'll be a dangerous fight regardless.

You don't need to dodge often against the Demon, but you can't afford to miss the mark when you do! This enemy has slow, heavy attacks that lay people out. Roll multiple times if you dodge too early, and hope that the timing works out well enough for the second dodge to avoid the hits.

You can get fairly greedy with your return combos after the Demon misses. Keep enough Stamina free to roll away from it, but otherwise go to town and get heavy damage while you can.

BOREAL OUTRIDER KNIGHT

Boreal Outrider Knights are uncommon enemies. You find them in a few locations throughout *Dark Souls III*, and they're always intended to be vicious combatants. In fact, they are unique targets that only need to be killed once per playthrough, so put everything into your skirmishes against them.

Boreal Outrider Knights have Frost effects on all of their attacks, which make it very difficult to stay mobile in longer fights. You're especially in bad shape if you try to engage in longer combos against them. Spells and ranged weapons are preferable.

Until you have the Boreal Outrider Knight at low health, keep defense as your primary focus. It's possible to be taken out from 100% health if you are hit by their combos, so only trade attacks if you're almost at the end of the fight and just need another hit or two for the kill.

If you're really having problems, use a few ranged attacks, pull the Boreal Outrider Knight back through cleared territory, and wait for them to give up the chase. Then, follow them and repeat this slow but effective tactic.

ROAD OF SACRIFICES

NAME	HP	SOULS	ITEM DROP	SPECIAL ABILITY	WEAKNESS	RESISTANT TO	INEFFECTIVE	TYPE & EFFECTIVE ITEMS
Cathedral Evangelist	804	380	Spiked Mace/Evangelist Hat/Evangelist Robe/Evangelist Gloves/Evangelist Trousers/Titanite Shard/Blessed Gem	Elemental Attack (Fire)	Thrust	Fire	None	Hollow/Alluring Skull/Rapport
Hollow Manservant	675	320	Great Machete/Titanite Shard/Rubbish	Ailment (Bleed)	None	None	None	Hollow/Alluring Skull/Rapport
Black Knight	640	900	Black Knight Greatsword/Black Knight Shield/ Black Knight Helm/Black Knight Armor/ Black Knight Gauntlets/Black Knight Leggings/ Ember	None	Dark/Frost	Poison & Toxic/Bleed	None	None
Crystal Sage	2723	8000	Soul of a Crystal Sage(Fixed)	Elemental Attack (Magic)	Physical Attack/Poison & Toxic	Magic	None	None
Lycanthrope	816	350	Titanite Shard/Ember	None	Slash/Bleed	Poison & Toxic	None	Hollow/Alluring Skull/Rapport
Lycanthrope Hunter	294	150	Pike/Titanite Shard	None	Poison & Toxic	None	None	Hollow/Alluring Skull/Rapport
Sage's Prentice	181	60	Long Sword or Light Crossbow or Broken Straight Sword or Dagger or Pike/ Wooden Shield/Throwing Knife/Firebomb/ Crystal Gem	Light Crossbow: Elemental Attack (Fire)	Poison & Toxic	None	None	Hollow/Alluring Skull/Rapport
Sage's Devout	499	280	Sorcerer's Staff/Crystal Gem	Elemental Attack (Magic)	Poison & Toxic	Magic	None	Hollow/Alluring Skull/Rapport
Starved Hound	204	80	None	None	Fire	None	None	Hollow/Alluring Skull
Festering Starved Hound	272	80	None	None	Fire	Poison & Toxic	None	Hollow/Alluring Skull
Crystal Lizard	97	0	Crystal Gem(Fixed)/Twinkling Titanite(Fixed)	None	None	Magic	Poison & Toxic/Bleed/Frost	None
Corvian	359	90	Corvian Greatknife or Great Corvian Scythe/Shriving Stone	Scythe: Ailment (Bleed)	Bleed	None	None	Alluring Skull/Rapport
Corvian Storyteller	359	360	Storyteller's Staff/Hollow Gem	Elemental Attack (Fire)/ Ailment (Poison)	Bleed	None	None	Alluring Skull/Rapport
Great Crab	1058	800	Great Swamp Ring(Fixed first time)/ Titanite Shard	Slows character's movement	Frost	Slash	Bleed	Alluring Skull
Lesser Crab	96	30	Bloodred Moss Clump/Purple Moss Clump	None	Frost	Slash	Bleed	Alluring Skull
Poisonhorn Bug	192	40	Rotten Pine Resin	Ailment (Poison)	Fire/Frost	None	Poison & Toxic	None

CORVIAN

Corvians are usually in small groups of 2-4 members. They are led by a Corvian Storyteller. Both types of these enemies are vulnerable for a short time as you meet them. They'll only become active after getting up and finishing a transformation. Corvian become berserk after that, and then they're nasty.

The typical method for winning these fights is to charge. Race into the group, kill the Corvian Storyteller first if at all possible, then get as many Corvian down as you can before they are ready for the real fight.

Once berserk, they'll attack with very fast combos. Find higher ground and use plunging attacks, ranged or thrown weapons, or melee weaponry with greater reach to kill them safely.

CORVIAN STORYTELLER

Corvian Storytellers have ranged, magical attacks. They'll support the Corvian in the area with slow but consistent shots from quite far away. This is why they're good targets to kill first, because that reduces the fights to a single type of enemy (Corvians only have melee attacks). Corvian Storytellers are rubbish at defending themselves up close.

LYCANTHROPE HUNTER

Lycanthrope Hunters are weaker undead that you only find in the marshes below the Road of Sacrifices. Jump them for fast kills, but watch out if you can't get initiative. Lycanthrope Hunters charge over a modest distance with their melee attacks, and they can sweep to catch you if you try to roll to their flanks. In each case, you want to roll and kill them or block and retreat because you'll lose a fair amount of Stamina.

LYCANTHROPE

Lycanthropes are vile. If you approach them from the flanks or rear, you often get a free series of attacks before the fight starts. In a stand up fight, Lycanthropes frequently land blows because they'll swing multiple times.

Make single hits or small combos, and roll away. Be conservative, even against single Lycanthropes.

BLACK KNIGHT

The Black Knight is a rare foe that guards an Ember near Farron Keep's entrance. Like all knights, you need to be focused when you face this target. It has deadly attacks, strong armor, and can do heavy damage if you leave yourself open.

Gather your full Stamina and either bait an attack or wait for the Black Knight to move around instead of standing still waiting for your strikes. Then, unleash an extended combo.

Alternatively, use parry or dodge and get small hits against the Black Knight after avoiding each attack. This takes time and requires precision, but it's also an effective way to win the encounter.

LESSER CRAB

Lesser Crabs are small enemies that do trivial damage and can't take much of a beating. Don't let them distract you while you're handling greater threats.

GREAT CRAB

Great Crabs are much worse than their smaller kin. They have high damage output, cause knock down very easily, and can't be comboed to death quickly early in the game. Even worse, they're usually located in areas where movement can be impeded by high water. You can't rely on sprinting to get you away from the fight.

Search for the areas where the water is low and doesn't influence your running or dodging. If you must fight Great Crabs, pull them to these safer spots and kill them there.

POISONHORN BUG

Poisonhorn Bugs don't have much health. Slaughter their groups before they start to spew poison all over the place. If they unleash their clouds, run away and leave them. These targets aren't worth many Souls, and being poisoned always raises the risk of dying.

SAGE'S DEVOUT

As you approach the Crystal Sage's area, you have to fight a few Sage's Devout; they have wonderful ranged attacks, but can't do much against an opponent who gets close to them. Sprint quickly to get through areas that are exposed to any Sage's Devout, and use pillars or walls to break line of sight so that they can't keep casting at you successfully.

Once you get a straight shot, sprint over to the Sage's Devout in question and use a full combo to bring them down immediately. Don't play the ranged game against these foes because it is slow and frustrating.

FARRON KEEP

NAME	HP	SOULS	ITEM DROP	SPECIAL ABILITY	WEAKNESS	RESISTANT TO	INEFFECTIVE	TYPE & EFFECTIVE ITEMS
Hollow Soldier	218	550	Long Sword or Light Crossbow or Pike or Dagger/Firebomb/Standard Bolt/ Crystal Gem	None	Poison & Toxic	None	None	Hollow/Alluring Skull/Rapport
Hollow Assassin	218	550	Dagger/Throwing Knife/Crystal Gem	None	Poison & Toxic	None	None	Hollow/Alluring Skull/Rapport
Rotten Slug	270	60	Poison Gem/Heavy Gem	Elemental Attack (Magic)	Thrust/Fire	Strike	Poison & Toxic	Alluring Skull
Ghru	436	350	Rotten Ghru Spear or Rotten Ghru Curved Sword/Ghru Rotshield/ Titanite Shard/Poison Gem/ Rotten Pine Resin/Wolf's Blood Swordgrass/Blue Bug Pellet	Ailment (Poison)	Fire	None	Poison & Toxic	Alluring Skull/Rapport
Ghru (Conjurator)	436	350	Rotten Ghru Dagger/ Titanite Shard/Heavy Gem/ Blue Bug Pellet/Wolf's Blood Swordgrass	Ailment (Poison)	Fire	None	Poison & Toxic	Alluring Skull/Rapport
Ghru (Mad)	635	600	Titanite Shard/Heavy Gem/ Blue Bug Pellet/Wolf's Blood Swordgrass	None	Fire	None	Poison & Toxic	Alluring Skull/Rapport .
Black Knight	640	900	Black Knight Greatsword/Black Knight Shield/ Black Knight Helm/Black Knight Armor/ Black Knight Gauntlets/Black Knight Leggings/ Ember	None	Dark/Frost	Poison & Toxic/Bleed	None	None
Basilisk	414	120	Mossfruit	Ailment (Curse)	None	None	Poison & Toxic	None
Crystal Lizard	117	0	Large Titanite Shard(Fixed)/ Heavy Gem(Fixed)/ Twinkling Titanite(Fixed)	None	None	Magic	Poison & Toxic/Bleed/Frost	None
Corvian	432	120	Corvian Greatknife or Great Corvian Scythe/Shriving Stone	Scythe: Ailment (Bleed)	Bleed	None	None	Alluring Skull/Rapport
Corvian Storyteller	432	440	Storyteller's Staff/Hollow Gem	Elemental Attack (Fire)/ Ailment (Poison)	Bleed	None	None	Alluring Skull/Rapport
Great Crab	1058	800	Lingering Dragoncrest Ring(Fixed first time)/Titanite Shard	Slows character's movement	Frost	Slash	Bleed	Alluring Skull
Abyss Watcher	1548	18000	Soul of the Blood of the Wolf(Fixed)/ Cinders of a Lord(Fixed)	Elemental Attack (Fire)	Lightning	Dark/Bleed	Poison & Toxic	None
Ravenous Crystal Lizard	1231	5000	Titanite Scale(Fixed)	Elemental Attack (Magic)	None	Magic	Poison & Toxic/Bleed/Frost	None
Elder Ghru	830	1600	Poison Gem//Heavy Gem/Ember/Stone Greatshield/Pharis's Hat (Fixed first time), Black Bow of Pharis (Fixed first time)	Elemental Attack (Magic)	Fire	None	Poison & Toxic	Alluring Skull
Darkwraith	692	2500	Dark Sword/ Dark Mask/Dark Armor/Dark Gauntlets/ Dark Leggings/ Pale Tongue/Cracked Red Eye Orb	None	None	Dark/Bleed/Frost	Poison & Toxic	Abyssal
Stray Demon	2004	5000	Soul of a Stray Demon(Fixed)	None	Strike	Fire/Lightning	Poison & Toxic/Bleed/Frost	Demon

GHRU

Ghrus are the rank and file enemies of Farron Keep. Pull them over to dry land so that you aren't fighting in the middle of poisonous muck, and destroy them. You don't usually have to worry about large groups, so the land itself is your real problem in Farron Keep. Ghru can appear as normal melee foes, Conjurators, or occasionally as Mad Ghru that wildly lunge and attempt to tackle you bodily.

BASILISK

Returning players know exactly what to expect from Basilisks! Lacking normal attacks, these enemies either can't hurt you at all, or they'll kill you outright by breathing thick clouds of Cursing gas. Roll past them as they breathe, kill them from behind, and sprint away before their clouds of death kill you.

ELDER GHRU

Elder Ghrus aren't seen often, but these massive evolved Ghru are dangerous. The slow, awkward footing of the area makes it really tough to avoid their attacks. The only good news is that they have less health than their size implies. Long combos or cautious ranged fire are both effective ways to kill these horrors.

It's a bad idea to take on a group of Elder Ghrus (exactly how they appear in a few places). Avoid this by shooting at maximum range to get the attention from one Elder Ghru and kill it separately.

CURSES

Don't mess with these cursing beasts. Either bring heavily Curse resistant armor, kill them from a distance, or avoid them entirely. Getting Cursed is not fun at all!

ROTTEN SLUG

Rotten Slugs appear in large groups, but they're still a petty threat. Use sweeping weaponry to clear them out. Run away if you have any trouble; Rotten Slugs are quite slow, so they won't be able to pursue you in a meaningful way.

CATHEDRAL OF THE DEEP

NAME	HP	SOULS	ITEM DROP	SPECIAL ABILITY	WEAKNESS	RESISTANT TO	INEFFECTIVE	TYPE & EFFECTIVE ITEMS
Knight of the Deep	556	550	Great Mace or Cathedral Knight Greatsword/Cathedral Knight Greatshield/Cathedral Knight Helm/Cathedral Knight Armor/Cathedral Knight Gauntlets/Cathedral Knight Leggings/Titanite Shard/Ember/Heavy Bolt	Miracle Enchant: Elemental Attack (Magic) Addition	Poison & Toxic/Bleed	Lightning/Frost	None	Hollow/Rapport
Hollow Slave	182	90	Thrall Axe or Flamberge/Thrall Hood/Deep Gem/Titanite Shard	None	Poison & Toxic	None	None	Hollow/Alluring Skull/Rapport
Reanimated Corpse	233	20	None	Ailment (Infesting with maggots: Bleed)	Fire	None	Poison & Toxic	Reanimated/Hollow/Alluring Skull/Rapport
Infested Corpse	233	200	None	Ailment (Infesting with maggots: Bleed)	Fire	None	Poison & Toxic	Reanimated/Hollow/Alluring Skull/Rapport
Cathedral Evangelist	830	380	Spiked Mace/Evangelist Hat/Evangelist Robe/Evangelist Gloves/Evangelist Trousers/Titanite Shard/Blessed Gem	Elemental Attack (Fire)	Thrust	Fire	None	Hollow/Alluring Skull/Rapport
Cathedral Grave Warden	707	750	Warden Twinblades/Grave Warden Hood/Grave Warden Robe/Grave Warden Wrap/Grave Warden Wrap/Bloodred Moss Clump	Elemental Attack (Fire)/Ailment (Bleed)	None	Poison & Toxic	None	Hollow/Alluring Skull/Rapport
Devout of the Deep	187	70	Long Sword or Spear or Light Crossbow or Dagger or Arbalest/Firebomb/Red Bug Pellet/Throwing Knife/Heavy Bolt	Elemental Attack (Fire)	Poison & Toxic	None	None	Hollow/Alluring Skull/Rapport
Devout of the Deep (Large)	556	350	Greataxe or Halberd/Crystal Gem	None	Poison & Toxic	None	None	Hollow/Alluring Skull/Rapport
Starved Hound	211	80	None	None	Fire	None	None	Hollow/Alluring Skull
Corpse-grub	680	600	Soul of a Deserted Corpse/Large soul of a Deserted Corpse	Ailment (Infesting with maggots: Bleed)	Fire	None	Poison & Toxic	Reanimated/Alluring Skull/Rapport
Avaricious Being	976	2000	Symbol of Avarice/Deep Braille Divine Tome (Fixed)	None	Dark	Lightning/Poison & Toxic/Bleed/Frost	None	Alluring Skull/Rapport
Writhing Rotten Flesh	227	20	Titanite Shard	None	Fire	Physical Attack/Magic/Lightning/Dark	Poison & Toxic/Bleed/Frost	Abyssal/Alluring Skull
Crystal Lizard	100	0	Twinkling Titanite(Fixed)	None	None	Magic	Poison & Toxic/Bleed/Frost	None
Man-grub	313	100	Undead Hunter Charm/Duel Charm/Red Sign Soapstone (fixed if you don't own one)	Ailment (Infesting with maggots: Bleed)	Slash/Thrust/Fire	None	Poison & Toxic	None
Giant Slave	1873	4000	Large Titanite Shard(Fixed)/Dung Pie(Fixed)	None	None	Slash/Thrust/Fire/Lightning	Poison & Toxic/Bleed/Frost	None
Ravenous Crystal Lizard	1231	5000	Titanite Scale(Fixed)	Elemental Attack (Magic)	None	Magic	Poison & Toxic/Bleed/Frost	None
Deep Accursed	800	1500	Aldrich's Sapphire(Fixed)	Ailment (Curse)	None	Poison & Toxic	None	Abyssal
Archdeacon Royce	4099	13000	Small Doll(Fixed)/Soul of the Deacons of the Deep(Fixed)	Elemental Attack (Dark)	Physical Attack	Magic/Dark/Poison & Toxic/Bleed	None	Hollow
Deacon of the Deep	292	150	Deacon Robe/Deacon Skirt/Deep Gem/Deep Ring (fixed when defeated for the first time)	Elemental Attack (Fire)	Physical Attack	Magic/Dark	None	Hollow/Rapport

DEVOUT OF THE DEEP

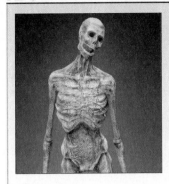

The Devout of the Deep are basic humanoid foes, much like Hollow Soldiers. Almost all of the tactics that you learn work well against them, but they serve as a distraction while you're also being attacked by more serious adversaries. Kill them while keeping your eyes out for ranged enemies with crossbows, or for any of the undead who are lighting themselves on fire.

REANIMATED CORPSE

Reanimated Corpses are pathetic targets. They are only any danger at all because they cannot be killed for long, reviving after falling. However, they aren't a major threat to you. Their attacks do minor damage and their health is poor. The only way they'll trouble you is by lurching forward to slow your progress when you're simply trying to run past them. Always assume that they can attack from greater range than expected, and watch your back if you cut them down. It doesn't take long for them to recover and stand back up.

DEVOUT BOMBER

Devout Bombers immolate themselves and sprint toward your direction. They'll throw themselves onto you and try to detonate. Though this kills them in the process, it deals plenty of damage to you, if it happens.

If you see a Devout Bomber starting their fiery animation, attack them immediately. They're defenseless while they put themselves to the torch, and it isn't hard to do enough damage to kill them. They won't explode.

Failing that, lead the Devout Bomber toward other enemies and then dodge soon after the undead jumps into the air. They'll likely miss, so you don't take damage. Even better, their explosion takes out everything nearby (and you still get Souls for their deaths).

INFESTED CORPSE

Infested Corpses are a worse form of Reanimated Corpses. They have a budding creature of maggots bursting out of them. They have massive Bleed capabilities, so make sure that your Resistance to Bleed is as high as possible. There are many maggot creatures in the area near the cathedral, so putting on equipment specifically for this purpose is worth your time.

Infested Corpses have more health compared to the Reanimated Corpses, and you need a very serious combo to kill them in a single run. Keep a shield out, lock on, and back off as soon as the Infested Corpses rear up for a two-handed blow. You should be able to avoid the hit just by backstepping. This leaves you with tons of Stamina left over for a lethal combo.

CORPSE-GRUB

Corpse-grubs are the worst of the maggoty bunch. They are larger, heavier, and meaner than the other two maggot foes near the graveyard. You have to bait their attacks, just like the Infested Corpses. Wait until they dedicate to their heaviest attacks, and then you can push forward, land a few blows, and then retreat.

Play conservatively, because even a single hit promises high damage and enough Bleed effect to make things difficult. Bring curatives.

CATHEDRAL GRAVE WARDEN

Cathedral Grave Wardens aren't seen too often, and that's a good thing. They have medium-range attacks, fast melee combos, and decent health. Keep a shield ready, because you can absorb much of their violence without losing all of your Stamina. Block, perform a short counter-combo, and then fade back.

WRITHING ROTTEN FLESH

Writhing Rotten Flesh is a disgusting slime that hangs on ceilings and attempt to ambush you from above. As long as you remember to look up, they're not much of a threat. After they fall, they attack slowly and exist just to soak up damage.

The biggest problem with Writhing Rotten Flesh is that they block narrow hallways if you don't take the time to kill them. Remember that the path is blocked if you hurry forward, and don't try to retreat through slime later on!

KNIGHT OF THE DEEP

Knights of the Deep aren't always as defensive as other knights in the game, but they know how to lay on the damage. Some of them have single-handed weaponry. These knights fight more like what you're used to from the early game. Use extended combos to knock aside their shields, and then get real damage in while they're briefly stunned.

The two-handed Knights of the Deep are damage dealers. Don't trade with them, because you are going to regret it (briefly).

A nice trick against all Knight of the Deeps is to back off and bait their spells. They'll buff themselves when you're far away, but you have enough time to close and attack before they finish.

DEEP ACCURSED

Deep Accursed are unique enemies. You meet one in the Cathedral of the Deep, and another later in Anor Londo. Both are large targets that look extremely intimidating. They have a Curse effect on their attacks, so any extended fighting can leave you in a difficult situation.

Therefore, take a more aggressive approach. Roll into the Deep Accursed and use long combos to deal maximum damage quickly. This trade gets you hurt every time, but the Estus Flasks that you drink restoring yourself are well spent. Because these are unique monsters, you just have to clear them once, return to a Bonfire, and then pass safely through the area in the future.

GIANT SLAVE

Giant Slaves are seen several times throughout the game. Most are unique (like the ones in the Cathedral of the Deep), but not all of them. Ranged weapons from a safe location are slow but effective at killing Giant Slaves. However, gutsy players should run under their feet and combo extensively to kill them. Don't get stepped on, and watch out for enemies that add to these fights, but the foot-stabbing method is very reliable.

There are smaller Giant Slaves located in Irithyll Valley, they are (slightly) faster than their massive brethren.

DEACONS OF THE DEEP

Deacons of the Deep are spellcasters with very long range. They rely on fire for damage, but have very weak melee attacks. Lure any knights that are protecting them away, kill those dangerous targets, and then return for an easy slaughter. They're defenseless if taken on directly. Roll under their fire spells on your approach, and close in for the kills.

AVARICIOUS BEING/MIMIC

Avaricious Beings/Mimics are false treasure chests. You learn where they are as you explore, or you can use the maps in the walkthrough chapter, but you can always check to see if a treasure chest is safe by swinging at it. Mimics only attack if you try to open them or if you go after them first. Take the initiative with a very long series of strikes, and try to kill the Mimic before it even stands up.

Roll backward if your combo doesn't finish the job, and try again in a few seconds. Mimics aren't very dangerous as long as you trigger them this way.

MAN-GRUB

Man-grubs are only seen near Rosaria's chamber. They use ranged fire attacks and are a moderate threat because of their numbers. Attack their groups and back away to break their line of sight. This lets you kill any of the members who follow.

CATACOMBS OF CARTHUS

NAME	HP	SOULS	ITEM DROP	SPECIAL ABILITY	WEAKNESS	RESISTANT TO	INEFFECTIVE	TYPE & EFFECTIVE ITEMS
Skeleton	249	120	Scimitar or Falchion or Longbow//Kukri/Carthus Rouge/Fire Arrow	None	Strike	Thrust/Lightning/Dark	Poison & Toxic/Bleed/Frost	Reanimated
Grave Warden Skeleton	249	120	Alluring Skull	Elemental Attack (Dark)	Strike	Thrust/Lightning/Dark	Poison & Toxic/Bleed/Frost	Reanimated
Skeleton Swordsman	582	320	Carthus Curved Sword or Carthus Curved Greatsword or Carthus Shotel/Carthus Shield/Titanite Shard/Large Titanite Shard/Sharp Gem/Vertebra Shackle/Carthus Rogue/Ember	Ailment (Bleed)/Reanimates once	Strike	Thrust/Lightning/Dark	Poison & Toxic/Bleed/Frost	Reanimated
Skeleton Wheel	249	280	Bonewheel Shield/Large Titanite Shard	None	Strike	Thrust/Lightning/Dark	Poison & Toxic/Bleed/Frost	Reanimated
Hound-rat	187	60	Large soul of a Deserted Corpse	None	Slash/Fire	Poison & Toxic	None	Alluring Skull
Writhing Rotten Flesh	302	40	Titanite Shard	None	Fire	Physical Attack/Magic/Lightning	Poison & Toxic/Bleed/Frost	Alluring Skull
Crystal Lizard	134	0	Twinkling Titanite(Fixed)/Fire Gem(Fixed)	None	None	Magic	Poison & Toxic/Bleed/Frost	None
Hound-rat (Large)	563	600	Soul of an Unknown Traveler	None	Slash/Fire	Poison & Toxic	None	Alluring Skull
High Lord Wolnir	7052	22000	Soul of High Lord Wolnir(Fixed)	Elemental Attack (Dark)	None	Dark	Poison & Toxic/Bleed/Frost	Reanimated/Abyssal

SKELETON SWORDSMAN

Skeleton Swordsmen are similar to Cathedral Grave Wardens. They have the health, combos, and range to kill you efficiently. Use a shield to blunt their initial attacks, and then counter with whatever Stamina you can afford to spend.

When you find Skeleton Swordsmen and regular Skeletons together, try to break line of sight and kill the targets as they close with you. They'll usually spread out a bit, and you won't be overwhelmed.

SKELETON WHEEL

Skeleton Wheels roll toward you at a decent clip and then knock you around so that you can't get a returning shot against them. Dodging works a little, but it leaves you rather far away from the Skeleton Wheel. Instead, use a shield to block their charge. You stop the Skeleton Wheel much closer to your position, making it easier to close, attack, and kill the pesky foes.

Stay near walls when you're fighting Skeleton Wheels. They always lose momentum if they smack into a hard surface, so you're in better shape when you fight near these obstacles.

RETURN OF THE WHEELS

Few enemies in the game are as likely to cause instant loathing for *Souls* veterans as these seemingly straightforward skeletal foes.

Getting run over and smashed into a fine paste by their rolling attack is a rite of passage for *Dark Souls* players. If you're new, join us in death!

If you're not, you should know that they are a *little* less brutal this time around.

SMOULDERING LAKE

NAME	HP	SOULS	ITEM DROP	SPECIAL ABILITY	WEAKNESS	RESISTANT TO	INEFFECTIVE	TYPE & EFFECTIVE ITEMS
Smoldering Ghru	635	140	Rotten Ghru Curved Sword or Rotten Ghru Spear/Ghru Rotshield/Titanite Shard/Large Titanite Shard	Ailment (Poison)	Physical Attack/Magic/Lightning/Dark	Fire	None	Alluring Skull/Rapport
Smoldering Ghru (Conjurator)	635	140	Rotten Ghru Dagger/Titanite Shard/Large Titanite Shard/Fire Gem	Ailment (Poison)	Physical Attack/Magic/Lightning/Dark	Fire	None	Alluring Skull/Rapport
Smoldering Ghru (Mad)	635	320	Titanite Shard/Large Titanite Shard/Fire Gem	None	Physical Attack/Magic/Lightning/Dark	Fire	None	Alluring Skull/Rapport
Smoldering Bastard Ghru	336	140	Titanite Shard/Large Titanite Shard	None	Physical Attack/Magic/Lightning/Dark	Fire	None	Alluring Skull/Rapport
Black Knight	931	1600	Black Knight Greatsword or Black Knight Greataxe/Black Knight Shield/Black Knight Helm/Black Knight Armor/Black Knight Gauntlets/Black Knight Leggings/Ember	None	Dark/Frost	Poison & Toxic/Bleed	None	None
Skeleton Wheel	317	280	Bonewheel Shield/Large Titanite Shard	None	Strike	Thrust/Lightning/Dark	Poison & Toxic/Bleed/Frost	Reanimated
Hound-rat	239	60	Soul of an Unknown Traveler	None	Slash/Fire	Poison & Toxic	None	Alluring Skull
Avaricious Being	1686	2000	Symbol of Avarice/Black Blade(Fixed)	None	Dark	Lightning/Poison & Toxic/Bleed/Frost	None	Alluring Skull/Rapport
Smoldering Rotten Flesh	385	20	Titanite Shard/Fire Gem	Elemental Attack (Fire)	None	Physical Attack	Fire/Poison & Toxic/Bleed/Frost	Alluring Skull
Basilisk	602	80	Mossfruit	Ailment (Curse)	None	None	Poison & Toxic	None
Crystal Lizard	171	0	Twinkling Titanite(Fixed)/Fire Gem(Fixed)	None	None	Magic	Poison & Toxic/Bleed/Frost	None
Carthus Sandworm	3180	6000	Lightning Stake(Fixed)/Undead Bone Shard(Fixed)	Elemental Attack (Lightning)	Thrust/Frost	Lightning/Bleed	Poison & Toxic	None
Great Crab	1539	1200	Large Titanite Shard/Titanite Shard(Fixed)	Slows character's movement	Frost	Slash/Fire	Bleed	Alluring Skull
Lesser Crab	168	80	Blooming Purple Moss Clump/Rime-blue Moss Clump	None	Frost	Slash	Bleed	Alluring Skull
Old Demon King	5301	25000	Soul of the Old Demon King(Fixed)	Elemental Attack (Fire)	None	Fire/Poison & Toxic	Bleed/Frost	Demon
Demon	2982	5000	Soul of a Demon(Fixed)	Elemental Attack (Fire)	None	Fire/Poison & Toxic	Bleed/Frost	Demon/Alluring Skull/Rapport
Demon Cleric	1425	900	Chaos Gem/Titanite Shard/Large Titanite Shard	Elemental Attack (Fire)	None	Poison & Toxic	None	Demon
Demon Statue	228	150	None	Elemental Attack (Fire)	None	Fire/Lightning/Dark	Poison & Toxic/Bleed/Frost	None

DEMON CLERIC

Demon Clerics are savage. A single one can be a serious problem, and any additional targets (whether Demon Clerics or Smouldering Ghrus) make them a very difficult encounter.

Take as much time as you need to pull everything else out of a Demon Cleric's room. Only attack after the enemy is fully isolated. Even then, you have to use walls to break line of sight any time that you need to heal or regain Stamina.

Melee combos get the job done, but it's always an ugly affair. You end up trading damage, so keep your supply of Estus Flasks high when you attack these monsters. After you've looted an Demon Cleric's room, consider sprinting through it in the future so that you don't spend so many resources every time you come through it.

SMOULDERING GHRU

Cousins to the Ghru in the swamp, Smouldering Ghrus have Poison and toxic damage in their melee attacks, and their shamans have a cloud attack that fills a huge area with these effects. When you're going through the Smouldering Ghru's area, wear armor with resistances geared specifically toward surviving this, because that and the Demon Clerics' Fire are the easiest ways to die down there.

Smouldering Ghrus come in groups. Each target has modest health and can be killed quickly. You need to capitalize on that, because these guys are horrible once they've gathered together. Rush each Smouldering Ghru you see and destroy them immediately, even if you have to take a little damage.

CARTHUS SANDWORM

The Carthus Sandworm is a unique encounter in the Smouldering Lake. A monstrous worm that can fire devastating blasts of Lightning, it is a serious threat. Sprint past the area where the monster emerges, and look for a ledge above, up and to the right from where you first see the enemy. Get onto that ledge to avoid the ballistas and the Carthus Sandworm. Fire arrows or bolts from that ledge to kill this mini-boss and clear the area for future exploration.

WAR MACHINE AND WORM

You're getting bombarded by a massive siege ballista, giant flaming crabs are trying to crush you, and then *this* thing roars out of the ground.

If you end up flattened the first time you venture down here and run into the worm, don't feel too bad, you're in good company. Also don't feel too bad about turning it into a pincushion from a distance.

DEMON STATUE

Demon Statues are almost immobile masses of flesh and Flame. They're easy to kill, but all of them do tremendous damage if you get caught in their extended breath attacks. Use their lack of mobility against them. Back away and kill any other types of defenders first. Then, charge up to the Demon Statues and attack furiously. Or, stay out of their range, and shoot them for safe kills.

8

IRITHYLL OF THE BOREAL VALLEY

NAME	HP	SOULS	ITEM DROP	SPECIAL ABILITY	WEAKNESS	RESISTANT TO	INEFFECTIVE	TYPE & EFFECTIVE ITEMS
Burning Stake Witch	792	1800	Immolation Tinder/Fire Witch Helm/Fire Witch Armor/Fire Witch Gauntlets/Fire Witch Leggings/Large Titanite Shard	Elemental Attack (Fire)	Dark/Frost	Bleed	None	None
Cathedral Evangelist	1608	800	Dorhys' Gnawing(Fixed)/Spiked Mace/ Evangelist Hat/Evangelist Robe/Evangelist Gloves/Evangelist Trousers	Elemental Attack (Fire)	Thrust	Fire	None	Hollow/Alluring Skull/Rapport
Irithyllian Slave	512	250	Blood Gem/Blue Bug Pellet	Elemental Attack (Magic)/ Hide	Physical Attack/Bleed	None	None	Hollow/Alluring Skull/Rapport
Irithyllian Soldier Slave	512	250	Claymore/Blood Gem	Elemental Attack (Magic)	Physical Attack/Bleed	None	None	Hollow/Alluring Skull/Rapport
Silver Knight	1099	2500	Dragonslayer Greatbow/Silver Knight Shield/Silver Knight Helm/Silver Knight Armor/Silver Knight Gauntlets/ Silver Knight Leggings/Dragonslayer Greatarrow/ Large Titanite Shard(Fixed first time)/ Divine Blessing(Fixed first time)	Elemental Attack (Lightning)	Dark/Frost	Physical Attack/Fire/ Lightning/Poison & Toxic/ Bleed	None	Hollow
Pontiff Knight	591	900	Pontiff Knight Curved Sword or Pontiff Knight Great Scythe/Pontiff Knight Shield/ Pontiff Knight Crown/Pontiff Knight Armor/ Pontiff Knight Gauntlets/ Pontiff Knight Leggings/Large Titanite Shard	Elemental Attack (Magic)/ Ailment (Frost)	Dark	Poison & Toxic/Frost	None	None
Sewer Centipede	478	750	Green Blossom/Budding Green Blossom	None	Strike	Thrust	Poison & Toxic	None
Crystal Lizard	164	0	Twinkling Titanite(Fixed)/Simple Gem(Fixed)	None	None	Magic	Poison & Toxic/Bleed/Frost	None
Corvian	719	120	Corvian Greatknife/Shriving Stone	None	Bleed	None	None	Alluring Skull/Rapport
Sulyvahn's Beast	2296	8000	Pontiff's Right Eye	Elemental Attack (Lightning)	Fire	Poison & Toxic	None	None
Sulyvahn's Beast	2721	12000	Ring of Favor(When the second one is defeated)	Elemental Attack (Lightning)	Fire	Poison & Toxic	None	None
Irithyllian Beast-hound	345	350	None	Ailment (Frost)	Fire	Dark	None	Reanimated/Alluring Skull
Pontiff Sulyvahn	5106	28000	Soul of Pontiff Sulyvahn	Elemental Attack (Fire/ Magic)	Thrust	Poison & Toxic/Bleed/Frost	None	None

SULYVAHN'S BEAST

There is one Beast in Irithyll that attacks you on the starting bridge that leads into the city. Later, you face two of them by the Water Reserve Bonfire.

All of Sulyvahn's Beasts are unique targets. Dedicated combos kill them quickly, but they have equally dangerous attacks of their own, and they can punish reckless behavior. It's hard to back away, roll, or even sprint away from Sulyvahn's Beasts, so you have to heal like you would in a boss fight (roll to avoid an attack, and use the enemy's recovery time as your healing window).

Roll sideways to stay close to these creatures when dodging, and come up swinging at them to get damage in before they attack again. Don't trade blows, and don't extend your combos. Use short groups of strikes, until the fight is almost over.

IRITHYLLIAN BEAST-HOUND

Irithyllian Beast-hounds behave exactly like the Starved Hounds that you are used to by this point in the game. However, these dogs are heavier targets and require more damage to kill, and a few of them have a Frost bite. Don't rely on single attacks to kill these foes. Back up while you're locked on, keep your shield raised, and hit each dog once after it bounces off of your shield.

PONTIFF KNIGHT

Pontiff Knights don't fight like the other varieties of knights that you encounter in *Dark Souls III*. They have their own timings and style of battle and it's hard to get used to initially. You may wish to employ a union of ranged attacks and then a sudden charge to kill each Pontiff Knight before it starts attacking. Blocking and dodging is very difficult against Pontiff Knights because their combos are fast.

Pull individuals to avoid getting a group of Pontiff Knights. These monsters patrol the Irithyll streets, so you never want to advance into your target.

BURNING STAKE WITCH

Beware the Burning Stake Witch. Few enemies have such a solid combination of ranged damage and melee potential. Burning Stake Witches cast spells that hit hard and don't give you much time to roll aside. Even worse, they're usually in a position that is difficult to reach. You have to sprint all the way around to get to your target. That's triply dangerous in Irithyll because of the patrolling enemies.

Even when you're close to a Burning Stake Witch you have to be careful. They can cast their spells when you're hitting them, and they have a throw that does massive damage. Strike quickly, dodge, and keep the pressure on these foes as much as possible.

IRITHYLLIAN SLAVE

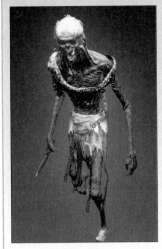

Irithyllian Slaves are plentiful in Irithyll. They are easy to see when they are out in the open, but become almost invisible when you are in dark places. Shields help to block their attacks and leave these weaker enemies vulnerable to any counterattack.

Because Irithyllian Slaves show up in numbers, you benefit more from sweeping weaponry rather than stabbing, single-target weapons.

Some Irithyllian Slaves use magical spells instead of melee weapons. They are a much more troublesome threat, and should be prioritized if you can reach them.

In dark areas of Irithyll, your shield should be held high almost all the time. This lets you avoid Irithyllian Slave attacks more often than not. Look for their burning eyes to spot them.

SEWER CENTIPEDE

The wet areas below Irithyll have Sewer Centipedes. Their hair stands out in the water as thick, dark strands. Use this feature to spot them and ambush these enemies before they wake. It's very easy to kill them with a few hits before they're able to get up.

If you see one Sewer Centipede, there are probably quite a few close by. They never appear by themselves in areas, but they're spread out enough for you to avoid being swarmed, as long as you're methodical about clearing all of them.

SILVER KNIGHT

Silver Knights use somewhat standard knight techniques, but they have Lightning attacks in addition to just physical attacks. This makes shield blocking less effective, because you're almost guaranteed to take damage even when you block successfully.

A two-handed weapon/stance can be much better for killing Silver Knights. The more damage you do per hit, the easier it is to take them out with one burst. These foes are very good at longer fights, so you want to end things quickly.

Ranged Silver Knights do high damage and and knock you back. They'll make each encounter extremely difficult if you're also being attacked by melee opponents. Hug the walls or use pillars for cover to break line of sight with them.

IRITHYLL DUNGEON

NAME	HP	SOULS	ITEM DROP	SPECIAL ABILITY	WEAKNESS	RESISTANT TO	INEFFECTIVE	TYPE & EFFECTIVE ITEMS
Reanimated Corpse	391	100	None	Ailment (Infesting with maggots: Bleed)	Fire	None	Poison & Toxic	Reanimated/Hollow/Alluring Skull/Rapport
Infested Corpse	391	500	None	Ailment (Infesting with maggots: Bleed)	Fire	None	Poison & Toxic	Reanimated/Hollow/Alluring Skull/Rapport
Peasant Hollow	445	180	Firebomb/Large Titanite Shard/Dung Pie	Elemental Attack (Fire)	Poison & Toxic	None	None	Hollow/Alluring Skull/Rapport
Lycanthrope	1413	500	None	None	Slash/Bleed	Poison & Toxic	None	Hollow/Alluring Skull/Rapport
Monstrosity of Sin	3946	2700	Eleonora(Fixed)/Dung Pie(Fixed)	Soul Absorption	Slash/Thrust/Bleed	Strike	Poison & Toxic	None
Corpse-grub	1898	450	Great Magic Shield(Fixed)	Ailment (Infesting with maggots: Bleed)	Fire	None	Poison & Toxic	Reanimated/Alluring Skull/Rapport
Wretch	496	250	Tailbone Spear or Tailbone Short Sword/Pale Pine Resin	Elemental Attack (Magic)/Equipment Breakage	Lightning	Slash/Strike/Fire/Poison & Toxic/Bleed	None	None
Sewer Centipede	490	750	Purging Stone	None	Strike	Thrust	Poison & Toxic	None
Hound-rat	236	80	Soul of an Unknown Traveler	None	Slash/Fire	Poison & Toxic	None	Alluring Skull
Avaricious Being	1572	2000	Symbol of Avarice/Dragonslayer Lightning Arrow(Fixed)/Titanite Scale(Fixed)/Rusted Gold Coin(Fixed)/Estus Shard(Fixed)/Dark Clutch Ring(Fixed)	None	Dark	Lightning/Poison & Toxic/Bleed/Frost	None	Alluring Skull/Rapport
Basilisk	595	130	Mossfruit	Ailment (Curse)	None	None	Poison & Toxic	None
Crystal Lizard	169	0	Titanite Chunk(Fixed)/Titanite Scale(Fixed)	None	None	Magic	Poison & Toxic/Bleed/Frost	None
Jailer	727	700	Soldering Iron/Aristocrat's Mask/Jailer Robe/Jailer Gloves/Jailer Trousers/Simple Gem	Elemental Attack (Fire)/Ailment(Lowers MAX HP)/Reduces healing power of Estus/Slows character's movement/Paralyzing by Soldering Iron	Poison & Toxic	None	None	None
Hound-rat (Large)	708	720	Soul of an Unknown Traveler	None	Slash/Fire	Poison & Toxic	None	Alluring Skull
Giant Slave	3141	5000	Titanite Chunk(Fixed)/Dung Pie(Fixed)	None	None	Slash/Thrust/Fire/Lightning	Poison & Toxic/Bleed/Frost	None
Cage Spider	287	90	Fading Soul	None	Thrust/Lightning	Slash	None	Hollow/Alluring Skull/Rapport

JAILER

Jailers are not normal enemies. They have several unique abilities, and you need to know how to fight them. Lure Jailers around corners; you never want to fight them at range or give them a clear view while they approach.

These enemies debuff your health while they're looking at you, and even if that doesn't kill you, it still counts as damage when the debuff eventually fades.

Jailers also have a Cursing gas attack. They'll do this when they're patrolling around. Listen for the "pssssshhh" sound effect so that you know when they're doing it. Don't rush into the cloud to attack the Jailer.

As long as you ambush Jailers while they're coming around corners, they can be dealt with.

WRETCH

Many Wretches are locked inside cells. They're twisted and strange beasts, but they're easy to kill when alone. Only the cells with multiple Wretches are worrisome. Wretches don't move quickly, so it's wise to rush them, attack, and score a fast kill before they can do anything.

Against groups, rush in and kill one Wretch. Then, back off, get Stamina, and fight whichever Wretch is the most aggressive about reaching you.

One thing to watch out for, Wretches can deal heavy Durability damage. This is rarely an issue in most of the game. Unless you are using a low Durability weapon, or you've been out in the field for a long time without returning to a Bonfire, Wretches can really give your equipment a beating.

PROFANED CAPITAL

NAME	HP	SOULS	ITEM DROP	SPECIAL ABILITY	WEAKNESS	RESISTANT TO	INEFFECTIVE	TYPE & EFFECTIVE ITEMS
Monstrosity of Sin	3946	2700	Eleonora(Fixed)/Dung Pie(Fixed)	Soul Absorption	Slash/Thrust/Bleed	Strike	Poison & Toxic	None
Sewer Centipede	490	750	Purging Stone	None	Strike	Thrust	Poison & Toxic	None
Avaricious Being	1572	2000	Symbol of Avarice/Court Sorcerer's Staff(Fixed)/Greatshield of Glory(Fixed)	None	Dark	Lightning/Poison & Toxic/Bleed/Frost	None	Alluring Skull/Rapport
Crystal Lizard	169	0	Twinkling Titanite(Fixed)	None	None	Magic	Poison & Toxic/Bleed/Frost	None
Headless Gargoyle	890	2500	Gargoyle Flame Hammer or Gargoyle Flame Spear	Flame Hammer: Elemental Attack (Fire)	Strike	Slash/Fire/Lightning	Poison & Toxic/Bleed/Frost	None
Jailer	727	850	Handmaid's Dagger/Rusted Coin/Rusted Gold Coin	Elemental Attack (Fire)	Poison & Toxic	Fire	None	None
Yhorm the Giant	27822	36000	Cinders of a Lord(Fixed)/Soul of Yhorm the Giant(Fixed)	Elemental Attack (Fire)	Lightning	Slash/Thrust	Fire/Poison & Toxic/Bleed/Frost	None

HEADLESS GARGOYLE

There are only a few Headless Gargoyles in the Profaned Capital. You also face them (with heads) in the Grand Archives.

Headless Gargoyles, if approached carefully, are often solitary targets. They have a lot of health and take damage well; they also choose their spots to attack you well. You never get to fight them on good ground. It's usually on a ledge or bridge, and dodging is very risky in those situations.

To defeat Headless Gargoyles, try to finish the fight quickly. Buff your Attack Power as much as you can (go into two-handed mode, switch to your most damaging weapon, use a weapon enchant, etc.). Trade with the Headless Gargoyle so that you kill it quickly and without much movement. Though costly, this is a better method then staying mobile and risking a lethal fall.

MONSTROSITY OF SIN

Several Monstrosities of Sin are lurking in a temple, on the eastern side of the capital. Each one has massive health. Although they are very slow, their attacks cover ground well and are very punishing.

No matter what position these targets get into, assume that they can flop, roll, or otherwise leap on top of you. As soon as they start moving, dodge backward and wait for them to whiff before resuming your attacks. Getting grabbed by one of these foul foes is extremely damaging and drains your Souls.

JAILER HANDMAID

Jailer Handmaids guard the hallway before you reach the boss of the Profaned Capital. They have a cursing gas attack, fire attacks at range, and are seen in high numbers. Use hit-and-run tactics to thin their numbers and escape. Each Jailer Handmaid is easy to kill, but you die if you stick around and try to get the entire group in attempt. To avoid this, pick a target or two, rush in to kill them, and then dash out of the area.

ANOR LONDO

A comparatively small area, Anor Londo only makes up a small part of Irithyll, and all of the foes encountered within its environs you have faced elsewhere.

NAME	HP	SOULS	ITEM DROP	SPECIAL ABILITY	WEAKNESS	RESISTANT TO	INEFFECTIVE	TYPE & EFFECTIVE ITEMS
Silver Knight	998	2500	Dragonslayer Greatbow/ Silver Knight Helm/Silver Knight Armor/ Silver Knight Gauntlets/Silver Knight Leggings/Dragonslayer Greatarrow/ Titanite Shard/Large Titanite Shard/Proof of a Concord Kept	Elemental Attack (Lightning)	Dark/Frost	Physical Attack/Fire/ Lightning/Poison & Toxic/ Bleed	None	Hollow
Avaricious Being	2015	3000	Symbol of Avarice/Golden Ritual Spear(Fixed)	None	Dark	Lightning/Poison & Toxic/ Bleed/Frost	None	Alluring Skull/Rapport
Rotten Flesh of Aldrich	440	80	Titanite Shard	None	Fire	Physical Attack/Magic/ Lightning/Dark	Poison & Toxic/Bleed/Frost	Abyssal/Alluring Skull
Giant Slave	852	3800	Stalk Dung Pie/Titanite Shard/Large Titanite Shard	None	None	Slash/Thrust/Fire/Lightning	Poison & Toxic/Bleed/Frost	None
Deep Accursed	2200	2500	Aldrich's Ruby(Fixed)	Ailment (Curse)	None	Poison & Toxic	None	Abyssal
Aldrich, Devourer of Gods	4727	50000	Soul of Aldrich(Fixed)/Cinders of a Lord(Fixed)	Elemental Attack (Magic)/ Lifedrain	Fire	Magic/Dark	Poison & Toxic	Abyssal
Deacon of the Deep	951	600	Deacon Robe/Deacon Skirt/Deep Gem/ Human Dregs	Elemental Attack (Fire)	Physical Attack	Magic/Dark	None	Hollow/Rapport

CONSUMED KING'S GARDEN

NAME	HP	SOULS	ITEM DROP	SPECIAL ABILITY	WEAKNESS	RESISTANT TO	INEFFECTIVE	TYPE & EFFECTIVE ITEMS
*Pus of Man	1937	2500	Dark Gem/Large Titanite Shard/Titanite Chunk/Ember	None	Fire	Dark/Frost	Poison & Toxic	Abyssal/Alluring Skull/Rapport
Rotten Slug	497	80	Dark Gem	Elemental Attack (Magic)	Thrust/Fire	Strike	Poison & Toxic	Alluring Skull
Consumed King's Knight	1194	2800	Great Mace or Cathedral Knight Greatsword/Cathedral Knight Greatshield/ Heavy Crossbow/ Cathedral Knight Helm/Cathedral Knight Armor/Cathedral Knight Gauntlets/ Cathedral Knight Leggings/ Large Titanite Shard/Titanite Chunk/ Ember/Magic Stoneplate Ring (Fixed first time)	Miracle Enchant: Elemental Attack (Magic) Addition	Poison & Toxic/Bleed	Lightning/Frost	None	Hollow/Rapport
Hollow Slave	391	80	Thrall Axe/Thrall Hood/Titanite Chunk	None	Poison & Toxic	None	None	Hollow/Alluring Skull/Rapport
Serpent-man	486	1500	Large Titanite Shard	Elemental Attack (Fire)	Lightning/Frost	Poison & Toxic	None	None
Lothric Priest	430	800	Blessed Gem	Healing Miracle/Buff Miracle	Poison & Toxic	None	None	Hollow/Alluring Skull/Rapport
Oceiros, the Consumed King	8087	58000	Soul of Consumed Oceiros(Fixed)	Elemental Attack (Magic)/ FP damage	Lightning	Magic/Bleed	Poison & Toxic	None

*The Pus of Man in the Garden are already active and quite ready to attack you, unlike the surprise ambushes long ago on the High Wall. Take them apart at a distance, or at the very least, away from the poisonous muck that coats the Garden.

CONSUMED KING'S KNIGHT

Consumed King's Knights are tough. They have the usual knight fighting style, but their stats are high and you don't get much room to maneuver when you're fighting them. The area's poisonous ground is bad enough, but there are also Pus of Man and other targets that you can back into while engaging in combat.

Bait the Consumed King's Knights from range to get them casting, or use extended combos to break their defense and leave them vulnerable.

SERPENT-MAN

Serpent-men are a smaller type of draconic foe. You find a few at the end of the Consumed King's Garden, but more lie in wait if you venture to their true home in Archdragon Peak. Block their fast attacks and respond with a few basic attacks to kill them.

UNTENDED GRAVES

No new foes here, and there are relatively few enemies in this darkened mirror of Firelink Shrine.

NAME	HP	SOULS	ITEM DROP	SPECIAL ABILITY	WEAKNESS	RESISTANT TO	INEFFECTIVE	TYPE & EFFECTIVE ITEMS
Pus of Man	1797	3500	Dark Gem/Large Titanite Shard/Titanite Chunk/Ember	None	Fire	Dark/Frost	Poison & Toxic	Abyssal/Alluring Skull/Rapport
Cathedral Grave Warden	1509	750	Warden Twinblades/Grave Warden Hood/Grave Warden Robe/Grave Warden Wrap/Grave Warden Wrap/Large Titanite Shard/Titanite Chunk	Elemental Attack (Fire)/Ailment (Bleed)	None	Poison & Toxic	None	Hollow/Alluring Skull/Rapport
Black Knight	1171	2000	Black Knight Greatsword or Black Knight Greataxe/Black Knight Shield/Black Knight Helm/Black Knight Armor/Black Knight Gauntlets/Black Knight Leggings/Ember	None	Dark/Frost	Poison & Toxic/Bleed	None	None
Grave Warden	399	160	Cleric's Sacred Chime/Large soul of a Deserted Corpse	None	Poison & Toxic	None	None	Hollow/Alluring Skull/Rapport
Starved Hound	450	180	None	None	Fire	None	None	Hollow/Alluring Skull
Corvian	792	150	Corvian Greatknife or Great Corvian Scythe/Shriving Stone	Scythe: Ailment (Bleed)	Bleed	None	None	Alluring Skull/Rapport
Corvian Storyteller	792	400	Storyteller's Staff/Hollow Gem	Elemental Attack (Fire)/Ailment (Poison)	Bleed	None	None	Alluring Skull/Rapport
Ravenous Crystal Lizard	2019	10000	Titanite Scale(Fixed)	Elemental Attack (Magic)	None	Magic	Poison & Toxic/Bleed/Frost	None
Champion Gundyr	4956	60000	Soul of Champion Gundyr(Fixed)	None	Lightning	Poison & Toxic/Bleed	None	None

LOTHRIC CASTLE

NAME	HP	SOULS	ITEM DROP	SPECIAL ABILITY	WEAKNESS	RESISTANT TO	INEFFECTIVE	TYPE & EFFECTIVE ITEMS
Pus of Man	1937	0	Dark Gem/Large Titanite Shard/Titanite Chunk/Ember	Elemental Attack (Dark)/Ailment (Curse)	Fire	Dark/Frost	Poison & Toxic	Abyssal/Alluring Skull/Rapport
*Hollow Soldier	552	400	Long Sword/Iron Round Shield/Steel Soldier Helm/Deserter Armor/Deserter Trousers/Firebomb/Large Titanite Shard/Titanite Chunk/Raw Gem	Elemental Attack (Fire)	Poison & Toxic	None	None	Hollow/Alluring Skull/Rapport
Hollow Assassin	430	400	Dagger/Deserter Trousers/Throwing Knife/Large Titanite Shard/Titanite Chunk/Raw Gem	None	Poison & Toxic	None	None	Hollow/Alluring Skull/Rapport
Hollow Soldier (Large)	1178	650	Greataxe or Halberd/Large Titanite Shard/Titanite Chunk/Raw Gem	None	Poison & Toxic	None	None	Hollow/Alluring Skull/Rapport
Lothric Knight	1079	2500	Lothric Knight Sword or Long Spear or Greatsword/Knight's Crossbow/Lothric Knight Shield/Lothric Knight Helm/Lothric Knight Armor/Lothric Knight Gauntlets/Lothric Knight Leggings/Large Titanite Shard/Titanite Chunk/Ember/Sunlight Medal	None	Lightning/Frost	Bleed	None	Hollow/Alluring Skull/Rapport
Winged Knight	1679	2600	Winged Knight Halberd or Twinaxes/Large Titanite Shard/Titanite Chunk/Blessed Gem	Elemental Attack (Magic)	Frost	Strike/Poison & Toxic/Bleed	None	Hollow/Rapport
Boreal Outrider Knight	1904	3000	Irithyll Rapier(Fixed)	Ailment (Frost)	Dark	Bleed	Poison & Toxic/Frost	None
Avaricious Being	2045	3000	Symbol of Avarice/Sunlight Straight Sword (Fixed)/Titanite Scale(Fixed)	None	Dark	Lightning/Poison & Toxic/Bleed/Frost	None	Alluring Skull/Rapport
Crystal Lizard	232	0	Twinkling Titanite(Fixed)	None	None	Magic	Poison & Toxic/Bleed/Frost	None
Lothric Wyvern	6471	15000	Titanite Chunk(Fixed)/Ember(Fixed) (both)	Elemental Attack (Fire)	Lightning/Frost	Poison & Toxic/Bleed	None	None
Dragonslayer Armour	4581	64000	Soul of Dragonslayer Armour(Fixed)	Elemental Attack (Lightning)	Frost	Lightning/Dark	Poison & Toxic/Bleed	Abyssal

*The Hollows here are noticeably tougher than the ones from long ago on the High Wall. Don't let them mob you!

LOTHRIC WYVERNS

The Lothric Wyverns are best killed with ranged weaponry from the Bonfire side of the bridge. Don't approach them, don't risk their flames, and accept that it takes many arrows to finish the job. Make sure to stock up before you start shooting at them, because running out of arrows when you're 70% through a dragon's health bar is more than counterproductive.

It *is* possible to kill the Wyverns in melee, both are controlled by an Abyssal infestation, not unlike Iudex Gundyr and the Pus of Man. If you make your way around the outskirts of the castle, you can reach their wings where the infestation manifests. Destroy it and the host Wyvern is slain instantly.

GRAND ARCHIVES

Quite a few foes reappear in the Grand Archives, all tougher than before.

NAME	HP	SOULS	ITEM DROP	SPECIAL ABILITY	WEAKNESS	RESISTANT TO	INEFFECTIVE	TYPE & EFFECTIVE ITEMS
Hollow Soldier (Royal Guard)	660	550	Long Sword or Spear or Light Crossbow/Iron Round Shield/Steel Soldier Helm/Deserter Armor/Deserter Trousers/Firebomb/Large Titanite Shard/Titanite Chunk	None	Poison & Toxic	None	None	Hollow/Alluring Skull/Rapport
Hollow Slave	501	900	Thrall Axe or Flamberge/Thrall Hood/Titanite Chunk/Crystal Gem	Elemental Attack (Fire)	Poison & Toxic	None	None	Hollow/Alluring Skull/Rapport
Lothric Knight	1289	4000	Lothric Knight Sword or Long Spear or Greatsword/Lothric Knight Shield/Lothric Knight Helm/Lothric Knight Armor/Lothric Knight Gauntlets/Lothric Knight Leggings/Refined Gem/Large Titanite Shard/Titanite Chunk/Ember	None	Lightning/Frost	Bleed	None	Hollow/Alluring Skull/Rapport
Gertrude's Knight	2420	13000	Winged Knight Halberd or Twinaxes/Large Titanite Shard/Titanite Chunk/Blessed Gem/Titanite Slab(Fixed)	Elemental Attack (Magic)	Dark/Frost	Strike/Poison & Toxic/Bleed	None	Hollow/Rapport
Boreal Outrider Knight	2274	15000	Outrider Knight Helm/Outrider Knight Armor/Outrider Knight Gauntlets/Outrider Knight Gauntlets	Ailment (Frost)	Dark	Bleed	Poison & Toxic/Frost	None
*Crystal Sage	4056	20000	Crystal Scroll(Fixed)	Elemental Attack (Magic)	Physical Attack/Poison & Toxic	Magic	None	None
Grand Archives Scholar	871	2700	Scholar's Candlestick/Scholar's Robe/Crystal Gem	Elemental Attack (Magic)	Fire	Magic/Frost	None	Hollow
Crystal Lizard	277	0	Chaos Gem, Crystal Gem, Heavy Gem, Sharp Gem, Refined Gem, Twinkling Titanite, Titanite Scale (all Fixed)	None	None	Magic	Poison & Toxic/Bleed/Frost	None
Man-grub	1350	900	Duel Charm	Elemental Attack (Magic)	Slash/Thrust/Fire	None	Poison & Toxic	None
Gargoyle	1676	4000	Gargoyle Flame Hammer or Gargoyle Flame Spear	Flame Hammer: Elemental Attack (Fire)	Strike	Slash/Fire/Lightning	Poison & Toxic/Bleed/Frost	None
Corvian	1020	1300	Corvian Greatknife or Great Corvian Scythe/Shriving Stone	Scythe: Ailment (Bleed)	Bleed	None	None	Alluring Skull/Rapport
Corvian Storyteller	1020	3200	Storyteller's Staff/Hollow Gem	Elemental Attack (Fire)/Ailment (Poison)	Bleed	None	None	Alluring Skull/Rapport
Lorian, Elder Prince	4294	0	None	Elemental Attack (Fire)/Elemental Attack (Magic)	Lightning/Frost	Dark	Poison & Toxic	None
Lorian, Elder Prince	3436	0	None	Elemental Attack (Fire)/Elemental Attack (Magic)	Lightning/Frost	Dark	Poison & Toxic	None
Lothric, Younger Prince	5799	85000	Cinders of a Lord/Soul of the Twin Princes	Elemental Attack (Magic)	Physical Attack	Dark	Poison & Toxic	None

*The Crystal Sage was a boss fight, here it's foe you have to battle as you work your way through the Archives!

GRAND ARCHIVES SCHOLAR

Many Grand Archives Scholars are inside the archives. They're normal casters when you're at long range, but they have a good trick if you get closer. These enemies spray you with wax, making it impossible to dodge for a short time. Instead, you wiggle in place and lose mobility while they cast spells at you.

First off, avoid the wax entirely. This is the best way to survive and kill them. Long-range shots work well because Grand Archives Scholars have low health. But, melee attacks are fine if you get in and score kills very quickly.

Second, walk away if you get wax onto your character. Don't try to dodge or fight in this state. Walk toward cover, heal if you need to, and come out once the wax fades.

GERTRUDE'S KNIGHT

Gertrude's Knights are the nastier versions of the Winged Knight. Tougher and harder hitting, they are still ponderous foes… until they take to the sky with their angelic wings!

Avoid their dangerous sweeping blows and holy magic. Use the available terrain to pick them off or back away as needed. There's plenty of open space where you encounter these winged knights, so make use of it.

ARCHDRAGON PEAK

The Serpent-men encountered in the Consumed King's Garden were partly a hint towards the existence of the Archdragon Peak. Unsurprisingly, they show up in considerably greater numbers at the Peak

NAME	HP	SOULS	ITEM DROP	SPECIAL ABILITY	WEAKNESS	RESISTANT TO	INEFFECTIVE	TYPE & EFFECTIVE ITEMS
Serpent-man Summoner	522	2400	Mendicant's Staff	None	Lightning/Frost	Poison & Toxic	None	None
Serpent-man	589	1500	Man Serpent Hatchet/Small Leather Shield/Large Titanite Shard/Titanite Chunk/Lightning Gem	Elemental Attack (Fire)	Lightning/Frost	Poison & Toxic	None	None
Serpent-man (Large)	1853	3600	Large Titanite Shard/Titanite Chunk/Lightning Gem	Elemental Attack (Fire)	Lightning/Frost	Poison & Toxic	None	None
Crystal Lizard	281	0	Twinkling Titanite(Fixed)	None	None	Magic	Poison & Toxic/Bleed/Frost	None
Ancient Wyvern	7846	36000	Titanite Chunk(Fixed)/Titanite Scale(Fixed)/Twinkling Titanite(Fixed) (both)	Elemental Attack (Fire)	Lightning/Frost	Poison & Toxic/Bleed	None	None
Ancient Wyvern	7873	70000	Dragon Head Stone(Fixed) (boss)	Elemental Attack (Fire)	Lightning/Frost	Poison & Toxic/Bleed	None	None
Rock Lizard	669	150	Titanite Scale/Twinkling Titanite	Elemental Attack (Fire)	None	Slash/Thrust/Fire/Lightning/Dark	Poison & Toxic/Bleed/Frost	Alluring Skull
Nameless King	7100	80000	Soul of the Nameless King(Fixed)	Elemental Attack (Lightning)	None	Lightning	Poison & Toxic	None
King of Storms	4577	0	None	Elemental Attack (Fire/Lightning)	Lightning	Fire/Poison & Toxic/Bleed	None	None

LARGE SERPENT-MAN

Large Serpent-men are burlier, tougher Serpent-men; you can spot them from far away, and this gives you time to prepare. Even though they're armed for melee combat, you need to be careful. They can throw their chains quite far, giving them medium range for some of their attacks.

Multiple blows are needed to kill each Large Serpent-man. Circle around them and get hits in while they recover from their slower attacks. If there are Serpent-men in the fight too, focus on them first to take out targets quickly and consolidate your problems.

ROCK LIZARD

There are Rock Lizards on a few hills and ledges. They're uncommon targets. Block or dodge if they roll toward you, and never stand with your back to a ledge when a Rock Lizard is close by, or you risk a fatal fall.

Rock Lizards are a sort of petrified Crystal Lizard, and a repeatable source of both Twinkling Titanite *and* Titanite Scales!

SERPENT-MAN SUMMONER

The sound of a chime periodically rings when you go into a room with a Serpent-man Summoner. When that happens, an Unkindled rises to come after you. These summoned enemies are worth their full Soul value, so you can farm them if you like. However, the battle won't end until you kill the Serpent-man Summoner. A fast run takes you past the Unkindled as they're forming. You usually get to kill the Serpent-man Summoner and then turn to take out the Unkindled.

Even if you wait, there will only be one Unkindled at a time. The Serpent-man Summoners just get themselves ready to call another one, but they won't complete the spell until you finish your target (they're polite).

The two Summoners here each summon a unique champion, one drops **Ricard's Rapier**, the other the **Drakeblood Greatsword**.

SPECIAL

DARK SPIRITS

Dark Spirits invade your world as red phantoms in some areas—these invasions are identical to an invasion by another player, with the obvious exception that these are AI controlled NPCs.

Because the specific challenge of the phantom depends on their loadout, you may find yourself facing a heavily armored melee tank, a lightweight ranged caster, or a nimble melee dodger.

The **Undead Hunter Charm** is of particular use against NPC Phantoms, it shuts down the use of Estus, which prevents these foes from healing! However, you can achieve the same goal with a simple Throwing Knife if you have one equipped and act fast, but keep the option in mind.

Phantoms block your ability to leave the area with fog doors, just like regular multiplayer invaders do, so you must defeat them before you can escape.

NPCS

In addition to the many types of enemies you can encounter throughout Lothric, there are also other foes of a more human (or undead) persuasion. You can encounter them out in the wild as allies, enemies, summonable phantoms, or invaders. This table summarizes all of the notable encounters, and any unique drops or special notes about them. **Be aware that, like the NPC chapter, reading this may spoil some NPC questlines, use on your first playthrough at your own risk!**

NPC	STATUS	LOCATION	ITEM DROP	NOTES
Anri of Astora	Summon player character as the host	Anor Londo	—	Summons you to battle Aldrich with him. Summon sign appears outside Aldrich's room. Only possible if you have progressed Anri's questline and slain the Pilgrim in the Church of Yorshka before killing Pontiff Sulyvahn.
Hawkwood the Deserter	White Phantom	Archdragon Peak	—	Sign is outside Great Belfry bonfire, at foot of steps.
Champion Spirit - Havel Knight	Adversary	Archdragon Peak	Dragon Tooth Havel's Greatshield	Encounter 14 in Archdragon Peak. Armor appears on Farron Keep bridge behind Stray Demon if you defeat him.
Champion Spirit - Drakeblood Knight	Adversary	Archdragon Peak	Drakeblood Greatsword	Encounter 8 in Archdragon Peak.
Champion Spirit - Vagabond Prince	Adversary	Archdragon Peak	Ricard's Rapier	Encounter 11 in Archdragon Peak.
Anri of Astora	Neutral	Catacombs of Carthus	Anri's Straight Sword	Appears on upper level of Catacombs first, then by rope bridge at lower level after talking to him.
Knight Slayer Tsorig	Dark Spirit	Catacombs of Carthus	My thanks! (gesture item) Knight Slayer's Ring	On lower level of catacombs, go down hall past Item 5 and return.
Sirris of the Sunless Realms	White Phantom	Cathedral of the Deep	—	Sign is immediately outside boss room.
Ringfinger Leonhard	Neutral	Cathedral of the Deep	Silver Mask Lift Chamber Key Cracked Red Eye Orb × 5	Appears after you pledge yourself to Rosaria's Fingers and offer or use a Pale Tongue.
Anri of Astora	Adversary	Cathedral of the Deep	Anri's Straight Sword	At the conclusion of Anri's questline, if you did not tell him of Horace's location.
Anri of Astora	White Phantom	Cathedral of the Deep	—	Sign is up the stairs from boss room.
Unbreakable Patches	Neutral	Cathedral of the Deep	Patches' Ashes Horsehoof Ring	Appears on second level, if you open the doors to the graveyard, then leave and return.
Unbreakable Patches	Neutral	Cathedral of the Deep	Patches' Ashes Horsehoof Ring	Appears across the central giant gate after talking with him near the doors to the graveyard.
Horace the Hushed	White Phantom	Cathedral of the Deep	—	Sign is up the stairs from boss room.
Brigand	Adversary	Cathedral of the Deep	Spider Shield	On stairs leading to the Cathedral graveyard.
Fallen Knight	Adversary	Cathedral of the Deep	—	Beside the initial bonfire.
Longfinger Kirk	Dark Spirit	Cathedral of the Deep	Barbed Straight Sword Spiked Shield	Downstairs in the giant's room. Armor appears in Rosaria's chamber after defeat.
Hawkwood the Deserter	White Phantom	Consumed King's Garden	—	Sign is directly on path to the boss, up the steps on the knight's platform.
Hawkwood the Deserter	Adversary	Farron Keep	Twinkling Dragon Head Stone	At the conclusion of Hawkwood's questline, after you receive Hawkwood's Swordgrass from the blacksmith.
Sirris of the Sunless Realms	White Phantom	Farron Keep	—	Sign is just outside boss door.
Yellowfinger Heysel	White Phantom	Farron Keep	—	Obtain the gesture, Proper bow, when summoning Yellowfinger Heysel. Sign is just outside the doors that are opened by extinguishing the flames in the swamp. Sign only appears if you have visited and offered a Pale Tongue to Rosaria.
Yellowfinger Heysel	Dark Spirit	Farron Keep	Heysel Pick Xanthous Crown	Invades in several locations, only drops items on first death.
Black Hand Gotthard	White Phantom	Farron Keep	—	Obtain the gesture, By my sword, when summoning Black Hand Gotthard. Sign is on stairs leading to boss room.
Londor Pale Shade	White Phantom	Farron Keep	—	Obtain the gesture, Duel bow, when summoning Londor Pale Shade. Sign is by Farron Keep Perimeter bonfire. Sign only appears if you are friendly with Yuria of Londor.
Londor Pale Shade	Dark Spirit	Farron Keep/Irithyll of the Boreal Valley	Manikin Claws	Attacks if you have angered Yuria of Londor. Pale Shade armor appears in Firelink if you defeat both him in both locations.
Greirat of the Undead Settlement	Neutral	Firelink Shrine	Greirat's Ashes	Found in a cell in the High Wall of Lothric.
Yuria of Londor	Neutral	Firelink Shrine	Yuria's Ashes Darkdrift	Hollow
Hawkwood the Deserter	Neutral	Firelink Shrine	Heavy Gem	Present in the shrine when you first reach it.
Sirris of the Sunless Realms	Neutral	Firelink Shrine	Sunless Talisman	Appears after you reach Farron Keep.
Sirris of the Sunless Realms	Dead	Firelink Shrine	—	By a grave outside Firelink near the Iudex doors, at the conclusion of her questline.
Ringfinger Leonhard	Neutral	Firelink Shrine	Silver Mask Lift Chamber Key Cracked Red Eye Orb × 5	Appears after reaching the Tower on the Wall bonfire, or defeating Vordt of the Boreal Valley.
Orbeck of Vinheim	Neutral	Firelink Shrine	Orbeck's Ashes	Found in the Road of Sacrifices
Cornyx of the Great Swamp	Neutral	Firelink Shrine	Cornyx's Ashes Old Sage's Blindfold Cornyx's Garb Cornyx's Wrap Cornyx's Skirt Pyromancy Flame	Found in a cage in the Undead Settlement
Karla	Neutral	Firelink Shrine	Karla's Ashes	Found in a cell in Irithyll Dungeon.
Irina of Carim	Neutral	Firelink Shrine	Irina's Ashes Tower Key	Found in a cell in the Undead Settlement
Eygon of Carim	Neutral	Firelink Shrine	Morne's Great Hammer Moaning Shield	Visits briefly to check on Irina (peaceful). Appears hostile if you attack Irina. Appears and kidnaps Irina if you corrupt her.
Unbreakable Patches	Neutral	Firelink Shrine	Patches' Ashes Horsehoof Ring	Appears outside the Firelink Tower if you go to the top and come back down after passing through the Cathedral of the Deep (whether you meet him there or not). Remains as a merchant on the upper floor.
Horace the Hushed	Neutral	Firelink Shrine	Llewellyn Shield Blue Sentinels	Visits briefly after Cathedral of the Deep with Anri.
Sword Master	Adversary	Firelink Shrine	Uchigatana Master's Attire Master's Gloves	Defeating the Sword Master here triggers his White Phantom appearing in High Wall and the Untended Graves.

NPC	STATUS	LOCATION	ITEM DROP	NOTES
Greirat of the Undead Settlement	Dead	Grand Archives	—	Dies if you send him to steal in Lothric Castle, even if you send Patches to attempt a rescue.
Sirris of the Sunless Realms	White Phantom	Grand Archives	—	Sign is outside the Twin Princes room.
Orbeck of Vinheim	Dead	Grand Archives	—	Expires (peacefully?) in a chair in the Grand Archives after aiding you in the Twin Princes battle at the end of his questline.
Orbeck of Vinheim	White Phantom	Grand Archives	—	Sign is outside the Twin Princes room.
Black Hand Gotthard	Adversary	Grand Archives	Onikiri and Ubadachi	Appears with his companions in a courtyard before the bridge to the Twin Princes.
Lion Knight Albert	Adversary	Grand Archives	Golden Wing Crest Shield	Appears with his companions in a courtyard before the bridge to the Twin Princes.
Daughter of Crystal Kriemhild	Adversary	Grand Archives	Sage's Crystal Staff	Appears with her companions in a courtyard before the bridge to the Twin Princes.
Greirat of the Undead Settlement	Neutral	High Wall of Lothric	Greirat's Ashes Blue Tearstone Ring	Can be recruited here.
Sword Master	White Phantom	High Wall of Lothric	—	Sign is in front of the boss door.
Lion Knight Albert	White Phantom	High Wall of Lothric	—	Sign is up the stairs from the boss near the Winged Knight room.
Karla	Neutral	Irithyll Dungeon	Karla's Ashes	Can be recruited here.
Siegward of Catarina	Neutral	Irithyll Dungeon	Storm Ruler Pierce Shield Catarina Helm Catarina Armor Catarina Gauntlets Catarina Leggings	Appears here twice if you have followed his questline, once locked in a cell, a second time to aid you against Yhorm the Giant.
Alva, Seeker of the Spurned	Dark Spirit	Irithyll Dungeon	Murakumo	Invades at the entrance to the dungeon.
Sirris of the Sunless Realms	Summon player character as the host	Irithyll of the Boreal Valley	—	Sirris of the Sunless Realms leaves a white summon sign, and Player Character can go into her world. Sign appears on the bridge into Irithyll, she summons you to battle Creighton the Wanderer.
Ringfinger Leonhard	Adversary*	Irithyll of the Boreal Valley	Soul of Rosaria Crescent Moon Sword Silver Mask	When invading him in Gwynevere's room past Aldrich in Anor Londo by using the Black Eye Orb.
Black Hand Gotthard	White Phantom	Irithyll of the Boreal Valley	—	Obtain the gesture, By my sword, when summoning Black Hand Gotthard. Sign is by a statue in front of Pontiff Sulyvahn's room.
Londor Pale Shade	White Phantom	Irithyll of the Boreal Valley	—	Obtain the gesture, Duel bow, when summoning Londor Pale Shade. Sign is by a statue in front of Pontiff Sulyvahn's room.
Creighton the Wanderer	Dark Spirit (In the world of Sirris)	Irithyll of the Boreal Valley	—	Battel against him with Sirris after she summons you.
Creighton the Wanderer	Dark Spirit	Irithyll of the Boreal Valley	Dragonslayer's Axe	Invades you in the small graveyard outside the Church of Yorskha after defeating him in Sirris realm. Causes his armor set to appear on the bridge into Irithyll if you defeat him here.
Greirat of the Undead Settlement	Dead	Irithyll of the Boreal Valley	—	If sent to Irithyll Valley alone. If Siegward is present, or if you tell Unbreakable Patches you sent Greirat, Greirat survives and returns with new items. If not, dies in sewers and leaves ashes.
Anri of Astora	Neutral	Irithyll of the Boreal Valley	Anri's Straight Sword	In Church of Yorshka.
Anri of Astora	Neutral	Irithyll of the Boreal Valley	Anri's Straight Sword	In hidden hallway for ceremony. Only appears if you progressed his storyline and did not kill the Pilgrim in the Church of Yorshka.
Anri of Astora	White Phantom	Irithyll of the Boreal Valley	—	Sign is in front of Pontiff Sulyvahn's room.
Siegward of Catarina	Neutral	Irithyll of the Boreal Valley	Storm Ruler Pierce Shield Catarina Helm Catarina Armor Catarina Gauntlets Catarina Leggings	Appears in the kitchen above the sewers if you returned his armor in the Cathedral of the Deep.
Aldrich Faithful - Drang Hammer Knight	Adversary	Irithyll of the Boreal Valley	—	In the courtyard just past Pontiff Sulyvahn's room.
Aldrich Faithful - Drang Spear Knight	Adversary	Irithyll of the Boreal Valley	Drang Twinspears	In the courtyard just past Pontiff Sulyvahn's room.
Yuria of Londor	White Phantom	Kiln of the First Flame	—	Sign only appears if you progressed her and Anri's storyline fully.
Londor Pale Shade	White Phantom	Kiln of the First Flame	—	Sign only appears if you progressed her and Anri's storyline fully.
Sirris of the Sunless Realms	White Phantom	Lothric Castle	—	Sign is outside Dragonslayer Armour's bridge.
Eygon of Carim	White Phantom	Lothric Castle	—	Sign is in a room just to the right of Dragonslayer Armour's bridge.
Court Sorcerer Eamon	Adversary	Profaned Capital	Logan's Scroll	On the roof of the chapel in the Profaned Capital.
Siegward of Catarina	Co-op*	Profaned Capital	—	If you progressed his story fully, he will join to help against Yhorm in human form.
Isabella the Mad	Adversary	Road of Sacrifices	Butcher Knife	Tucked away on a small path on the road leading from the Undead Settlement.
Orbeck of Vinheim	Neutral	Road of Sacrifices	Orbeck's Ashes	Can be recruited here.
Eygon of Carim	White Phantom	Road of Sacrifices	—	Sign is hidden behind a pillar in the room leading up to the Crystal Sage's room.
Anri of Astora	Neutral	Road of Sacrifices	Anri's Straight Sword	First meet Anri here.
Horace the Hushed	Neutral	Road of Sacrifices	Llewellyn Shield Blue Sentinels	Standing beside Anri, gives the Blue Sentinels Covenant sigil the first time you meet him.
Yellowfinger Heysel	Dark Spirit	Road of Sacrifices	Heysel Pick Xanthous Crown	Defeating Yellowfinger in the Road of Sacrifices or Farron Keep drops his items the first time he is defeated.
Holy Knight Hodrick	White Phantom (Purple)	Road of Sacrifices	—	He will attack allies and foes alike including the host who summons him.
Watchdog of Farron - Exile	Adversary	Road of Sacrifices	Exile Greatsword	Guards the entrance to Farron Keep.
Watchdog of Farron - Cleric Exile	Adversary	Road of Sacrifices	Great Club	Guards the entrance to Farron Keep.
Anri of Astora	Dead	Smouldering Lake	Anri's Straight Sword	If you tell him of Horace's location and do not kill Horace.
Anri of Astora	Adversary	Smouldering Lake	Anri's Straight Sword	At the conclusion of Anri's questline, if you told him of Horace's location and did kill Horace.
Horace the Hushed	Adversary	Smouldering Lake	Llewellyn Shield Blue Sentinels	In a small hidden chamber far below the rope bridge.
Great Swamp Cuculus	White Phantom	Smouldering Lake	—	Sign is just down the stairs from the Old Demon King's room.
Knight Slayer Tsorig	Adversary	Smouldering Lake	Fume Ultra Greatsword Black Iron Greatshield	Hidden deep in the Izalith ruins by a pool of lava.
Knight Slayer Tsorig	White Phantom	Smouldering Lake	—	Sign is in the small cave near the bonfire by the Old Demon King's room.
Sirris of the Sunless Realms	Summon player character as the host	Undead Settlement	—	Summon sign appears just outside the Curse-Rotted Greatwood's room, near the end of her questline.
Sirris of the Sunless Realms	Adversary	Undead Settlement	Sunless Talisman	Appears mad and hollow in the Pit of Hollows if you refuse her allegiance near the end of her questline.
Cornyx of the Great Swamp	Neutral	Undead Settlement	Cornyx's Ashes Old Sage's Blindfold Cornyx's Garb Cornyx's Wrap Cornyx's Skirt Pyromancy Flame	Can be recruited here.
Irina of Carim	Neutral	Undead Settlement	Irina's Ashes	Can be recruited here.
Eygon of Carim	Neutral	Undead Settlement	Morne's Great Hammer Moaning Shield	Outside Irina's cell, peaceful when encountered.
Eygon of Carim	Dead	Undead Settlement	—	If you do not anger him and protect Irina, appears dead in Irina's cell after his last fight against the Dragonslayer Armour as a White Phantom.
Siegward of Catarina	Neutral	Undead Settlement	Storm Ruler Pierce Shield Catarina Helm Catarina Armor Catarina Gauntlets Catarina Leggings	First meet Siegward here. Can battle with him cooperatively against a Demon beside the tower where you meet him.
Holy Knight Hodrick	Adversary (In the world of Sirris)	Undead Settlement	Mound-makers	When appearing as an adversary NPC in the world of Sirris of the Sunless Realms.
Holy Knight Hodrick	Dark Spirit (Purple)*	Undead Settlement	Vertebra Shackle	Returns to his world when he defeats the host or at least one white phantom.
Holy Knight Hodrick	Neutral	Undead Settlement	Homeward Bone	Can be encountered peacefully only by traveling to the Pit of Hollows via a Hollow Manservant's cage before the Curse-Rotted Greatwood is killed.
Sword Master	White Phantom	Untended Graves	—	Sign is just outside Champion Gundyr's room.
Daughter of Crystal Kriemhild	Dark Spirit	Untended Graves	—	Invades on the route to Champion Gundyr.

NPC White Phantom and Co-op Appearances

NAME	STATUS	AREA
Yuria of Londor	White Phantom	Kiln of the First Flame
Hawkwood the Deserter	White Phantom	Consumed King's Garden
Hawkwood the Deserter	White Phantom	Archdragon Peak
Sirris of the Sunless Realms	Summon player character as the host	Undead Settlement
Sirris of the Sunless Realms	Summon player character as the host	Irithyll of the Boreal Valley
Sirris of the Sunless Realms	White Phantom	Cathedral of the Deep
Sirris of the Sunless Realms	White Phantom	Farron Keep
Sirris of the Sunless Realms	White Phantom	Lothric Castle
Sirris of the Sunless Realms	White Phantom	Grand Archives
Orbeck of Vinheim	White Phantom	Grand Archives
Eygon of Carim	White Phantom	Road of Sacrifices
Eygon of Carim	White Phantom	Lothric Castle
Anri of Astora	Summon player character as the host	Anor Londo

NAME	STATUS	AREA
Anri of Astora	White Phantom	Anor Londo
Anri of Astora	White Phantom	Cathedral of the Deep
Siegward of Catarina	Co-op	Undead Settlement
Siegward of Catarina	Co-op	Profaned Capital
Horace the Hushed	White Phantom	Cathedral of the Deep
Sword Master	White Phantom	High Wall of Lothric
Sword Master	White Phantom	Untended Graves
Yellowfinger Heysel	White Phantom	Farron Keep
Black Hand Gotthard	White Phantom	Farron Keep
Black Hand Gotthard	White Phantom	Irithyll of the Boreal Valley
Great Swamp Cuculus	White Phantom	Smouldering Lake
Londor Pale Shade	White Phantom	Farron Keep
Londor Pale Shade	White Phantom	Irithyll of the Boreal Valley
Londor Pale Shade	White Phantom	Kiln of the First Flame
Lion Knight Albert	White Phantom	High Wall of Lothric
Knight Slayer Tsorig	White Phantom	Smouldering Lake

ANDRE THE BLACKSMITH

Andre the Blacksmith begins in the Firelink
Shrine and stays there the entire time. He serves
multiple functions, with most of them allowing your
character to become more powerful and to survive
greater dangers.

Bring him upgrade materials to improve your
weapons and shields. Special, named Coals give
him the ability to Infuse equipment in additional
ways; he'll be able to make them scale to different
attributes, or to gain special aspects (e.g. Bleed,
Frost, Poison).

Take Estus Shards to Andre so that you get even
more uses out of your Flasks for each time you stop
at a Bonfire. He'll also let you decide how many of
yours Flasks go toward Health or FPs.

Andre returns to the shrine if you kill him, but he
won't craft anything for you, or serve any of his other
functions. That's fair, he doesn't like being murdered!
To get his loyalty back, go to the Undead Settlement.
Near the Dilapidated Bridge Bonfire is a sewer area.
Down there you find an altar to Velka. Bring plenty of
Souls, pay for your sins, and be absolved.

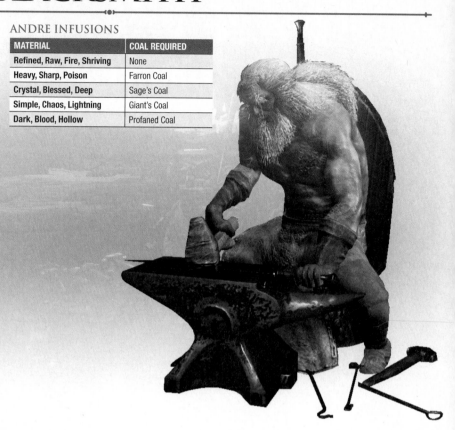

ANDRE INFUSIONS

MATERIAL	COAL REQUIRED
Refined, Raw, Fire, Shriving	None
Heavy, Sharp, Poison	Farron Coal
Crystal, Blessed, Deep	Sage's Coal
Simple, Chaos, Lightning	Giant's Coal
Dark, Blood, Hollow	Profaned Coal

ANRI AND HORACE

Anri is a very important NPC that you meet as you start working your way
through the Road of Sacrifices. This NPC is going to be a man if you're playing a
female character, or a woman if you're playing a male.

Anri is a good person who is traveling with Horace, a quiet Knight. Anri seems
like an honorable Unkinkled. Talk to Anri and Horace when you meet them.
Horace gives you the Blue Sentinels Covenant item, and Anri will move on and be
found elsewhere in the future. Anri's chain of events is incredibly elaborate, so
bear with us while we explain how to follow them.

If you are aiming for the Hollow Lord ending, look up Yuria in this chapter so
that you make sure that she is summoned in your
playthrough. You can't complete the Hollow Lord story
without Yuria.

ANRI'S STORY

❖ Halfway Fortress Bonfire: Talk to Anri several times
❖ After Killing Deacons of the Deep: Return after beating the Deacons and
   search around the shrine. You find Anri there, to the left of the thrones.
   Talk to Anri a couple of times to advance the quest. This is not required.
❖ Catacombs of Carthus, Upper Level: Meet Anri not too far from the front of
   the Catacombs. From the entrance bridge, look for a staircase below and
   to your right. The hallway you want is on the other side of those stairs is
   has a visible entrance from where you are. Talk to Anri
   and say nothing when asked if you've seen Horace.
   Exhaust this dialogue.

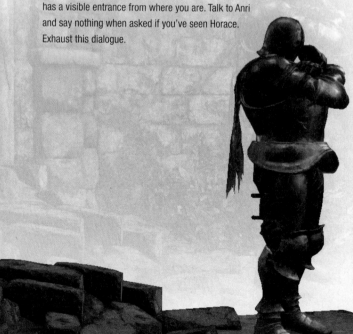

CORNYX THE PYROMANCER

Cornyx is a mage who is trapped in the Undead Settlement. Search for him in a cage that is above the road through town. You can't get to it without finding a way up to the rooftops. Ironically, this means that you need to look for a path below the main road. As you cross a stone bridge Peasant Hollows ahead begin to throw Firebombs at you. That's the right area.

CORNYX INVENTORY

SPELL/ITEM	COST	QUANTITY	PYROMANCY TOME REQUIRED
Fireball	1000	1	None
Fire Surge	1000	1	None
Great Combustion	3000	1	None
Flash Sweat	1500	1	None
Fire Orb	3000	1	Great Swamp Pyromancy Tome
Bursting Fireball	5000	1	Great Swamp Pyromancy Tome
Poison Mist	2000	1	Great Swamp Pyromancy Tome
Profuse Sweat	2000	1	Great Swamp Pyromancy Tome
Acid Surge	6000	1	Carthus Pyromancy Tome
Carthus Beacon	8000	1	Carthus Pyromancy Tome
Carthus Flame Arc	10000	1	Carthus Pyromancy Tome
Great Chaos Fire Orb	10000	1	Izalith Pyromancy Tome
Chaos Storm	12000	1	Izalith Pyromancy Tome
Pyromancer Crown	500	-	-
Pyromancer Garb	800	-	-
Pyromancer Wrap	500	-	-
Pyromancer Trousers	500	-	-

Drop off the side of the pathway to get onto a ledge beneath that village. You soon discover a Bonfire, and the path leads through a basement and up to the rooftops from the other side. Cornyx is easy to find from there. Let him join your cause, and he'll teleport to the Firelink Shrine.

Once there, he'll sell you Pyromancy spells. You find Tomes to expand his repertoire throughout the game. Bring them to him to improve his inventory.

If slain, he drops Ashes of Cornyx and Cornyx's Armor Set.

Unlike the other elaborate questlines here, Cornyx is remarkably straightforward. The only unusual secret he is connected to involves the White Phantom Great Swamp Cuculus in the Smouldering Lake. If you summon that phantom and defeat the Old Demon King, you can then journey to Cornyx's original imprisonment site, where you can find the **Spotted Whip**, and a set of Cornyx's garb.

❖ Catacombs of Carthus, Second Level: Anri is on a side ledge, close to the collapsing bridge that divides the area between the upper Catacombs and the lower area of Smouldering Lake. Anri is still looking for Horace. You can't say anything about Horace at first. He is directly underneath that position, though the fall would be fatal. You have to go down to the Smouldering Lake and find him down a side tunnel, off of the main cavern. When you return, after seeing him, you have the option to tell Anri.
To keep Anri alive, don't say anything. Or, travel down there and kill Horace the Hushed before speaking with Anri about it. Horace is in a distant side chamber, past a Crystal Lizard. It's a somewhat tough fight.
Regardless of what you choose to do, Anri gives you the **Ring of the Evil Eye** if you mention where you saw Horace. This is a very nice item that helps with keep your health high after battles (though you get it during the next step if you don't tell Anri anything).
Horace drops the **Llewellyn Shield** if you kill him.
If you do not kill Horace, but tell Anri of his whereabouts, Anri perishes in the lake at his chamber, dropping his blade there.

❖ Irithyll: Go to the Church of Yorshka Bonfire and look for Anri on the right side of the room. Talk Anri and get the Ring of the Evil Eye now. Complete the rest of the region, and summon Anri to help fight Pontiff Sulyvahn.

❖ Return to the Firelink Shrine and talk to Yuria several times. She'll let you know that the marriage ceremony is ready.

❖ Find the tower at the end of Irithyll (just a few steps away from Anor Londo). A secret wall disappears if you arrive here for the marriage ceremony. Go down that side hallway and talk to a Pilgrim. She gives you the **Sword of Avowal**. Keep going down the hall and use the sword for a ritual inside the next room. This grants the final three Dark Sigils needed to complete the Hollow Lord ending. However… if you do not wish to become such a Lord, there is another way.

❖ **Before** you defeat Pontiff Sulyvahn, there is a chance to save Anri, at least for the moment. When you meet Anri in the Church of Yorshka, hidden in the room are a group of statues. One of those statues is the Pilgrim of Londor, spying on the intended bride (or groom). Attack and kill the Pilgrim here and now to stop the ceremony! If you fail to kill the Pilgrim here, even if you have not encountered (or have angered) Yuria, Anri will still end up dead in the ceremony chamber, someone in some other world has wed Anri.
Killing the Pilgrim allows you to use Anri as a White Phantom against Sulyvahn as usual, but later, when you go to face Aldrich in Anor Londo, Anri places a summoning sign outside the door. Use the sign and you can join Anri to fight his/her version of Aldrich.
If you do so and successfully aid him/her in defeating Aldrich, Anri leaves the blade with Ludleth for you, and departs.
Where Anri departs to depends on if you told Anri of Horace's death. If you did, Anri travels to the grave site in the Smouldering Lake. If not, Anri travels to the graves in the Cathedral of the Deep near the entrance. Unfortunately, either way, Anri finishes this long journey maddened, and attacks you on sight. Anri's death anywhere along this chain results in the Shrine Handmaid selling the **Elite Knight** armor set, while Horace leaves the **Executioner's Armor**.

GREIRAT

Greirat is locked in a small cell underneath the High Wall of Lothric. You find this dungeon by going to the Tower on the Wall Bonfire, climbing to the bottom of its tower, and exploring the hallway down there.

To unlock Greirat, look for a Cell Key as you make your way toward the Winged Knight from Tower on the Wall, past the shapechanging cultist, down a ladder, and into a building at the bottom. Search it for the Cell Key.

Unlock Greirat the next time you see him. He'll ask you to find a friend of his, named Loretta. She's in the Undead Settlement, supposedly. He'll hand you a **Blue Tearstone Ring** to take to her. Agree to do this to win his friendship.

After being freed, Greirat goes to the Firelink Shrine. He'll be a merchant there. Loretta's Bones are in the Undead Settlement, not far from the Undead Settlement Bonfire. Bring her bones back to Greirat. He'll let you keep the ring.

With these things done, Greirat continues as a merchant but also offers to go out into the world. He'll pillage from various areas to improve his selection. You can prevent him from doing this, or allow him to collect as he sees fit.

Allowing him to pillage the Undead Settlement is safe. If you let him Pillage Irithyll without either Siegward present there, or telling Unbreakable Patches where he went, he will die in Irithyll, leaving his Ashes in the sewer.

If you send him to pillage Lothric Castle, he dies regardless of whether you tell Patches where he went.

If you kill Greirat, he'll drop Ashes of Greirat and a Bandit's Knife.

GRIERAT STANDARD INVENTORY

ITEM	COST	QUANTITY
Ember	2000	3
Bloodred Moss Clump	500	-
Throwing Knife	20	-
Firebomb	50	-
Rope Firebomb	50	-
Bandit's Knife	1500	-
Long Sword	1000	-
Bastard Sword	3000	-
Mace	600	-
Spear	600	-
Light Crossbow	1000	-
Buckler	2000	-
Elkhorn Round Shield	1500	-
Round Shield	1000	-
Kite Shield	4000	-
Standard Helm	1500	-
Hard Leather Armor	2500	-
Hard Leather Gauntlets	1000	-
Hard Leather Boots	1000	-
Thief Mask	400	-
Standard Arrow	10	-
Fire Arrow	100	-
Standard Bolt	30	-

GREIRAT SENT TO PILLAGE UNDEAD SETTLEMENT

ITEM	COST	QUANTITY
Ember	2000	4
Divine Blessing	8000	1
Repair Powder	300	-
Lightning Urn	700	6
Zweihander	6000	-
Pontiff Knight Curved Sword	6000	-
Estoc	3000	-
Warpick	1500	-
Glaive	3500	-
Short Bow	1000	-
Priest's Chime	4000	-
Target Shield	2500	-
Knight Shield	1500	-
Pontiff Knight Shield	3000	-
Knight Helm	2000	-
Knight Armor	3000	-
Knight Gauntlets	2000	-
Knight Leggings	3000	-
Assassin Hood	1500	-
Assassin Armor	1500	-
Assassin Gloves	1500	-
Assassin Trousers	1500	-
Large Arrow	50	-
Heavy Bolt	100	-
Sniper Bolt	150	-

GREIRAT SENT TO PILLAGE IRITHYLL

ITEM	COST	QUANTITY
Divine Blessing	8000	1
Hidden Blessing	8000	1
Twinkling Titanite	12000	3
Titanite Slab	16000	3
Scholar's Candlestick	3500	-
Lothric Knight Sword	4000	-
Lothric Knight Greatsword	7000	-
Lothric Knight Long Spear	4500	-
Knight's Crossbow	3000	-
Lothric Knight Shield	3000	-
Lothric Knight Greatshield	5000	-
Moonlight Arrow	500	-
Dragonslayer Greatarrow	500	-
Dragonslayer Lightning Arrow	750	-
Lightning Bolt	300	-

HAWKWOOD THE DESERTER

Hawkwood is a desolate man who stays in the Firelink Shrine. You meet him at the beginning of the game, when you first arrive at the shrine. He likes to hang out near the thrones, sitting with his legs kicked over the side of a ledge.

Speak with Hawkwood after defeating the Greatwood or Crystal Sage bosses to acquire a **Heavy Gem**. Defeat the Abyss Watchers and speak with him to acquire the **Farron Ring**.

You may occasionally find Hawkwood paying his respects to a grave outside the shrine on the right side…

After you have exhausted Hawkwood's dialogue and defeated all three of the above bosses, Hawkwood departs, leaving **Hawkwood's Shield** at the grave. At this point, you won't see Hawkwood for a long time. He'll appear again as a White Phantom sign in the Consumed King's Garden.

After that, if you find your way to Archdragon Peak, his White Phantom sign can be found not far from the third bonfire. Activating it causes Hawkwood to travel up to the shrine at the end of the trail, where he prays and vanishes.

If you follow suit and use the Path of the Dragon gesture at the shrine and acquire the Twinkling Dragon Torso Stone, Hawkwood leaves a message with Blacksmith Andre in the shrine, challenging you to a duel. If you travel to the Abyss Watcher's room in Farron Keep and face Hawkwood, defeating him earns you the **Twinkling Dragon Head Stone**, but losing loses the Torso stone.

IRINA OF CARIM

Irina starts in the Undead Settlement, toward the very end of the region. She's locked behind a door that can only be opened if you take the sewers all the way under the area. To open this, you need the Grave Key.

Explore the cemetery, by the white birch. This is where the gigantic arrows strike. You find Ashes there that should be taken back to Firelink Shrine. Give them to the Shrine Handmaid, buy the Grave Key from her, and return to the sewers.

On the far side, you meet Irina (and then Eygon as well). When you meet Irina, show her some warmth and then agree to take her into your service. She'll travel to Firelink Shrine and act as your teacher for Miracles. To expand her inventory, bring Braille Tomes back to her.

Learning Dark Miracles from Irina has consequences. If you give her the Deep or Londor Tomes and then purchase any Dark Miracles from her, she falls to darkness, and Eygon will kidnap her to try to save her from your corruption.

If you buy all of the Dark Miracles, she falls completely to darkness and no longer acts as a vendor. Interact with her for some sad dialogue. Or interact with her while wearing Eygon's gauntlets for some truly sad dialogue.

However, there is a brighter path. If you purchase all of the holy Miracles instead, she becomes a Fire Keeper, and moves to the basement of the tower just outside the Firelink Shrine!

If you had previously given her the dark Tomes (but did not buy any Dark Miracles), she will leave both of them on the ground beside her, and you can retrieve them to teach Karla instead.

IRINA INVENTORY

SPELL/ITEM	COST	QUANTITY	DIVINE TOME REQUIRED
Heal	1000	1	None
Replenishment	1000	1	None
Caressing Tears	1500	1	None
Homeward	3000	1	None
Med Heal	3500	1	Braille Divine Tome of Carim
Tears of Denial	10000	1	Braille Divine Tome of Carim
Force	1000	1	Braille Divine Tome of Carim
Bountiful Light	5000	1	Braille Divine Tome of Lothric
Blessed Weapon	8000	1	Braille Divine Tome of Lothric
Magic Barrier	5000	1	Braille Divine Tome of Lothric
Deep Protection	4000	1	Deep Braille Divine Tome
Gnaw	2000	1	Deep Braille Divine Tome
Dark Blade	10000	1	Londor Braille Divine Tome
Vow of Silence	15000	1	Londor Braille Divine Tome
Dead Again	5000	1	Londor Braille Divine Tome
Saint's Ring	300	1	-

EYGON OF CARIM

Eygon is a warrior who is charged with guarding Irina. He's a terse individual, and isn't very friendly. However, he'll do his job. If you release Irina from her cell (in the Undead Settlement), Eygon will agree to let her travel to the Firelink Shrine. Should you harm Irina, he'll turn aggressive on you.

If you purchase any Dark Miracles from Irina, she will fall to darkness, and Eygon will kidnap her. You can encounter him just outside the Iudex Gundyr bonfire when this occurs. If you do not anger Eygon, his last appearance is as a White Phantom for the Dragonslayer Armour battle, after which his corpse appears in Irina's original cell in the Undead Settlement.

KARLA THE WITCH

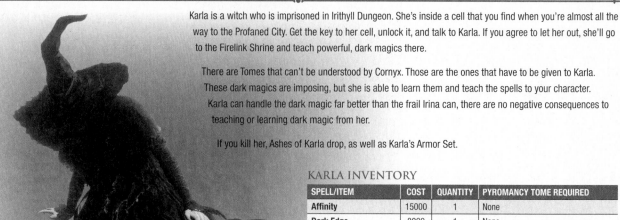

Karla is a witch who is imprisoned in Irithyll Dungeon. She's inside a cell that you find when you're almost all the way to the Profaned City. Get the key to her cell, unlock it, and talk to Karla. If you agree to let her out, she'll go to the Firelink Shrine and teach powerful, dark magics there.

There are Tomes that can't be understood by Cornyx. Those are the ones that have to be given to Karla. These dark magics are imposing, but she is able to learn them and teach the spells to your character. Karla can handle the dark magic far better than the frail Irina can, there are no negative consequences to teaching or learning dark magic from her.

If you kill her, Ashes of Karla drop, as well as Karla's Armor Set.

KARLA INVENTORY

SPELL/ITEM	COST	QUANTITY	PYROMANCY TOME REQUIRED
Affinity	15000	1	None
Dark Edge	8000	1	None
Dark Blade	10000	1	Londor Braille Divine Tome
Vow of Silence	15000	1	Londor Braille Divine Tome
Dead Again	5000	1	Londor Braille Divine Tome
Deep Protection	4000	1	Deep Braille Divine Tome
Gnaw	2000	1	Deep Braille Divine Tome
Fire Whip	10000	1	Quelana Pyromancy Tome
Firestorm	15000	1	Quelana Pyromancy Tome
Rapport	7000	1	Quelana Pyromancy Tome
Black Flame	10000	1	Grave Warden Pyromancy Tome
Black Fire Orb	10000	1	Grave Warden Pyromancy Tome

LEONHARD, THE RINGFINGER

Leonhard usually spends time near the thrones for the Lords of Cinder (in Firelink Shrine). He first appears after you light the Tower on the Wall bonfire in the High Wall, or after defeating Vordt. Speak with him to acquire 5 Cracked Red-Eye Orbs, which can be used to invade other players as a hostile Red Phantom.

Once you light the Cliff Underside bonfire in the Undead Settlement, or defeat the Curse Rotted Greatwood and you have a Pale Tongue in your inventory, Leonhard reappears in the shrine. Speak with him to acquire the Lift-Chamber Key. You can use this key to descend through a locked door in the High Wall of Lothric, beneath the Tower on the Wall bonfire. Deep in the chamber is a Darkwraith. Defeat it, and you can acquire a full **Red Eye Orb**, which can be used for unlimited invasions of other players. Defeating the Darkwraith also causes Leonhard to appear once more in the shrine.

Your next encounter with Leonhard only occurs if you join Rosaria's Fingers in the Cathedral of the Deep and offer or use at least one Pale Tongue (though be aware that doing so antagonizes Sirris of the Sunless Realm if you are pursuing her questline). Leonhard appears at the exit to her chamber after you do so.

Still later, after you have joined Rosaria's Fingers and you have reached the Profaned Capital bonfire or defeated Yhorm the Giant, Leonhard slays Rosaria. Return to her body to find the **Black Eye Orb**. Take the Orb to the highest room in Anor Londo, it will activate, allowing you to invade Leonhard and slay him to recover **Rosaria's Soul**, as well as the **Crescent Moon Sword** and the **Silver Mask**. This also causes the Shrine Handmaid to sell **Leonhard's Armor** set.

LUDLETH OF COURTLAND

TRANSPOSITION KILN

ITEM	COST	BOSS SOUL REQUIRED
Giant's Chain	0	Champion Gundyr
Crystal Hai	1500	Crystal Sage
Crystal Sage's Rapier	0	Crystal Sage
Soothing Sunlight	5000	Dancer
Dancer's Enchanted Swords	0	Dancer
Deep Soul	0	Deacons of the Deep
Cleric's Candlestick	0	Deacons of the Deep
Demon's Greataxe	0	Demon
Demon's Fist	0	Demon
Dragonslayer Greataxe	0	Dragonslayer Armour
Dragonslayer Greatshield	0	Dragonslayer Armour
Lightning Storm	5000	Nameless King
Storm Curved Sword	5000	Nameless King
Dragonslayer Swordspear	5000	Nameless King
White Dragon Breath	10000	Oceiros
Moonlight Greatsword	10000	Oceiros
Chaos Bed Vestiges	5000	Old Demon King
Old King's Great Hammer	0	Old Demon King
Hollowslayer Greatsword	1000	Rotted Greatwood
Arstor's Spear	1000	Rotted Greatwood
Sunlight Spear	10000	Soul of the Lords
Firelink Greatsword	15000	Soul of the Lords
Boulder Heave	0	Stray Demon
Havel's Ring	5000	Stray Demon
Greatsword of Judgment	3000	Sulyvahn
Profaned Greatsword	3000	Sulyvahn
Lothric's Holy Sword	5000	Twin Princes
Lorian's Greatsword	0	Twin Princes
Vordt's Great Hammer	0	Vordt
Pontiff's Left Eye	0	Vordt
Black Serpent	0	Wolnir
Wolnir's Holy Sword	0	Wolnir
Yhorm's Great Machete	0	Yhorm
Yhorm's Greatshield	0	Yhorm

Ludleth is one of the Lords of Cinder. He sits on top of his throne, in the Firelink Shrine. Talk to him early on to see how the small but ominous fellow is doing.

Once you kill the Curse-rotted Greatwood, you should return to Ludleth and give him the Transposition Kiln that you receive from that boss. This lets Ludleth turn the special souls that you get from bosses into special items. Many are weapons, but spells and rings are in that bunch as well! If you don't see things that you like, you can still convert the boss' materials into Souls later to try and buy others things or to raise your level.

If you kill Ludleth, you get the Skull Ring (it makes you easier to detect). Ludleth returns from the dead, and he takes the whole thing in stride.

Should you progress Anri's storyline far into the game, he will leave **Anri's Straight Sword** with Ludleth for you to retrieve.

HOLY KNIGHT HODRICK

Hodrick is a mad Hollow knight, a servant of the Mound Makers Covenant. It is possible to encounter him in a few locations throughout the game, as a Mound Maker PvP summon, or if you pursue Sirris questline, as a foe in her world.

Reaching Hodrick in your world alive is tricky, to say the least. He resides in the Pit of Hollows, beneath the Rotted Greatwood. However, if you kill that boss, the floor collapses during the battle, killing Hodrick.

The only way to meet Hodrick alive is to locate a Hollow Manservant wearing a cage on its back, just north of **Item 12** on our Undead Settlement map. Approach it quietly from behind and you can press the use key on the cage to enter the cage and you will be deposited in the Pit of Hollows!

ORBECK OF VINHEIM

Orbeck is a mage and an assassin. He is studying near the Crystal Sage boss fight, in the Road of Sacrifices. If you have at least 10 Intelligence, he'll offer to join you and travel to Firelink Shrine.

Orbeck's pact with you is a promise to deliver him scrolls for study. Fail to do so by killing four bosses without giving him a single scroll and he departs forever.

You can obtain the **Young Dragon Ring** and the **Slumbering Dragon Ring** by speaking with Orbeck.

For the Young ring, buy at least three sorceries, give him one scroll and be playing any non-Sorcerer starting class (though he gives this ring on New Game+ to any starting class). For the Slumbering ring, purchase Aural Decoy, Farron Flashsword, and Pestilent Mercury.

Finally, if you manage to provide him with all of the scrolls in the game and buy all of the spells, he speaks with you politely before departing. You can then find his White Phantom summon sign on the battlements near the Twin Princes battle in the Grand Archives.

After defeating the Twin Princes, you can find Orbeck dead in the Grand Archives, where you can pick up his ashes. At least he died surrounded by his favored books of sorcery…

Yuria of Londor may task you with eliminating Orbeck. Do so, and she rewards you with the **Morion Blade**.

ORBECK STANDARD INVENTORY

SPELL/ITEM	COST	QUANTITY	SCROLL REQUIRED
Soul Arrow	1000	1	None
Great Soul Arrow	3000	1	None
Heavy Soul Arrow	2000	1	None
Great Heavy Soul Arrow	4000	1	None
Farron Dart	1000	1	None
Great Farron Dart	2000	1	Sage
Farron Hail	5000	1	Sage
Homing Soulmass	6000	1	Logan
Homing Crystal Soulmass	18000	1	Crystal
Soul Spear	5000	1	Logan
Crystal Soul Spear	15000	1	Crystal
Soul Greatsword	5000	1	None
Farron Flashsword	3000	1	None
Magic Weapon	3000	1	None
Crystal Magic Weapon	10000	1	Crystal
Magic Shield	3000	1	None
Spook	2000	1	None
Aural Decoy	2000	1	None
Pestilent Mercury	1000	1	Sage
Cast Light	1000	1	Golden
Repair	2000	1	Golden
Hidden Weapon	1500	1	Golden
Hidden Body	3000	1	Golden
Twisted Wall of Light	6000	1	Golden

SHRINE HANDMAID

The Shrine Handmaid will always be at the Firelink Shrine. She serves as a major merchant for the area throughout all of your playthroughs. You can't kill her, at least, not for long. Attacking her gets you very little. In fact, she'll raise her prices by 20% when she returns, so you're really hurting yourself no matter how you look at it.

As with the Smith, you can restore the Handmaid's prices by visiting the altar to Velka (in the Undead Settlement). Pay your Souls for absolution and the Shrine Handmaid will return to her regular prices.

The Shrine Handmaid acquires new inventory by providing her with Ashes. She also sells new equipment after you defeat certain bosses and enemies, and complete various NPC questlines (or kill them!).

This table covers all items she normally sells, plus items for giving her Ashes. If you spot an armor set in the Equipment chapter with its location as the Shrine Handmaid, you need to kill the NPC or boss associated with that set to unlock it.

There is a second Shrine Handmaid hidden in the game, located in the Untended Graves, she sells a few unique items.

Placing all of the Lord's Ashes upon their thrones causes the Handmaid to sell a single Titanite Slab.

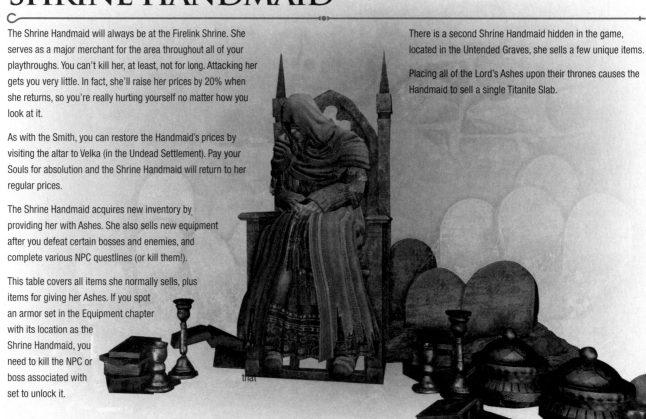

SHRINE HANDMAID STANDARD INVENTORY

SPELL/ITEM	COST	#	ASHES REQUIRED
Ember	2500	3	Multiple Ashes Yield This
Hidden Blessing	1000	1	Dreamchaser
Green Blossom	1000	-	Dreamchaser
Repair Powder	600	-	None
Blue Bug Bellet	1500	-	Excrement Covered
Red Bug Pellet	1000	-	Patches
Yellow Bug Pellet	1500	-	Paladin
Black Bug Pellet	1500	-	Dreamchaser
Mossfruit	1500	-	Dragon Chaser
Bloodred Moss Clump	500	-	Greirat
Purple Moss Clump	500	6	None
Blooming Purple Moss Clump	1000	-	Excrement Covered
Rime-Blue Moss Clump	500	-	Prisoner Chief
Purging Stone	4500	-	Yuria
Throwing Knife	20	-	Greirat
Poison Throwing Knife	100	-	Yuria
Kukri	50	-	Grave Warden
Firebomb	100	-	None
Rope Firebomb	300	-	Greirat
Black Firebomb	300	-	Patches
Rope Black Firebomb	300	-	Patches
Dung Pie	50	-	Grave Warden
Stalk Dung Pie	50	-	Grave Warden
Charcoal Pine Resin	500	-	Mortician
Charcoal Pine Bundle	300	-	Mortician
Gold Pine Resin	1000	3	Dreamchaser
Gold Pine Bundle	600	6	Dreamchaser
Pale Pine Resin	1000	-	Prisoner Chief
Human Pine Resin	1500	-	Patches
Rotten Pine Resin	500	-	Dreamchaser
Carthus Rouge	1000	-	Grave Warden
Alluring Skull	800	-	Patches
Undead Hunter Charm	500	-	Paladin
Duel Charm	500	-	Paladin
Rusted Coin	200	-	Patches
Young White Branch	1000	-	Xanthous
Rubbish	200	-	Patches
Prism Stone	10	-	None
Homeward Bone	500	-	None
White Sign Soapstone	500	1	None
Titanite Shard	800	-	Dreamchaser
Large Titanite Shard	4000	-	Easterners
Titanite Chunk	13000	-	Dragon Chaser
Twinkling Titanite	15000	-	Dragon Chaser
Titanite Scale	20000	-	Dragon Chaser
Dried Finger	2000	1	None
Tower Key	20000	1	None
Grave Key	1500	1	Mortician

SPELL/ITEM	COST	#	ASHES REQUIRED
Londor Braille Divine Tome	50	1	Yuria
Soul Arrow	2000	1	None
Great Soul Arrow	3000	1	Orbeck
Heavy Soul Arrow	2000	1	Orbeck
Great Heavy Soul Arrow	4000	1	Orbeck
Farron Dart	1000	1	None
Soul Greatsword	5000	1	Orbeck
Farron Flashsword	3000	1	Orbeck
Magic Weapon	3000	1	Orbeck
Magic Shield	3000	1	Orbeck
Spook	2000	1	Orbeck
Aural Decoy	2000	1	Orbeck
Affinity	15000	1	Karla
Dark Edge	8000	1	Karla
Fireball	1000	1	Cornyx
Fire Surge	1000	1	Cornyx
Great Combustion	3000	1	Cornyx
Poison Mist	2000	1	Cornyx
Flash Sweat	1500	1	Cornyx
Heal Aid	500	1	None
Heal	1000	1	Irina
Replenishment	1000	1	Irina
Caressing Tears	1500	1	Irina
Homeward	3000	1	Irina
Dagger	300	-	None
Parrying Dagger	2000	-	Patches
Bandit's Knife	1500	-	Greirat
Shortsword	600	-	None
Longsword	1000	-	Greirat
Bastard Sword	3000	-	Greirat
Scimitar	600	-	None
Shotel	4000	2	Patches
Washing Pole	7500	1	Easterners
Mace	600	-	Greirat
Morningstar	2500	-	Paladin
Spear	600	-	Greirat
Winged Spear	1500	-	Patches
Halberd	1500	-	None
Crescent Axe	4000	-	Paladin
Dark Hand	12000	1	Yuria
Composite Bow	3500	-	Dreamchaser
Light Crossbow	1000	-	Greirat
Sorcerer's Staff	500	-	None
Talisman	500	-	None
Canvas Talisman	3000	-	Paladin
Torch	300	-	None
Buckler	2000	-	Greirat
Leather Shield	500	-	None
Crimson Parma	800	-	None
Elkhorn Round Shield	1500	-	Greirat
Warrior's Round Shield	600	-	None
Large Leather Shield	800	-	None

SPELL/ITEM	COST	#	ASHES REQUIRED
Round Shield	1000	-	Greirat
Kite Shield	4000	-	Greirat
Chain Helm	500	-	None
Chain Armor	800	-	None
Leather Armor	800	-	Greirat
Leather Gloves	500	-	Greirat
Leather Boots	500	-	Greirat
Standard Helm	1500	-	Greirat
Hard Leather Armor	2500	-	Greirat
Hard Leather Gauntlets	1000	-	Greirat
Hard Leather Boots	1000	-	Greirat
Chain Helm	500	-	Greirat
Chain Armor	800	-	Greirat
Leather Gauntlets	500	-	None
Chain Leggings	500	-	None
Eastern Helm	5000	1	Easterners
Eastern Armor	8000	1	Easterners
Eastern Gauntlets	5000	1	Easterners
Eastern Leggings	5000	1	Easterners
Thief Mask	400	-	Greirat
Black Leather Armor	2500	-	Patches
Black Leather Gloves	2000	-	Patches
Black Leather Boots	2000	-	Patches
Karla's Pointed Hat	5000	1	Prisoner Chief
Karla's Coat	8000	1	Prisoner Chief
Karla's Gloves	5000	1	Prisoner Chief
Karla's Trousers	5000	1	Prisoner Chief
Xanthous Overcoat	10000	1	Xanthous
Xanthous Gloves	7000	1	Xanthous
Xanthous Trousers	7000	1	Xanthous
Pyromancer Crown	500	-	Cornyx
Pyromancer Garb	800	-	Cornyx
Pyromancer Wrap	500	-	Cornyx
Pyromancer Trousers	500	-	Cornyx
Wood Arrow	5	-	None
Feather Arrow	100	-	Dreamchaser
Fire Arrow	100	-	Greirat
Poison Arrow	120	-	Patches
Dark Arrow	200	-	Easterners
Onislayer Greatarrow	600	-	Easterners
Wood Bolt	10	-	None
Standard Bolt	30	-	Greirat
Life Ring	1500	1	Dreamchaser
Replenishment	1000	1	Irina
Saint's Ring	300	1	None
Wood Grain Ring	3000	1	Excrement Covered
Lloyd's Shield Ring	2500	1	Paladin
Untrue Dark Ring	5000	1	Yuria
Untrue White Ring	5000	1	Yuria
Ring of Sacrifice	5000	3	Yuria

UNBREAKABLE PATCHES

Patches is a disreputable sort who you can first encounter in the Cathedral of the Deep. If you open the front doors leading out to the graveyard, then leave and return, he appears on the second floor by the large gate leading to the pool of slime. You may find your interactions with him end poorly, but if you forgive him, you can eventually acquire his services as a merchant back in the shrine. You can find and speak with him a second time in the cathedral by using the rafters to cross over to Rosaria's side of the second floor, where he is waiting.

However, if you bypass the front door route (or don't leave and return) and travel over the rafters above the cathedral to reach Rosaria, you won't encounter Patches in the Cathedral.

Either way, to meet him a second time, return to the Firelink Shrine, purchase the Tower Key and head up to the top of the tower where the Firekeeper's Soul rests. When you come back down the lift, you will find Patches has locked the door. Descend through the tower and emerge out the door at the bottom.

Again, if you forgive him, you can retain his services as a merchant. He resides up on the upper level of the Firelink Shrine. Patches sells Siegward's armor set, and indeed, you need to purchase it to save Siegward from being trapped down a well without it outside the Cathedral of the Deep's Cleansing Chapel!

Finally, Patches has a fair bit of respect for Greirat, the thief. Should you attack Greirat, this will enrage Patches and he will attack. If you send Greirat to pillage Irithyll and tell Patches, he will travel there to rescue him (assuming Siegward isn't already there, as Siegward can also save Greirat). If you send Greirat to pillage Lothric Castle, Patches will try to save him, but fail…

ITEM	COST	QUANTITY
Ember	5000	4
Red Bug Pellet	1000	—
Black Firebomb	300	—
Rope Black Firebomb	300	—
Human Pine Resin	1500	—
Alluring Skull	800	—
Rusted Coin	200	—
Rubbish	200	—
Parrying Dagger	2000	—
Shotel	4000	2
Winged Spear	1500	—

ITEM	COST	QUANTITY
Pierce Shield	3000	1
Catarina Helm	3500	1
Catarina Armor	4500	1
Catarina Gauntlets	3500	1
Catarina Leggings	3500	1
Black Leather Armor	2500	—
Black Leather Gloves	2000	—
Black Leather Boots	2000	—
Poison Arrow	120	—
Horsehoof Ring	500	1

ROSARIA

Rosaria is the Covenant leader for Rosaria's Fingers, the PvP Covenant. Located in the Cathedral of the Deep, her room can only be reached by climbing over the rafters high above the cathedral floor.

Rosaria also acts as the only source of a few very special services. You can respec your attributes completely by visiting her, and you can change your appearance. Both require Pale Tongues. You are limited to five respecs or rebirths on a single playthrough, but if you venture into new game territory, you can do so again.

There is a subplot involving Ringfinger Leonhard and his relationship with both you and Rosaria. If you follow Leonhard's story up to the point of retrieving the Red Eye Orb from the Darkwraith in High Wall and then come to the Cathedral and join Rosaria's Fingers, he appears just outside her chambers to greet you.

Later, after reaching the Profaned Capital bonfire or defeating Yhorm, if you return here, you will find Rosaria dead! Pick up the **Black Eye Orb** from her body and carry it with you to Anor Londo. In the room at the top of the cathedral there, past the Aldrich boss fight, the Black Eye Orb triggers, allowing you to invade Leonhard and slay him to recover **Rosaria's Soul**. Return her soul and she revives as though nothing occurred.

Finally, joining Rosaria's Fingers angers Sirris' of the Sunless Realms. If you are pursuing her story fully, you cannot join Rosaria in the same playthrough.

SIEGWARD OF CATARINA

Siegward is a knight of Catarina. You first meet him in the Undead Settlement. He'll come up a lift as you prepare to finish the region and leave for the Road of Sacrifices. Talk to Siegward a few times to finish his dialogue there.

He'll move to a balcony slightly higher along that same lift. Roll off of the lift when it's on its way up, and talk to him more to find out what he's going there. He wants to stop the arrows that are coming from that tower. If you befriend the Giant up top, this will succeed.

Either way, Siegward will join you as an ally in battle if you descend from his balcony and go toward the town that's close by. There is a powerful Demon there that can (and should) be killed. Help Siegward in that fight and then talk with him a few times afterward. You get his Siegbrau as a reward, and he'll teach you Toast and Sleep gestures too.

Siegward is next found in a bind in the Cathedral of the Deep. Trapped down a well just outside the Cleansing Shrine bonfire chapel, you need to recover his full Catarina armor from Patches and give it to him there. Do so and he'll teach you the Rejoice gesture and venture on to Irithyll Valley.

Meeting Siegward in Irithyll Valley is rewarding, as he grants you the Emit Force miracle, another gesture, and, should you send Greirat to pillage Irithyll while Siegward is present, he automatically saves the little thief from death. You can find him resting by the pot of Estus Soup in the kitchen just above the sewers.

Finally, in Irithyll Dungeon, you find Siegward in another bind. He's been captured and locked in a cell. Find the Key to unlock and release him. This is well rewarded, because Siegward gives you a Titanite Slab for your efforts! If you help Siegward through all of that, he'll be able to return the favor when you go against Yhorm the Giant at the end of the Profaned Capital. After the battle, you can return to Yhorm's room and retrieve the full **Catarina Armor** set from Siegward, as well as a second **Storm Ruler** sword, and his shield.

SIRRIS OF THE SUNLESS REALMS

This valorous Blade of the Darkmoon appears in Firelink Shrine after you reach Farron Keep. Speak to her, and then explore Farron Keep to find the Dreamchaser's Ashes. Deliver those to the Shrine Handmaid, and Sirris will appear again, offering the Darkmoon Loyalty gesture.

At this point, her White Phantom sign appears in Farron Keep and the Cathedral of the Deep.

When you reach Irithyll Valley after you battle Sulyvahn's Beast on the bridge at the entrance to the town, leave and return to check the front of the bridge. There you can find a summoning sign from Sirris. Enter her world and aid her against the invader Creighton the Wanderer. Successfully defend Sirris and she'll show up in the shrine again to thank you, and give you a **Blessed Mail Breaker**. In addition, Creighton now invades you later in Irithyll Valley, and after defeating him for his **Dragonslayer's Axe**, **Creighton's Armor** set appears in the middle of the bridge at the entrance to the town.

Finally, she has one last summoning event directly in front of the Curse Rotted Greatwood's room. To trigger it, you must defeat both the Greatwood and Aldrich in Anor Londo. Because slaying the Greatwood causes Hodrick to perish, you may wish to visit him before killing the Greatwood.

Successfully aid her in her battle when she summons you to acquire the **Sunset Armor** set, and she returns to the Shrine and asks to swear an oath of knighthood to you. In addition, she leaves the **Sunset Shield** by the grave of her grandfather. To find it, look off the right side of the cliff, just past the doors from Iudex Gundyr's room.

If you accept her vow, she appears as a White Phantom for Dragonslayer Armour and the Twin Princes battles in Lothric Castle and the Grand Archives. Complete those battles, and you later find her corpse by her grandfather's grave, along with the **Sunless Talisman**.

Should you refuse her offer of knighthood however, she is found Hollow and aggressive in the Pit of Hollows.

Fully completing her storyline, or killing her causes the Shrine Handmaid to sell the **Sunless Armor** set.

THE FIRE KEEPER

The Fire Keeper lives in the Firelink Shrine. She'll allow you to spend Souls to improve your character. Talk to her to learn a bit more about her purpose, but don't try to harm her. When slain, she'll simply return. If you perform an emote in front of the Fire Keeper, she may respond with a gesture of her own. Try them all...

CHOICES, CHOICES

The Fire Keeper can be given Eyes of a Fire Keeper and the Soul of a Fire Keeper. The Soul is found on the tower above the shrine. Buy the Tower Key from the Shrine Handmaid, unlock the tower, and follow that route up to get the Fire Keeper Soul. Give the Fire Keeper that soul; she gains the power to remove the Dark Sigil from you. This costs many Souls, but can be done at any time as long as you can afford it. To get the Eyes of a Fire Keeper look up the Untended Graves section of the walkthrough. Go to that area and search for a hidden door in that region (it's in the spot where Irina would be if you were in the real Firelink Shrine).

To use the Eyes of a Fire Keeper, talk to the Fire Keeper and give them to her. Talk to her twice afterward to hear everything about them. Then, talk to the Fire Keeper again when you're at the end of the game. She'll say to summon her instead of Linking the First Flame.

Beat the final boss normally, and then approach the First Flame (the Bonfire that appears). Instead of lighting it, look for a white summoning sign on the group. Use that sign to summon the Fire Keeper and get the dark ending to the game, or summon and attack her when you regain control for an alternate ending.

Until you actually do all of this, you can change your mind. Slaying the Fire Keeper lets you take the Eyes back, preventing the alternate ending from occurring. Also, Linking the First Flame gets you the standard ending even if you've given the Fire Keeper her eyes.

THE GIANT OF THE UNDEAD SETTLEMENT

A Giant lives on top of a fort in the Undead Settlement. This massive creature shoots arrows down toward a white birch far away. When you're traveling through the Undead Settlement, you might get hit or even killed by these arrows. Your enemies are also targeted, though that's only of marginal help because you're so busy trying not to get splattered.

To stop the arrows, go to the fort and take the lift that goes to the top of the building. Meet the Giant and either talk to him or kill him. If you're friendly and give him one of the branches from the white birch, he'll stop shooting his bow at you when you're down in the valley. If you kill him, that works as a long-term solution as well.

Remaining friendly with him can help you in a few places later, there are white birch trees in both Faron Keep's swamp, and in the graveyard outside the Cathedral of the Deep.

He'll shoot at any foes near any of the three trees, and won't target you if you carry a white branch, or wear either the Worker's Hat or Evangelist's Hat.

If you pick up all of the white tree branches and return, you find the Giant has peacefully expired, leaving the **Hawk Ring**. Or you can kill him to take it, you monster.

THE NESTLING OF FIRELINK SHRINE (SNUGGLY THE CROW)

A Nestling, rumored to be named Snuggly, lives on top of the Firelink Shrine. Get onto the bridge above the shrine, using a key that you can purchase from the Shrine Handmaid. Jump off of the bridge, onto the roof, and look for a nest close by. Stand inside the nest and look at your inventory. Select an item, "Leave" it, and then see if the Nestling will exchange that item for something more interesting.

Each playthrough only allows you to trade one of each item type on the list. In New Game Plus, you can go back and start trading again, so remember to do that! Many of these trades are quite advantageous, so keep an eye out for these opportunities.

ORIGINAL ITEM	EXCHANGED ITEM
Alluring Skull	Hello Carving
Hidden Blessing	Thank you Carving
Divine Blessing	Very good! Carving
Shriving Stone	I'm sorry Carving
Yorshka's Chime	Help Me! Carving
Cleric's Sacred Chime	Help Me! Carving
Priest's Chime	Help Me! Carving
Saint-Tree Bellvine	Help Me! Carving
Caitha's Chime	Help Me! Carving
Crystal Chime	Help Me! Carving
Lightning Urn	Iron Helm
Siegbräu	Armor of the Sun
Homeward Bone	Iron Bracelets
Seed of a Giant Tree	Iron Leggings
Firebomb	Large Titanite Shard
Rope Firebomb	Large Titanite Shard
Black Firebomb	Titanite Chunk
Rope Black Firebomb	Titanite Chunk
Undead Bone Shard	Porcine Shield
Blacksmith Hammer	Titanite Scale
Avelyn	Titanite Scale
Prism Stone	Twinkling Titanite
Large Leather Shield	Twinkling Titanite
Xanthous Crown	Lightning Gem
Moaning Shield	Blessed Gem
Eleonora	Hollow Gem
Vertebra Shackle	Lucatiel's Mask
Loretta's Bone	Ring of Sacrifice
Coiled Sword Fragment	Titanite Slab
Mendicant's Staff	Sunlight Shield

YOEL OF LONDOR

Yoel is discovered in the earliest part of the Undead Settlement. From the Foot of the High Wall, you descend to a road with Starved Hounds and weaker undead. Kill these targets and look along a desolate stretch to your left. Many petrified pilgrims are there. Look around until you find one that is alive. He'll talk to you. Agree to let him enter your service and he'll travel to the Firelink Shrine. There, he'll help you learn magic. Speak to Yoel in the shrine and he can use Draw Out True Power. This lets you gain a 'free' level, but beware, nothing is without cost. Each time he draws out your power you acquire a Dark Sigil item. While in possession of these sigils, each time you die, you gain Hollowing Points, and your appearance becomes ever more corpse-like.

The only way to cure the Dark Sigil is to give the Fire Keeper the Firekeeper's Soul and pay her in Souls to remove the Sigils. The cost can become extremely expensive, you must pay the cost of your next Level times the number of Dark Sigils you are carrying. Hollowing points (and the curse of your undead appearance) can be reversed by using a Purging Stone, but doing so does not remove the Dark Sigils, only the Fire Keeper can cleanse them.

To fully draw out your strength, you must gain a certain amount of Hollowing. The fastest way to do this is simply jump to your death repeatedly at the shrine and return to speak to Yoel at 2, 6, and 12 Hollowing to gain more Dark Sigils (and levels). Once your Hollowing is progressed enough, he grants you the fifth Dark Sigil. Three more Dark Sigils can be acquired by completing Anri's wedding questline, and finishing the game with all eight in your possession triggers the Hollow Lord ending.

However, your time with Yoel is limited. Whether you take him home or leave him here, he will not survive deep into the playthrough. If you reach the Catacombs of Carthus, or use Draw Out True Strength five times, Yoel expires. Even leaving him out in the wild will change little, save the location of his corpse. Some things can't be changed.

YORSHKA

There is a massive tower near Anor Londo that you can't reach easily. Start at the Anor Londo Bonfire and backtrack to the highest tower in Irithyll; it's just a few steps away. Use the mechanism of that tower to lower the walkway where you're positioned.

From the tower's lower setting, walk out onto the edge of the walkway. It looks like it's hovering over nothing. Just empty air. Trust in the fates and step onto that nothingness. It's an invisible bridge. Walk from there over to a tower that's close by, but a bit lower than where you're standing. Hop off to get onto the balcony of that tower and use a Bonfire there.

Yorshka, a Covenant leader, is around the corner. Talk to her and pledge yourself to her Covenant if you wish. Also, drop through the broken supports and beams inside that tower to get extra loot!

YURIA OF LONDOR

Yuria of Londor is a key NPC for reaching the Hollow Lord ending. She only appears in the Firelink Shrine if you use Draw Out True Strength from Yoel of Londor five times to acquire five Dark Sigils. This must be done before reaching the Catacombs of Carthus, as Yoel passes away when you do.

If Anri dies early or Yoel dies before you draw out all sigils, Yuria leaves and the Pale Shade of Londor invades in Farron Keep and Irithyll Valley. Defeating it in both places causes the Pale Shade armor set to appear in the room where Yoel and Yuria reside.

Yuria also becomes angered if you heal the Dark Sigil, or you kill the Pilgrim of Londor in Irithyll Valley before the ceremony is complete. While Yuria is friendly, the Pale Shade of Londor appears as a White Phantom in Farron Keep and Irithyll Valley.

YURIA INVENTORY

ITEM	COST	QUANTITY
Purging Stone	4500	-
Poison Throwing Knife	100	-
Londor Braille Divine Tome	50	1
Soul Arrow	1000	1
Heavy Soul Arrow	2000	1
Soul Greatsword	5000	1
Magic Weapon	4500	1
Magic Shield	4500	1
Dark Hand	12000	1
Untrue Dark Ring	5000	1
Untrue White Ring	5000	1
Ring of Sacrifice	5000	3

If you progress all the way to the end game after the ceremony with Yuria still friendly, both her and the Pale Shade leave White Phantom signs for the final battle. Defeating the final boss with her still alive causes her to leave her armor and weapon where she stood in Firelink Shrine.

TROPHIES AND ACHIEVEMENTS

ACHIEVEMENT	DESCRIPTION	GAMERSCORE	TROPHY TYPE
The Dark Soul	Complete all achievements.	70	Platinum
To Link the First Flame	Reach "To Link the First Flame" ending.	50	Gold
The End of Fire	Reach "The End of Fire" ending.	50	Gold
The Usurpation of Fire	Reach "The Usurpation of Fire" ending.	50	Gold
Lords of Cinder: Abyss Watchers	Defeat the Abyss Watchers, Lords of Cinder.	30	Gold
Lord of Cinder: Yhorm the Giant	Defeat Yhorm the Giant, Lord of Cinder.	30	Gold
Lord of Cinder: Aldritch, Devourer of Gods	Defeat Aldritch, Devourer of Gods, Lord of Cinder.	30	Gold
Lord of Cinder: Lothric, Younger Prince	Defeat Lothric, Younger Prince, Lord of Cinder.	30	Gold
Supreme Weapon Reinforcement	Reinforce any weapon to the highest level.	30	Gold
Master of Infusion	Perform all forms of infusion.	30	Gold
Master of Sorceries	Acquire all sorceries.	30	Gold
Master of Pyromancies	Acquire all pyromancies.	30	Gold
Master of Miracles	Acquire all miracles.	30	Gold
Master of Rings	Acquire all rings.	30	Gold
Master of Expression	Learn all gestures.	30	Gold
Ultimate Bonfire	Reinforce a bonfire to the highest level.	30	Gold
Ultimate Estus	Reinforce the Estus Flask to the highest level.	30	Gold
Covenant: Warrior of Sunlight	Discover Warrior of Sunlight covenant.	15	Bronze
Covenant: Way of Blue	Discover Way of Blue covenant.	15	Bronze
Covenant: Blue Sentinels	Discover Blue Sentinels covenant.	15	Bronze
Covenant: Blade of the Darkmoon	Discover Blade of the Darkmoon covenant.	15	Bronze
Covenant: Rosaria's Fingers	Discover Rosaria's Fingers covenant.	15	Bronze
Covenant: Mound-makers	Discover Mound-makers covenant.	15	Bronze
Covenant: Watchdogs of Farron	Discover Watchdogs of Farron covenant.	15	Bronze
Covenant: Aldritch Faithful	Discover Aldritch Faithful covenant.	15	Bronze
Untended Graves	Reach the Untended Graves.	15	Bronze
Archdragon Peak	Reach Archdragon Peak.	15	Bronze
Iudex Gundyr	Defeat Iudex Gundyr.	15	Bronze
Vordt of the Boreal Valley	Defeat Vordt of the Boreal Valley.	15	Bronze
Curse-rotted Greatwood	Defeat the Curse-rotted Greatwood.	15	Bronze
Crystal Sage	Defeat Crystal Sage.	15	Bronze
Deacons of the Deep	Defeat the Deacons of the Deep.	15	Bronze
High Lord Wolnir	Defeat High Lord Wolnir.	15	Bronze
Pontiff Sulyvahn	Defeat Pontiff Sulyvahn.	15	Bronze
Dancer of the Boreal Valley	Defeat Dancer of the Boreal Valley.	15	Bronze
Dragonslayer Armour	Defeat Dragonslayer Armour.	15	Bronze
Old Demon King	Defeat Old Demon King.	15	Bronze
Oceiros, the Consumed King	Defeat Oceiros, the Consumed King.	15	Bronze
Champion Gundyr	Defeat Champion Gundyr.	15	Bronze
Ancient Wyvern	Defeat Ancient Wyvern.	15	Bronze
The Nameless King	Defeat Nameless King.	15	Bronze
Enkindle	Light a bonfire flame for the first time.	15	Bronze
Embrace the Flame	Become a Host of Embers for the first time.	15	Bronze